Lecture Notes in Compute

T0238847

Commenced Publication in 1973
Founding and Former Series Editors:
Gerhard Goos, Juris Hartmanis, and Jan van Leeuwen

Lecture Notes in Computer Science 4711

Cliff B. Jones Zhiming Liu
Jim Woodcock (Eds.)

Theoretical Aspects of Computing – ICTAC 2007

4th International Colloquium
Macao, China, September 26-28, 2007
Proceedings

Springer

Volume Editors

Cliff B. Jones
Newcastle University
School of Computing Science
Newcastle upon Tyne, NE1 7RU, UK
E-mail: cliff.jones@ncl.ac.uk

Zhiming Liu
United Nations University
International Institute for Software Technology
Macao, China
E-mail: lzm@iist.unu.edu

Jim Woodcock
University of York
Department of Computer Science
Heslington, York YO10 5DD, UK
E-mail: jim@cs.york.ac.uk

Library of Congress Control Number: 2007935596

CR Subject Classification (1998): F.1, F.3, F.4, D.3, D.2, C.2.4

LNCS Sublibrary: SL 1 – Theoretical Computer Science and General Issues

ISSN 0302-9743
ISBN-10 3-540-75290-0 Springer Berlin Heidelberg New York
ISBN-13 978-3-540-75290-5 Springer Berlin Heidelberg New York

Springer is a part of Springer Science+Business Media

springer.com

Printed in Germany

Typesetting: Camera-ready by author, data conversion by Scientific Publishing Services, Chennai, India
Printed on acid-free paper SPIN: 12167203 06/3180 5 4 3 2 1 0

Preface to *Colloquium* Proceedings

This volume contains the papers presented at ICTAC 2007: *The 4th International Colloquium on Theoretical Aspects of Computing* held during 26th–28th September 2007 in Macao. There were 69 submissions, and each was reviewed by at least three programme committee members; the committee decided to accept 29 papers. The programme also included four invited talks by Dines Bjørner, He Jifeng, Zohar Manna, and Zhou Chaochen. Online conference management was provided by EasyChair.

The *International Colloquia on Theoretical Aspects of Computing* (*ICTAC*) is a series of annual events founded in 2003 by the United Nations University International Institute for Software Technology (UNU-IIST). The three previous *ICTAC* events were held in Guiyang (2004), Hanoi (2005), and Tunis (2006). The aim of each colloquium is twofold:

Scholarship. To bring together the leading international practitioners and researchers from academia, industry, and government to present their research results, and exchange experience, ideas, and solutions for their problems in theoretical aspects of computing.

Cooperation. To promote cooperation in research and education between participants and their institutions, from developing and industrial countries, as in the mandate of the United Nations University.

We are happy to acknowledge the generous sponsorship that this year's *Colloquium* has received from the following organisations.

- Formal Methods Europe, who kindly funded Zohar Manna's participation.
- The Macao Foundation.
- Macao Polytechnic Institute, who generously provided the conference venue.
- United Nations University International Institute for Software Technology, who provided local support and conference planning.
- University of York who provided editorial and secretarial support.

As mentioned above, this year's *ICTAC* was specially dedicated to Dines Bjørner and Zhou Chaochen. It was also associated with two other events.

- The *School on Domain Modelling and the Duration Calculus*, held in Shanghai during 17th–21st September 2007.
- The *Festschrift Symposium* held in Macao on the 24th–25th September 2007.

A further event was timed to coincide with *ICTAC*:

- *1st Workshop on Harnessing Theories for Tool Support in Software.*

July 2007 J.C.P.W.

Organisation

Programme Chairs

Cliff Jones
Zhiming Liu
Jim Woodcock

Programme Committee

Mícheál Mac an Airchinnigh
Farhad Arbab
Jonathan Bowen
Andrew Butterfield
Ana Cavalcanti
Antonio Cerone
Dang Van Hung
Jim Davies
David Déharbe
Jin Song Dong
Lindsay Groves
Stefan Hallerstede
Michael Hansen
Ian Hayes
Mathai Joseph
Joseph Kiniry
Peter Gorm Larsen
Xuandong Li
Shaoying Liu
Ali Mili
Joe Morris
Leonor Prensa
Anders Ravn
Augusto Sampaio
Emil Sekerinski
Natarajan Shankar
Ji Wang
Hongseok Yang
Naijun Zhan
Huibiao Zhu

Local Organisation

Kitty Chan
Wendy Hoi
Chris George
Violet Pun

External Reviewers

Benjamin Bedregal
Giampaolo Bella
Adalberto Cajueiro
Chunqing Chen
Robert Colvin
Brijesh Dongol
Pascal Fontaine
Robin Green
Radu Grigore
Haifeng Guo
Thai Son Hoang
Mikolas Janota
Padmanabhan Krishnan
Jing Li
Yuan Fang Li
Yang Liu
Ana Matos
Farhad Mehta
Larissa Meinicke
Michal Moskal
Gethin Norman
Joseph Okika
Anjolina Oliveira
Jun Pang
Dirk Pattinson
Cong Vinh Phan
Rodrigo Ramos
Peter Robinson
Rudolf Schlatte
Jeffrey Sanders
Regivan Santiago
Shaikh Siraj
Sergio Soares
Volker Stolz
Martin Strecker
Meng Sun
Francois Terrier
Cao Son Tran
Malcolm Tyrrell
Phan Cong Vinh
James Welch
Min Zhang
Jianhua Zhao
Daniel Zimmerman
Jianhua Zhao

Table of Contents

Domain Theory: Practice and Theories*
A Discussion of Possible Research Topics

Dines Bjørner**

Department of Computer Science and Engineering
Institute of Informatics and Mathematical Modelling
Technical University of Denmark
DK-2800 Kgs. Lyngby, Denmark***

Abstract. By a domain we mean a universe of discourse.

Typical examples are (partially) man-made universes of discourse - such as Air Traffic, Airports, Financial Services (banks, insurance companies, securities trading [brokers, traders, stock exchanges]), Health Care (hospitals etc.), Secure IT Systems (according to Intl. ISO/IEC Standard 17799), The Market (consumers, retailers, wholesalers, producers, "the supply chain"), Transportation (road, air, sea and/or rail transport), etc.

We shall outline how one might describe such (infrastructure component) domains, informally and formally - what the current descriptional limitations appear to be, and, hence, the prospects for future research as well as practice.

The current paper is based on Part IV, Chaps. 8–16 of [3]. The volume is one of [1,2,3].

The aim of this paper is to suggest a number of areas of domain theory and methodology research.

Maybe the title of the paper need be explained: The second part of the title: 'Practice and Theories' shall indicate that there is an engineering practice (i.e., methodology) of developing domain descriptions and that any such domain description forms the basis for a specific domain theory. The first part of the title: 'Theories' shall indicate that we need support the practice, i.e., the methodology, by theoretical insight, and that there probably are some theoretical insight that applies across some or all domain theories.

1 Introduction

1.1 A Preamble

This paper is mostly a computing science paper. This paper is less of a computer science paper. Computer science is the study and knowledge about the "things"

* Invited paper for ICTAC 2007, The 4th International Colloquium on Theoretical Aspects of Computing, 26–28 September 2007, Macau SAR, China: http://www.iist.unu.edu/ictac07/

** Prof. Emeritus.

*** Home address: Fredsvej 11, DK-2840 Holte, Denmark.

C.B. Jones, Z. Liu, J. Woodcock (Eds.): ICTAC 2007, LNCS 4711, pp. 1–17, 2007.

that can exist "inside" computers, and of what computing is. Computing science is the study and knowledge about how to construct computers and the "things" that can exist "inside" computers. Although the main emphasis of 'Domain Theory and Practice' is computing science, some of the research topics identified in this paper have a computer science nature.

1.2 On Originality

Since this paper is an invited paper and since it basically builds on and extends a certain part (Part IV Domain Engineering) of Vol. 3, [3], of my book [1,2,3], I shall not bring a lot of motivation nor putting my possible contributions in a broader context other that saying this: as far as I can see from the literature my concept of domain engineering is new. It may have appeared in rudimentary forms here and there in the literature, but in the nine chapters (Chaps. 8–16) of Part IV, [3], it receives a rather definitive and fully comprehensive treatment. But even that treatment can be improved. The present paper is one such attempt.

1.3 Structure of Paper

In a first semi-technical section we briefly express the triptych software engineering dogma, its consequences and its possibilities. We relate software verification to the triptych and present a first research topic. Then we list some briefly explained domains, and we present three more research topics. In the main technical section of this paper we present five sets of what we shall call domain facets (intrinsics, support technology, management and organisation, rules and regulations, and human behaviour). Each of these will be characterised but not really exemplified. We refer to [3] for details. But we will again list corresponding research topics. The paper ends first with some thoughts about what a 'domain theory' is, then on relations to requirements, and finally on two rather distinct benefits from domain engineering. In that final part of the paper we discuss a programming methodology notion of 'requirements specific development models' and its research topics.

2 Domain Engineering: A Dogma and Its Consequences

2.1 The Dogma

First the dogma: Before software can be designed its requirements must be understood. Before requirements can be prescribed the application domain must be understood.

2.2 The Consequences

Then the "idealised" consequences: In software development we first describe the domain, then we prescribe the requirements, and finally we design the software.

As we shall see: major parts of requirements can be systematically "derived"[1] from domain descriptions. In engineering we can accommodate for less idealised consequences, but in science we need investigate the "ideals".

2.3 The Triptych Verification

A further consequence of this triptych development is that

$$\mathcal{D}, \mathcal{S} \models \mathcal{R},$$

which we read as: in order to prove that $\mathcal{S}$oftware implements the $\mathcal{R}$equirements the proof often has to make assumptions about the $\mathcal{D}$omain.

2.4 Full Scale Development: A First Suggested $\mathfrak{R}$esearch Topic

Again, presupposing much to come we can formulate a first research topic.

$\mathfrak{R}$ 1. **The $\mathcal{D}, \mathcal{S} \models \mathcal{R}$ Relation**: Assume that there is a formal description of the $\mathcal{D}$omain, a formal prescription of the $\mathcal{R}$equirements and a formal specification of the $\mathcal{S}$oftware design. Assume, possibly, that there is expressed and verified a number of relations between the $\mathcal{D}$omain description and the $\mathcal{R}$equirements prescription. Now how do we express the assertion: $\mathcal{D}, \mathcal{S} \models \mathcal{R}$ — namely that the software is correct? We may assume, without loss of generality, that this assertion is in some form of a pre/post condition of $\mathcal{S}$ — and that this pre/post condition is supported by a number of assertions "nicely spread" across the $\mathcal{S}$oftware design (i.e., the code). The research topic is now that of studying how, in the pre/post condition of $\mathcal{S}$ (the full code) and in the (likewise pre/post condition) assertions "within" $\mathcal{S}$, the various components of $\mathcal{R}$ and $\mathcal{D}$ "appear", and of how they relate to the full formal pre- and descriptions, respectively.

2.5 Examples of Domains

The Examples. Lest we loose contact with reality it is appropriate here, however briefly, to give some examples of (application) domains.

Air Traffic: A domain description includes descriptions of the entities, functions, events and behaviours of aircraft, airports (runways, taxi-ways, apron, etc.), air lanes, ground, terminal, regional, and continental control towers, of (national [CAA, CAAC, FAA, SLV, etc.] and international [JAA, CAO]) aviation authorities, etc.

Airports: A domain description includes descriptions of the flow of people (passengers, staff), material (catering, fuel, baggage), aircraft, information (boarding cards, baggage tags) and control; of these entities, of the operations performed

[1] By "derivation" we here mean one which is guided by humans (i.e., the domain and requirements engineers in collaboration with the stakeholders).

by or on them, the events that may occur (cancellation or delay of flights, lost luggage, missing passenger), and, hence, of the many concurrent and intertwined (mutually "synchronising") behaviours that entities undergo.

Container Shipping: A domain description includes descriptions of containers, container ships, the stowage of containers on ships and in container yards, container terminal (ports), the loading and unloading of containers between ships and ports and between ports and the "hinterland" (including crances, port trucking and feeder trucks, trains and barges), the container bills of lading (or way bills), the container transport logistics, the (planning and execution, scheduling and allocation) of voyages, the berthing (arrival and departure) of container ships, customer relations, etc.

Financial Service Industry: A domain description includes descriptions of banks (and banking: [demand/deposit, savings, mortgage] accounts, [opening, closing, deposit, withdrawal, transfer, statements] operations on accounts), insurance companies (claims processing, etc.), securities trading (stocks, bonds, brokers, traders, exchanges, etc.), portfolio management, IPOs, etc.

Health care: A domain description includes descriptions of the entities, operations, events and behaviours of healthy people, patients and medical staff, of private physicians, medical clinics, hospitals, pharmacies, health insurance, national boards of health, etc.

The Internet: The reader is encouraged to fill in some details here!

Manufacturing: Machining & Assembly: The reader is encouraged to also fill in some details here!

"The" Market: A domain description includes descriptions of the entities, operations, events and behaviours of consumers, retailers, wholesalers, producers, the delivery chain and the payment of (or for) merchandise and services.

Transportation: A domain description includes descriptions of the entities, functions, events and behaviours of transport vehicles (cars/trucks/busses, trains, aircraft, ships), [multimodal] transport nets (roads, rail lines, air lanes, shipping lanes) and hubs (road intersections [junctions], stations, airports, harbours), transported items (people and freight), and of logistics (scheduling and allocation of transport items to transport vehicles, and of transport vehicles to transport nets and hubs). Monomodal descriptions can focus on just air traffic or on container shipping, or on railways.

The Web: The reader is encouraged to "likewise" fill in some details here!

There are many "less grand" domains: railway level crossings, the interconnect cabling between the oftentimes dozens of "boxes" of some electronic/mechanical/acoustical measuring set-up, a gas burner, etc. These are all, rather onesidedly, examples of what might be called embedded, or real-time, or safety critical systems.

We can refer to several projects at UNU-IIST which have produced domain specifications for railway systems (China), ministry of finance (Vietnam), telephone systems (The Philippines), harbours (India), etc.; and to dozens of MSc projects which have likewise produced domain specifications for airports, air traffic, container shipping, health care, the market, manufacturing, etc. I give many, many references in [3]. I also refer the reader to http://www.railwaydomain.org/ for documents, specifically http://www.railwaydomain.org/book.pdf for domain models of railway systems.

Some Remarks. A point made by listing and explaining the above domains is the following: They all display a seeming complexity in terms of multitude of entities, functions, events and interrelated behaviours; and they all focus on the reality of "what is out there": no mention is (to be) made of requirements to supporting computing systems let alone of these (incl. software).

2.6 Domains: Suggested ℜesearch Topics

From the above list we observe that the 'transportation item' "lifts" those of 'air traffic' and 'container shipping'. Other examples could be shown. This brings us, at this early stage where we have yet to really outline what domain engineering is, to suggest the following research topics:

ℜ 2. **Lifted Domains and Projections**: We observe, above, that the 'transportation' domain seems to be an abstraction of at least four more concrete domains: road, rail, sea and air transportation. We could say that 'transportation' is a commensurate "lifting" of each of the others, or that these more concrete could arise as a result of a "projection" from the 'transportation' domain. The research topic is now to investigate two aspects: a computing science cum software engineering aspect and a computer science aspect. The former should preferably result in principles, techniques and tools for choosing levels of "lifted" abstraction and "projected" concretisation. The latter should study the implied "lifting" and "projection" operators.

ℜ 3. **What Do We Mean by an Infrastructure ?** We observe, above, that some of the domains exemplify what is normally called infrastructure[2] components. According to the World Bank: *'Infrastructure' is an umbrella term for many activities referred to as 'social overhead capital' by some development economists, and encompasses activities that share technical and economic features (such as economies of scale and spillovers from users to nonusers)*. The research is now to study whether we can reformulate the sociologically vague World Bank definition in precise mathematical terms.

[2] Winston Churchill is quoted to have said, during a debate in the House of Commons, in 1946: ... *The young Labourite speaker that we have just listened to, clearly wishes to impress upon his constituency the fact that he has gone to Eton and Oxford since he now uses such fashionable terms as 'infra-structures'. [I have recently been in communication with the British House of Commons information office enquiries manager, Mr. Martin Davies in order to verify and, possibly pinpoint, this statement. I am told that "as the Hansard debates in question are not available electronically, it could only be found via a manual search of hard copy Hansard". So there it stands.]*

ℜ 4. **What Is an Infrastructure Component ?** We observe, above, that not all of the domains exemplified are what is normally called infrastructure components.[3] The research is now to study whether we can formulate and formalise some "tests" which help us determine whether some domain that we are about to model qualifies as part of one or more infrastructure components.

We bring these early research topic suggestions so that the reader can better judge whether domain engineering principles and techniques might help in establishing a base for such research. Throughout the paper we shall "spice it" with further suggestions of research topics.

•••

We do not cover the important methodological aspects of stakeholder identification and liaison, domain acquisition and analysis, domain model verification and validation. For that we refer to Vol. 3 Chaps. 9–10 and 12–14 [3].

3 Domain Facets

The rôle, the purpose, of domain engineering is to construct, to develop, and research domain descriptions. It is both an engineering and a scientific task. It is engineering because we do know, today, a necessary number of principles, techniques and tools with which to create domain models. It is scientific, i.e., of research nature, because, it appears, that we do not necessarily know, today, whether what we know is sufficient.

3.1 Stages of Domain Development

By domain development we mean a process, consisting of a number of reasonably clearly separable stages which when properly conducted leads to a domain description, i.e., a domain model. We claim that the following are meaningful and necessary domain development stages of development, each with their attendant principles, techniques and tools: (i) identification of stakeholders, (ii) rough domain identification, (iii) domain acquisition, (iv) analysis of rough domain description units, (v) domain modelling, (vi) domain verification, (vii) domain validation and (viii) domain theory formation. We shall focus on domain modelling emphasising the modelling concept of domain facets.

3.2 The Facets

By domain modelling we mean the construction of both an informal, narrative and a formal domain description.

[3] 'Manufacturing' and 'The Market' appear, in the above list to not be infrastructure components, but, of course, they rely on the others, the infrastructure components.

We claim that the following identified facets (i.e., "steps") (later to be briefly explained) are necessary parts of the domain modelling process: (i) intrinsics, (ii) support technologies, (iii) management and organisation, (iv) rules and regulations, (v) and human behaviour. Ideally speaking one may proceed with these "steps" in the order listed. Engineering accommodates for less ideal progressions. Each "step" produces a partial domain description. Subsequent "steps" 'extend' partial descriptions into partial or even (relative) complete descriptions.

In this section, Sect. 3, we will not give concrete examples but will rely on such already given in Chap. 11 of [3].

3.3 Intrinsics

By the intrinsics of a domain we shall understand those phenomena and concepts, that is, those entities, functions, events and behaviours in terms of which all other facets are described.

The choice as to what constitutes the intrinsics of a domain is often determined by the views of the stakeholders. Thus it is a pragmatic choice, and the choice cannot be formalised in the form of an **is_intrinsics** predicate that one applies to phenomena and concepts of the domain.

Intrinsics: Suggested $\Re$esearch Topic

$\Re$ 5. **Intrinsics**: We refer to Sect. 11.3 in [3]. What is, perhaps, needed, is a theoretically founded characterisation of "being intrinsic".

3.4 Support Technology

By a support technology of a domain we shall understand either of a set of (one or more) alternative entities, functions, events and behaviours which "implement" an intrinsic phenomenon or concept. Thus for some one or more intrinsic phenomena or concepts there might be a technology which supports those phenomena or concepts.

Sampling Behaviour of Support Technologies. Let us consider intrinsic **A**ir **T**raffic as a continuous function ($\rightarrow$) from **T**ime to **F**light **L**ocations:

type
  T, F, L
  iAT = T $\rightarrow$ (F $\overrightarrow{m}$ L)

But what is observed, by some support technology, is not a continuous function, but a discrete sampling (a map $\overrightarrow{m}$):

  sAT = T $\overrightarrow{m}$ (F $\overrightarrow{m}$ L)

There is a support technology, say in the form of **radar** which "observes" the intrinsic traffic and delivers the sampled traffic:

value
  radar: iAT $\rightarrow$ sAT

Probabilistic cum Statistical Behaviour of Support Technologies. But even the radar technology is not perfect. Its positioning of flights follows some probabilistic or statistical pattern:

type
  P = {|r:**Real** • 0≤r≤1|}
  ssAT = P $\overrightarrow{m}$ sAT-**infset**
value
  radar′: iAT $\stackrel{\sim}{\rightarrow}$ ssAT

The radar technology will, with some probability produce either of a set of samplings, and with some other probability some other set of samplings, etc.[4]

Support Technology Quality Control, a Sketch. How can we express that a given technology delivers a reasonable support ? One approach is to postulate intrinsic and technology states (or observed behaviours), Θ_i, Θ_s, a support technology τ and a "**close**ness" predicate:

type
  Θ_i, Θ_s
value
  τ: Θ_i $\rightarrow$ P $\overrightarrow{m}$ Θ_s-**infset**
  close: Θ_i × Θ_s $\rightarrow$ **Bool**

and then require that an experiment can be performed which validates the support technology.

The experiment is expressed by the following axiom:

value
  p_threshhold:P
axiom
  ∀ θ_i:Θ_i •
    let pθ_ss = τ(θ_i) **in**
    ∀ p:P • p>p_threshhold ⇒
      θ_s:Θ_s • θ_s ∈ pθ_ss(p) ⇒ close(θ_i,θ_s) **end**

The p_threshhold probability has to be a-priori determined as one above which the support technology renditions of the intrinsic states (or behaviours) are acceptable.

[4] Throughout this paper we omit formulation of type well-formedness predicates.

Support Technologies: Suggested $\mathfrak{R}$esearch Topics.

$\mathfrak{R}$ 6. **Probabilistic and/or Statistical Support Technologies**: Some cases should be studied to illuminate the issue of probability versus statistics. More generally we need more studies of how support technologies "enter the picture", i.e., how "they take over" from other facet. And we need to come up with precise modelling concepts for probabilistic and statistical phenomena and their integration into the formal specification approaches at hand.

$\mathfrak{R}$ 7. **A Support Technology Quality Control Method**: The above sketched a 'support technology quality control' procedure. It left out the equally important 'monitoring' aspects. Develop experimentally two or three distinct models of domains involving distinct sets of support technologies. Then propose and study concrete implementations of 'support technology quality monitoring and control' procedures.

3.5 Management and Organisation

By the management of an enterprise (an institution) we shall understand a (possibly stratified, see 'organisation' next) set of enterprise staff (behaviours, processes) authorised to perform certain functions not allowed performed by other enterprise staff (behaviours, processes) and where such functions involve monitoring and controlling other enterprise staff (behaviours, processes). By organisation of an enterprise (an institution) we shall understand the stratification (partitioning) of enterprise staff (behaviours, processes) with each partition endowed with a set of authorised functions and with communication interfaces defined between partitions, i.e., between behaviours (processes).

An Abstraction of Management Functions. Let **E** designate some enterprise state concept, and let **stra_mgt, tact_mgt, oper_mgt, wrkr** and **merge** designate strategic management, tactical management, operational management and worker actions on states such that these actions are "somehow aware" of the state targets of respective management groups and or workers. Let **p** be a predicate which determines whether a given target state has been reached, and let **merge** harmonise different state targets into an agreeable one. Then the following behaviour reflects some aspects of management.

type
  E
value
  stra_mgt, tact_mgt, oper_mgt, wrkr, merge: $E \times E \times E \times E \rightarrow E$
  p: $E^* \rightarrow$ **Bool**
  mgt: $E \rightarrow E$
  mgt(e) $\equiv$
    let $e' = \text{stra\_mgt}(e,e'',e''',e'''')$,
      $e'' = \text{tact\_mgt}(e,e'',e''',e'''')$,

```
    e''' = oper_mgt(e,e'',e''',e''''),
    e'''' = wrkr(e,e'',e''',e'''') in
  if p(e,e'',e''',e'''')
    then skip
    else mgt(merge(e,e'',e''',e''''))
  end end
```

The recursive set of $e^{\cdot\cdot\prime}$ = *f(e, e'', e''', e'''')* equations are "solved" by iterative communication between the management groups and the workers. The arrangement of these equations reflect the organisation and the various functions, **stra_mgt, tact_mgt, oper_mgt** and **wrkr** reflect the management. The frequency of communication between the management groups and the workers help determine a quality of the result.

The above is just a very crude, and only an illustrative model of management and organisation.

We could also have given a generic model, as the above, of management and organisation but now in terms of, say, CSP processes. Individual managers are processes and so are workers. The enterprise state, $e : E$, is maintained by one or more processes, separate from manager and worker processes. Etcetera.

Management and Organisation: Suggested ℜesearch Topics

ℜ 8. **Strategic, Tactical and Operation Management**: We made no explicit references to such "business school of administration" "BA101" topics as 'strategic' and 'tactical' management. Study Example 9.2 of Sect. 9.3.1 of Vol. 3 [3]. Study other sources on 'Strategic and Tactical Management'. Question Example 9.2's attempt at delineating 'strategic' and 'tactical' management. Come up with better or other proposals, and/or attempt clear, but not necessarily computable predicates which (help) determine whether an operation (above they are alluded to as 'stra' and 'tact') is one of strategic or of tactical concern.

ℜ 9. **Modelling Management and Organisation Applicatively or Concurrently**: The abstraction of 'management and organisation' on Page 3.5 was applicative, i.e., a recursive function — whose auxiliary functions were hopefully all continuous. Suggest a CSP rendition of "the same idea" ! Relate the applicative to the concurrent models.

3.6 Rules and Regulations

By a rule of an enterprise (an institution) we understand a syntactic piece of text whose meaning apply in any pair of actual present and potential next states of the enterprise, and then evaluates to either true or false: the rule has been obeyed, or the rule has been (or will be, or might be) broken. By a regulation of an enterprise (an institution) we understand a syntactic piece of text whose meaning, for example, apply in states of the enterprise where a rule has been broken, and when applied in such states will change the state, that is, "remedy" the "breaking of a rule".

Abstraction of Rules and Regulations. Stimuli are introduced in order to capture the possibility of rule-breaking next states.

type
  Sti, Rul, Reg
  RulReg = Rul $\times$ Reg
  Θ
  STI = $\Theta \rightarrow \Theta$
  RUL = $(\Theta \times \Theta) \rightarrow$ **Bool**
  REG = $\Theta \rightarrow \Theta$
value
  meaning: Sti $\rightarrow$ STI, Rul $\rightarrow$ RUL, Reg $\rightarrow$ REG
  valid: Sti $\times$ Rul $\rightarrow \Theta \rightarrow$ **Bool**
  valid(sti,rul)$\theta \equiv$ (meaning(rul))(θ,meaning(sti)θ)
axiom
  $\forall$ sti:Sti,(rul,reg):RulReg,θ:Θ $\bullet$
    $\sim$valid(sti,rul)$\theta \Rightarrow$ meaning(rul)(θ,meaning(reg)θ)

Quality Control of Rules and Regulations. The axiom above presents us with a guideline for checking the suitability of (pairs of) rules and regulations in the context of stimuli: for every proposed pair of rules and regulations and for every conceivable stimulus check whether the stimulus might cause a breaking of the rule and, if so, whether the regulation will restore the system to an acceptable state.

Rules and Regulations Suggested $\mathfrak{R}$esearch Topic

$\mathfrak{R}$ 10. **A Concrete Case**: The above sketched a quality control procedure for 'stimuli, rules and regulations'. It left out the equally important 'monitoring' aspects. Develop experimentally two or three distinct models of domains involving distinct sets of rules and regulations. Then propose and study concrete implementations of procedures for quality monitoring and control of 'stimuli, rules and regulations'.

3.7 Human Behaviour

By human behaviour we understand a "way" of representing entities, performing functions, causing or reacting to events or participating in behaviours. As such a human behaviour may be characterisable on a per phenomenon or concept basis as lying somewhere in the "continuous" spectrum from (i) diligent: precise representations, performances, event (re)actions, and behaviour interactions; via (ii) sloppy: occasionally imprecise representations, performances, event (re)actions, and behaviour interactions; and (iii) delinquent: repeatedly imprecise representations, performances, event (re)actions, and behaviour interactions; to (iv) criminal: outright counter productive, damaging representations, performances, event (re)actions, and behaviour interactions.

Abstraction of Human Behaviour. We extend the formalisation of rules and regulations.

Human actions (**ACT**) lead from a state (Θ) to any one of possible successor states (Θ**-infset**) — depending on the human behaviour, whether diligent, sloppy, delinquent or having criminal intent. The **human interpretation** of a rule (**Rul**) usually depends on the current state (Θ) and can be any one of a possibly great number of semantic rules (**RUL**). For a delinquent (...) user the rule must yield truth in order to satisfy "being delinquent (...)".

type
  ACT = $\Theta \rightarrow \Theta$**-infset**
value
  hum_int: Rul $\rightarrow \Theta \rightarrow$ RUL-**infset**
  hum_behav: Sti $\times$ Rul $\rightarrow$ ACT $\rightarrow \Theta \rightarrow \Theta$**-infset**
  hum_behav(sti,rul)(α)(θ) **as** θs
    post θs = $\alpha(\theta) \wedge$
      $\forall\, \theta'$:Θ • $\theta' \in \theta$s $\Rightarrow$
        $\exists$ se_rul:RUL • se_rul $\in$ hum_int(rul)(θ) $\Rightarrow$ se_rul(θ,θ')

Human behaviour is thus characterisable as follows: It occurs in a context of a **stimulus**, a **rule**, a present state (θ) and (the choice of) an action (α:**ACT**) which may have either one of a number of outcomes (θ**s**). Thus let θ**s** be the possible spread of diligent, sloppy, delinquent or outright criminal successor states. For each such successor states there must exist a rule interpretation which satisfies the pair of present an successor states. That is, it must satisfy being either diligent, sloppy, delinquent or having criminal intent and possibly achieving that!

Human Behaviour Suggested ℜesearch Topics. Section 11.8 of Vol. 3 [3] elaborates on a number of ways of describing (i.e., modelling) human behaviour.

ℜ 11. **Concrete Methodology**: Based on the abstraction of human behaviour given earlier, one is to study how one can partition the set, $\alpha(\theta)$, of outcomes of human actions into 'diligent', 'sloppy', 'delinquent' and 'criminal' behaviours — or some such, perhaps cruder, perhaps finer partitioning — and for concrete cases attempt to formalise these for possible interactive "mechanisation".

ℜ 12. **Monitoring and Control of Human Behaviour**: Based on possible solutions to the previous research topic one is to study general such interactive "mechanisation" of the monitoring and control of human behaviour.

3.8 Domain Modelling: Suggested ℜesearch Topic

ℜ 13. **Sufficiency of Domain Facets**: We have covered five facets: intrinsics, support technology, management and organisation, rules and regulations and human behaviour. The question is: are these the only facets, i.e., views on the domain that are relevant and can be modelled? Another question is: is there an altogether different set of facets, "cut up", so-to-speak, "along other lines of sights", using which we could likewise cover our models of domains?

One might further subdivide the above five facets (intrinsics, support technology, management and organisation, rules and regulations and human behaviour) into "sub"-facets. A useful one seems to be to separate out from the facet of rules and regulations the sub-facet of scripts.

• • •

We have finished our overview of domain facets.

4 Domains: Miscellaneous Issues

4.1 Domain Theories

- *By a* **domain theory** *we shall understand a domain description together with lemmas, propositions and theorems that may be proved about the description — and hence can be claimed to hold in the domain.*

To create a domain theory the specification language must possess a proof system. It appears that the essence of possible theorems of — that is, laws about — domains can be found in laws of physics. For a delightful view of the law-based nature of physics — and hence possibly also of man-made universes we refer to Richard Feynman's Lectures on Physics [4].

Example Theorem of Railway Domain Theory. Let us hint at some domain theory theorems: **Kirchhoff's Law for Railways:** Assume regular train traffic as per a modulo κ hour time table. Then we have, observed over a κ hour period, that the number of trains arriving at a station minus the number of trains ending their journey at that station plus the number of trains starting their journey at that station equals the number of trains departing from that station.

Why Domain Theories ? Well, it ought be obvious ! We need to understand far better the laws even of man-made systems.

Domain Theories: Suggested $\Re$esearch Topics:.

$\Re$ 14. **Domain Theories**: We need to experimentally develop and analyse a number of suggested theorems for a number of representative domains in order to possibly 'discover' some meta-theorems: laws about laws !

4.2 Domain Descriptions and Requirements Prescriptions

From Domains to Requirements. Requirements prescribe what "the machine", i.e., the hardware + software is expected to deliver. We show, in Vol. 3, Part V, Requirements Engineering, and in particular in Chap. 19, Sects. 19.4–19.5 how to construct, from a domain description, in collaboration with the requirements stakeholders, the domain (i.e., functional) requirements, and the interface (i.e., user) requirements.

Domain requirements are those requirements which can be expressed only using terms from the domain description. Interface requirements are those requirements which can be expressed only using terms from both the domain description and the machine — the latter means that terms of computers and software are also being used.

Domain requirements are developed as follows: Every line of the domain description is inspected by both the requirements engineer and the requirements stakeholders. For each line the first question is asked: *Shall this line of description prescribe a property of the requirements ?* If so it is "copied" over to the requirements prescription. If not it is "projected away". In similar rounds the following questions are then raised: *Shall the possible generality of the description be instantiated to something more concrete ? Shall possible non-determinism of the description be made less non-deterministic, more deterministic ? Shall the domain be "extended" to allow for hitherto infeasible entities, functions, events and behaviours ? Shall the emerging requirements prescription be "fitted" to elsewhere emerging requirements prescriptions ?* Similar "transformation" steps can be applied in order to arrive at (data initialisation and refreshment, GUI, dialogue, incremental control flow, machine-to-machine communication, etc.) interface requirements.

Domain and Interface Requirements: Suggested ℜesearch Topics

ℜ 15. **Domain and Interface Requirements**: Vol. 3, Part V, Sects. 19.4–19.5 give many examples of requirements "derivation" principles and techniques. But one could wish for more research in this area: more detailed principles and techniques, on examples across a wider spectrum of problem frames.

4.3 Requirements-Specific Domain Software Development Models

A long term, that one: 'requirements-specific domain software development models' ! The term is explained next.

Software "Intensities". One can speak of 'software intensity'. Here are some examples. Compilers represent 'translation' intensity. 'Word processors', 'spread sheet systems', etc., represent "workpiece" intensity. Databases represent 'information' intensity. Real-time embedded software represent 'reactive' intensity. Data communication software represent connection intensity. Etcetera.

"Abstract" Developments. Let $''\mathcal{R}''$ denote the "archetypal" requirements for some specific software 'intensity'. Many different domains $\{\mathcal{D}_1, \mathcal{D}_2, \ldots, \mathcal{D}_i, \ldots, \mathcal{D}_j, \ldots\}$ may be subject to requirements $''\mathcal{R}''$-like prescriptions. For each such a set of possible software may result. The "pseudo-formula" below attempts, albeit informally, to capture this situation:

$$\left\{\begin{array}{c}\mathcal{D}_1\\ \mathcal{D}_2\\ \ldots\\ \mathcal{D}_i\\ \ldots\\ \mathcal{D}_k\\ \ldots\end{array}\right\} \sim \; ''\mathcal{R}'' \; \mapsto \left[\begin{array}{c}\{\mathcal{S}_{1_1}, \mathcal{S}_{1_2}, \ldots, \mathcal{S}_{1_{j_1}}, \ldots\}\\ \{\mathcal{S}_{1_1}, \mathcal{S}_{1_2}, \ldots, \mathcal{S}_{1_{j_2}}, \ldots\}\\ \ldots\\ \{\mathcal{S}_{i_1}, \mathcal{S}_{i_2}, \ldots, \mathcal{S}_{i_{j_i}}, \ldots\}\\ \ldots\\ \{\mathcal{S}_{k_1}, \mathcal{S}_{k_2}, \ldots, \mathcal{S}_{k_{j_k}}, \ldots\}\\ \ldots\end{array}\right]$$

Several different domains, to wit: road nets and railway nets, can be given the "same kind" of (road and rail) maintenance requirements leading to information systems. Several different domains, to wit: road nets, railway nets, shipping lanes, or air lane nets, can be given the "same kind" of (bus, train, ship, air flight) monitoring and control requirements (leading to real-time embedded systems). But usually the specific requirements skills determine much of the requirements prescription work and especially the software design work.

Requirements-Specific Devt. Models: Suggested ℜesearch Topics

ℜ 16_j. **Requirements-Specific Development Models,** $\mathcal{RSDM}_j$: We see these as grand challenges: to develop and research a number of requirements-specific domain (software) development models $\mathcal{RSDM}_j$.

The "pseudo-formal" $\prod(\sum_i^{\cdots} \mathcal{D}_i)\ ''\mathcal{R}''\ \sum_{i,j}^{\cdots} \mathcal{S}_{i_j}$ expression attempts to capture an essence of such research: The $\prod$ "operator" is intended to project (that is, look at only) those domains, $\mathcal{D}_i$, for which $''\mathcal{R}''$ may be relevant. The research explores the projections $\prod$, the possible $''\mathcal{R}''$s and the varieties of software $\sum_{i,j}^{\cdots} \mathcal{S}_{i_j}$.

4.4 On Two Reasons for Domain Modelling

Thus there seems to be two entirely different, albeit, related reasons for domain modelling: one justifies domain modelling on engineering grounds, the other on scientific grounds.

An Engineering Reason for Domain Modelling. In an e-mail, in response, undoubtedly, to my steadfast, perhaps conceived as stubborn insistence, on domain engineering, Sir Tony Hoare summed up his reaction, in summer of 2006, to domain engineering as follows, and I quote[5]:

"There are many unique contributions that can be made by domain modelling.

[5] E-Mail to Dines Bjørner, CC to Robin Milner et al., July 19, 2006.

1. The models describe all aspects of the real world that are relevant for any good software design in the area. They describe possible places to define the system boundary for any particular project.
2. They make explicit the preconditions about the real world that have to be made in any embedded software design, especially one that is going to be formally proved.
3. They describe[6] the[7] whole range of possible designs for the software, and the whole range of technologies available for its realisation.
4. They provide a framework for a full analysis of requirements, which is wholly independent of the technology of implementation.
5. They enumerate and analyse the decisions that must be taken earlier or later in any design project, and identify those that are independent and those that conflict. Late discovery of feature interactions can be avoided."

All of these issues are dealt with, one-by-one, and in some depth, in Vol. 3 [3] of my three volume book.

A Science Reason for Domain Modelling. So, inasmuch as the above-listed issues of Sect. 4.4, so aptly expressed in Tony's mastery, also of concepts (through his delightful mastery of words), are of course of utmost engineering importance, it is really, in our mind, the science issues that are foremost: We must first and foremost understand. There is no excuse for not trying to first understand. Whether that understanding can be "translated" into engineering tools and techniques is then another matter. But then, of course, it is nice that clear and elegant understanding also leads to better tools and hence better engineering. It usually does.

Domains Versus Requirements-Specific Development Models. Sir Tony's five statements are more related, it seems, to the concept of requirements-specific domain software development models than to merely the concept of domain models. His statements help us formulate the research programme $\Re$16 of requirements specific domain software development models. When, in his statements, you replace his use of the term 'models' with our term 'requirements-specific development models *based on domain models*', then "complete harmony" between the two views exists.

5 Conclusion

5.1 What Has Been Achieved ?

I set out to focus on what I consider the crucial modelling stage of describing domain facets and to identify a number of their research issues. I've done that. Cursorily, the topic is "near-holistic", so an overview is all that can be done. The issue is that of that of a comprehensive methodology. Hence the "holism" challenge.

[6] read: imply.
[7] read: a.

5.2 What Needs to Be Achieved ?

Well, simply, to get on with that research. There are two sides to it: the 16 research topics mentioned above, and the ones mentioned below. The latter serves as a carrier for the former research.

Domain Theories: Grand Challenge $\Re$esearch Topics. The overriding research topic is that of:

$\Re$ 17_i. **Domain Models:** $\mathcal{D}_i$: We see this as a set of grand challenges: to develop and research a family of domain models $\mathcal{D}_i$.

Acknowledgements

I thank the organisers for inviting me to present a (this ?) talk. I thank UNU-IIST for inviting me and my wife back to Macau to a place where I spent great years. I consider UNU/IIST (as we spelled it in those days) one of my main achievements, so I also thank all those people who made it possible. They may have suffered then. But they too can be very proud now. I thank Sir Tony for fruitful discussions during the writing of this paper.

References

1. Bjørner, D.: Software Engineering. In: Abstraction and Modelling. Texts in Theoretical Computer Science, the EATCS Series, vol. 1, Springer, Heidelberg (2006)
2. Bjørner, D.: Software Engineering. In: Specification of Systems and Languages. Texts in Theoretical Computer Science, the EATCS Series, vol. 2, pp. 12–14. Springer, Heidelberg (2006) (Chapters 12–14 are primarily authored by Madsen, C.K.)
3. Bjørner, D.: Software Engineering. In: Domains, Requirements and Software Design. Texts in Theoretical Computer Science, the EATCS Series, vol. 3, Springer, Heidelberg (2006)
4. Feynmann, R., Leighton, R., Sands, M.: The Feynmann Lectures on Physics, vol. I–II–II. Addison-Wesley, California Institute of Technology (1963)

Linking Semantic Models

He Jifeng*

Software Engineering Institute
East China Normal University, Shanghai

Abstract. A theory of programming is intended to help in the construction of programs that provably meet their specifications. It starts with a complete lattice of specifications, used as a domain for the semantics of the programming language. The operators of the language are defined as monotonic functions over this domain. This paper presents a method which enables us to derive an enriched semantics for the imperative languages. We show that the new definition of the primitive commands can be recast as the weakest solution of the embedding equation, and demonstrate how the operators of the programming language are redefined from the homomorphic property of the embedding and the healthiness conditions imposed on "real" programs.

1 Introduction

How are we to understand complicated programming languages, and thereby use them with greater reliability? Surely the answer is to start with the core of a language and simply add to it, one at a time, a number of new features that are required. Ideally, the properties of programs established in the simpler theories of programming can remain valid in the enriched ones. In this way, our understanding of complexity is cumulative; nothing that has been learnt in the simpler cases needs to be unlearnt for the most complex combinations.

The most general possible way of defining a link between theories of programming is as a function which maps all elements from one theory into a subset of the elements from the other. An example familiar in computing is a *compiler*, which translates a program in a high level language to one expressed in a lower level language, executed directly by the hardware of a machine. In addition to these practical purposes, the link can reveal a lot about the structure of the theories which it is used to compare.

The general case of a link is a function that maps between disjoint semantic domains. Since the domains are usually lattices, monotonicity is still an important property. Suppose that **D1** and **D2** are two semantic domains, and **L** a programming language. Let

$$sem1 : \mathbf{L} \rightarrow \mathbf{D1} \qquad \text{and} \qquad sem2 : \mathbf{L} \rightarrow \mathbf{D2}$$

be semantic functions. A link $*$ from **D1** to **D2** is required to satisfy

* This work was supported by the National Basic Research Program of China (Grant No. 2005CB321904).

C.B. Jones, Z. Liu, J. Woodcock (Eds.): ICTAC 2007, LNCS 4711, pp. 18–33, 2007.

$$sem2(P) \quad = \quad sem1(P)^* \qquad \text{for all the program } P \text{ of } \mathbf{L} \qquad (1)$$

In order to preserve the algebraic laws that have already been proved in the domain **D1**, we require $*$ to be a homomorphism, i.e., for all the operators op

$$(sem1(P)\ op\ sem1(Q))^* \quad = \quad sem2(P)\ op\ sem2(Q) \qquad (2)$$

For decades, the relational model has been used widely in formalising the imperative sequential languages [3,4,6]. Each extension of the languages usually elaborates the structure of the underlying observation space. The following tables exemplifies how to model the behaviour of assignment and non-deterministic choice in a variety of semantic frameworks

	Definition of $x := 0$
States of variables	$x' \ = \ 0$ where x and x' denote the initial and final values of program variable x.
Termination	$ok \Rightarrow \ (ok' \ \wedge \ (x' = 0))$ where ok' is true if and only when a program terminates.
Probability	$ok \Rightarrow \ (ok' \ \wedge \ prob'(\{x \mapsto 0\}) = 1)$ where $prob'$ is a distribution over the final states.
	Definition of $x := 0 \ \sqcap \ x := 1$
States of variables	$x' = 0 \ \vee \ x' = 1$
Termination	$ok \Rightarrow (ok' \ \wedge \ (x' = 0 \vee x' = 1))$
Probability	$ok \Rightarrow (ok' \ \wedge \ (prob'(\{x \mapsto 0\} \cup \{x \mapsto 1\}) = 1))$

This paper presents an equation-solving approach to derivation of enriched semantics, which consists of two steps

1. Let **D1** be the family of binary relations over the base type S

$$\mathbf{D1} \ =_{df} \ S \leftrightarrow S$$

and $sem1$ a semantic function of the language **L** over the domain **D1**. To introduce a new feature to **L** we construct an enriched type

$$T =_{df} extend(S)$$

and its link with the original type S

$$\rho : S \leftrightarrow T$$

Let $\mathbf{D2} =_{df} T \leftrightarrow T$. The semantic function $sem2 : \mathbf{L} \rightarrow \mathbf{D2}$ is required to establish the commuting diagram

$$sem1(P); \rho = \rho; sem2(P) \quad (3)$$

2. The second step is to characterise the defining properties of programs in the enriched domain **D2**. Such algebraic laws, often called *healthiness conditions*, are only valid for real programs. $sem2(P)$ is selected among the healthy solutions of the equation (3).

The rest of this paper illustrates how to calculate $sem2$ directly from the equation (3) and the healthiness conditions by investigating a number of well-known programming features, including nontermination, deadlock, communication and probability.

2 Linear Equation and Its Solution

This section deals with two issues related to the equation (3) of Section 1:

1. Under which condition on the relation P, the linear equation

$$P; X = R$$

has solutions.
2. Properties of solutions of linear equations

Let P, Q and R be predicates with free variables s and s' of the type S, representing binary relations over the set S. The notation id_S denotes the identity relation on S. We use $\breve{P}$ to denote the converse of the relation P

$$\breve{P} =_{df} P[s, s'/s', s]$$

We use $P \lhd Q \rhd R$ to stand for the conditional

$$(P \wedge Q) \vee (\neg Q \wedge R)$$

The notation $P; Q$ stands for the sequential composition of P and Q

$$P; Q =_{df} \exists m \bullet (P[m/s'] \wedge Q[m/s])$$

where the substitution $P[m/s']$ gives a version of P where all occurrences of s' have been replaced by the free variable m. The notation $P \backslash R$ denotes the *weakest postspecification* [5] of P with respect to R, which is defined by the Galois connection

$$(P; X) \Rightarrow R \quad \text{if and only if} \quad X \Rightarrow P \backslash R \qquad \text{for all } X : S \leftrightarrow S$$

where the symbol $\Rightarrow$ stands for logical implication, i.e., validity for all values of free variables contained in either side. The weakest prespecification R/P is defined in a dual way

$$(X;P) \Rightarrow R \quad \text{if and only if} \quad X \Rightarrow R/P \qquad \text{for all } X: S \leftrightarrow S$$

Theorem 2.1 (Existence of solution of linear equation)

$P;X = R$ has solutions if and only if $P;(P\backslash R) = R$

Proof.

$$\begin{array}{ll} P;X = R & \{\text{Def of } P\backslash R\} \\ \Rightarrow X \Rightarrow P\backslash R & \{;\ \text{is monotonic}\} \\ \Rightarrow (P;X) \Rightarrow (P;(P\backslash R)) & \{P;X = R\} \\ \Rightarrow R \Rightarrow (P;(P\backslash R)) & \{P;(P\backslash R) \Rightarrow R\} \\ \Rightarrow P;(P\backslash R) = R & \square \end{array}$$

Theorem 2.2

If there exists Q such that $P;Q;R = R$, then $P;(P\backslash R) = R$

Proof.

$$\begin{array}{ll} (P;Q;R) = R & \{\text{Def of } \backslash\} \\ \Rightarrow (Q;R) \Rightarrow (P\backslash R) & \{;\ \text{is monotonic}\} \\ \Rightarrow P;(Q;R) \Rightarrow P;(P\backslash R) & \{P;Q;R = R\} \\ \Rightarrow R \Rightarrow P;(P\backslash R) & \{P;(P\backslash R) \Rightarrow R\} \\ \Rightarrow R = P;(P\backslash R) & \square \end{array}$$

Corollary. $\forall R \bullet\ P;(P\backslash R) = R$ if and only if $P;(P\backslash id_S) = id_S$

Proof. ($\Longrightarrow$): Let $R =_{df} id_S$

($\Longleftarrow$): From Theorem 2.2 and the fact that for all R

$$P;(P\backslash id_S);R = R \qquad \square$$

Theorem 2.3

If $P;(P\backslash id_S) = id_S$ then

$$P\backslash R = \neg(\breve{P};true) \vee (\breve{P};R)$$

Proof. From the assumption it follows that $P;\breve{P} = id_S$, i.e. $\breve{P}$ represents an injective function

$$\breve{P};true \Rightarrow \exists!\, s' \bullet \breve{P} \qquad (\spadesuit)$$

$$\begin{array}{ll} P\backslash R & \{\text{Def of } \backslash\} \\ = \forall t \bullet\ (P(t,s) \Rightarrow R(t,s')) & \{\text{case analysis}\} \\ = (\breve{P};true) \wedge \forall t \bullet (P(t,s) \Rightarrow R(t,s')) \vee & \\ \quad \neg(\breve{P};true) \wedge \forall t \bullet P(t,s) \Rightarrow R(t,s') & \{;\ \text{is monotonic}\} \end{array}$$

$$= (\breve{P}; true) \;\wedge\; \forall t \bullet (P(t,\, s) \Rightarrow R(t,\, s')) \;\vee$$
$$\neg(\breve{P}; true) \qquad \{\text{Conclusion } (\spadesuit)\}$$
$$= \breve{P}; R \;\vee\; \neg(\breve{P}; true) \qquad \Box$$

Corollary. (Disjunctivity)

If $P; (P \backslash id_S) \;=\; id_S$, then for any nonempty set I

$$P \backslash (\bigvee_{i \in I} R_i) \;=\; \bigvee_{i \in I} (P \backslash R_i)$$

Proof. From Theorem 2.3 and the disjunctivity of sequential composition. $\Box$

Theorem 2.4. (Distributivity)

If $P; (P \backslash id_S) \;=\; id_S$, then

$$P \backslash (R1; R2; P) \;=\; (P \backslash (R1; P)); (P \backslash (R2; P))$$

Proof.
$$RHS \qquad \{\text{Theorem 2.3}\}$$
$$= (\neg(\breve{P}; true) \vee \breve{P}; R1; P);$$
$$(\neg(\breve{P}; true) \vee \breve{P}; R2; P) \qquad \{P; \neg(\breve{P}; true) \;=\; false\}$$
$$= \neg(\breve{P}; true) \;\vee\; \breve{P}; R1; P; \breve{P}; R2; P \qquad \{P; \breve{P} \;=\; id_S\}$$
$$= \neg(\breve{P}; true) \;\vee\; \breve{P}; R1; R2; P \qquad \{\text{Theorem 2.3}\}$$
$$= LHS \qquad \Box$$

Beware that

$$(P; Q)^{\smile} \;=\; \breve{Q}; \breve{P}$$

which leads to the observation that the equation $X; P \;=\; R$ has solutions if and only if $\breve{P}; X \;= \breve{R}$ does so.

Theorem 2.5

The equation $X; P \;=\; R$ has solutions if and only if $(R/P); P \;=\; R$

Proof.
$$X; P \;=\; R \text{ has solutions} \qquad \{(P; Q)^{\smile} \;=\; \breve{Q}; \breve{P}\}$$
$$\equiv \breve{P}; X \;=\; \breve{R} \text{ has solutions} \qquad \{\text{Theorem 2.1}\}$$
$$\equiv \breve{P}; (\breve{P} \backslash \breve{R}) \;=\; \breve{R} \qquad \{P \backslash R \;=\; \neg(\breve{P}; \neg R)\}$$
$$\equiv \breve{P}; \neg(P; \neg\breve{R}) \;=\; \breve{R} \qquad \{(P; Q)^{\smile} \;=\; \breve{Q}; \breve{P}\}$$
$$\equiv \breve{P}; \neg(\neg R; \breve{P})^{\smile} \;=\; \breve{R} \qquad \{R/P \;=\; \neg(\neg R; \breve{P})\}$$
$$\equiv (R/P); P \;=\; R \qquad \Box$$

Theorem 2.6

$\forall R \bullet (R/P); P \;=\; R$ if and only if $((id_S/P); P) \;=\; id_S$

Proof. From the duality between $\backslash$ and $/$ we conclude that

$$\breve{R}/\breve{P} \;=\; (P \backslash R)^{\smile}$$

$$\begin{aligned} &\forall R \bullet (R/P);P = R && \{(P;Q)^{\smile} = \breve{Q};\breve{P}\} \\ &\equiv \forall R \bullet \breve{P};(\breve{P}\backslash R) = R && \{\text{Theorem 2.2}\} \\ &\equiv \breve{P};(\breve{P}\backslash id_S) = id_S && \{\breve{id_S} = id_S\} \\ &\equiv (id_S/P);P = id_S && \square \end{aligned}$$

Theorem 2.7

If $(id_S/P);P = id_S$ then

$$R/P = \neg(true;\breve{P}) \vee R;\breve{P} \qquad \square$$

Theorem 2.8. (Distributivity)

If $(id_S/P);P = id_S$, then

(1) $(R1 \lhd b(s) \rhd R2)/P = (R1/P) \lhd b(s) \rhd (R2/P)$

(2) $(\bigvee_{i\in I} R_i)/P = \bigvee_{i\in I}(R_i/P)$ for all nonempty set I $\square$

3 Termination

Let $S =_{df} (VAR \rightarrow VAL)$ be the base type. A program can be modelled by a predicate which represents a binary relation on S identifying the relationship between the initial and final states of program variables. The following table gives the definition of a simple programming language in this framework

Program	Meaning
$x := e$	$x' = e \wedge y' = y \wedge ... \wedge z' = z$
skip	$x' = x \wedge y' = y \wedge ... \wedge z' = z$
$P \sqcap Q$	$P \vee Q$
$P \lhd b(x) \rhd Q$	$P \wedge b(x) \vee \neg b(x) \wedge Q$
$P;Q$	$\exists m \bullet (P[m/s'] \wedge Q[m/s])$

where

- x and x' are used to represent the initial and final values of program variable x respectively.
- The execution of $x := e$ assigns the value of e to variable x and leaves other variables unchanged.
- The empty command **skip** has no effect at all. It leaves the values of all variables unchanged.

- The program $P \sqcap Q$ is executed by executing either P or Q.
- The conditional $P \lhd b \rhd Q$ behaves like P if the initial value of b is true, or like Q if the initial value of b is false.
- $P; Q$ is executed by first executing P, and when P is finished then Q is started. The final state of P is passed on as the initial state of Q, but this is only an intermediate state of $(P; Q)$, and cannot be directly observed. All we know is that it exists.

This simple model can not distinguish the terminating execution of a program from the non-terminating ones. To specify non-termination behaviour we introduce a pair of Boolean variables to denote the relevant observation:

1. *ok* records the observation that the program has been started.
2. *ok'* records the observation that the program has terminated. When the program fails to terminate, the value of *ok'* is not determinable.

We extend the base type S by adding the logical variable *ok*

$$T1 \;=_{df}\; S \times (\{ok\} \rightarrow Bool)$$

The original state of S will be seen as a terminating state in the extended type $T1$, and we thereby define the embedding ρ from S to $T1$ by

$$\rho \;=_{df}\; ok' \;\wedge\; (x' = x) \;\wedge\; ... \;\wedge\; (z' = z)$$

Let P and Q be predicates not containing *ok* and *ok'*. For notational convenience we use $P \vdash Q$ to represent the predicate

$$(ok \wedge P) \Rightarrow (ok' \wedge Q)$$

which called a *design* [6].

We mention here some logical properties of designs that will be useful in later calculation; they are proved elsewhere [6]

Theorem 3.1

(1) $(b1 \vdash R1); (b2 \vdash R2) \;=\; (b \wedge \neg(R1; \neg b2)) \vdash (R1; R2)$

(2) $(b1 \vdash R1) \vee (b2 \vdash R2) \;=\; (b1 \wedge b2) \vdash (R1 \vee R2)$

(3) $(b1 \vdash R1) \wedge (b2 \vdash R2) \;=\; (b1 \vee b2) \vdash ((b1 \Rightarrow R1) \wedge (b2 \Rightarrow R2))$

(4) $(b1 \vdash R1) \lhd b \rhd (b2 \vdash R2) \;=\; (b1 \lhd b \rhd b2) \vdash (R1 \lhd b \rhd R2)$ □

For any predicate P representing a binary relation on S, we define its image P^* on the enriched domain $T \leftrightarrow T$ as the weakest solution of the equation

$$\rho; X \;=\; P; \rho$$ □

Theorem 3.2 (Weakest solution)

The equation $\rho; X \;=\; P; \rho$ has the weakest solution

$$P^* \;=\; true \vdash P$$

Proof. It is clear that

$$\rho; (x' = x \ \wedge \ ... \ \wedge \ z' = z) \ = \ (x' = x \ \wedge \ ... \ \wedge \ z' = z)$$

¿From Theorems 2.1 and 2.2 it follows that the weakest solution of the equation is

$$\begin{aligned} & \rho \backslash (P; \rho) && \{\text{Def of ; }\} \\ = \ & \rho \backslash (P \wedge ok') && \{\text{Theorem 2.3}\} \\ = \ & \neg(\breve{\rho}; true) \ \vee \ \breve{\rho}; (P \wedge ok') && \{\text{Def of ; }\} \\ = \ & \neg ok \ \vee \ (P \wedge ok') && \{\text{Def of } P \vdash Q\} \\ = \ & true \vdash P && \square \end{aligned}$$

The new definition of primitive commands of our programming language is given by the following table.

Program	Meaning
skip	$(x' = x \ \wedge \ ... \ \wedge \ z' = z)^* \ = \ true \vdash (x' = x \ \wedge \ ... \ \wedge \ z' = z)$
$x := e$	$(x' = e \ \wedge \ ... \wedge \ z' = z)^* \ = \ true \vdash (x' = e \ \wedge \ ... \ \wedge \ z' = z)$

The linking function $*$ is a homomorphism from the original domain $S \leftrightarrow S$ to the enriched domain $T1 \leftrightarrow T1$

Theorem 3.3

(1) $(P; Q)^* \ = \ P^*; Q^*$

(2) $(P \vee Q)^* \ = \ P^* \vee Q^*$

(3) $(P \wedge Q)^* \ = \ P^* \wedge Q^*$

(4) $(P \lhd b \rhd Q)^* \ = \ P^* \lhd b \rhd Q^*$

Proof (1) : From Theorem 1.4.

(2) : From Corollary of Theorem 1.3.

(3) : From the conjunctivity of $\backslash$ and the fact that

$$(P \ \wedge \ Q); \rho \ = \ (P; \rho) \ \wedge \ (Q; \rho)$$

(4) : From the fact that

$$\breve{\rho}; (P \lhd b \rhd Q) \ = \ (\breve{\rho}; P) \lhd b \rhd (\breve{\rho}; Q) \qquad \square$$

4 Deadlock

For reactive programming paradigms (such as shared-variable concurrency), we are required to distinguish a complete terminated computation from an incomplete one that is suspended. The former is used to specify the case where the program has finished its execution, but the latter suggests that the program cannot proceed further without an interaction with its environment. For example, a synchronisation command

$$\mathbf{wait}(v = 0)$$

can not be executed unless the value of v is set to zero, perhaps by some other programs in its environment.

We introduce a Boolean variable *wait* into the type $T1$ defined in Section 3,

$$T2 \ =_{df} \ T1 \times (\{wait\} \to Bool)$$

The variable *wait* takes the value false if and only when the program has completed its execution.

The introduction of waiting states has implication for sequential composition: all the waiting observation of P are of course also waiting observations of $P; Q$. Control can pass from P to Q when P is in final state, distinguished by the fact that $wait'$ is false. Rather than change the definition of sequential composition of our programming language, we enforce these rules by means of a healthiness condition. If a program Q is asked to start in a waiting state of its predecessor, it leaves the state unchanged.

$$Q \ = \ II \lhd wait \rhd Q \qquad \textbf{(H1)}$$

where the predicate II adopts the following meaning in this section

$$II \ =_{df} \ true \vdash (wait' = wait \ \wedge \ x' = x \ \wedge \ ... \ \wedge \ z' = z)$$

A predicate representing a binary relation on $T2$ is *healthy* it it satisfies the condition (**H1**).

The embedding from $T1$ to $T2$ is defined by

$$\rho \ =_{df} \ true \vdash (\neg wait' \ \wedge \ x' = x \ \wedge \ ... \ \wedge \ z' = z)$$

which leaves divergent observation unchanged and maps terminating states to complete ones in the extended space $T2$.

For any design $d \ = \ b(v) \vdash R(v, v')$ in the domain $T1 \leftrightarrow T1$, we define its image d^* in the extended domain $T2 \leftrightarrow T2$ as the weakest healthy solution of the equation

$$\rho; X \ = \ d; \rho \qquad \square$$

Theorem 4.1

$d^* \ = \ II \lhd wait \rhd (\rho \backslash (d; \rho))$

Proof. Let $I =_{df} true \vdash (x' = x \ \wedge ... \wedge \ z' = z)$. We can show using Theorem 3.1 that

$$\rho; I; d \ = \ I; d \ = \ d$$

from which and Theorem 2.2 we conclude that

$$\rho; (\rho \backslash (d; \rho)) \ = \ d; \rho \qquad (\clubsuit)$$

Furthermore

$$\begin{aligned} & \rho; d^* && \{\text{Def of } d^*\} \\ =\ & \rho; (II \lhd wait \rhd \rho \backslash (d; \rho)) && \{\text{assignment distributes over } \lhd b \rhd\} \\ =\ & (\rho; II) \lhd false \rhd (\rho; (\rho \backslash (d; \rho))) && \{\text{Conclusion } (\clubsuit)\} \\ =\ & d; \rho \end{aligned}$$

which indicates d^* is the weakest healthy solution of the equation. □

Corollary

$(b \vdash R)^* \ = \ II \lhd wait \rhd (b \vdash (R \wedge \neg wait'))$

Proof. From Theorems 2.3 and 4.1. □

The link $*$ is also a homomorphism.

Theorem 4.2

(1) $(d1; d2)^* \ = \ d1^*; d2^*$

(2) $(d1 \vee d2)^* \ = \ d1^* \vee d2^*$

(3) $(d1 \wedge d2)^* \ = \ d1^* \wedge d2^*$

(4) $(d1 \lhd b \rhd d2)^* \ = \ d1^* \lhd b \rhd d2^*$

Proof. The conclusion follows from Corollary of Theorem 4.1 and Theorem 3.1. □

5 Communication

A communicating sequence process may perform many successive actions and we assume that they can be recorded sequentially in the order in which they occur. We use $\mathcal{A}$ to represent the set of all actions which are logically possible for the processes. The sequence of interactions recorded to some given moment in time in called a *trace*; this is abbreviated to tr and is included in the state space

$$T3 =_{df} T1 \times (\{tr\} \rightarrow \mathbf{seq}(\mathcal{A}))$$

We use $<>$ to represent the empty trace. For s, $t \in \mathbf{seq}(\mathcal{A})$, we use $s \cdot t$ to denote the catenation of s and t, and $s \leq t$ to indicate s is a prefix of t.

Since the execution of a process can never *undo* any action performed previously, the trace can only get longer. The current value of tr must therefore be an extension of its initial value. The predicate which describes a communicating process must therefore imply this fact. So it satisfies the healthiness condition

$$P \;=\; P \wedge (tr \leq tr') \qquad \textbf{(H2)}$$

Note that the sequence $tr' - tr$ represents the trace of actions in which the process itself has engaged from the moment that it starts to the moment of observation.

The purpose of the undashed variable tr is to permit reuse in the theory of communicating processes of the same definition of sequential composition as in the models of the previous sections. In fact this variable plays no other significant role. In particular it has no inference on the behaviour of the process. So a communicating process also satisfies a second healthiness condition

$$P(tr,\, tr') \;=\; P(<>,\, (tr' - tr)) \qquad \textbf{(H3)}$$

A predicate representing a binary relation on $T3$ is *healthy* if it satisfies the conditions (**H2**) and (**H3**).

The embedding from $T1$ to $T3$ is defined by

$$\rho =_{df} true \vdash (tr' = <> \;\wedge\; x' = x \;\wedge\; ... \;\wedge\; z' = z)$$

which ascribes tr to the empty sequence, and keeps the values of program variables unchanged.

For any design $d \;=\; b(v) \vdash R(v,\, v')$ in the domain $T1 \leftrightarrow T1$, we define its image d^* in the extended domain $T2 \leftrightarrow T2$ as the weakest healthy solution of the equation

$$\rho; X \;=\; d; \rho \qquad \square$$

Theorem 5.1

$(b \vdash R)^* \;=\; (b \vdash (R \wedge tr = tr')) \;\wedge\; (tr \;\leq\; tr')$

Proof. It is routine to show that the predicate $U \;=_{df}\; (b \vdash (R \wedge tr = tr')) \wedge (tr \leq tr')$ is a healthy solution of the equation $\rho; X \;=\; (b \vdash R); \rho$. We are going to prove that it is the weakest healthy solution. Let P be a healthy solution of the equation, and $V \;=\; b \vdash (R \wedge (tr' = tr))$, and $W \;=\; (b \wedge tr = <>) \vdash (R \wedge tr' = <>)$.

$$
\begin{array}{ll}
\rho; P \;=\; (b \vdash R); \rho & \{\text{Def of } \backslash\} \\
\Rightarrow P(tr,\, tr') \Rightarrow \rho \backslash ((b \vdash R); \rho) & \{X \backslash Y \;=\; \neg(\breve{X}; \neg Y)\} \\
\equiv P(tr,\, tr') \Rightarrow W & \{\text{Let } tr,\, tr' \;=\; <>,\, tr' - tr\} \\
\Rightarrow P(<>,\, tr' - tr) \Rightarrow V & \{P \text{ satisfies } \textbf{H2}\} \\
\Rightarrow P(<>,\, tr' - tr) \Rightarrow U & \{P \text{ satisfies } \textbf{H3}\} \\
\Rightarrow P(tr,\, tr') \Rightarrow U & \square
\end{array}
$$

The link $*$ enjoys the same properties as the links presented in the previous sections.

Theorem 5.2

(1) $(d1; d2)^* \;=\; d1^*; d2^*$

(2) $(d1 \vee d2)^* \;=\; d1^* \vee d2^*$

(3) $(d1 \wedge d2)^* \;=\; d1^* \wedge d2^*$

(4) $(d1 \lhd b \rhd d2)^* \;=\; d1^* \lhd b \rhd d2^*$

Proof. Similar to Theorem 4.2. □

6 Probability

For probabilistic programming, an observation is a probability distribution over the final states of program variables. The set of all distribution functions is

$$T4 \;=_{df}\; \{prob : S \rightarrow [0,\, 1] \mid \Sigma_{s \in S}\, prob(s) = 1\}$$

The difference between the model of Section 3 and the probabilistic semantics is that the former tells us which final states are or are not possible, whereas the latter tells us the probability with which they may occur. To relate these frameworks we take the view that a final state is possible in the relational description of a program in Section 3 if it has positive probability of occurrence in the probabilistic model. The mapping χ from $T4$ to $T1$ relates a probabilistic distribution *prob* to a set of standard states s' according to the definition

$$\chi(ok,\, prob,\, ok',\, s') \;=_{df}\; true \vdash prob(s') > 0$$

For any design $d \;=\; b \vdash R$ representing a binary relation on $T1$, its embedding d^* is defined as the weakest solution of the equation

$$X \,;\, \chi \;=\; d$$ □

Theorem 6.1

$(b \vdash R)^* \;=\; b \vdash (prob'(R) = 1)$

where $prob'(R)$ abbreviates $prob'(\{t \mid R(s,t)\})$.

Proof.

LHS	{Theorem 2.6}
$= (b \vdash R)/\chi$	$\{(b \vdash R)/(true \vdash Q) \;=\; b \vdash (R/Q)\}$
$= b \vdash (R/prob(s') > 0)$	$\{X/Y \;=\; \neg(\neg X; \check{Y})\}$
$= b \vdash prob'(t \mid R(s,\, t)) = 1$	

□

The new definition of primitive commands is given by calculation

Primitive command	Meaning
skip	$true \vdash prob'(s) = 1$
$x := e$	$true \vdash prob'(s[e/x]) = 1$

The linking function $*$ distributes over conditional.

Theorem 6.2

$(d1 \lhd b \rhd d2)^* \;=\; d1^* \lhd b \rhd d2^*$

Proof. From Theorem 2.8. □

We now use the linking function $*$ to discover the appropriate definition for demonic choice between probabilistic programs.

Theorem 6.3. (New definition for demonic choice)

$(d1 \;\vee\; d2)^* \;=\; d1^* \;\vee\; d2^* \;\vee\; \bigvee_{0<r<1}(d1^* \|_{M_r} d2^*)$

where M_r is a coupling predicate in the style of [6] used in this case as

$$(b1 \vdash R1)\|_{M_r}(b2 \vdash R2) \;=_{df}$$
$$((b1 \wedge b2) \vdash (R1(s,\, 1.prob') \wedge R1(s,\, 2.prob')) \;;\; M_r$$

and $M_r \;=_{df}\; true \vdash (prob' \;=\; r \times 1.prob + (1-r) \times 2.prob)$.

Proof. Let $d1 \;=\; b1 \vdash R1$ and $d2 \;=\; b2 \vdash R2$, and $R \;=\; R1 \vee R2$.

$$\begin{array}{ll}
RHS & \{\text{Theorem 3.1}\} \\
= b1 \vdash (prob'(R1) = 1) \;\vee\; (b2 \vdash prob'(R2) = 1) \;\vee & \\
\quad \bigvee_{0<r<1}(b1 \wedge b2) \vdash \exists 1.prob,\, 2.prob \,\bullet & \\
= 1.prob(R1) = 1 \;\wedge\; 2.prob(R2) = 1 \;\wedge & \\
\quad prob' \;=\; r \times 1.prob + (1-r) \times 2.prob & \{prob'(R) = 1\} \\
\Rightarrow b1 \vdash (prob'(R1) = 1) \;\vee\; (b2 \vdash prob'(R2) = 1) \;\vee & \\
\quad (b1 \wedge b2) \vdash prob'(R) = 1 & \{\text{Theorem 3.1}\} \\
= (b1 \wedge b2) \vdash prob'(R) = 1 & \{\text{Theorem 6.1}\} \\
= ((b1 \wedge b2) \vdash R)^* & \{\text{Theorem 3.1}\} \\
= LHS & \{\text{Theorem 6.1}\}
\end{array}$$

$$
\begin{array}{ll}
= (b1 \wedge b2) \vdash & \{\text{let } r = \alpha/(\alpha+\beta) \\
\quad (prob'(R1) = 1 \ \vee \ prob'(R2) = 1 \ \vee & 1.prob(R1 \wedge \neg R2) = \alpha + \beta \\
\quad \exists \alpha, \beta > 0 \ \bullet \ prob'(R) = 1 \ \wedge & 1.prob(R1 \wedge R2) = 1 - (\alpha+\beta) \\
\quad prob'(R1 \wedge \neg R2) = \alpha \ \wedge & 2.prob(R2 \wedge \neg R1) = \alpha + \beta \\
\quad prob'(R2 \wedge \neg R1) = \beta & 2.prob(R1 \wedge R2) = 1 - (\alpha+\beta)\} \\
\Rightarrow (b1 \wedge b2) \vdash & \\
\quad (prob'(R1) = 1 \ \vee \ prob'(R2) = 1 \ \vee & \\
\quad \exists r \in (0,1),\, 1.prob, 2.prob \bullet & \\
\quad 1.prob(R1) = 1 \ \wedge \ 2.prob(R2) = 1 \ \wedge & \\
\quad prob' \ = \ r \times 1.prob + (1-r) \times 2.prob & \{\text{Def of } \|_M\} \\
= RHS & \Box
\end{array}
$$

For sequential composition we follow the Kleisli-triple approach to semantics of programming languages [8], introducing a function $\uparrow$ to deal with sequential composition, which maps a predicate representing a member of $T1 \leftrightarrow T4$ to a 'lifted' one representing a binary relation on $T4$

$$
\begin{array}{l}
\uparrow (b(s) \vdash U(s,\, prob')) \ =_{df} \\
(prob(b) = 1) \ \vdash \exists Q \in (S \rightarrow T4) \bullet \\
\forall s \bullet \ (prob(s) > 0 \Rightarrow \ U(s,\, Q(s)) \ \wedge \ prob' = \Sigma_{t \in S}\, (prob(t) \times Q(t))
\end{array}
$$

Theorem 6.4. (Distributivity of the linking function)
$(d1; d2)^* \ = \ d1^* \,;\, \uparrow d2^*$

Proof. Let $d1 \ = \ b1 \vdash R1$, $d2 \ = \ b2 \vdash R2$, and define

$$V(s,\, t,\, v) \ =_{df} \ R1(s,\, t) \wedge R2(t,\, v)$$

$$
\begin{array}{ll}
\quad RHS & \{\text{Theorem 6.1}\} \\
= (b1 \vdash prob'(\{t \mid R1(s,t)\}) = 1)\,; & \\
\quad prob(b2) = 1 \vdash \exists Q \ \bullet & \\
\quad \forall t \bullet (prob(t) > 0 \Rightarrow Q(t)(\{s' \mid R2(t,\, s')\}) = 1) \ \wedge & \\
\quad prob' = \Sigma_t(prob(t) \times Q(t))) & \{\text{Theorem 3.1}\} \\
= b1 \ \wedge \ \neg(prob'(\{t \mid R1(s,t)\}) = 1\,;\, prob(b2) < 1) & \\
\quad \vdash & \\
\quad \exists \phi \bullet \ \phi(\{t \mid R1(s,t)\}) = 1 \ \wedge & \\
\quad prob' = \Sigma_s\{\phi(t) \times Q(t) \mid & \\
\quad \phi(t) > 0 \ \wedge \ Q(t)(\{s' \mid R1(t,s')\}) = 1\} & \{\text{Simplification}\}
\end{array}
$$

$= b1 \wedge \neg(R1; \neg b2) \vdash$

$\exists \phi \bullet \phi(\{t \mid R1(s,t)\}) = 1 \wedge$

$prob' = \Sigma_s\{\phi(t) \times Q(t) \mid$ $\quad\{prob'(R1; R2) =$

$\phi(t) > 0 \wedge$ $\quad\Sigma_t\{\phi(t) \times Q(t)(\{s' | R2(t, s')\}) \mid$

$Q(t)(\{s' \mid R1(t, s')\}) = 1\}$ $\quad R1(s, t) \wedge \phi(t) > 0\}\}$

$\Rightarrow b1 \wedge \neg(R1; \neg b2) \vdash$

$prob'(R1; R2) = 1$ $\quad$ {Theorem 6.1}

$= LHS$ $\quad\{\text{let } f(u, v) = prob'(v)/(\#\{t|V(s, t, v)\}) \lhd V(u) \rhd 0,$

$\phi(u) = \Sigma_v f(u, v),$

$Q(u)(v) = f(u, v)/\phi(u) \text{ if } \phi(u) > 0\}$

$\Rightarrow b1(s) \wedge \neg(R1; \neg b2) \vdash$

$\exists \phi \bullet \phi(\{t \mid R1(s,t)\}) = 1 \wedge$

$prob' = \Sigma_s\{\phi(t) \times Q(t) \mid$

$\phi(t) > 0 \wedge$

$Q(t)(\{s' \mid R2(t, s')\}) = 1\}$ $\quad$ {Theorems 3.1 and 6.1}

$= RHS$ $\quad\square$

7 Conclusion

The commuting diagram approach has been used for support of data refinement in the state-oriented development methods [1,7,9,10], where the embedding ρ is designed to connect abstract data type with its concrete representation. It is also used for data abstraction in model checking by dramatically reducing the size of state space. This paper illustrates another way of using the commuting diagram to derive enriched semantics.

References

1. Back, R.-J.R.: A calculus for program derivations. Acta Informatica 25, 593–624 (1988)
2. Jifeng, H., Seidel, K., McIver, A.: Probabilistic models for the Guarded Command Language. Science of Computer Programming 28, 171–192 (1997)
3. Hehner, E.C.R.: Predicative Programming: Part 1 and 2. Communications of the ACM 27(2), 134–151 (1984)
4. Hehner, E.C.R., Hoare, C.A.R.: A more complete model of communicating processes. Theoretical Computer Sciences 26(1), 105–120 (1983)
5. Hoare, C.A.R., Jifeng, H.: Weakest prespecifications. Fundamenta Informaticae IX, 51–84, 217–252 (1986)
6. Hoare, C.A.R., Jifeng, H.: Unifying theories of programming. Prentice-Hall, Englewood Cliffs (1998)

7. Jones, C.B.: Systematic Software Development Using VDM. Prentice-Hall, Englewood Cliffs (1986)
8. Moggi, E.: Notations of computation and monads. Information and Computation 93, 55–92 (1986)
9. Morris, J.M.: A theoretical basis for stepwise refinement and the programming calculus. Science of Computer Programming 9(3), 287–306 (1987)
10. de Roever, W.P., Engelhardt, K.: Data Refinement: Model-oriented Proof Methods and Their Comparison. Cambridge University Press, Cambridge (1998)

Discovering Non-linear Ranking Functions by Solving Semi-algebraic Systems*

Yinghua Chen[1], Bican Xia[1], Lu Yang[2], Naijun Zhan **,[3], and Chaochen Zhou[3]

[1] LMAM & School of Mathematical Sciences, Peking University
[2] Institute of Theoretical Computing,, East China Normal University
[3] Lab. of Computer Science, Institute of Software, Chinese Academy of Sciences

Abstract. Differing from [6] this paper reduces non-linear ranking function discovering for polynomial programs to semi-algebraic system solving, and demonstrates how to apply the symbolic computation tools, DISCOVERER and QEPCAD, to some interesting examples.

Keywords: Program Verification, Loop Termination, Ranking Function, Polynomial Programs, Semi-Algebraic Systems, Computer Algebra, DISCOVERER, QEPCAD.

1 Introduction

The design of reliable software is a grand challenge in computer science [17] in the 21st century, as our modern life becomes more and more computerized. One of the bases for designing reliable software is the correctness of programs. The dominant approach to automatic program verification is the so-called *Floyd-Hoare-Dijkstra's inductive assertion method* [8,10,11], by using *pre-* and *post-* conditions, loop invariants and proving loop termination through ranking functions, etc. Therefore, the discovery of loop invariants and ranking functions plays a central role in proving the correctness of programs and is also thought of as the most challenging part of the approach.

The classical method for establishing termination of a program is the use of well-founded domain together with so-called ranking function that maps the state space of the program to the domain. Termination is then concluded by demonstrating that each step as the program moves forwards decreases the measure assigned by the ranking function. As there can be no infinite descending chain of elements in a well-founded domain, any execution of the program must eventually terminate. Clearly, the existence of such a ranking function for any given program implies its termination. Recently, the synthesis of ranking functions draws increasing attention, and some heuristics concerning how to automatically generate linear ranking functions for linear programs have been proposed

* The work is in part supported by the projects NKBRPC-2002cb312200, 2004CB318003, 2005CB321902, and NSFC-60493200, 60421001, 60573007.

** The corresponding author: South Fourth Street, No. 4, Zhong Guan Cun, Beijing, 100080, P.R. China, `znj@ios.ac.cn`

C.B. Jones, Z. Liu, J. Woodcock (Eds.): ICTAC 2007, LNCS 4711, pp. 34–49, 2007.

[7,5,13]. [7] proposed a heuristic strategy to synthesize a linear ranking function according to the syntax of a linear program. Since in many cases there does not exist obvious correlation between the syntax of a program and its ranking functions, this approach is very restrictive. Notably, [5] utilized the theory of polyhedra to synthesize linear ranking function of linear programs, and [13] first presented a complete method to find out linear ranking functions for a class of linear programs that have only single path without nested loop, in the sense that if there exists a linear ranking function for a program in the class, then the method can eventually discover it.

Existence of ranking function is only a sufficient condition on the termination of a program. It is easy to construct programs that terminate, but have no ranking functions. Furthermore, even if a (linear) program has ranking functions, it may not have a linear ranking function. we will show this point by an example later in the paper. Besides, it is well-known that the termination of programs is undecidable in general, even for the class of linear programs [16] or a simple class of polynomial programs [2]. In contrast to the above approach, [16,1] tried to identify decidable subclasses and proved the decidability of the termination problem for a special class of linear programs over reals and integers, respectively. [27] further developed the work of [16] by calculating symbolic (sufficient) conditions for the termination of its subclasses through computer algebra tool, DISCOVERER.

Linear programs with linear ranking functions compose a very small class of programs. As to polynomial programs, [2] proposed an incomplete method to decide whether a polynomial program terminates by using the technique of finite difference tree. However, [2] can only tackle very simple polynomial programs, that have 'polynomial behaviour'.

In 2005, [6] presented a very general approach to ranking function discovery as well as invariant generation of polynomial programs by parametric abstraction, Lagrangian relaxation and semidefinite programming. The basic idea of the approach is: first the program semantics is expressed in polynomial form; then the unknown ranking function and invariants are abstracted in parametric form; the verification conditions are abstracted as numerical constraints of the parameters through Lagrangian relaxation; the remaining universal quantifications are handled by semidefinite programming; finally the parameters are computed using semidefinite programming solvers. [6] does not directly use the first-order quantifier elimination method due to its bad complexity of doubly exponential[1]. Therefore the approach of [6] is incomplete in the sense that for some program that may have ranking functions and invariants of the predefined form, however applying the approach cannot find them, as Lagrangian relaxation and over-approximation of the positive semi-definiteness of a polynomial are applied.

We here use *semi-algebraic transition system* (SATS), which is an extension of algebraic transition systems in [14], to represent polynomial programs. Then, for a loop in a given SATS (i.e. a given polynomial program), we can first assume

[1] [6] does not provide information about complexity of its own approach. But we are afraid that the complexity of the semidefinite programming, in particular, when the Gram Matrix method is involved, is also bad.

to be a ranking function a polynomial in its program variables with parametric coefficients. In order to determine the parameters, we translate the definition of ranking functions in regard with the predefined polynomial into several SASs, and prove that the polynomial is a ranking function of the loop if and only if each of these SASs has no real solutions. After the translation we apply the functions of root classification for parametric SASs [22,23,24] (and real root isolation for constant SASs [20] if needed) of DISCOVERER to each of these SASs to generate conditions on the parameters. If some universally quantified program variables remain in the resulted conditions, in order to acquire a condition only on the parameters, we can apply QEPCAD to eliminate the remaining quantifiers. In case that the final condition on parameters is still very complicated, applying PCAD (partial cylindrical algebra decomposition [4]) included in both DISCOVERER and QEPCAD, we can conclude whether the condition can be satisfied. If yes, we can further apply PCAD to get the instantiations of these parameters, and therefore achieve a specific polynomial ranking function as necessary. If not, we can define another polynomial template and repeat the above procedure. So our approach does not compromise its completeness. As to the complexity of the approach, DISCOVERER functions on root classification and real root isolation for SASs include algorithms, such as Wu's triangularization [18], to eliminate variables through equalities in SASs with a cost of singly exponential in the number of variables and parameters. Hence, the application of these algorithms can dramatically ease the application of other algorithms of DISCOVERER, QEPCAD and/or PCAD, although they still cost doubly exponential but in the number of *remaining* variables and parameters. A detailed analysis of the complexity will be published in a later paper. In this paper, by briefing the theories behind DISCOVERER we show why the tool works and by applying to examples we show how the tool discovers ranking functions for polynomial programs.

The rest of this paper is structured as follows: Section 2 presents a brief review of the theories and tools of semi-algebraic systems, in particular, the theories on root classification of parametric semi-algebraic systems and on real root isolation of constant SASs, and their implementations in the computer algebra tool DISCOVERER; We extend the notion of algebraic transition systems of [14] to semi-algebraic transition system to represent polynomial programs in Section 3; In Section 4, we use examples to illustrate the reduction of non-linear ranking function discovering to SAS solving; and Section 5 draws a summary and discusses future work.

2 Theories and Tools on Solving Semi-algebraic Systems

In this section, we introduce the theories and the tool DISCOVERER [2] on solving SASs.

---

[2] DISCOVERER can be downloaded at http://www.is.pku.edu.cn/~xbc/ discoverer.html

2.1 Semi-algebraic Systems

Let $\mathcal{K}$ be a field, $X = \{x_1, \cdots, x_n\}$ a set of indeterminates, and $\mathcal{K}[x_1, ..., x_n]$ the ring of polynomials in the n indeterminates with coefficients in $\mathcal{K}$, ranged over $p(x_1, \ldots, x_n)$ with possible subscription and superscription. Let the variables be ordered as $x_1 \prec x_2 \prec \cdots \prec x_n$. Then, the *leading variable* of a polynomial p is the variable with the biggest index which indeed occurs in p. If the leading variable of a polynomial p is x_k, p can be collected w.r.t its leading variable as $p = c_m x_k^m + \cdots + c_0$ where m is the *degree* of p w.r.t. x_k and c_is are polynomials in $\mathcal{K}[x_1, ..., x_{k-1}]$. We call $c_m x_k^m$ the *leading term* of p w.r.t. x_k and c_m the *leading coefficient*. For example, let $p(x_1, \ldots, x_5) = x_2^6 x_3 + 2x_1^4 x_4^4 + (3x_2 x_3 + x_1)x_4^5$, so, its leading variable, term and coefficient are x_4, $(3x_2x_3 + x_1)x_4^5$ and $3x_2x_3 + x_1$, respectively.

An*atomic polynomial formula* over $\mathcal{K}[x_1, ..., x_n]$ is of the form $p(x_1, \ldots, x_n) \rhd 0$, where $\rhd \in \{=, >, \geq, \neq\}$, while a *polynomial formula* over $\mathcal{K}[x_1, ..., x_n]$ is constructed from atomic polynomial formulae by applying the logical connectives. Conjunctive polynomial formulae are those that are built from atomic polynomial formulae with the logical operator $\wedge$. We will denote by $PF(\{x_1, \ldots, x_n\})$ the set of polynomial formulae and by $CPF(\{x_1, \ldots, x_n\})$ the set of conjunctive polynomial formulae, respectively.

In what follows, we will use $\mathbb{Q}$ to stand for rationales and $\mathbb{R}$ for reals, and fix $\mathcal{K}$ to be $\mathbb{Q}$. In fact, all results discussed below can be applied to $\mathbb{R}$.

In the following, the n indeterminates are divided into two groups: $\mathbf{u} = (u_1, ..., u_d)$ and $\mathbf{x} = (x_1, ..., x_s)$, which are called parameters and variables, respectively, and we sometimes use "," to denote the conjunction of atomic formulae for simplicity.

Definition 1. *A semi-algebraic system is a conjunctive polynomial formula of the following form:*

$$\begin{cases} p_1(\mathbf{u}, \mathbf{x}) = 0, ..., p_r(\mathbf{u}, \mathbf{x}) = 0, \\ g_1(\mathbf{u}, \mathbf{x}) \geq 0, ..., g_k(\mathbf{u}, \mathbf{x}) \geq 0, \\ g_{k+1}(\mathbf{u}, \mathbf{x}) > 0, ..., g_t(\mathbf{u}, \mathbf{x}) > 0, \\ h_1(\mathbf{u}, \mathbf{x}) \neq 0, ..., h_m(\mathbf{u}, \mathbf{x}) \neq 0, \end{cases} \tag{1}$$

where $r > 1, t \geq k \geq 0, m \geq 0$ and all p_i's, g_i's and h_i's are in $\mathbb{Q}[\mathbf{u}, \mathbf{x}] \setminus \mathbb{Q}$. An SAS of the form (1) is called parametric *if $d \neq 0$, otherwise* constant.

An SAS of the form (1) is usually denoted by a quadruple $[\mathbb{P}, \mathbb{G}_1, \mathbb{G}_2, \mathbb{H}]$, where $\mathbb{P} = [p_1, ..., p_r], \mathbb{G}_1 = [g_1, ..., g_k], \mathbb{G}_2 = [g_{k+1}, ..., g_t]$ and $\mathbb{H} = [h_1, ..., h_m]$.

For a constant SAS S, interesting questions are how to compute the number of real solutions of S, and if the number is finite, how to compute these real solutions. For a parametric SAS, the interesting problem is so-called *real solution classification*, that is to determine the condition on the parameters such that the system has the prescribed number of distinct real solutions, possibly infinite.

2.2 Real Solution Classification

In this subsection, we give a sketch of our theory for real root classification of parametric SASs. For details, please be referred to [23,26].

A finite set of polynomials $\mathbb{T}: [T_1, ..., T_k]$ is called a *triangular set* if it is in the following form

$$\begin{aligned} T_1 &= T_1(x_1, ..., x_{i_1}), \\ T_2 &= T_2(x_1, ..., x_{i_1}, ..., x_{i_2}), \\ &\cdots\cdots \\ T_k &= T_k(x_1, ..., x_{i_1}, ..., x_{i_2}, ..., x_{i_k}), \end{aligned}$$

where x_i is the leading variable of T_i and $x_1 \preceq x_{i_1} \prec x_{i_2} \prec \cdots \prec x_{i_k} \preceq x_s$. For any given SAS S in the form of (1), where the variables in the order $x_1 \prec \cdots \prec x_s$ and all polynomials in S are viewed as polynomials in $\mathbb{Q}(\mathbf{u})[\mathbf{x}]$, we first decompose the equations in S into triangular sets, that is, we transform the polynomial set $\mathbb{P} = [p_1, ..., p_r]$ into a finite set $\mathcal{T} = \{\mathbb{T}_1, ..., \mathbb{T}_e\}$ where each $\mathbb{T}_i$ is a triangular set. Furthermore, this decomposition satisfies $\mathrm{Zero}(\mathbb{P}) = \bigcup_{i=1}^{e} \mathrm{Zero}(\mathbb{T}_i/J_i)$, where $\mathrm{Zero}(\mathbb{P})$ denotes the set of *common zeros* (in some extension of the field of rational numbers) of $p_1, ..., p_r$, $\mathrm{Zero}(\mathbb{T}_i/J_i) = \mathrm{Zero}(\mathbb{T}_i) \setminus \mathrm{Zero}(\{J_i\})$, where J_i is the product of *leading coefficients* of the polynomials in $\mathbb{T}_i$ for each i. It is well-known that the decomposition can be realized by some triangularization methods such as Wu's method [18].

Example 1. Consider an SAS $RS : [\mathbb{P}, \mathbb{G}_1, \mathbb{G}_2, \mathbb{H}]$ in $\mathbb{Q}[a, x, y, z]$ with $\mathbb{P} = [p_1, p_2, p_3]$, $\mathbb{G}_1 = [a - 1], \mathbb{G}_2 = \emptyset, \mathbb{H} = \emptyset$, where

$$p_1 = x^2 + y^2 - xy - 1,\ p_2 = y^2 + z^2 - yz - a^2,\ p_3 = z^2 + x^2 - zx - 1,$$

The equations $\mathbb{P}$ can be decomposed into three triangular sets in $\mathbb{Q}(a)[x, y, z]$

$$\begin{aligned} &\mathbb{T}_1 : [x^2 - ax + a^2 - 1, y - a, z - a], \\ &\mathbb{T}_2 : [x^2 + ax + a^2 - 1, y + a, z + a], \\ &\mathbb{T}_3 : [2x^2 + a^2 - 3, 2y(x - y) + a^2 - 1, (x - y)z + xy - 1]. \end{aligned}$$

To simplify our description, let us suppose the number of polynomials in each triangular set is equal to the number of variables as in the above example. For discussion on the other cases of $\mathcal{T}$, please be referred to [19]. That is to say, we now only consider triangular system

$$\begin{cases} f_1(\mathbf{u}, x_1) = 0, \\ \quad \vdots \\ f_s(\mathbf{u}, x_1, ..., x_s) = 0, \\ \mathbb{G}_1,\ \mathbb{G}_2,\ \mathbb{H}. \end{cases} \tag{2}$$

Second, we compute a so-called *border polynomial* from the resulting systems $[\mathbb{T}_i, \mathbb{G}_1, \mathbb{G}_2, \mathbb{H}]$. We need to introduce some concepts. Suppose F and G are polynomials in x with degrees m and l, respectively. Thus, they can be written in the following forms

$$F = a_0x^m + a_1x^{m-1} + \cdots + a_{m-1}x + a_m,\ G = b_0x^l + b_1x^{l-1} + \cdots + b_{l-1}x + b_l.$$

The following $(m+l) \times (m+l)$ matrix (those entries except a_i, b_j are all zero)

$$\left.\begin{pmatrix} a_0 & a_1 & \cdots & a_m & & & \\ & a_0 & a_1 & \cdots & a_m & & \\ & & \ddots & \ddots & & \ddots & \\ & & & a_0 & a_1 & \cdots & a_m \\ b_0 & b_1 & \cdots & b_l & & & \\ & b_0 & b_1 & \cdots & b_l & & \\ & & \ddots & \ddots & & \ddots & \\ & & & b_0 & b_1 & \cdots & b_l \end{pmatrix}\begin{matrix} \left.\vphantom{\begin{matrix}a\\a\\a\\a\end{matrix}}\right\} l \\ \left.\vphantom{\begin{matrix}a\\a\\a\\a\end{matrix}}\right\} m \end{matrix}\right. ,$$

is called the *Sylvester matrix* of F and G with respect to x. The determinant of the matrix is called the *Sylvester resultant* or *resultant* of F and G with respect to x and is denoted by $\operatorname{res}(F, G, x)$.

For system (2), we compute the resultant of f_s and f_s' *w.r.t.* x_s and denote it by $\operatorname{dis}(f_s)$ (it has the leading coefficient and discriminant of f_s as factors). Then we compute the *successive resultant* of $\operatorname{dis}(f_s)$ and the triangular set $\{f_{s-1}, ..., f_1\}$. That is, we compute $\operatorname{res}(\operatorname{res}(\cdots \operatorname{res}(\operatorname{res}(\operatorname{dis}(f_s), f_{s-1}, x_{s-1}), f_{s-2}, x_{s-2}) \cdots), f_1, x_1)$ and denote it by $\operatorname{res}(\operatorname{dis}(f_s); f_{s-1}, ..., f_1)$ or simply R_s. Similarly, for each i $(1 < i \leq s)$, we compute $R_i = \operatorname{res}(\operatorname{dis}(f_i); f_{i-1}, ..., f_1)$ and $R_1 = \operatorname{dis}(f_1)$.

For each of those inequalities and inequations, we compute the successive resultant of g_j (or h_j) w.r.t. the triangular set $[f_1, ..., f_s]$ and denote it by Q_j (resp. Q_{t+j}).

Definition 2. *For an SAS T as defined by (2), the* border polynomial *of T is*

$$BP = \prod_{i=1}^{s} R_i \prod_{j=1}^{t+m} Q_j.$$

Sometimes, with a little abuse of notation, we also use BP to denote the square-free part or the set of square-free factors of BP.

Example 2. For the system RS in Example 1, the border polynomial is

$$BP = a(a-1)(a+1)(a^2-3)(3a^2-4)(3a^2-1).$$

From the result in [23,26], we may assume $BP \not\equiv 0$. In fact, if any factor of BP is a zero polynomial, we can further decompose the system into new systems with such a property. For a parametric SAS, its border polynomial is a polynomial in the parameters with the following property.

Theorem 1. *Suppose S is a parametric SAS as defined by (2) and BP its border polynomial. Then, in each connected component of the complement of $BP = 0$ in parametric space $\mathbb{R}^d$, the number of distinct real solutions of S is constant.*

Third, $BP = 0$ decomposes the parametric space into a finite number of connected region. We then choose sample points in each connected component of the complement of $BP = 0$ and compute the number of distinct real solutions of S at each sample point. Note that sample points can be obtained by the partial cylindrical algebra decomposition (PCAD) algorithm [4].

Example 3. For the system RS in Example 1, $BP = 0$ gives $a = 0, \pm 1, \pm \frac{\sqrt{3}}{3}, \pm \frac{2\sqrt{3}}{3}, \pm \sqrt{3}$. The reals are divided into several open intervals by these points. Because $a \geq 1$, we only need to choose, for example, $9/8, 3/2$ and 2 from $(1, \frac{\sqrt{3}}{3}), (\frac{\sqrt{3}}{3}, \frac{2\sqrt{3}}{3})$ and $(\frac{2\sqrt{3}}{3}, \sqrt{3})$, respectively. Then, we substitute each of the three values for a in the system, and compute the number of distinct real solutions of the system, consequently obtain the system has respectively $8, 4$ and 0 distinct real solutions.

The above three steps constitute the main part of the algorithm in [23,26,19], which, for any input SAS S, outputs the so-called border polynomial BP and a quantifier-free formula Ψ in terms of polynomials in parameters $\mathbf{u}$ (and possible some variables) such that, provided $BP \neq 0$, Ψ is the necessary and sufficient condition for S to have the given number (possibly infinite) of real solutions.

Finally, if we want to discuss the case when parameters are on the "boundary" $BP = 0$, we put $BP = 0$ (or some of its factors) into the system and apply a similar procedure to handle the new SAS.

Example 4. By the steps described above, we obtain the necessary and sufficient condition for RS to have 4 distinct real solutions is $3a^2 - 4 > 0 \wedge a^2 - 3 < 0$ provided $BP \neq 0$. Now, if $3a^2 - 4 = 0$, adding the equation into the system, we obtain a new SAS $[\ [3a^2 - 4, p_1, p_2, p_3], [a - 1], [\ ], [\ ]\ ]$. By the algorithm in [20,21], we know the number of distinct real solutions of the system is 6.

2.3 DISCOVERER

In this section, we will give a short description of the main functions of DISCOVERER which includes an implementation of the algorithms presented in the previous subsection with Maple. The reader can refer to [23,26] for details. The prerequisite to run the package is Maple 7.0 or a later version of it.

The main features of DISCOVERER include

Real Solution Classification of Parametric Semi-algebraic Systems

For a parametric SAS T of the form (1) and an argument N, where N is one of the following three forms:

- a non-negative integer b;
- a range $b..c$, where b, c are non-negative integers and $b < c$;
- a range $b..w$, where b is a non-negative integer and w is a name without value, standing for $+\infty$,

DISCOVERER can determine the conditions on $\mathbf{u}$ such that the number of the distinct real solutions of T equals to N if N is an integer, otherwise falls in the scope N. This is by calling

$$\textbf{tofind}([\mathbb{P}], [\mathbb{G}_1], [\mathbb{G}_2], [\mathbb{H}], [x_1, ..., x_s], [u_1, ..., u_d], N),$$

and results in the necessary and sufficient condition as well as the *border polynomial* BP of T in u such that the number of the distinct real solutions of T exactly equals to N or belongs to N provided $BP \neq 0$. If T has infinite real solutions for generic value of parameters, BP may have some variables. Then, for the "boundaries" produced by "**tofind**", i.e. $BP = 0$, we can call

$$\textbf{Tofind}([\mathbb{P}, BP], [\mathbb{G}_1], [\mathbb{G}_2], [\mathbb{H}], [x_1, ..., x_s], [u_1, ..., u_d], N)$$

to obtain some further conditions on the parameters.

Real Solution Isolation of Constant Semi-algebraic Systems

For a constant SAS T (i.e., $d = 0$) of the form (1), if T has only a finite number of real solutions, DISCOVERER can determine the number of distinct real solutions of T, say n, and moreover, can find out n disjoint cubes with rational vertices in each of which there is only one solution. In addition, the width of the cubes can be less than any given positive real. The two functions are realized through calling

$$\textbf{nearsolve}([\mathbb{P}], [\mathbb{G}_1], [\mathbb{G}_2], [\mathbb{H}], [x_1, ..., x_s]) \text{ and}$$
$$\textbf{realzeros}([\mathbb{P}], [\mathbb{G}_1], [\mathbb{G}_2], [\mathbb{H}], [x_1, ..., x_s], w),$$

respectively, where w is optional and used to indicate the maximum size of the output cubes.

Comparing with other well-known computer algebra tools like REDLOG [9] and QEPCAD [4], DISCOVERER has distinct features on solving problems related to root classification and isolation of SASs through the *complete discrimination system* [24].

3 Polynomial Programs

A polynomial program takes polynomials of $\mathbb{R}[x_1, \ldots, x_n]$ as its only expressions, where $x_1, \ldots, x_n$ stands for the variables of the program. Polynomial programs include expressive class of loops that deserves a careful analysis.

For technical reason, similar to [14], we use algebraic transition systems (ATSs) to represent polynomial programs. An ATS is a special case of standard transition system, in which the initial condition and all transitions are specified in terms of polynomial equations. The class of polynomial programs considered in this paper is more general than the one given in [14] by allowing each assignment inside a loop body to have a guard and its initial and loop conditions possibly with polynomial inequalities. We therefore accordingly extend the notion of algebraic transition systems in [14] by associating with each transition a conjunctive polynomial formula as guard and allowing the initial condition possibly to contain polynomial inequalities. We call such an extension *semi-algebraic transition system* (SATS). It is easy to see that ATS is a special case of SATS.

Definition 3. *A semi-algebraic transition system is a quintuple $\langle V, L, T, \ell_0, \Theta\rangle$, where V is a set of program variables, L is a set of locations, and T is a set of transitions. Each transition $\tau \in T$ is a quadruple $\langle \ell_1, \ell_2, \rho_\tau, \theta_\tau\rangle$, where ℓ_1 and ℓ_2 are the pre- and post- locations of the transition, $\rho_\tau \in CPF(V, V')$ is the transition relation, and $\theta_\tau \in CPF(V)$ is the guard of the transition. Only if θ_τ holds, the* *transition can take place. Here, we use V' (variables with prime) to denote the next-state variables. The location ℓ_0 is the initial location, and $\Theta \in CPF(V)$ is the initial condition.*

Note that in the above definition, for simplicity, we require that each guard should be a conjunctive polynomial formula. In fact, we can drop such a restriction, as for any transition with a disjunctive guard we can split it into multiple transitions, each of which takes a disjunct of the original guard as its guard.

A state is an evaluation of the variables in V and all states are denoted by $Val(V)$. Without confusion we will use V to denote both the variable set and an arbitrary state, and use $F(V)$ to mean the (truth) value of function (formula) F under the state V. The semantics of SATSs can be explained through state transitions as usual.

A transition is called *separable* if its relation is a conjunctive formula of equations which define variables in V' equal to polynomial expressions over variables in V. It is easy to see that the composition of two separable transitions is equivalent to a single separable one. An SATS is called separable if each transition of the system is separable. In a separable system, the composition of transitions along a path of the system is also equivalent to a single separable transition. We will only concentrate on separable SATSs as any polynomial program can easily be represented by a separable SATS (see [12]. Any SATS in the rest of the paper is always assumed separable.

For convenience, by $l_1 \overset{\rho_\tau,\theta_\tau}{\rightarrow} l_2$ we denote the transition $\tau = (l_1, l_2, \rho_\tau, \theta_\tau)$, or simply by $l_1 \overset{\tau}{\rightarrow} l_2$. A sequence of transitions $l_{11} \overset{\tau_1}{\rightarrow} l_{12}, \ldots, l_{n1} \overset{\tau_n}{\rightarrow} l_{n2}$ is called *composable* if $l_{i2} = l_{(i+1)1}$ for $i = 1, \ldots, n-1$, and written as $l_{11} \overset{\tau_1}{\rightarrow} l_{12}(l_{21}) \overset{\tau_2}{\rightarrow} \cdots \overset{\tau_n}{\rightarrow} l_{n2}$. A composable sequence is called *transition circle* at l_{11}, if $l_{11} = l_{n2}$. For any composable sequence $l_0 \overset{\tau_1}{\rightarrow} l_1 \overset{\tau_2}{\rightarrow} \cdots \overset{\tau_n}{\rightarrow} l_n$, it is easy to show that there is a transition of the form $l_0 \overset{\tau_1;\tau_2;\cdots;\tau_n}{\rightarrow} l_n$ such that the composable sequence is equivalent to the transition, where $\tau_1;\tau_2 \cdots ;\tau_n$, $\rho_{\tau_1;\tau_2;\cdots;\tau_n}$ and $\theta_{\tau_1;\tau_2;\cdots;\tau_n}$ are the compositions of $\tau_1, \tau_2, \ldots, \tau_n$, $\rho_{\tau_1}, \ldots, \rho_{\tau_n}$ and $\theta_{\tau_1}, \ldots, \theta_{\tau_n}$, respectively. The composition of transition relations is defined in the standard way, for example, $x' = x^4 + 3; x' = x^2 + 2$ is $x' = (x^4 + 3)^2 + 2$; while the composition of transition guards have to be given as a conjunction of the guards, each of which takes into account the past state transitions. In the above example, if we assume the first transition with the guard $x + 7 = x^5$, and the second with the guard $x^4 = x + 3$, then the composition of the two guards is $x + 7 = x^5 \wedge (x^4 + 3)^4 = (x^4 + 3) + 3$. That is,

Theorem 2. *For any composable sequence $l_0 \overset{\tau_1}{\rightarrow} l_1 \overset{\tau_2}{\rightarrow} \cdots \overset{\tau_n}{\rightarrow} l_n$, it is equivalent to the transition $l_0 \overset{\tau_1;\tau_2;\cdots;\tau_n}{\rightarrow} l_n$.*

Example 5. Consider the SATS $P \triangleq \{V = \{x\}, L = \{l_0, l_1\}, T = \{\tau_1 = \langle l_0, l_1, x' = x^2 + 7, x = 5\rangle, \tau_2 = \langle l_1, l_0, x' = x^3 + 12, x = 12\rangle\}, l_0, \Theta = x = 5\}$. According to the definition, P is separable and $l_0 \overset{\tau_1}{\rightarrow} l_1 \overset{\tau_2}{\rightarrow} l_0$ is a composable transition circle, which is equivalent to $\langle l_0, l_0, x' = (x^2 + 7)^3 + 12, x = 5 \wedge x^2 + 7 = 12\rangle$.

Definition 4 (Ranking Function). *Assume $P = \langle V, L, T, l_0, \Theta\rangle$ is an SATS. A ranking function is a function $\gamma : Val(V) \rightarrow \mathbb{R}^+$ such that the following conditions are satisfied:*

Initial Condition: $\Theta(V_0) \models \gamma(V_0) \geq 0$.

Decreasing Condition: *There exists a constant $C \in \mathbb{R}^+$ such that $C > 0$ and for any transition circle at l_0 $l_0 \xrightarrow{\tau_1} l_1 \xrightarrow{\tau_2} \cdots \xrightarrow{\tau_{n-1}} l_{n-1} \xrightarrow{\tau_n} l_0$,*

$$\rho_{\tau_1;\tau_2;\cdots;\tau_n}(V, V') \wedge \theta_{\tau_1;\tau_2;\cdots;\tau_n}(V) \models \gamma(V) - \gamma(V') \geq C \wedge \gamma(V') \geq 0,$$

where V, V' denote the starting and ending states of the transition circle, respectively.

Condition 1 says that for any initial state satisfying the initial condition, its image under the ranking function must be no less than 0; Condition 2 expresses the fact that the value of the ranking function decreases at least c as the program moves back to the initial location along any transition circle, and is still greater than or equal to 0.

According to Definition 4, for any SATS, if we can find such a ranking function, the system will not go through l_0 infinitely often.

4 Discovering Non-linear Ranking Function

In Definition 4, if γ is a polynomial, we call it a *polynomial ranking function.* In this section, we show how to synthesize polynomial ranking functions of an SATS with the techniques for solving SASs.

We will not present a rigorous proof of the approach to synthesize polynomial ranking function, but use the following program as a running example to demonstrate this. We believe, readers can follow the demonstration to derive a proof by their own if interested in.

Example 6. Consider a program shown in Fig.1 (a).

(a)

```
     x = m,  m > 0
l0 : while x ≠ 0 do
        if x > 0 then
            x := m1 − x
        else
            x := −x − m2
        end if
     end while
     where m, m1, m2 are integers.
```

(b)

$P = \{$
$\quad V = \{x\}$
$\quad L = \{l_0\}$
$\quad T = \{\tau_1, \tau_2\}$
$\quad \Theta = \{x = m,\ m > 0\}$
$\quad$ where
$\quad\quad \tau_1 : \langle l_0, l_0, x' + x - m_1 = 0, x \geq 1\rangle$
$\quad\quad \tau_2 : \langle l_0, l_0, x' + x + m_2 = 0, x \leq -1\rangle\}$
$\}$

Fig. 1.

We can transform the program to an SATS as in Fig.1 (b).

Step 1. Predetermine a template of ranking functions. For example, we can assume a template of ranking functions of P in Example 6 in the form $\gamma(\{x\}) = ax + b$, where a, b are parameters.

Step 2– Encoding Initial Condition. According to the initial condition of ranking function, we have $\Theta \models \gamma \geq 0$ which means that each real solution of Θ must satisfy $\gamma \geq 0$. In other words, $\Theta \wedge \gamma < 0$ has no real solution. It is easy to see that $\Theta \wedge \gamma < 0$ is a semi-algebraic system according to Definition 1. Therefore, applying the tool DISCOVERER, we get a necessary and sufficient condition of the derived SAS having no real solution. The condition may contain the occurrences of some program variables. In this case, the condition should hold for any instantiations of these variables. Thus, by introducing universal quantifications of these variables (we usually add a scope to each of these variables according to different situations) and then applying QEPCAD, we can get a necessary and sufficient condition only on the presumed parameters.

Example 7. In Example 6, $\Theta \models \gamma(\{x\}) \geq 0$ is equivalent to that the following parametric SAS has no real solution

$$x = m, m > 0, \gamma(\{x\}) < 0. \tag{3}$$

By calling

$$\textbf{tofind}([x-m],[\,],[-\gamma(\{x\}),m],[\,],[x],[m,a,b],0),$$

we get that (3) has no real solution iff

$$b + ma \geq 0. \tag{4}$$

By using QEPCAD to eliminate $\forall m > 0$ over (4), we get

$$a \geq 0 \wedge b \geq 0. \tag{5}$$

Step 3–Encoding Decreasing Condition. From Definition 4, there exists a positive constant C such that for any transition circle $l_0 \xrightarrow{\tau_1} l_1 \xrightarrow{\tau_2} \cdots \xrightarrow{\tau_n} l_0$,

$$\rho_{\tau_1;\tau_2;\cdots;\tau_n} \wedge \theta_{\tau_1;\tau_2;\cdots;\tau_n} \models \gamma(V) - \gamma(V') \geq C \wedge \gamma(V') \geq 0. \tag{6}$$

(6) is equivalent to

$$\rho_{\tau_1;\tau_2;\cdots;\tau_n} \wedge \theta_{\tau_1;\tau_2;\cdots;\tau_n} \wedge \gamma(V') < 0 \qquad \text{and} \tag{7}$$

$$\rho_{\tau_1;\tau_2;\cdots;\tau_n} \wedge \theta_{\tau_1;\tau_2;\cdots;\tau_n} \wedge \gamma(V) - \gamma(V') < C \tag{8}$$

both have no real solution. It is easy to see that (7) and (8) are parametric SASs according to Definition 1, so applying the tool DISCOVERER, we obtain some conditions on the parameters. Subsequently, similar to Step 2, we may need to exploit the quantifier elimination tool QEPCAD to simplify the resulted condition in order to get a necessary and sufficient condition only on the presumed parameters.

Example 8. In Example 6, suppose $C > 0$ such that

- For the transition circle $l_0 \xrightarrow{\tau_1} l_0$,
  - firstly, $\rho_{\tau_1} \wedge \theta_{\tau_1} \models \gamma(\{x'\}) \geq 0$ iff

$$x' + x - m_1 = 0, x - 1 \geq 0, \gamma(\{x'\}) < 0 \quad (9)$$

has no solution. Calling

$$\textbf{tofind}([x' + x - m_1], [x - 1], [-\gamma(\{x'\})], [\,], [x'], [x, m_1, a, b], 0),$$

it follows that (9) has no real solution iff

$$b + am_1 - ax \geq 0. \quad (10)$$

(10) should hold for any $x \geq 1$. Thus, by applying QEPCAD to eliminate the quantifier $\forall x \geq 1$ over (10), we get

$$a \leq 0 \wedge am_1 + b - a \geq 0. \quad (11)$$

  - secondly, $\rho_{\tau_1} \wedge \theta_{\tau_1} \models \gamma(\{x\}) - \gamma(\{x'\}) \geq C$ iff

$$x' + x - m_1 = 0, x - 1 \geq 0, \gamma(\{x\}) - \gamma(\{x'\}) < C \quad (12)$$

has no solution. By calling

$$\textbf{tofind}([x' + x - m_1], [x - 1], [\gamma(\{x'\}) - \gamma(\{x\}) + C, C], [\,], [x'], [x, m_1, a, b, C], 0),$$

it results that (12) has no real solution iff

$$2ax - C - am_1 \geq 0. \quad (13)$$

Also, (13) should hold for any $x \geq 1$. Thus, by applying QEPCAD to eliminate the quantifier $\forall x \geq 1$ over (13), we get

$$a \geq 0 \wedge C + am_1 - 2a \leq 0 \wedge C > 0. \quad (14)$$

- Similarly, by encoding the decreasing condition w.r.t. the transition circle $l_0 \xrightarrow{\tau_2} l_0$, we get a condition

$$a \geq 0 \wedge am_2 - b - a \leq 0 \wedge a \leq 0 \wedge C - am_2 + 2a \leq 0. \quad (15)$$

Step 4. According to the results obtained from Steps 1, 2 and 3, we can get the final necessary and sufficient condition only on the parameters of the ranking function template. If the condition is still complicated, we can utilize the function of PCAD of DISCOVERER or QEPCAD to prove whether the condition can be satisfied. If yes, the tool can produce instantiations of these parameters. Thus, we can get a specific ranking function of the predetermined form by replacing the parameters with the instantiations, respectively.

Example 9. Obviously, for any positive constant C, $C > 0$ always contradicts to (14) and (15). This means that there is no linear ranking functions for the program P.

Note that the above procedure is *complete* in the sense that for any given template of ranking function, the procedure can always give you an answer: yes or no, while an incomplete one (such as the one proposed in [6]) is lack of the ability to produce a negative conclusion.

Example 10. Now, let us consider nonlinear ranking functions of the program in Example 6 in the form $\gamma = ax^2 + bx + c$. For simplicity, we assume $C = 1$.

Applying the the above procedure, we get the condition on m_1, m_2, a, b, c as

$$\begin{aligned} a \geq 0 \wedge c \geq 0 \wedge (b \geq 0 \vee 4ac - b^2 \geq 0) \wedge am_1^2 + bm_1 - 2am_1 + c - b + a \geq 0 \wedge \\ (4ac - b^2 \geq 0 \vee 2am_1 + b - 2a \leq 0) \wedge am_1^2 + bm_1 - 2am_1 - 2b + 1 \leq 0 \wedge \\ am_2^2 - bm_2 - 2am_2 + c + b + a \geq 0 \wedge (4ac - b^2 \geq 0 \vee 2am_2 - b - 2a \leq 0) \wedge \\ am_1 + b \geq 0 \wedge am_2 - b \geq 0 \wedge am_2^2 - bm_2 - 2am_2 + 2b + 1 \leq 0. \end{aligned} \quad (16)$$

For (16), according to m_1 and m_2, we can discuss as follows:

- Let $m_1 = m_2 = 1$, there are quadratic ranking functions for the program, for example $\gamma = x^2$ or $\gamma = 4x^2 + x + 2$;
- Let $m_1 = 1, m_2 = 2$, it is clear that (16) does not hold from its last conjunct. Therefore, the program has no quadratic ranking functions. In fact, the program does not terminate e.g. initializing $m = 2$.
- In the case where $m = 3n \vee m = 3n + 1$ for any positive integer n, the program terminates, and we can also compute a quadratic ranking function $4x^2 - x + 2$ for it.

In the following, we show how to apply this approach to finding ranking functions of a non-linear program.

Example 11. Find a polynomial ranking function for the polynomial program given in Fig.2 (a).

```
     Real x = A
         where 1 < A < 10
l0 : while x > 1 ∧ x < 10 do
         if x > 1 ∧ x < 3 then
             x := x(5 − x)
         else
             x := x + 1
         end if
     end while
```

(a)

```
P = {
    V = {x}
    L = {l0}
    T = {τ1, τ2}
    Θ = x = A ∧ A > 1 ∧ A < 10
    where
        τ1 : ⟨l0, l0, x' − 5x + x² = 0, x > 1 ∧ x < 3⟩
        τ2 : ⟨l0, l0, x' − x − 1 = 0, x ≥ 3 ∧ x < 10⟩
}
```

(b)

Fig. 2.

In order to find a ranking function of the program, we first transform the program to an SATS represented in Fig.2 (b). Then, assume a ranking function template with degree 1 in the form $\gamma(\{x\}) = ax + b$.

After encoding the initial condition and then applying DISCOVERER and QEPCAD, we get a condition on a and b is

$$b + 10\,a \geq 0 \wedge b + a \geq 0. \tag{17}$$

Afterwards, encoding the decreasing condition w.r.t. the transition circle $l_0 \xrightarrow{\tau_1} l_0$ and then applying DISCOVERER and QEPCAD, we obtain

$$b + 4\,a \geq 0 \wedge 4\,b + 25\,a \geq 0 \wedge C + 4\,a \leq 0 \wedge C + 3\,a \leq 0. \tag{18}$$

Similarly, encoding the decreasing condition w.r.t. the transition circle $l_0 \xrightarrow{\tau_2} l_0$ and then applying DISCOVERER and QEPCAD, we get a condition

$$b + 11\,a \geq 0 \wedge b + 4\,a \geq 0 \wedge C + a \leq 0. \tag{19}$$

Thus, a necessary and sufficient condition on these parameters is obtained as

$$C > 0 \wedge a + C \leq 0 \wedge b + 11\,a \geq 0.$$

So, if we assume $C = 1$, we can get a linear ranking function $11 - x$.

For this example, if we assume a ranking function template with degree 2 in the form $\gamma(\{x\}) = ax^2 + bx + c$, and let $C = 1$, we get a necessary and sufficient condition on a, b, c as

$$\begin{aligned} c + 10\,b + 100\,a \geq 0 \wedge c + b + a \geq 0 \wedge b + 9\,a + 1 \leq 0 \wedge b + 21\,a + 1 \leq 0 \wedge \\ (b + 2\,a \geq 0 \vee b + 20\,a \leq 0 \vee 4\,ac - b^2 \geq 0) \wedge 16\,c + 100\,b + 625\,a \geq 0 \wedge \\ c + 4\,b + 16\,a \geq 0 \wedge (b + 8\,a \geq 0 \vee 2\,b + 25\,a \leq 0 \vee 4\,ac - b^2 \geq 0) \wedge \\ 3\,b + 15\,a + 1 \leq 0 \wedge c + 11\,b + 121\,a \geq 0 \wedge c + 4\,b + 16\,a \geq 0 \wedge \\ (b + 8\,a \geq 0 \vee b + 22\,a \leq 0 \vee 4\,ac - b^2 \geq 0) \wedge b + 7\,a + 1 \leq 0. \end{aligned} \tag{20}$$

For (20), applying PCAD in DISCOVERER we get a sample point $(1, -22, 150)$, we therefore obtain a non-linear ranking function $x^2 - 22x + 150$.

5 Conclusions and Future Work

This paper uses the techniques on solving semi-algebraic systems to discover non-linear ranking functions of polynomial programs. This paper also shows how to use computer algebra tools, DISCOVERER and QEPCAD, to synthesize ranking functions for two interesting programs.

The paper represents a part of the authors' efforts to use DISCOVERER to verify programs. We have used it to verify reachability of linear hybrid systems and generate symbolic termination conditions for linear programs in [27], and to discover ranking functions for polynomial programs here. Similar to Cousot's approach [6], DISCOVERER can also be applied to invariant generation for polynomial programs. We will report this in another paper.

Comparing with the well-known tools REDLOG and QEPCAD, DISCOVERER has distinct features on solving problems related to root classification and isolation of SASs through the complete discrimination system. We will analyze its complexity in another paper. The results of the efforts to apply DISCOVERER to program verification are encouraging so far, and we will continue our efforts. The successful story of TERMINATOR [3] also encourages us to develop a program verification tool based on DISCOVERER when we have sufficient experience.

References

1. Braverman, M.: Termination of integer linear programs. In: Ball, T., Jones, R.B. (eds.) CAV 2006. LNCS, vol. 4144, pp. 372–385. Springer, Heidelberg (2006)
2. Bradley, A., Manna, Z., Sipma, H.: Terminaition of polynomial programs. In: Cousot, R. (ed.) VMCAI 2005. LNCS, vol. 3385, pp. 113–129. Springer, Heidelberg (2005)
3. Cook, B., Podelski, A., Rybalchenko, A.: TERMINATOR: Beyond safety. In: Ball, T., Jones, R.B. (eds.) CAV 2006. LNCS, vol. 4144, pp. 415–418. Springer, Heidelberg (2006)
4. Collins, G.E., Hong, H.: Partial cylindrical algebraic decomposition for quantifier elimination. J. of Symbolic Computation 12, 299–328 (1991)
5. Colón, M., Sipma, H.B.: Synthesis of linear ranking functions. In: Margaria, T., Yi, W. (eds.) ETAPS 2001 and TACAS 2001. LNCS, vol. 2031, pp. 67–81. Springer, Heidelberg (2001)
6. Cousot, P.: Proving program invariance and termination by parametric abstraction, Langrangian Relaxation and semidefinite programming. In: Cousot, R. (ed.) VMCAI 2005. LNCS, vol. 3385, pp. 1–24. Springer, Heidelberg (2005)
7. Dams, D., Gerth, R., Grumberg, O.: A heuristic for the automatic generation of ranking functions. In: Workshop on Advances in Verification (WAVe'00), pp. 1–8 (2000)
8. Dijkstra, E.W.: A Discipline of Programming. Prentice-Hall, Englewood Cliffs (1976)
9. Dolzman, A., Sturm, T.: REDLOG: Computer algebra meets computer logic. ACM SIGSAM Bulletin 31(2), 2–9
10. Floyd, R.W.: Assigning meanings to programs. In: Proc. Symphosia in Applied Mathematics, vol. 19, pp. 19–37 (1967)
11. Hoare, C.A.R.: An axiomatic basis for computer programming. Comm. ACM 12(10), 576–580 (1969)
12. Manna, Z., Pnueli, A.: Temporal Verification of Reactive Systems: Safety. Springer, Heidelberg (1995)
13. Podelski, A., Rybalchenko, A.: A complete method for the synthesis of linear ranking functions. In: Steffen, B., Levi, G. (eds.) VMCAI 2004. LNCS, vol. 2937, pp. 239–251. Springer, Heidelberg (2004)
14. Sankaranarayanan, S., Sipma, H.B., Manna, Z.: Non-linear loop invariant generation using Gröbner bases. In: ACM POPL'04, pp. 318–329 (2004)
15. Tarski, A.: A Decision for Elementary Algebra and Geometry. University of California Press, Berkeley (1951)
16. Tiwari, A.: Termination of linear programs. In: Alur, R., Peled, D.A. (eds.) CAV 2004. LNCS, vol. 3114, pp. 70–82. Springer, Heidelberg (2004)

17. International Conference on Verified Software: Theories, Tools and Experiments, ETH Zürich (October 10-13, 2005)
18. Wu, W.-T.: Basic principles of mechanical theorem proving in elementary geometries. J. Syst. Sci. Math. 4, 207–235 (1984)
19. Xia, B., Xiao, R., Yang, L.: Solving parametric semi-algebraic systems. In: Pae, S.-i., Park, H. (eds.) ASCM 2005. Proc. the 7th Asian Symposium on Computer Mathematics, Seoul, December 8-10, pp. 8–10 (2005)
20. Xia, B., Yang, L.: An algorithm for isolating the real solutions of semi-algebraic systems. J. Symbolic Computation 34, 461–477 (2002)
21. Xia, B., Zhang, T.: Real Solution Isolation Using Interval Arithmetic. Comput. Math. Appl. 52, 853–860 (2006)
22. Yang, L.: Recent advances on determining the number of real roots of parametric polynomials. J. Symbolic Computation 28, 225–242 (1999)
23. Yang, L., Hou, X., Xia, B.: A complete algorithm for automated discovering of a class of inequality-type theorems. Sci. in China (Ser. F) 44, 33–49 (2001)
24. Yang, L., Hou, X., Zeng, Z.: A complete discrimination system for polynomials. Science in China (Ser. E) 39, 628–646 (1996)
25. Yang, L., Xia, B.: Automated Deduction in Real Geometry. In: Chen, F., Wang, D. (eds.) Geometric Computation, pp. 248–298. World Scientific, Singapore (2004)
26. Yang, L., Xia, B.: Real solution classifications of a class of parametric semi-algebraic systems. In: Proc. of Int'l Conf. on Algorithmic Algebra and Logic, pp. 281–289 (2005)
27. Yang, L., Zhan, N., Xia, B., Zhou, C.: Program verification by using DISCOVERER. In: Proc. VSTTE'05, Zürich (October 10-October 13, 2005) (to appear)

Mobile Ambients with Timers and Types

Bogdan Aman[2] and Gabriel Ciobanu[1,2]

[1] "A.I.Cuza" University, Faculty of Computer Science
Blvd. Carol I no.11, 700506 Iaşi, Romania
[2] Romanian Academy, Institute of Computer Science
Blvd. Carol I no.8, 700505 Iaşi, Romania
baman@iit.tuiasi.ro, gabriel@info.uaic.ro

Abstract. Mobile ambients calculus is a formalism for mobile computing able to express local communications inside ambients. Ambients mobility is controlled by capabilities: *in, out*, and *open*. We add timers to communication channels, capabilities and ambients, and use a typing system for communication. The passage of time is given by a discrete global time progress function. We prove that structural congruence and passage of time do not interfere with the typing system. Moreover, once well-typed, an ambient remains well-typed. A timed extension of the cab protocol illustrates how the new formalism is working.

1 Introduction

Ambient calculus is a formalism for describing distributed and mobile computing in terms of ambients. In contrast with other formalisms for mobile systems such as CCS and π-calculus [12] whose computation model is based on *communication*, the ambient calculus is based on the notion of *movement*. An ambient, which is a named location, is the unit of movement. Ambients mobility is controlled by capabilities: *in, out*, and *open*. Inside an ambient we have processes which may exchange messages.

The definition of mobile ambients is related in [4] to the network communication. Ambient calculus can model communication protocols. So far the timing properties have not been considered in the framework of mobile ambients. However timing properties are important in network communication. For instance, a *Time to Live* (TTL) value is used to indicate the timeout for a communication package before it should be discarded. Servers do not apply a single fixed timeout for all the communication packages. Simple Network Manage Protocol (SNMP) could implement its own strategy for timeout and retransmission in TCP/IP.

TTL value and strategies for retransmission in TCP/IP protocol provide a good motivation to add timers to ambients. In this paper we associate timers not only to ambients, but also to capabilities and communication channels. The resulting formalism is called mobile ambients with timers (tMA), and represent a conservative extension of the ambient calculus. Inspired by [5] we introduce types for ambients in tMA. The type system associates to each ambient a set of types in order to control its communication by allowing only well-typed messages. For

C.B. Jones, Z. Liu, J. Woodcock (Eds.): ICTAC 2007, LNCS 4711, pp. 50–63, 2007.

instance, if a process inside an ambient sends a message of a type which is not included in the type system of the ambient, then the process fails. In mobile ambients with timers, by using timers, the process may continue its execution after the timer of the corresponding output communication expires.

The structure of the paper is as follows. Section 2 presents the mobile ambients. Section 3 gives the description of the mobile ambients with timers and types. First we provide a static semantic given by a typing system, and an operational semantics of the new calculus given by a reduction relation. The passage of time is given by a discrete global time progress function. We prove that structural congruence and passage of time do not interfere with the typing system. A subject reduction result ensures that once well-typed, a timed mobile ambient remains well-typed. In Section 4 a cab protocol with timers illustrates some of the timing features of the new formalism. Conclusion and references end the paper.

2 Mobile Ambients

In this section we provide a short description of the mobile ambients; more details could be found in [4]. The following table describes the syntax of mobile ambients.

Table 1. *Mobile Ambients Syntax*

c		channel name		P, Q	$::=$	processes	
n, m		ambient names			$\mathbf{0}$		inactivity
x		variable			$M.P$		movement
M	$::=$	capabilities			$n[P]$		ambient
	$in\ n$		can enter n		$P \mid Q$		composition
	$out\ n$		can exit n		$(\nu n)P$		restriction
	$open\ n$		can open n		$c!\langle m\rangle.P$		output action
					$c?(x).P$		input action
					$*P$		replication

Process $\mathbf{0}$ is an inactive process (it does nothing). A movement $M.P$ is provided by the capability M, followed by the execution of process P. An ambient $n[P]$ represents a bounded place labelled by n in which a process P is executed. $P \mid Q$ is a parallel composition of processes P and Q. $(\nu n)P$ creates a new unique name n within the scope of process P. An output action $c!\langle m\rangle.P$ releases a name m on channel c, and then behaves as process P. An input action $c?(x).P$ captures a name from channel c, and binds it to a variable x within the scope of process P. $*P$ denotes the unbounded replication of a process P, producing as many parallel replicas of process P as needed.

The semantics of the ambient calculus is given by two relations: structural congruence and reduction. The *structural congruence* $P \equiv Q$ relates different syntactic representations of the same process; it is also used to define the reduction relation. The *reduction relation* $P \to Q$ describes the evolution of processes. We denote by $\to^*$ the reflexive and transitive closure of $\to$.

The structural congruence is defined as the least relation over processes satisfying the axioms presented in Table 2. The rules from the left side of the table describe the commuting/association of parallel components, unfolding recursion, stretching of a restriction scope, renaming of bounded names. The rules from the right side describe how structural congruence is propagated across processes.

Table 2. *Structural Congruence*

$P \mid Q \equiv Q \mid P$	$P \equiv P \qquad P \equiv Q$ implies $Q \equiv P$
$(P \mid Q) \mid R \equiv P \mid (Q \mid R)$	$P \equiv Q$, $Q \equiv R$ implies $P \equiv R$
$*P \equiv P \mid *P$	$P \equiv Q$ implies $(\nu n)P \equiv (\nu n)Q$
$(\nu n)(\nu m)P \equiv (\nu m)(\nu n)P$ if $n \neq m$	$P \equiv Q$ implies $P \mid R \equiv Q \mid R$
$(\nu n)(P \mid Q) \equiv P \mid (\nu n)Q$ if $n \notin fn(P)$	$P \equiv Q$ implies $*P \equiv *Q$
$(\nu n)m[P] \equiv m[(\nu n)P]$ if $n \neq m$	$P \equiv Q$ implies $n[P] \equiv n[Q]$
$P \mid \mathbf{0} \equiv P$	$P \equiv Q$ implies $M.P \equiv M.Q$
$(\nu n)\mathbf{0} \equiv \mathbf{0} \qquad *\mathbf{0} \equiv \mathbf{0}$	$P \equiv Q$ implies $c?(x).P \equiv c?(x).Q$

The set $fn(P)$ of free names of a process P is defined as:

$$fn(P) = \begin{cases} \emptyset & \text{if } P = \mathbf{0} \\ fn(R) \cup \{n\} & \text{if } P = in\ n.R \text{ or } P = out\ n.R \text{ or } P = open\ n.R \\ & \text{or } P = n[R] \text{ or } P = c!\langle n\rangle.R \\ fn(R) \cup fn(Q) & \text{if } P = R \mid Q \\ fn(R) - \{n\} & \text{if } P = (\nu n)R \\ fn(R) & \text{if } P = c?(x).R \text{ or } P = *R \end{cases}$$

The reduction relation is defined as the least relation over processes satisfying the following set of axioms:

Table 3. *Reduction Rules*

(In)	$n[in\ m.\,P \mid Q] \mid m[R] \to m[n[P \mid Q] \mid R]$
(Out)	$m[n[out\ m.\,P \mid Q] \mid R] \to n[P \mid Q] \mid m[R]$
(Open)	$open\ n.\,P \mid n[Q] \to P \mid Q$
(Com)	$c!\langle m\rangle.\,P \mid c?(x).\,P' \to P \mid P'\{m/x\}$
(Res)	$P \to Q$ implies $(\nu n)P \to (\nu n)Q$
(Amb)	$P \to Q$ implies $n[P] \to n[Q]$
(Par)	$P \to Q$ implies $P \mid R \to Q \mid R$
(Struct)	$P' \equiv P,\ P \to Q,\ Q \equiv Q'$ implies $P' \to Q'$

The first four rules are the one-step reductions for *in, out, open* and *communication.* In the rule **(Com)** we write $P'\{m/x\}$ for the substitution of name m for each free occurrence of variable x in process P'. The next three rules propagate reductions across scopes, ambient nesting and parallel composition. The final rule allows the use of structural congruence during reduction.

3 Mobile Ambients with Timers and Types

In mobile ambients with timers (shortly, tMA) communication channels (input and output channels), capabilities and ambients are used as temporal resources.

A timer Δt of each temporal resource makes the resource available only for a period of time t.

The novelty of this approach results from the fact that a location, represented by an ambient, can disappear. We denote by $n^{\Delta t}[P]^{\mu}$ the fact that an ambient n has a timer Δt, while the tag μ is a neutral tag that indicates if an ambient is active or passive. If $t > 0$, the ambient $n^{\Delta t}[P]^{\mu}$ behaves exactly as the untimed ambient $n[P]$. Since the timer Δt can expire (i.e., $t = 0$) we use a pair $(n^{\Delta t}[P]^{\mu}, Q)$, where Q is a *safety process.* If no *open* n capability appears in t units of time, the ambient $n^{\Delta t}[P]^{\mu}$ is dissolved, the process P is cancelled, and the safety process Q is executed. If $Q = \mathbf{0}$ we can simply write $n^{\Delta t}[P]^{\mu}$ instead of $(n^{\Delta t}[P]^{\mu}, Q)$. If we want to simulate the behaviour of an untimed mobile ambient, then we use ∞ instead of Δt, i.e., $n^{\infty}[P]^{\mu}$.

Similarly, we add a safety process for the input and output communications and the movement processes. The process $open^{\Delta t}n.(P, Q)$ evolves to process P if before the timer Δt expires, the capability $open^{\Delta t}n$ is consumed; otherwise evolves to process Q. The process $c^{\Delta t}!\langle m\rangle.(P, Q)$ evolves to process P if before the timer Δt expires, a process captures name m from channel c; otherwise evolves to process Q.

Since messages are undirected, it is possible for a process $c^{\Delta t}!\langle m\rangle.(P, Q)$ to send a message which is not appropriate for any receiver. To restrict the communication and be sure that m reaches an appropriate receiver, we add types expressed by $Amb[\Gamma]$ and write $c^{\Delta t}!\langle m : Amb[\Gamma]\rangle.(P, Q)$. We use types inspired by [5]; the set of types is defined in Table 4. We use types for communication in order to validate the exchange of messages, namely that if we expect to communicate integers, then we cannot communicate boolean values. $\mathcal{B}$ represents a set of *base types.* The intuitive meaning of the subtyping relation is that $<:$ represents the inverse the set inclusion relation ($\Gamma <: \Gamma'$ for types means $\Gamma \supset \Gamma'$ for sets and $\Gamma \sqcap \Gamma'$ for types means $\Gamma \cup \Gamma'$ for sets).

Table 4. *Types*

Set of types:	
$\Gamma ::= \mathcal{B} \mid Amb[\Gamma] \mid \Gamma \sqcap \Gamma'$	
$Amb[\Gamma]$	ambient name allowing Γ exchanges

If an appropriate message is received before the timer Δt expires, then process $c^{\Delta t}?(x : Amb[\Gamma]).(P, Q)$ evolves to process P; otherwise evolves to process Q. According to the syntax of tMA presented in Table 5, $Amb[\Gamma]$ can be used in a restriction $(\nu n : Amb[\Gamma])P$, which means that n of type $Amb[\Gamma]$ is new in process P. A variable x is bounded only in process P when we consider the process $c^{\Delta t}?(x : Amb[\Gamma]).(P, Q)$.

If it does not matter if an ambient is passive or active, we simple use μ as the tag of the ambient. When we describe initially the ambients, we consider that all ambients are active, and we associate the tag a to them.

Table 5. *Syntax of Mobile Ambients with Timers and Types*

a, p	ambient tags	$P, Q ::=$	processes
c	channel name	$\mathbf{0}$	inactivity
n, m	ambient names	$M^{\Delta t}.(P, Q)$	movement
x	variable	$(n^{\Delta t}[P]^{\mu}, Q)$	ambient
M ::=	capabilities	$P \mid Q$	composition
$in\ n$	can enter n	$(\nu n : Amb[\Gamma])P$	restriction
$out\ n$	can exit n	$c^{\Delta t}!\langle m : Amb[\Gamma]\rangle.(P, Q)$	output action
$open\ n$	can open n	$c^{\Delta t}?(x : Amb[\Gamma]).(P, Q)$	input action
		$*P$	replication

3.1 Operational Semantics

The passage of time is described by a discrete global time progress function ϕ_Δ defined over the set $\mathcal{P}$ of mobile ambients with timers. The actions are performed at every tick of a universal clock. The opened ambients, the channels involved in a communication and the consumed capabilities disappear together with their timers. If a channel, capability or ambient has the timer equal to ∞ we use the equality $\infty - 1 = \infty$ when applying the function ϕ_Δ. This function modifies a process accordingly with the global passage of time. Another property of the function ϕ_Δ is that the passive ambients can become active in the next unit of time in order to participate in other reductions.

Definition 1. *(Global time progress function) We define* $\phi_\Delta : \mathcal{P} \to \mathcal{P}$*, by:*

$$\phi_\Delta(P) = \begin{cases} M^{\Delta(t-1)}.(R, Q) & \text{if } P = M^{\Delta t}.(R, Q),\ t > 0 \\ Q & \text{if } P = M^{\Delta t}.(R, Q),\ t = 0 \\ c^{\Delta(t-1)}!\langle m : Amb[\Gamma]\rangle.(R, Q) & \text{if } P = c^{\Delta t}!\langle m : Amb[\Gamma]\rangle.(R, Q),\ t > 0 \\ Q & \text{if } P = c^{\Delta t}!\langle m : Amb[\Gamma]\rangle.(R, Q),\ t = 0 \\ c^{\Delta(t-1)}?(x : Amb[\Gamma]).(R, Q) & \text{if } P = c^{\Delta t}?(x : Amb[\Gamma]).(R, Q),\ t > 0 \\ Q & \text{if } P = c^{\Delta t}?(x : Amb[\Gamma]).(R, Q),\ t = 0 \\ \phi_\Delta(R) \mid \phi_\Delta(Q) & \text{if } P = R \mid Q \\ (\nu n : Amb[\Gamma])\phi_\Delta(R) & \text{if } P = (\nu n : Amb[\Gamma])R \\ (n^{\Delta(t-1)}[\phi_\Delta(R)]^a, Q) & \text{if } P = (n^{\Delta t}[R]^{\mu}, Q),\ t > 0 \\ Q & \text{if } P = (n^{\Delta t}[R]^{\mu}, Q),\ t = 0 \\ P & \text{if } P = *R \text{ or } P = \mathbf{0} \end{cases}$$

For the processes $c^{\Delta t}!\langle m : Amb[\Gamma]\rangle.(P, Q)$, $c^{\Delta t}?(x : Amb[\Gamma]).(P, Q)$ and $M^{\Delta t}.(P, Q)$, the timer of process P is activated only after the consumption of $c^{\Delta t}!\langle m : Amb[\Gamma]\rangle$, $c^{\Delta t}?(x : Amb[\Gamma])$ and $M^{\Delta t}$ (in at most t units of time). Reduction rules (Table 7) shows how the time function ϕ_Δ is used.

Processes are grouped into equivalence classes by the equivalence relation $\equiv$ called structural congruence. This relation provides a way of rearranging expressions such that interacting parts can be brought together.

Table 6. *Structural Congruence*

(S-Refl)	$P \equiv P$
(S-Sym)	$P \equiv Q$ implies $Q \equiv P$
(S-Trans)	$P \equiv R,\ R \equiv Q$ implies $P \equiv Q$
(S-Res)	$P \equiv Q$ implies $(\nu n : Amb[\Gamma])P \equiv (\nu n : Amb[\Gamma])Q$
(S-Par)	$P \equiv Q$ implies $P \mid R \equiv Q \mid R$
(S-Repl)	$P \equiv Q$ implies $*P \equiv *Q$
(S-Amb)	$P \equiv Q$ and $R \equiv S$ implies $(n^{\Delta t}[P]^{\mu}, R) \equiv (n^{\Delta t}[Q]^{\mu}, S)$
(S-Cap)	$P \equiv Q$ and $R \equiv S$ implies $M^{\Delta t}.(P, R) \equiv M^{\Delta t}.(Q, S)$
(S-Input)	$P \equiv Q$ and $R \equiv S$ implies $c^{\Delta t}?(x : Amb[\Gamma]).(P, R) \equiv c^{\Delta t}?(x : Amb[\Gamma]).(Q, S)$
(S-Output)	$P \equiv Q$ and $R \equiv S$ implies $c^{\Delta t}!\langle m : Amb[\Gamma]\rangle.(P, R) \equiv c^{\Delta t}!\langle m : Amb[\Gamma]\rangle.(Q, S)$
(S-Par Com)	$P \mid Q \equiv Q \mid P$
(S-Par Assoc)	$(P \mid Q) \mid R \equiv P \mid (Q \mid R)$
(S-Res Res)	$(\nu n : Amb[\Gamma])(\nu m : Amb[\Gamma'])P \equiv (\nu m : Amb[\Gamma'])(\nu n : Amb[\Gamma])P$ if $\Gamma \neq \Gamma'$
(S-Res Par)	$(\nu n : Amb[\Gamma])(P \mid Q) \equiv P \mid (\nu n : Amb[\Gamma])Q$ if $(n : Amb[\Gamma]) \notin fn(P)$
(S-Res Amb Dif)	$(\nu n : Amb[\Gamma])(m^{\Delta t}[P]^{\mu}, Q) \equiv (m^{\Delta t}[(\nu n : Amb[\Gamma])P]^{\mu}, Q)$ if $m \neq n$ and $n \notin fn(Q)$
(S-Res Amb Eq)	$(\nu n : Amb[\Gamma])(m^{\Delta t}[P]^{\mu}, Q) \equiv (m^{\Delta t}[(\nu n : Amb[\Gamma])P]^{\mu}, Q)$ if $m = n$, $n \notin fn(Q)$ and $\Gamma \neq \Gamma'$ where $m : Amb[\Gamma']$
(S-Zero Par)	$P \mid \mathbf{0} \equiv P$
(S-Repl Par)	$*P \equiv P \mid *P$
(S-Zero Res)	$(\nu n : Amb[\Gamma])\mathbf{0} \equiv \mathbf{0}$
(S-Zero Repl)	$*\mathbf{0} \equiv \mathbf{0}$

The rule **(S-Res Amb Eq)** states that if an ambient $n : Amb[\Gamma']$ is in the scope of a restriction $(\nu n : Amb[\Gamma])$ and $\Gamma \neq \Gamma'$, then the scope of $(\nu n : Amb[\Gamma])$ is restricted to the process running inside ambient $n : Amb[\Gamma']$. This rule is able to distinguish between two ambients having the same name ($m = n$), but different types.

We denote by $\not\rightarrow$ the fact that none of the rules **(R-In)**, **(R-Out)**, **(R-Open)**, **(R-Com)** can be applied. The behaviour of processes is given by the reduction rules:

Table 7. *Reduction Rules*

(R-GTProgress)
$$\frac{P \not\rightarrow}{P \rightarrow \phi_{\Delta}(P)}$$

(R-In)
$$(n^{\Delta t'}[in^{\Delta t} m.(P, P') \mid Q]^{a}, S') \mid (m^{\Delta t''}[R]^{\mu}, S'') \rightarrow (m^{\Delta t''}[(n^{\Delta t'}[P \mid Q]^{p}, S') \mid R]^{\mu}, S'')$$

(R-Out)
$$(m^{\Delta t'}[(n^{\Delta t''}[out^{\Delta t} m.(P, P') \mid Q]^{a}, S'') \mid R]^{\mu}, S') \rightarrow (n^{\Delta t''}[P \mid Q]^{p}, S'') \mid (m^{\Delta t'}[R]^{\mu}, S')$$

(R-Com)
$$c^{\Delta t}!\langle m : Amb[\Gamma]\rangle.(P, Q) \mid c^{\Delta t}?(x : Amb[\Gamma]).(P', Q') \rightarrow P \mid P'\{m/x\}$$

(R-Open)
$$\frac{n : Amb[\Gamma'],\ m : Amb[\Gamma],\ \Gamma <: \Gamma'}{(m^{\Delta t'}[open^{\Delta t} n.\,(P, P') \mid (n^{\Delta t''}[Q]^{\mu}, S'')], S') \rightarrow (m^{\Delta t'}[P \mid Q]^{\mu}, S')}$$

(R-Res)
$$\frac{P \rightarrow Q}{(\nu n : Amb[\Gamma])P \rightarrow (\nu n : Amb[\Gamma])Q}$$

(R-Amb)
$$\frac{P \rightarrow Q}{(n^{\Delta t}[P]^{\mu}, R) \rightarrow (n^{\Delta t}[Q]^{\mu}, R)}$$

(R-Par1)
$$\frac{P \rightarrow Q}{R \mid P \rightarrow R \mid Q}$$

(R-Par2)
$$\frac{P \rightarrow P',\ Q \rightarrow Q'}{P \mid Q \rightarrow P' \mid Q'}$$

(R-Struct)
$$\frac{P' \equiv P,\ P \rightarrow Q,\ Q \equiv Q'}{P' \rightarrow Q'}$$

In the rules **(R-In)**, **(R-Out)**, **(R-Open)** ambient m can be *passive* or *active*, while in the rules , **(R-In)**, **(R-Out)** ambient n is *active*. The difference between *passive* and *active* ambients is that the *passive* ambients can be used in several reductions in a unit of time, while the *active* ambients can be used in at most one reduction in a unit of time, by consuming their capabilities. In the rules **(R-In)**, **(R-Out)** the *active* ambient n becomes *passive*, forcing it to consume only one capability in one unit of time. In **(R-Open)** we imposed the condition $\Gamma <: \Gamma'$ to avoid releasing an unwanted set of types inside the surrounding ambient m. The ambients which are tagged as *passive*, become *active* again by applying the global time-stepping function **(R-GTProgress)**.

In mobile ambients with timers, if one process evolves by one of the rules **(R-In)**, **(R-Out)**, **(R-Open)**, **(R-Com)**, while another one does not perform any reduction, then the rule **(R-Par1)** should be applied. We define only the left composition **(R-Par1)**, because the right composition results from **(R-Struct)** and **(R-Par1)**. If more than one process evolve in parallel by applying one of the rules **(R-In)**, **(R-Out)**, **(R-Open)**, **(R-Com)** then the rule **(R-Par2)** should be applied. The rule **(R-GTProgress)** is applied to simulate the global passage of time, changing all the p tags to a, and so permitting the ambients to participate in new reductions in the next unit of time.

Even if we consider types for ambients as in [5], we do not take into account the environment parameter. Instead, we consider that each ambient has its own set of types Γ, which control the communication of processes inside that ambient as it results from Table 7.

3.2 Subject Reduction

Well-typedness of a process is defined by a set of rules regarding only the communication inside ambients. The typing rules of Table 8 express the conditions which must be satisfied for each syntactic construction of a process in order to be well-typed. These rules describe the relationship of a process to its types, providing the static semantics of tMA. We write $P : \Gamma$ and say that a *process P is well-typed with respect to the set of types Γ*, meaning that process P can exchange only messages of types from set Γ; usually Γ represents the set of types valid in the ambient containing process P.

Table 8. *Typing Rules*

$$\textbf{(T-Null)}\ \mathbf{0} : \Gamma \quad \textbf{(T-Write)}\ \frac{P : \Gamma,\ Q : \Gamma,\ \Gamma <: Amb[\Gamma']}{c^{\Delta t}!\langle m : Amb[\Gamma']\rangle.\,(P, Q) : \Gamma} \quad \textbf{(T-Par)}\ \frac{P : \Gamma,\ Q : \Gamma}{P \,|\, Q : \Gamma}$$

$$\textbf{(T-Read)}\ \frac{P : \Gamma \sqcap Amb[\Gamma'],\ Q : \Gamma}{c^{\Delta t}?(x : Amb[\Gamma']).\,(P, Q) : \Gamma \sqcap Amb[\Gamma']} \quad \textbf{(T-New)}\ \frac{P : \Gamma \sqcap Amb[\Gamma']}{(\nu n : Amb[\Gamma'])P : \Gamma}$$

$$\textbf{(T-Amb)}\frac{n : Amb[\Gamma],\ P : \Gamma,\ Q : \Gamma'}{(n^{\Delta t}[P]^{\mu}, Q) : \Gamma'} \quad \textbf{(T-Cap)}\ \frac{P : \Gamma,\ Q : \Gamma}{M^{\Delta t}.(P, Q) : \Gamma} \quad \textbf{(T-Repl)}\ \frac{P : \Gamma}{*P : \Gamma}$$

Since process $\mathbf{0}$ cannot communicate, $\mathbf{0}$ is well-typed under any set of types, this being expressed in rule **(T-Null)**. Rule **(T-Write)** states that only messages of types from the set Γ can be sent. Similar reasoning is expressed in rule **(T-Read)**. An ambient has only internal communication, meaning that it cannot send messages to sibling processes; therefore an ambient is well-typed under any set of types, and this is expressed in rule **(T-Amb)**. If P and Q are sibling processes which can exchange messages of types from the set Γ, then $P \mid Q$ is also such a process. Rule **(T-New)** states that if a process can exchange messages of types from the set $\Gamma \sqcap Amb[\Gamma']$, then the restricted process $(\nu n : Amb[\Gamma'])P$ cannot exchange messages of type $Amb[\Gamma']$ with sibling processes. By adding a capability to a process we do not affect the well-typedness of that process as it results from rule **(T-Cap)**.

Lemma 1. *If* $(\nu n : Amb[\Gamma'])P : \Gamma$ *and* $n \notin fn(P)$ *then* $P : \Gamma$.

Lemma 2. *If* $P : \Gamma \sqcap Amb[\Gamma']$, $x, m : Amb[\Gamma']$, $x \in bn(P)$ *and* $m \notin fn(P)$ *then* $P\{m/x\} : \Gamma \sqcap Amb[\Gamma']$.

In order to say that $c^{\Delta t}!\langle m : amb[\Gamma']\rangle.(P, Q)$ is well-typed with respect to the set of types Γ, the following statements should hold:

(i) $m : Amb[\Gamma']$, which means that ambient m contains the set of types Γ';

(ii) $\Gamma <: Amb[\Gamma']$, which means that Γ contains the type $Amb[\Gamma']$;

(iii) $P : \Gamma$; $Q : \Gamma$, which means that P and Q are well-typed with respect to the set of types Γ. If one of the statements is not true, the process $c^{\Delta t}!\langle m : Amb[\Gamma']\rangle.(P, Q)$ can still be well-typed, if the alternative process Q is well-typed, with respect to the same set of types Γ.

The following proposition states that the application of the global time progress function ϕ_Δ to a process P does not change its property of being well-typed.

Proposition 1 (Time Passage). *If* $P : \Gamma$ *then* $\phi_\Delta(P) : \Gamma$.

Proof. We take into account all the cases which enter in the definition of ϕ_Δ. *We present only one case the other being treated in a similar manner.*

Case *inferred from* $P = M^{\Delta t}.(R, Q)$, $t > 0$. *The syntax is a general notation to capture all the capabilities because their behaviour is the same in this context. As a consequence, the rule* **(T-Cap)** *is applied and the expected result* $M^{\Delta(t-1)}.(R, Q) : \Gamma$ *is obtained which is the same as* $\phi_\Delta(P) : \Gamma$.

The following proposition states that if a process P is well-typed, then all the processes from its equivalence class are well-typed.

Proposition 2 (Subject Congruence). *If* $P \equiv Q$ *then* $P : \Gamma$ *iff* $Q : \Gamma$.

Proof. We proceed by structural induction. We present only one case the other being treated in a similar manner.

(S-Res Amb Dif) *We have that* $P = (\nu n : Amb[\Gamma'])(m^{\Delta t}[P']^{\mu}, P'')$ *and* $Q = (m^{\Delta t}[(\nu n : Amb[\Gamma'])P']^{\mu}, P'')$ *with* $n \neq m$. *Assume* $P : \Gamma$. *This must have been derived from* **(T-New)** *and* **(T-Amb)** *with* $P'' : \Gamma \sqcap Amb[\Gamma']$. *Because n does not affect the process* P'' *by applying the rule Lemma 1 we have that* $P'' : \Gamma$. *By applying* **(T-Amb)** *we obtain that* $Q : \Gamma$.

The following proposition states that if a process P is well-typed, then the process obtained after applying a reduction rule is well-typed.

Proposition 3 (Subject Reduction). *If $P \to Q$ then $P : \Gamma$ iff $Q : \Gamma$.*

Proof. We proceed by induction on the derivation of $P \to Q$. We present only one case the other being treated in a similar manner.
(R-Com) *We have that $P = c^{\Delta t}!\langle m \rangle.(P,Q) \,|\, c^{\Delta t'}?(x : Amb[\Gamma']).(P',Q')$ and $Q = P \,|\, P'\{m/x\}$. Assume $P : \Gamma$. This must have been derived from* **(T-Par)** *with $c^{\Delta t}!\langle m \rangle.(P,Q) : \Gamma$ and $c^{\Delta t'}?(x).(P',Q') : \Gamma$ and by applying the rules* **(T-Write)** *and* **(T-Read)** *we obtain that $P : \Gamma$, $P'\Gamma$ and $\Gamma <: Amb[\Gamma']$. By applying the Lemma 2 and the rule* **(T-Par)** *we obtain that $P \,|\, P'\{m/x\} : \Gamma$.*

In Table 9 we describe the error system of tMA, where by $\xrightarrow{err}$ we denote the fact that an error occurred. An error can occur only when a process tries to exchange a message of a wrong type. Note that if a process wants to communicate a message of a wrong type, it can still be well-typed if the alternative process Q is well-typed.

Table 9. *Error System*

$$\textbf{(E-Com)}\ \frac{\Gamma \neq \Gamma'}{c^{\Delta t}!\langle m : Amb[\Gamma'] \rangle.(P,Q) \,|\, c^{\Delta t}?(x : Amb[\Gamma]).(P',Q') \xrightarrow{err}}$$

$$\textbf{(E-Open)}\ \frac{n : Amb[\Gamma'],\ m : Amb[\Gamma],\ \Gamma \not<: \Gamma'}{(m^{\Delta t'}[open^{\Delta t} n.(P,P') \,|\, (n^{\Delta t''}[Q]^{\mu}, S'')]^{\mu}, S') \xrightarrow{err}} \qquad \textbf{(E-Par)}\ \frac{P \xrightarrow{err}}{P \,|\, Q \xrightarrow{err}}$$

$$\textbf{(E-Amb)}\ \frac{P \xrightarrow{err}}{(n^{\Delta t}[P]^{\mu}, Q) \xrightarrow{err}} \quad \textbf{(E-New)}\ \frac{P \xrightarrow{err}}{(\nu n : Amb[\Gamma])P \xrightarrow{err}} \quad \textbf{(E-Str)}\ \frac{P \equiv Q \quad Q \xrightarrow{err}}{P \xrightarrow{err}}$$

Rule **(E-Com)** states that a process can receive only messages of a certain type. In Rule **(E-Open)** we express the fact that if in an ambient n are exchanged messages of types from Γ', by opening the ambient, in order for the processes to exchange messages of types from Γ', the ambient m containing ambient n should allow exchange of messages of types from Γ'. The rest of the rules are obvious and state the fact that if a process generates an error then including it in another process, the error does not disappear.

Proposition 4. *If a process is well typed, then it does not generate errors: $P : \Gamma$ implies $P \not\xrightarrow{err}$.*

Proof. The proof considers the opposite of the fact that if P gives rise to a runtime error ($P \xrightarrow{err}$), then P cannot be well-typed under any set of types Γ ($P \not: \Gamma$, for all Γ). We use induction on the structure of P and consider a proof cases for each rule in Table 9. We present only one case the other being treated in a similar manner.

(E-Com) *We consider that there exist a set of types Γ such that $R : \Gamma$, where $R = c^{\Delta t}!\langle m \rangle.(P,Q) \,|\, c^{\Delta t'}?(x : Amb[\Gamma']).(P',Q')$. This must have been derived* *from* **(T-Par)** *with* $c^{\Delta t}!\langle m\rangle.(P,Q) : \Gamma$ *and* $c^{\Delta t'}?(x : Amb[\Gamma']).(P',Q') : \Gamma$. *Applying* **(T-Write)**, **(T-Read)** *we have that* $\Gamma <: Amb[\Gamma']$ *and* $n : Amb[\Gamma']$, *which is in contradiction with the hypothesis of the rule* **(E-Com)**, *and so we have that* $R \not\xrightarrow{err}$.

We denote by $P \xrightarrow{t} Q$ the fact that process P evolves to process Q after applying the rule **(R-GTProgress)** for $t \geq 0$ times, and with $t\phi_\Delta(R)$ the fact that function ϕ_Δ is applied t times to process R. We denote by $\cong$ the relation which respects all the rules of Table 6 except replication, namely rule **(S-Repl Par)**. The following result claims that if two processes are structurally congruent and both idle for t units of time, then the obtained processes are also structural congruent.

Proposition 5. *Time passage cannot cause a nondeterministic behaviour:*

$$\text{if } P \cong Q,\ P \xrightarrow{t} P' \text{ and } Q \xrightarrow{t} Q' \text{ then } P' \cong Q'.$$

Proof. We proceed by structural induction and present only one case the other being treated in a similar manner.
(S-Res) *We have* $P = (\nu n : Amb[\Gamma'])P'$ *and* $Q = (\nu n : Amb[\Gamma'])Q'$ *with* $P \cong Q$. *By induction we have that if* $P' \cong Q'$, $P' \xrightarrow{t} P''$ *and* $Q' \xrightarrow{t} Q''$ *then* $P'' \cong Q''$. *By applying* **(R-Res)** *to both* $P' \xrightarrow{t} P''$ *and* $Q' \xrightarrow{t} Q''$ *we obtain that* $P \xrightarrow{t} (\nu n : Amb[\Gamma])P''$ *and* $Q \xrightarrow{t} (\nu n : Amb[\Gamma])Q''$. *By applying* **(S-Res)** *to* $P'' \cong Q''$ *we obtain that* $(\nu n : Amb[\Gamma])P'' \cong (\nu n : Amb[\Gamma])Q''$.

The following example motivates why we remove replication. Let $P = in^{\Delta 5}n$. Then we have $*P \equiv P \mid *P$. By applying the function ϕ_Δ, we obtain

$$\phi_\Delta(P \mid *P) = in^{\Delta 4}n \mid *P \not\equiv *P = \phi_\Delta(*P).$$

4 Cab Protocol with Timers

We extend the cab protocol described in [10] by introducing new operations which describe a recall for a taxi when a certain period of time has passed, and the payment of the trip. Roughly speaking, the cab protocol is about a city with various sites, cabs and clients willing to go from one site to another. At http://www-sop.inria.fr/mimosa/ambicobjs/taxis.html, a graphical implementation of the cab protocol is presented. The implementation is written in Java, and presents the ambients as named and coloured circles, whose limits act as boundaries for what is inside. A capability *in c* is described by an anchor which remains in the ambient *a*, and an arrow outside which is linked to any ambient with name *c*. When such an arrow finds an ambient *c*, the ambient *a* is entirely moved inside *c*. A capability *out c* is described by an anchor pointing outside. A capability *open c* is represented as a small square trying to find an ambient with the same name. If it does, the boundaries are dissolved and the content of that ambient is released. A snapshot of the cab protocol is presented in the following figure:

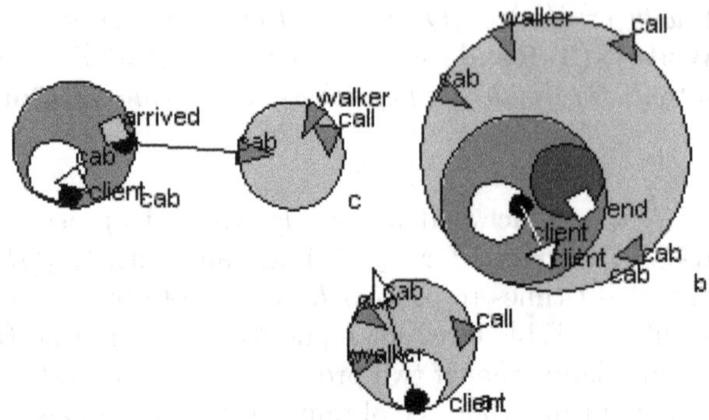

The whole system consists of one city, n sites, and several cabs and clients. The cabs can be empty waiting in a precise site or can have clients and be anywhere in the city, while the clients can be either on some sites waiting for a free cab to arrive, or ar already traveling with a cab. In order to initiate a trip a client must achieve a cab, and it does this by sending a request for an empty cab. In what follows we use this protocol to illustrate how the mobile ambients with timers are working, emphasizing on the timing aspects. It is worth to note that each ambient of the system is well-typed because we do not consider communication. Considering the fact that we have only ambients with no internal communication, all the processes are well-typed under any set of types Γ.

A message emitted by a *client* located at a site *from* in order to call a *cab* is described by

$load\ client = loading^{\Delta t_1}[out^{\Delta t_2} cab.\ in^{\Delta t_3} client]^{\mu}$
$call = call^{\Delta t_7}[out^{\Delta t_8} client.\ out^{\Delta t_9} from.\ in^{\Delta t_{10}} cab.\ in^{\Delta t_{11}} from.\ load\ client]^{\mu}$
$recall = recall^{\Delta t_{12}}[out^{\Delta t_{13}} cab.\ in^{\Delta t_{14}} from.\ in^{\Delta t_{15}} client]^{\mu}$
$call\ from\ client = (call,\ recall)$

This ambient must enter a *cab*, where it gets opened and releases the process *load client*. After it exits the ambient *client* and successively the ambient *from* it looks for a *cab* to enter. If it founds a *cab* then it enters it by applying a **(R-In)**:

$$(call^{\Delta t_7}[in^{\Delta t_{10}} cab.in^{\Delta t_{11}} from. \ldots]^{a}, recall) \mid cab^{\infty}[\ ]^{\mu}$$
$$\rightarrow cab^{\infty}[call^{\Delta t_7}[in^{\Delta t_{11}} from. \ldots]^{p}, recall]^{\mu}$$

If the timer Δt_7 of the ambient *call* expires before it enters a *cab*, then an ambient *recall* is released. This would be possible if no *cab* ambient becomes sibling with the ambient *call* in the period of time represented by the timer Δt_7. To discard the ambient *call* with the expired timer we apply a **(R-GTProgress)** rule which launches the safety process *recall*:

$$(call^{\Delta t_7}[in^{\Delta t_{10}} cab.in^{\Delta t_{11}} from. \ldots]^{a}, recall) \rightarrow recall$$

The *recall* ambient enters the ambient *client*, and announces that he can make another call. This process of recalling is repeated until the process *load client* is released. The process *load client* is launch by opening the ambient *call* using a **(R-Open)** rule:

$$cab^{\infty}[(call^{\Delta t_7}[load\ client]^{\mu}, recall) \mid open^{\Delta t_{44}} call.open^{\Delta t_{45}} trip. \ldots]^{\mu}$$
$$\rightarrow cab^{\infty}[load\ client \mid open^{\Delta t_{45}} trip. \ldots]^{\mu}$$

As a consequence, the *cab* goes to *from* in order to meet its *client*, and it releases an ambient *loading*. All the steps necessary for a correct evolution of the trip, are performed by applying the appropriate reduction rules. Once *loading* has been released, it enters the ambient *client*.

The address given to the *driver* by a *client* to go from the current location *from* to address *to*, as well as the payment of the trip are described by

$trip\ from\ to\ c = trip^{\Delta t_{20}}[out^{\Delta t_{21}} client.\, out^{\Delta t_{22}} from.\, in^{\Delta t_{23}} to.\, pay\ driver]^{\mu}$

$pay\ driver = pay^{\Delta_{16}}[in^{\Delta t_{17}} c.\, in^{\Delta t_{18}} wallet.\, in^{\Delta t_{19}} money]^{\mu}$

Whenever the *client* opens *loading* it means that the *cab* is present, and therefore the *client* may enter it. Consequently, the *client* enters the *cab* and releases an ambient *trip*, which the *cab* receives and opens. The process which is released moves the *cab* to its destination where it releases another synchronization ambient *pay* to inform the *client* to pay the trip. An ambient *pay* enters the *client wallet* and moves an ambient *money* to the *driver wallet*.

$paid\ driver = paid^{\Delta t_{28}}[out^{\Delta t_{29}} money.\, out^{\Delta t_{30}} wallet.\, out^{\Delta t_{31}} driver.\, in^{\Delta t_{32}} c]^{\mu}$

$money\ client = money^{\infty}[open^{\Delta t_{33}} pay.\, out^{\Delta t_{34}} wallet.\, out^{\Delta t_{35}} c.\, in^{\Delta t_{36}} driver.$
$\quad in^{\Delta t_{37}} wallet.\, paid\ driver]^{\mu}$

$wallet\ client = wallet^{\infty}[money\ client \mid \ldots \mid money\ client]^{\mu}$

$bye\ cab = bye^{\Delta t_{24}}[out^{\Delta t_{25}} c.\, in^{\Delta t_{26}} cab.\, out^{\Delta t_{27}} to]^{\mu}$

$client\ from\ to = (\nu c)c^{\infty}[*(open^{\Delta t_{38}} recall.\, call\ from\ c) \mid recall^{\Delta t_{39}}[\,]^{\mu} \mid$
$\quad open^{\Delta t_{40}} loading.\, in^{\Delta t_{41}} cab.\, trip\ from\ to\ c \mid open^{\Delta t_{42}} paid.$
$\quad out^{\Delta t_{43}} cab.\, bye\ cab \mid wallet\ client]^{\mu}$

Once the ambient *money* enters the *driver wallet*, an ambient *paid* is released and send to the *client* telling him to get out from the *cab*. The *client* opens it, leaves the *cab*, and sends the last synchronization ambient *bye* to the *cab*, instructing it to leave the current location *to*.

The *cab* and the *city* are described by

$driver = driver^{\infty}[wallet^{\infty}[money^{\infty}[\,]^{\mu} \mid \ldots \mid money^{\infty}[\,]^{\mu}]^{\mu}]^{\mu}$

$cab = cab^{\infty}[rec\ X.\, open^{\Delta t_{44}} call.\, open^{\Delta t_{45}} trip.\, open^{\Delta t_{46}} bye.\, X \mid driver]^{\mu}$

$city = city^{\infty}[cab \mid \ldots \mid cab \mid site_1^{\infty}[client\ site_1\ site_i \mid client\ site_1\ site_j \mid \ldots]^{\mu}$
$\quad \mid \ldots \mid site_i^{\infty}[\ldots]^{\mu}]^{\mu}$

In the discussion above we have supposed that only the timer Δt_7 of the ambient *call* expires, and this may produce the execution of the safety process *recall*. This was made only for the sake of simplicity. In order to simulate other possible scenarios, we can suppose that other timers may also expire:

- Δt_1 - means that the *loading* ambient does not reach the ambient *client*, and a safety process should be released in order to announce *cab* to create another *loading* ambient;
- Δt_{16} - means that the *pay* ambient does not reach the ambient *client*, and a safety process should be released in order to announce *cab* to create another *pay* ambient;
- Δt_{20} - means that the *trip* ambient does not reach the ambient *cab*, and a safety process should be released in order to announce the *client* to create another *trip* ambient;

- Δt_{28} - means that the *paid* ambient does not reach the ambient *client*, and a safety process should be released in order to announce *cab* to create another *paid* ambient;
- Δt_{24} - means that the *bye* ambient does not reach the ambient *cab*, and a safety process should be released in order to announce the *client* to create another *bye* ambient;
- various other scenarios can be simulated by introducing several other timers over capabilities and ambients.

5 Conclusion

Process algebra is the general study of distributed concurrent systems in an algebraic framework. In the last decades, some successful models have been introduced within this framework: ACP [3], CSP [11], CCS and π-calculus [12], distributed π-calculus [9], mobile ambients [4]. Each of these approaches are not able to naturally describe properties of timing, probability and priority of events performed by the components of the system being modelled. Process algebra with timing features are presented in [1,7,8,13]. In [1] it is presented a process algebra (CIPA) with local clocks where duration is attached to actions. A global clock, eager actions and static durations are presented in [8]. A closer approach is presented in [7], where the actions are durationless, and the author uses both a relative and an absolute time over TCCS [13] and CIPA. An important difference between these papers and our approach is that they work with process algebras like CSP, TCCS, CIPA and we work with mobile ambients. We do not know about another timed approach over mobile ambients. We have extended the mobile ambients by adding time constraints to channels, capabilities and ambients. A similar extension with timers for π-calculus is presented in [2], and for distributed π-calculus in [6]. A difference comes from the fact that a location may disappear together with its processes.

Our work is motivated by the existence of timers in TCP/IP communication protocols; the timers fit very well to the description of messages as mobile ambients. We extend with time restrictions a formalism designed for mobility in order to study various aspects related to time. The formalism used is the ambient calculus. The novelty comes from the fact that the ambients can also expire, simulating in this way the maximum amount of time any package can exist in a network before being discarded. We have provided a static semantic given by a typing system, and an operational semantics by a reduction relation. To describe passage of time we have given a discrete global time progress function. We proved that the structural congruence and passage of time do not interfere with the typing system. A subject reduction results ensures that once well-typed, an ambient remains well-typed.

This paper is a first attempt to incorporate timing information on a simple semantics without any significant contradiction. Time-related design decisions follow standard ones for Timed CCS-like languages but their embedding in ambients make the construction of syntax and semantics more involved because of structural semantics, reduction rules and typing systems for which mobile ambients rely on.

To illustrate how the new formalism works, we have presented a timed extension of the cab protocol. In this example we emphasize the use of timers. For the sake of simplicity we have presented a variant of the protocol in which only one timer can expire. Other scenarios where other timers may expire are briefly described.

References

1. Aceto, L., Murphy, D.: Timing and Causality in Process Algebra. Acta Informatica 33(4), 317–350 (1996)
2. Berger, M.: Basic Theory of Reduction Congruence for Two Timed Asynchronous pi-Calculi. In: Gardner, P., Yoshida, N. (eds.) CONCUR 2004. LNCS, vol. 3170, pp. 115–130. Springer, Heidelberg (2004)
3. Bergstra, J.A., Klop, J.W.: Process Theory based on Bisimulation Semantics. In: de Bakker, J.W., de Roever, W.-P., Rozenberg, G. (eds.) Linear Time, Branching Time and Partial Order in Logics and Models for Concurrency. LNCS, vol. 354, pp. 50–122. Springer, Heidelberg (1989)
4. Cardelli, L., Gordon, A.: Mobile Ambients. In: Nivat, M. (ed.) ETAPS 1998 and FOSSACS 1998. LNCS, vol. 1378, pp. 140–155. Springer, Heidelberg (1998)
5. Cardelli, L., Gordon, A.: Types for Mobile Ambients. In: ACM Symposium on Principles of Programming Languages, pp. 79–92. ACM Press, New York (1999)
6. Ciobanu, G., Prisacariu, C.: Timers for Distributed Systems. Electronic Notes in Theoretical Computer Science 164(3), 81–99 (2006)
7. Corradini, F.: Absolute versus relative time in process algebras. Information and Computation 156(1), 122–172 (2000)
8. Gorrieri, R., Roccetti, M., Stancampiano, E.: A Theory of Processes with Durational Actions. Theoretical Computer Science 140(1), 73–94 (1995)
9. Hennessy, M., Riely, J.: Resource access control in systems of mobile agents. Information and Computation 173(1), 82–120 (2002)
10. Hirschkoff, D., Teller, D., Zimmer, P.: Using ambients to control resources. In: Brim, L., Jančar, P., Křetínský, M., Kucera, A. (eds.) CONCUR 2002. LNCS, vol. 2421, pp. 288–303. Springer, Heidelberg (2002)
11. Hoare, C.A.R.: Communicating Sequential Processes. Prentice-Hall, Englewood Cliffs (1989)
12. Milner, R.: Communicating and mobile systems: the π-calculus. Cambridge University Press, Cambridge (1999)
13. Moller, F., Tofts, C.: A Temporal Calculus of Communicating Systems. In: Groote, J.F., Baeten, J.C.M. (eds.) CONCUR 1991. LNCS, vol. 527, pp. 401–415. Springer, Heidelberg (1991)

Automatic Refinement of Split Binary Semaphore

Damián Barsotti and Javier O. Blanco

Fa.M.A.F., Universidad Nacional de Córdoba,
Córdoba 5000, Argentina

Abstract. Binary semaphores can be used to implement conditional critical regions by using the split binary semaphore (SBS) technique. Given a specification of a conditional critical regions problem, the SBS technique provides not only the resulting programs but also some invariants which ensure the correctness of the solution. The programs obtained in this way are generally not efficient. However, they can be optimized by strengthening these invariants and using them to eliminate unnecessary tests.

We present a mechanical method to perform these optimizations. The idea is to use the backward propagation technique over a guarded transition system that models the behavior of the programs generated by the SBS. This process needs proving heavy implications and simplifying growing invariants. Our method automatically entrusts these tasks to the Isabelle theorem prover and the CVC Lite validity checker. We have tested our method on a number of classical examples from concurrent programming.

1 Introduction

Split Binary Semaphores (SBS) are used to implement conditional critical regions [1,2]. Since the method is fairly general, the solutions obtained often perform some unnecessary tests when leaving a critical region. This work focuses on the mechanical elimination of these unnecessary tests in the programs.

The SBS technique provides not only the programs implementing conditional critical regions, but also some invariants which ensure its correctness. Starting from them, we find stronger invariants from which it can be automatically deduced that certain tests will always be false and hence can be eliminated.

In order to achieve these optimizations, we model programs as guarded transition systems, for which many invariant generation techniques are well-known. In this work we mainly use the backward propagation technique [3] which provides invariants that are quantifier-free formulae. The proofs involved in their manipulation can be dealt with fully automated provers[1] such as CVC Lite [4].

[1] Some provers (like CVC Lite and Simplify) include some support for first-order quantifiers elimination. Nevertheless, these provers work better and faster on quantifier-free formulae since support for quantifiers is not complete.

C.B. Jones, Z. Liu, J. Woodcock (Eds.): ICTAC 2007, LNCS 4711, pp. 64–78, 2007.

This validity checker also supports several interpreted theories (including rational and integer linear arithmetic, arrays, tuples, etc.) which are appropriate for obtaining assertions on programs.

The propagation techniques (backward and forward) are based on the calculus of a fixed point of a formula transformer. One of the advantages of the backward propagation technique is that the sequence of approximations is usually finite. Unfortunately, the formulae produced during this process are large. We use some simplification techniques implemented in CVC Lite and in the Isabelle theorem prover [5] to tackle this problem. Isabelle is an interactive theorem prover that offers efficient tactics for simplification. Besides, we implement other simplification methods using CVC Lite.

The paper is structured as follows. In Sec. 2 we explain the SBS technique. Sec. 3 and 4 present the theoretical framework for constructing the guarded transition system and the method for obtaining the invariants. The guarded transition system that results from the programs generated by SBS technique is developed in Sec. 5 and the refinement procedure in Sec. 6. In Sec. 7 we show some optimizations applied on the refinement procedure. Finally, we show some examples in Sec. 8 and expose our conclusions and suggestions for further work in Sec. 9.

2 Split Binary Semaphores

It is well-known that binary semaphores can easily ensure mutual exclusion and are suitable to implement critical regions. Moreover, they can be used in a systematic way to implement conditional critical regions. We briefly present the solution and refer to the literature for a justification of the method [1,6,2,7].

A set $\{s_0, \ldots, s_n\}$ of binary semaphores is called a *split binary semaphore* if at any time at most one of them equals 1, i.e. the following property is a global invariant for the (multi)program:

$$0 \leq \langle \sum i : 0 \leq i \leq n : s_i \rangle \leq 1 \ .$$

In the execution of the program, every critical region begins with a P on some semaphore, and ends with a V operation on some semaphore (not necessarily the same one). Hence, the invariant ensures mutual exclusion between *any* pair P-V.

Besides ensuring mutual exclusion, SBS satisfies the following *domino rule* [7]. In an execution of the program, if the last V operation is over semaphore s, then the next P operation will be on the same semaphore (notice that there may be more than one P on s). This means that the precondition of a V operation can be taken as the postcondition of any corresponding P operation since shared variables can only be modified inside critical sections. This rule can be formulated as the global invariant $\varphi_{SBS} : \langle \forall s :: s = 0 \vee I_s \rangle$ where I_s is the assertion that holds before every V.s statement and after every corresponding P.s statement.

In order to implement conditional critical regions, the SBS can be used in the following way. To every different condition, a binary semaphore of the SBS is associated, and another "neutral" semaphore is used for the case in which no condition holds. Then, every critical region will be prefixed by a P operation on the semaphore associated with its precondition. Some care should be taken to introduce V operations to ensure progress. We illustrate the method with two conditional critical regions.

Suppose we want to execute statements S_o, S_1 atomically under conditions B_0, B_1 respectively. Furthermore, the critical regions must preserve a global invariant I. We use binary semaphores s_0, s_1 for each condition and two counters b_0, b_1 which will be used to count the number of processes committed to execute P.s_0, P.s_1 respectively. These counters are necessary to avoid deadlocks. Another semaphore m is used for the case in which no condition holds or there is no process waiting.

The following invariant characterizes the SBS solution for the critical region problem.

$$\begin{aligned}\varphi_{SBS} : \; & (s_0 = 0 \vee (B_0 \wedge 0 < b_0 \wedge I)) \wedge \\ & (s_1 = 0 \vee (B_1 \wedge 0 < b_1 \wedge I)) \wedge \\ & (m = 0 \vee ((\neg B_0 \vee 0 = b_0) \wedge (\neg B_1 \vee 0 = b_1) \wedge I)) \;.\end{aligned}$$

Fig. 1 shows the (fully annotated) component obtained by the application of the SBS technique for the atomic execution of S_o.

$\underline{\text{SCC}_o}$

$$\begin{array}{l}
\text{P}.m \;; \\
\{I \wedge (\neg B_0 \vee b_0 = 0) \wedge (\neg B_1 \vee b_1 = 0)\} \\
\underline{\text{if}}\;\; B_0 \rightarrow \{I \wedge B_0 \wedge b_0 = 0 \wedge (\neg B_1 \vee b_1 = 0)\} \\
\qquad\qquad \text{skip} \\
\Box\; \neg B_0 \rightarrow \{I \wedge \neg B_0 \wedge (\neg B_1 \vee b_1 = 0)\} \\
\qquad\qquad b_0 := b_0 + 1 \;; \\
\qquad\qquad \{I \wedge (\neg B_0 \vee b_0 = 0) \wedge (\neg B_1 \vee b_1 = 0)\} \\
\qquad\qquad \text{V}.m \;; \\
\qquad\qquad \text{P}.s_0 \;; \\
\qquad\qquad \{I \wedge B_0 \wedge b_0 > 0\} \\
\qquad\qquad b_0 := b_0 - 1 \\
\underline{\text{fi}}; \\
\{I \wedge B_0\} \\
\text{S}_o \;; \\
\{I\} \\
\underline{\text{if}}\;\; B_0 \wedge b_0 > 0 \rightarrow \{I \wedge B_0 \wedge b_0 > 0\}\; \text{V}.s_0 \\
\Box\; B_1 \wedge b_1 > 0 \rightarrow \{I \wedge B_1 \wedge b_1 > 0\}\; \text{V}.s_1 \\
\Box\; (\neg B_0 \vee b_0 = 0) \wedge (\neg B_1 \vee b_1 = 0) \\
\qquad \rightarrow \{I \wedge (\neg B_0 \vee b_0 = 0) \wedge (\neg B_1 \vee b_1 = 0)\}\; \text{V}.m \\
\underline{\text{fi}}
\end{array}$$

Fig. 1. SBS generated component

For some examples on the use of this method see the extended version of this article [8] and [1].

3 Guarded Transition System

The following definitions are taken from [9,3]. Let Σ be a first-order language containing interpreted symbols for concrete domains like booleans, integers and reals. Let $\mathcal{F}$ be the set of first-order formulas with free (typed) variables contained in a finite set $\mathcal{V} = \{x_1, \cdots, x_n\}$ over Σ. We shall denote the sequence of variables $x_1, \cdots, x_n$ by $\bar{x}$.

The usual way to model reactive systems is by using a *guarded transition system* $\mathcal{S} = \langle \mathcal{V}, \Theta, \mathcal{T} \rangle$ where $\Theta \in \mathcal{F}$ is its *initial condition* and $\mathcal{T}$ is a finite set of *guarded transitions.* Each $\tau \in \mathcal{T}$ can be specified as follows:

$$\gamma_\tau \longmapsto \bar{x} := \bar{e}_\tau(\bar{x})$$

where $\gamma_\tau \in \mathcal{F}$ is the *transition guard* and $\bar{e}_\tau(\bar{x})$ is a sequence of expressions in Σ whose free variables are taken from $\mathcal{V}$; both sequences should have equal length. The formula γ_τ denotes the condition that should hold in order to execute the transition, $\bar{x} := \bar{e}_\tau(\bar{x})$ is a simultaneous assignment which indicate the transformation of the state produced by the transition.

Usually, a transition system has a control variable $vc \in \mathcal{V}$ which ranges over a finite set $\mathcal{L}$ of *locations.* This variable acts as a program counter and the locations act as source and target of each transition. Hence, any $\tau \in \mathcal{T}$ can be written as:

$$vc = l_\tau \wedge \gamma_\tau \longmapsto \bar{x} := \bar{e}_\tau(\bar{x})\,; vc := l'_\tau$$

where $l_\tau, l'_\tau \in \mathcal{L}$, γ_τ is a predicate with variables in $\mathcal{V}/\{vc\}$ and $\bar{x} := \bar{e}_\tau(\bar{x})$ is a simultaneous assignment with variables in $\mathcal{V}/\{vc\}$. For a given transition τ we define the functions $src(\tau) = l_\tau$ and $tgt(\tau) = l'_\tau$.

For each transition, we define a predicate Φ_τ as follows:

$$\Phi_\tau(\bar{x}, \bar{x}') \triangleq \gamma_\tau(\bar{x}) \wedge \bar{x}' = \bar{e}_\tau(\bar{x})$$

where $\bar{x}'$ is the renaming of variables x_i in $\bar{x}$ as x'_i. Note that Φ_τ is a formula with free variables in $\mathcal{V} \cup \mathcal{V}'$ where $\mathcal{V}'$ is the set of variables obtained by renaming the variables x to x' in $\mathcal{V}$. These predicates denote the relation between the values of the variables before execution of the transitions (in a given location $src(\tau)$), with the values of the same variables after its execution (in location $tgt(\tau)$). Hence, we can define the *transition predicate* Φ of a guarded transition system $\mathcal{S}$ as follows:

$$\Phi(\bar{x}, vc, \bar{x}', vc') \triangleq \bigvee_{\tau \in \mathcal{T}} vc = src(\tau) \wedge vc' = tgt(\tau) \wedge \Phi_\tau(\bar{x}, \bar{x}') \ .$$

The formula transformer *weakest precondition*[3,9] of a transition τ, denoted by $wp(\Phi_\tau)$, is defined as follows:

$$wp(\Phi_\tau)(\varphi(\bar{x})) \triangleq \forall \bar{x}'. (\Phi_\tau(\bar{x}, \bar{x}') \rightarrow \varphi(\bar{x}')) \ .$$

The universal quantifier can be eliminated using substitution:

$$wp(\Phi_\tau)(\varphi(\bar{x})) = \gamma_\tau(\bar{x}) \rightarrow \varphi(\bar{e}_\tau(\bar{x})) \ . \tag{1}$$

In general, the weakest precondition transformer for the whole transition system $\mathcal{S}$, denoted by $WP(\Phi)$, is defined as follows:

$$WP(\Phi)(\phi(\bar{x}, vc)) \triangleq \forall\, \bar{x}', vc'. (\Phi(\bar{x}, vc, \bar{x}', vc') \rightarrow \phi(\bar{x}', vc')) \ .$$

Since the set of location $\mathcal{L}$ is finite, the predicate ϕ can be written as:

$$\phi(\bar{x}, vc) = \bigwedge_{l \in \mathcal{L}} vc = l \rightarrow \phi(\bar{x}, l) \ . \tag{2}$$

If we define the predicates $\phi_l(\bar{x}) = \phi(\bar{x}, l)$ for each location $l \in \mathcal{L}$ then the weakest precondition of the whole system is equivalent to:

$$WP(\Phi)(\phi(\bar{x}, vc)) = \bigwedge_{\tau \in \mathcal{T}} vc = src(\tau) \rightarrow wp(\Phi_\tau)(\phi_{tgt(\tau)}(\bar{x})) \tag{3}$$

or, using (1):

$$WP(\Phi)(\phi(\bar{x}, vc)) = \bigwedge_{\tau \in \mathcal{T}} (vc = src(\tau) \wedge \gamma_\tau(\bar{x})) \rightarrow \phi_{tgt(\tau)}(\bar{e}_\tau(\bar{x})) \ . \tag{4}$$

4 Invariants

Let $\mathcal{S} = \langle \mathcal{V}, \Theta, \mathcal{T} \rangle$ be a guarded transition system and $\mathfrak{R}$ a first-order theory over the language Σ. A formula $\varphi \in \mathcal{F}$ is an *inductive invariant* if $\mathfrak{R} \models \Theta \rightarrow \varphi$ and $\mathfrak{R} \models \varphi \rightarrow WP(\Phi)(\varphi)$, with Φ the transition predicate of the guarded transition system. Since the theory $\mathfrak{R}$ is fixed, we shall not mention it explicitly when we talk about satisfiability and validity in $\mathfrak{R}$. Thus, validity in $\mathfrak{R}$ is denoted by $\models$.

A formula $\phi \in \mathcal{F}$ is an invariant if there exists an inductive invariant φ such that $\models \varphi \rightarrow \phi$. This characterization is sound and relative complete[2].

For a monotone formula transformer $\Gamma : \mathcal{F} \mapsto \mathcal{F}$, such as WP, we write the greatest fixed point as $\nu X.\Gamma(X)$. Its meaning is the usual [3].

Given a formula ϕ, we define the monotone formula transformer $\mathcal{B}$ by

$$\mathcal{B}(Y) \triangleq \phi \wedge WP(\Phi)(Y) \ . \tag{5}$$

The greatest fixed point $\varphi_\mathcal{B} : \nu X.\mathcal{B}(X)$ provides the weakest formula $\varphi_\mathcal{B}$ satisfying $\models \varphi_\mathcal{B} \rightarrow \phi$ and $\models \varphi_\mathcal{B} \rightarrow WP(\Phi)(\varphi_\mathcal{B})$. Therefore, if $\models \Theta \rightarrow \varphi_\mathcal{B}$ then ϕ is an invariant and $\varphi_\mathcal{B}$ is an inductive invariant of the system.

Since $\mathcal{B}$ is monotone, if the sequence starting from *True*

$$\underbrace{True}_{\varphi^0} \leftarrow \underbrace{\mathcal{B}(\varphi_0)}_{\varphi^1} \leftarrow \underbrace{\mathcal{B}(\varphi_1)}_{\varphi^2} \leftarrow \cdots \tag{6}$$

converges in finitely many steps, then its limit is $\varphi_\mathcal{B}$. From this property we can explore the state space using the *backward propagation technique* [3]: given a candidate invariant ϕ, we can find the fixed point $\varphi_\mathcal{B}$ if the sequence converges in finitely many steps. Then, proving $\models \Theta \rightarrow \varphi_\mathcal{B}$ we can verify if ϕ is an invariant of the system.

[2] Completeness is here understood relative to the expressibility of the first-order language.

5 SBS as a Transition System

In this section we explain how to obtain a transition system for a set of processes executing the programs generated by the implementation of conditional critical regions using the SBS technique.

There is a common way to construct transition systems which model the behavior of concurrent programs [10]. The main idea is to first obtain a transition system for every individual thread or sequential component (in a standard way) and then construct their parallel composition as a product, relying on the interleaving semantics of concurrency. In this new transition system there is a variable vc which ranges over sets of locations instead of a single one. The value of this variable is a subset of $\mathcal{L}$ and it denotes all the locations in which control currently resides.

Note, however, that for SBS programs, the number of threads may grow unboundedly (we only model access to a shared resource, in principle it may be accessed by many different components). Establishing a bound for these components is unnecessary and artificial. Instead, we construct a different transition system in which the transitions represent coarser atomic actions. This will be possible given certain peculiarities of SBS programs.

Mutual exclusion: as mentioned in Sec. 2 any process executing these programs begins with a P operation and ends with a V operation. Moreover, all the statements between them are executed in mutual exclusion. This is a characteristic of the method: split binary semaphores ensure mutual exclusion between any pair of P and V operations, i.e. at most one semaphore is on at any point of the execution. Mutual exclusion is therefore ensured[3]. From this property it follows that we can consider any sequence of the form $\mathrm{P}.s_i; c_1; \cdots ; c_n; \mathrm{V}.s_j$ as atomic. Such sequence will be called section S_p^{ij}. Execution of programs can be seen as the execution of a set $\{S_1^{i_1 j_1}, \cdots , S_n^{i_n j_n}\}$ of such sections.

Domino rule: by the semaphore's semantics we can assert that every V operation is followed by a corresponding P operation applied on the same semaphore, i.e. after a S_p^{ij} ends, only a section S_q^{jk} can begin.

Locality of the variables: the variables used in the SBS programs cannot be modified by other programs, i.e. the system is closed.

The mutual exclusion property implies that the sections S_p^{ij} are executed one-at-a-time for each isolated thread. The possible interleavings among different threads are performed outside these sections, which can be considered atomic. Considering also the other two properties, the behavior of the system can be regarded as the execution of a sequence of sections $S_{p_1}^{i_{p_1} j_{p_1}}; S_{p_2}^{i_{p_2} j_{p_2}}; \cdots ; S_{p_n}^{i_{p_n} j_{p_n}}; \cdots$ with $j_{p_k} = i_{p_{k+1}}$. This gives these sort of systems a sequential flavor.

These characteristics allows us to define coarse grained transition systems which are much more suitable for simplification. These systems can be seen as

[3] For further discussions and an operational consideration, we refer to [1].

sequential processes with non-deterministic jumps (goto sentences) between V's and P's applied to the same semaphore.

From these facts, each section S_p^{ij} will be modeled as a transition and the locations identify which semaphore is active before and after the section is executed (i.e. s_i and s_j for the section S_p^{ij}). Loosely speaking, each transition will be associated with a sequence of actions executed inside a critical region by a thread.

In the general case, the SBS technique takes as input a set $\{S_0, \cdots, S_{m-1}\}$ of programs with its corresponding conditions $\{B_0, \cdots, B_{m-1}\}$, an initial condition Θ' and a global invariant I. Here, m refers to the number of critical regions. For each program S_i the technique generates a component SCC_i implementing its corresponding critical region as shown in Fig. 2.

```
SCCi

 P.sm ; (inm)
 if Bi    → skip
 □ ¬Bi   → bi := bi + 1 ;
            V.sm ; (out'm)
            P.si ; (ini)
            bi := bi − 1
 fi;
  Si ;
 if B0 ∧ b0 > 0                  → V.s0       (out0)
    ⋮                               ⋮          ⋮
 □ Bm−1 ∧ bm−1 > 0               → V.s(m−1)  (outm−1)
 □ ⋀0≤j<m ¬Bj ∨ bj = 0           → V.sm      (outm)
 fi
```

Fig. 2. Component with labels

Only temporarily, we annotate each entry and exit point in a given component SCC_i to identify the sections S_p^{jk} (these labels will not identify nodes of the transition system): the entry points are marked with labels prefixed by "in" and the exit points are prefixed by "out". The former are associated with P operations and the later with V operations. The subscripts of the labels indicate which is the semaphore involved. For example, a section (S_p^{mm}) starting with in_m may end in out'_m (if condition $\neg B_i$ holds) or in one of the out_j, with $j \in \{0, \cdots, m\}$ (if B_i holds). On the other hand, the sections (S_p^{ij} with $j \in \{0, \cdots, m\}$) starting in in_i should end in one of the exit points out_j (if its corresponding guard is on).

Given the shape of the guarded transition systems, we need to calculate the condition under which a trace can be executed. This can be done by propagating the classical weakest precondition transformer [11] for every guard inside a section S_p^{jk} to the beginning of the section. We enumerate all possible transitions:

- From (in_m) to (out'_m): Each transition is executed if the condition $\neg B_i$ holds and the state changes only with the increment of b_i. Hence, we have the following m transitions (one for each component SCC_i):

$$vc = s_m \wedge \neg B_i \longmapsto b_i := b_i + 1\,; vc := s_m$$

with $i \in \{0, \cdots, m-1\}$.

- From (in_m) to (out_j): These transitions are executed if B_i holds and $B_j \wedge b_j > 0$ holds in the final guarded command. To calculate γ we apply wp on the guard $B_j \wedge b_j > 0$. We have then $m \times m$ transitions as follows:

$$vc = s_m \wedge B_i \wedge wp(S_i)(B_j \wedge b_j > 0) \longmapsto S_i\,; vc := s_j$$

with $i \in \{0, \cdots, m-1\}$, $j \in \{0, \cdots, m-1\}$.

- From (in_m) to (out_m): These transitions execute the same program as before but only when the last guard of the final guarded command holds for each SCC_i. To calculate the guard γ we apply again wp but this time on guard $\bigwedge_{0 \le j < m} \neg B_j \vee b_j = 0$:

$$vc = s_m \wedge B_i \wedge wp(S_i)(\textstyle\bigwedge_{0 \le j < m} \neg B_j \vee b_j = 0) \longmapsto S_i\,; vc := s_m$$

with $i \in \{0, \cdots, m-1\}$.

- From (in_i) to (out_j): These transitions are executed when $B_j \wedge b_j > 0$ holds in the last guarded command. To calculate the guard for the transition we apply wp, using as program the decrement of b_i followed by program S_i, on the guard $B_j \wedge b_j > 0$. We obtain then $m \times m$ transitions as follows:

$$\begin{aligned} vc = s_i \wedge wp(b_i := b_i - 1; S_i)(B_j \wedge b_j > 0) \\ \longmapsto b_i := b_i - 1\,; S_i\,; vc := s_j \end{aligned}$$

with $i \in \{0, \cdots, m-1\}$, $j \in \{0, \cdots, m-1\}$.

- From (in_i) to (out_m): These transitions are analogous to the ones considered in the previous item, but are executed when the last guard of the final guarded command holds for each SCC_i. We now apply wp on these guards:

$$\begin{aligned} vc = s_i \wedge wp(b_i := b_i - 1; S_i)(\textstyle\bigwedge_{0 \le j < m} \neg B_j \vee b_j = 0) \\ \longmapsto b_i := b_i - 1\,; S_i\,; vc := s_m \end{aligned}$$

with $i \in \{0, \cdots, m-1\}$.

These transitions form the set $\mathcal{T}$ of a transition system $\mathcal{S} = \langle \mathcal{V}, \Theta, \mathcal{T} \rangle$ that model the behavior of the SBS-based process. $\mathcal{V}$ is the set of program variables in $\{\mathrm{S}_0, \cdots, \mathrm{S}_{m-1}\}$ adding the auxiliary variables $\{b_0, \cdots, b_{m-1}\}$ and the control variable vc. The initial condition Θ is:

$$\Theta : vc = s_m \wedge (\textstyle\bigwedge_{0 \le i < m} b_i = 0) \wedge \Theta' \ .$$

The SBS technique also provides an inductive invariant for the system:

$$\varphi_{SBS} : \bigwedge_{0 \le i \le m} vc = s_i \rightarrow \varphi_{s_i} \tag{7}$$

with $\varphi_{s_i} \ : \ B_i \wedge b_i > 0 \wedge I$, $0 \le i < m$ and $\varphi_{s_m} \ : \ (\bigwedge_{0 \le j < m} \neg B_j \vee b_j = 0) \wedge I$.

6 Automatic Refinement

We describe the process that automatically performs the required simplifications. In particular, we focus on the elimination of some guards in the final conditional statement of each component.

To check the possibility of elimination of a given guard, we use the backward propagation technique on a candidate invariant ϕ (5) which models the impossibility of the execution of this guard while the correction of the critical regions is preserved.

For example, if we want to eliminate guard $B_k \wedge b_k > 0$ (for some $k \in \{0, \cdots, m-1\}$) in program SCC$_i$ (Fig. 2) we strengthen the invariant to ensure that any transition with source (in$_m$) and target (out$_k$) or with source (in$_i$) and target (out$_k$), is never executed. This is achieved by strengthening the inductive invariant φ_{SBS} (7) with the propagation (using wp) of the negation of the guard for each program SCC$_i$:

$$\phi : \varphi_{SBD} \wedge F_m \wedge F_i \tag{8}$$

with
$$F_m : vc = s_m \wedge B_i \;\rightarrow\; wp(S_i)(\neg B_k \vee b_k = 0)$$
$$F_i \;: vc = s_i \;\rightarrow\; wp(b_i := b_i - 1; S_i)(\neg B_k \vee b_k = 0)$$

the strengthening of the transitions with source (in$_m$) and target (out$_k$), and with source (in$_i$) and target (out$_k$) respectively.

Since we have a finite number of locations, we represent the set $\mathcal{L}$ as $\{0, \cdots, m\}$. Furthermore, with (2), every assertion ϕ over the transition system can be represented by arrays indexed over $\mathcal{L}$. That is, a formula $\phi(\bar{x}, vc) = \bigwedge_{l \in \mathcal{L}} vc = l \rightarrow \phi(\bar{x}, l)$ will be represented by $[\phi(\bar{x}, 0), \cdots, \phi(\bar{x}, m)]$.

Given the formula ϕ and a formula φ (both represented as arrays) we implement the formula transformer $\mathcal{B}$:

function $\mathcal{B}(\phi, \mathcal{T}, \varphi)$
  for every $i \in \mathcal{L}$ **do**
    $\mathcal{T}_i := \{\tau \in \mathcal{T} : src(\tau) = i\}$;
    $\varphi[i] := \phi[i] \;\wedge\; \bigwedge_{\tau \in \mathcal{T}_i} wp(\Phi_\tau)(\varphi[tgt(\tau)])$;
    $\varphi[i] := \mathfrak{R}$-simplify$(\varphi[i])$;
  end for
  return φ ;

In each iteration the function obtains $\mathcal{B}(\varphi)$ calculating the set $\{\tau \in \mathcal{T} : src(\tau) = i\}$ for each location. The result of the function is calculated using the formula

$$WP(\Phi)(\varphi(\bar{x}, vc)) = \bigwedge_{s \in \mathcal{L}} vc = s \;\rightarrow \bigwedge_{\substack{\tau \in \mathcal{T} \wedge \\ src(\tau) = s}} wp(\Phi_\tau)(\varphi_{tgt(\tau)}(\bar{x}))$$

which is equivalent to (3).

The function $\mathfrak{R}$-simplify performs simplifications in the theory $\mathfrak{R}$ and always returns equivalent formulae. We implement them using CVC Lite and Isabelle. These are described in Sec. 7.

Using the function $\mathcal{B}$ we can implement the algorithm for the fixed point:

function backPropagation($\phi, \mathcal{T}$)
  $\varphi := [\mathit{True}, \cdots, \mathit{True}]$;
  loop
    if $\not\models \Theta \rightarrow \mathcal{B}(\phi, \mathcal{T}, \varphi)$ **then**
      return unsat($\mathcal{B}(\phi, \mathcal{T}, \varphi)$) ;
    else if $\models \varphi \rightarrow \mathcal{B}(\phi, \mathcal{T}, \varphi)$ **then**
      return converge(φ) ;
    else
      $\varphi := \mathcal{B}(\phi, \mathcal{T}, \varphi)$;
    end if
  end loop

This function has a main loop which calculates the values φ_i in (6). The variable φ stores these values. If the value $\mathcal{B}(\phi, \mathcal{T}, \varphi)$ does not satisfy $\models \Theta \rightarrow \mathcal{B}(\phi, \mathcal{T}, \varphi)$, then the function returns the value unsat($\mathcal{B}(\phi, \mathcal{T}, \varphi)$). In this case the method cannot find an inductive invariant for the formula ϕ. In the other case, the method checks if it has reached the fix point. If it is the case, it returns the value converge(φ) which stores the fix point. We use CVC Lite in order to implement the verifications of these conditions.

7 Method Optimizations

During the execution of the procedure described in Sec. 6, the size of the formulae grows in each iteration. This is due to substitutions in the calculation of *WP* (4) performed by the $\mathcal{B}$ transformer. In order to optimize the procedure, we try to keep the size of the formulae as short as possible. We carry out this task in two ways: by eliminating and simplifying transitions and the candidate invariant before the execution of the method and applying simplification strategies over the formulae obtained in the fix point calculation.

Transition Simplification. The transitions from (in_m) to (out_j) in program SCC_i (Fig. 2) are

$$vc = s_m \wedge B_i \wedge wp(S_i)(B_j \wedge b_j > 0) \;\longmapsto\; S_i\,; vc := s_j$$

with $i \in \{0, \cdots, m-1\}$, $j \in \{0, \cdots, m-1\}$. When $i = j$ the transition is never executed. This is proven by showing that the term corresponding to this transition in (3) is weaker than the candidate invariant ϕ, and hence can be absorbed in the fix point calculation. Then, these transitions will be:

$$vc = s_m \wedge B_i \wedge wp(S_i)(B_j \wedge b_j > 0) \;\longmapsto\; S_i\,; vc := s_j$$

with $i \in \{0, \cdots, m-1\}$, $j \in \{0, \cdots, m-1\}$ and $i \neq j$. The proof is in the extended version of this paper [8].

We can eliminate other transitions considering the strength in the candidate invariant ϕ (8). If we try to eliminate the guard $B_k \wedge b_k > 0$ in the program SCC_i, the transitions from (in_m) to (out_k) and from (in_i) to (out_k)

$$vc = s_m \wedge B_i \wedge wp(S_i)(B_k \wedge b_k > 0) \longmapsto S_i \,;vc := s_k \quad \text{and}$$
$$vc = s_i \wedge wp(b_i := b_i - 1; S_i)(B_k \wedge b_k > 0) \longmapsto b_i := b_i - 1 \,; S_i \,; vc := s_k$$

can be eliminated. This fact is proven by showing that the terms generated by these transitions are absorbed in the fix point calculation. The proofs are in the extended version of this paper [8].

We can also simplify the transition going from (in_m) to (out_m):

$$vc = s_m \wedge B_i \wedge wp(S_i)(\textstyle\bigwedge_{0 \le j < m} \neg B_j \vee b_j = 0) \longmapsto S_i \,; vc := s_m$$

with $i \in \{0, \cdots, m-1\}$. These transitions are simplified by eliminating a conjunction term in the subformula $\bigwedge_{0 \le j < m} \neg B_j \vee b_j = 0$:

$$vc = s_m \wedge B_i \wedge wp(S_i)(\textstyle\bigwedge_{\substack{0 \le j < m \\ i \ne j}} \neg B_j \vee b_j = 0) \longmapsto S_i \,; vc := s_m$$

with $i \in \{0, \cdots, m-1\}$. The proof is in the extended version of this paper [8].

Candidate Invariant Simplification. If we try to eliminate the guard $B_i \wedge b_i > 0$ in the program SCC_i (i.e. eliminating the guard that releases the same kind of process) the strengthening of F_m in (8) is not necessary. The proof is in the extended version of this paper [8].

Formulae Simplifications. We implement some simplification strategies over the formulae. The function $\mathfrak{R}$-simplify (Sec. 6) implements these strategies over the formulae $\varphi[i]$ in the algorithm. These are quantifier-free formulae due to substitution in (4). Hence we can store them in conjunctive normal form. If some term in the normalized formulae is weaker than the conjunction of the others, this term can be eliminated. The process is applied over all terms in the formula. Also, a similar tactic is applied over the disjunctions inside the conjunctions; if a subterm is stronger than the disjunction of other subterms (in the same conjunctive term), it can be eliminated. The testing of these implications is done with the CVC Lite Validity Checker.

Moreover, other simplifications are implemented using the Isabelle theorem prover. This tool implements default tactics of simplification and the function $\mathfrak{R}$-simplify uses them in order to reduce the size of the formulae.

8 Examples

We test the method over some classical problems. From a given problem, the generation of the transition system and the candidate invariant was done automatically from its specification. The specification consists of a set $\{S_0, \cdots, S_{m-1}\}$ of programs with its corresponding conditions $\{B_0, \cdots, B_{m-1}\}$, an initial condition Θ' and a global invariant I, as described in Sec. 5.

We develop a transition system generator that takes a text specification of the problem as input and returns a textual representation of the transition system with the candidate invariant. In this section we show the input and the result for each example in a formatted form.

The method and the transition system generator was programmed in the SML language. These programs and the specifications of the examples can be found at `http://www.cs.famaf.unc.edu.ar/ damian/publications/sbdinv/programs/`

Example 1 (Bounded Buffer). Consider the classical *Producer/Consumer* problem through a bounded buffer. The component called *Producer* produces some elements and sends them to the *Consumer* component which will use them. Some synchronization is needed to avoid writing on a full buffer or reading from an empty one. The programs are $S_0 : n := n + 1$ (producer component) and $S_1 : n := n - 1$ (consumer component), the conditions are $B_0 : n < N$ and $B_1 : n > 0$, the initial condition is $\Theta' : n = 0 \wedge N > 0$ and the global invariant is $I : 0 \leq n \wedge n \leq N$.

First we test the method without any guard elimination. This case is for testing purposes only (we do not attempt to eliminate any guard). After performing the system simplifications the set of transitions generated is shown in Fig. 3. In this

$$
\begin{aligned}
&vc = 2 \wedge \neg n < N \longmapsto b_0 := b_0 + 1; vc := 2\ , \\
&vc = 2 \wedge \neg n > 0 \longmapsto b_1 := b_1 + 1; vc := 2\ , \\
&vc = 2 \wedge n < N \wedge b_1 > 0 \wedge n + 1 > 0 \longmapsto n := n + 1; vc := 1\ , \\
&vc = 2 \wedge n > 0 \wedge b_0 > 0 \wedge n - 1 < N \longmapsto n := n - 1; vc := 0\ , \\
&vc = 2 \wedge n < N \wedge (b_1 = 0 \vee \neg n + 1 > 0) \longmapsto n := n + 1; vc := 2\ , \\
&vc = 2 \wedge n > 0 \wedge (b_0 = 0 \vee \neg n - 1 < N) \longmapsto n := n - 1; vc := 2\ , \\
&vc = 0 \wedge b_0 - 1 > 0 \wedge n + 1 < N \longmapsto b_0, n := b_0 - 1, n + 1; vc := 0\ , \\
&vc = 0 \wedge b_1 > 0 \wedge n + 1 > 0 \longmapsto b_0, n := b_0 - 1, n + 1; vc := 1\ , \\
&vc = 1 \wedge b_0 > 0 \wedge n - 1 < N \longmapsto b_1, n := b_1 - 1, n - 1; vc := 0\ , \\
&vc = 1 \wedge b_1 - 1 > 0 \wedge n - 1 > 0 \longmapsto b_1, n := b_1 - 1, n - 1; vc := 1\ , \\
&vc = 0 \wedge (b_0 - 1 = 0 \vee \neg n + 1 < N) \wedge (b_1 = 0 \vee \neg n + 1 > 0) \\
&\qquad\qquad \longmapsto b_0, n := b_0 - 1, n + 1; vc := 2\ , \\
&vc = 1 \wedge (b_0 = 0 \vee \neg n - 1 < N) \wedge (b_1 - 1 = 0 \vee \neg n - 1 > 0) \\
&\qquad\qquad \longmapsto b_1, n := b_1 - 1, n - 1; vc := 2
\end{aligned}
$$

Fig. 3. Bounded Buffer transitions

figure the locations are represented by the semaphore index as the transitions generator does. Note that after performing the system simplifications we obtain fewer transitions than those developed in Sec. 5.

The candidate invariant is also automatically generated and is the same SBS invariant of the problem φ_{SBS} because we do not attempt to do any guard elimination:

$$
\begin{aligned}
\phi : &(vc = 0 \rightarrow 0 \leq n \wedge n < N \wedge b_0 > 0) \wedge \\
&(vc = 1 \rightarrow 0 < n \wedge n \leq N \wedge b_1 > 0) \wedge \\
&(vc = 2 \rightarrow (\neg n < N \vee b_0 = 0) \wedge (\neg n > 0 \vee b_1 = 0) \wedge 0 \leq n \wedge n \leq N)\ .
\end{aligned}
$$

Furthermore, the initial condition generated is:

$$\Theta : vc = 2 \wedge n = 0 \wedge b_0 = 0 \wedge b_1 = 0 \wedge N > 0 \ .$$

After a few seconds of execution time the method converges in one iteration, returning the same invariant ϕ.

In the second test we attempt to eliminate the producer's guard $n < N \wedge b_0 > 0$. This guard releases the producer that waits in the semaphore. The resulting set of transitions is different from the previous one (for the details see the extended version of the article [8]) and the candidate invariant is

$$\begin{aligned} \phi : & (vc = 0 \rightarrow 0 \leq n \wedge n < N \wedge b_0 > 0 \wedge (b_0 = 1 \vee \neg n + 1 < N)) \wedge \\ & (vc = 1 \rightarrow 0 < n \wedge n \leq N \wedge b_1 > 0) \wedge \\ & (vc = 2 \rightarrow (\neg n < N \vee b_0 = 0) \wedge (\neg n > 0 \vee b_1 = 0) \wedge 0 \leq n \wedge n \leq N) \ . \end{aligned}$$

After a few seconds the method converges in four iterations, returning the following inductive invariant:

$$\begin{aligned} \varphi : & (vc = 0 \rightarrow 0 \leq n \wedge n < N \wedge b_0 > 0 \wedge (n < N - 1 \rightarrow b_0 = 1) \\ & \qquad \wedge (n > 0 \rightarrow b_0 \leq 2 \vee b_1 \leq 1)) \wedge \\ & (vc = 1 \rightarrow 0 < n \wedge n \leq N \wedge b_1 > 0) \wedge (n > 1 \rightarrow b_0 \leq 1 \vee b_1 = 1) \\ & \qquad \wedge (n < N \rightarrow b_0 \leq 1)) \wedge \\ & (vc = 2 \rightarrow (\neg n < N \vee b_0 = 0) \wedge (\neg n > 0 \vee b_1 = 0) \\ & \qquad \wedge 0 \leq n \wedge n \leq N) \end{aligned}$$

which is implied by the initial condition Θ. Hence we can eliminate this guard.

We also try to eliminate the consumer's guard $n > 0 \wedge b_1 > 0$ obtaining a similar positive result.

For the rest of guards ($n > 0 \wedge b_1 > 0$ in producer and $n < N \wedge b_0 > 0$ in consumer) the method detects the unsatisfiability of the formula $\Theta \rightarrow \mathcal{B}(\phi, \mathcal{T}, \varphi)$ in the first iteration.

Example 2 (Greedy Bounded Buffer). This example is a modified version of the bounded buffer problem, where the consumer is greedy and consumes two elements instead of one. The programs are $S_0 : n := n + 1$ (producer) and $S_1 : n := n - 2$ (greedy consumer), $B_0 : n < N$ and $B_1 : n > 1$ are the conditions, $\Theta' : n = 0 \wedge N > 1$ is the initial condition, and the global invariant is $I : 0 \leq n \wedge n \leq N$.

For this problem the only guard that can be removed is $n > 2 \wedge b_1 > 0$ in the consumer program. This guard releases a consumer process waiting in his semaphore.

The transition system generated has 11 transitions and the fix point calculation converges in 6 iterations to the invariant:

$$
\begin{aligned}
\varphi : (vc = 0 \rightarrow 0 \leq n \wedge 0 < b_0 \wedge n < N \\
&\wedge (3 \leq n \rightarrow b_1 = 1 \vee \neg 0 < b_1) \\
&\wedge (2 + n < N \wedge 1 \leq n \rightarrow (0 < b_1 \rightarrow (0 < -2 + b_0 \rightarrow b_1 = 1))) \\
&\wedge (3 + n < N \rightarrow (0 < b_1 \rightarrow b_1 = 1 \vee \neg 0 < -3 + b_0)) \\
&\wedge (n + 1 < N \wedge 2 \leq n \rightarrow (0 < b_1 \rightarrow b_1 = 1 \vee \neg 0 < b_0 - 1))) \wedge \\
(vc = 1 \rightarrow n \leq N \wedge 0 < b_1 \wedge 1 < n \\
&\wedge (3 < n \rightarrow b_1 = 1) \\
&\wedge (n < N \wedge 3 \leq n \rightarrow (0 < b_1 - 1 \rightarrow (b_1 = 2 \vee \neg 0 < -2 + b_0)))) \\
&\wedge (1 + n < N \rightarrow (0 < b_1 - 1 \rightarrow (0 < -3 + b_0 \rightarrow b_1 = 2))) \wedge \\
(vc = 2 \rightarrow n \leq N \wedge 0 \leq n \wedge (b_1 = 0 \vee \neg 1 < n) \wedge (b_0 = 0 \vee \neg n < N))
\end{aligned}
$$

For the others guards the method finishes detecting the unsatisfiability of the formula $\Theta \rightarrow \mathcal{B}(\phi, \mathcal{T}, \varphi)$.

Example 3 (Readers and Writers). The last example is the classical readers and writers problem. The specification has the programs $S_0 : w := w + 1$ (writer's entrance), $S_1 : w := w - 1$ (writer's exit), $S_2 : r := r + 1$ (reader's entrance) and $S_3 : r := r - 1$ (reader's exit). The corresponding conditions are $B_0 : w = 0 \wedge r = 0$, $B_1 : \mathit{True}$, $B_2 : w = 0$ and $B_3 : \mathit{True}$.

In order to achieve the simplifications we need to add two kinds of assertions to the programs. First, given the topology of the programs (i.e. every exit is preceded by an entry), we can add the preconditions of the specification. This means that all the transitions in the writer's exit will have the predicate $w > 0$ as extra precondition and similarly for the reader's exit with $r > 0$. Furthermore, since the conditions for the execution of both exit procedures are always true, variables b_2 and b_3 will be invariantly equal to 0. Hence, these two predicates are added to the global invariant.

With these additions, the method finds all superfluous guards of all SBS programs in a few seconds. It also detects all the cases where the simplification is not possible (for the details see the extended version of the article [8]).

9 Conclusions and Further Work

Conditional critical regions are a high level design pattern for concurrent programming. Unfortunately, since they are expensive to implement, most programming languages do not provide them as primitives. The SBS technique allows a nice implementation which can be further improved by axiomatic methods. This work provides a tool for performing such simplifications automatically. Since many problems can be solved with conditional critical regions, this method may have a wide range of applications. We performed some experiments with classical concurrent programs and variants of them (e.g. readers and writers, bounded buffer where the consumer is greedy and consume more than one element).

The examples suggest that in many cases the strengthening process terminates. However, until now we were unable to prove a termination theorem which would be of great importance since in this case the simplification could even be implemented in a compiler. Given that SBS was early considered as a valid alternative for implementation of conditional critical regions and monitors [12], these improvements may give a much more efficient implementation of monitors with conditional wait, which are easier to handle than other kinds of monitors.

Whereas the transition systems considered are generated by a SBS program, many of these results can be extended to other kinds of programs in which each transition models an atomic sequence of actions.

Although it works only for a very specific case, this work can be seen as a step towards the use of theorems provers not only for a posteriori verification of systems, but also for their formal construction and optimization.

Acknowledgements. We would like to thank Leonor Prensa Nieto and the referees for their helpful comments.

References

1. Dijkstra, E.W.: A tutorial on the split binary semaphore (March 1979), `http://www.cs.utexas.edu/users/EWD/ewd07xx/EWD703.PDF`
2. Schneider, F.B.: On Concurrent Programming. Graduate texts in computer science. Springer, New York, Inc. (1997)
3. Bjorner, N., Browne, A., Manna, Z.: Automatic generation of invariants and intermediate assertions. Theor. Comput. Sci. 173(1), 49–87 (1997)
4. Barrett, C., Berezin, S.: CVC Lite: A new implementation of the cooperating validity checker. In: Alur, R., Peled, D.A. (eds.) CAV 2004. LNCS, vol. 3114, pp. 515–518. Springer, Heidelberg (2004)
5. Paulson, L.C.: The Isabelle reference manual (2004), `http://isabelle.in.tum.de/doc/ref.pdf`
6. Andrews, G.: Foundations of Multithreaded, Parallel, and Distributed Programming. Addison-Wesley, Reading, Massachusetts, USA (1999)
7. Martin, A., van de Snepscheut, J.: Design of synchronization algorithms. Constructive Methods in Computing Science, pp. 445–478 (1989)
8. Barsotti, D., Blanco, J.O.: (Im)proving split binary semaphores. Tecnical Report (2007), Available at `http://www.cs.famaf.unc.edu.ar/ damian/publicaciones/sbdinv/SBDwip_ext.pdf`
9. Tiwari, A., Rueß, H., Saïdi, H., Shankar, N.: A technique for invariant generation. In: Margaria, T., Yi, W. (eds.) ETAPS 2001 and TACAS 2001. LNCS, vol. 2031, pp. 113–127. Springer, Heidelberg (2001)
10. Manna, Z., Pnueli, A.: On the faithfulness of formal models. In: Mathematical Foundations of Computer Science, pp. 28–42 (1991)
11. Dijkstra, E.W., Scholten, C.S.: Predicate calculus and program semantics. Springer, New York, Inc. (1990)
12. Kessels, J.L.W.: An alternative to event queues for synchronization in monitors. Commun. ACM 20(7), 500–503 (1977)

Stepwise Development of Simulink Models Using the Refinement Calculus Framework*

Pontus Boström[1], Lionel Morel[2], and Marina Waldén[1]

[1] Åbo Akademi University, Department of Information Technologies
Turku Centre for Computer Science
Joukahaisenkatu 3-5, 20520 Turku, Finland
{pontus.bostrom,marina.walden}@abo.fi
[2] INRIA/IRISA - Campus universitaire de Beaulieu
35042 Rennes Cedex, France
lionel.morel@irisa.fr

Abstract. Simulink is a popular tool for model-based development of control systems. However, due to the complexity caused by the increasing demand for sophisticated controllers, validation of Simulink models is becoming a more difficult task. To ensure correctness and reliability of large models, it is important to be able to reason about model parts and their interactions. This paper provides a definition of contracts and refinement using the action system formalism. Contracts enable abstract specifications of model parts, while refinement offers a framework to reason about correctness of implementation of contracts, as well as composition of model parts. An example is provided to illustrate system development using contracts and refinement.

1 Introduction

Simulink / Stateflow [16] is a domain specific programming and simulation language that has become popular for development of control- and signal-processing systems. It enables model-based design of control systems, where a (continuous) model of the plant can be constructed together with the (discrete) controller. Simulink offers a wide range of simulation tools, which enables simulation and evaluation of the performance of the controller. However, it lacks good tools and development methodologies for reasoning about correctness of models. In particular, it fails to enforce a structured stepwise development method that becomes necessary when developing large control systems.

A goal of our work is to establish such a development method by studying the application of formal analysis techniques to help validate models. The work is based on the use of assume-guarantee (called pre-post in this paper) contracts as a form of local specifications. Analysis techniques rely on a notion of refinement of Simulink models. The refinement calculus [6] gives a good theoretical

* This work is carried out in the context of the project ITCEE (Improving Transient Control and Energy Efficiency by digital hydraulics) funded by the Finnish funding agency TEKES

C.B. Jones, Z. Liu, J. Woodcock (Eds.): ICTAC 2007, LNCS 4711, pp. 79–93, 2007.

framework for developing formal stepwise design methodologies in which abstract specifications are refined into detailed ones. The advantage with refinement is that it allows for a *seamless design flow* where every step in the development process can be formally validated by comparing the refined model to the more abstract one. The final implementation is then formally guaranteed to exhibit the behaviour described by the original specification.

Design-by-contract for embedded controllers. Contract-based design [18] is a popular software design technique in object-oriented programming. It is based on the idea that every method in each object is accompanied by (executable) pre- and post- conditions. The approach has also been successfully applied to reactive programs in [15]. There, a contract is described as a pair of monitors (A, G) and is associated to each component. The meaning of such a contract is that "*as long as input values satisfy A, the outputs should satisfy G*".

Contracts in Simulink consists of such pre- and post-conditions for model fragments [8]. To get a formal semantics of contracts we translate the Simulink models to action systems. Action systems [5,7] is a formalism based on the refinement calculus [6] for reasoning about reactive systems. Contracts are here viewed as non-deterministic abstract specifications. They cannot be simulated in Simulink, but they can be analysed by other tools e.g. theorem provers. Conformance of an implementation to a specification can be validated by model checking or testing. The aim to provide an easy to use and lightweight reasoning framework for correctness of models. Contracts together with the refinement definition also enable compositional reasoning [1] about correctness of models.

Other formalisations of Simulink exist [3,10,11,21,22]. Each one of these take into account different subsets of Simulink. Refinement of Simulink diagrams has also been considered by Cavalcanti et al. [10]. However, they deal mostly with refinement of models into code. We are interested in refinement and stepwise development of models from abstract specifications, which is not the concern of any of those works. Instead of action systems, a definition of refinement [19] for Lustre [13] could also be used in conjunction with the translation from Simulink to Lustre [22]. However, that formalisation can only accommodate discrete models. Treating continuous models using refinement of continuous action systems [17] is a rather natural extension of our formalisation. Furthermore, general formal description and refinement rules for process nets (block-diagrams) has also been investigated [14]. However, we focus specifically on rules for Simulink.

Here we only consider Simulink models that are discrete and use only one single sampling time. We do not consider all types of blocks, e.g., non-virtual subsystems or Stateflow. The action system formalism and refinement calculus is, however, very versatile [6] and can accommodate these features as well.

2 Action Systems

Action systems [4,5,7] are used for describing reactive and distributed systems. The formalism was invented by Back and Kurki-Sounio and later versions of it use the refinement calculus [6].

Table 1. Program statements with their predicate transformer semantics

$\langle f \rangle.q.\sigma$	$= q.f.\sigma$	(Functional update)
$\{p\}.q$	$= p \wedge q$	(Assertion)
$[p].q$	$= p \Rightarrow q$	(Assumption)
$(S_1; S_2).q$	$= S_1.(S_2.q)$	(Sequential composition)
$[R].q.\sigma$	$= \forall \sigma'.(R.\sigma.\sigma' \Rightarrow q.\sigma')$	(Demonic relational update)
$(S_1 \sqcap S_2).q$	$= S_1.q \wedge S_2.q$	(Demonic choice)
skip.q	$= q$	(Skip)
abort.q	$=$ false	(Aborted execution)
magic.q	$=$ true	(Miraculous execution)

Before introducing action systems, a short introduction to the refinement calculus [6] is needed. The refinement calculus is based on Higher Order Logic (HOL) and lattice theory. The state-space of a program in the refinement calculus is assumed to be of type Σ. Predicates are functions from the state-space to the type Boolean, $p : \Sigma \to bool$. A predicate corresponds to the subset of Σ where p evaluates to true. Relations can be thought of as functions from elements to set of elements, $R : \Sigma \to (\Sigma \to bool)$. A program statement is a predicate transformer from predicates on the output state-space Σ to predicates on the input state-space Γ, $S : (\Sigma \to bool) \to (\Gamma \to bool)$. Here we will only consider conjunctive predicate transformers [6,7]. Note also that conjunctivity implies monotonicity. A list of conjunctive predicate transformers are given in Table 1.The functional update consists of assignments of the type $(\langle f \rangle \mathrel{\hat{=}} x := e)$, where the value of variable x in state-space σ is replaced by e. The relational update R is given in the form $R \mathrel{\hat{=}} (x := x' | P.x.x')$. The predicate P gives the relation between the old values of variable x in σ and the new values x' in σ'. Other variables than x in σ remains unchanged in the updated state-space σ'.

An action system has the form:

$$\mathcal{A} \mathrel{\hat{=}} |[\ \textbf{var}\ x;\ \textbf{init}\ A_0;\ \textbf{do}\ A\ \textbf{od}\ ]| : \langle z \rangle$$

Here x (resp. z) denotes the local (resp. global) variables. A_0 is a predicate giving the initialisation action. All actions can be grouped as one single action A that consists of conjunctive predicate transformers, without loss of generality [7].

2.1 Trace Semantics

The execution of an action system gives rise to a sequence of states, called behaviours [5,7]. Behaviours can be finite or infinite. Finite behaviours can be aborted or miraculous, since we do not consider action systems that can terminate normally. In order to only consider infinite behaviours, aborted or miraculous behaviours are extended with infinite sequences of $\bot$ or $\top$, respectively. These states are referred to as *improper states.*

Action A can be written as $\{tA\}; [nA]$, where tA is a predicate and nA is a relation that relates the old and the new state-spaces. This can again be done without loss of generality [7]. Then $\sigma = \sigma_0, \sigma_1, \ldots$ is a possible behaviour of $\mathcal{A}$ if the following conditions hold [5,7]:

- The initial state satisfies the initialisation predicate, $A_0.\sigma_0$
- if σ_i is improper then σ_{i+1} is improper
- if σ_i is proper then either:

- the action system aborts, $\neg tA.\sigma_i$ and $\sigma_{i+1} = \perp$, or
- it behaves miraculously, $tA.\sigma_i \wedge (nA.\sigma_i = \varnothing)$ and $\sigma_{i+1} = \top$, or
- it executes normally, $tA.\sigma_i \wedge nA.\sigma_i.\sigma_{i+1}$

Behaviours contain local variables that cannot be observed. Only a trace of a behaviour consisting of global variables can be observed. Furthermore, all finite stuttering has been removed from the result and finally all infinite stuttering (internal divergence) has been replaced with an infinite sequence of $\perp$. Stuttering refers to steps where the global variables are left unchanged. The semantics of action system $\mathcal{A}$ is now a set of observable traces [5,7].

2.2 Refinement

Refinement of an action system $\mathcal{A}$ means replacing it by another system that is indistinguishable from $\mathcal{A}$ by the environment [5,7]. An ordering of traces σ and τ, $\sigma \leq \tau$, is first defined on the extended state-space $\Sigma \cup \{\perp, \top\}$ as:

$$(\sigma_0, \sigma_1, \ldots) \leq (\tau_0, \tau_1, \ldots) \mathrel{\hat{=}} (\forall i \cdot \sigma_i = \perp \vee \sigma_i = \tau_i \vee \tau_i = \top)$$

Consider two action systems $\mathcal{A}$ and $\mathcal{A}'$. Refinement is then defined as:

$$\mathcal{A} \sqsubseteq \mathcal{A}' \mathrel{\hat{=}} (\forall \sigma' \in tr(\mathcal{A}') \Rightarrow (\exists \sigma \in tr(\mathcal{A}) \cdot \sigma \leq \sigma'))$$

This means that for each trace in the refined system $\mathcal{A}'$ there exists a corresponding trace in the abstract system $\mathcal{A}$. Data refinement rules corresponding to this refinement semantics can be found in [5,7].

3 Encoding Simulink Diagrams in the Refinement Calculus

The structure of a Simulink *block diagram* can be described as a set of *blocks* containing *ports*, where ports are related by *signals*. Simulink has a large library of different blocks for mathematical and logical functions, blocks for modelling discrete and continuous systems, as well as blocks for structuring diagrams. Simulink diagrams can be hierarchical, where subsystem blocks are used for structuring.

3.1 The Steam Boiler Example

To illustrate the formalisation and stepwise development of Simulink, we use a simplified version of the steam boiler case study [2] as a running example throughout the paper. This system consists of a boiler for producing steam. Water is delivered to the system using a pump that can be switched on or off. Steam is taken from the boiler using a valve that is either fully opened or fully closed. The goal of the controller is to maintain the water level between the lower limit L_1 and upper limit L_2. It can read the current water level using the sensor *w_level* and it controls both the pump and the out-valve of the boiler through the actuators *pump_on* and *out_open*.

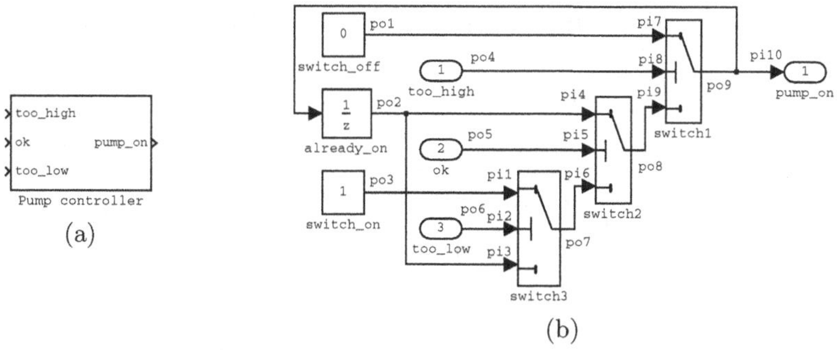

Fig. 1. A simple Simulink model consisting of a part from the steam boiler example. Diagram (b) shows the content of subsystem (a).

3.2 Translating Simulink Model Elements

To introduce the Simulink diagram notation, a small example is shown in Fig. 1. The diagram contains the part of the steam boiler controller that controls if the pump is switched on or off. The diagram contains source blocks *switch_on* and *switch_off* for defining constants giving the state of the pump. There are three in-blocks that provides Booleans stating whether the water level is *too high*, *ok* or *too low*. If the water level is too low the pump is switched on and if it is too high the pump is switched off by the switch-blocks, *switch1*, *switch2* and *switch3*. If the water level is between the limits, the current state of the pump is maintained using the memory in the block *already_on*. The desired state of the pump is delivered from the subsystem by the out block *pump_on*.

A Simulink model is defined as a tuple $\mathcal{M} = (B, root, \mathsf{subh}, P, \mathsf{blk}, \mathsf{ndep}, C)$.

- B is the set of blocks in the model. We can distinguish between the following types of blocks; subsystem blocks B^s, in-blocks in subsystems B^i, out-blocks in subsystems B^o and blocks with memory B^{mem}. When referring to other types of "basic" blocks, B^b is used in this paper. Subsystems B^s, in-blocks B^i and out-blocks B^o are referred to as *virtual blocks*, since they are used purely for structuring and have no effect on the behavioural semantics.
- $root \in B^s$ is the root subsystem.
- $\mathsf{subh} : B \rightarrow B^s$ is a function that describes the subsystem hierarchy. For every block b, $\mathsf{subh}.b$ gives the subsystem b is in;
- P is the set of ports for input and output of data to and from blocks. The ports P^i is the set of in-ports and P^o is the set of out-ports, $P = P^i \cup P^o$;
- $\mathsf{blk} : P \rightarrow B$ is a relation that maps every port to the block it belongs to;
- $\mathsf{ndep} : P^i \nrightarrow P^o$ is a partial function that maps in-ports in non-virtual blocks to the ports in other non-virtual blocks they depend on. An in-port depends on an out-port, if there is a signal or sequence of ports in virtual blocks connected by signals between them. Since we need to be able to analyse model fragments, all in-ports in non-virtual blocks are not necessarily connected. This function can be defined in terms of signals and ports, but for brevity it is given directly.

Table 2. Overview of the translation from Simulink to refinement calculus

Simulink construct	Requirements	Refinement calculus translation
Port, p:	$p \in P \wedge$ $\mathsf{blk}.p \notin (B^i \wedge B^o \wedge B^s)$	$\nu.p$
Constant, c:	$true$	c
Dependency, ndep:	$p_1 = \mathsf{ndep}.p_2$	$\nu.p_2 := \nu.p_1$
Normal block, b:	$b \in B^b \wedge \mathsf{blk}.p^o = b \wedge p^o \in P^o \wedge$ $\mathsf{blk}.p^i = b \wedge p^i \in P^i$	$\nu.p^o := f_b.(\nu.p^i).c_b$
Memory block, b:	$b \in B^{mem} \wedge \mathsf{blk}.p^o = b \wedge p^o \in P^o \wedge$ $\mathsf{blk}.p^i_f = b \wedge p^i_f \in P^i \wedge$ $\mathsf{blk}.p^i_g = b \wedge p^i_g \in P^i$	$\nu.p^o := f_b.p^i_f.x_b.c_b$ $x_b := g_b.p^i_g.x_b.c_b$

– C is the set of block parameters of the model. The block parameters are a set of constants defined in the Matlab workspace of the model.

There are several constraints concerning these functions and relations in order to only consider valid Simulink models, e.g., valid hierarchy of subsystems. In this paper we assume that we only deal with syntactically correct Simulink models (ones that can be drawn).

Consider the Simulink block diagram given in Fig. 1. The blocks are defined as $B \mathrel{\hat{=}} \{root, Pump\ controller,\ too\_high,\ ok,\ too\_low,\ switch1, \ldots\}$. The subsystems are given as $B^s \mathrel{\hat{=}} \{Pump\ controller, root\}$ and the hierarchy as $\mathsf{subh} \mathrel{\hat{=}} \{(Pump\ controller,\ root),\ (too\_high,\ Pump\ controller), \ldots\}$. Names of ports are usually not shown in diagrams. Here we have the following ports, $P \mathrel{\hat{=}} \{pi1, \ldots, pi10\} \cup \{po1, \ldots, po9\}$. The function describing to which block each port belongs to is then given as $\mathsf{blk} \mathrel{\hat{=}} \{(po1,\ switch\_off), (po2,\ already\_on),$ $(po3,\ switch\_on), \ldots\}$. The connections between the ports are defined as ndep $\mathrel{\hat{=}} \{(pi1, po3), (pi3, po2), (pi4, po2), \ldots\}$. Note that e.g. $(pi2, po6)$ is not in ndep, since $pi2$ is only connected to a virtual block. There are no configurable parameters C in this diagram.

To reason about Simulink models in the refinement calculus framework, all Simulink constructs are mapped to a corresponding construct in the refinement calculus, as shown in Table 2. The column *requirements* gives the required condition for a construct to be translated, while the column *refinement calculus translation* gives the actual translation.

Ports in Simulink corresponds to variables in the refinement calculus framework. The function $\nu : P \rightarrowtail V$ describes this mapping, where V is a set of variable names. Only necessary ports are translated to variables, i.e., ports that can be in $(\mathrm{dom}\,.\mathsf{ndep} \cup \mathrm{ran}\,.\mathsf{ndep})$. The constant block parameters are translated directly to variables c. The connections between blocks, $p_1 = \mathsf{ndep}.p_2$, are modelled as assignments. A block can contain in-ports, out-ports, and block parameters. Each block $b \in B^b$ is associated with a function f_b that updates its out-ports based on the value of the in-ports p^i and the parameters of the block c_b. In blocks that contain memory $b \in B^{mem}$, the value on the out-ports depends also on the memory in the block x_b. The memory is updated (using a function g_b). These functions do not need to depend on all in-ports.

3.3 Ordering the Assignments Obtained from Simulink

Now that the translation of the individual constructs have been determined we can give the order in which to execute them. There are several different orderings, since diagrams can have blocks that do not depend on each other. To find an ordering, the dependency between ports in the Simulink diagram need to be determined. We define a relation totdep that describes this.

$$\begin{aligned}\mathsf{totdep} \mathrel{\hat{=}} \; & \lambda p_1 : P \cdot \{p_2 \in P | \\ & ((p_1 \in P^i \Rightarrow p_2 \in \mathsf{ndep}.p_1) \wedge \\ & (p_1 \in P^o \Rightarrow p_2 \in \mathsf{fdep}.p_1))\}\end{aligned}$$

The relation totdep considers both the relation between ports as given by the signals and subsystem hierarchy (ndep), as well as the relations between out-ports and in-ports inside blocks (fdep). The relation fdep, $\mathsf{fdep} : P^o \to \mathcal{P}(P^i)$, can sometimes not be determined syntactically on the graphical part of the Simulink diagram. However, the data dependency for different blocks is documented in the Simulink documentation [16]. The relation totdep need to be a partial order that forms a directed acyclic graph for *deterministic models*. Hence, we can always find an order in which to update the ports in the model and ensure predictable behaviour and execution time. This is automatically ensured by Simulink, if the check for algebraic loops is activated. The order in which the translated Simulink model elements are executed can now be defined.

Definition 1 (Ordering of assignments). *Consider two ports p_1 and p_2 such that p_1 depends on p_2, $p_2 \in \mathsf{totdep}^*.p_1$. In the refinement calculus representation $\nu.p_1$ is updated in the substitution S_1 and $\nu.p_2$ in S_2. Then there exists a (possibly empty) sequence of substitutions S such that $S_2; S; S_1$.*

The ordering given in Def. 1 can be achieved by topologically sorting the assignments to ports. Note that this ensures that a port is never read before it has been updated.

Consider again the model in Fig. 1. The data dependency inside blocks is given by $\mathsf{fdep} \mathrel{\hat{=}} \{(po7, pi1), (po7, pi2), (po7, pi3), (po8, pi4), \ldots\}$, since the output of a switch block depends on all its inputs and the output of the memory block *already_on* does not depend on its input. The complete ordering of ports is then, $\mathsf{totdep} \mathrel{\hat{=}} \mathsf{ndep} \cup \mathsf{fdep}$. The refinement calculus representation $\mathsf{refCalc}.M$ of model M becomes:

$$\begin{aligned}\mathsf{refCalc}.M \mathrel{\hat{=}} \; & \nu.po1 := 0; \nu.pi7 := \nu.po1; \nu.po2 := x; \nu.pi3 := \nu.po2; \\ & \nu.po3 := 1; \nu.pi1 := \nu.po3; \nu.po7 := (\textbf{if } \nu.pi2 \textbf{ then } \nu.pi1 \textbf{ else } \nu.pi3 \textbf{ end}); \ldots \\ & x := \nu.po9\end{aligned}$$

Here x denotes the memory in block *already_on*. The memories are updated after the ports in the diagram have been updated. Hence, $\mathsf{refCalc}.M$ returns the sequential composition of a permutation satisfying the ordering rules of the individual translated statements, as well as the memory updates. Note that all in-ports are not assigned, since some in-ports are not connected to non-virtual blocks.

Table 3. Refinement calculus semantics of contract conditions

Contract condition	Refinement calculus semantics
$Q^{param}(c)$	$Q^{param}(c)$
$Q^{pre}(p^i, c)$	$\{Q^{pre}(\nu.p^i, c)\}$
$Q^{post}(p^o, p^i, c)$	$[\nu.p^o := v_o \mid Q^{post}(v_o, \nu.p^i, c)]$

4 Specification of Simulink Models

When developing Simulink models, we want to start with an abstract overview of the system that is then refined in a stepwise manner. We use contracts to give this abstract description.

The blocks in a Simulink diagram usually use parameters from the Matlab workspace. These parameters are required to have certain properties, here described by the predicate Q^{param}. In the refinement calculus this translates (see 3) into a condition describing the valid parameter values.

A contract for a Simulink model fragment consists of a pre-condition and a post-condition that state properties about its inputs and outputs. In practise this means that we give a *specification block* that can then be refined to a desired implementation. A specification block, M_s, contains in-ports (p^i), out-ports (p^o), a pre-condition (Q^{pre}) and a post-condition (Q^{post}). The semantics of the specification M_s is given by its translation to the refinement calculus shown in Table 3. Statements with this semantics cannot be simulated by the solvers in Simulink. However, other tools can be used to analyse these abstract specifications. The fact that an implementation satisfies its specification can be tested also in Simulink.

Consider again the steam boiler example. An overview of the complete system is given in Fig. 2. This model consists of a specification of the controller, *Controller*, and a specification of the plant, *Steam boiler.* The model has block parameters giving the maximum and minimum water levels L_1 and L_2, respectively. Water levels are positive and the upper level L_2 is higher than the lower level L_1, $Q^{param} \triangleq L_1 > 0 \wedge L_2 > L_1$. The following safety requirements are then given for the water level in the controller:

- When it is above L_2, the pump is switched off and the out valve is opened.
- When it is below L_1, the pump is switched on and the valve is closed.

The contract of the controller is then derived from the safety requirements.

$$\begin{aligned} Q_c^{pre} &\triangleq true \\ Q_c^{post} &\triangleq (w\_level > L_2 \Rightarrow \neg pump\_on \wedge out\_open) \wedge \\ &\quad\ (w\_level < L_1 \Rightarrow pump\_on \wedge \neg out\_open) \end{aligned}$$

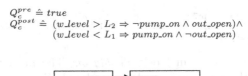

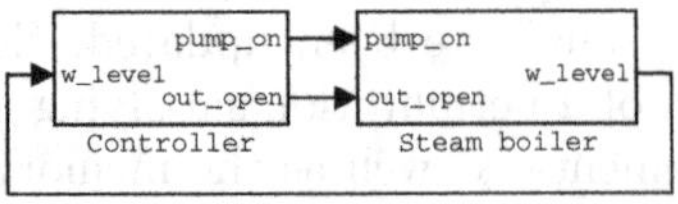

Fig. 2. The diagram in gives an overview of the complete steam boiler system

The plant has no pre-condition, $Q_p^{pre} \hat{=} true$, and it can assign any positive value to the current water level, $Q_p^{post} \hat{=} w\_level \geq 0$.

Since the ordering rules for statements in Def. 1 only concerns statements that updates variables, the assert statement needs a separate rule.

Definition 2 (Ordering of assert statements). *Consider an arbitrary assert statement $\{Q(p_1, \ldots, p_n)\}$. The assert statement is evaluated as soon as possible. This means that all statements S_j that updates $\nu.p_j$, where $p_j \in \{p_1, \ldots, p_n\}$, have already been evaluated. Furthermore, the last such update statement S is directly followed by the assert statement, $S; \{Q(p_1, \ldots, p_n)\}$.*

The diagram in Fig. 2 contains cyclic dependencies between blocks, i.e., feedback. Since this is a common pattern for connections between specification blocks, we also deal with it here. A cycle can be treated as a fix-point [14].

Definition 3 (Cyclic dependencies). *Assume that M_s is any specification block in a cycle. Let the in-port p_s^i of M_s be connected to the out-port p^o of another block in the same cycle. In order to be able to use the ordering rules in Definitions 1 and 2, this connection is considered broken when ordering statements. The refinement calculus translation of M_s gives the statements $([\nu.p_s^i := v|true], [\nu.p_s^o := v|Q^{post}])$. The rest of the constructs in the cycle are translated as in Tables 2 and 3. These statements are then followed by the assumption that the value of p_s^i and the value of p^o are equal and by the translated pre-condition Q^{pre} of the specification, $[\nu.p_s^i = \nu.p^o]; \{Q^{pre}\}$.*

The treatment of feedback here is similar to the one by Mahony [14]. It enables us to prove that the pre-condition is guaranteed by its preceding blocks. Using this technique, the diagram in Fig. 2 can now be translated:

$$\begin{array}{l}\mathsf{refCalc}.System \hat{=} \\ \quad [w\_level' := v|true]; [pump\_on, out\_open := v_p, v_o|Q_c^{post}]; pump\_on' := pump\_on; \\ \quad out\_open' := out\_open; \{Q_p^{pre}\};\ [w\_level := v|Q_p^{post}]; [w\_level' = w\_level]; \{Q_c^{pre}\}\end{array}$$

Cycles are not allowed in the implementation and new features have to be added during the refinement process to make the cyclic dependencies disappear.

4.1 Action System Semantics of Simulink Models

We have now given the semantics of all the needed parts of Simulink in the refinement calculus framework. The behaviour of the complete diagram is given as an action system. Assume that the constructs in the Simulink model is translated to the refinement calculus statements $(S_1, \ldots, S_n)$. This involves both standard Simulink constructs and contract statements. However, the execution order of these statements given in Def. 1-3 is not unique. Consider two arbitrarily chosen execution orders $S_k; \ldots; S_l$ and $S_r; \ldots; S_s$ satisfying the ordering constraints. The following results are then possible:

1 $(S_k; \ldots; S_l).false \wedge \neg(S_r; \ldots; S_s).true$
2 $\neg(S_k; \ldots; S_l).true \wedge (S_r; \ldots; S_s).false$
3 $\forall q \cdot (S_k; \ldots; S_l).q = (S_r; \ldots; S_s).q$

Due to the different order of statements, one sequence of statements might execute a miraculous statement before an abort statement or vice-versa (cases 1 and 2). Otherwise, the result is the same for both orderings (case 3).

Since a model should be non-terminating both miraculous and aborting behaviour are considered erroneous and should be avoided. Hence, we can consideran arbitrary ordering of the statements. The action system is then:

$$\begin{array}{l} \mathcal{M} \hat{=} \;|[\; \mathbf{var}\; x_1, \ldots, x_m, c; \\ \quad\quad \mathbf{init}\; Q^{param}(c) \wedge Init(x_1, \ldots, x_m); \\ \quad\quad \mathbf{do} \\ \quad\quad\quad S_k; \ldots; S_l; R_1; \ldots; R_m; t := t + t_s \\ \quad\quad \mathbf{od} \\ \quad]| : \langle \nu.p_1, \ldots, \nu.p_n, t \rangle \end{array}$$

The global variables giving the observable behaviour are given by the ports, $p_1, \ldots, p_n$, in the model. This way it is possible to track that the behaviour of the initial model is preserved. The time t is considered to be a global variable, to ensure that we have no infinite stuttering. The memory of the blocks, $x_1, \ldots, x_m$, and constant block parameters c are local variables to the action system. The action consists of a sequence of statements $S_k; \ldots; S_l$ satisfying the ordering rules in Def. 1-3 that updates ports. This sequence is followed by statements $R_1; \ldots; R_m$ updating the memory variables $x_1, \ldots, x_m$. The order is not important, since these statements are deterministic and independent of each other. The system is correct, if all pre- and post-conditions are satisfied at all times. Correctness can be verified by checking that the system is non-terminating, $\forall t \cdot t \in tr(\mathcal{M}^V) \Rightarrow t \notin \{\bot, \top\}$.

4.2 Correctness of Simulink Models

The aim of this paper is to be able to define and verify correctness properties of Simulink models. Furthermore, since proofs might not always be feasible, we like to be able to have correctness criteria that can be model checked or tested.

Assume that we have a Simulink model M with a pre-condition Q^{pre} that should maintain a condition Q^{post}. Assume further that p_f^i denotes in-ports that are free and p_b^i denotes in-ports in Q^{pre} that are already connected. The translation of constructs of M with the pre-condition Q^{pre} and post-condition Q^{post} is given by the refinement calculus statements $(S_1, \ldots, S_n, \{Q^{pre}\}, \{Q^{post}\}, R_1, \ldots, R_m)$:

$$\mathsf{refCalc}.M = S_k; \ldots; S_j; \ldots; \{Q^{post}\}; \ldots; S_l; R_1; \ldots; R_m \;, \quad \text{for } k, j, l \in 1..n$$

The assert $\{Q^{pre}\}$ cannot be included, since not all in-ports are connected. Model M is therefore a *partial model*. However, we are interested in the model behaviour in the environment where it is used, i.e., for inputs, where the pre-condition holds. We create a *validation model* for obtaining a complete model that provides the most general environment of such type.

Definition 4 (Validation model). *A validation model is created by adding a non-deterministic assignment to the model that assigns the free in-ports* p_f^i *in*

M values satisfying the precondition. The model contains the refinement calculus statements: $(S_1, \ldots, S_n, \{Q^{pre}\}, \{Q^{post}\}, [\nu.p^i_f := v | Q^{pre}], R_1, \ldots, R_m)$*. The validation model for M is given as*

$$\mathsf{refCalc}.M^V \;\hat{=}\; S_k; \ldots; [\nu.p^i_f := v|Q^{pre}]; \ldots; \{Q^{pre}\}; \ldots; S_j; \ldots; \{Q^{post}\}; \ldots; S_l; R_1; \ldots; R_m$$

The behaviour of the validation model $\mathsf{refCalc}.M^V$ is given as an action system. The model M is correct, if the action system $\mathcal{M}^V$ has no improper traces.

If the model M is deterministic, the correctness of the validation model can be checked using model checking, other verification tools or testing. A test case for M is a model where the statement $[\nu.p^i_f := v|Q^{pre}(v, \nu.p^i_b)]$ has been refined to a deterministic statement. Note that we need to show that there is always a test case in order to ensure that the validation model does not behave miraculously.

If the model M is given as a set of specification blocks $M_1, \ldots, M_m$, where all the models M_j consists of a pre-condition Q^{pre}_j and post-condition Q^{post}_j, the correctness constraints can be simplified. In this case, there is no need to iterate the system over time, since the execution of the graph is independent of the number of times it has been executed before (see Def. 1-3). This lead to compositional reasoning about correctness for different model fragments similar to composition of specifications in [1], i.e., we do not have to know anything about the implementation of the specifications to prove that the connections between them are correct. We need to verify that 1) the validation model does not behave miraculously, $\neg M^V.false$ and that 2) the pre-conditions are not violated, $M^V.true$.

We can then derive a condition of the following type for checking pre-conditions in the model M^V using the refinement calculus:

$$\begin{array}{l}([Q^{param}(c)]; [\nu.p^i_f := v|Q^{pre}]; \{Q^{pre}_1\}; [\nu.p^o_1 := v|Q^{post}_1]; \ldots; \\ \{Q^{pre}_m\}; [\nu.p^o_m := v|Q^{post}_m]; \{Q^{post}\}).true\end{array}$$

Hence, the post-conditions of the predecessors have to imply the pre-condition of the successors and the final post-condition Q^{post}. Using weakest precondition calculations simple conditions can be derived. To show the absence of miraculous behaviour is similar.

5 Refinement

To get a definition of refinement we use the translation of Simulink to the Action Systems formalism. The abstract specifications given by contracts are refined to more concrete models. The properties of the block parameters were stated using an initialisation condition. Refinement of the block parameters follow standard rules for refinement of initialisation [5,7] and is not discussed here.

Consider specification block M_s with in-ports P^i_s, out-ports P^o_s, pre-condition Q^{pre} and post-condition Q^{post} in a model $M = (B, root, \mathsf{subh}, P, \mathsf{blk}, \mathsf{ndep}, C)$. This specification is refined by the model fragment $M_n = (B_n, root_n, \mathsf{subh}_n, P_n, \mathsf{blk}_n, \mathsf{ndep}_n, C_n)$ with pre-condition Q^{pre}_n. The refinement is illustrated in Fig. 3.

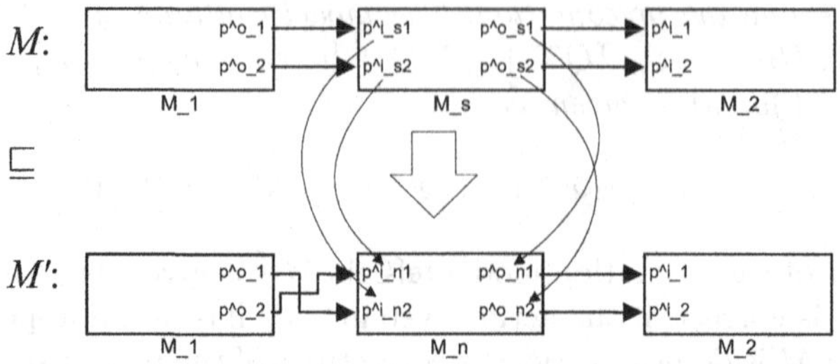

Fig. 3. Illustration of refinement of abstract specification M into refinement M'

The specification M_s is replaced by M_n, while the ports P_s^i and P_s^o of M_s are replaced by ports from M_n.

First we need to determine how ports in the old model M relates to ports in the new model M', in order to relate the variables refCalc.M to the variables in refCalc.M'. The mapping of ports to variables is denoted by ν in the abstract model and by ν' in the refined model.

1. Every block except M_s in M is preserved in M'. Hence, each port p from these blocks are also preserved, which means that they are mapped to the same variables in the refinement calculus representation, $\nu'.p = \nu.p$.
2. For every in-port p from M_s in M there is an in-port p_n from M_n in M' such that they depend on the same port, ndep.p = ndep$'.p_n$ (see Fig. 3). The port p_n that replaces port p is mapped to the same variable in the refinement calculus representation, $\nu'.p_n = \nu.p$.
3. For every in-port p such that it depends on an out-port p_s in the specification block M_s there is a corresponding port p_n in M_n that p depends on, $p_s =$ ndep.$p \wedge p_n =$ ndep$'.p$ (see Fig. 3). The port p_n that replaces port p_s is mapped to the same variable as before in the refinement calculus representation, $\nu'.p_n = \nu.p_s$.

We need to show that the replacement of M_s with pre-condition Q_n^{pre} and model fragment M_n is a correct refinement. First we note that we can add an assert statement $\{Q^{post}\}$ after the statement $[\nu.p_{s1}^o, \ldots, \nu.p_{sn}^o := v | Q^{post}]$ in the abstract specification. In the refinement, the contract statements ($\{Q^{pre}\}$, $[\nu.p_{s1}^o, \ldots, \nu.p_{sn}^o := v | Q^{post}]$) are replaced by the translated Simulink model constructs ($\{Q_n^{pre}\}, S_1, \ldots, S_m, R_1, \ldots, R_t$) obtained from M_n. We use a validation model to check the correctness of this refinement. This validation model uses the refinement calculus statements ($[\nu.p_{s1}^i, \ldots, \nu.p_{sm}^i := v | Q^{pre}], \{Q^{post}\}, \{Q_n^{pre}\}, S_1, \ldots, S_m, R_1, \ldots, R_t$). This model, refCalc.$M_n^V$, is constructed of the statements above ordered according to the rules in Def. 1-3. Note that statement $[\nu.p_{s1}^i, \ldots, \nu.p_{sm}^i := v | Q^{pre}]$ assign the in-ports and, hence, appears in the beginning of the translation. The assert statement $\{Q^{post}\}$ that depends on the out-ports is placed towards the end.

$$\text{refCalc}.M_n^V \triangleq S_k; [\nu.p_{s1}^i, \ldots, \nu.p_{sm}^i := v | Q^{pre}]; \ldots; \{Q_n^{pre}\}; \ldots; S_l; \{Q^{post}\}; R_1; \ldots; R_t$$

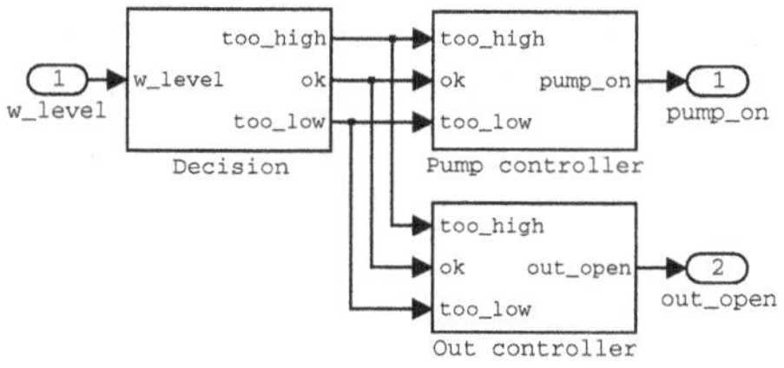

Fig. 4. This diagram shows the refinement of the controller

Theorem 1 (Correctness of refinement). *The model M_n refines M_s, $M_s \sqsubseteq M_n$, if $\forall t \cdot t \in tr(\mathcal{M}_n^V) \Rightarrow t \neq \bot$ and M_n does not behave miraculously.*

Proof. There are two constructs to consider $\{Q^{pre}\} \sqsubseteq \{Q_n^{pre}\}$ and $[\nu.p_{s1}^o, \ldots, \nu.p_{sn}^o := v|Q^{post}] \sqsubseteq \mathsf{refCalc}.M_n$.

- If $\{Q^{pre}\} \sqsubseteq \{Q_n^{pre}\}$ does not hold $\{Q_n^{pre}\}$ will contribute with aborted traces, due to the assignment to in-ports, $[\nu'.p_{s1}^i, \ldots, \nu'.p_{sm}^i := v|Q^{pre}]$.
- If $[\nu.p_{s1}^o, \ldots, \nu.p_{sn}^o := v|Q^{post}] \sqsubseteq \mathsf{refCalc}.M_n$ does not hold, then either,
  - the model fragment $\mathsf{refCalc}.M_n$ aborts, or
  - the output from $\mathsf{refCalc}.M_n$ does not satisfy Q^{post}.

  Both cases contribute with aborted traces.

Since we show that $\mathcal{M}_n^V$ does not abort we can conclude that $\{Q^{pre}\} \sqsubseteq \{Q_n^{pre}\}$ and $[\nu.p_{s1}^o, \ldots, \nu.p_{sn}^o := v|Q^{post}] \sqsubseteq \mathsf{refCalc}.M_n$ must hold. □

Due to monotonicity we have $M_s \sqsubseteq M_n \Rightarrow M \sqsubseteq M'$.

The controller in the steam boiler example is refined in a stepwise manner to obtain an implementation. Here we do the development in one single model, such that each level in the subsystem hierarchy is a new refinement step. Each subsystem is associated with a contract. When the system is refined, the details of the subsystem are added. First we refine the specification of the controller into three different subsystem as shown in Fig. 4. The first one, *Decision*, decides if the water level is too high (*too_high*), suitable (*ok*) or too low (*too_low*). The second one, *Pump Controller*, computes if the pump should be on, while the third one, *Out Controller*, computes if the out valve should be opened. The contract for the specification *Decision* states that the water level should be between L_1 and L_2 to be acceptable, otherwise it is too high or too low.

$$\begin{aligned} Q_d^{pre} &\mathrel{\hat{=}} true \\ Q_d^{post} &\mathrel{\hat{=}} (w\_level > L_2 \Rightarrow too\_high \wedge \neg ok \wedge \neg too\_low) \wedge \\ &\quad (w\_level < L_1 \Rightarrow \neg too\_high \wedge \neg ok \wedge too\_low) \wedge \\ &\quad (w\_level \geq L_1 \wedge w\_level \leq L_2 \Rightarrow \neg too\_low \wedge ok \wedge \neg too\_high) \end{aligned}$$

The specification block *Pump Controller* requires that the water level is either too low, acceptable or too high. It guarantees that the pump is switched on if the water level is too low and switched off if it is too high.

$$\begin{aligned} Q_{pump}^{pre} &\mathrel{\hat{=}} too\_high \vee ok \vee too\_low \\ Q_{pump}^{post} &\mathrel{\hat{=}} (too\_high \Rightarrow \neg pump\_on) \wedge (too\_low \Rightarrow pump\_on) \end{aligned}$$

The contract for the last specification, *Out Controller*, is defined similarly. Note that we do not say anything about the situation when the level is between L_1 and L_2. The implementation can choose the best alternative in that case.

To validate that the system in Fig. 4 refines the specification *Controller* we create a validation model:

$$\begin{aligned}&\mathsf{refCalc}.Controller^V \triangleq\\ &\quad [w\_level := v|Q_c^{pre}(v)]; \{Q_d^{pre}\}; [too\_high, ok, too\_low := v_h, v_o, v_l|Q_d^{post}];\\ &\quad \{Q_{pump}^{pre}\}; [pump\_on := v|Q_{pump}^{post}]; \{Q_{out}^{pre}\}; [out\_open := v|Q_{out}^{post}]; \{Q_c^{post}\}\end{aligned}$$

We first need to show that the validation model does not behave miraculously, $\neg(\mathsf{refCalc}.Controller^V).false$. It is easy to see that values can always be given to the in-ports and that the post-conditions are feasible. The refinement is then correct if the validation model does not abort. By systematically computing the weakest precondition $(\mathsf{refCalc}.Controller^V).true$ from this program we get the following conditions:

$$\begin{aligned}&(Q^{param} \wedge Q_c^{pre} \Rightarrow Q_d^{pre})\wedge\\ &(Q^{param} \wedge Q_c^{pre} \wedge Q_d^{post} \Rightarrow Q_{pump}^{pre})\wedge\\ &(Q^{param} \wedge Q_c^{pre} \wedge Q_d^{post} \Rightarrow Q_{out}^{pre})\wedge\\ &(Q^{param} \wedge Q_c^{pre} \wedge Q_d^{post} \wedge Q_{pump}^{post} \wedge Q_{out}^{post} \Rightarrow Q_c^{post})\end{aligned}$$

The refinement of the *Controller* is still abstract and not executable. To illustrate the final implementation consider the implementation of the specification *Pump Controller* in Fig. 1. Here we have taken the approach to only switch on or off the pump when a water level limit is reached. Other control strategies can also be used. The implementation of *Pump Controller* uses memory and we have to validate its behaviour over time to ensure correct behaviour. This is again done by creating a validation model.

6 Conclusions and Future Work

In this paper we have presented a definition of refinement of Simulink diagrams using contracts and an action systems semantics. First we gave a translation from Simulink to refinement calculus and provided a definition of contracts using pre- and post-conditions in *specification blocks*. The action systems formalism provided semantics to these contracts. We then showed how an abstract specification given as a contract could be refined into an implementation satisfying the contract. Furthermore, validation of the refinement can be performed by model checking or testing a *validation model*. These ideas have been tried on a larger case study [8] and the initial experience with contracts and Simulink are positive. An extended version of the paper is also available as a technical report [9].

We believe this refinement-based development provides a convenient design method even for developers not familiar with formal methods. These methods are not limited to Simulink: they can be applied to other similar languages like SCADE [12] and Scicos [20] as well.

References

1. Abadi, M., Lamport, L.: Conjoining specifications. ACM Transactions on Programming Languages and Systems 17(3), 507–534 (1995)
2. Abrial, J.-R., Börger, E., Langmaack, H.: The steam boiler case study: Competition of formal program specification and development methods. In: Abrial, J.-R., Börger, E., Langmaack, H. (eds.) Formal Methods for Industrial Applications. LNCS, vol. 1165, pp. 1–12. Springer, Heidelberg (1996)
3. Arthan, R., Caseley, P., O'Halloran, C., Smith, A.: ClawZ: Control laws in Z. In: Proceedings of ICFEM 2000, pp. 169–176. IEEE Press, Los Alamitos (2000)
4. Back, R.-J.R., Kurki-Suonio, R.: Decentralization of process nets with centralized control. In: Proceedings of the 2nd ACM SIGACT-SIGOPS Symposium of Principles of Distributed Computing, pp. 131–142. ACM Press, New York (1983)
5. Back, R.-J.R., von Wright, J.: Trace refinement of action systems. In: Jonsson, B., Parrow, J. (eds.) CONCUR 1994. LNCS, vol. 836, pp. 367–384. Springer, Heidelberg (1994)
6. Back, R.-J.R., von Wright, J.: Refinement Calculus: A Systematic Introduction. Graduate Texts in Computer Science. Springer, Heidelberg (1998)
7. Back, R.-J.R., von Wright, J.: Compositional action system refinement. Formal Aspects of Computing 15, 103–117 (2003)
8. Boström, P., Linjama, M., Morel, L., Siivonen, L., Waldén, M.: Design and validation of digital controllers for hydraulics systems. In: The 10th Scandinavian International Conference on Fluid Power, Tampere, Finland (2007)
9. Boström, P., Morel, L., Waldén, M.: Stepwise development of Simulink models using the refinement calculus framework. Technical Report 821, TUCS (2007)
10. Cavalanti, A., Clayton, P., O'Halloran, C.: Control law diagrams in Circus. In: Fitzgerald, J.A., Hayes, I.J., Tarlecki, A. (eds.) FM 2005. LNCS, vol. 3582, pp. 253–268. Springer, Heidelberg (2005)
11. Chen, C., Dong, J.S.: Applying timed interval calculus to Simulink diagrams. In: Liu, Z., He, J. (eds.) ICFEM 2006. LNCS, vol. 4260, pp. 74–93. Springer, Heidelberg (2006)
12. Esterel Technologies. SCADE (2006), `http://www.esterel-technologies.com/`
13. Halbwachs, N., Caspi, P., Raymond, P., Pilaud, D.: The synchronous dataflow programming language lustre. Proceedings of the IEEE 79(9), 1305–1320 (1991)
14. Mahony, B.: The DOVE approach to design of complex dynamic processes. In: Theorem Proving in Higher Order Logic, NASA conf. publ., CP-2002-211736 (2002)
15. Maraninchi, F., Morel, L.: Logical-time contracts for reactive embedded components. In: ECBSE'04. 30th EUROMICRO Conference on Component-Based Software Engineering Track, Rennes, France (2004)
16. Mathworks Inc., Simulink/Stateflow (2006), `http://www.mathworks.com`
17. Meinicke, L., Hayes, I.: Continuous action system refinement. In: Uustalu, T. (ed.) MPC 2006. LNCS, vol. 4014, pp. 316–337. Springer, Heidelberg (2006)
18. Meyer, B.: Object-Oriented Software Construction, 2nd edn. Prentice-Hall, Englewood Cliffs (1997)
19. Mikáč, J., Caspi, P.: Temporal refinement for Lustre. In: SLAP 2005. Proceedings of Synchronous Languages, Applications and Programming, Edinburgh, Scotland. ENTCS, Elsevier, Amsterdam (2005)
20. Scilab Consortium. Scilab/Scicos (2006), `http://www.scilab.org`
21. Tiwari, A., Shankar, N., Rushby, J.: Invisible formal methods for embedded control systems. Proceedings of the IEEE 91(1), 29–39 (2003)
22. Tripakis, S., Sofronis, C., Caspi, P., Curic, A.: Translating discrete-time Simulink to Lustre. ACM Trans. on Embedded Computing Systems 4(4), 779–818 (2005)

Bisimulations for a Distributed Higher Order π-Calculus*

Zining Cao

Department of Computer Science and Technology
Nanjing University of Aero. & Astro., Nanjing 210016, P. R. China
caozn@nuaa.edu.cn

Abstract. In this paper we design a distributed variant of higher order π-calculus which takes distributed location into account. Furthermore, we present three bisimulations for such a distributed higher order π-calculus, called distributed context bisimulation, distributed normal bisimulation and distributed reduction bisimulation respectively. We prove that the three distributed bisimulations are equivalent.

1 Introduction

Higher order π-calculus was proposed and studied intensively in Sangiorgi's dissertation [14]. In higher order π-calculus, processes and abstractions over processes of arbitrarily high order, can be communicated. Some interesting equivalences for higher order π-calculus, such as barbed equivalence, context bisimulation and normal bisimulation, were presented in [14]. The relation between the three equivalences was studied in [12,14].

Process calculi can be enriched with localities that explicitly describe the distribution of processes. There are various proposals for distributed process calculi, including distributed *CCS* [3,7], distributed π-calculus [13], *Seal* calculus [17], distributed higher order calculus [18], *M*-calculus [16], *Kell*-calculus [15], *Homer*-calculus [8,9] etc. For these process calculi, localities may represent physical machines, or more generally distribution units where processes are grouped according to some criterion like the sharing of resources. In a concurrent process, localities are naturally associated with parallel components. These localities then intervene in the semantics of processes and become part, to some extent, of their observable behaviour.

In this paper we design a distributed higher order π-calculus which allows the observer to see the distributed nature of processes. For this distributed higher order π-calculus, the processes under observation are considered to be distributed in nature and locations are associated with parallel components which represent sites. So, the observer not only can test the process by communicating with it but also can observe or distinguish that part of the distributed process which reacted to the test. Furthermore, three general notions of bisimulation related to this

* This work was supported by the National Natural Science Foundation of China under Grant 60473036.

C.B. Jones, Z. Liu, J. Woodcock (Eds.): ICTAC 2007, LNCS 4711, pp. 94–108, 2007.

observation of distributed systems are introduced. The equivalence between the distributed bisimulations is proved, which generalizes the equivalence between barbed equivalence, normal bisimulation and context bisimulation to distributed process calculus. Concretely, a distributed context bisimulation is presented via a generalization of context bisimulation to the case of distributed processes. Processes are equated if they present behaviours which are viewed as equivalent for context bisimulation, and furthermore these behaviours happened at the same location or between the same locations. Similarly, a distributed normal bisimulation is presented as a very economic form of distributed bisimulation. We also propose a new reduction bisimulation for our distributed process calculus, called distributed reduction bisimulation, which is based on the move of messages among components of process rather than observables such as actions or barbs. Roughly speaking, for distributed reduction bisimulation, K and L are said to be strong distributed reduction bisimilar if given an arbitrary distributed process M, any distributed communication $\{\tau\}_{i,j}$ between K and M can be matched by the same distributed communication $\{\tau\}_{i,j}$ between L and M, where $\{\tau\}_{i,j}$ denotes the communication between locations i and j. This is essentially different from original barbed equivalence because the barb testing is not needed. We study the property of these distributed bisimulations and prove the equivalence between the three distributed bisimulations.

This paper is organized as follows: In Section 2 we briefly review higher order π-calculus. In Section 3, we introduce the corresponding syntax, labelled transition system for distributed higher order π-calculus. In Section 4, we present the notions of distributed context bisimulation, distributed normal bisimulation and distributed reduction bisimulation. In Section 5, we study the relation between distributed reduction bisimulation and distributed context bisimulation. In Section 6, we study the relation between distributed normal bisimulation and distributed context bisimulation. In Section 7, we give a characterisation theorem. The paper is concluded in Section 8.

2 An Overview of Higher Order π-Processes

In this section we briefly recall the syntax, labelled transition system and bisimulations of the higher order π-calculus. We only focus on a second-order fragment of the higher order π-calculus [12], i.e., there is no abstraction in this fragment.

We assume a set N of names, ranged over by $a, b, c,...$ and a set Var of process variables, ranged over by $X, Y, Z, U, ...$ We use $E, F, P, Q,...$ to stand for processes. Pr denotes the set of all processes.

We first give the grammar for the higher order π-calculus processes as follows:
$P ::= 0 \mid U \mid \pi.P \mid P_1|P_2 \mid (\nu a)P \mid !P$

π is called a prefix and can have one of the following forms:

$\pi ::= \tau \mid l \mid \bar{l} \mid a(U) \mid \overline{a}\langle P\rangle$, here τ is a tau prefix; l is a first order input prefix; $\bar{l}$ is a first order output prefix; $a(U)$ is a higher order input prefix and $\overline{a}\langle P\rangle$ is a higher order output prefix.

In each process of the form $(\nu y)P$ the occurrence of y is bound within the scope of P. An occurrence of y in a process is said to be free iff it does not lie within the scope of a bound occurrence of y. The set of names occurring free in P is denoted $fn(P)$. An occurrence of a name in a process is said to be bound if it is not free, we write the set of bound names as $bn(P)$. $n(P)$ denotes the set of names of P, i.e., $n(P) = fn(P) \cup bn(P)$. The definition of substitution in process terms may involve renaming of bound names when necessary to avoid name capture.

Higher order input prefix $a(U).P$ binds all free occurrences of U in P. The set of variables occurring free in P is denoted $fv(P)$. We write the set of bound variables as $bv(P)$. A process is closed if it has no free variable; it is open if it has free variables. Pr^c is the set of all closed processes.

Processes P and Q are α-convertible, $P \equiv_\alpha Q$, if Q can be obtained from P by a finite number of changes of bound names and variables. For example, $(\nu c)(\overline{b}\langle c(U).U\rangle.0) \equiv_\alpha (\nu d)(\overline{b}\langle d(U).U\rangle.0)$.

The operational semantics of higher order processes is given in Table 1. We have omitted the symmetric rules of the parallelism and communication.

$$ALP: \frac{P \xrightarrow{\alpha} P'}{Q \xrightarrow{\alpha} Q'} P \equiv_\alpha Q, P' \equiv_\alpha Q' \qquad TAU: \tau.P \xrightarrow{\tau} P$$

$$OUT1: \overline{l}.P \xrightarrow{\overline{l}} P \qquad IN1: l.P \xrightarrow{l} P$$

$$OUT2: \overline{a}\langle E\rangle.P \xrightarrow{\overline{a}\langle E\rangle} P \qquad IN2: a(U).P \xrightarrow{a\langle E\rangle} P\{E/U\}$$

$$PAR: \frac{P \xrightarrow{\alpha} P'}{P|Q \xrightarrow{\alpha} P'|Q} bn(\alpha) \cap fn(Q) = \emptyset$$

$$COM1: \frac{P \xrightarrow{\overline{l}} P' \quad Q \xrightarrow{l} Q'}{P|Q \xrightarrow{\tau} P'|Q'}$$

$$COM2: \frac{P \xrightarrow{(\nu\widetilde{b})\overline{a}\langle E\rangle} P' \quad Q \xrightarrow{a\langle E\rangle} Q'}{P|Q \xrightarrow{\tau} (\nu\widetilde{b})(P'|Q')} \widetilde{b} \cap fn(Q) = \emptyset$$

$$RES: \frac{P \xrightarrow{\alpha} P'}{(\nu a)P \xrightarrow{\alpha} (\nu a)P'} a \notin n(\alpha) \qquad REP: \frac{P|!P \xrightarrow{\alpha} P'}{!P \xrightarrow{\alpha} P'}$$

$$OPEN: \frac{P \xrightarrow{(\nu\widetilde{c})\overline{a}\langle E\rangle} P'}{(\nu b)P \xrightarrow{(\nu b,\widetilde{c})\overline{a}\langle E\rangle} P'} a \neq b,\ b \in fn(E) - \widetilde{c}$$

Table 1

In [12,14], Sangiorgi presented some interesting equivalences for higher order π-calculus such as context bisimulation, normal bisimulation and barbed equivalence. These equivalences were proved to be coincident. In the following, we use $\overset{\varepsilon}{\Longrightarrow}$ to abbreviate the reflexive and transitive closure of $\xrightarrow{\tau}$, use $\overset{\alpha}{\Longrightarrow}$ to abbreviate $\overset{\varepsilon}{\Longrightarrow}\xrightarrow{\alpha}\overset{\varepsilon}{\Longrightarrow}$.

A symmetric relation $R \subseteq Pr^c \times Pr^c$ is a weak context bisimulation if P R Q implies: (1) whenever $P \overset{\varepsilon}{\Longrightarrow} P'$, then there exists Q' such that $Q \overset{\varepsilon}{\Longrightarrow} Q'$ and P' R Q'; (2) whenever $P \overset{l}{\Longrightarrow} P'$, then there exists Q', such that $Q \overset{l}{\Longrightarrow} Q'$ and P' R Q'; (3) whenever $P \overset{\overline{l}}{\Longrightarrow} P'$, then there exists Q', such that $Q \overset{\overline{l}}{\Longrightarrow} Q'$ and

$P'\ R\ Q'$; (4) whenever $P \stackrel{a\langle E\rangle}{\Longrightarrow} P'$, there exists Q' such that $Q \stackrel{a\langle E\rangle}{\Longrightarrow} Q'$ and $P'\ R\ Q'$; (5) whenever $P \stackrel{(\nu\widetilde{b})\overline{a}\langle E\rangle}{\Longrightarrow} P'$, there exist Q', F, $\widetilde{c}$, such that $Q \stackrel{(\nu\widetilde{c})\overline{a}\langle F\rangle}{\Longrightarrow} Q'$ and for all $C(U)$ with $fn(C(U)) \cap \{\widetilde{b},\widetilde{c}\} = \emptyset$, $(\nu\widetilde{b})(P'|C\langle E\rangle)\ R\ (\nu\widetilde{c})(Q'|C\langle F\rangle)$.

We write $P \approx_{Ct} Q$ if P and Q are weakly context bisimilar.

A symmetric relation $R \subseteq Pr^c \times Pr^c$ is a weak normal bisimulation if $P\ R\ Q$ implies: (1) whenever $P \stackrel{\varepsilon}{\Longrightarrow} P'$, then there exists Q' such that $Q \stackrel{\varepsilon}{\Longrightarrow} Q'$ and $P'\ R\ Q'$; (2) whenever $P \stackrel{l}{\Longrightarrow} P'$, then there exists Q', such that $Q \stackrel{l}{\Longrightarrow} Q'$ and $P'\ R\ Q'$; (3) whenever $P \stackrel{\overline{l}}{\Longrightarrow} P'$, then there exists Q', such that $Q \stackrel{\overline{l}}{\Longrightarrow} Q'$ and $P'\ R\ Q'$; (4) whenever $P \stackrel{a\langle\overline{m}.0\rangle}{\Rightarrow} P'$, here m is a fresh name, there exists Q' such that $Q \stackrel{a\langle\overline{m}.0\rangle}{\Rightarrow} Q'$ and $P'\ R\ Q'$; (5) whenever $P \stackrel{(\nu\widetilde{b})\overline{a}\langle E\rangle}{\Rightarrow} P'$, there exist Q', F, $\widetilde{c}$, such that $Q \stackrel{(\nu\widetilde{c})\overline{a}\langle F\rangle}{\Rightarrow} Q'$ and for a fresh name m, $(\nu\widetilde{b})(P'|!m.E)\ R\ (\nu\widetilde{c})(Q'|!m.F)$.

We write $P \approx_{Nr} Q$ if P and Q are weakly normal bisimilar.

A symmetric relation $R \subseteq Pr^c \times Pr^c$ is a weak barbed bisimulation if $P\ R\ Q$ implies:

(1) whenever $P \stackrel{\tau}{\Longrightarrow} P'$ then there exists Q', such that $Q \stackrel{\tau}{\Longrightarrow} Q'$ and $P'\ R\ Q'$;

(2) for any channel n, if $P \Downarrow n$, then also $Q \Downarrow n$. Here $P \Downarrow n$ means $\exists P'$, $P \stackrel{\alpha}{\Longrightarrow} P'$, here $\alpha = n$ or $\overline{n}$ or $n\langle E\rangle$ or $(\nu\widetilde{a})\overline{n}\langle E\rangle$..

Two processes P and Q are weakly barbed equivalent, if there is a weak barbed bisimulation R, such that $P|C\ R\ Q|C$ for any process C.

3 Syntax and Labelled Transition System of Distributed Higher Order π-Calculus

In this section, a variant of process calculus is presented which incorporates indexing as a means of identifying process distribution. We now introduce the concept of distributed process. Given a location set *Loc*, w.l.o.g., let *Loc* be the set of natural numbers, the syntax for distributed processes allows the parallel composition of located process $\{P\}_i$, which may share defined name a, using the construct $(\nu a)-$. The class of the distributed processes is denoted as DPr, ranged over by $K, L, M, N, \ldots$.

The formal definition of distributed process is given as follows:

$M ::= \{P\}_i \mid M_1|M_2 \mid (\nu a)M$, here $i \in Loc$ and $P \in Pr$.

Intuitively, $\{P\}_i$ represents process P residing at location i. The actions of such a process will be observed to occur "within location i". $M_1|M_2$ represents the parallel composition of two distributed systems M_1 and M_2. $(\nu a)M$ is the restriction operator, which makes name a local to system M.

For example, $\{(\nu l)(\overline{b}\langle l.0|!\tau.0\rangle.0|\overline{l}.0)\}_0|\{b(U).U\}_1$, $(\nu l)(\{\overline{l}.0\}_0|\{l.0|!\tau.0\}_1)$, $\{\overline{b}\langle !\tau.0\rangle.0\}_0|\{b(U).U\}_1$ and $\{0\}_0|\{!\tau.0\}_1$ are distributed processes, here intuitively $\{(\nu l)(\overline{b}\langle l.0|!\tau.0\rangle.0|\overline{l}.0)\}_0|\{b(U).U\}_1$ represents $(\nu l)(\overline{b}\langle l.0|!\tau.0\rangle.0|\overline{l}.0)$ and $b(U).U$ running at locations 0 and 1 respectively, $(\nu l)(\{\overline{l}.0\}_0|\{l.0|!\tau.0\}_1)$ rep resents the parallel of $\{\overline{l}.0\}_0$ and $\{l.0|!\tau.0\}_1$ with a private name l.

Similar to the original higher order π-calculus, in each distributed process of the form $(\nu a)M$ the occurrence of a is a bound within the scope of M. An occurrence of a in M is said to be free iff it does not lie within the scope of a bound occurrence of a. The set of names occurring free in M is denoted $fn(M)$. An occurrence of a name in M is said to be bound if it is not free, we write the set of bound names as $bn(M)$. $n(M)$ denotes the set of names of M, i.e., $n(M) = fn(M) \cup bn(M)$. We use $n(M,N)$ to denote $n(M) \cup n(N)$. Higher order input prefix $\{a(U).P\}_i$ binds all free occurrences of U in P. The set of variables occurring free in M is denoted as $fv(M)$. We write the set of bound variables in M as $bv(M)$. A distributed process is closed if it has no free variable; it is open if it has free variables. DPr^c is the set of all closed distributed processes.

Processes M and N are α-convertible, $M \equiv_\alpha N$, if N can be obtained from M by a finite number of changes of bound names and bound variables.

Structural congruence is a congruence relation including the following rules:

$\{P\}_i|\{Q\}_i \equiv \{P|Q\}_i$; $M|N \equiv N|M$; $(L|M)|N \equiv L|(M|N)$; $M|0 \equiv M$; $(\nu a)0 \equiv 0$; $(\nu a)(\nu b)M \equiv (\nu b)(\nu a)M$; $(\nu a)(M|N) \equiv M|(\nu a)N$ if $a \notin fn(M)$; $M \equiv N$ if $M \equiv_\alpha N$.

The distributed actions are given by

$I\alpha ::= \{\tau\}_{i,j} \mid \{l\}_i \mid \{\overline{l}\}_i \mid \{a\langle E\rangle\}_i \mid \{\overline{a}\langle E\rangle\}_i \mid \{(\nu\widetilde{b})\overline{a}\langle E\rangle\}_i$

We write $bn(I\alpha)$ for the set of names bound in $I\alpha$, which is $\{\widetilde{b}\}$ if $I\alpha$ is $\{(\nu\widetilde{b})\overline{a}\langle E\rangle\}_i$ and $\emptyset$ otherwise. $n(I\alpha)$ denotes the set of names that occur in $I\alpha$.

Similar to Table 1, we give the operational semantics of distributed processes in Table 2. We have omitted the symmetric rules of the parallelism and communication. The main feature of Table 2 is that the label $I\alpha$ on the transition arrow is of the form $\{\alpha\}_i$ or $\{\tau\}_{i,j}$, where α is an input or output action, i and j are locations. From the distributed view, $\{\alpha\}_i$ can be regarded as an input or output action performed at location i, and $\{\tau\}_{i,j}$ can be regarded as a communication between locations i and j. In the following, we view $\{\alpha\}_i$ as a distributed input or output action, and $\{\tau\}_{i,j}$ as a distributed communication.

$$ALP: \frac{M \xrightarrow{I\alpha} M'}{N \xrightarrow{I\alpha} N'} M \equiv N, M' \equiv N' \qquad TAU: \frac{P \xrightarrow{\tau} P'}{\{P\}_i \xrightarrow{\{\tau\}_{i,i}} \{P'\}_i}$$

$$OUT1: \frac{P \xrightarrow{\overline{l}} P'}{\{P\}_i \xrightarrow{\{\overline{l}\}_i} \{P'\}_i} \qquad IN1: \frac{P \xrightarrow{l} P'}{\{P\}_i \xrightarrow{\{l\}_i} \{P'\}_i}$$

$$OUT2: \frac{P \xrightarrow{(\nu\widetilde{b})\overline{a}\langle E\rangle} P'}{\{P\}_i \xrightarrow{\{(\nu\widetilde{b})\overline{a}\langle E\rangle\}_i} \{P'\}_i} \qquad IN2: \frac{P \xrightarrow{a\langle E\rangle} P'}{\{P\}_i \xrightarrow{\{a\langle E\rangle\}_i} \{P'\}_i}$$

$$PAR: \frac{M \xrightarrow{I\alpha} M'}{M|N \xrightarrow{I\alpha} M'|N} bn(I\alpha) \cap fn(N) = \emptyset$$

$$COM1: \frac{M \xrightarrow{\{\overline{l}\}_i} M' \quad N \xrightarrow{\{l\}_j} N'}{M|N \xrightarrow{\{\tau\}_{i,j}} M'|N'}$$

$$COM2: \frac{M \stackrel{\{(\nu\widetilde{b})\overline{a}\langle E\rangle\}_i}{\longrightarrow} M' \quad N \stackrel{\{a\langle E\rangle\}_j}{\longrightarrow} N'}{M|N \stackrel{\{\tau\}_{i,j}}{\longrightarrow} (\nu\widetilde{b})(M'|N')} \widetilde{b} \cap fn(N) = \emptyset$$

$$RES: \frac{M \stackrel{I\alpha}{\longrightarrow} M'}{(\nu a)M \stackrel{I\alpha}{\longrightarrow} (\nu a)M'} a \notin n(I\alpha)$$

$$OPEN: \frac{M \stackrel{\{(\nu\widetilde{c})\overline{a}\langle E\rangle\}_i}{\longrightarrow} M'}{(\nu b)M \stackrel{\{(\nu b,\widetilde{c})\overline{a}\langle E\rangle\}_i}{\longrightarrow} M'} a \neq b,\ b \in fn(E) - \widetilde{c}$$

Table 2

Remark: In the above table, transition $M \stackrel{\{\alpha\}_i}{\longrightarrow} M'$ means that distributed process M performs an action at location i, then continues as M'; and transition $M \stackrel{\{\tau\}_{i,j}}{\longrightarrow} M'$ means that after a communication between locations i and j, distributed process M continues as M'.

4 Distributed Bisimulations

In our distributed calculus, processes contain locations, and actions in the scope of locations will be observed at those locations. For such distributed processes, some new distributed bisimulations - distributed context bisimulation, distributed normal bisimulation and distributed reduction bisimulation, will be proposed. The new semantics we give to distributed processes additionally takes the distribution in space into account.

For distributed calculus, two distributed processes are equated if not only the actions, but also the locations, where the actions happen, can be matched each other. So we get the following definition of distributed context bisimulation. In the following, we abbreviate $P\{E/U\}$ as $P\langle E\rangle$.

We first give the weak distributed context bisimulation, weak distributed normal bisimulation and the weak distributed reduction bisimulation. Then we give their congruence property and the equivalence between these three bisimulations.

Before giving the weak distributed bisimulations, let us compare communication $\{\tau\}_{i,i}$ with $\{\tau\}_{i,j}$, where $i \neq j$. For weak distributed bisimulations, it seems natural to view $\{\tau\}_{i,i}$ as an invisible communication and $\{\tau\}_{i,j}$ as a visible communication, since for an observer who can distinguish between sites, $\{\tau\}_{i,i}$ is an internal communication at location i, and $\{\tau\}_{i,j}$ represents an external communication between two different locations i and j. Therefore in the following, we regard $\{\tau\}_{i,i}$ as a private event at location i, and $\{\tau\}_{i,j}$ as a visible event between locations i and j.

For example, let us consider a system consisting of a satellite and an earth station. It is clear that in this system, the satellite is physically far away from the earth station. If the program controlling the satellite has to be changed, either because of a program error or because the job of the satellite is to be changed, then a new program will be send to the satellite. The satellite is ready to receive a new program. After reception it acts according to this program until it is "interrupted" either by a new job or because a program error has occurred or because the program has finished.

In this example, the satellite and the earth can be specified in our distributed calculus syntax as follows:

$Sat \stackrel{def}{=} \{!a(U).U|satsys\}_S$, where $_S$ represents location *satellite*.

$Earth \stackrel{def}{=} \{\overline{a}\langle newprg_1\rangle.\overline{a}\langle newprg_2\rangle...\}_E$, where $_E$ represents location *earth*.

Now the system is specified as:

$Sys \stackrel{def}{=} (\nu a)(\{!a(U).U|satsys\}_S|\{\overline{a}\langle newprg_1\rangle.\overline{a}\langle newprg_2\rangle...\}_E)$

The earth can send a new program to the satellite, then in the satellite, this program interacts with the old satellite system:

$Sys \stackrel{\{\tau\}_{S,E}}{\longrightarrow} (\nu a)(\{!a(U).U|newprg_1|satsys\}_S|\{\overline{a}\langle newprg_2\rangle...\}_E) \stackrel{\{\tau\}_{S,S}}{\Longrightarrow} (\nu a)(\{!a(U).U|newsatsys\}_S|\{\overline{a}\langle newprg_2\rangle...\}_E)$

In this transition sequence, $\{\tau\}_{S,E}$ is a communication between locations *satellite* and *earth*, $\{\tau\}_{S,S}$ is an internal action at location *satellite*. Intuitively, we can consider $\{\tau\}_{S,E}$ as an external communication and it is visible; meanwhile, $\{\tau\}_{S,S}$ can be viewed as an internal action of satellite and it is private. Therefore, from view of distributed calculus, we can neglect internal communication such as $\{\tau\}_{S,S}$ but $\{\tau\}_{S,E}$ is treated as a visible action.

Firstly we give the definition of weak distributed context bisimulation. The difference from strong distributed context bisimulation is that in the case of weak bisimulation we neglect $\{\tau\}_{i,i}$ since from distributed view $\{\tau\}_{i,i}$ happens internally at location i.

In the following, we use $M \stackrel{\varepsilon}{\Longrightarrow} M'$ to abbreviate $M \stackrel{\{\tau\}_{i_1,i_1}}{\longrightarrow} ... \stackrel{\{\tau\}_{i_n,i_n}}{\longrightarrow} M'$, and use $M \stackrel{I\alpha}{\Longrightarrow} M'$ to abbreviate $M \stackrel{\varepsilon}{\Longrightarrow}\stackrel{I\alpha}{\longrightarrow}\stackrel{\varepsilon}{\Longrightarrow} M'$.

Definition 1. Weak distributed context bisimulation

Let $M, N \in DPr^c$, we write $M \approx^d_{cxt} N$, if there is a symmetric relation R, M R N implies:

(1) whenever $M \stackrel{\varepsilon}{\Longrightarrow} M'$, there exists N' such that $N \stackrel{\varepsilon}{\Longrightarrow} N'$ and M' R N';

(2) whenever $M \stackrel{\{\tau\}_{i,j}}{\Longrightarrow} M'$, there exists N' such that $N \stackrel{\{\tau\}_{i,j}}{\Longrightarrow} N'$ with M' R N', where $i \neq j$;

(3) whenever $M \stackrel{\{l\}_i}{\Longrightarrow} M'$, there exists N' such that $N \stackrel{\{l\}_i}{\Longrightarrow} N'$ with M' R N';

(4) whenever $M \stackrel{\{\overline{l}\}_i}{\Longrightarrow} M'$, there exists N' such that $N \stackrel{\{\overline{l}\}_i}{\Longrightarrow} N'$ with M' R N';

(5) whenever $M \stackrel{\{a\langle E\rangle\}_i}{\Longrightarrow} M'$, there exists N' such that $N \stackrel{\{a\langle E\rangle\}_i}{\Longrightarrow} N'$ and M' R N';

(6) whenever $M \stackrel{\{(\nu\widetilde{b})\overline{a}\langle E\rangle\}_i}{\Longrightarrow} M'$, there exist N', F, $\widetilde{c}$, such that $N \stackrel{\{(\nu\widetilde{c})\overline{a}\langle F\rangle\}_i}{\Longrightarrow} N'$, and for any distributed process $C(U)$ with $fn(C(U)) \cap \{\widetilde{b}, \widetilde{c}\} = \emptyset$, $(\nu\widetilde{b})(M'|C\langle E\rangle)$ R $(\nu\widetilde{c})(N'|C\langle F\rangle)$.

Definition 2. Weak distributed normal bisimulation

Let $M, N \in DPr^c$, we write $M \approx^d_{nor} N$, if there is a symmetric relation R, M R N implies:

(1) whenever $M \stackrel{\varepsilon}{\Longrightarrow} M'$, there exists N' such that $N \stackrel{\varepsilon}{\Longrightarrow} N'$ and $M'\ R\ N'$;

(2) whenever $M \stackrel{\{\tau\}_{i,j}}{\Longrightarrow} M'$, there exists N' such that $N \stackrel{\{\tau\}_{i,j}}{\Longrightarrow} N'$ with $M'\ R\ N'$, where $i \neq j$;

(3) whenever $M \stackrel{\{l\}_i}{\Longrightarrow} M'$, there exists N' such that $N \stackrel{\{l\}_i}{\Longrightarrow} N'$ with $M'\ R\ N'$;

(4) whenever $M \stackrel{\{\bar{l}\}_i}{\Longrightarrow} M'$, there exists N' such that $N \stackrel{\{\bar{l}\}_i}{\Longrightarrow} N'$ with $M'\ R\ N'$;

(5) whenever $M \stackrel{\{a\langle\overline{m}.0\rangle\}_i}{\Longrightarrow} M'$, there exists N' such that $N \stackrel{\{a\langle\overline{m}.0\rangle\}_i}{\Longrightarrow} N'$ and M' $R\ N'$, where m is a fresh name;

(6) whenever $M \stackrel{\{(\nu\widetilde{b})\overline{a}\langle E\rangle\}_i}{\Longrightarrow} M'$, there exist N', F, $\widetilde{c}$, such that $N \stackrel{\{(\nu\widetilde{c})\overline{a}\langle F\rangle\}_i}{\Longrightarrow} N'$, and for a fresh name m and fresh location k, $(\nu\widetilde{b})(M'|\{!m.E\}_k)$ $R\ (\nu\widetilde{c})(N'|\{!m.F\}_k)$.

In the following definition of weak distributed reduction bisimulation, we also neglect $\{\tau\}_{i,i}$ since $\{\tau\}_{i,i}$ represents an internal communication at location i, and regard $\{\tau\}_{i,j}$ as a visible event, where $i \neq j$, since for an observer who can distinguish between sites, $\{\tau\}_{i,j}$ represents an external communication between locations i and j.

Definition 3. Weak distributed reduction bisimulation

Let $K,\ L \in DPr^c$, we write $K \approx^d_{red} L$, if there is a symmetric relation R, such that whenever $K\ R\ L$ then for any distributed process M,

(1) $K|M \stackrel{\varepsilon}{\Longrightarrow} K'$ implies $L|M \stackrel{\varepsilon}{\Longrightarrow} L'$ for some L' with $K'\ R\ L'$;

(2)$K|M \stackrel{\{\tau\}_{i,j}}{\Longrightarrow} K'$, where $i \neq j$, implies $L|M \stackrel{\{\tau\}_{i,j}}{\Longrightarrow} L'$ for some L' with $K'\ R\ L'$.

From the above definitions, we can see that barbed equivalence and distributed reduction bisimulation are both reduction-based bisimulations. On the other hand, for barbed equivalence, an observer can test channels through which process can interact with environment, whereas for distributed reduction bisimulation, an observer need not to test channels but only has capability to distinguish between locations where communication happens. Therefore our distributed reduction bisimulation is more simple than barbed equivalence in the case of distributed calculi.

5 The Relation Between Distributed Context and Reduction Bisimulations

We firstly give the congruence property of weak distributed context bisimulation, i.e., such bisimulation is preserved by parallel and restriction operators of the language.

Proposition 1 (Congruence of $\approx^d_{cxt}$). For all $M,\ N,\ S \in DPr^c$, $M \approx^d_{cxt} N$ implies:

(1) $M|S \approx^d_{cxt} N|S$;

(2) $(\nu a)M \approx^d_{cxt} (\nu a)N$.

Now, we study the relation between distributed context bisimulation and distributed reduction bisimulation.

Proposition 2. $M \approx^d_{cxt} N \Rightarrow M \approx^d_{red} N$.

Proposition 3. $M \approx^d_{red} N \Rightarrow M \approx^d_{nor} N$.

6 The Relation Between Distributed Context and Normal Bisimulations

6.1 Syntax and Labelled Transition System of Distributed Higher Order π-Calculus with Location Variables

In [12,14], the equivalence between weak context bisimulation and weak normal bisimulation was proved. In the proof, the factorisation theorem was firstly given. It allows us to factorise out certain subprocesses of a given process. Thus, a complex process can be decomposed into the parallel composition of simpler processes. Then the concept of triggered processes was introduced, which is the key step in the proof. Triggered processes represent a sort of normal form for the processes. Most importantly, there is a very simple characterisation of context bisimulation on triggered processes, called triggered bisimulation. By the factorisation theorem, a process can be transformed to a triggered process. The transformation allows us to use the simpler theory of triggered processes to reason about the set of all processes. In [12,14], weak context bisimulation was firstly proved to be equivalent to weak triggered bisimulation on triggered processes, then by the mapping from general processes to triggered processes, the equivalence between weak context bisimulation and weak normal bisimulation was proved. The aim of this section is to extend Sangiorgi's proof to cover also the correspondence between distributed context bisimulation and distributed normal bisimulation.

But some central technical results in Sangiorgi's proof, like the factorisation theorem and full abstraction of the mapping to triggered processes, cannot be generalized to distributed processes directly. For example, let us have a look at the process $\overline{a}\langle b.0\rangle$. Its triggered mapping result is $(\nu m)(\overline{a}\langle\overline{m}.0\rangle|!m.b.0)$ and we have $\overline{a}\langle b.0\rangle \approx_{Ct} (\nu m)(\overline{a}\langle\overline{m}.0\rangle|!m.b.0)$. For the distributed process $\{\overline{a}\langle b.0\rangle\}_i$, a possible triggered mapping result is $(\nu m)(\{\overline{a}\langle\overline{m}.0\rangle\}_i|!\{m.b.0\}_i)$. But unfortunately, $\{\overline{a}\langle b.0\rangle\}_i \not\approx^d_{cxt} (\nu m)(\{\overline{a}\langle\overline{m}.0\rangle\}_i|!\{m.b.0\}_i)$. Roughly speaking, if we assume tested processes $\overline{a}\langle\overline{m}.0\rangle$ and $!m.b.0$ are located at i and testing process $a(U).U$ is located at j, then they can communicate between i and j, then continue as $!m.b.0$ at location i and $\overline{m}.0$ at location j respectively, where m is their private name. $!m.b.0$ and $\overline{m}.0$ can communicate again between i and j; hence there are two communications between i and j. But tested process $\overline{a}\langle b.0\rangle$ at location i and testing process $a(U).U$ at location j can communicate only once between i and j, then continue as 0 at location i and $b.0$ at location j respectively. Therefore processes $\{\overline{a}\langle b.0\rangle\}_i$ and $(\nu m)(\{\overline{a}\langle\overline{m}.0\rangle\}_i|!\{m.b.0\}_i)$ are not distributed context bisimilar.

Similarly, for any fixed location k, $\{\overline{a}\langle b.0\rangle\}_i$ and $(\nu m)(\{\overline{a}\langle\overline{m}.0\rangle\}_i|!\{m.b.0\}_k)$ are not distributed context bisimilar. But if we allow location variables and add some rule in the operational semantics, then this problem can be solved. For example, let us see $\{\overline{a}\langle b.0\rangle\}_i$ and $(\nu m)(\{\overline{a}\langle\overline{m}.0\rangle\}_i|!\{m.b.0\}_x)$. We have $\{\overline{a}\langle b.0\rangle\}_i|\{a(U).U\}_j \stackrel{\{\tau\}_{i,j}}{\longrightarrow} \{b.0\}_j$, and $(\nu m)(\{\overline{a}\langle\overline{m}.0\rangle\}_i|!\{m.b.0\}_x)|\{a(U).U\}_j$ can simulate it by the following transition: $(\nu m)(\{\overline{a}\langle\overline{m}.0\rangle\}_i|!\{m.b.0\}_x)|\{a(U).U\}_j \stackrel{\{\tau\}_{i,j}}{\longrightarrow}$ $(\nu m)(!\{m.b.0\}_x|\{\overline{m}.0\}_j) \stackrel{\{\tau\}_{j,j}}{\longrightarrow} (\nu m)(!\{m.b.0\}_j|\{b.0\}_j) \equiv \{b.0\}_j$, where we assume $!\{m.b.0\}_x \stackrel{\{m\}_j}{\longrightarrow} !\{m.b.0|b.0\}_j$, i.e., when $\{P\}_x$ communicates with $\{Q\}_j$, P can be viewed as in location j.

Now to give the correct concepts of distributed triggered processes and distributed triggered mapping, we should first generalize distributed processes to the ones with location variables.

We usually use x, y, z to denote location variables. Let lv be the set of location variables.

The formal definition of distributed processes with location variables is given as follows:

$M ::= \{P\}_i \mid M_1|M_2 \mid (\nu a)M \mid !M$, where $i \in loc \cup lv$ and $P \in Pr$.

Furthermore, the labelled transition system of distributed processes with location variables consists of the following rules:

All rules of the labelled transition system of distributed processes (All rules in Table2)

$$INS: \frac{P \stackrel{\alpha}{\longrightarrow} P'}{\{P\}_x \stackrel{\{\alpha\}_{x\rightarrow i}}{\longrightarrow} \{P'\}_i} \alpha \text{ is in the form of } l$$

$$COMV: \frac{M \stackrel{\{\overline{l}\}_i}{\longrightarrow} M' \quad N \stackrel{\{l\}_{x\rightarrow i}}{\longrightarrow} N'}{M|N \stackrel{\{\tau\}_{i,i}}{\longrightarrow} M'|N'}$$

$$REP: \frac{M|!M \stackrel{I\alpha}{\longrightarrow} M'}{!M \stackrel{I\alpha}{\longrightarrow} M'}$$

Table 3

Remark: In this labelled transition system, the distributed actions are given by: $I\alpha ::= \{\tau\}_{i,j} \mid \{l\}_i \mid \{\overline{l}\}_i \mid \{l\}_{x\rightarrow i} \mid \{a\langle E\rangle\}_i \mid \{\overline{a}\langle E\rangle\}_i \mid \{(\nu\widetilde{b})\overline{a}\langle E\rangle\}_i$, where $\{l\}_{x\rightarrow i}$ represents distributed first order input actions with a location variable x instantiated by i.

In the rule INS we let α be only a first order input action, because in the following discussion, we only need to consider this case. The rule INS means that location variables can be instantiated by any location when processes perform a first order input action. An example is $\{m.Q\}_x \stackrel{\{m\}_{x\rightarrow i}}{\longrightarrow} \{Q\}_i$. $COMV$ means that if N communicates with a component in location i through a first order input action, then location variable x in N should be instantiated by i and the communication is viewed as an internal tau action in i. For example, we have $(\nu m)(\{\overline{m}.P\}_i|\{m.Q\}_x) \stackrel{\{\tau\}_{i,i}}{\longrightarrow} \{P\}_i|\{Q\}_i$, but $(\nu m)(\{\overline{m}.P\}_i|\{m.Q\}_x) \stackrel{\{\tau\}_{i,j}}{\longrightarrow}$ $\{P\}_i|\{Q\}_j$ is not admitted since there is no rule such as $\dfrac{M \stackrel{\{\overline{l}\}_i}{\longrightarrow} M' \quad N \stackrel{\{l\}_{x\rightarrow j}}{\longrightarrow} N'}{M|N \stackrel{\{\tau\}_{i,j}}{\longrightarrow} M'|N'}$.

We exclude such a rule because otherwise the distributed version of the factorisation theorem will not hold (see Lemma 1). For example, if we admit $(\nu m)(\{\overline{m}.0\}_i|!\{m.b.0\}_x)\{\tau\}_{i,j}\longrightarrow(\nu m)(\{0\}_i|\{b.0\}_j|!\{m.b.0\}_x)$ then $(\nu m)(\{\overline{m}.0\}_i|$

$!\{m.b.0\}_x) \not\approx^d_{cxt} \{b.0\}_i$. In addition, the transition $(\nu m)(\{\overline{m}.0\}_x|!\{m.b.0\}_y) \xrightarrow{\{\tau\}_{i,j}} (\nu m)(\{0\}_i|\{b.0\}_j|!\{m.b.0\}_j)$ is also not admitted since there is no rule such as $\dfrac{M \xrightarrow{\{\overline{l}\}_{x\to i}} M' \quad N \xrightarrow{\{l\}_{y\to j}} N'}{M|N \xrightarrow{\{\tau\}_{i,j}} M'|N'}$. This rule is excluded because for us, only some special distributed processes with location variables are interesting, which are called distributed triggered processes defined in the next section. For distributed triggered processes, there is no case that one component in location variable x can communicate with another component in location variable y.

Distributed context bisimulation $\approx^d_{cxt}$ and distributed normal bisimulation $\approx^d_{nor}$ can be generalized to distributed processes with location variables.

6.2 Distributed Triggered Processes, Distributed Triggered Mapping and Distributed Triggered Bisimulation

The concept of triggered processes was introduced in [12,14] for the proof of the equivalence between context bisimulation and normal bisimulation. For technical reasons, the proof goes through an intermediate step that puts processes into a kind of normal form (triggered processes). The distinguishing feature of triggered processes is that every communication among them is an exchange of a trigger, where a trigger is an elementary process whose only functionality is to activate a copy of another process. In this section, we introduce the distributed version of triggered processes. Similar to triggered processes, distributed triggered processes can also be seen as a sort of "normal form" for the distributed processes, and every communication among them is the exchange of a distributed trigger. We shall use distributed triggers to perform distributed process transformations which make the treatment of the constructs of distributed higher order processes easier.

Now we introduce the concept of distributed triggered processes. The class of the distributed triggered processes $DTPr$ is built similar to DPr, except that every higher order output process is in the form of trigger.

We first give the following definition:

$M ::= \{Q\}_i \mid M_1|M_2 \mid (\nu a)M \mid (\nu m)(M|!\{m.Q\}_x)$ where $i \in loc$ and $x \in lv$.

$Q ::= 0 \mid U \mid \tau.Q \mid l.Q \mid \overline{l}.Q \mid a(U).Q \mid \overline{a}\langle\overline{m}.0\rangle.Q \mid Q_1|Q_2 \mid (\nu a)Q \mid !Q$

We say that M is a distributed triggered process if M is defined as above. $DTPr^c$ is the set of all closed distributed triggered processes. For example, $(\nu m)\{\overline{a}\langle \overline{m}.0\rangle.0\}_i|!\{m.0\}_x$, $(\nu n)(\{\overline{a}\langle\overline{m}.0\rangle.0\}_i|!\{n.\overline{b}\langle\overline{c}.0\rangle.0\}_x)$, $\{\overline{a}\langle\overline{m}.0\rangle.0\}_i$ and $(\nu m,n)(\{\overline{a}\langle\overline{m}.0\rangle.0\}_i|!\{m.\overline{b}\langle\overline{n}.0\rangle.0\}_x|!\{n.\tau.0\}_y)$ are closed distributed triggered processes.

Location variables in M are denoted as $lv(M)$. $lv(M) \cup lv(N)$ is abbreviated as $lv(M,N)$. Please note that in this paper, the concept of distributed processes with location variables is introduced only for giving the definition of distributed triggered processes. Hence processes in $DTPr$ may contain location variables, but processes in DPr have no location variables, i.e., for any process M in DPr, $lv(M) = \emptyset$.

In [12,14], triggered mapping was defined inductively, but for distributed processes, things are different. For example, let $M = \{(\overline{a}\langle\tau.0\rangle.0|\overline{b}\langle l.0\rangle.0)\}_0$, if we define triggered mapping as in [12,14], then the triggered process is $\{(\nu m,n)(\overline{a}\langle\overline{m}.0\rangle.0|!m.\tau.0|\overline{b}\langle\overline{n}.0\rangle.0|!n.l.0)\}_0$. But $\{(\overline{a}\langle\tau.0\rangle.0|\overline{b}\langle l.0\rangle.0)\}_0 \not\approx^d_{cxt}$ $\{(\nu m,n)(\overline{a}\langle\overline{m}.0\rangle.0|!m.\tau.0|\overline{b}\langle\overline{n}.0\rangle.0|!n.l.0)\}_0$. Therefore we have to present a new definition of triggered mapping for distributed processes.

For $\{(\overline{a}\langle\tau.0\rangle.0|\overline{b}\langle l.0\rangle.0)\}_0$, in order to preserve the correctness of mapping we want to transform it to $(\nu m,n)(\{\overline{a}\langle\overline{m}.0\rangle.0|\overline{b}\langle\overline{n}.0\rangle.0\}_0|!\{m.\tau.0\}_x|!\{n.l.0\}_x)$. We do this by two steps, firstly we replace all output processes in $\{(\overline{a}\langle\tau.0\rangle.0|\overline{b}\langle l.0\rangle.0)\}_0$ by fresh variables and get $\{(\overline{a}\langle X\rangle.0|\overline{b}\langle Y\rangle.0)\}_0$, then we replace all output variables in $\{(\overline{a}\langle X\rangle.0|\overline{b}\langle Y\rangle.0)\}_0$ by triggers and get $(\nu m,n)(\{\overline{a}\langle\overline{m}.0\rangle.0|\overline{b}\langle\overline{n}.0\rangle.0\}_0|$ $!\{m.\tau.0\}_x|!\{n.l.0\}_x)$.

Definition 4. We give a mapping Vr which transforms every process P into a process which is the same as P but where every output process is replaced by a process variable.

(1) $Vr[0] ::= 0$;
(2) $Vr[U] ::= U$;
(3) $Vr[\tau.P] ::= \tau.Vr[P]$;
(4) $Vr[l.P] ::= l.Vr[P]$;
(5) $Vr[\overline{l}.P] ::= \overline{l}.Vr[P]$;
(6) $Vr[a(U).P] ::= a(U).Vr[P]$;
(7) $Vr[\overline{a}\langle E\rangle.P] ::= \overline{a}\langle X\rangle.Vr[P]$, where X is a fresh variable;
(8) $Vr[P_1|P_2] ::= Vr[P_1]|Vr[P_2]$;
(9) $Vr[(\nu a)P] ::= (\nu a)Vr[P]$;
(10) $Vr[!P] ::= !Vr[P]$;

Definition 5. We give a mapping Tr^x which transforms every distributed process M into the distributed triggered process $Tr^x[M]$ with respect to a location variable x. The mapping is defined inductively on the structure of M.

(1) $Tr^x[\{P\}_i] ::= (\nu m_1,...,m_n)(\{Vr[P]\{\overline{m}_1.0/X_1,...,\overline{m}_n.0/X_n\}\}_i|$ $Tr^x[!\{m_1.E_1\}_x]|...|Tr^x[!\{m_n.E_n\}_x])$, where $m_1,...,m_n$ are fresh names, $X_1,...,$ X_n are all variables that occur in higher order output prefixes of $Vr[P]$ and $E_1,...,$ E_n satisfy $P \equiv Vr[P]\{E_1/X_1,...,E_n/X_n\}$;
(2) $Tr^x[M_1|M_2] ::= Tr^x[M_1]|Tr^x[M_2]$;
(3) $Tr^x[(\nu a)M] ::= (\nu a)Tr^x[M]$;

It is useful to see the operational correspondence between M and $Tr^x[M]$. Transformation $Tr^x[\,]$ may expand the number of $\{\tau\}_{j,j}$ steps in a process. But the behaviour is otherwise the same. The expansion is due to the fact that if in M a process E is transmitted and used k times then, in $Tr^x[M]$ k additional $\{\tau\}_{j,j}$ interactions are required to activate the copies of E.

For example, let $M \stackrel{def}{=} \{\overline{a}\langle E\rangle.0\}_i|\{a(U).(U|U)\}_j$, then $M \stackrel{\{\tau\}_{i,j}}{\longrightarrow} 0|\{E|E\}_j \stackrel{def}{=}$ M'.

In $Tr^x[M]$, this is simulated using two additional $\{\tau\}_{j,j}$ interactions:

$$Tr^x[M] = (\nu m)(\{\overline{a}\langle\overline{m}.0\rangle.0\}_i|Tr^x[!\{m.E\}_x]|\{a(U).(U|U)\}_j)$$
$$\stackrel{\{\tau\}_{i,j}}{\longrightarrow} (\nu m)(\{0\}_i|Tr^x[!\{m.E\}_x]|\{\overline{m}.0|\overline{m}.0\}_j)$$
$$\stackrel{\{\tau\}_{j,j}}{\longrightarrow}\stackrel{\{\tau\}_{j,j}}{\longrightarrow} (\nu m)(\{0\}_i|Tr^x[\{E\}_j]|Tr^x[\{E\}_j]|Tr^x[!\{m.E\}_x])$$

$= \{0\}_i | Tr^x[\{E\}_j] | Tr^x[\{E\}_j]$ since m is a fresh name
$= Tr^x[M']$.

It is worthy to note that for any process in $DTPr$, it cannot perform any action of the form $\{m\}_{x \to i}$ because by the definition of $DTPr$, every location variable occurs in processes of the form $(\nu m)(M|!\{m.Q\}_x)$, where m is bounded by the restriction (νm), and by the rules in Table 3, it cannot perform $\{m\}_{x \to i}$. Therefore for any process in $DTPr$, the actions it can perform are all in the form of:

$\{\tau\}_{i,j} \mid \{l\}_i \mid \{\overline{l}\}_i \mid \{a\langle E\rangle\}_i \mid \{\overline{a}\langle E\rangle\}_i \mid \{(\nu\widetilde{b})\overline{a}\langle E\rangle\}_i$

Now we can give the distributed version of triggered bisimulation as follows.

Definition 6. Let M, N be two closed distributed triggered processes, we write $M \approx^d_{tr} N$, if there is a symmetric relation R:

(1) whenever $M\ R\ N$ and $M \stackrel{\varepsilon}{\Longrightarrow} M'$, there exists N' such that $N \stackrel{\varepsilon}{\Longrightarrow} N'$ and $M'\ R\ N'$;

(2) whenever $M\ R\ N$ and $M \stackrel{I\alpha}{\Longrightarrow} M'$, there exists N' such that $N \stackrel{I\alpha}{\Longrightarrow} N'$ and $M'\ R\ N'$, where $I\alpha \neq \{\tau\}_{i,i}$ for any $i \in loc$, $I\alpha$ is not a distributed higher order action;

(3) whenever $M\ R\ N$ and $M \stackrel{\{a\langle\overline{m}.0\rangle\}_i}{\Longrightarrow} M'$, where m is a fresh name, there exists N' such that $N \stackrel{\{a\langle\overline{m}.0\rangle\}_i}{\Longrightarrow} N'$ and $M'\ R\ N'$;

(4) whenever $M\ R\ N$ and $M \stackrel{\{(\nu m)\overline{a}\langle\overline{m}.0\rangle\}_i}{\Longrightarrow} M'$, there exists N' such that $N \stackrel{\{(\nu m)\overline{a}\langle\overline{m}.0\rangle\}_i}{\Longrightarrow} N'$ and $M'\ R\ N'$.

We say M and N are distributed triggered bisimilar if $M \approx^d_{tr} N$.

6.3 Distributed Normal Bisimulation Implies Distributed Context Bisimulation

Now we study the relation between the distributed context bisimulation and distributed normal bisimulation. The main result is that: $M \approx^d_{nor} N \Rightarrow Tr^x[M] \approx^d_{tr} Tr^x[N] \Rightarrow M \approx^d_{cxt} N$, where x is an arbitrary location variable. We achieve this result by proving several propositions including distributed factorisation theorem (Lemma 1), full abstraction of the mapping to distributed triggered processes (Lemma 2), the relation between distributed triggered bisimulation and distributed normal bisimulation (Proposition 5), and the relation between distributed triggered bisimulation and distributed context bisimulation (Proposition 6).

Firstly, we give the congruence of $\approx^d_{tr}$.

Proposition 4. (Congruence of $\approx^d_{tr}$) For all $M, N, K \in DTPr^c$, $M \approx^d_{tr} N$ implies:

1. $M|K \approx^d_{tr} N|K$;
2. $(\nu a)M \approx^d_{tr} (\nu a)N$.

Now we give the distributed version of the factorisation theorem, which states that, by means of distributed triggers, a distributed subprocess of a given distributed process can be factorised out.

Lemma 1. For arbitrary distributed process M and process E with $m \notin fn(M, E)$, it holds that $M\{E/U\} \approx_{cxt}^{d} (\nu m)(M\{\overline{m}.0/U\}|!\{m.E\}_x)$.

Note: We do not have $M\{E/U\} \approx_{cxt}^{d} (\nu m)(M\{\overline{m}.0/U\}|\{!m.E\}_x)$. A counter example is: $M = \{U\}_i|\{U\}_j$, $E = a.0$. This shows why we introduce the replication operator in distributed processes with location variables.

The correctness of $Tr^x[\,]$ is stated as Lemma 2:

Lemma 2. For each $M \in DPr^c$:

1. $Tr^x[M]$ is a distributed triggered process;
2. $Tr^x[M] \approx_{cxt}^{d} M$;
3. $Tr^x[M] \approx_{tr}^{d} M$, if M is a distributed triggered process.

Proposition 5 below states the relation between $\approx_{nor}^{d}$ and $\approx_{tr}^{d}$:

Proposition 5. For any M, $N \in DPr^c$, $M \approx_{nor}^{d} N \Rightarrow Tr^x[M] \approx_{tr}^{d} Tr^x[N]$, where x is an arbitrary location variable.

Proposition 6 below states the relation between $\approx_{cxt}^{d}$ and $\approx_{tr}^{d}$:

Proposition 6. For arbitrary $M, N \in DPr^c$, $Tr^x[M] \approx_{tr}^{d} Tr^x[N] \Rightarrow M \approx_{cxt}^{d} N$, where x is an arbitrary location variable.

The following proposition is the main result of this section, which states the equivalence between distributed normal and context bisimulations.

Proposition 7. $M \approx_{nor}^{d} N \Rightarrow M \approx_{cxt}^{d} N$.

7 A Characterisation Theorem

In this section, we give the equivalence between weak distributed normal bisimulation, weak distributed context bisimulation and weak distributed reduction bisimulation.

Proposition 8. $M \approx_{nor}^{d} N \Leftrightarrow M \approx_{cxt}^{d} N \Leftrightarrow M \approx_{red}^{d} N$.
These distributed bisimulations naturally bring new equivalences on regular processes as follows: two higher order π-calculus processes P and Q are consider to be equivalent if the distributed processes $\{P\}_l$ and $\{Q\}_l$ runing at the same location l are distributed bisimilar.

8 Conclusions

This paper presents an extension of the higher order π-calculus with very simple distributed features. Three new locality-based bisimulations were proposed in this paper. These distributed bisimulations are proved to be equivalent.

Traditionally, the distributed structure of processes can be made explicit by assigning different locations to their parallel components. The assignment of locations may be done statically, or dynamically as the execution proceeds. The static approach was studied first by Aceto [1], by assigning different locations to parallel components. The dynamic approach was developed first, by Boudol et al. [2], by associating locations with actions, as it appeared more convenient for defining notions of location equivalence and preorder. We adopt the static approach in this paper, which is more natural from an intuitive point of view, and more manageable for verification purposes.

References

1. Aceto, L.: A static view of localities. Formal Aspects of Computing 6(2), 201–222 (1994)
2. Boudol, G., Castellani, I., Hennessy, M., Kiehn, A.: A theory of processes with localities. Formal Aspects of Computing 6, 165–200 (1994)
3. Boudol, G., Castellani, I., Hennessy, M., Kiehn, A.: Observing localities. Theoretical Computer Science 114, 31–61 (1993)
4. Castellani, I.: Process Algebras with Localities. In: Bergstra, J., Ponse, A., Smolka, S. (eds.) Handbook of Process Algebra, ch. 15, North-Holland, Amsterdam (2001)
5. Castellani, I.: Observing distribution in processes: static and dynamic localities. Int. Journal of Foundations of Computer Science 6(4), 353–393 (1995)
6. Castellani, I., Hennessy, M.: Distributed Bisimulations. Journal of the ACM 36(4), 887–911 (1989)
7. Corradini, F., De Nicola, R.: Locality based semantics for process algebras. Acta Informatica 34, 291–324 (1997)
8. Godskesen, J.C., Hildebrandt, T., Sassone, V.: A Calculus of Mobile Resources. In: Brim, L., Jančar, P., Křetínský, M., Kucera, A. (eds.) CONCUR 2002. LNCS, vol. 2421, pp. 272–287. Springer, Heidelberg (2002)
9. Hildebrandt, T., Godskesen, J.C., Bundgaard, M.: Bisimulation Congruences for Homer - a Calculus of Higher Order Mobile Embedded Resources. Technical Report TR-2004-52, IT University of Copenhagen (2004)
10. Hennessy, M., Rathke, J., Yoshida, N.: SafeDpi: a language for controlling mobile code. In: Walukiewicz, I. (ed.) FOSSACS 2004. LNCS, vol. 2987, pp. 241–256. Springer, Heidelberg (2004)
11. Riely, J., Hennessy, M.: A typed language for distributed mobile processes. In: Proceedings of POPL98 (1998)
12. Sangiorgi, D.: Bisimulation in higher-order calculi. Information and Computation 131(2) (1996)
13. Sangiorgi, D.: Locality and interleaving semantics in calculi for mobile processes. In: Hagiya, M., Mitchell, J.C. (eds.) TACS 1994. LNCS, vol. 789, Springer, Heidelberg (1994)
14. Sangiorgi, D.: Expressing mobility in process algebras: first-order and higher-order paradigms, Ph.D thesis, University of Einburgh (1992)
15. Schmitt, A., Stefani, J.: The Kell calculus: A family of higher order distributed process calculi. In: Priami, C., Quaglia, P. (eds.) GC 2004. LNCS, vol. 3267, Springer, Heidelberg (2005)
16. Schmitt, A., Stefani, J.: The M-calculus: a higher-order distributed process calculus. ACM SIGPLAN Notices 38(1), 50–61 (2003)
17. Vitek, J., Castagna, G.: Seal: A framework for secure mobile computations. In: Tsichritzis, D. (ed.) Workshop on Internet Programming Languages (1999)
18. Yoshida, N., Hennessy, M.: Subtyping and locality in distributed higher order processes. In: Baeten, J.C.M., Mauw, S. (eds.) CONCUR 1999. LNCS, vol. 1664, Springer, Heidelberg (1999)

A Complete and Compact Propositional Deontic Logic

Pablo F. Castro and T.S.E. Maibaum

McMaster University
Department of Computing & Software
Hamilton, Canada
castropf@mcmaster.ca, tom@maibaum.org

Abstract. In this paper we present a propositional deontic logic, with the goal of using it to specify fault-tolerant systems, and an axiomatization of it. We prove several results about this logic: completeness, soundness, compactness and decidability. The main technique used during the completeness proof is based on standard techniques for modal logics, but it has some new characteristics introduced for dealing with this logic. In addition, the logic provides several operators which appear useful for use in practice, in particular to model fault-tolerant systems and to reason about their fault tolerance properties.

Keywords: Modal Logic, Deontic Logic, Temporal Logic, Fault tolerance, Software Specification.

1 Introduction

Deontic logics have been a field of research in formal logic for many years; the first deontic formal systems were given by Ernst Mally in the 1920's. Since then, several different systems have been developed; in particular, the use of modal systems enjoyed great success in the deontic community (see [1]). Though the most important research was done by philosophers and logicians, in the last 25 years computer scientists have adopted deontic logics as a field of research. The utility of these logics to formalize concepts such as *violation*, *obligation*, *permission* and *prohibition*, is very useful for system specification, where these concepts arise naturally. Examples of the application of deontic systems can be found in several places: in [2] Broersen develops several deontic frameworks to reason about real-time systems; in [3], Maibaum and Khosla use deontic notions to distinguish between prescription and description of systems; and several deontic logics have been developed to deal with agents (for example: [4]). Deontic logics seem to be very useful to formalize fault-tolerant systems (as argued in [5]): they allow us to distinguish between normal and non-normal states, and therefore between bad and good actions.

In this paper we present our own version of deontic logic; we include some operators which are not so common in the literature (the *done* operator, the relative complement on actions and two versions of permission), and we describe

C.B. Jones, Z. Liu, J. Woodcock (Eds.): ICTAC 2007, LNCS 4711, pp. 109–123, 2007.

some of its properties. The important point to make about this logic is that it has a complete and sound axiomatization; we give a proof of this in section 2. Also, we outline a temporal extension of this logic. An important characteristic of our framework is that we use a *relative* complement over actions (that is, the complement is with respect to the other actions, and not with respect to the universal relation). Moreover, the operators on actions that we consider are exactly those of boolean algebras, and the novel feature of the axiomatization is that it is compact. In several places (e.g., see [2]) it is shown that modal boolean logics (modal logics with boolean operators) with relative complement are not compact; we shall explain why this is not true in the logic described later on.

Our main goal is to use this logic to reason about fault-tolerant systems; we provide some examples of applications in this paper. However, our intention here is to focus on the theoretical properties of the logic.

The paper is organized as follows: in section 2 we describe the propositional version of the logic and we prove the completeness and soundness theorems. We give an example of its application in section 3, and, finally, we describe some future work.

2 A Propositional Ought-to-Do Deontic Logic

We shall present a logic, which can be considered as an *ought-to-do logic* in the sense that deontic operators are applied to actions. Using greek letters: α, β, γ, ... to denote actions, we can describe informally the constructions of our logic:

- $\alpha =_{act} \beta$: *actions* α *and* β *are equals.*
- $[\alpha]$: *after any possible execution of* α, φ *is true.*
- $[\alpha \sqcup \beta]\varphi$: *after the non-deterministic execution of* α *or* β, φ *is true.*
- $[\alpha \sqcap \beta]\varphi$: *after the parallel execution of* α *and* β, φ *is true.*
- $[\mathbf{U}]\varphi$: *after the non-deterministic choice of any possible action,* φ *is true.*
- $[\emptyset]\varphi$: *after executing an impossible action,* φ *becomes true.*
- $[\overline{\alpha}]$: *after executing an action different from* α, φ *is true.*
- $\mathsf{P}(\alpha)$: *every way of executing* α *is allowed.*
- $\mathsf{P}_\mathsf{w}(\alpha)$: *some way of executing* α *is allowed.*

As usual we consider the logical connectives: $\vee, \wedge, \neg$ and $\rightarrow$. The dual of the box modality can be defined in the standard way: $\langle\alpha\rangle\varphi \stackrel{\mathsf{def}}{\iff} \neg[\alpha]\neg\varphi$.

Note that, as common in deontic logics, we have the notion of permission; the operator $\mathsf{P}(\alpha)$ tells us if an action is allowed to be performed or not. We can call it a *strong permission* since it requires that every way of performing an action has to be allowed. For example, if we say that *driving* is allowed, we also mean that *driving while drinking beer* is allowed. Of course, permission has been a polemical notion since the beginning of deontic logic. Some people (for example: [6]) have proposed a weak version, where to be allowed to perform an action means that this action is allowed only in some contexts. We shall use both notions of permission; the latter is denoted by the operation $\mathsf{P}_\mathsf{w}(\alpha)$, and it should be read as: α *is weakly allowed.* The two versions differ in their properties, as we shall show later on.

It is usual to define the notion of obligation using the notion of permission (although these two are not necessarily related!), some versions include (see [6]): $\mathsf{O}(\alpha) \equiv \neg\mathsf{P_w}(\overline{\alpha})$. This can give us some problems; for example this definition enables Ross's paradox: $\mathsf{O}(\alpha) \rightarrow \mathsf{O}(\alpha \sqcup \alpha')$. This can be read as: *if you are obliged to send a letter, then you are obliged to send it or burn it.* Trying to keep the definition of obligation simple, we use a variant of the above definition, but using both versions of permission: $\mathsf{O}(\alpha) \stackrel{\mathsf{def}}{\Longleftrightarrow} \mathsf{P}(\alpha) \wedge \neg\mathsf{P_w}(\overline{\alpha})$. That is, an action is obligated if and only if it is strongly permitted and no other action is weakly permitted. Ross's paradox is avoided as the reader can check for himself.

A vocabulary (or language) $\langle \Phi_0, \Delta_0 \rangle$, is a tuple where $\Phi_0 = \{p, q, s, ...\}$ is a (enumerable) set of propositions, and $\Delta_0 = \{\alpha_0, .., \alpha_n\}$ is a finite set of "*atomic*" (or *primitive*) actions. Using a vocabulary we can define the set Φ of formulae; the inductive definition is straightforward.

Let us introduce the notion of deontic structures.

Definition 1 (models). *Given a language* $L = \langle \Phi_0, \Delta_0 \rangle$*, an L-Structure is a tuple:* $M = \langle \mathcal{W}, \mathcal{R}, \mathcal{E}, \mathcal{I}, \mathcal{P} \rangle$ *where:*

- $\mathcal{W}$*, is a set of worlds.*
- $\mathcal{R}$*, is an* $\mathcal{E}$*-labeled relation between worlds. We require that, if* $(w, w', e) \in \mathcal{R}$ *and* $(w, w'', e) \in \mathcal{R}$*, then* $w' = w''$*, i.e.,* $\mathcal{R}$ *is functional.*
- $\mathcal{E}$*, is a non-empty set of (names of) events.*
- $\mathcal{I}$*, is a function:*
  - *For every* $p \in \Phi_0 : \mathcal{I}(p) \subseteq \mathcal{W}$
  - *For every* $\alpha \in \Delta_0 : \mathcal{I}(\alpha) \subseteq \mathcal{E}$.

  In addition, the interpretation $\mathcal{I}$ *has to satisfy the following properties:*

  I.1 *For every* $\alpha_i \in \Delta_0$*:* $|\mathcal{I}(\alpha_i) - \bigcup\{\mathcal{I}(\alpha_j) \mid \alpha_j \in (\Delta_0 - \{\alpha_i\})\}| \leq 1$.

  I.2 *For every* $e \in \mathcal{E}$*: if* $e \in \mathcal{I}(\alpha_i) \cap \mathcal{I}(\alpha_j)$*, where* $\alpha_i \neq \alpha_j \in \Delta_0$*, then:* $\bigcap\{\mathcal{I}(\alpha_k) \mid \alpha_k \in \Delta_0 \wedge e \in \mathcal{I}(\alpha_k)\} = \{e\}$.

  I.3 $\mathcal{E} = \bigcup_{\alpha_i \in \Delta_0} \mathcal{I}(\alpha_i)$.
- $\mathcal{P} \subseteq \mathcal{W} \times \mathcal{E}$*, is a relation which indicates which event is permitted in which world.* ■

We can extend the function $\mathcal{I}$ to well-formed action terms and formulas, as follows:

- $\mathcal{I}(\neg\varphi) \stackrel{\mathsf{def}}{=} \mathcal{W} - \mathcal{I}(\varphi)$.
- $\mathcal{I}(\varphi \rightarrow \psi) \stackrel{\mathsf{def}}{=} \mathcal{I}(\neg\varphi) \cup \mathcal{I}(\psi)$.
- $\mathcal{I}(\alpha \sqcup \beta) \stackrel{\mathsf{def}}{=} \mathcal{I}(\alpha) \cup \mathcal{I}(\beta)$.
- $\mathcal{I}(\alpha \sqcap \beta) \stackrel{\mathsf{def}}{=} \mathcal{I}(\alpha) \cap \mathcal{I}(\beta)$.
- $\mathcal{I}(\overline{\alpha}) \stackrel{\mathsf{def}}{=} \mathcal{E} - I(\alpha)$.
- $\mathcal{I}(\emptyset) \stackrel{\mathsf{def}}{=} \emptyset$.
- $\mathcal{I}(\mathbf{U}) \stackrel{\mathsf{def}}{=} \mathcal{E}$.

We are following the approach given in [7] for the semantics, in the sense that we interpret an action as a set of events. Intuitively, an action *produces* a set of events during its execution.

Conditions **I.1**, **I.2** and **I.3** in definition 1 express topological requirements on the possible interpretations of atomic actions. **I.1** says that *the isolated application of an action always generates at most one event*; otherwise we will have an undesired nondeterminism in our models, as the different ways of executing an atomic action arise because you can execute it together with other actions (perhaps environmental actions). **I.2** establishes that *if an event is a result of the execution of two or more actions, then the concurrent execution of all the actions which generate it will give us only this event.* **I.3** only says that *every event is produced by some atomic action.* It is a kind of *standard model* requirement.

Now, we can introduce the relation $\vDash$ between models and formulae. Some notation is needed for dealing with the relational part of the structure: we will use the notation $w \xrightarrow{e} w'$ when $(w, w', e) \in \mathcal{R}$.

Definition 2 ($\vDash$). *Given a vocabulary* $L = \langle \Phi_0, \Delta_0 \rangle$ *and a* L*-structure* $M = \langle \mathcal{W}, \mathcal{R}, \mathcal{E}, \mathcal{I}, \mathcal{P} \rangle$, *we define the relation* $\vDash$ *between worlds and formulas as follows:*

- $w, M \vDash p \overset{\text{def}}{\Longleftrightarrow} w \in \mathcal{I}(p)$
- $w, M \vDash \alpha =_{act} \beta \overset{\text{def}}{\Longleftrightarrow} \mathcal{I}(\alpha) = \mathcal{I}(\beta)$
- $w, M \vDash \neg\varphi \overset{\text{def}}{\Longleftrightarrow}$ *not* $w \vDash \varphi$.
- $w, M \vDash \varphi \to \psi \overset{\text{def}}{\Longleftrightarrow} w \vDash \neg\varphi$ *or* $w \vDash \psi$ *or both.*
- $w, M \vDash [\alpha]\phi \overset{\text{def}}{\Longleftrightarrow}$ *for all* $w' \in \mathcal{W}$ *and* $e \in \mathcal{I}(\alpha)$ *if* $w \xrightarrow{e} w'$ *then* $w', M \vDash \phi$.
- $w, M \vDash \mathsf{P}(\alpha) \overset{\text{def}}{\Longleftrightarrow}$ *for all* $e \in \mathcal{I}(\alpha)$, $\mathcal{P}(w, e)$ *holds.*
- $w, M \vDash \mathsf{P_w}(\alpha) \overset{\text{def}}{\Longleftrightarrow}$ *there exists some* $e \in \mathcal{I}(\alpha)$ *such that* $\mathcal{P}(w, e)$ ■

Some explanation about the semantics of complement is needed. Note that for interpreting $[\overline{\alpha}]\varphi$, we are only taking into account the events which are not *produced* by the action α and which can be executed in the actual state. In other words, we are not using the complement with respect to the universal relation. If we used the latter notion, non reachable worlds would become reachable.

2.1 A Deductive System

In this section we present a deductive system; this is a normal modal system (in the sense that the **K**-axiom can be deduced from it) and the axioms for the modal part of the logic are similar to those given at [8] and [9]. We assume the standard definition of the relation $\vdash \subseteq \wp(\Phi) \times \Phi$. And we will say: $\vdash_{DPL} \varphi$, if φ is a theorem of the following axiomatic system (we shall omit the subscript DPL when there is no confusion).

An important characteristic of our set of axioms (which, to the authors' knowledge, is not shared with other related work) is that it establishes a deep connection between the weak version of permission and the strong version of it. Actually, one of these axioms can be seen as a kind of "compactness" property that our models satisfy. This property is implied by the restrictions assumed about them. This is a key fact exploited in the completeness proof. Before going into details, we need to introduce the notions of *canonical action terms* and *boolean algebra of action terms.* For the following definitions, we consider the following fixed vocabulary:

$$\Phi_0 = \{p_1, p_2, p_3, ...\} \quad \Delta_0 = \{\alpha_1, ..., \alpha_n\}$$

This language induces the set Δ of boolean terms; we denote by Φ_{BA} some axiomatization of boolean algebras (note that there exist complete axiomatizations, see [10]). Then, the set Δ/Φ_{BA} is the quotient set of the boolean terms by $=_{act}$; the point is that using this set we can define the (atomic) boolean algebra $\langle \Delta/\Phi_{BA}, \sqcup_{[]}, \sqcap_{[]}, -_{[]}, [\emptyset]_{BA}, [U]_{BA} \rangle$ as follows:

- $-_{[]}[\alpha]_{BA} = [\overline{\alpha}]_{BA}$
- $[\alpha]_{BA} \sqcup_{[]} [\beta]_{BA} = [\alpha \sqcup \beta]_{BA}$
- $[\alpha]_{BA} \sqcap_{[]} [\beta]_{BA} = [\alpha \sqcap \beta]_{BA}$

It is straightforward to prove that this is a boolean algebra. Furthermore, since the terms in Δ are generated by a finite set Δ_0 of atomic actions, the quotient boolean algebra is finite, and therefore atomic. We call $at(\Delta/\Phi_{BA})$ (or $at(\Delta)$ when no confusions arises) the set of atoms of the quotient boolean algebra of terms. Note also that we can define $\sqsubseteq_{[]}$ in the usual way.

It will be useful to recall the following theorems about atomic boolean algebras (their proofs can be found in [11], for example).

Theorem 1. *For every finite boolean algebra $\langle A, \cup, \cap, -, 0, 1 \rangle$, the following holds: for all $x \in A$, there exist atoms $a_1, ..., a_n$ such that: $x = a_1 \cup ... \cup a_n$.* ∎

Theorem 2. *For every finite boolean algebra $B = \langle A, \cup, \cap, -, 0, 1 \rangle$, and considering $A = \{a \mid a$ is an atom of $B\}$, there exists an isomorphism between B and the boolean algebra $\langle \wp(A), \cup, \cap, -, \emptyset, A \rangle$. The isomorphism is defined by $f(x) = \{a \mid a \leq x\}$.* ∎

It is important to keep in mind these facts for the proofs given below. At this point we are ready to present our axiomatic system.

Definition 3 (Axioms for DPL). *Given a vocabulary $\langle \Phi_0, \Delta_0 \rangle$, where $\Delta_0 = \{\alpha_1, ..., \alpha_n\}$. The axiomatic system is composed of the following axioms:*

1. *The set of propositional tautologies.*
2. *A set of axioms for boolean algebras for action terms (a complete one), including standard axioms for equality.*
3. *The following set of axioms*
   A1. $\langle \alpha \rangle \bot \leftrightarrow \bot$
   A2. $[\emptyset]\varphi$
   A3. $\langle \alpha \rangle \varphi \wedge [\alpha]\psi \rightarrow \langle \alpha \rangle (\varphi \wedge \psi)$
   A4. $[\alpha \sqcup \alpha']\varphi \leftrightarrow [\alpha]\varphi \wedge [\alpha']\varphi$
   A5. $[\alpha]\varphi \rightarrow [\alpha \sqcap \alpha']\varphi$
   A6. $\mathsf{P}(\emptyset)$
   A7. $\mathsf{P}(\alpha \sqcup \beta) \leftrightarrow \mathsf{P}(\alpha) \wedge \mathsf{P}(\beta)$
   A8. $\mathsf{P}(\alpha) \vee \mathsf{P}(\beta) \rightarrow \mathsf{P}(\alpha \sqcap \beta)$

A9. $\neg \mathsf{P_w}(\emptyset)$
A10. $\mathsf{P_w}(\alpha \sqcup \beta) \leftrightarrow \mathsf{P_w}(\alpha) \vee \mathsf{P_w}(\beta)$
A11. $\mathsf{P_w}(\alpha \sqcap \beta) \leftrightarrow \mathsf{P_w}(\alpha) \wedge \mathsf{P_w}(\beta)$
A12. $\mathsf{P}(\alpha) \wedge \alpha \neq_{act} \emptyset \rightarrow \mathsf{P_w}(\alpha)$
A13. $(\bigwedge_{[\alpha]_{BA} \wedge \alpha \sqsubseteq \alpha'} (P_w(\alpha) \vee (\alpha =_{act} \emptyset))) \rightarrow \mathsf{P}(\alpha')$
A14. $\mathsf{P}(\alpha) \wedge \neg \mathsf{P_w}(\overline{\alpha}) \leftrightarrow \mathsf{O}(\alpha)$
A15. $\langle \alpha \rangle \varphi \leftrightarrow \neg [\alpha] \neg \varphi$
A16. $(\alpha_1 \sqcup ... \sqcup \alpha_n) =_{act} \mathbf{U}$
A17a. $\alpha =_{act} \alpha' \rightarrow [\beta](\alpha =_{act} \alpha')$
A17b. $\langle \beta \rangle (\alpha =_{act} \alpha') \rightarrow \alpha =_{act} \alpha'$

and the following deduction rules:

$$\mathsf{MP}: \frac{\varphi \quad \varphi \rightarrow \psi}{\psi} \qquad \mathsf{GN}: \frac{\varphi}{[\alpha]\varphi} \qquad \mathsf{BA}: \frac{\alpha =_{act} \alpha' \quad \varphi[\alpha]}{\varphi[\alpha/\alpha']}$$

■

Some explanation is needed for the axioms. **A1** and **A3** are basic axioms of normal modal logics. **A2** says that *after an impossible action everything becomes possible.* **A4** tells us that *if something is true after the execution of a nondeterministic choice between two actions, then this has to be true after the execution of one of these actions.* **A5** says that parallel execution preserves properties; one can think of some scenario where this is not true, but this happens when we execute two actions not consistent with each other, and this is just an impossible action in our framework. **A6**, **A7** and **A8** are similar axioms for strong permission, and **A9**, **A10** and **A11** are the duals for weak permission. Here the important point is to establish a relationship between both versions of permissions; because of the nature of deontic predicates (they predicate on actions), we cannot use the standard technique that we use for modal operators (that is, define one of them as the dual of the other). Axioms **A12** and **A13** express the relation between the two versions of permission. The former says that strong permission implies weak permission for "*non-impossible*" actions. The latter one says that *if every way of executing an action* α *is weakly permitted, then* α *is strongly permitted.* Or, by the contrapositive, *if an action is not strongly allowed, then some way of executing it is not weakly permitted.* As the reader can deduce, this is a kind of compactness property which relates both versions of permission. Note that the given formula is finite because the underlying canonical term algebra (modulo action equality) is finite; in this way we can avoid second order quantifiers. Unfortunately, in a first order extension of this axiomatic system we cannot use the same trick. Axioms **A14** and **A15** define obligation and the box modality, respectively. Finally, formula **A16** says that the union of all actions gives us the universal action and axioms **A17a** and **A17b** express that equality is not affected by modalities.

Now, we can prove the soundness of our axiomatic system. We only show the proofs of the most important axioms; the other proofs are similar.

Theorem 3 (soundness). *The axiomatic system defined in definition 3 is sound with respect to the models defined in definition 1, that is:*

$$\vdash \varphi \Rightarrow \models \varphi$$

Proof. *We have to prove that each axiom is valid, and that the deduction rules preserve validity. Axioms 1-3 and the deduction rules* MP *and* GN *are very standard and their soundness proofs can be found in the literature. On the other hand, it is clear that boolean algebra axioms are valid, since the interpretation of action operators are given by means of set operators. We prove the validity of axioms 4-17 and that the deduction rule* BA *preserves validity.*
Axiom 4: *Straightforward by first order properties. See axiom 7's proof.*
Axiom 5: *Direct using subset properties and "for all" properties.*
Axiom 6: *Straightforward by definition of* $\models$ *and vacuous domain.*
Axiom 7: *Suppose* $w, M \models \mathsf{P}(\alpha \sqcup \beta)$, *for arbitrary model* M *and world* w. *This means that:* $\forall e \in \mathcal{I}(\alpha \sqcup \beta) : \mathcal{P}(w,e)$; *using first order logic we get:* $(\forall e \in \mathcal{I}(\alpha) : \mathcal{P}(w,e)) \wedge (\forall e \in \mathcal{I}(\alpha) : \mathcal{P}(w,e))$, *and this implies:* $w, M \models \mathsf{P}(\alpha) \wedge \mathsf{P}(\beta)$.
Axiom 8: *Similar reasoning as before, but using the fact that:* $\mathcal{I}(\alpha \sqcap \beta) = \mathcal{I}(\alpha) \cap \mathcal{I}(\beta)$.
Axiom 9: *For every model* M *and world* w, *by logic we have:* $\neg(\exists e \in I(\emptyset) : \mathcal{P}(w,e))$, *and this means:* $\models \neg \mathsf{P}_{\mathsf{w}}(\emptyset)$.
Axiom 10: *Suppose* $w, M \models \mathsf{P}_{\mathsf{w}}(\alpha \sqcup \beta)$; *by definition we obtain:* $\exists e \in \mathcal{I}(\alpha \sqcup \beta) : \mathcal{P}(w,e)$ *and using the definition of* $\mathcal{I}$ *and properties of* $\exists$ *we get:* $w, M \models \mathsf{P}_{\mathsf{w}}(\alpha) \vee \mathsf{P}_{\mathsf{w}}(\beta)$.
Axiom 11: *Similar to* Axiom 10.
Axiom 12: *Suppose that* $w, M \models \mathsf{P}(\alpha) \wedge \alpha \neq \emptyset$; *this means:* $\forall e \in I(\alpha) : e \in \mathcal{P}_w$ *and* $I(\alpha) \neq \emptyset$; *by basic first order reasoning we get:* $\exists e \in I(\alpha) : \mathcal{P}(w,e)$, *but this implies* $w, M \models \mathsf{P}_{\mathsf{w}}(\alpha)$.
Axiom A13: *Suppose that for some* w:

$$w, M \models \bigwedge_{[\alpha]_{BA} \wedge \alpha \sqsubseteq \alpha'} (\mathsf{P}_{\mathsf{w}}(\alpha) \vee \alpha =_{act} \emptyset)$$

and:

$$w, M \not\models \mathsf{P}(\alpha')$$

The last formula implies: $\exists e \in \mathcal{I}(\alpha') : \neg\mathcal{P}(w,e)$. *Now, using condition* ***I.1*** *and* ***I.2***, *we can reason by cases:*

- $e \in \mathcal{I}(\alpha_i) - \bigcup_{j \neq i}(\mathcal{I}(\alpha_j))$, *for some* α_i. *Therefore, by condition* ***I.1***, *we get:* $\mathcal{I}(\alpha_i \sqcap (\overline{\bigsqcup_{j\neq i} \alpha_j})) = \{e\}$. *And then* $w, M \not\models \mathsf{P}_{\mathsf{w}}(\alpha_i \sqcap (\bigsqcap_{j \neq i} \overline{\alpha_j}))$. *This gives us a contradiction.*
- $e \in \mathcal{I}(\alpha_i) \cap \mathcal{I}(\alpha_j)$, *for some* $i \neq j$. *Then, let* $\alpha^1_1, ..., \alpha^1_m$ *be all the atomic action such that:* $e \in \mathcal{I}(\alpha^1_k)$, *for* $1 \leq k \leq m$. *Then by condition* I2, *we get:* $\bigcap_{1 \leq k \leq m} \mathcal{I}(\alpha^1_k) = \{e\}$. *And then* $w, M \not\models \mathsf{P}_{\mathsf{w}}(\alpha^1_1 \sqcap ... \sqcap \alpha^1_m)$, *giving a contradiction, the result follows.*

Axiom A14, Axiom A15, Axiom16: Straightforward.
Axiom A17: The result follows from the fact that action interpretations are fixed, and they do not depend on states.
BA: The result is straightforward from the fact that, if we have $\alpha =_{act} \alpha'$, then $I(\alpha) = I(\alpha')$; here using the Leibniz equality property deduce that, if $\models \varphi[\alpha]$, then $\models \varphi[\alpha']$. ■

The following theorems of the axiomatic system just defined are used in the completeness proof; actually in [8] theorem T3 is used for axiomatizing the modal part of boolean logic, and it should be enough for the modal part of our logic. Because we are taking an algebraic view of the logic, in our axiomatic system we focused on operational properties.

Theorem 4. *The following are theorems of DPL; we do not include the proofs here, but they can be found in [12].*

T1. $\mathsf{P}(\alpha) \wedge \alpha' \sqsubseteq \alpha \rightarrow \mathsf{P}(\alpha')$
T2. $\mathsf{P_w}(\alpha') \wedge \alpha' \sqsubseteq \alpha \rightarrow \mathsf{P_w}(\alpha)$
T3. $[\alpha]\varphi \wedge (\alpha' \sqsubseteq \alpha) \rightarrow [\alpha']\varphi$
T4. $[\alpha]\varphi \wedge [\alpha']\psi \rightarrow [\alpha \sqcup \alpha'](\varphi \vee \psi)$
T5. $[\alpha]\varphi \wedge [\alpha']\psi \rightarrow [\alpha \sqcap \alpha'](\varphi \wedge \psi)$

For the completeness proof, we introduce the following canonical model:

Definition 4 (canonical model). $\mathcal{C} = \langle \mathcal{E}_\mathcal{C}, \mathcal{W}_\mathcal{C}, \mathcal{R}_\mathcal{C}, \mathcal{P}_\mathcal{C}, \mathcal{I}_\mathcal{C} \rangle$ *where:*

- $\mathcal{E}_\mathcal{C} \stackrel{\mathsf{def}}{=} at(\Delta)$
- $\mathcal{W}_\mathcal{C} \stackrel{\mathsf{def}}{=} \{\Gamma \mid \Gamma \text{ is a maximal consistent set of formulae}\}$
- $\mathcal{R}_\mathcal{C} \stackrel{\mathsf{def}}{=} \bigcup\{\mathcal{R}_{\alpha,w,w'} \mid w, w' \in \mathcal{W}_\mathcal{C} \wedge \alpha \in \Delta \wedge (\forall \varphi \in \Phi : [\alpha]\varphi \in w \Rightarrow \varphi \in w')\}$, *where* $R_{\alpha,w,w'} \stackrel{\mathsf{def}}{=} \{w \stackrel{[\alpha']_{BA}}{\rightarrow} w' \mid \forall [\alpha']_{BA} \in \mathcal{I}_\mathcal{C}(\alpha)\}$
- $\mathcal{P}_\mathcal{C} \stackrel{\mathsf{def}}{=} \bigcup\{\mathcal{P}_{w,\alpha} \mid w \in \mathcal{W}_\mathcal{C} \wedge \mathsf{P}(\alpha) \in w\}$, *where:* $\mathcal{P}_{w,\alpha} \stackrel{\mathsf{def}}{=} \{(w, [\alpha']_{BA}) \mid [\alpha']_{BA} \in \mathcal{I}_\mathcal{C}(\alpha)\}$
- $\mathcal{I}_\mathcal{C}(\alpha_i) \stackrel{\mathsf{def}}{=} \{[\alpha']_{BA} \in \mathcal{E}_\mathcal{C} \mid \vdash_{\Phi_{BA}} \alpha' \sqsubseteq \alpha\}$
- $\mathcal{I}_\mathcal{C}(p_i) \stackrel{\mathsf{def}}{=} \{w \in \mathcal{W}_\mathcal{C} \mid p_i \in w\}$ ■

It is important to explain the basic intuition behind this canonical model. We use the set of atoms in the underlying term algebra (modulo equality) for the set of events. Analyzing the atoms of the term algebra, we note that they are quite suitable for defining the events, each of them having the form: $\alpha_i \sqcap ... \sqcap \alpha_{i+n} \sqcap \overline{\alpha_k} \sqcap ...\overline{\alpha_{k+m}}$, where the first sequence of actions can be thought of as the *primitive* actions executed by the action (which this event belongs to) and the rest are the actions not executed when the event takes effect. The worlds, as usual, are maximal consistent sets of formulae, and the relationship between them is defined as is common in modal logics (see [13]); the novel point is that we label the relationship with the corresponding atoms. In a similar way we define the relation $\mathcal{R}_\mathcal{C}$; if a formula $\mathsf{P}(\alpha)$ exists in a given world w, then we add to the relation the pairs (w, γ), where γ is an atom of the term algebra. Our axioms ensure that this is safe.

Keeping these facts in mind, we can prove the completeness of the system, that is; *each consistent set of formulas has a model.* First, for the proof we need the following lemma whose proof is straighforward using boolean algebra properties.

Lemma 1. $\forall \alpha \in \Delta, \forall [\alpha']_{BA} \in \mathcal{I}_{\mathcal{C}}(\alpha) : \vdash_{\Phi_{BA}} \alpha' \sqsubseteq \alpha$

Now, we can prove a fundamental lemma.

Lemma 2 (truth lemma). $w, \mathcal{C} \vDash \varphi \Leftrightarrow \varphi \in w$.

Proof. *The proof is by induction on φ; we only describe the most important steps.*

Base Case. Using the definition we get

$$w, \mathcal{C} \vDash p_i \Leftrightarrow w \in \mathcal{I}_{\mathcal{C}}(p_i) \Leftrightarrow p_i \in w$$

Inductive Case. We have several cases:

CASE I. we have to prove $w, \mathcal{C} \vDash [\alpha]\varphi \Leftrightarrow [\alpha]\varphi \in w$.
$\Rightarrow$) Suppose $w, \mathcal{C} \vDash [\alpha]\varphi$, this means:

$$\begin{array}{ll} \forall [\gamma]_{BA} \in \mathcal{I}_{\mathcal{C}}(\alpha), \forall w' \in \mathcal{W}_{\mathcal{C}} : w \stackrel{[\gamma]_{BA}}{\rightarrow} w' \Rightarrow w', \mathcal{C} \vDash \varphi & \\ \equiv & \textit{[inductive hypothesis]} \\ \forall [\gamma]_{BA} \in \mathcal{I}_{\mathcal{C}}(\alpha), \forall w' \in \mathcal{W}_{\mathcal{C}} : w \stackrel{[\gamma]_{BA}}{\rightarrow} w' \Rightarrow \varphi \in w' \quad (*) & \end{array}$$

On the other hand, suppose $[\alpha]\varphi \notin w$, then (recalling properties of maximal consistent sets) $\langle\alpha\rangle\neg\varphi \in w$. Now, consider the set: $\Gamma = \{\neg\varphi\} \cup \{\psi \mid [\alpha]\psi \in w\}$. We claim that this set is consistent, for if not:

$$\exists \psi_1, ..., \psi_n \in \Gamma : \{\psi_1, ..., \psi_n, \varphi\} \vdash \bot$$

by definition of contradiction. But using this we can deduce:

$$\begin{array}{ll} \langle\alpha\rangle\neg\varphi \wedge [\alpha]\psi_1 \wedge ... \wedge [\alpha]\psi_n \in w & \\ \Rightarrow & \textit{[axiom 3 and maximal consistent set properties]} \\ \langle\alpha\rangle(\neg\varphi \wedge \psi_1 \wedge ... \wedge \psi_n) \in w & \\ \Leftrightarrow & \textit{[hypothesis]} \\ \langle\alpha\rangle\bot \in w & \\ \Leftrightarrow & \textit{[axiom 1]} \\ \bot \in w\ ! & \end{array}$$

Then Γ has to be consistent, and therefore it has a maximal consistent extension (by Zorn's lemma) Γ^*. But by definition of $\mathcal{R}_{\mathcal{C}}$:

$$\forall [\gamma]_{BA} \in \mathcal{I}_{\mathcal{C}}(\alpha) : w \stackrel{[\gamma]_{BA}}{\rightarrow} \Gamma^* \wedge \Gamma^* \vDash \neg\varphi$$

which contradicts (*) and therefore $[\alpha]\varphi \in w$.

$\Leftarrow$) *Suppose* $[\alpha]\varphi \in w$; *we have to prove* $w \vDash [\alpha]\varphi$. *Suppose that* $w \nvDash [\alpha]\varphi$, *then this means:*

$$\exists[\gamma]_{BA} \in \mathcal{I}_{\mathcal{C}}(\alpha), \exists w' \in \mathcal{W}_{\mathcal{C}} : w \overset{[\gamma]_{BA}}{\rightarrow} w' \wedge w', \mathcal{C} \nvDash \varphi$$

which is equivalent to (by ind.hyp.):

$$\exists[\gamma]_{BA} \in \mathcal{I}_{\mathcal{C}}(\alpha), \exists w' \in \mathcal{W}_{\mathcal{C}} : w \overset{[\gamma]_{BA}}{\rightarrow} w' \wedge \varphi \notin w' \quad (**)$$

But, by definition of $\mathcal{R}_{\mathcal{C}}$, *this means:*

$\exists w' \in \mathcal{W}_{\mathcal{C}} : (\forall \psi : [\gamma]\psi \in w \Rightarrow \psi \in w') \wedge \varphi \notin w'$
$\Rightarrow$ *[logic]*
$\neg([\gamma]\varphi) \in w$
$\Leftrightarrow$ *[max.cons.set properties]*
$[\gamma]\varphi \notin w$ *(***)*

But we know by lemma 1 that $\gamma \sqsubseteq \alpha$. *From here and using the hypothesis* ($[\alpha]\varphi \in w$) *and using theorem T3, we obtain:* $[\gamma]\varphi \in w$*!. And therefore:* $w, \mathcal{C} \vDash [\alpha]\varphi$.

<u>CASE II.</u> *We have to prove:* $w, \mathcal{C} \vDash \mathsf{P}(\alpha) \Leftrightarrow \mathsf{P}(\alpha) \in w$.
$\Rightarrow$) *Suppose* $w, \mathcal{C} \vDash \mathsf{P}(\alpha)$; *this means:*

$$\forall[\gamma]_{BA} \in \mathcal{I}_{\mathcal{C}}(\alpha) : \mathcal{P}_{\mathcal{C}}(w, [\gamma]_{BA})$$

Because of lemma 1, this implies (using definition of $\mathcal{P}_{\mathcal{C}}$*) that either* $\mathsf{P}(\alpha)$ *or* $\mathsf{P}(\beta)$ *where* $\vdash_{\Phi_{BA}} \alpha \sqsubseteq \beta$, *since there is no other way to introduce this relation in the canonical model. In both cases the result follows, in the first trivially, in the second one by using T1.*
$\Leftarrow$) *Suppose that* $\mathsf{P}(\alpha) \in w$; *by definition of* $\mathcal{P}_{\mathcal{C}}$ *this means:*

$$\forall[\gamma]_{BA} \in \mathcal{I}_{\mathcal{C}}(\alpha) : \mathcal{P}_{\mathcal{C}}(w, [\gamma]_{BA})$$

But using the definition of $\vDash$ *we get:* $w, \mathcal{C} \vDash P(\alpha)$.

<u>CASE III.</u> $w, \mathcal{C} \vDash \mathsf{P_w}(\alpha) \Leftrightarrow \mathsf{P_w}(\alpha) \in w$.
For the case $\alpha =_{act} \emptyset$ *the equivalence is trivial; let us prove the other case* ($\alpha \neq_{act} \emptyset$).
$\Rightarrow$) *Suppose* $w, \mathcal{C} \vDash \mathsf{P_w}(\alpha)$; *this means:*

$$\exists[\gamma]_{BA} \in \mathcal{I}_{\mathcal{C}} : \mathcal{P}_{\mathcal{C}}(w, [\gamma]_{BA})$$

By definition of $\mathcal{P}_{\mathcal{C}}$, *this only happens if for some* β: $\gamma \sqsubseteq \beta$ *and* $\mathsf{P}(\beta) \in w$. *Then by theorem T1 this implies* $\mathsf{P}(\gamma) \in w$, *and therefore, using axiom A12, we get:* $\mathsf{P_w}(\gamma) \in w$; *from this, by theorem T2, we obtain* $\mathsf{P_w}(\alpha) \in w$.
$\Leftarrow$) *Suppose* $\mathsf{P_w}(\alpha) \in w$. *We know by properties of atomic boolean algebras that:*

$[\alpha]_{BA} = [\gamma_1]_{BA} \sqcup_{[]} ... \sqcup_{[]} [\gamma_n]_{BA}$ *for some* $[\gamma_1]_{BA}, ..., [\gamma_n]_{BA}$ *atoms in* Δ/Φ_{BA}
$\Leftrightarrow$ *[def. of* Δ/Φ_{BA}*]*
$[\alpha]_{BA} = [\gamma_1 \sqcup ... \sqcup \gamma_n]_{BA}$

But this implies by deduction rule BA that $\mathsf{P_w}(\gamma_1 \sqcup ... \sqcup \gamma_n) \in w$*. By axiom A10, this implies:*

$$\mathsf{P_w}(\gamma_1) \vee ... \vee \mathsf{P_w}(\gamma_n) \in w$$

Let γ_i *be some of these action terms such that* $\mathsf{P_w}(\gamma_i) \in w$*; since* $\gamma_i \in at(\Delta)$*, we have:*

$$\bigwedge_{[\alpha]_{BA} \wedge \alpha \sqsubseteq \gamma_i} (\mathsf{P_w}(\alpha) \vee (\alpha =_{act} \emptyset)) \in w$$

Then by MP and A13 we get $\mathsf{P}(\gamma_i) \in w$*. By definition of* $\mathcal{P}_\mathcal{C}$*, this implies that:*

$$\exists [\gamma]_{BA} \in \mathcal{I}_\mathcal{C}(\alpha) : \mathcal{P}_\mathcal{C}([\gamma]_{BA}, w)$$

and this is just the definition of $w \vDash \mathsf{P_w}(\alpha)$*.* ■

Note that we have to prove that the defined interpretation $\mathcal{I}_\mathcal{C}$ holds with the restrictions **I.1** and **I.2** (**I.3** is satisfied by definition). The following theorem does this.

Theorem 5. *The function* $\mathcal{I}_\mathcal{C}$ *satisfies the conditions **I.1**,**I.2**.*
Proof. *First note that all the atoms of the boolean algebra* Δ/Φ_{BA} *(the Lindenbaum-Tarski algebra [10]) have the following form (or are equivalent to it):*

$$\alpha_1^1 \sqcap ... \sqcap \alpha_m^1 \sqcap \alpha_1^2 \sqcap ... \sqcap \alpha_k^2$$

Where for all $\alpha_i \in \Delta_0$*:* $\alpha_i = \alpha_j^1$ *or* $\overline{\alpha_i} = \alpha_j^2$*, for some* j*. That is, the atoms in the Lindenbaum algebra can be represented by terms which are composed of "intersections" of atomic actions or their negations.*

That $\mathcal{I}_\mathcal{C}$ *satisfies conditions **I.1**, **I.2** is implied by the underlying structure of the generated Lindenbaum Algebra:*
***I.1**: If* $[\gamma] \in \mathcal{I}_\mathcal{C}(\alpha_i) - \bigcup_{j \neq i}(\mathcal{I}_\mathcal{C}(\alpha_j))$*, then* $\gamma =_{act} \alpha_i \sqcap (\bigsqcap_{j \neq i}(\overline{\alpha_j}))$*, where* $\bigsqcap$ *is used to denote the application of* $\sqcap$ *to a finite sequence of boolean terms.*
***I.2**: We have to show that if* $[\gamma] \in \mathcal{I}(\alpha_i) \cap \mathcal{I}(\alpha_j)$*, for some* $i \neq j$*. Then:*

$$\bigcap \{\mathcal{I}(\alpha_k) \mid [\gamma] \in \mathcal{I}(\alpha_k)\} = \{[\gamma]\} \quad (1)$$

In this case it is easy to see that:

$$\gamma =_{act} \alpha_1^1 \sqcap ... \sqcap \alpha_m^1 \sqcap \overline{\alpha_1^2} \sqcap ... \sqcap \overline{\alpha_{m'}^2} \quad (2)$$

where α_i^1 *are the atomic actions which have the equivalence class* $[\gamma]$ *in its interpretation, and* α_i^2 *are the rest. Since the right term in equation 2 is an atom, every other* $[\gamma']$ *that satisfies condition 1 also satisfies:* $[\gamma'] = [\gamma]$*. The theorem follows.* ■

We have proved that the canonical model has the correct behavior; the completeness follows:

Corollary 1. *For every consistent set* Γ *of DPL, there is a model which satisfies it.*

Proof. *If* Γ *is consistent, then there exists a maximal extension of it which is a maximal consistent set, and therefore this set is a world* w *in the canonical model. By the definition of canonical model we know* $w, \mathcal{C} \vDash \Gamma$*; this finalizes the proof.* ■

Compactness is a corollary of strong completeness:

Corollary 2. *If every finite subset of a set Γ of formulae is satisfable, then Γ is satisfable.*

On the other hand, decidability can be proved using a selection argument (see [13]).

Theorem 6 (decidability). *Satisfability is decidable in DPL.*

Proof. *Suppose that for a formula φ: $w, M \vDash \varphi$, for some model M and world w. Let $d(\varphi) = m$ be the degree of φ (that is, the maximal depth of nested modalities), and let n be the number of primitive actions in the language.*

First, note that for every world in M we have at most $\sum_{i=1}^{n} \binom{n}{i} = 2^n - 1$ possible relationships with other worlds (that is, the maximum number of events in the model). Let M' be the model obtained from M ruling out those worlds do not reachable from w in m "steps". Clearly, $M', w \vDash \varphi$, and M' has at most $m * (2^n - 1)$ worlds, where $m = d(\varphi)$ and n is the number of primitive actions.

This gives us a decidability method: given φ, build all the models up to size $m * (2^n - 1)$ and check if φ is true in everyone of them. Obviously, this method is exponential in complexity. ∎

3 Extensions and Applications of DPL

The notion of time is useful for specifying fault-tolerant systems; using temporal constructs we can formalize, for example, error recovery (which without doubt, is a temporal property). Several temporal formalism have been proposed in the literature; it seems that for our formalism a CTL logic (see [14]) is the most appropriate. This is mainly because branching is inherent in our approach to system specification. Here we only present the syntactic extension of the logic; both the semantics (using traces) and an axiomatic system are described in [12].

We define the temporal formulae as follows.

Definition 5 (Temporal Formulae). *Given a DPL vocabulary $\langle \Phi_0, \Delta_0 \rangle$, the set of temporal deontic formulae (Φ_T) is defined as follows:*

- $\Phi_0 \subseteq \Phi_T$.
- $\top, \bot \in \Phi_T$.
- *if* $\alpha, \beta \in \Delta$, *then* $\alpha =_{act} \beta \in \Phi_T$
- *if* $\varphi_1, \varphi_2 \in \Phi_T$, *then* $\varphi_1 \rightarrow \varphi_2 \in \Phi_T$.
- *if* $\varphi \in \Phi_T$, *then* $\neg\varphi \in \Phi_T$.
- *if* $\varphi \in \Phi_T$ *with no temporal operators and* $\alpha \in \Delta$, *then* $\langle\alpha\rangle\phi \in \Phi_T$.
- *if* $\alpha \in \Delta$ *then* $\mathsf{P}(\alpha) \in \Phi_T$ *and* $\mathsf{P_w}(\alpha) \in \Phi_T$.
- *If* $\alpha \in \Delta$, *then* $\mathsf{Done}(\alpha) \in \Phi_T$.
- *If* $\varphi_1, \varphi_2 \in \Phi$, *then* $\mathsf{AN}\varphi$, $\mathsf{AG}\varphi$, $\mathsf{A}(\varphi_1 \,\mathcal{U}\, \varphi_2)$, $\mathsf{E}(\varphi_1 \,\mathcal{U}\, \varphi_2) \in \Phi_T$.

The temporal operators are the classic ones in CTL logics; intuitively, the predicate $\mathsf{AN}\varphi$ means *in all possible executions φ is true at the next moment*, $\mathsf{AG}\varphi$ means *in all executions* φ *is always true*, $\mathsf{A}(\varphi_1\ \mathcal{U}\ \varphi_2)$ means *for every possible execution* φ_1 *is true until* φ_2 *becomes true* and $\mathsf{E}(\varphi_1\ \mathcal{U}\ \varphi_2)$ says there *exists some execution where* φ_1 *is true until* φ_2 *becomes true.* As usual, using these operators we can define the dual versions of them. The $\mathsf{Done}(-)$ operator is a bit uncommon, it is used to predicate about the past execution of an action. Intuitively, $\mathsf{Done}(\alpha)$ means *the last action executed was* α. Some properties of $\mathsf{Done}(-)$ are:

Done1. $\mathsf{Done}(\alpha) \wedge \alpha \sqsubseteq \alpha' \rightarrow \mathsf{Done}(\alpha')$
Done2. $\mathsf{Done}(\alpha \sqcup \beta) \rightarrow \mathsf{Done}(\alpha) \vee \mathsf{Done}(\beta)$
Done3. $\mathsf{Done}(\alpha \sqcap \beta) \leftrightarrow \mathsf{Done}(\alpha) \wedge \mathsf{Done}(\beta)$
Done4. $\mathsf{Done}(\alpha \sqcup \beta) \wedge \mathsf{Done}(\overline{\alpha}) \rightarrow \mathsf{Done}(\beta)$
Done5. $[\alpha]\varphi \wedge [\beta]\mathsf{Done}(\alpha) \rightarrow [\beta]\varphi$

All these properties are intuitive; the last of them is a kind of subsumption property: *if after doing* α φ *is true, and after doing* β *we have also done* α, *then after* β φ *is true.* We can use the $\mathsf{Done}(-)$ operator to introduce a $\mathsf{Do}(\alpha)$ operator: $\mathsf{Do}(\alpha) \overset{\mathsf{def}}{\Longleftrightarrow} \mathsf{ANDone}(\alpha)$, which means: *the next action to be performed is* α. It is in particular useful to specify recovery actions and model restrictions.

Using these new constructions we can show an example of application of this formalism. We take again the dining philosophers problem ([15]), but we add the possibility of processes crashing. This is introduced in the model saying that a philosopher can feel sick and then he has to go to the bathroom (perhaps holding onto some fork). The complete example is shown in [12] and here we only describe the part where we model fault-tolerance. Consider the following formulae :

DO $i.eating \rightarrow \mathsf{Do}(i.getthk \sqcup i.getbad)$
O1. $i.eating \leftrightarrow \mathsf{O}(i.down_L \sqcap i.down_R)$
V1. $\neg i.v_1 \wedge \mathsf{O}(i.down_L \sqcap i.down_R) \rightarrow$
$$([\overline{i.down_L \sqcap i.down_R}]i.v_1) \wedge ([i.down_L \sqcap i.down_R]\neg i.v_1)$$
V2. $\neg i.v_1 \wedge \neg\mathsf{O}(i.down_L \sqcap i.down_R) \rightarrow [\mathbf{U}]\neg i.v_1$
V3. $i.v_2 \leftrightarrow i.v_1 \wedge (\neg i.has_L \veebar \neg i.has_R)$
V4. $(i.v_1 \rightarrow [i.down_L \sqcap i.down_R]\neg i.v_1) \wedge$
$$(i.v_1 \wedge \neg i.v_2 \rightarrow [\overline{i.down_L \sqcap i.down_R}]i.v_1)$$
V5. $i.v_2 \rightarrow [\overline{i.down_L \sqcup i.down_R}]i.v_2$
V6. $((i.v_2 \wedge \neg i.has_L) \rightarrow [i.down_R]\neg(\neg i.v_2 \wedge \neg i.v_1)) \wedge$
$$((i.v_2 \wedge \neg i.has_R) \rightarrow [i.down_R](\neg i.v_2 \wedge \neg i.v_1))$$

where $0 \leq i \leq n$. The predicate $i.v_1$ is used to note when a violation occurs (i.e., when philosopoher i goes with some forks to the bathroom). $i.v_2$ is a refinement of it; it is only true when philosopher i went to the bathroom with only one fork. Predicates $i.has_L$ and $i.has_R$ allow us to know if philosopher i has his left or right fork, respectively. Actions $i.down_L, i.down_R$ model the actions of philosopher i putting down the corresponding fork. The predicate $i.eating$ tells us if a philosopher is eating or not. The actions $i.getthk$ and $i.getbad$ are used when philosopher i goes to thinking again (he puts down the forks) or he goes to the bathroom, respectively. The two actions are disjoint between them ($i.getthk \sqcap i.getbad = \emptyset$).

It is interesting to analyze the formulae given above. **DO** is a model restriction; it says that, after eating, a philosopher has to go thinking or he can get a stomachache and then he goes to the bathroom. **O1** tells us that if a philosopher is eating, then he is obligated to put down both forks after eating. Formula **V1** specifies when a violation becomes possible, that is, when the philosopher does not put both forks down. **V2** describe those scenarios where a violation is not possible. **V3** defines $i.v_2$. **V4** tell us that returning both forks to the table is a recovery action. In a similar way, **V5** and **V6** define how we can recover from a violation of type v_2.

Several properties can now be proven. For example, we can prove that a violation $i.v_2$ is less dangerous than a $i.v_1 \wedge \neg i.v_2$ violation, in the sense that the first type of violation allows neighbors to progress in some cases (under the hypothesis of no more crashes occurring).

$$\vdash \mathsf{AG}(((i+1).v_2 \wedge \neg(i+1).has_R) \wedge \neg i.bath \wedge \neg(i-1).bath) \rightarrow \mathsf{EF}i.eating$$

We show some of these properties in [12]. The important point to make is the way in which we can specify different kinds of violations (faults having occurred in the system) and the relationships between them. As we have shown, recovery actions can be described using modalities; furthermore, deontic constructions are important to differentiate between normative and non-normative states. In addition, more complicated constructions (e.g., obligations bounded by some time limit) can be expressed using the temporal operators. We leave this for further work.

4 Conclusion and Further Work

In this paper we presented the propositional part of a deontic logic; an axiomatic system was described and some of its properties were proved. As shown in an example, this logic provides some constructs which seem useful to formalize fault-tolerance concepts. Our ultimate goal is to use this logic for developing a more inclusive framework; modularization is a key factor in such a framework. However, some important problems have to be solved to modularize the logic, e.g, how the deontic operators associated with different modules can be distributed and composed is an important point here.

On the other hand, it is well-known that propositional logics are not expressive enough to deal with some problems. It seems possible to extend this logic with first-order logic constructs, although it is not straightforward that all the properties (like compactness) will be preserved in such an extension.

The decidability method described in section 2 is very inefficient. However, other (still exponential) methods are possible; in particular tableaux methods are known to be useful in dynamic logics; from the axiomatic system described it is likely to be possible to develop a tableaux method and we leave this as further work.

References

1. Meyer, J.J., Wieringa, R.J.: Deontic logic: A concise overview. In: DEON 91. First International Workshop on Deontic Logic (1991)
2. Broersen, J.: Modal Action Logics for Reasoning about Reactive Systems. PhD thesis, Vrije University Amsterdam (2003)

3. Maibaum, T.S.E., Khosla, S.: The prescription and description of state-based systems. In: Barringer, H.B., Pnueli, A. (eds.) Temporal Logic in Computation, Springer, Heidelberg (1985)
4. Meyer, J.J.: Dynamic logic for reasoning about actions and agents. In: Workshop on Logic-Based Artificial Intelligence, Washington, DC, June 14–16 (1999)
5. Magee, J., Maibaum, T.S.E.: Towards specification, modelling and analysis of fault tolerance in self managed systems. In: Proceeding of the 2006 international workshop on self-adaptation and self-managing systems (2006)
6. Meyer, J.J.: A different approach to deontic logic: Deontic logic viewed as variant of dynamic logic. Notre Dame Journal of Formal Logic 29 (1988)
7. Kent, S., Quirk, B., Maibaum, T.S.E.: Specifying deontic behavior in modal action logic. Technical report, Forest Research Project (1991)
8. Gargov, G., Passy, S.: A note on boolean logic. In: Petkov, P.P. (ed.) Proceedings of the Heyting Summerschool, Plenum Press, New York (1990)
9. Harel, D., Kozen, D., Tiuryn, J.: Dynamic Logic. MIT Press, Cambridge (2000)
10. Sikorski, R.: Boolean Algebras. Springer, Heidelberg (1969)
11. Monk, J.D.: Mathematical Logic. Graduate Texts in Mathematics. Springer, Heidelberg (1976)
12. Castro, P.F., Maibaum, T.S.E.: Torwards a deontic logic for fault tolerance. Technical Report SQRL39, McMaster, Department of Computing & Software, Software Quality Research Laboratory (2007)
13. Blackburn, P., Rijke, M., Venema, Y.: Modal Logic. Cambridge Tracts in Theoretical Computer Science, vol. 53 (2001)
14. Emerson, E.A., Halpern, J.Y.: Decision procedures and expressiveness in the temporal logic of branching time. In: STOC. 14th Annual Symposiun on Theory of Computing (1982)
15. Dijkstra, E.W.: Hirarchical ordering of sequential processes. In: Acta Informatica, vol. 1, pp. 115–138. Springer, Heidelberg (1971)

Verifying Lock-Freedom Using Well-Founded Orders

Robert Colvin and Brijesh Dongol

ARC Centre for Complex Systems
School of Information Technology and Electrical Engineering
University of Queensland
{robert,brijesh} @itee.uq.edu.au

Abstract. Lock-free algorithms are designed to improve the performance of concurrent programs by maximising the potential for processes to operate in parallel. Lock-free algorithms guarantee that within the system as a whole, *some* process will eventually complete its operation (as opposed to guaranteeing that *all* operations will eventully complete). Since lock-free algorithms potentially allow a high degree of interference between concurrent processes, and because their progress property is non-trivial, it is difficult to be assured of their correctness without a formal, machine-checked verification. In this paper we describe a method for proving the lock-free progress property. The approach is based on the construction of a well-founded ordering on the set of processes. The method is demonstrated using a well-known lock-free stack algorithm as an example, and we describe how the proof was checked using a theorem prover.

1 Introduction

The lock-free property may be expressed informally as "eventually *some* process will complete an operation". Hence, the system as a whole will make progress, even if some processes never complete their operation [HLM03,Don06a]. Lock-free algorithms are designed to avoid problems associated with lock-based algorithms (such as deadlock and priority inversion) and to increase the potential for concurrent execution (for improved performance). However, lock-free algorithms tend to be more complex than lock-based programs and due to this complexity, some published lock-free algorithms have been proved to be incorrect, despite being presented alongside informal proofs [CG05,Doh03].

Formal verification of lock-free algorithms has so far focussed on their safety properties [CGLM06,CDG05,CG05,DGLM04]. This is for two reasons: firstly, until recently lock-freedom had not been formalised; and secondly, because techniques for proving complex progress properties, such as lock-freedom, can be difficult to apply [Don06a]. In this paper, we complement the formal verification of safety properties of lock-free algorithms with a technique for formally verifying their progress property. The technique is designed to be intuitive and amenable to tool support.

C.B. Jones, Z. Liu, J. Woodcock (Eds.): ICTAC 2007, LNCS 4711, pp. 124–138, 2007.

The paper is structured as follows. In Sect. 2 we describe lock-free algorithms, and the formal framework used to describe programs and progress properties. In Sect. 3 we describe the proof method and demonstrate it on a well-known lock-free stack algorithm. In Sect. 4 we show how the framework and proofs were encoded in the PVS theorem prover [ORR+96].

2 Preliminaries

In this section we give our formal framework: in Sect. 2.1 we describe lock-free algorithms, and in Sect. 2.2 we descibe how we represent them as transition systems. In Sect. 2.3 we give a formal definition of lock-freedom and in Sect. 2.4 we give a theorem for proving lock-freedom.

2.1 Lock-Free Algorithms

The typical structure of a lock-free operation on a shared data G is to take a snapshot of G, construct a new value for G locally, then attempt to update G to this new value. If no interference has occurred, i.e., G has not been modified since the snapshot was taken, the operation completes, whereas if interference has occurred, a new snapshot of G is taken and the steps above are repeated. This can be more efficient than lock-based approaches, since each operation is executed mostly independently. The risk is that an operation may be continually interfered with, hence unable to complete. However, a lock-free program must only ensure that *some* operation will eventually complete, even if other operations never do. In the rest of this section we formalise the general structure of lock-free algorithms using a lock-free stack algorithm as an example.

The general structure of a program that implements a lock-free data structure consists of a finite set of processes, $PROC$, each of which executes operations on the data structure from the set OP. A process may either be *active* (currently executing an operation) or *idle* (not executing any operation). An idle process becomes active by starting a new operation, while an active process becomes idle by completing the operation it is currently executing. An operation is a sequential statement (implicitly parameterised by the calling process) and is non-blocking, i.e., no atomic statement of the operation exhibits blocking behaviour. In this paper, we assume each operation $op \in OP$ is of the form in Fig. 1.

$$\begin{array}{rcl} op & \mathrel{\widehat=} & op.preloop;\ op.loop;\ op.postloop \\ \mathcal{P}(PROC, OP) & \mathrel{\widehat=} & \|\ p{:}\ PROC \bullet \texttt{while true}\ \{\sqcap\ op{:}\ OP \bullet op\}\ \texttt{end} \end{array}$$

Fig. 1. Structure of lock-free algorithms

The code corresponding to *op.loop* is a potentially infinite retry-loop, while the code corresponding to both *op.preloop* and *op.postloop* is assumed not to contain any potentially infinite loops, i.e., is guaranteed to terminate in a finite number of steps regardless of interference. Note that *op.preloop* and *op.postloop* may be empty for some operations. The lock-free programs in [MS98,DDG+04], [CG05] all conform to the structure in Fig. 1.

Each atomic statement has a unique *label*, and each process p has a *program counter* (pc) whose value is the label of the next statement p will execute. We assume the existence of a special label idle to identify idle processes, i.e., p is idle iff $pc_p = \mathsf{idle}$. We use PC to denote the set of all labels in the program (including idle).

The general structure of a lock free program is summarised by the program, $\mathcal{P}$, in Fig. 1. The processes execute in parallel, and are initially idle; from this state a process p non-deterministically chooses an operation op from OP for execution. When execution of op is completed, the process executing op returns to the idle state, and may once again choose a new operation for execution.

Example: Treiber's stack. To understand how typical lock-free operations are implemented, consider the code in Fig. 3, which is based on a lock-free stack algorithm presented by Michael and Scott [MS98] and attributed to Treiber [Tre86]. The labels ps1 ... ps6 and pp1 ... pp9, in addition to idle, form the set PC. The program uses the Compare-and-Swap (CAS) primitive (Fig. 2), which combines a test and update of a variable within a single atomic statement. A procedure call $CAS(G, ss, n)$ operates as follows: if (shared) variable G is the same as (snapshot) variable ss, then G is updated to the value of n and *true* is returned; otherwise no update occurs and *false* is returned.

```
CAS(G, ss, n)  ≙  if G = ss then G := n ; return true
                  else return false
```

Fig. 2. Compare-and-Swap

It is well known that CAS-based implementations can suffer from the "ABA problem" [MS98]. This can be manifested in the following way: a process p takes a snapshot, say ss_p, of the shared variable G when G's value is A; then another process modifies G to B, then back again to A. Process p has been interfered with, but the CAS that compares G and ss_p cannot detect this since $G = ss_p$ after the interference has taken place. If value A is a pointer, this is a potentially fatal problem, as the contents of the location pointed to by A may have changed. A work-around is to store a *modification count* with each global variable, and to increment the count each time the variable is modified. Modification counts do not constitute a full solution to the ABA problem, since in a real system, modification counts will be bounded. However, in practice, the likelihood of the ABA problem occurring is reduced to a tolerably small level [Moi97]. In the stack implementation in Fig. 3, the ABA problem can occur because pointers may be reused after they are freed by the pop operation (pp8), hence, a modification count is added to the shared variable pointer (for a full explanation, see Michael and Scott [MS98]).

The stack is represented as a linked list of nodes (of type `node`). A `push(v)` operation, where `v` is of some type `Value`, adds a new node with value `v` to the

```
struct node { val: Value; next: *node }
struct node_ptr { ptr: *node; count: int }
node_ptr Top = (null, 0)

     push(v: Value) ≙
ps1  n := new node()
ps2  n->val := v
ps3  repeat
ps4     ss := Top
ps5     n->next := ss.ptr
ps6  until CAS(Top, ss, (n, ss.count + 1))

     pop : Value ≙
pp1  repeat
pp2     ss := Top
pp3     if ss.ptr = NULL then
pp4       return EMPTY
pp5     n := ss.ptr->next
pp6  until CAS(Top, ss, (n, ss.count + 1))
pp7  pvalue := ss.ptr->val
pp8  free(ss.ptr)
pp9  return pvalue
```

Fig. 3. Treiber's stack

front of the list, while a `pop` operation returns `EMPTY` if the stack is empty and otherwise removes a node from the front of the list and returns its value (we assume `EMPTY` is a member of type `Value` which is never pushed). Each node consists of a value field (`val` of type `Value`) and a next pointer (`next` of type `*node`). The first node in the list is stored in shared variable `Top`, of special type `node_ptr`: it contains a pointer to the top of the stack (`Top.ptr`) which is null if the stack is empty, and a modification count (`Top.count`) which is used to detect interference as described above.

A process executing `push(v)` first allocates a new node, `n` (ps1), and sets the value field of `n` to the pushed value, `v` (ps2). These two statements constitute `push`.*preloop*. It then enters `push(v)`.*loop*, in which it takes a snapshot, `ss`, of the top of the stack (ps4), then sets the next field of `n` to `ss.ptr` (ps5). Assuming that the snapshot `ss` is still accurate, i.e., the value of `Top` (which includes its modification count) is the same as when the snapshot was taken at ps4, the stack may be updated by setting `Top.ptr` to `n` and incrementing its modification count (ps6). A successful execution of the CAS at ps6 marks a successful push operation, therefore the executing process exits `push(v)`.*loop* and returns to an idle state. In this case, `push(v)`.*postloop* is empty. If `CAS(Top, ss, (n, ss.count + 1))` fails (ps6), then `Top` has been modified by another process and `push(v)`.*loop* is retried.

The pop operation is similarly structured. In this case `pop`.*preloop* is empty, so it immediately enters `pop`.*loop* in which it takes a snapshot, `ss`, of `Top` (pp2). If the snapshot is null (pp3), the pop operation completes and returns `Empty` to indicate an empty stack was observed (pp4). If the snapshot is non-null, local variable `n` is set the next pointer of `ss` (pp5), then a CAS is used to update `Top` (pp6) and `pop`.*postloop* is executed. If the CAS is unsuccessful, the loop is retried. Execution of `pop`.*postloop* stores the value of the popped node (pp7) in `pvalue`, frees the popped node (pp8) and returns the value of `pvalue` (pp9). This completes the pop operation and thus the executing process returns to an idle state.

We now argue informally why Treiber's stack is lock-free. A push operation will not complete if it is stuck forever inside `push`.*loop*, i.e., retries the loop an infinite number of times. Because each retry occurs when some other operation has modified `Top`, this implies that an infinite number of processes have successfully executed a CAS. Because both `push`.*postloop* and `pop`.*postloop* have only a finite number of steps, and because we assume there are a finite number of processes, an infinite number of successful CASs implies an infinite number of operations complete, hence, there will always be some process that completes its operation. Similar reasoning holds for the pop operation.

2.2 Transition Systems and Trace-Based Reasoning

We model programs as labelled transition systems. The variables of a program may either be *shared* or *local* (a local variable of type T is modelled as a function of type $PROC \to T$). The system also includes a program counter for each process ($PROC \to PC$). A program $\mathcal{P}$ is defined by: $states(\mathcal{P})$, the set of allowable states of $\mathcal{P}$, each of which is a mapping from variables of $\mathcal{P}$ to their values; a nonempty set $start(\mathcal{P}) \subseteq states(\mathcal{P})$, the initial states of $\mathcal{P}$; $actions(\mathcal{P})$, a set of labels for transitions – there is one action for each atomic statement of code per process; and $trans(\mathcal{P})$: $states(\mathcal{P}) \times actions(\mathcal{P}) \times states(\mathcal{P})$, the transitions of the system, each of which corresponds to an individual action. A *predicate* of $\mathcal{P}$ has type $states(\mathcal{P}) \to \mathbb{B}$, thus, for a predicate Q and state s, $Q.s$ denotes that s satisfies Q. For convenience, we represent the transitions of an action α as an atomic guard/effect pair, where the guard (denoted **grd**) is a predicate on $states(\mathcal{P})$ that defines the states in which α is enabled, and the effect (denoted **eff**) atomically updates the values of the variables of the current state. For example, the statement ps4 for process p is represented by the transition

$push4_p$:
  grd: $pc_p = \mathsf{ps4}$
  eff: $ss_p, pc_p := Top, \mathsf{ps5}$

This transition is enabled in any state in which process p is ready to execute the code at ps4, and the effect of this transition is to atomically update local variable ss_p to the value held by the shared variable Top and to advance the pc value for p to ps5.

The transitions corresponding to the CAS at pp6 is represented by the two transitions below, corresponding to the succeed/fail cases, respectively.

$pop6Suc_p$:
grd: $pc_p = \mathsf{pp6} \wedge Top = ss_p$
eff: $Top, pc_p := (n_p, ss_p.count + 1), \mathsf{pp7}$

$pop6Fail_p$:
grd: $pc_p = \mathsf{pp6} \wedge Top \neq ss_p$
eff: $pc_p := \mathsf{pp2}$

A *trace*, t, of a program $\mathcal{P}$ is a sequence of states $s_0, s_1, ...$, such that $s_0 \in start(\mathcal{P})$, and for each i, there exists an action $\alpha \in actions(\mathcal{P})$ such that $(s_i, \alpha, s_{i+1}) \in trans(\mathcal{P})$ (written $s_i \xrightarrow{\alpha} s_{i+1}$). We use $traces(\mathcal{P})$ to denote the set of all *complete* traces of $\mathcal{P}$, i.e., each $t \in traces(\mathcal{P})$ represents a terminating or infinite execution of $\mathcal{P}$. We assume the presence of *minimal progress* [Mis01], i.e., *some* enabled action is chosen for execution, although this may always be an action of the same process. For a program, $\mathcal{P}$, of the form outlined in Fig. 1, under the minimal progress assumption, each $t \in traces(\mathcal{P})$ is infinite, i.e., $dom(t) = \mathbb{N}$.

To describe properties of traces we use the temporal operators *always*, *eventually* and *next*, represented by $\Box$, $\Diamond$ and $\bigcirc$, respectively. The notation $(t, i) \vdash F$ states that formula F is satisfied by trace t at index i. If F is a predicate on a single state, i.e., does not contain any temporal operators, then $(t, i) \vdash F$ iff $F.t_i$. The meaning of the three operators are defined below, following Manna and Pnueli [MP92].

$$\begin{array}{lcl} (t,i) \vdash \Box F & \Leftrightarrow & (\forall j{:}\mathbb{N} \bullet j \geq i \Rightarrow (t,j) \vdash F) \\ (t,i) \vdash \Diamond F & \Leftrightarrow & (\exists j{:}\mathbb{N} \bullet j \geq i \wedge (t,j) \vdash F) \\ (t,i) \vdash \bigcirc F & \Leftrightarrow & (t, i+1) \vdash F \end{array}$$

A trace t satisfies temporal formula F, written $t \vdash F$, if $(t, 0) \vdash F$, i.e., F holds in the initial state. For a program $\mathcal{P}$ and a temporal formula F, $\mathcal{P}$ satisfies F, written $\mathcal{P} \models F$, iff $(\forall t{:}\, traces(\mathcal{P}) \bullet t \vdash F)$.

2.3 Formalising Lock-Freedom

Lock-freedom is a system-wide property that guarantees *some* active process will eventually complete an operation. That is, in Fig. 1, some processes may get stuck executing *op.loop* forever, but at least one other process will always be able to complete. The definition of lock-freedom is formalised by Dongol [Don06a], but because it is designed to be as general as possible, it is not easily amenable to proof. Our definition of lock-freedom is based on [Don06a], but specialised for the class of lock-free operations outlined in Sect. 2.1.

Definition 1 (Lock-freedom). *A program $\mathcal{P}$ of the form outlined in Sect. 2.1 is lock-free iff it satisfies the following property*

$$\mathcal{P} \models \Box\Diamond(\exists p{:}\, PROC \bullet pc_p \neq \mathsf{idle} \wedge \bigcirc(pc_p = \mathsf{idle})). \qquad (1)$$

That is, a program $\mathcal{P}$ with a finite number of processes for which every trace of $\mathcal{P}$ is infinite is lock free iff from any reachable state, there is a point in the future where some active process transitions to the idle state, i.e., some active process completes its operation. In the case of Treiber's stack, lock-freedom is satisfied if there will always eventually be a successful execution of the CAS at ps6, a pop operation that returns `Empty` at pp4, or a pop operation that returns a value at pp9.

2.4 Proving Always-Eventually Properties

To prove a property of the form $\Box\Diamond F$ we utilise a common technique of identifying a well-founded ordering on program states and showing that each transition in the system either reduces the well-founded ordering or establishes F. Using a well-founded ordering ensures a finite bound the number of intermediate states before F is established. Well-founded orders are used to develop methods for proving *leads-to* properties [CM88] and *until* properties [FG96].

Theorem 1. *Let $\mathcal{P}$ be a program where all traces in $traces(\mathcal{P})$ are infinite in length; $(\mathcal{W}, \prec)$ be a well-founded ordering; P_p and Q_p be predicates parameterised by process p; and δ be a total function from program states to $\mathcal{W}$. If*

$$(\forall \alpha{:}\, actions(\mathcal{P});\ s, s'{:}\, states(\mathcal{P}) \bullet s \xrightarrow{\alpha} s' \Rightarrow \\ \delta(s') \prec \delta(s) \vee (\exists p{:}\, PROC \bullet P_p.s \wedge Q_p.s') \tag{2}$$

then

$$\mathcal{P} \models \Box\Diamond(\exists p{:}\, PROC \bullet P_p \wedge \bigcirc Q_p). \tag{3}$$

Proof. First note that by the definition of $\Box$, $\Diamond$ and $\bigcirc$, expanding and simplifying (3) gives

$$(\forall t{:}\, traces(\mathcal{P}) \bullet (\forall i{:}\, \mathbb{N} \bullet (\exists j{:}\, \mathbb{N} \bullet j \geq i \wedge (\exists p{:}\, PROC \bullet P_p.t_j \wedge Q_p.t_{j+1})))). \tag{4}$$

Assume arbitrary $t \in traces(\mathcal{P})$ and $i \in \mathbb{N}$. By (2) and the definition of a trace, either $\delta(t_{i+1}) \prec \delta(t_i)$ holds, or (4) is satisfied because some process that is active in state t_i becomes idle in state t_{i+1}. Since $(\mathcal{W}, \prec)$ is well-founded, we will eventually reach a state t_k such that $k \geq i$ and $\delta(t_k)$ is the base of $(\mathcal{W}, \prec)$. Since each trace is infinite, state t_{k+1} must exist and furthermore, $\delta(t_{k+1})$ cannot be smaller than $\delta(t_k)$. By (2), some process that satisfies $P_p.t_k$ satisfies $Q_p.t_{k+1}$; k is therefore the witness for j in (4). $\square$

By instantiating P_p to $pc_p \neq \mathsf{idle}$ and Q_p to $pc_p = \mathsf{idle}$, we may apply Theorem 1 to reduce a proof of a temporal formula such as (1) to the construction of a well-founded ordering followed by case analysis on all transitions in the system.

3 Proving Lock-Freedom

In this section we outline how we prove lock-freedom and demonstrate the technique using Treiber's stack as an example. The proof consists of the following steps:

1. Identify the transitions from *op.loop* to *op.postloop*, and show that an infinite number of such transitions implies lock-freedom.
2. Define a well-founded ordering on program states.
3. Apply Theorem 1 to show lock-freedom by case analysis on transitions.

3.1 Identifying Transitions from *op.loop* to *op.postloop*

Definition 1 describes lock-freedom for programs of the form outlined in Sect. 2.1. While this is an appropriate definition, it is generally easier to show that eventually, either a process becomes idle or it exits *op.loop* (and therefore reaches *op.postloop*). For the Treiber stack, we therefore show that a process eventually either transitions to idle (which satisfies (1)) or to pp7 (the start of pop.*postloop*). Note that a push operation exiting `push(v)`.*loop* and a pop operation returning `Empty` directly transition to idle. It then remains to show that this implies lock-freedom.

Theorem 2 (Lock-freedom for Treiber). *If the following holds for the program in Fig. 3*

$$\mathcal{P} \models \Box\Diamond(\exists p{:}\, PROC \bullet pc_p \notin \{\mathsf{idle}, \mathsf{pp7}\} \wedge \bigcirc(pc_p \in \{\mathsf{idle}, \mathsf{pp7}\})) \qquad (5)$$

then (1) holds, i.e., the Treiber stack is lock-free.

Proof: Assume $\mathcal{P}$ satisfies (5). Then an arbitrary trace t in $traces(\mathcal{P})$ must contain an infinite number of transitions to idle or to pp7. If t contains an infinite number of transitions to idle then (1) holds. If t contains an infinite number of transitions to pp7, then, because there are a finite number of processes, at least one process, say p, must be responsible for an infinite number of these transitions. Between any two transitions to pp7 by process p a transition to idle by p must occur. Hence, t must contain an infinite number of transitions to idle, and (1) holds. □

3.2 Defining the Well-Founded Ordering

The straightforward approach to defining a well-founded ordering on program states is to base it purely on PC, i.e., the labels of the program statements [DM06,DM07]. However, this does not work for lock-free operations because each retry of *op.loop* will break the well-founded ordering on PC. Furthermore, the guard of the loop is not suited for defining a loop variant.

To give the intuition behind the ordering we use, we note that a process executing *op.loop* is in one of two "states": either its snapshot of the global variable is accurate, in which case its "goal" is to successfully execute the CAS and exit *op.loop*; or its snapshot is inaccurate, in which case its goal is to take a new snapshot to obtain an accurate one. We consider a simple hierarchy between these two "states": having an accurate snapshot is better than having an inaccurate snapshot, thus, taking a new snapshot constitutes an improvement in the status of each process.

Note that a successful execution of the CAS allows the process to exit *op.loop*. Thus, each step a process p takes within *op.loop* takes it closer to its goal of exiting *op.loop* or renewing its snapshot. The difficulty arises when another process q interferes with p by modifying the shared variable thereby rendering p's snapshot inaccurate. This is clearly a step of the system which is not an improvement for p. However, crucially, the step that regresses p also establishes that process q has made progress, i.e., has reached a point from which it will complete within a finite number of steps. So each step of the system improves the position for the process that executed the step, but may simultaneously "regress" other processes; however these regressive steps are exactly the ones that ensure progress of the system as a whole.

In the Treiber stack, a process p performing a push operation proceeds by entering push(v).*loop* and taking a snapshot. If p is not interfered with, it will go on to successfully execute the CAS at ps6 and complete. However, if between taking the snapshot and executing the CAS some other process q interferes with p (and therefore makes progress), then from *this point* process p will proceed back to statement ps4 (where it will take another snapshot of Top). Execution of ps4 improves the status of process p by renewing the snapshot then proceeding as before.

We now formalise this intuition for the Treiber stack and construct two orderings on pc values, one for an accurate snapshot, $\prec^{\checkmark}$, and one for an inaccurate snapshot, $\prec^{\times}$. The ordering in the case where the snapshot is accurate is a straightforward progression from being idle through to being ready to execute the CAS (ps6). We underline the labels that are contained within push(v).*loop*. So that the labels may be presented in the same order they appear in the program, for labels a and b we define, $(b \succ^{\checkmark} a) \Leftrightarrow (a \prec^{\checkmark} b)$ and $(b \succ^{\times} a) \Leftrightarrow (a \prec^{\times} b)$.

$$\mathsf{idle} \succ^{\checkmark} \mathsf{ps1} \succ^{\checkmark} \mathsf{ps2} \succ^{\checkmark} \underline{\mathsf{ps4} \succ^{\checkmark} \mathsf{ps5} \succ^{\checkmark} \mathsf{ps6}}$$

The ordering for an inaccurate snapshot is similar, except that the base of the ordering is statement ps4 where another snapshot is taken.

$$\mathsf{idle} \succ^{\times} \mathsf{ps1} \succ^{\times} \mathsf{ps2} \succ^{\times} \underline{\mathsf{ps5} \succ^{\times} \mathsf{ps6} \succ^{\times} \mathsf{ps4}}$$

Notice that outside push(v).*loop* the orderings $\prec^{\checkmark}$ and $\prec^{\times}$ are identical; the accuracy of the snapshot is irrelevant at this stage. For practical reasons, it is simpler to include all pc values in both $\prec^{\checkmark}$ and $\prec^{\times}$.

We may follow the same pattern for the pop operation, except that in this case, the labels corresponding to pop.*postloop* precede those in pop.*loop* because the label corresponding to the CAS (pp6) is the base.

$$\mathsf{pp7} \succ^{\checkmark} \mathsf{pp8} \succ^{\checkmark} \mathsf{pp9} \succ^{\checkmark} \mathsf{idle} \succ^{\checkmark} \underline{\mathsf{pp2} \succ^{\checkmark} \mathsf{pp3} \succ^{\checkmark} \mathsf{pp4} \succ^{\checkmark} \mathsf{pp5} \succ^{\checkmark} \mathsf{pp6}}$$

The ordering for an inaccurate snapshot is again similar, except that the label at the base corresponds to the statement that updates the snapshot of *Top* (pp2).

$$\mathsf{pp7} \succ^{\times} \mathsf{pp8} \succ^{\times} \mathsf{pp9} \succ^{\times} \mathsf{idle} \succ^{\times} \underline{\mathsf{pp3} \succ^{\times} \mathsf{pp4} \succ^{\times} \mathsf{pp5} \succ^{\times} \mathsf{pp6} \succ^{\times} \mathsf{pp2}}$$

This ordering is more constrained than it needs to be, for instance, pp4 precedes pp5, though this is not necessary – they are unrelated. However, for presentation purposes it is easier to give the values in a strict order.

We have defined orderings $\prec^{\checkmark}$ and $\prec^{\times}$ on *PC* for an accurate and inaccurate snapshot of *Top*, respectively. To determine which is the appropriate ordering to use for a particular process p we must observe the status of p's snapshot via the predicate $Top = ss_p$. We define the type $ProcM: \mathbb{B} \times PC$, such that for each process p, its corresponding value in *ProcM* is $(Top = ss_p, pc_p)$. We may now define an ordering on processes via *ProcM*, corresponding to our earlier intuition.

Definition 2 ($\prec^p$). *Let b_1, b_2 be booleans; and pc_1, pc_2 be program labels. Given the ordering on booleans $\prec^{\mathbb{B}}$, where true $\prec^{\mathbb{B}}$ false, the ordering $\prec^p$ on ProcM is defined as follows:*

$$\begin{aligned}(b_1, pc_1) \prec^p (b_2, pc_2) \;\widehat{=}\;\; & b_1 \prec^{\mathbb{B}} b_2 \lor \\ & (b_1 = b_2 \land (b_1 \Rightarrow pc_1 \prec^{\checkmark} pc_2) \land (\neg\, b_1 \Rightarrow pc_1 \prec^{\times} pc_2))\end{aligned}$$

Hence, a process can improve its position by turning an inaccurate snapshot into an accurate one ($b_1 \prec^{\mathbb{B}} b_2$), or, if no change is made to the snapshot, by making progress within the appropriate ordering on pc values, either $\prec^{\checkmark}$ or $\prec^{\times}$. Note that the ordering $\prec^p$ is not lexicographic (for details see [Don06b]).

To apply Theorem 1, we must instantiate the well-founded ordering $(\mathcal{W}, \prec)$ and define a function δ. We choose the set $\mathcal{W}$ to be a function from processes to their *ProcM* value, i.e., $\mathcal{W}: PROC \to ProcM$. Therefore, for a state s, δ is defined as follows:

$$\delta(s) = (\lambda\, p: PROC \bullet (s.Top = s.ss_p, s.pc_p)) \tag{6}$$

It remains to give an ordering on type $\mathcal{W}$. We call this ordering $\prec^s$, which we define below; we first define the non-strict version $\preceq^s$.

Definition 3 ($\preceq^s$). *Let s_1 and s_2 be states. The non-strict ordering, $\preceq^s$, on $\delta(s_1)$ and $\delta(s_2)$ is defined as:*

$$\delta(s_1) \preceq^s \delta(s_2) \;\widehat{=}\; (\forall r: PROC \bullet \delta(s_1).r \preceq^p \delta(s_2).r).$$

Hence, state s_1 is no worse than s_2 if each process is no worse with respect to $\preceq^p$. We use Definition 3 to define $\prec^s$ as follows:

Definition 4 ($\prec^s$). *Suppose s_1 and s_2 are states.*

$$\delta(s_1) \prec^s \delta(s_2) \;\widehat{=}\; \delta(s_1) \preceq \delta(s_2) \land \delta(s_1) \neq \delta(s_2).$$

Thus, at least one process must have improved its position with respect to $\prec^p$.

Theorem 3. *The ordering $\prec^s$ is well-founded.*

Proof: The definition of $\prec^s$ requires at least one process in the state to be better placed with respect to $\prec^p$, and the other processes to be no worse. Hence $\prec^s$ is well-founded if $\prec^p$ is well founded. For $\prec^p$ to be well-founded, the three orderings $\prec^{\mathbb{B}}$, $\prec^{\checkmark}$ and $\prec^{\times}$ must be well-founded, which follows from inspection. □

In Sect. 4 we outline a machine-checked proof of Theorem 3.

3.3 Case Analysis

We now complete the proof that the Treiber stack is lock-free.

Theorem 4. *The Treiber stack (Fig. 3) is lock-free.*

Proof: By Theorem 2, the Treiber stack is lock-free if (5) holds. We utilise Theorem 1, with the following instantiations: $pc_p \notin \{\mathsf{idle}, \mathsf{pp7}\}$ and $pc_p \in \{\mathsf{idle}, \mathsf{pp7}\}$ for P_p and Q_p, respectively; $(PROC \to ProcM, \prec^s)$ for $(\mathcal{W}, \prec)$; and instantiating δ as defined in (6). The proof of (5) is therefore reduced to showing the following instantiation of (2), for all states s and all actions α.

$$\begin{aligned} s \xrightarrow{\alpha} s' \Rightarrow\ & \delta(s') \prec^s \delta(s) \lor \\ & (\exists p{:}\, PROC \bullet (pc_p \notin \{\mathsf{idle}, \mathsf{pp7}\}).s \land (pc_p \in \{\mathsf{idle}, \mathsf{pp7}\}).s') \end{aligned} \tag{7}$$

We split the actions into three (mutually exhaustive) classes: those that modify *Top*, those that modify ss_p, (since these two classes will affect the first element of the *ProcM* pairs), and then the rest of the actions.

1. **Transitions which modify** *Top*
We strengthen the quantified property in Definition 7 by choosing a witness for p; the obvious choice is the process, say p_α, that is responsible for transition α

$$\begin{aligned} & s \xrightarrow{\alpha} s' \Rightarrow \\ & \quad \delta(s') \prec^s \delta(s) \lor (s.pc_{p_\alpha} \notin \{\mathsf{idle}, \mathsf{pp7}\} \land s'.pc_{p_\alpha} \in \{\mathsf{idle}, \mathsf{pp7}\}) \end{aligned}$$

The actions corresponding to a successful CAS at ps6 and pp6 (the only transitions that modify *Top*) also establish $pc_p \in \{\mathsf{idle}, \mathsf{pp7}\}$. Hence (7) holds for this class of transitions.
2. **Transitions which modify** ss_p
The only actions that alter ss_p are $push4_p$ and $pop2_p$; and their effect is to set $ss_p = Top$ to true. Hence, for $push4_p$, $\delta(s').p = (true, \mathsf{ps5})$. If $\delta(s).p = (false, \mathsf{ps4})$, i.e., p's snapshot is inaccurate, then $\delta(s').p \prec^p \delta(s).p$ by Definition 2 since $true \prec^{\mathbb{B}} false$. If $\delta(s).p = (true, \mathsf{ps4})$, then then $\delta(s').p \prec^p \delta(s).p$ by Definition 2 because $\mathsf{ps5} \prec^{\checkmark} \mathsf{ps4}$. Similar reasoning applies to the transition $pop2_p$, hence (7) holds for this class of transitions.
3. **All other transitions**
Actions that do not modify *Top* or ss_p do not affect any other process: their improvement is based purely on the relationship between pc_p in the pre and post states of the corresponding transition. We have carefully chosen the well-founded orderings $\prec^{\checkmark}$ and $\prec^{\times}$ to contain the pair of pc values associated with almost all of the transitions that do not modify *Top* or ss_p, hence (7) is trivially satisfied in these cases. The only exception is the transition corresponding to line pp4, where a pop operation returns `Empty` to indicate that an empty stack was observed. However, (7) in this case is also trivially satisfied, since it is a transition from active to idle. Hence, (7) hold for this class of transitions.

Since (7) holds, by Theorem 3 and Theorem 1, (5) holds; therefore by Theorem 2, the Treiber stack is lock-free. □

4 Mechanising Proofs of Lock-Freedom

In this section, we describe how our proof of lock-freedom for the Treiber stack was checked using the PVS theorem prover [ORR+96]. The encoding of the Treiber program as a transition system was straightforward, and follows similar encodings as described in, e.g., [CG05]. The PVS theory, proof and strategies files are available online from [CD]. The PVS encoding of (7) is given below; as expected, the proof is trivial, and was automatically proved by a single application of the built-in PVS proof strategy "`grind`". For an action `alpha`, `proc(alpha)` is the process that executes `alpha`, and for a label `pc`, `progress(pc)` holds if `pc` = `idle` or `pc` = `pp7`.

```
treiber-lf: LEMMA
  FORALL alpha, s0, s: trans(s0)(alpha)(s) IMPLIES
         LT(delta(s), delta(s0)) OR
         (not progress(s0'pc(proc(alpha))) and
              progress(s'pc(proc(alpha))))
```

The more difficult aspect of the lock-freedom proof is proving Theorem 3, i.e., that the relation $\prec^s$ ("LT" above) is well-founded. This proof was constructed by first showing the underlying relations $\prec^{\mathbb{B}}$, $\prec^{\checkmark}$ and $\prec^{\times}$ are well-founded, with respect to the appropriate theorem from the underlying PVS theories. This theorem states that a relationship on type T is well founded if there exists a least element in every non-empty subset of T. The proofs were conducted by selecting an arbitrary subset of T, and doing a case analysis, in turn, on whether a particular element of PC or $\mathbb{B}$ was or was not a member of that set. To simplify proofs of this form, we developed a specialised proof strategy `prove-wf` which takes a list of values (the elements of T) and performs the case analysis in turn. Assuming the values are given in the correct order, the strategy can automatically show well-foundedness, e.g., the well-foundedness of $\prec^{\checkmark}$ was shown by

```
(prove-wf ("ps6" "ps5" "ps4" "ps2" "ps1"
           "pp6" "pp5" "pp4" "pp3" "pp2" "idle"
                 "pp9" "pp8" "pp7"))
```

The ordering of the pc values corresponds to the (combined) ordering for $\prec^{\checkmark}$ given earlier: if $a \prec^{\checkmark} b$ then a must appear to the left of b in the list.

The ordering on processes, $\prec^{p}$, was straightforwardly encoded as follows, where, if `p1` is a tuple, the expressions `p1'1` and `p1'2` access the the first and second elements of `p1`, respectively, and where `LT_bool`, `LT_pcT` and `LT_pcF` encode $\prec^{\mathbb{B}}$, $\prec^{\checkmark}$ and $\prec^{\times}$, respectively.

```
LT_pair(p1:ProcM, p2:ProcM): boolean =
   LT_bool(p1'1, p2'1) or
   (p1'1 = p2'1 AND
       (p1'1 implies LT_pcT(p1'2, p2'2)) and
       (NOT p1'1 implies LT_pcF(p1'2, p2'2)))
```

However, proving the minimal-element definition of well-foundedness for such an ordering is not convenient, since enumerating each element of type *ProcM* is time-consuming and error-prone. Instead we used the alternate *decreasing finite chain* property of well-founded relations. (see, e.g., Gries and Schneider [GS93, Sect. 12.4] for a comparison of different well-foundedness characterisations). For a finite set T, to show that every descending chain in T is finite, it is sufficient to show that for all elements y of T, it is not the case that $y \prec^* y$. That is, we used the following definition[1] for relation `r` on finite type `T`.

```
well_founded_finite?(r): bool =
     forall (y:T): not trans_closure(r)(y, y)
```

Using this more convenient formulation of the well-foundedness, Theorem 3 was proved. As expected, the bulk of the proof effort was spent on this (and supporting) theorems.

5 Conclusion

Programs which exhibit lock-freedom have been demonstrated to have performance advantages over lock-based algorithms [MS98]. In this paper we have outlined a general approach for formally proving lock-freedom, using a well-known lock-free stack algorithm as a case study. Although applied to a relatively straightforward lock-free algorithm, the same principles, particularly in designing the well-founded ordering, apply to the general class of lock-free algorithms outlined in Sect. 2.1, including those of Michael and Scott [MS98] and algorithms with more complex memory models [Mic04,HLM02]. Formally proving lock-freedom is difficult because (1) idle process can always begin a new operation, hence there is no final "end-point" that we can appeal to (2) all synchronisation is not lock-based, hence there is a high degree of interference (3) the reasoning must be based on the system as a whole, as opposed to a single process.

In contrast to techniques for proving progress properties which analyse all possible interleavings of the processes, our technique is based on a well-founded ordering on the state of a single process and the shared variables. Our technique does not compare the states of two processes, hence it scales because it is independant of the number of processes in the system. The bulk of the work is in desribing the ordering and proving it to be well-founded. The rest of the proof is a case analysis on transitions, which is trivial and can be automatically verified, as we demonstrated with the theorem prover PVS.

In [Don06a], where lock-freedom, along with other classes of nonblocking algorithms, is formalised, a proof of lock-freedom for a simple algorithm is presented. However, the technique used is not amenable to tool support and does not scale

---

[1] We postulated, but did not prove, that a relation `r` on a finite type `T` that satisfies this definition is well-founded – a proof of this theorem in PVS is beyond the scope of this work.

well. Gao and Hesselink [GH07] have formalised lock-freedom, but their proofs remain informal and furthermore, they assume stronger system properties such as weak fairness.

In future work we will extend the theory and tool support to more complex lock-free algorithms such as (1) the linked list queue algorithm of Michael and Scott [MS98] where updating the queue requires two steps, and, because of this, operations may have to retry the loop twice to complete an operation even in the absence of interference (2) the array-based queue algorithm in [CG05], which requires up to three iterations of its loop to complete an operation. We plan on extending our PVS proof strategies for proving well-foundedness, particularly as the case studies become more complex.

Acknowledgements. The authors wish to thank Ian Hayes and three anonymous reviewers for helpful suggestions on this paper.

References

CD. Colvin, R., Dongol, B.: PVS files for lock-freedom of the Treiber stack, `http://www.itee.uq.edu.au/~nbverif/Lockfreedom_Proofs/Treiber/`

CDG05. Colvin, R., Doherty, S., Groves, L.: Verifying concurrent data structures by simulation. In: Proceedings of the REFINE 2005 Workshop. Electronic Notes in Theoretical Computer Science, vol. 137, pp. 93–110 (2005)

CG05. Colvin, R., Groves, L.: Formal verification of an array-based nonblocking queue. In: 10th International Conference on Engineering of Complex Computer Systems, pp. 507–516. IEEE Computer Society Press, Los Alamitos (2005)

CGLM06. Colvin, R., Groves, L., Luchangco, V., Moir, M.: Formal verification of a lazy concurrent list-based set algorithm. In: Ball, T., Jones, R.B. (eds.) CAV 2006. LNCS, vol. 4144, pp. 475–488. Springer, Heidelberg (2006)

CM88. Chandy, K.M., Misra, J.: Parallel Program Design: A Foundation. Addison-Wesley Longman Publishing Co., Inc., Redwood City, CA, USA (1988)

DDG$^+$04. Doherty, S., Detlefs, D., Groves, L., Flood, C.H., Luchangco, V., Martin, P.A., Moir, M., Shavit, N., Steele, Jr., G.L.: DCAS is not a silver bullet for nonblocking algorithm design. In: Gibbons, P., Adler, M. (eds.) Proceedings of the 16th Annual ACM Symposium on Parallel Algorithms, pp. 216–224. ACM Press, New York (2004)

DGLM04. Doherty, S., Groves, L., Luchangco, V., Moir, M.: Formal verification of a practical lock-free queue algorithm. In: de Frutos-Escrig, D., Núñez, M. (eds.) FORTE 2004. LNCS, vol. 3235, pp. 97–114. Springer, Heidelberg (2004)

DM06. Dongol, B., Mooij, A.J.: Progress in deriving concurrent programs: Emphasizing the role of stable guards. In: Uustalu, T. (ed.) MPC 2006. LNCS, vol. 4014, pp. 140–161. Springer, Heidelberg (2006)

DM07. Dongol, B., Mooij, A.J.: Streamlining progress-based derivations of concurrent programs. Formal Aspects of Computing (to appear)

Doh03. Doherty, S.: Modelling and verifying non-blocking algorithms that use dynamically allocated memory. Master's thesis, Victoria University of Wellington (2003)

Don06a. Dongol, B.: Formalising progress properties of non-blocking programs. In: Liu, Z., He, J. (eds.) ICFEM 2006. LNCS, vol. 4260, pp. 284–303. Springer, Heidelberg (2006)

Don06b. Dongol, B.: Towards simpler proofs of lock-freedom. In: AWCVS'06. 1st International Workshop - Asian Working Conference on Verified Software, October 2006, pp. 136–147 (2006)

FG96. Fix, L., Grumberg, O.: Verification of temporal properties. J. Log. Comput. 6(3), 343–361 (1996)

GH07. Gao, H., Hesselink, W.H.: A general lock-free algorithm using compare-and-swap. Inf. Comput. 205(2), 225–241 (2007)

GS93. Gries, D., Schneider, F.B.: A logical approach to discrete math. Springer-Verlag New York, Inc., New York, NY, USA (1993)

HLM02. Herlihy, M., Luchangco, V., Moir, M.: The repeat offender problem: A mechanism for supporting dynamic-sized, lock-free data structures. In: Malkhi, D. (ed.) DISC 2002. LNCS, vol. 2508, pp. 339–353. Springer, Heidelberg (2002)

HLM03. Herlihy, M., Luchangco, V., Moir, M.: Obstruction-free synchronization: Double-ended queues as an example. In: 23rd IEEE International Conference on Distributed Computing Systems, p. 522. IEEE Computer Society Press, Los Alamitos (2003)

Mic04. Michael, M.M.: Hazard pointers: Safe memory reclamation for lock-free objects. IEEE Trans. Parallel Distrib. Syst. 15(6), 491–504 (2004)

Mis01. Misra, J.: A Discipline of Multiprogramming. Springer, Heidelberg (2001)

Moi97. Moir, M.: Practical implementations of non-blocking synchronization primitives. In: PODC, pp. 219–228 (August 1997)

MP92. Manna, Z., Pnueli, A.: Temporal Verification of Reactive and Concurrent Systems: Specification. Springer, New York, Inc. (1992)

MS98. Michael, M.M., Scott, M.L.: Nonblocking algorithms and preemption-safe locking on multiprogrammed shared memory multiprocessors. J. Parallel Distrib. Comput. 51(1), 1–26 (1998)

ORR+96. Owre, S., Rajan, S., Rushby, J.M., Shankar, N., Srivas, M.K.: PVS: Combining specification, proof checking, and model checking. In: Alur, R., Henzinger, T.A. (eds.) CAV 1996. LNCS, vol. 1102, pp. 411–414. Springer, Heidelberg (1996)

Tre86. Treiber, R.K.: Systems programming: Coping with parallelism, Technical Report RJ 5118, IBM Almaden Res. Ctr. (1986)

Tree Components Programming: An Application to XML*

Pascal Coupey, Christophe Fouqueré, and Jean-Vincent Loddo

LIPN – UMR7030
CNRS – Université Paris 13
99 av. J-B Clément, F–93430 Villetaneuse, France
firstname.lastname@lipn.univ-paris13.fr

Abstract. We present a new programming approach based on a contextual component specification. The language we propose integrates XML and functional aspects in a coherent and homogeneous framework. This enables us to fully have static typing and to specify formal properties with respect to interactions.

Our language FICX, Functional Interactive and Compositional XML, defines a new kind of data structure called Xobjects and relies on a statically typed functional language (currently OCaml). An Xobject is an abstract structure made in two parts: the Xdata part is an XML structure extended by means of triggers dedicated to interactions, the reaction part gives the code associated to triggers that is evaluated on demand. The modularity is ensured by a parameterization of Xobjects: compound Xobjects form a tree structure, rendering a complex XML tree together with appropriate reactions for triggers. A program is a set of structures, each structure being a tree of Xobjects.

Keywords: web programming language, static typing, tree components, XML.

1 Introduction

Classic object oriented programming languages offer class/subclass relationship with inheritance mechanism. It is not well suited when applications need "part-of" relationship. Of course, this may be encoded using the object paradigm but no facility is given to the programmer since she has to build by herself the partonomy beside the class/-subclass hierarchy. This is true in the semi-structured data field and in particular XML-like languages where many recent works extend XML language in order to describe documents as a composition of various parts (pure XML, scripts, database requests, web service requests [11,13,5]). Our purpose is to propose a programming language whose core principle is that basic objects are components of a tree and to apply it to XML language. In fact, tree structures may be obtained by merging partial trees (instead of just composing them). Such (partially defined) structures are first-class citizens in our programming language. They encapsulate static and dynamic contents to allow for interactivity and expressiveness. Moreover the whole language is strongly typed to ensure error-free executions. This programming paradigm is applied here to XML programming. Examples are given wrt the web as this domain has at least the following

* This work is supported by the Marie Curie action n. 29849 Websicola.

C.B. Jones, Z. Liu, J. Woodcock (Eds.): ICTAC 2007, LNCS 4711, pp. 139–153, 2007.

features: use of semi-structured data, interactivity, needs for modular and safe programming. Our language FICX, Functional Interactive and Compositional XML, defines a new kind of data structure called *Xobjects* and relies on a statically typed functional language (currently OCaml). An Xobject is an abstract structure made of two parts: the *Xdata* part is an XML structure extended by means of triggers dedicated to interactions, the *reaction* part gives the code associated to triggers and that is evaluated on request. A *Request* is a first-citizen expression of the language. Its value is the result of a reaction selected by a trigger. To take advantage of the tree structure of compound Xobjects, a delegation mechanism is offered: a request may contain an (abstract) path to be followed to find an adequate reaction. FICX uses in fact extensively the concept of *abstract path*. An abstract path is a sequence of labels for addressing Xobjects in a tree, e.g. the root, the value at label Y of a parent, ... To summarize, FICX has the main following characteristics:

Modularity: Compound Xobjects form a tree structure, rendering a complex XML tree together with appropriate reactions for triggers. A program is a set of *Xstructures*. Each Xstructure is a fully defined tree of Xobjects and plays the role of an entry point to the program.

Interaction: Each reaction describes a possible evolution: the result of requesting a reaction to some Xobject is a new Xobject (possibly with new Xdata, new triggers, new reactions).

Static typing: The type of an Xobject is given by the type of its Xdata part together with the type of its reactions. An Xobject defines a set of triggers (usable for interaction) and a set of reactions (called either by an expression of the language or by means of an interaction). These two sets should coincide in case of Xstructures: the type of reaction patterns should cover the type of the XML structure associated to a trigger (soundness), and, a reaction being given, a corresponding trigger should have been defined for interaction (completeness).

These peculiarities offer the user means to develop modular and type checked programs. In the framework of web applications, triggers may be viewed as web service names or anchors in web sites. However, contrarily to most web languages, triggers and reactions should be related in a program in such a way that controls may occur. The toy example given in Ex. 1 on the left defines the variable `link` to be a function with one parameter `msg` which returns an Xobject[1] and `home` whose value is an Xobject with one parameter `Y`. The Xdata part is written in CDuce style [2] and is extended with a trigger `T`. The corresponding XML structure in `home` Xobject declaration is given on the right. The Xobject `link` has two reactions with trigger tag `T`. The first one creates a new Xobject `link` with the string `"Bonjour"` if the parameter given with the trigger contains the string `"Hello"`, the second reaction has the converse behaviour. The evolution consists in creating Xobjects that alternates `"Bonjour"` and `"Hello"` messages. `website` is a

[1] For the sake of simplicity, we consider that `link = xobject <> (msg:string) ...` is syntactic sugar for `link = fun (msg:string)→xobject <> ...` then collapsing the name of the function which returns the Xobject with the name of the Xobject itself.

```
link = fun (msg:string) →
    xobject <>
        T<h1 align="center">[msg]
    ▶
        T(<h1 align="center">["Hello"])
            ⇒ (link "Bonjour")
        T(<h1 align="center">["Bonjour"])
            ⇒ (link "Hello")
    xend;

home = xobject <Y>
        <html>[
            <head>[<title>["Welcome"]]
            <body>[Y]
        ]
    ▶ xend;

website = home[Y ↦ (link "Hello")];
otherwebsite = Y.T("Hello")@website;
```

Data extracted from `website` in standard XML style:

```
<html>
    <head>
        <title>"Welcome"</title>
    </head>
    <body>
        <a href=
            URL_encoding_of(
                Y.T("Hello")@website
            )>
        <h1 align="center">["Hello"]
        </a>
    </body>
</html>
```

Ex. 1. Xobject definitions and XML data

(compound) Xobject giving a value to the parameter `Y` in a copy of Xobject `home`. Note that Xobject `home` is unchanged. Its standard HTML presentation is given on the right (where $URL\_encoding\_of()$ is a built-in function). The interactive request has the same shape as the expression for defining `otherwebsite`. Its operational semantics uses the delegation mechanism. In `Y.T("Hello")@website`, `website` is called the *initial concrete receiver* as it is the Xobject that should at first react. As it has no appropriate reaction, the request is delegated wrt the path, here `Y`. Let o be the value of `(link "Hello")`, o responds by `(link "Bonjour")`. The Xobject `otherwebsite` may then have been defined equivalently by the expression `home[Y↦(link "Bonjour")]`. This is also the result sent back in case of interactive request.

We present in the next section the syntax and the operational semantics of the language FICX, focussing on its main features: abstract paths, Xobjects, requests. We define in particular a specific class of trees and show in which extent a set of abstract paths is a representation of such a tree. We give in section 3 the type system . We end comparing FICX to other works in this domain and present a few extensions under study.

2 Language FICX: Syntax and Operational Semantics

We use a functional programming language, currently OCaml, as a core language for functions, definitions, ... that we do not detail here (the reader may find descriptions of OCaml in [6]). This core is extended by means of an *Xobject* data type that integrates an extended XML structure called *Xdata* to publish data and triggers, and a functional part called *reaction* intended to answer requests built from triggers. Moreover Xobjects may be parameterized by *abstract paths* defined in the following subsection. Finally, an *Xstructure* is a specific top-level definition that is used to declare interactive data and functionalities. The grammar of the language FICX, specific to our aim, is given in

Program			
P	$::= \epsilon$		*empty program*
	$\mid S\,P \mid d\,P$		*Xstructure or definition followed by a program*
Xstructure			
S	$::=$ `xstruc` d `begin` $w = e$		*where d is a definition, w an identifier, e an expression*
Xobject			
e	$::=$ `xobject`$\langle Y_1,\ldots,Y_n\rangle$		*Xobject definition with abstract paths parameters*
	$e \blacktriangleright sr$		*Xdata* ▶ *reactions*
	`xend`		
	$\mid e_1[Y \mapsto e_2]$		*parameter assignment*
	$\mid \tau(e_2)@e_1$		*request evaluation*
	$\mid Y$		*Abstract path name Y*
Reactions			
sr	$::= \epsilon$	$r\ ::=\ \tau_p(p) \Rightarrow e$	*reaction conditioned by trigger and parameter patterns*
	$\mid r\ sr$		
Triggers			
τ	$::= Y.C$		*abstract path followed by a tag*

Fig. 1. Grammar of FICX

Fig. 1. We use the following notations throughout the paper: e is an expression and p is a pattern, a, A, C, x, y are identifiers, τ is a trigger, Y, Z are abstract paths, finally r states for a reaction.

The operational semantics follows standard functional programming operational semantics: it is given as an evaluation judgment on programs, expressions, ... to be computed with respect to a given environment. An environment is an *evaluation environment* together with a *handler environment*. An evaluation environment is a partial function from the set of variable names and abstract paths to values, either ground values or handlers to such values (supposing a domain of handlers). A handler environment is a partial function from the set of handlers to values. Handlers are used to denote Xobject parameter values. The evaluation judgment for expressions is of the following form:

$$\mathcal{E}, \mathcal{H} \vdash e \Downarrow v, \mathcal{H}'$$

read as: the evaluation of expression e in an evaluation environment $\mathcal{E}$ with a handler environment $\mathcal{H}$ leads to a value v together with a new handler environment $\mathcal{H}'$.

2.1 Abstract Paths

Abstract paths are defined according to the following grammar, where y is an identifier, `parent`, `root` and `self` are keywords:

Y ::= `parent` | `root` | `self` | `y` | Y.Y

We suppose further that abstract paths (and abstract path patterns or path types in the same way) are always in normal form with respect to the rewriting $\rightarrow_{AP}$ applied to `self`.Y, where Y is the abstract path to be normalized ($y \neq$ `self`, `root`, `parent`):

y.`parent` $\rightarrow_{AP} \epsilon$ Y.`root` $\rightarrow_{AP}$ `root`   Y.`self` $\rightarrow_{AP}$ `self`

Let $\phi = \{\texttt{root}.r, \texttt{self}.a.c, \texttt{self}.a.d, \texttt{self}.b.e\}$
and $\psi = \{\texttt{root}.s, \texttt{self}.g, \texttt{self.parent}.f\}$,
ϕ and ψ represent the following pairs of trees:

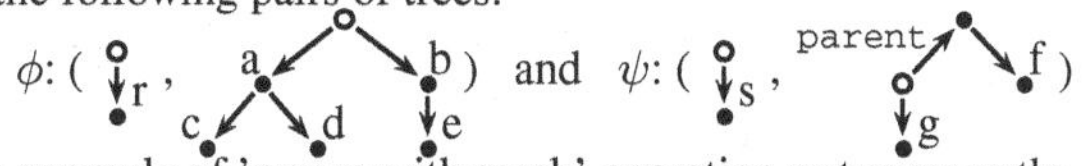

The following is an example of 'merge with mask' operation wrt some path:

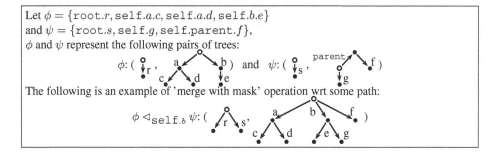

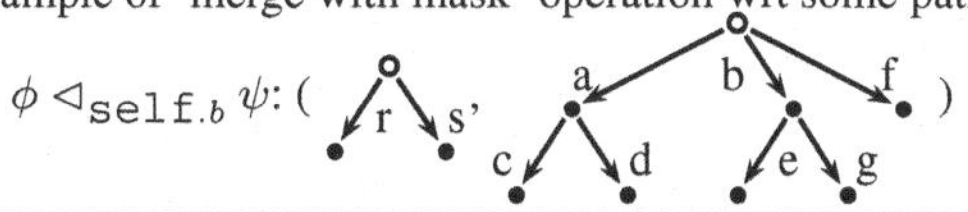

Ex. 2. Abstract paths and trees

Thus $\rightarrow_{AP}$ gives rise to two kinds of normal forms: `root`.Y and `self`.Y with `self` and `root` not in Y. The intended meaning is that a set of such abstract paths should partially define two rooted trees, one with abstract root `root` and another 'centered' on `self` where `self.parent....parent` should represent a path 'up' to some concrete root (see Ex. 2 where orientation is given as the root is not always at top). Abusively, `self` may be omitted in the following from abstract paths writings. We give below a few simple definitions and properties that characterize the particular trees and operations we need. We then relate such trees to a specification given by abstract paths. We do not first consider values (say Xdata and reactions) attached to nodes and we fix a non-empty set of symbols $\mathcal{L}$.

Definition 1

- *An* unambiguous rooted $\mathcal{L}$-edge-labelled tree *is a tree with a root node, edges labelled by elements in $\mathcal{L}$, and such that for each node two distinct edges have distinct labels. Let $\mathcal{T}_\mathcal{L}$ be the set of such trees.*
- *Let $T_1, T_2 \in \mathcal{T}_\mathcal{L}$, $T_1 \leq T_2$ if there exists an injective mapping f from T_1 to T_2 such that if r is the root node of T_1 then $f(r)$ is the root node of T_2, and if (n_1, n_2) is an edge of T_1 labelled l, then $(f(n_1), f(n_2))$ is an edge of T_2 labelled l.*

Proposition 1. *Let $\mathcal{L}^*$ be the set of finite sequences of elements of $\mathcal{L}$ and $\mathcal{P}(\mathcal{L}^*)$ be the powerset of $\mathcal{L}^*$, $(\mathcal{T}_\mathcal{L}, \leq)$ is faithfully represented by $(\mathcal{P}(\mathcal{L}^*), \subset)$, hence $(\mathcal{T}_\mathcal{L}, \leq)$ is a lattice.*

Let us now consider the set $\mathcal{T}_\mathcal{L}^-$ of *partially defined unambiguous rooted $\mathcal{L}$-edge-labelled trees*, where a special symbol '_' plays the role of a variable:

Definition 2. *Let _ be a symbol not in $\mathcal{L}$, $\mathcal{T}_\mathcal{L}^-$ is the set of unambiguous rooted $\mathcal{L} \cup \{\_\}$-edge-labelled trees such that paths Y.l._ cannot appear, where $l \in \mathcal{L}$. Let $T_1, T_2 \in \mathcal{T}_\mathcal{L}^-$, $T_1 \leq T_2$ if there exists an injective mapping f from T_1 to T_2 such that if r is the root node of T_1 then $f(r)$ is the root node of T_2, if (n_1, n_2) is an edge of T_1, then $(f(n_1), f(n_2))$ is an edge of T_2, moreover if the label of (n_1, n_2) is in $\mathcal{L}$ then it is also the label of $(f(n_1), f(n_2))$.*

Proposition 2. *$(\mathcal{T}_\mathcal{L}^-, \leq)$ is a poset, $(\mathcal{T}_\mathcal{L}, \leq)$ embeds in $(\mathcal{T}_\mathcal{L}^-, \leq)$, $(\mathcal{T}_\mathcal{L}^-, \leq)$ is not a lattice.*

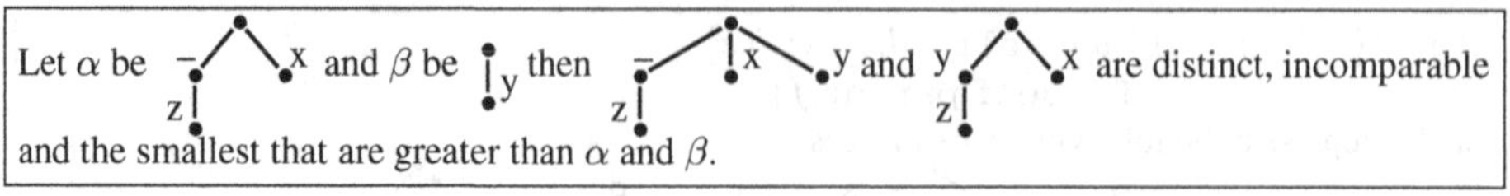
Let α be
_
x
z
and β be
y
then
_
x
y
z
and
y
x
z
are distinct, incomparable
and the smallest that are greater than α and β.

Ex. 3. Trees in $\mathcal{T}_{\bar{\mathcal{L}}}$

In Ex.3, a counter-example for $(\mathcal{T}_{\bar{\mathcal{L}}}, \leq)$ to be a lattice is given. However the following proposition serves to control Xobject composition validity:

Proposition 3. *Let $T_1, T_2 \in \mathcal{T}_{\bar{\mathcal{L}}}$, (T_1, T_2) has a least upper bound (lub) iff either $T_1 = T_2$, or $T_1, T_2 \in \mathcal{T}_{\mathcal{L}}$, or if $T_1 \notin \mathcal{T}_{\mathcal{L}}$ then $T_2 \in \mathcal{T}_{\mathcal{L}}$ and the set of labels of edges from the root of T_2 is included in the set of labels of edges from the root of T_1, or the same last property interchanging T_1 and T_2.*

The proof follows a structural definition of these trees. The key element comes from the fact that if the two roots have each a daughter labelled _ then there are always at least two distinct minima: one merging the two edges labelled _, the other putting separately two branches, one labelled _, the other labelled by some element of $\mathcal{L}$ (that is a non-empty set).

Let us now add to nodes values, i.e. values necessary for the operational semantics or the typing system. For simplicity, we keep notation $\mathcal{T}_{\bar{\mathcal{L}}}$ and we define a lub of two valued trees as the lub of the trees obtained forgetting the values. We consider moreover the following definitions: If $T \in \mathcal{T}_{\bar{\mathcal{L}}}$ and Z is a path in T then $Z(T)$ is the subtree of T at path Z, $val(T)$ is the value associated to the root node of T, $self(T)$ is defined as the subtree ending the _ path: $self(T) = T$ if $T \in \mathcal{T}_{\mathcal{L}}$, $self(T) = self(\_(T))$ otherwise. Taking care of previous properties, we define the following partial operations on $\mathcal{T}_{\bar{\mathcal{L}}}$:

Definition 3. *Let $T_1, T_2 \in \mathcal{T}_{\bar{\mathcal{L}}}$,*

- *'Merge with mask' operation $\lhd$: $T = T_1 \lhd T_2$ has the structure of the lub of T_1 and T_2 if it exists and, forall path Y, $val(Y(T)) = val(Y(T_2))$ if defined, $val(Y(T)) = val(Y(T_1))$ otherwise.*
- *'Merge with mask' operation wrt some path. $T = T_1 \lhd_Y T_2$ is defined in the following way: let n be the longest path including only _ in T_2 (i.e. the depth of $self(T_2)$ in T_2),*
    - *if $|Y| \geq n$, let Z be the prefix of Y of length $|Y| - n$ and T_1' be the tree T_1 after deleting the subtree $Z(T_1)$, if $Z(T_1) \lhd T_2$ exists, T is the tree T_1' appending $Z(T) \lhd T_2$ at the leaf Z, otherwise T is not defined ;*
    - *if $|Y| < n$, let Z be a sequence of _ of length $n - |Y|$ and T_2' be the tree T_2 after deleting the subtree $Z(T_2)$, if $T_1 \lhd Z(T_2)$ exists, T is the tree T_2' appending $T_1 \lhd Z(T_2)$ at the leaf Z, otherwise T is not defined.*

Note that, thanks to proposition 3, the safety of previous operations may be statically checked as soon as labels are known. The following proposition shows that such trees may be used to design an operational model for our language (and also a typing system as soon as a typing system is available for Xdata and reactions).

```
xstruc
link =  xobject <root.H1> (x:string)
        root.H1.T<a>[x]
    ▶ xend;
message = xobject <> (msg:string)
        <h1 align="center">[msg]
    ▶ xend;
phandler = xobject <M1> (k:int)
        M1 <p>["Visits for this session (cs): " k]
    ▶
        T(<a>[x]) ⇒ (let y=(if (x = "Hello") then "Salut" else "Hello") in
                        (phandler (k + 1))[M1↦(message y)])
    xend;
home = xobject <L1, L2, H1>
        <html>[ <head>[ <title>["Welcome"]] <body>[ H1 <br> L1 <br> L2]]
    ▶ xend;

m1 = (message "Hello");
h1 = (phandler 0)[M1 ↦ m1];
l1 = (link "Increment cs and reload with Hello");
l2 = (link "Increment cs and reload with Salut");
o = home[L1 ↦ l1][L2 ↦ l2][H1 ↦ h1];

begin website = o
```

Ex. 4. Xobjects with components

Proposition 4. *A finite set of abstract paths represents two trees: a tree in $\mathcal{T}_{\mathcal{L}}$ we called 'with abstract root* `root`*', and one in $\mathcal{T}_{\bar{\mathcal{L}}}$, we called 'centered on* `self`*'.*

In the following, we freely use the abstract path notation for operations on $\mathcal{T}_{\bar{\mathcal{L}}}$.

2.2 *Xobjects*

An *Xobject* is structured in two parts: an *Xdata* structure together with *reactions*, and is parameterized by means of abstract paths. Parameterization is a convenient way to refer to yet unknown Xobjects while parameter assignment merges partial trees of components. Abstract paths that are used in an Xobject body are declared in the header: in Ex. 4, Xobject `home` expects three subcomponents `L1,L2,H1`. Note the reference to `root.H1` in the definition of `link`: this Xobject is expected to be in a tree whose Xobject root has at least a subcomponent for label `H1`.

In Ex. 4, `website` is declared as an entry point. The tree of components is rooted at `o`, that has two links `l1` and `l2` and one phandler `h1` as subcomponents, `h1` having a child `m1`. Two triggers are declared, posted in `l1` and `l2`, authorizing interactive requests of the form `H1.T(x)@website`.

We are now able to precise the operational model. We extend a domain, supposed given for basic types and that includes handlers, by the following kinds of values:

- $\mathbb{T}$ called a *handler tree value* is a map from abstract paths to handlers. It is a pair of trees $(U,V) \in \mathcal{T}_{\mathcal{L}} \times \mathcal{T}_{\bar{\mathcal{L}}}$, one rooted at abstract path `root` and one centered at `self` with the following partial operations:
  - An 'identifier' operation: let $\mathbb{T} = (U,V)$, if $V \in \mathcal{T}_{\mathcal{L}}$ and $U \lhd V$ is defined then $\updownarrow\mathbb{T} = (U \lhd V, U \lhd V)$.

$$\frac{m \ \texttt{fresh}, \mathbb{T} = \{self \mapsto m\}}{\mathcal{E},\mathcal{H} \vdash \texttt{xobject}\langle Y_1,\ldots,Y_n\rangle{\rightarrow}e \blacktriangleright sr \ \texttt{xend} \Downarrow \mathbb{T}, \mathcal{H} \cup \{m \mapsto xval(\mathcal{E}, e \blacktriangleright sr)\}}$$

$$\frac{\mathcal{E},\mathcal{H} \vdash e_2 \Downarrow \mathbb{T}_2, \mathcal{H}_2 \quad \mathcal{E},\mathcal{H}_2 \vdash e_1 \Downarrow \mathbb{T}_1, \mathcal{H}_1}{\mathcal{E},\mathcal{H} \vdash e_1[Y{\mapsto}e_2] \Downarrow \mathbb{T}_1 \lhd_Y \mathbb{T}_2, \mathcal{H}_1}$$

$$\frac{\mathcal{E},\mathcal{H} \vdash d \Downarrow_d \mathcal{E}_1, \mathcal{H}_1 \quad \mathcal{E}_1,\mathcal{H}_1 \vdash e \Downarrow \mathbb{T}_2, \mathcal{H}_2}{\mathcal{E},\mathcal{H} \vdash \texttt{xstruc}\ d\ \texttt{begin}\ w = e \Downarrow_d \mathcal{E}_2 \cup \{w \mapsto \updownarrow\mathbb{T}_2\}, \mathcal{H}_2}$$

Fig. 2. Operational semantics for Xobject and Xstructure declarations

- A 'merge with mask' operation $\lhd$: let $\mathbb{T}_1 = (U_1, V_1)$ and $\mathbb{T}_2 = (U_2, V_2)$ be handler tree values, $\mathbb{T} = \mathbb{T}_1 \lhd \mathbb{T}_2$ is the handler tree value (U, V) such that $U = U_1 \lhd U_2$ and $V = V_1 \lhd V_2$.
- A 'merge with mask' operation wrt some path: let $\mathbb{T}_1 = (U_1, V_1)$ and $\mathbb{T}_2 = (U_2, V_2)$ be handler tree values, Y be an abstract path in normal form, $\mathbb{T} = \mathbb{T}_1 \lhd_Y \mathbb{T}_2$ is the handler tree value (U, V) such that
  - ∗ if Y has form $self.Z$, $U = U_1 \lhd U_2$ and $V = V_1 \lhd_Y V_2$,
  - ∗ if Y has form $root.Z$, $V = V_1$ and $U = U_1 \lhd_Y W$ where $\updownarrow\mathbb{T}_2 = (W, W)$.

- $xval(\mathcal{E}, e \blacktriangleright r)$ serves to denote Xobject closures, where r is a sequence of values of the form $\tau_p(p) \Rightarrow e$, e is an expression and $\mathcal{E}$ is an evaluation environment.

A handler tree value $\mathbb{T}$ may also be part of an evaluation environment as it is a map from abstract paths to values. $dom(\mathbb{T})$ is then the set of abstract paths of $\mathbb{T}$. We consider available in that case an operation $\mathbb{T}^{Y \rightarrow Y'}$ that changes the reference frame of the domain of $\mathbb{T}$ wrt the change from Y to Y'.

The operational semantics of Xobjects is given in Fig. 2. The semantics corresponding to an Xobject declaration is straightforwardly a closure (as for functions) and assignment of abstract path parameters is similar to the standard treatment of handlers in functional programming: the rule is nothing else but a new value given for the reference (the typing system should ensure that v_2 is an Xobject value). The semantics of an Xstructure declaration follows the semantics of a (top level) definition ($\Downarrow_d$ evaluates definitions).

2.3 *Xdata* and *Reactions*

The language for the Xdata part extends XML. XML is basically expressed by means of tree structures where nodes are of the form $<a\ \ l_e>[s]$ where a is the markup of the node, l_e is a list of attribute-value pairs (the value may be the result of the evaluation of an expression), and s is a sequence of XML constituents. XML syntax is extended in the following way: an abstract path may be used in place of an XML node and each node in an XML structure may be labelled by a trigger τ. A trigger τ has the general form $Y.C$ where C is an *interaction tag* (tag for short) and the abstract path Y is the path to the *abstract last possible receiver*. Setting down a trigger means that a functionality should be available, as a GET in HTML or the description of a service. In case of Xstructures, a

$$\frac{\mathcal{E},\mathcal{H} \vdash e_2 \Downarrow v_2,\mathcal{H}_2 \quad \mathcal{E},\mathcal{H}_2 \vdash e_1 \Downarrow \mathbb{T}_1,\mathcal{H}_1 \quad \mathcal{H}_1(self(\mathbb{T}_1)) = xval(\mathcal{E}_1, e \blacktriangleright sr) \quad match(\tau, v_2, sr) = (e_0, \mathcal{E}_0) \quad \mathcal{E}_1 \backslash (dom(\mathcal{E}_0) \cup dom(\mathbb{T}_1)) \cup \mathcal{E}_0 \cup \mathbb{T}_1, \mathcal{H}_1 \vdash e_0 \Downarrow \mathbb{T}_0, \mathcal{H}_0}{\mathcal{E},\mathcal{H} \vdash \tau(e_2)@e_1 \Downarrow \mathbb{T}_0,\mathcal{H}_0}$$

$$\frac{\mathcal{E},\mathcal{H} \vdash e_2 \Downarrow v_2,\mathcal{H}_2 \quad \mathcal{E},\mathcal{H}_2 \vdash e_1 \Downarrow \mathbb{T}_1,\mathcal{H}_1 \quad \mathcal{H}_1(self(\mathbb{T}_1)) = xval(\mathcal{E}_1, e \blacktriangleright sr) \quad match(y.Z.C, v_2, sr) = undef \quad \mathcal{E}_1 \cup \mathbb{T}_1^{y \to self}, \mathcal{H}_1 \vdash Z.C(e_2)@\mathtt{self} \Downarrow \mathbb{T}_0, \mathcal{H}_0}{\mathcal{E},\mathcal{H} \vdash y.Z.C(e_2)@e_1 \Downarrow \mathbb{T}_1 \lhd_y \mathbb{T}_0,\mathcal{H}_0}$$

where the function $match(\_,\_,\_)$ checks if a trigger fires a reaction and in this case sends back the expression to be evaluated together with the capture variables given by a standard pattern matching function $matchPatt$ (not given here):

$match(Y.C, v, \epsilon) = undef,$

$match(Y.C, v, Z.D \Rightarrow e\ sr) = match(Y.C, v, sr)$ $\mathtt{if}\ Y \neq Z\ \mathtt{or}\ C \neq D\ \mathtt{or}\ matchPatt(v,p) = undef$

$match(Y.C, v, Y.C(p) \Rightarrow e\ sr) = (e, \Gamma)\ \mathtt{if}\ matchPatt(v,p) = \Gamma$

Fig. 3. Operational semantics of requests

built-in function `get_Xdata` is available that extracts the Xdatum to build a (standard) XML structure that can be sent interactively. When encountering an abstract path in place of an XML node, the function is recursively called on the value at the abstract path. In case of a trigger, a request is prepared that includes the address of the value of `root` (called the *initial concrete receiver*[2]), the abstract path from it to the last possible receiver, the interaction tag and an XML structure (the parameter of the request). Note that the abstract path to the last possible receiver is now given from `root`, then may be different from the abstract path set up in the Xdata. Such an interactive request is at first received (and executed) by the initial concrete receiver. In fact a request is a first-class citizen that has the general form $\tau(e_2)@e_1$: e_1 is the concrete receiver of the request, $\tau(e_2)$ gives the trigger and the parameter value for the request. The operational semantics is given in Fig. 3. Due to lack of space, the second rule considers only an identifier beginning the abstract path but similar rules may be given with keywords `parent`, `root` and `self`. The semantics may be rephrased in the following way: if the concrete receiver has an adequate reaction (the reaction matches trigger and parameter of the request), the reaction is evaluated ; otherwise the request is delegated following the path to the last possible receiver until some Xobject has an adequate reaction. It is the type system that is responsible for checking that there cannot be run-time errors. Note that an Xobject value is rebuilt when a delegation occurs. In this paper, we suppose that capture variables are available in standard and XML patterns. However, this may be extended to tag and abstract paths patterns.

Going back to Ex. 4, a tag `T` is set down in the Xdata part of `link`: `root.H1.T<a>[x]` states that the tag `T` is an anchor. Requests available in this case may be for example `T("Hello")@h1` or `H1.T("Hello")@website`. This last request is the only one that can be used interactively. As `website` has no appropriate reaction, the request is delegated to `h1`, value

[2] This is generalized in section 4 where the initial receiver may be different from `root`.

Xdata			
t^s	$::= [\tau]$<$a\ l_t$>$[r_t]$		*Xdata tree*
	$\mid\ Y$		*abstract path type name*
Xobjects			
t^o	$::= \mathbb{T} \mid Y$		*abstract tree and path name types*
vn	$::= t^s \blacktriangleright \rho$		*type of a $\mathbb{T}$ node value*
ρ	$::= \epsilon$		*sequence of Xobject types*
	$\mid\ \tau_{p1} \rightarrow t^s_{p1}\ [\rightarrow t^o_1]; \ldots ;\tau_{pn} \rightarrow t^s_{pn}\ [\rightarrow t^o_n]$		*for a pattern type for trigger type*

Fig. 4. Type language of FICX (except XML and functional type language)

of `H1` as it is given in `website`. The reaction part of this phandler contains a reaction that is fired with result the Xobject `(phandler 1)[M1↦(message "Salut")]`. The final value sent back to the requester is `home[L1↦l1][L2↦l2][H1↦(phandler 1)[M1↦(message "Salut")]]`.

3 Language FICX: The Type System

FICX is strongly typed: the static typing offers the programmer a way to check its program before execution. Besides the usual benefits, it allows to check the completeness and soundness of the program with respect to interactions as given by requests expressions. Obviously, requests included in the program are checked at compile time and interactive requests are checked only on the fly. However, one may control interactive requests by studying available triggers and reactions: e.g. clicks in a browser generate requests and are allowed by triggers set up on some Xdata, web services should answer to declared services. We refer in the later to completeness and soudness with respect to the cover of triggers and reactions in an Xstructure, i.e. a fully defined tree of Xobjects.

The type language is in two parts (see Fig. 4): t^s stands for standard or Xdata expressions, t^o for Xobjects. The type system for functional expressions is standard, it is extended for Xdata expressions by mimicking the structure. Abstract path variables are also defined as types (these are sequences of constants). The type of an Xobject is an abstraction of a handler tree value as defined in the operational semantics: it is a pair of trees in $\mathcal{T}_{\mathcal{L}} \times \mathcal{T}_{\bar{\mathcal{L}}}$ with abstract paths as labels and nodes valued by the type of its Xdata together with types for the reactions (pattern and result), these values are noted vn in the figure. ρ defines the types for possible reactions (supposed if given as triggers, explicit if given as reactions): this is a sequence possibly empty associating to a trigger pattern and a pattern type the type of the result if it is defined (summing over the sets of patterns types, and of result types). Taking into account reactions in the type is possible because of subtyping, and the fact that a program may only include a finite number of Xobject types. However, as reactions and triggers may not be defined in the same Xobject, the type system should propagate pieces of information and when possible merge them to satisfy coherence properties when an Xobject is used as a parameter value for another Xobject.

Due to lack of space, we limit the description of type judgments to Xobjects. The remainder is quite easy to define as it takes up technics used for functional programming, XML, ... Note that in the following we suppose that variables newly typed were not typed before (type clash with respect to the environment is supposed implicit). Let Δ be a type environment, i.e. a partial function $\mapsto$ from the set of variable names (including abstract path variables) to types, judgments for an expression and a sequence of reactions are given as follows:

$\Delta \vdash e : t$ where e is an expression and t its type

$\Delta \vdash_r sr : \rho$ where sr is a sequence of reactions with type ρ

3.1 Expression Judgment Rules: Xobjects

The type of an Xobject is of type $\mathbb{T}$ (`YJoin` builds the pair of trees) whose `self` node value summarizes types of reactions and of triggers set up in the Xdata part. These two data are merged in a single type ρ' considering that triggers not covered by reactions give 'partially defined' types. `Trig` computes the set of triggers set up in its argument. `RIT` (Reaction Intersection Type) retracts triggers (in its second argument) for which reactions are given in its first argument (a reaction type). Parameter assignment is typed by means of a merge and mask operation wrt an abstract path.

$$\frac{\Delta, \overrightarrow{Y_i \mapsto Y_i} \vdash e : t \quad \Delta, \overrightarrow{Y_i \mapsto Y_i} \vdash_r sr : \rho \qquad \mathtt{RIT}(\rho, \mathtt{Trig}(t)) = \rho' \qquad t_1^o = \mathtt{YJoin}(Y_1, \ldots, Y_n, \mathtt{self} {\mapsto} t {\blacktriangleright} \rho')}{\Delta \vdash \mathtt{xobject}\ {<}Y_1, \ldots, Y_n{>} {\rightarrow} e \blacktriangleright sr\ \mathtt{xend} : t_1^o}$$

$$\frac{\Delta \vdash e_1 : \mathbb{T}_1 \quad \Delta \vdash e_2 : \mathbb{T}_2}{\Delta \vdash e_1[Y {\mapsto} e_2] : \mathbb{T}_1 \lhd_Y \mathbb{T}_2}$$

Auxiliary functions for type computation:

$\mathtt{Trig}({<}a\ l_t{>}[r_t]) = \mathtt{Trig}(r_t)$

$\mathtt{Trig}(\tau{<}a\ l_t{>}[r_t]) = \{\tau {\rightarrow} {<}a\ l_t{>}[r_t]\} \cup \mathtt{Trig}(r_t)$

$\mathtt{Trig}(r_{t1}\ r_{t2}) = \mathtt{Trig}(r_{t1}) \cup \mathtt{Trig}(r_{t2})$

$\mathtt{Trig}(t) = \emptyset \quad \mathtt{otherwise}$

$\mathtt{RIT}(\rho, \emptyset) = \rho$

$\mathtt{RIT}(\rho, \{\tau \rightarrow t^s\} \cup T) = \mathtt{RIT}(\mathtt{RIT1}(\rho, \tau \rightarrow t^s), T)$

$\mathtt{RIT1}(\epsilon, \tau \rightarrow t^s) = \tau \rightarrow t^s$

$\mathtt{RIT1}(\tau_1 \rightarrow t_1^s\ [\rightarrow t_1^o];\rho, \tau \rightarrow t^s) = \tau_1 \rightarrow t_1^s\ [\rightarrow t_1^o];\mathtt{RIT1}(\rho, \tau \rightarrow t^s \setminus \tau_1 \rightarrow t_1^s)$

3.2 Expression Judgment Rules: Requests

A request $\tau(e_2)@e_1$ has a type given by the result of the fired reaction. This reaction should be on the path (given in the trigger τ) beginning from the receiver (value of e_1). If the type of e_1 includes a compatible reaction (function *testreac*), then the request has the type of the result:

$$\frac{\Delta \vdash e_1 : \mathbb{T}_1 \quad \Delta \vdash e_2 : t_2 \quad testreac(\tau, t_2, \rho(\mathtt{self}(\mathbb{T}_1))) = \mathbb{T}_2}{\Delta \vdash \tau(e_2)@e_1 : \mathbb{T}_1 \lhd_y \mathbb{T}_2}$$

otherwise the request is delegated to the first part of the trigger. The following rule concerns the case where this first part is some child y. The fact that the type of an Xobject is a global environment (not limited to local constituents) allows for similar rules when the first element of the path is `parent`, or `root`.

$$\frac{\Delta \vdash e_1 : \mathbb{T}_1 \quad \Delta \vdash e_2 : t_2 \quad \mathit{testreac}(y.Y.C, t_2, \rho(\texttt{self}(\mathbb{T}_1))) = \texttt{undef} \quad \mathit{val}(y(\mathbb{T}_1)) \textit{ defined} \quad \Delta \setminus \mathit{dom}(\mathbb{T}_1) \cup \mathbb{T}_1{}^{y \to \texttt{self}} \vdash Y.C(e_2)@\texttt{self} : \mathbb{T}_2}{\Delta \vdash y.Y.C(e_2)@e_1 : \mathbb{T}_1 \lhd_y \mathbb{T}_2}$$

where

$\mathit{testreac}(\tau, t, \epsilon) = \texttt{undef}$

$\mathit{testreac}(\tau, t, \tau_p \to t_1 \to t_2^o\,; \rho) = t_2^o \texttt{ if } \tau <:_\tau \tau_p \texttt{ and } t <: t_1$

$\mathit{testreac}(\tau, t, \tau_p \to t_1 \to t_2^o\,; \rho) = \mathit{testreac}(\tau, t, \rho) \texttt{ otherwise}$

It is not too difficult to prove a safety theorem stating that well-typed expressions are evaluable, i.e. there cannot be evaluation errors (provided for the functional language part an operational semantics safe with respect to a classic typing):

Theorem 1. *Let e be an expression of the language, if* $\vdash e : t$ *is provable, then there exist* $v, \mathcal{H}'$ *such that* $\vdash e \Downarrow v, \mathcal{H}'$ *is provable.*

The proof results from a careful study of the various rules. Note that the typing rules ensure that the Xobject parameters of a request have appropriate reactions, and that the operational semantics rules are in correspondence with the typing ones.

3.3 Xobject Evolution and Completeness

Interactive requests may be controlled by means of a static study of Xstructures: interactive requests that correspond to declared triggers on Xobjects may be executed without errors. This is particularly the case with web sites when requests are built by the browser after a user click, it is also the case with web services if clients conform a WSDL or BPEL declaration. However, a dynamic type checking has to be added as one cannot be sure that requests are well-formed with respect to some declaration. Besides this soundness property, the completeness stands for checking that reactions given in Xobjects are correctly declared. The typing rule for the Xstructure expression is given in Fig. 5 ($\Delta \vdash_d d : \Gamma$ is a type judgment for definitions, Γ is a type environment, $\vdash_S$ is used for top-level type judgments). The complexity of the rule comes from the fact that the pair of trees have now to be merged. This is done by the function `FDX` that also ensures that soundness and completeness properties are satisfied:

- 1st line does an 'identifier' operation,
- 2nd line ensures that reactions cover triggers (ρ is fully defined), and recursively through reactions,
- 3rd line ensures that Xobjects in the environment are known.

3.4 Subtyping

A subtyping system is supposed to be given for the XML part of the language. It is extended for XML and trigger patterns. The subtyping system for Xobjects has the following characteristics: let t_1^o and t_2^o be two Xobject types, $t_1^o <: t_2^o$ (t_1^o extends t_2^o) if

- For each abstract path Y, possibly with type t_Y in t_2^o, Y is present in t_1^o, if required with a type $t'_Y <: t_Y$.

Xstructure

$$\frac{\Delta \vdash_d d : \Gamma \quad \Gamma \vdash e : t^o \quad \texttt{FDX}(t^o) = t'^o}{\Delta \vdash_S \texttt{xstruc}\ d\ \texttt{begin}\ w = e : w \mapsto t'^o}$$

where

$\texttt{FDX}(\mathbb{T} <: t^o)$	$= \mathbb{T}' <: t^o$ iff	$\mathbb{T}' = \updownarrow \mathbb{T}$ and $\rho(\texttt{self}(\mathbb{T}')) = \texttt{FDX}_\rho(\rho(\texttt{self}(\mathbb{T})))$ and $\texttt{FDX}_T(\mathbb{T}')$ is true
$\texttt{FDX}_\rho(\epsilon)$	$= \epsilon$	
$\texttt{FDX}_\rho(\tau_p \rightarrow t_p^s \rightarrow t^o;\rho)$	$= \tau_p \rightarrow t_p^s \rightarrow \texttt{FDX}(t^o);\texttt{FDX}_\rho(\rho)$	
$\texttt{FDX}_T(\mathbb{T})$	is true	iff forall node n of $\mathbb{T}$, n has a value

Fig. 5. Soundness and completeness of Xstructures (entry points)

- XML subtyping should be satisfied as well as subtyping with respect to triggers (triggers in t_2^o should appear in t_1^o).
- Each reaction defined in t_2^o has its counterpart in t_1^o.

Typing constraints may then be added to the language as usual.

4 Extensions

In the current setting, requests should initially be sent to the (concrete) root of a tree of components, and, if necessary, delegated to some adequate Xobject wrt an abstract path to a final receiver. However, this constraint is neither formally necessary nor practically wishful. In fact, this delegation mechanism is safe as soon as the concrete receiver is known and the nodes in the abstract path have each a value. Moreover, sending a request directly to some node in a tree of components allows for an Ajax-like mechanism. Ajax [3] is a web development technique for creating interactive web applications and is intended to increase the web page's interactivity, speed, and usability. A response may be given as a part of an HTML document and it is the client responsability to replace the old value by the new one at the right place (a DOM-based mechanism generally), avoiding the page to be completely reloaded. This mechanism may be modelled in our framework as a request to some specific Xobject maybe different from a root, this Xobject being specified when setting up a trigger. To take care of this generalization, the syntax of a request does not change and a trigger should be set up as $Y'{:}Y.C{<}a \;\; l_e{>}[s]$ where the initial receiver is such that Y' is the path from `self` to it.

Let us replace the definition of `link` in Ex. 4 by:

```
link = xobject <parent.H1> (x:string)
        root.H1.M1:self.parent.H1.T<a>[x]
    ▶ xend;
```

The trigger `root.H1.M1:self.parent.H1.T<a>[x]` in `link` states that the initial (resp. final) receiver for the tag `T` should be the value at `self.parent.H1` (resp. `root.H1.M1`). A request corresponding to such a tag could be `root.H1.M1.T("Hello")@h1`. Operational and typing rules are slightly more complex as one should manage delegation not only wrt direct subcomponents (daughters in the component tree) but also to parents of a node. Using such a mechanism interactively requires more theoretical and practical investigations. When a request is received at first by the root of a tree of components, a new tree of components is created for the response, hence the tree structure is fully defined. This is no more the case when a request is initially sent to a node different from the root: either the tree is rebuilt but efficiency is lost, or a replacement is done but completeness and soundness wrt reactions may not be guaranteed.

More generally, we currently study carefuly the theoretical meaning of interaction, i.e. setting up triggers as a dual to requesting reactions. An operational semantics of interaction may be given in terms of processus calculus while keeping the semantics of the delegation process described in this paper. This may be fruitful for extending expressivity of interaction. For instance, associating multiple receivers to the same tag could be useful in pratice. In example 4, one would desire to increment the handler at each change in the welcome message: requests `root.L1.T("Hello")@m1` and `root.L1.T("Hello")@h1` are sent. However, the operational semantics is not obvious if order of execution matters. This is not the case when replies concern disjoint parts of the concrete tree of components.

5 Related Works

Our work concerns two different communities: object and XML programming as the real novelties of FICX are program modularity through Xobject component trees and static typing for structures that mix XML and functional parts. However our approach is uneasily comparable to the standard object-oriented paradigm in that modularity is got by partonomy rather than inheritance. Moreover Xobjects are in fact immutable as parameter instantiation and requests create each time new Xobjects. It is easier to relate our work to different areas in semi-structured data field (embedded calls, type checking, web services).

Embedded calls in XML documents: Concepts of triggers and reactions in FICX are close to the (not new) idea of embedded calls in XML structures. Previous works from this area can be classified in two categories: data oriented and code oriented. In the data-oriented approach, the XML structure is enriched with intensional data. In Macromedia [10], Appache Jelly [14], AXML [1,5], database or web service queries help to dynamically complete XML documents and a declaration of services may be available. Including expressions and triggers in Xdata has the same objectives even if we do not focus on the problems of distributed stream data. The difference mainly relies on the fact that our language is strongly type-checked although works just cited extend loosely XML types or schemas. For example, type checking in AXML is based on an extension of XML schemas in order to describe data types needed in an exchange. The code-oriented approach, as popularized by PHP [13], JSP [12], ASP [11], tries to introduce code in XML structures in order to allow parameterization and dynamicity of websites. However, no static checking is proposed so there is no guarantee the resulting XML structure is correct before run-time.

Typed XML processing languages: Many works (see [9]) for a general survey) exist that propose strongly typed languages for manipulating XML data: Xact [7] (an extension of JAVA), CDUCE [2] (a ML-like language), XSTATIC [4] (an extension of C#). These programming languages allow to manipulate, to create and to check XML documents thanks to a powerful parser and a type inference system. They extend a programming language by means of a typed language for XML document manipulation. However they do not support code integration in XML data. On the other hand XMλ [8] is closer to our concerns. It uses a Haskell-like syntax and treats XML documents as native values. It allows to include typed expressions and embedded functions calls in XML documents while proposing a powerful type-checking. All these systems lack a general framework able to design software in a modular and homogeneous way.

6 Conclusion

FICX is a programming language that focuses on designing trees of components, close to part-of relationship. FICX is well suited to XML-like languages by integrating static and dynamic aspects in an homogeneous framework. A powerful delegation process for interactions is defined thanks to the tree structure. The study of FICX (type checking, operational semantics) is facilitated by the fact that XML data and Xobject evolutions are encoded in the same language. Such a tree components programming paradigm increases expressivity with respect to other works where XML values may be computed only by means of direct calls.

References

1. Abiteboul, S., Benjelloun, O., Milo, T.: Positive active xml. In: ACM SIGMOD/PODS 2004 Conference (June 2004)
2. Benzaken, V., Castagna, G., Frisch, A.: Cduce: An xml-centric general purpose language. In: ICFP 2003. Proc. 8th ACM SIGPLAN International Conference on Functional Programming, Uppsala, Sweden, ACM Press, New York (2003)
3. Crane, D., Pascarello, E., James, D.: Ajax in Action. Manning Publications (2005)
4. Gapeyev, V., Levin, M.Y., Pierce, B.C., Schmitt, A.: XML goes native: Run-time representations for Xtatic. In: 14th International Conference on Compiler Construction (April 2005)
5. Active XML homepage, `http://activexml.net`
6. Objective CAML homepage, `http://caml.inria.fr/ocaml/index.en.html`
7. Kirkegaard, C., Møller, A.: Type checking with XML Schema in Xact. Technical Report RS-05-31, BRICS (September 2005)
8. Meijer, E., Shields, M.: XMλ: A functional language for constructing and manipulating XML documents (Draft) (1999)
9. Møller, A., Schwartzbach, M.I.: The design space of type checkers for XML transformation languages. In: Eiter, T., Libkin, L. (eds.) ICDT 2005. LNCS, vol. 3363, pp. 17–36. Springer, Heidelberg (2004)
10. Macromedia Coldfusion MX, `http://www.macromedia.com/software/coldfusion`
11. Active Server pages, `http://www.asp.net/`
12. Sun's, J.A.V.A.: Server Pages, `http://java.sun.com/products/jsp`
13. The PHP Hypertext Preprocessor, `http://www.php.net`
14. Jelly: Executable XML, `http://jakarta.apache.org/commons/jelly`

A Framework for Incorporating Trust into Formal Systems Development

Fredrik Degerlund[1,2] and Kaisa Sere[2]

[1]Turku Centre for Computer Science &
[2]Åbo Akademi University, Dept. of Information Technologies
Joukahainengatan 3-5
FIN-20520 Åbo, Finland
{Fredrik.Degerlund, Kaisa.Sere}@abo.fi

Abstract. Formal methods constitute a means of developing reliable and correctly behaving software based on a specification. In scenarios where information technology is used as a foundation to enable human communication, this is, however, not always enough. Successful interaction between humans often depends on the concept of trust, which is different from program correctness. In this paper, we present a framework for integrating trust into a formal development process, allowing for the construction of formally correct programs for communication, embracing trust as a central concept. We present a coordination language for use with action systems, taking a modular approach of separating trust aspects from other functionality. We also believe that our work can be adapted to modelling other aspects beside trust. Throughout the paper, we employ a case study as a testbed for our concepts.

1 Introduction

Formal methods for stepwise refinement of programs [1,2,6] provide for a strict mathematical framework of developing provably correct software. These methods allow for the refinement of an initial specification into a more concrete one and, finally, into an executable program. The underlying reasoning of the procedure can be based, for example, on the states of program variables and the operations operating on this state space. As such, they are mathematical-logical in nature and constitute a firm foundation for precise reasoning about computer programs.

However, in an environment where computer programs interact with humans, correctness of the automated algorithms involved is not enough. The behaviour of people not always being predictable, irrational behaviour has to be taken into account, as well as malicious intents of specific individuals. Scenarios of this type include, but are not limited to, mobile ad hoc networks (MANETs), peer-to-peer systems, on-line auctions and virtual communities. A property that all these scenarios have in common is that they rely on people being able to have confidence in each other, even when individuals who have no prior relationships are involved. A typical approach to dealing with these issues is introducing the notion of *trust* [5,9].

C.B. Jones, Z. Liu, J. Woodcock (Eds.): ICTAC 2007, LNCS 4711, pp. 154–168, 2007.

We believe that the solution to this problem is to integrate reasoning about trust into the formal development process. This is, technically speaking, already possible to do using today's modelling languages. In practice, however, trust relationships are often complex and difficult to describe using standard computing statements. The main contribution of this paper is to extend modelling languages with new constructs facilitating treatment of trust during the formal development process. Our model has its roots in the idea that trust can be *provided* as well as *required* in order to perform certain operations. By proposing a number of clauses and special variables describing the trust scenario, as well as the trust relationships necessary to perform specific operations, we introduce a special *coordination language* dedicated to handling trust aspects of formal systems. Our goal is to develop a framework within which we can reason about trust related functionality and other functionality in a modular fashion. We also show how our constructs translate into a corresponding traditional modelling language. This translation serves two purposes. First, it gives a strict definition of the new concepts, in terms of traditional ones, as well as a theoretical framework to reason about them. Second, it shows how much more complicated the translation into traditional constructs renders the system, demonstrating the practical usefulness of our concepts. We also believe that the models we propose in this paper can be adapted to other purposes beside trust.

The rest of the paper is structured as follows. In section 2, we describe some of the main background concepts that our framework is built upon. More specifically, section 2.1 gives a short presentation of the modelling language involved (Action systems), whereas 2.2 presents the mathematical concepts (Subjective logic) that we use as our foundation when combining trust values. At this point, we also introduce a demo scenario that will constitute a running example throughout the paper. In section 3, we give an initial presentation of how trust concepts can be used in formal systems. The integration of trust into formal systems will be made more sophisticated and elegant in section 4, where we introduce a coordination language providing direct support for trust concepts. Finally, in section 5, we make conclusions about the most significant contributions of the paper, as well as present some related work.

2 Background Concepts

2.1 Modelling Languages

Several formal methods for development of correct programs have been well studied over the years, including the Action Systems formalism [2] and the B-Method [1]. The Action Systems formalism is based on Dijkstra's guarded command language [8], and the refinement calculus [4] is used to develop programs according to the correct-by-construction approach. Based on state transformers, the basic form of the formalism is suited primarily for programs taking a number of values as input, performing a set of computations on them and giving one or several output values, as well as for describing reactive behaviour. The formalism is inherently suitable for development of concurrent software.

The B-Method is another successful approach to formal program development. In contrast to the Action Systems formalism, it was not initially designed for concurrency. More recent approaches have, however, adapted the method for this purpose. The Event B [12] formalism is heavily influenced by Action Systems. As a result of this work, modern approaches to B can tackle approximately the same development tasks as action systems. There is, however, one crucial difference when choosing which formalism to use. The Action Systems formalism has more expressive power, making it convenient to use for pen-and-paper sketches of a system. The syntax used in B (called AMN, Abstract Machine Notation) is, in contrast, quite limited, but as a result more suitable for actual implementation of systems, and even more so for mechanization. For example, there is tool support readily available for the B-Method, whereas there is none for action systems. In this paper, we will use the Action Systems formalism because of its typographic convenience. We do, however, wish to stress that the extensions we make could also be done correspondingly to the AMN notation of the B-Method.

A traditional action system can be written according to the following structure:

$\mathcal{A} = |[$
  var *var_list*
  const *const_list*
  imports *imp_list*
  exports *exp_list*
  proc *list of procname(param_names_list)* = {<*implementation*>}
  S_0;
  do
    $g_1 \rightarrow S_1$ [] ... [] $g_n \rightarrow S_n$
  od
$]|$

The lists *var_list* and *const_list* contain the local variables, and the constants, respectively. Furthermore, *import_list* lists all non-local variables that should be accessible from the system, and are exported by another action system. The list *exp_list* represents non-local variables that are introduced by the system and can be imported by other ones. The *proc* clause contains procedures, including procedure headers used as names to refer to a particular procedure, as well as the bodies containing the implementation. The rest of the system contains its *guards* and the *statements*. When the system starts, the initial statement S_0 is executed, followed sequentially by a loop containing elements of the form $g_i \rightarrow S_i$. These guard-statement pairs are called the *actions* of the system, hence the name action systems. The guards are boolean expressions, and in case the guard of an action evaluates to true, the action is said to be *enabled.* An action, or more precisely the statement of the action, can be executed if and only if enabled. Enabled actions are executed in nondeterministic order, and they are always considered to be atomic. In practice, the actions can often be executed in parallel, but in this case, they must be scheduled in such a way that they generate the same result as if they were executed in a (nondeterministic) sequence. For example, actions that have no variables in common, or actions that have variables in common but only have read access to these variables, can be scheduled to run in parallel without the risk of illegal interference. The action system terminates when there are no longer any enabled actions left. In this paper, we will, however, assume that there is always some action enabled, so that our systems will not terminate.

2.2 Subjective Logic

We base the mathematical-logical process of reasoning about trust on the *subjective logic* introduced by Jøsang [9]. We find that this logic suits our purposes well by providing a means of computing a single trust value from a chain of values. In subjective logic, trust is expressed as triples of the form (b, d, i), where b represents belief, d stands for disbelief, and i is ignorance. Values ranging from 0 to 1 are used, i.e. $b, d, i \in [0..1]$, and their sum should add up to 1, i.e. $b+d+i=1$. Each person can express his trust in another entity, for example another person, by using a trust triple. If entity A trusts entity B with belief b_B^A, disbelief d_B^A and ignorance i_B^A, we use the notation $\pi_B^A = (b_B^A, d_B^A, i_B^A)$. Intuitively, the belief and disbelief portions of the triple represent previous experience in the entity for which the triple is given, and ignorance represents the lack of knowledge in the entity. For example, when evaluating an entity of which you have no previous experience whatsoever, belief, disbelief and ignorance would be 0, 0 and 1, respectively.

Trust triples can be operated on by using a number of algebraic operators, resulting in a framework called *subjective logic*. Jøsang suggests a number of operators, of which only some will be important for the purpose of this paper. We will use the following ones knows as *consensus* and *recommendation*.

Consensus can intuitively be described as the operator computing the collective opinion of two entities, A and B, about a third entity, C, of which both A and B already have a personal opinion. Formally, it is defined as:

Definition 1. *Let $\pi_C^A = (b_C^A, d_C^A, i_C^A)$ and $\pi_C^B = (b_C^B, d_C^B, i_C^B)$ be opinions on entity C, held by entity A and entity B, respectively. Let $\pi_C^{A,B} = (b_C^{A,B}, d_C^{A,B}, i_C^{A,B})$ be the consensus opinion held by entities A and B about entity C. The consensus opinion relates to the individual opinions of A and B as follows:*

1. $b_C^{A,B} = (b_C^A i_C^B + b_C^B i_C^A)/\kappa$
2. $d_C^{A,B} = (d_C^A i_C^B + d_C^B i_C^A)/\kappa$
3. $i_C^{A,B} = (i_C^A i_C^B)/\kappa$
4. $\kappa = i_C^A + i_C^B - i_C^A i_C^B$

The symbol $\oplus$ will be used to denote consensus, so that $\pi_C^{A,B} = \pi_C^A \oplus \pi_C^B$.

Recommendation is the operator computing the entity A's opinion on C, given that A provides his opinion on B, and B's opinion on C is known.

Definition 2. *Let $\pi_B^A = (b_B^A, d_B^A, i_B^A)$ be an opinion held by entity A on entity B, and $\pi_C^B = (b_C^B, d_C^B, i_C^B)$ an opinion held by entity B on entity C.*

Let $\pi_C^{AB} = (b_C^{AB}, d_C^{AB}, i_C^{AB})$ be the recommendation opinion held by entity A about entity C by recommendation of B. The recommendation opinion π_C^{AB} relates to the opinions π_B^A and π_C^B as follows:

1. $b_C^{AB} = b_B^A b_C^B$
2. $d_C^{AB} = b_B^A d_C^B$
3. $i_C^{AB} = d_B^A + i_B^A + b_B^A i_C^B$

The symbol $\otimes$ will be used to denote recommendation, so that $\pi_C^{AB} = \pi_B^A \otimes \pi_C^B$.

The consensus and recommendation operations can together be used to compute the trust of one entity in another entity when these are connected via other entities in a directed graph. This concept is described in detail by Jøsang [10], but for the purpose of this paper, we will demonstrate the method for a simple example graph, which will also constitute a running example throughout the rest of this paper. Consider a number of entities: A, B, ..., H. These entities correspond to the nodes of the graph in figure 1. The directed arcs represent the trust relations, and the numbers given are trust triples. For example, the directed arc from node A to node F denotes that entity A trusts entity F according to the triple (0.6, 0.1, 0.3), i.e. belief is 0.6, disbelief is 0.1 and ignorance is 0.3.

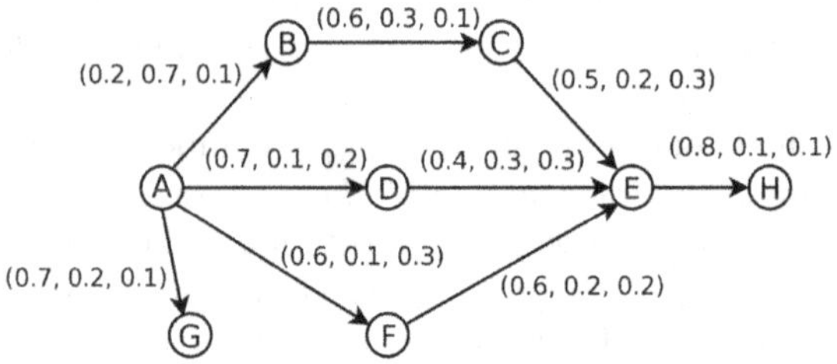

Fig. 1. Directed graph describing trust relationships

Now assume that we want to know how much entity A trusts H. As can be seen from the graph, A has no direct experience of H, and, hence, does not have any trust triple regarding H (other than (0, 0, 1), i.e. total ignorance). Instead, the trust triple can be derived indirectly from the trust relationships in the graph using subjective logic. In this particular scenario, the graph (excluding the dead-end path (A,G)), is a DSPG (Directed Series-Parallel Graph), for which a trust value can be computed by combining the consensus and recommendation operators as in the expression below. The details on how to derive the expression, as well as how to handle more complex scenarios (non-DSPG graphs) can be found in Jøsang's work [9,10]. The main principle is, however, that recommendation is used to form a trust chain from A to H. When branches occur, the consensus operator is used over the various alternative paths to acquire a combined trust value. In our case, the expression we acquire is:

$$((\pi_B^A \otimes \pi_C^B \otimes \pi_E^C) \oplus (\pi_D^A \otimes \pi_E^D) \oplus (\pi_F^A \otimes \pi_E^F)) \otimes \pi_H^E$$

When inserting the values given in the graph into the expression, we get the result (0.35, 0.044, 0.60). We interpret this as entity A having moderate reason to trust entity H, the belief value being 0.35. On the other hand, there is very little reason to explicitly distrust H, since disbelief is only 0.044. The reason why there is only a fair amount of explicit trust in H, even though distrust is minimal, is the fact that there is quite a high degree of ignorance, 0.60, involved.

3 Trust in Formal Systems

In this section, we will demonstrate how to express trust relationships, trust requirements etc. in formal systems. We will use the Action Systems formalism from section 2.1 to describe the systems, and we will reason about trust using the subjective logic as presented in 2.2. In this section we will only use standard action systems notation, whereas in section 4 we will render the syntax more sophisticated by adding direct support for trust aspects to the formalism.

Let us consider an on-line auction scenario, where one person, Anna, is interested in buying a used car from a seller, Harald. First, we will disregard trust issues. The transaction can take place if the following three conditions are met:

- Anna is *ready to buy* the car.
- Harald is *ready to sell* the car.
- Anna has *enough money* to buy the car. (Harald decides the price.)

The action systems representing the scenario would look as follows. Anna and Harald are represented by $\mathcal{A}$ and $\mathcal{H}$, respectively, and the communication between the two parties takes place via exported/imported variables.

$\mathcal{A} = |[$
  var *AMoney* : Nat, *AReadyToBuy* : Set of String
  imports *HReadyToSell*, *HItemPrices*
  proc *ABuyFromH*(*item* : String) = {<*impl.*>}
  ...
  do
    "car" $\in$ *AReadyToBuy* $\wedge$ "car" $\in$ *HReadyToSell*
    $\wedge$ *AMoney* $\geq$ *HItemPrices*("car")
    $\rightarrow$ *ABuyFromH*("car")
    ...
  od
$]|$

$\mathcal{H} = |[$
  ...
  exports *HReadyToSell* : Set of String,
    HItemPrices : Function (String$\rightarrow$Nat)
  ...
$]|$

We assume that there are other actions present ("..." in the **do-od** loop) that keep the system running when the purchase action in disabled, i.e. some action should be enabled at any time so that the system will not terminate. Those actions are also responsible for keeping track of e.g. money and related functionality. Further details on these actions are irrelevant for our purposes, and will be omitted here.

Now suppose that Anna wants to buy the car only if she has enough reason to trust Harald. Even though a program would technically be correctly refined, there is no guarantee that Harald really delivers the car after he has received the payment. This constitutes a particularly serious problem if Anna has only recently met Harald online, and has no experience of his trustworthiness. On the other hand, she might have previous experience of other persons, who in turn have done business with someone who knows Harald. In this manner, a chain or network of trust can be derived. For this reason we introduce trust handling into the model. Let us recall the example in section 2.2, and assume that this network of trust is represented by the directed graph in figure 1. In this graph, we let nodes A and H represent Anna and Harald, respectively. According to the graph, Anna has previous experience of Ben (B), Daniel (D), Fredrik (F) and Gwyneth (G), but none of these persons know Harald directly, either. Fortunately, Ben, Daniel and Fredrik, in turn, know other people, and it turns out that chains of trust can be formed, which include Anna as source and Harald as the destination. As a result, Anna can derive indirect trust in Harald using subjective logic. Anna might set a *threshold* trust triple, that her derived trust in Harald must exceed in order for the transaction to take place. We recognize that this can be done by extending the guard of the action triggering the transaction, so in addition to the previous requirements ("ready to sell", "ready to buy", "has enough money"), we now add a trust condition:

- Anna has *enough trust* in Harald

What we do is technically a *superposition refinement* [3], which will be discussed further in section 4. Anna's action system could now be expressed as:

$\mathcal{A} = |[$

var *AMoney* : Nat, *AReadyToBuy* : Set of String,

π^A_B : TrustTriple,
π^A_D : TrustTriple,
π^A_F : TrustTriple,
threshold : TrustTriple

imports *HReadyToSell*, *HItemPrices*,

π^B_C, π^C_E, π^D_E,
π^F_E, π^E_H

proc *ABuyFromH*(*item* : String) = {<*impl.*>}

threshold := (0.3, 0.3, 0.7);
π^A_B:= (0.2, 0.7, 0.1);
π^A_D:= (0.7, 0.1, 0.2);
π^A_F:= (0.6, 0.1, 0.3);

...
do
"car" $\in$ *AReadyToBuy* $\wedge$ "car" $\in$ *HReadyToSell*
$\wedge$ *AMoney* $\geq$ *HItemPrices*("car")
$\wedge\ ((\pi_B^A \otimes \pi_C^B \otimes \pi_E^C) \oplus (\pi_D^A \otimes \pi_E^D) \oplus (\pi_F^A \otimes \pi_E^F)) \otimes \pi_H^E > \mathit{threshold}$
$\rightarrow$ *ABuyFromH*("car")
...
od
]|

The parts of the system that have been added are marked with a box. As can be seen, an additional part evaluating the amount of trust has been added to the guard, i.e. the guard has been *strengthened.* The trust values used in the trust calculation formula have been added as local and imported variables. The values that Anna herself is responsible for deciding, i.e. her own direct trust in other persons, are modelled as local variables, whereas other persons' trust values are imported. These variables should be exported by the systems representing the respective persons. To represent these trust values, we have introduced a new type, TrustTriple, which is simply a short hand notation for ([0..1], [0..1], [0..1]). This type is also used for the threshold variable, which contains Anna's limits on what she considers to be enough trust to carry out the transaction. In the guard, we use comparison (">") between the calculated trust value and the threshold triple. To be able to do this, we must define what we mean by using a comparison relation on TrustTriple variables. We define equality in the following manner, which corresponds well to intuition:

Definition 3. *Consider two trust triples* $t_1 = (b_1, d_1, i_1)$ *and* $t_2 = (b_2, d_2, i_2)$. *These triples are equal* ($t_1 = t_2$) *if* $b_1 = b_2$ *and* $d_1 = d_2$ *and* $i_1 = i_2$.

Furthermore, we define the "less than or equal" and "greater than or equal" relations, "$\leq$" and "$\geq$", respectively, as follows:

Definition 4. *Consider two trust triples* $t_1 = (b_1, d_1, i_1)$ *and* $t_2 = (b_2, d_2, i_2)$.
t_1 *is less than or equal to* t_2 ($t_1 \leq t_2$) *if* $b_1 \leq b_2$ *and* $d_1 \geq d_2$ *and* $i_1 \geq i_2$.
t_1 *is greater than or equal to* t_2 ($t_1 \geq t_2$) *if* $b_1 \geq b_2$ *and* $d_1 \leq d_2$ *and* $i_1 \leq i_2$.

Finally, the "less than" and "greater than" relations, "$<$" and "$>$", respectively, are defined in the same manner as "$\leq$" and "$\geq$", with the additional condition that $t_1 \neq t_2$.

Now, we want to point out especially three things. First, in def. 4, the comparison of disbelief and ignorance values is done the other way than in the comparison of belief values. This is because less disbelief/ignorance is considered "better", whereas less belief is considered to be "worse". Second, we want to stress that these relations do not constitute total orders. For example, for the trust triples $t_1 = (0.5, 0.4, 0.1)$ and $t_2 = (0.3, 0.2, 0.5)$, neither $t_1 \leq t_2$ nor $t_2 \leq t_1$ is true. Third, the sum of the elements of threshold trust triples need not be 1, since it makes perfect sense to match a trust value against, for example, (0.8,

0.5, 0.3). The reason is that the threshold triples can be regarded as boundaries for the individual belief, disbelief and ignorance values in normal trust triples. In normal trust triples, both direct (given) and indirect (derived) ones, the elements must, however, sum up to exactly 1.

Let us consider our running example again. We have taken a first step towards introducing trust aspects into the system, but there are still a number of obstacles in the way. One of the problems is the fact that it is certainly not convenient to manually write the whole trust formula as part of the guard - let alone to derive the expression. From an aesthetical point of view, we would also like to keep the guards short and simple, and try to avoid long expressions such as those of trust computations. Another problem is that the paths of the trust value computations are fixed, i.e. the formula is immutable. While our solutions do take changed trust values into account (the trust value is recalculated each time), it cannot handle changes to the actual trust paths such as adding new persons and their respective paths, since the formula itself would have to be changed. A related restriction in our current approach is the fact that the expression can only be used to compute the value for Anna's trust in Harald. In case Anna wished to do business with Fredrik, another expression would have to be derived. Now, we will try to address these problem, i.e.:

- Clean up the guard.
- Take trust path changes into account.
- Make changing business partners possible.

To make the guard more convenient, we move the trust computation to a separate procedure, and simply make a function call from the guard. This helps keeping the main **do-od** loop shorter, while the work is moved outside into workhorse procedures. The new procedure could simply be expressed as:

proc *Trust*() = {
return $((\pi_B^A \otimes \pi_C^B \otimes \pi_E^C) \oplus (\pi_D^A \otimes \pi_E^D) \oplus (\pi_F^A \otimes \pi_E^F)) \otimes \pi_H^E$
} : TrustTriple

The comparison part of the guard would now simply be expressed as "Trust() > *threshold*". The procedure does, however, still contain a hard-coded expression and does not address the problem of path updates at all, neither does it support any other business partner than Harald. To achieve this kind of flexibility, we replace the predefined expression with an algorithm that dynamically derives the trust expression and, then, evaluates the expression. The algorithm to be used is, for example, the one presented by Jøsang [10], which was also used in the first place to derive our hard-coded expression above. Here, we will not list the algorithm, but simply refer to our new trust computation procedure as a black box. This far we have only taken those trust values which we have actually needed into account. For example, π_B^A has been present in our variables clause, but not π_G^A, since it has not been needed in our particular expression. The fact that it has not been needed is, in turn, a result of Harald being Anna's only business partner in conjunction with the lack of a path from node A to H via G in the graph. When taking arbitrary partners as well as arbitrary paths into account, all trust values have to be included. With n partners, the total number of trust variables will be $n^2 - n$ (an all-to-all relationship, except for oneself-to-oneself). 8 persons being present in our example, there will be 56 trust variables. The relationships for which there is currently no arc in the graph represent total ignorance, i.e. (0, 0, 1). These variables, such as π_D^E, still have to be included in the system, since they are included in the trust algorithm in case such a relationship is formed in the future. Since any other person might also need Anna's trust values in other nodes, we will move these from the **var** clause to **exports**. *The principle is that each person's trust values should be visible to everybody else.* Our algorithm being able to compute trust relationships between *any* two persons, not just Anna to Harald, the source as well as destination nodes should also be taken as input to the trust computation procedure.

When incorporating our new concepts, the structure of Anna's action system can be written as follows. The highlighted parts of the system are those that are related to the trust mechanisms:

$\mathcal{A} = ||[$

var *AMoney* : Nat, *AReadyToBuy* : Set of String,
[*threshold* : TrustTriple]

imports *HReadyToSell*, *HItemPrices*,
[$\pi_A^B, \pi_C^B, \pi_D^B, \pi_E^B, \pi_F^B, \pi_G^B, \pi_H^B,$
...
$\pi_A^H, \pi_B^H, \pi_C^H, \pi_D^H, \pi_E^H, \pi_F^H, \pi_G^H$]

exports [$\pi_B^A, \pi_C^A, \pi_D^A$: TrustTriple,
$\pi_E^A, \pi_F^A, \pi_G^A$: TrustTriple,
π_H^A : TrustTriple]

proc *ABuyFromH*(*item* : String) = {<*impl.*>},
[Trust(*src* : Char, *dest* : Char) = {<*impl.*>} : TrustTriple]

...

[*threshold* := (0.3, 0.3, 0.7);
π_B^A:= (0.2, 0.7, 0.1); π_C^A:= (0, 0, 1); π_D^A:= (0.7, 0.1, 0.2);
π_E^A:= (0, 0, 1); π_F^A:= (0.6, 0.1, 0.3); π_G^A:= (0, 0, 1);
π_H^A:= (0, 0, 1)]

...

do

"car" ∈ *AReadyToBuy* ∧ "car" ∈ *HReadyToSell*
∧ *AMoney* ≥ *HItemPrices*("car")
[∧ Trust('A', 'H') > *threshold*]
→ *ABuyFromH*("car")

...

od

$]|$

4 Trust-Coordinated Action Systems

As shown in the previous section, it is possible to express trust requirements and relationships in action systems. However, they are not originally designed for that purpose and provide no syntactic support. In this section, we introduce a coordination language for action systems, providing for a convenient way to reason about trust in the formal development process. While the expressibility of coordinated action system is the same as that of classic ones, they provide higher-level constructs for expressing trust-related properties. We first introduce the new syntax into our case study scenario:

$\mathcal{A} = |[$
  var *AMoney* : Nat, *AReadyToBuy* : Set of String
  imports *HReadyToSell*, *HItemPrices*
  proc *ABuyFromH*(*item* : String) = {<*impl.*>}
  ...
  do
    "car" $\in$ *AReadyToBuy* $\wedge$ "car" $\in$ *HReadyToSell*
    $\wedge$ *AMoney* $\geq$ *HItemPrices*("car")
    $\rightarrow$ *ABuyFromH*("car") [@*AHPurchase*]
    ...
  od
$]|$ [@$\mathcal{T}$]

$\mathcal{T} = |[$
  proc *Trust*(*src* : Char, *dest* : Char) = {<*impl.*>} : TrustTriple
  entities *A*, *B*, *C*, *D*, *E*, *F*, *G*, *H*
  transactions *AHPurchase*
  π_B^A:= (0.2, 0.7, 0.1); π_C^A:= (0, 0, 1); ...; π_H^A:= (0, 0, 1);
  ...
  π_A^H:= (0, 0, 1); π_B^H:= (0, 0, 1); ...; π_G^H:= (0, 0, 1);
  ...
  do
    AHpurchase: *Trust*('*A*', '*H*') > (0.3, 0.3, 0.7) $\rightarrow$ skip;
  od
  ...
$]|$

We have *decomposed* the system by abstracting away trust aspects from the rest of the functionality. While we previously expressed all trust aspects in the action systems themselves ($\mathcal{A}$, ..., $\mathcal{H}$), we now have the coordination system $\mathcal{T}$ dedicated to coordinating trust. As in the previous section, we have marked the parts of the systems related to trust by boxes. While the whole coordination system is trust-related, the action system $\mathcal{A}$ only contains two short references related to trust. The reference ("@$\mathcal{T}$") specifies which coordination system should be used for describing trust aspects. Furthermore, the reference "@*AHPurchase*" implies that the *AHPurchase* transaction should be applied to the car purchase action. The transaction *AHPurchase* itself is declared in the **transactions** clause of the coordination system, and we have also moved the trust computation procedure to the coordination system. The trust variables (π_j^i) are implicit. By identifying all entities involved, achieved by listing them in the **entities** clause, we can unambiguously conclude which the $n^2 - n$ trust variables are. In our example, with the entities A, ..., H, the trust variables are π_B^A, π_C^A, ..., π_G^H. By examining the action system $\mathcal{A}$, we conclude that it is almost identical to the first action system in section 3, i.e. before introducing trust aspects. The only difference is the fact the we now have two references to the trust coordination system. In a sense, we have done a full circle, returning back to the roots. We have succeeded in achieving a modular approach of abstracting away trust into a separate system. In fact, the version of the system incorporating trust is a refinement of the initial system (given that the trust computation procedure terminates).

Up to this point, we have introduced a coordination system without giving a strict definition. We intend to do this by showing how a general coordination system translates into standard action systems syntax. Consider the following schematic view of an action system, $\mathcal{A}$, and a similar schematic view of a trust coordination system, $\mathcal{T}$:

$\mathcal{A} = |[$
    var *var_list*
    const *const_list*
    imports *imp_list*
    exports *exp_list*
    proc *list of procname(param_names_list)* = {<*impl.*>}
    S_0;
    do
        $g_1 \rightarrow S_1@trans_1$ [] ... [] $g_n \rightarrow S_n@trans_n$
        ...
    od
$]|@\mathcal{T}$

$\mathcal{T} = |[$
    proc *list of trustproc(src* : Char, *dest* : Char) = {<*impl.*>} : TrustTriple
    entities e_1, ..., e_k
    transactions t_1, ..., t_m
    $\pi_{e_2}^{e_1}$:= <*triple*>; $\pi_{e_3}^{e_1}$:= <*triple*>; ...; $\pi_{e_{k-2}}^{e_k}$:= <*triple*>; $\pi_{e_{k-1}}^{e_k}$:= <*triple*>
    do
        t_1: $h_1 \rightarrow T_1$ [] ... [] t_m: $h_m \rightarrow T_m$
    od
$]|$

The action system $\mathcal{A}$ is quite similar to the schematic view in section 2.1. We do, however, assume that there are always some additional enabled action that prevents the system from terminating, i.e. the same assumption as in our example. Furthermore, there are references to $\mathcal{T}$ present, as well as the references $trans_1$, ..., $trans_n$. These should be replaced with one of the transactions t_1, ..., t_m listed in the **transactions** clause of $\mathcal{T}$, or simply ignored if the action in question has no trust requirements. The trust coordination system $\mathcal{T}$ contains two more clauses in addition to the **transactions** clause already mentioned, as well as variable initializations. The clause **proc** simply contains a list of procedures containing algorithms for computing trust between the *src* and *dest* nodes/entities, which are taken as input. The purpose of the **entities** clause is to list all the entities available.

The **do-od** part contains the implementations of the transactions. These can be considered labelled actions, whose purpose is to express trust requirements. The guards h_1, ..., h_m will typically be of the form $trustproc_i(src_i, dest_i)\bullet(b_i, d_i, i_i)$, where the symbol • stands for any one of the operators $=, <, >, \leq$ or $\geq$, i.e. a procedure call and a comparison of the result against some threshold triple. The statements T_1, ..., T_m are executed whenever the transaction is performed. If there is an action $g \rightarrow S$ @B in the action system $\mathcal{A}$ and a transaction B: $h \rightarrow T$ in the coordination system $\mathcal{T}$, this is defined to be the action $g \wedge h \rightarrow S;T$ in standard Action Systems theory. These T_i statements can be used to implement additional trust related functionality, but if not needed they can perform *skip* (no-op). As an example, they can be used to implement a counter tracking how many times a transaction has been performed.

The transactions (incl. the statements T_i) are never executed as such, but always in conjunction with an action from an action system. This is because the coordination system is never executed on its own. It can rather be considered a parasite, appending its functionality to the host system, i.e. the action system that it coordinates. Furthermore, the coordination system has the $k^2 - k$ trust variables $(\pi^{e1}_{e2}, \pi^{e1}_{e3}, ..., \pi^{ek}_{ek-2}, \pi^{ek}_{ek-1})$, which are not explicitly declared since they can be derived from the list of entities. They do, however, have to be initialized, which is done in conjunction with the initialization in the host system.

We now translate the above $\mathcal{A}$@$\mathcal{T}$ system into a standard action system to achieve a strict definition of coordination systems. We define the meaning of the system $\mathcal{A}$@$\mathcal{T}$ to be equivalent to the following standard action system:

$\mathcal{A}_{standard} = |[$
  var *var_ list*, $\pi^{e1}_{e2}, \pi^{e1}_{e3}, ..., \pi^{ek}_{ek-2}, \pi^{ek}_{ek-1}$
  const *const_ list*
  imports *imp_ list*
  exports *exp_ list*
  proc *list of procname(param_ names_ list)* = {<*impl.*>},
    list of trustproc(src : Char, *dest* : Char) = {<*impl.*>} : TrustTriple
  S_0; π^{e1}_{e2} := <*triple*>; π^{ek}_{ek-1} := <triple>;
  do
    $g_1 \wedge g_{trans_1} \rightarrow S_1; T_{trans_1}$ [] ... [] $g_n \wedge g_{trans_n} \rightarrow S_n; T_{trans_n}$
    ...
  od
$]|$

The $trans_i$ indices in $\mathcal{A}_{standard}$ refer to the corresponding references in $\mathcal{A}$. To make things clear, if there is an action $g_1 \rightarrow S_1$@$trans_1$ in $\mathcal{A}$ and $trans_1$ was chosen to correspond to the transaction t_j: $h_j \to T_j$ in $\mathcal{T}$, that would in $\mathcal{A}_{standard}$ translate to the action $g_i \wedge h_j \to S_i; T_j$.

Finally, we compare the above schematic view with an action system lacking any notion of trust (see section 2.1), but which is still non-terminating. We especially note that: *(1) No new actions have been added*, and *(2) The guards of the actions have been strengthened.* As for exit conditions, neither the old nor the new system will terminate, since we assumed the presence of actions that prevent the system as a whole from terminating. If we, in addition, assume that the individual trust computation procedures do terminate, and the T_i statements refine *skip*, all the prerequisites in action systems theory of $\mathcal{A}_{standard}$ being a valid superposition refinement [3] are fulfilled. We conclude that our method of introducing trust aspects constitutes a superposition refinement step, provided that the algorithms used for trust computation terminate and all T_i statements are refinements of *skip*. We have achieved *modularity* and the ability to refine trust aspects ($\mathcal{T}$) separately from the rest of the functionality ($\mathcal{A}$).

5 Conclusions and Related Work

In this paper, we have shown how to systematically introduce reasoning about trust requirements into formal systems development. We have used subjective logic [9] for operating on trust values, and the Action Systems formalism [2] has served as formal modelling language. Throughout the paper, we have used an online auction scenario as a running example, into which we have systematically introduced reasoning about trust. Furthermore, we have suggested a modular approach by showing how to separate trust requirements from other functionality, and, finally, we proposed a trust coordination language for use with action systems. By doing so, we allow for the possibility to keep the action systems clean of trust functionality, allowing the developer to concentrate on other aspects. The trust requirements can then be superposed onto the system in a superposition refinement step [3]. Although we have used action systems in the paper, our work can in principle be incorporated into other modelling languages as well. Finally, we believe that our concepts can be adapted to applications outside the field of trust. This is due to our modelling of weighted graphs which, in this paper, have been used to represent trust. Other problems involving similar graphs could, however, also benefit from the framework presented in this paper.

We have found inspiration in the theory of context aware action systems [17], which in turn is related to topological systems [15]. Trust can be considered a kind of context, and the mechanism for providing/requiring trust is founded on the corresponding method for context information [13]. Although the integration of trust into formal systems seems to be quite an unexplored field of study, it has been discussed at least in a position paper by Butler et al. [5], as well as by Degerlund and Sere [7]. Work has also been done in formalizing trust, unrelated to program refinement [16]. Furthermore, our scenario of study has a similar set-up to that of Byzantine agreement [11,14], but we concentrate on building trust relationships to specific persons instead of reaching a common agreement.

References

1. Abrial, J.-R.: The B-Book: assigning programs to meanings. Cambridge University Press, New York, USA (1996)
2. Back, R.J.R., Kurki-Suonio, R.: Decentralization of process nets with centralized control. In: PODC '83. Proceedings of the second annual ACM symposium on Principles of distributed computing, pp. 131–142. ACM Press, New York, NY, USA (1983)
3. Back, R.J.R., Sere, K.: Superposition refinement of reactive systems. Formal Aspects of Computing 8(3), 324–346 (1996)
4. Back, R.J.R., von Wright, J.: Refinement Calculus: A Systematic Introduction. Springer, New York (1998)
5. Butler, M., Leuschel, M., Lo Presti, S., Turner, P.: The use of formal methods in the analysis of trust (position paper). In: Jensen, C., Poslad, S., Dimitrakos, T. (eds.) iTrust 2004. LNCS, vol. 2995, pp. 333–339. Springer, Heidelberg (2004)
6. Chandy, K.M., Misra, J.: Parallel Program Design: A Foundation. Addison-Wesley Publishing Company, Reading (1988)
7. Degerlund, F., Sere, K.: A framework for incorporating trust into the action systems formalism (work in progress). In: Aceto, L., Ingólfsdóttir, A. (eds.) NWPT'06. Proceedings for the 18th Nordic Workshop on Programming Theory, oct 2006, Reykjavík Univerity, Reykjavík, Iceland (2006) (abstract)
8. Dijkstra, E.: A Discipline of Programming. Prentice-Hall, Englewood Cliffs (1976)
9. Jøsang, A.: Artificial reasoning with subjective logic. In: Proceedings of the 2nd Australian Workshop on Commonsense Reasoning (1997)
10. Jøsang, A., Hayward, R., Pope, S.: Trust network analysis with subjective logic. In: ACSC '06. Proceedings of the 29th Australasian Computer Science Conference, pp. 85–94 (2006)
11. Lamport, L., Shostak, R., Pease, M.: The byzantine generals problem. ACM Transactions on Programming Languages and Systems 4(3), 382–401 (1982)
12. Métayer, C., Abrial, J.-R., Voisin, L.: Event-b language, Rodin Deliverable D7. EU-project RODIN (IST-511599) (2005), `http://rodin.cs.ncl.ac.uk/deliverables.htm`
13. Neovius, M., Sere, K., Yan, L., Satpathy, M.: A formal model of context-awareness and context-dependency. In: SEFN '06. Proceedings of the Fourth IEEE International Conference on Software Engineering and Formal Methods, Washington, DC, USA, pp. 177–185. IEEE Computer Society Press, Los Alamitos (2006)
14. Pease, M., Shostak, R., Lamport, L.: Reaching agreement in the presence of faults. Journal of the ACM 27(2), 228–234 (1980)
15. Petre, L., Sere, K., Waldén, M.: A topological approach to distributed computing. In: Proceedings of WDS'99 - Workshop on Distributed Systems, September 1999. Electronic Notes in Theoretical Computer Science, vol. 28, pp. 97–118. Elsevier, Amsterdam (1999)
16. Wagealla, W., Carbone, M., English, C., Terzis, S., Lowe, H., Nixon, P.: A formal model for trust lifecycle management. In: FAST'03. Workshop on Formal Aspects in Security and Trust, pp. 181–192 (2004)
17. Yan, L., Sere, K.: A formalism for context-aware mobile computing. In: ISPDC '04. Proceedings of the Third International Symposium on Parallel and Distributed Computing/Third International Workshop on Algorithms, Models and Tools for Parallel Computing on Heterogeneous Networks (ISPDC/HeteroPar'04), Washington, DC, USA, pp. 14–21. IEEE Computer Society Press, Los Alamitos (2004)

A Higher-Order Demand-Driven Narrowing Calculus with Definitional Trees

Rafael del Vado Vírseda

Dpto. de Sistemas Informáticos y Computación
Universidad Complutense de Madrid
rdelvado@sip.ucm.es

Abstract. We generalize the *Constructor-based ReWriting Logic* CRWL to the setting of the simply typed λ-calculus, where theories are presented by conditional overlapping fully extended pattern rewrite systems. We claim that this logic is useful for higher-order functional-logic programming, and propose a *Higher-Order Lazy Narrowing calculus* $\mathrm{HOLN}^{\mathrm{DT}}$ for answering joinability and reducibility queries, in which a variant of *Definitional Trees* is used to efficiently control the demand-driven narrowing strategy. The calculus $\mathrm{HOLN}^{\mathrm{DT}}$ is shown to be sound and strongly complete with respect to this higher-order conditional rewriting logic.

1 Introduction

The effort to identify suitable computational models for higher-order functional logic programming has grown in recent years. Functional-logic languages with a sound and complete operational semantics are mainly based on *narrowing*, a transformation rule which combines the basic execution mechanisms of functional and logic languages, namely *rewriting* with *unification*. All serious attempts to generalize narrowing for higher-order functional-logic programs (see, for example, [5,7,9]) must address issues such as identifying suitable notions of *value* and *equality*, and reducing the huge search space for bindings of higher order variables.

The *Constructor-based ReWriting Logic* CRWL [4] provides a suitable framework for rule-based declarative (functional and logic) programming with non deterministic non-strict functions with *call-time choice* semantics, where programs are *Constructor-Based Conditional Term Rewrite Systems* (CB-CTRSs for short). Since the classical notion of rewriting is not suitable in this setting, a new notion of rewriting is adopted as the basis of *proof calculi* for joinability and reduction statements. An important result is the existence of sound and complete *lazy narrowing calculi* [4,2,3] for solving goals in first-order CRWL-theories presented by CB-CTRSs. Moreover, a higher-order extension of CRWL is presented in [5] but using applicative rewrite rules instead of λ-abstractions and higher-order unification.

In this paper, we propose a higher-order rewriting logic for declarative programming with higher-order functions and λ-terms as data structures to obtain more of the expressivity of higher-order functional programming. More precisely,

C.B. Jones, Z. Liu, J. Woodcock (Eds.): ICTAC 2007, LNCS 4711, pp. 169–184, 2007.

we adopt the framework of simply typed λ-calculus in which terms are in $\beta\eta$-normal form and theories are presented by conditional overlapping inductively sequential pattern rewrite systems. These are a subclass of fully-extended conditional pattern rewrite systems whose rules can be arranged in a variant of the classical *definitional trees*, a useful tool introduced by Antoy [1] for achieving a reduction strategy which avoids unneeded steps. Compared to CRWL, the distinctive features of our new higher-order conditional rewriting logic are:

- *values* are terms which do not match the left hand side of any rewrite rule. In the first-order case [4,2], values are constructor-based terms, but this notion is too weak in a higher-order setting. Still, our notion of value is decidable because matching against a pattern is decidable.
- *equality* is interpreted as joinability to a common value.

We prove the existence of a sound and strongly complete lazy narrowing calculus for higher-order functional-logic programming in such a logic, generalizing and improving previous higher-order narrowing calculi [5,9] and strategies [7]. Moreover, as the main novelty w.r.t. [7] and following the ideas introduced in [2,3] for the first-order case, we show that definitional trees can be used to efficiently control the narrowing strategy in the setting of our higher-order rewriting logic.

The paper is structured as follows. In Section 2 we introduce the basic notions and notations of our theoretical framework. In Subsection 2.2 we propose a higher-order conditional rewriting logic characterized by a *proof system* called GHRC, a generalization of the proof system GORC which underlies the constructor-based rewriting logic CRWL of [4]. In Section 3 we propose a higher-order demand-driven narrowing calculus with definitional trees called HOLN^{DT}. Section 4 is devoted to proving the main properties which guarantee the usefulness of HOLN^{DT} — soundness and strong completeness. Section 5 concludes.

2 Preliminaries

We assume the reader is familiar with the notions and notations pertaining to higher-order narrowing and term rewriting with definitional trees (see, e.g., [7] and [2]). The set of types for the simply typed λ-terms is generated by a set $\mathcal{B}$ of base types (e.g., `nat`, `bool`) and the function type constructor "$\rightarrow$". Simply typed λ-terms are generated in the usual way from a signature $\mathcal{F}$ of function symbols and a countably infinite set $\mathcal{V}$ of variables by successive operations of abstraction and application. We also consider the enhanced signature $\mathcal{F}_\perp = \mathcal{F} \cup$ `Bot`, where `Bot` $= \{\perp_b \mid b \in \mathcal{B}\}$ is a set of distinguished $\mathcal{B}$-typed constants. The constant $\perp_b$ is intended to denote an undefined value of type b. We employ $\perp$ as a generic notation for a constant from `Bot`. In this paper, we assume the following conventions of notation: X, Y, Z, R, H, possibly primed or with subscripts, denote free variables; f, f' denote defined function symbols, g denotes a data constructor or defined function symbol, and a a (free or bound) variable or a constant from $\mathcal{F}$; l, r, s, t, u, possibly primed or with subscript, denote terms; $\pi, \pi', \pi_1, \pi_2, \ldots$ denote terms of base type.

A sequence of syntactic objects $o_1, \ldots, o_n$, where $n \geq 0$, is abbreviated by $\overline{o_n}$. For instance, the simply typed λ-term $\lambda x_1.\ldots\lambda x_k.(\cdots(a\ t_1)\ \cdots\ t_n)$ is abbreviated by $\lambda\overline{x_k}.a(\overline{t_n})$. Substitutions are finite type-preserving mappings from variables to terms, denoted by $\{\overline{X_n \mapsto t_n}\}$, and extend homomorphically from terms to terms. The set of free variables of a term t is denoted by $\mathcal{FV}(t)$.

The long $\beta\eta$-normal form of a term, denoted by $t\updownarrow_\beta^\eta$, is the η-expanded form of the β-normal form of t. It is well-known that $s =_{\alpha\beta\eta} t$ if $s\updownarrow_\beta^\eta =_\alpha t\updownarrow_\beta^\eta$ [8]. Since $\beta\eta$-normal forms are always defined, we will in general assume that terms are in long $\beta\eta$-normal form and are identified modulo α-conversion. For brevity, we may write variables and constants from $\mathcal{F}$ in η-normal form, e.g., X instead of $\lambda\overline{x_k}.X(\overline{x_k})$. We assume that the transformation into long $\beta\eta$-normal form is an implicit operation, e.g., when applying a substitution to a term. With these conventions, every term t has an unique long $\beta\eta$-normal form $\lambda\overline{x_k}.a(\overline{t_n})$, where $a \in \mathcal{F}_\bot \cup \mathcal{V}$ and $a()$ coincides with a. The symbol a is called the **root** of t and is denoted by $hd(t)$. We distinguish between the set $\mathcal{T}(\mathcal{F}_\bot, \mathcal{V})$ of **partial** terms (**terms** for short), the set $\mathcal{T}(\mathcal{F}, \mathcal{V})$ of **total** terms, and the set $\mathcal{T}(\mathcal{F}_\bot, \mathcal{V})^* = \mathcal{T}(\mathcal{F}_\bot, \mathcal{V}) \setminus \{\lambda\overline{x_k}.\bot \mid k \geq 0\}$ of partially defined terms. $\mathcal{T}(\mathcal{F}_\bot, \mathcal{V})$ is a poset with respect to the **approximation ordering** $\sqsubseteq$, defined as the least partial ordering such that:

$$\lambda\overline{x_k}.\bot \sqsubseteq \lambda\overline{x_k}.t \qquad t \sqsubseteq t \qquad \frac{s_1 \sqsubseteq t_1\ \ldots\ s_n \sqsubseteq t_n}{\lambda\overline{x_k}.a(\overline{s_n}) \sqsubseteq \lambda\overline{x_k}.a(\overline{t_n})}$$

We adopt the convention that the free and bound variables inside a term are kept disjoint, and assume that bound variables with different binders have different names. We define $Dom(\gamma)=\{X\in\mathcal{FV} \mid X\gamma\neq X\}$. Two substitutions γ_1 and γ_2 are equal on a set W of variables, written as $\gamma_1 = \gamma_2\ [W]$, iff $X\gamma_1=X\gamma_2$ for all $X\in W$, and we write $\gamma_1\leq\gamma_2\ [W]$ iff there is a substitution σ with $\gamma_2 = \sigma\gamma_1\ [W]$. The restriction $\gamma\restriction_W$ of a substitution γ to a set W of variables is defined by $X\gamma\restriction_W=X\gamma$ if $X\in W$ and $X\gamma\restriction_W=X$ otherwise. To manipulate terms, we define:

- the set of positions in t: $Pos(\lambda\overline{x_k}.a(\overline{t_n})) = \{1^i \mid 0 \leq i \leq k\} \cup \{1^k.j.q \mid 1 \leq j \leq n,\ q \in Pos(t_j)\}$, where "." denotes sequence concatenation and 1^k is the sequence of 1 repeated k times. The empty sequence is denoted by ϵ. Note that, with this convention, we have $1^0 = \epsilon$.
- the subterm $t|_p$ of t at some position $p \in Pos(t)$:

$$(\lambda\overline{x_k}.a(\overline{t_n}))|_p = \begin{cases} \lambda x_{i+1}\ldots x_k.a(\overline{t_n}) & \text{if } p = 1^i \text{ with } 0 \leq i \leq k, \\ t_i|_q & \text{if } p = 1^k.i.q \text{ and } 1 \leq i \leq n. \end{cases}$$

  A position p is maximal in t if $t|_p$ is of base type. The set of maximal positions in a term t is denoted by $MPos(t)$.
- the sequence of variables abstracted on the path to position $p \in Pos(t)$:

$$seq_{bv}(t,p) = \begin{cases} \epsilon & \text{if } p = \epsilon, \\ x.seq_{bv}(s,q) & \text{if } t = \lambda x.s \text{ and } p = 1.q, \\ seq_{bv}(t_i,q) & \text{if } t = a(\overline{t_n}),\ 0 < i \leq n, \text{ and } p = i.q. \end{cases}$$

The set of variables abstracted on the path to position $p \in Pos(t)$ is $\mathcal{BV}(t,p) = \{seq_{bv}(t,p)\}$, and the set of variables with bound occurrences in t is $\mathcal{BV}(t) = \bigcup_{p \in Pos(t)} \mathcal{BV}(t,p)$. We also find it convenient to define $t\upharpoonleft_p = \lambda\overline{x_k}.(t|_p)$, where $\overline{x_k} = seq_{bv}(t,p)$.

A **pattern** [10] is a term t for which all subterms $t|_p = X(\overline{t_n})$, with $X \in \mathcal{FV}(t)$ and $p \in MPos(t)$, satisfy the condition that $t_1\downarrow_\eta, \ldots, t_n\downarrow_\eta$ is a sequence of distinct elements of $\mathcal{BV}(t,p)$. Moreover, if all such subterms of t satisfy the additional condition $\mathcal{BV}(t,p) \setminus \{t_1\downarrow_\eta, \ldots, t_n\downarrow_\eta\} = \emptyset$, then the pattern t is **fully extended**.

An **equality statement** is a multiset $\{\!\{s,t\}\!\}$, written $s == \mathtt{t}$, where $s,t \in \mathcal{T}(\mathcal{F}_\perp, \mathcal{V})$ are terms of the same type.

Definition 1. *A* **Conditional Pattern Rewrite System** *(***CPRS** *for short) is a finite set of conditional rewrite rules of the form $f(\overline{l_n}) \to r \Leftarrow C$, where*

- *$f(\overline{l_n})$ and r are total terms of the same base type,*
- *$f(\overline{l_n})$ is a fully extended linear pattern, and*
- *C is a (possibly empty) finite sequence of equality statements between total terms. In symbols, $C \equiv \overline{s_m == \mathtt{t_m}}$, with $s_i, t_i \in \mathcal{T}(\mathcal{F}, \mathcal{V})$ for $i = 1, \ldots, m$.*

The term $f(\overline{l_n})$ is called the left hand side (lhs), r is the right hand side (rhs), and C is the conditional part of the rewrite rule.

A CPRS $\mathcal{R}$ induces a partition of $\mathcal{F}$ into $\mathcal{F}_d$ (*defined symbols*) and $\mathcal{F}_c$ (*constructors*):

$$\mathcal{F}_d = \{f \in \mathcal{F} \mid \exists (f(\overline{l_n}) \to r \Leftarrow C) \in \mathcal{R}\}, \quad \mathcal{F}_c = \mathcal{F} \setminus \mathcal{F}_d.$$

$\mathcal{R}$ is a **Constructor-Based** CPRS (**CB-CPRS** for short) if each rewrite rule $f(\overline{l_n}) \to r \Leftarrow C$ satisfies the additional condition that $l_1, \ldots, l_n \in \mathcal{T}(\mathcal{F}_c, \mathcal{V})$.

Definition 2 (Lifter). *Given a term t, a subset V of $\mathcal{FV}(t)$, and a sequence $\overline{x_k}$ of distinct variables with no occurrences in t, the* $\overline{x_k}$**-lifter of** t **with respect to** V *is the term $t^{\uparrow\overline{x_k}\restriction_V}$, defined recursively as follows:*

$$t^{\uparrow\overline{x_k}\restriction_V} = \begin{cases} \lambda\overline{y_l}.(\pi^{\uparrow(\overline{y_l},\overline{x_k})\restriction_V}) & \text{if } t \equiv \lambda\overline{y_l}.\pi, \\ a\left(\overline{t_n^{\uparrow\overline{x_k}\restriction_V}}\right) & \text{if } t \equiv a(\overline{t_n}) \text{ with } a \notin V, \\ X\left(\overline{x_k}, \overline{t_n^{\uparrow\overline{x_k}\restriction_V}}\right) & \text{if } t \equiv X(\overline{t_n}) \text{ with } X \in V. \end{cases}$$

The $\overline{x_k}$**-lifter of a term** t *is the term $t^{\uparrow\overline{x_k}} = t^{\uparrow\overline{x_k}\restriction_{\mathcal{FV}(t)}}$. We also define $t^{\updownarrow\overline{x_k}} = \lambda\overline{x_k}.(t^{\uparrow\overline{x_k}})$.*

For example, $(\lambda x.Y(f(x,Z(x))))^{\uparrow y,z} = \lambda x.Y(y,z,f(x,Z(y,z,x)))$, whereas $(\lambda x.\, Y(x,Z(x)))^{\updownarrow y,z} = \lambda y,z,x.Y(y,z,x,Z(y,z,x))$. If $C = \overline{s_m == \mathtt{t_m}}$ is a sequence of equality statements then we write $C^{\updownarrow\overline{x_k}}$ for the sequence $\overline{s_m^{\updownarrow\overline{x_k}} == \mathtt{t_m^{\updownarrow\overline{x_k}}}}$.

For later use, we introduce the notation $\mathcal{R}_f$ for the subset of $\mathcal{R}$ consisting of the rewrite rules whose left-hand sides have head f.

It is well known that unification of patterns is decidable and unitary [10]. Therefore, for every $t \in \mathcal{T}(\mathcal{F}_\perp, \mathcal{V})$ and pattern π, there exists at most one matcher between t and π, which we denote by $matcher(t, \pi)$.

A position $p \in MPos(t)$ is **rigid** in t if $hd(t|_q) \in \mathcal{BV}(t, q) \cup \mathcal{F}$ for all $q \leq p$. $p \in MPos(t)$ is **safe** in t if $hd(t|_q) \in \mathcal{BV}(t, q) \cup \mathcal{F}_c$ for all $q \leq p$. t is **flex** if $hd(t) \in \mathcal{FV}(t)$, and **rigid** otherwise. We denote by $Pos_r(t)$ the set of rigid positions of t, and by $Pos_s(t)$ the set of safe positions of t.

Example 1. If $t = \lambda x, y.g(f(x(X(a, y)), \perp))$, where $f \in \mathcal{F}_d$, $a, g \in \mathcal{F}_c$, and y is a bound variable of base type, then $MPos(t) = \{1^i \mid 2 \leq i \leq 6\} \cup \{1^5.2, 1.1.2\}$, $Pos_r(t) = \{1^2, 1^3, 1^4\}$, and $Pos_s(t) = \{1.1\}$. □

2.1 Higher-Order Overlapping Definitional Trees

The following definitions generalize the higher-order definitional trees introduced in [7]. There, neither conditional rewrite rules nor overlapping left hand sides were considered. The definitions also generalize Antoy's ODTs [1] and del Vado Vírseda's ODTs [2] for the first-order case.

Definition 3. *$\mathcal{T}$ is an* **Overlapping Definitional Tree** *(***ODT** *for short) with fully extended linear pattern π iff $\mathcal{T}$ can be built in finitely many steps by using the following two construction rules:*

1. *$\mathcal{T} \equiv \underline{rule}(\pi, \{r_1 \Leftarrow C_1, \ldots, r_m \Leftarrow C_m\})$, abbreviated $\underline{rule}(\pi, \{r_i \Leftarrow C_i\}_{1 \leq i \leq m})$, where $\pi \to r_i \Leftarrow C_i$ are called the rewrite rules offered by $\mathcal{T}$.*
2. *$\mathcal{T} \equiv \underline{case}(\pi, p, \{\pi_1 : \mathcal{T}_1, \ldots, \pi_m : \mathcal{T}_m\})$, abbreviated $\underline{case}(\pi, p, \{\pi_i : \mathcal{T}_i\}_{1 \leq i \leq m})$, where $p \in MPos(\pi)$, $\pi|_p = X(\overline{y_n})$, each π_i is a term of the form $a_i(\overline{X_{q_i}})^{\uparrow \overline{y_n}}$, with $a_i \in \mathcal{F}_c \cup \{\overline{y_n}\}$ such that $a(\overline{X_{q_i}})^{\updownarrow \overline{y_n}}$ is of the same type as X, $\overline{X_{q_i}}$ is a sequence of distinct fresh variables, $a_i \neq a_j$ whenever $i \neq j$, and each $\mathcal{T}_i$ is an ODT with linear pattern $\pi\{X \mapsto a(\overline{X_{q_i}})^{\updownarrow \overline{y_n}}\}$.*

Let $\mathcal{R}[\mathcal{T}]$ be the set of all rewrite rules in $\mathcal{R}$ offered by the $\underline{rule}$-nodes of the ODT $\mathcal{T}$. A **call pattern** for an n-ary function symbol f is any fully extended linear pattern $f(\overline{t_n})$ such that $t_1, \ldots, t_n \in \mathcal{T}(\mathcal{F}_c, \mathcal{V})$. Note that, if $\mathcal{T}$ is an ODT with pattern π, then π is a call pattern for some $f \in \mathcal{F}_d$. An **ODT for** $f \in \mathcal{F}_d$ is an ODT whose pattern is a call pattern for f.

Definition 4. *A CB-CPRS $\mathcal{R}$ is a* **Conditional Overlapping Inductively Sequential System** *(***COISS** *for short) if every $f \in \mathcal{F}_d$ has an ODT $\mathcal{T}$ with pattern $f(\overline{X_n})$ such that $\mathcal{R}[\mathcal{T}] = \mathcal{R}_f$.*

Example 2. We consider the set of data constructors

$$\mathcal{F}_c = \{0 : \texttt{nat}, \quad s : \texttt{nat} \to \texttt{nat}, \quad \texttt{true}, \texttt{false} : \texttt{bool}\}$$

and the set of defined symbols

$$\mathcal{F}_d = \{f, g : \texttt{nat} \to \texttt{nat} \to \texttt{nat}, \quad \texttt{leq} : (\texttt{nat} \to \texttt{nat}) \to (\texttt{nat} \to \texttt{nat}) \to \texttt{bool}\}$$

defined by the CB-CPRS

$$\mathcal{R} = \{\ f(X,Y) \to s(0), \quad g(X,Y) \to 0,$$
$$\texttt{leq}(\lambda x.0, F) \to \texttt{true},$$
$$\texttt{leq}(\lambda x.s(F(x)), \lambda x.0) \to \texttt{false},$$
$$\texttt{leq}(\lambda x.s(F(x)), \lambda x.s(G(x))) \to \texttt{leq}(\lambda x.F(x), \lambda x.G(x))\}.$$

It is easy to check that $\mathcal{R}$ is a COISS. For example, the defined symbol leq has the ODT

$$\begin{aligned}\mathcal{T} = \underline{case}(\,&\texttt{leq}(\lambda x.X(x), \lambda x.Y(x)), 1.1, \{\\ &0 : \underline{rule}(\texttt{leq}(\lambda x.0, \lambda x.Y(x)), \{\texttt{true} \Leftarrow \{\}\}),\\ &s(F(x)) : \underline{case}(\,\texttt{leq}(\lambda x.s(F(x)), \lambda x.Y(x)), 2.1, \{\\ &\quad 0 : \underline{rule}(\texttt{leq}(\lambda x.s(F(x)), \lambda x.0), \{\texttt{false} \Leftarrow \{\}\}),\\ &\quad s(G(x)) : \underline{rule}(\,\texttt{leq}(\lambda x.s(F(x)), \lambda x.s(G(x))),\\ &\qquad \{\texttt{leq}(\lambda x.F(x), \lambda x.G(x)) \Leftarrow \{\}\})\})\})\end{aligned}$$

and $\mathcal{R}[\mathcal{T}] = \mathcal{R}_{\texttt{leq}}$. Note that the variables in the ODT have been written in long $\beta\eta$-normal form, in order to show that the ODT is built properly. □

We find it convenient to define the $\overline{x_k}$-lifter of an ODT as follows:

Definition 5. *The* **$\overline{x_k}$-lifter** $\mathcal{T}^{\uparrow \overline{x_k}}$ *of an ODT* $\mathcal{T}$ *is defined recursively as follows:*

– $\underline{rule}(\pi^{\uparrow \overline{x_k}}, \{r_i^{\uparrow \overline{x_k}} \Leftarrow C_i^{\uparrow \overline{x_k}}\}_{1 \le i \le m})$ *if* $\mathcal{T} \equiv \underline{rule}(\pi, \{r_i \Leftarrow C_i\}_{1 \le i \le m})$,
– $\underline{case}(\pi^{\uparrow \overline{x_k}}, p, \{\pi_i^{\uparrow \overline{x_k}} : \mathcal{T}_i^{\uparrow \overline{x_k}}\}_{1 \le i \le m})$ *if* $\mathcal{T} \equiv \underline{case}(\pi, p, \{\pi_i : \mathcal{T}_i\}_{1 \le i \le m})$.

The $\overline{x_k}$-lifted term $\pi^{\uparrow \overline{x_k}}$ is called the **pattern of** $\mathcal{T}^{\uparrow \overline{x_k}}$ *and is denoted by* $patt(\mathcal{T}^{\uparrow \overline{x_k}})$, *and the position p is called the* **choice position** *of* $\mathcal{T}^{\uparrow \overline{x_k}}$ *and is denoted by* $Pos(\mathcal{T}^{\uparrow \overline{x_k}})$.

We note that, if $\mathcal{T} \equiv \underline{case}(\pi^{\uparrow \overline{x_k}}, p, \{\pi_i^{\uparrow \overline{x_k}} : \mathcal{T}_i^{\uparrow \overline{x_k}}\}_{1 \le i \le m})$, then the terms $\pi^{\uparrow \overline{x_k}}|_p$, $\pi_i^{\uparrow \overline{x_k}}$ and $patt(\mathcal{T}_i^{\uparrow \overline{x_k}})|_p$ are of the same base type, and $hd(\pi_i^{\uparrow \overline{x_k}}) = hd(patt(\mathcal{T}_i^{\uparrow \overline{x_k}})|_p)$.

From now on, assume we are given a COISS $\mathcal{R}$ together with a predefined association of an ODT $\mathcal{T}_f$, with $\mathcal{R}[\mathcal{T}_f] = \mathcal{R}_f$ to every $f \in \mathcal{F}_d$. We extend the notion $\mathcal{R}[\mathcal{T}]$ to $\overline{x_k}$-lifted ODTs by defining $\mathcal{R}[\mathcal{T}^{\uparrow \overline{x_k}}] = \mathcal{R}[\mathcal{T}]$. If $\mathcal{T}_1, \mathcal{T}_2$ are $\overline{x_k}$-lifted ODTs, then we write $\mathcal{T}_1 \ll \mathcal{T}_2$ if $\mathcal{T}_1$ is a proper subtree of $\mathcal{T}_2$.

Definition 6. *Let* $t \equiv \lambda \overline{x_k}.f(\overline{s_n})$ *and* $p = 1^k.q \in MPos(t)$. *p is a* **demanded position** *of t (i.e.,* $p \in dmd(t)$*) if there exists* $\mathcal{T} \ll \mathcal{T}_f^{\uparrow \overline{x_k}}$ *with* $Pos(\mathcal{T}) = q$, *and* $\forall \mathcal{T}'.\ \mathcal{T}' \ll \mathcal{T} \wedge q' = Pos(\mathcal{T}') \Rightarrow hd(f(\overline{s_n})|_{q'}) = hd(patt(\mathcal{T})|_{q'})$.

2.2 A Higher-Order Conditional Rewriting Logic

In this section, we propose a (conditional) higher-order rewriting logic for declarative programming with non-strict and non-deterministic functions with *call time choice* semantics, as a generalization of the first-order rewriting logic CRWL [4]. We propose this logic as the basis of a proof calculus, called GHRC, for reduction and joinability statements to a common value. The GHRC proof calculus provides a declarative semantic for a COISS $\mathcal{R}$, and will be used to prove the soundness and completeness properties of our narrowing calculus with definitional trees HOLN^{DT} in Section 4. First, we need to define the suitable notion of *value* that is used in our setting.

Definition 7. *A* **value** *is a partial term t which has the following property:*

$$\forall p \in MPos(t), \forall(\pi \to r \Leftarrow C) \in \mathcal{R} : \nexists matcher(t\,|_p, \pi^{\updownarrow seq_{bv}(t,p)})^1$$

A **total value** *is a value which is a total term. A* **value substitution** *is a substitution which binds variables to values. We write $Val(\mathcal{F}_\perp, \mathcal{V})$ (resp. $Val(\mathcal{F}, \mathcal{V})$) for the set of values (resp. total values), and $VSubst(\mathcal{F}_\perp, \mathcal{V})$ for the set of substitutions which bind variables to values.*

For a given COISS $\mathcal{R}$, we want to derive statements of the following kind:

- *reduction* statements: $s \twoheadrightarrow t$, where $s, t \in \mathcal{T}(\mathcal{F}_\perp, \mathcal{V})$ are of the same type.
- *equality* statements: $s == t$, which holds iff reduction statements $s \twoheadrightarrow u$ and $t \twoheadrightarrow u$ can be derived for some total value $u \in Val(\mathcal{F}, \mathcal{V})$.

The provability relation is defined by the following proof system:

Definition 8 (GHRC proof calculus).

B *Bottom:* $\lambda\overline{x_k}.\pi \twoheadrightarrow \lambda\overline{x_k}.\perp$

MN *Monotonicity:* $\dfrac{\lambda\overline{x_k}.s_1 \twoheadrightarrow \lambda\overline{x_k}.t_1 \;\ldots\; \lambda\overline{x_k}.s_n \twoheadrightarrow \lambda\overline{x_k}.t_n}{\lambda\overline{x_k}.a(\overline{s_n}) \twoheadrightarrow \lambda\overline{x_k}.a(\overline{t_n})}$

RF *Reflexivity:* $s \twoheadrightarrow s$

OR *Outermost reduction:*

$$\frac{\lambda\overline{x_k}.s_1 \twoheadrightarrow l_1^{\updownarrow\overline{x_k}}\theta \;\ldots\; \lambda\overline{x_k}.s_n \twoheadrightarrow l_n^{\updownarrow\overline{x_k}}\theta \quad C^{\updownarrow\overline{x_k}}\theta \quad r^{\updownarrow\overline{x_k}}\theta \twoheadrightarrow u}{\lambda\overline{x_k}.f(\overline{s_n}) \twoheadrightarrow u}$$

for any $u \neq \lambda\overline{x_k}.\perp$, $\theta \in VSubst(\mathcal{F}_\perp, \mathcal{V})$, and $(f(\overline{l_n}) \to r \Leftarrow C) \in \mathcal{R}$.

J *Join:* $\dfrac{s \twoheadrightarrow u \quad t \twoheadrightarrow u}{s == \mathtt{t}}$ *if $u \in Val(\mathcal{F}, \mathcal{V})$.*

Thus, we interpret equality as joinability to a common total value. Detailed examples of derivations in the form of *proof trees* in this kind of rewriting logics can be found in [4] and [2]. We write $\mathcal{R} \vdash A$ if A is provable with GHRC for $\mathcal{R}$, and $\mathcal{R} \vdash \{\!\{A_1, \ldots, A_n\}\!\}$ if $\mathcal{R} \vdash A_i$ for $i = 1, \ldots, n$. We denote by $\mathcal{PT}(A)$ the set of proof trees for a statement A, $\mathcal{PT}_L(A)$ for the proof trees of $\mathcal{PT}(A)$ which end with the application of inference rule $L \in \{\mathbf{B}, \mathbf{MN}, \mathbf{RF}, \mathbf{OR}, \mathbf{J}\}$, and by $|\mathcal{P}|_{OR}$ the number of applications of **OR** in a proof tree $\mathcal{P}$. We also write $\mathcal{R} \vdash_L A$ if there exists a proof of $\mathcal{R} \vdash A$ which ends with application of rule L, and $\mathcal{R} \nvdash_L A$ if there is no such a proof. In the sequel, we will also consider the distinguished statement `false`, which denotes an unprovable statement.

In our study of GHRC it is relevant to tell more about the set from which we pick up the rewrite rule employed in an **OR** step. For this purpose, we assume in the sequel that Ω, Ω' range over sets of rewrite rules, and define the set $\mathcal{PT}_{OR}^{\Omega}(A)$ of proof trees $P \in \mathcal{PT}_{OR}(A)$, which employ a rewrite rule from Ω in the last proof step. We also write $\mathcal{R} \vdash_{OR}^{\Omega} A$ if there exists $P \in \mathcal{PT}_{OR}^{\Omega}(A)$, where Ω ranges over sets of rewrite rules of $\mathcal{R}$. Obviously, $\mathcal{PT}_{OR}^{\Omega'}(A) \subseteq \mathcal{PT}_{OR}^{\Omega}(A)$ whenever $\Omega' \subseteq \Omega$. We also define the set $\mathcal{PT}_J^u(s == \mathtt{t})$ of proof trees, which are of the form $\frac{\mathcal{P}_1 \; \mathcal{P}_2}{s == \mathtt{t}}(\mathrm{J})$, where $\mathcal{P}_1 \in \mathcal{PT}(s \twoheadrightarrow u)$ and $\mathcal{P}_2 \in \mathcal{PT}(t \twoheadrightarrow u)$.

In the remainder of this subsection we give two results, generalizing useful known properties of CRWL-deductions for the first-order case (see [4,2] for more

[1] Note: in this definition, we assume $\mathcal{FV}(t) \cap \mathcal{FV}(\pi) = \emptyset$.

details), which characterize the semantics proofs built with GHRC and which are relevant to our further development of a demand-driven narrowing calculus.

Lemma 1 (Approximation Property). *Let* $s \in Val(\mathcal{F}_\perp, \mathcal{V})$. *If* $\mathcal{R} \vdash s \twoheadrightarrow t$ *then* $t \in Val(\mathcal{F}_\perp, \mathcal{V})$, $s \sqsupseteq t$, *and* $\mathcal{R} \nvdash_{\mathbf{OR}} s \twoheadrightarrow t$. *Moreover, if* $t \in Val(\mathcal{F}, \mathcal{V})$ *then* $s = t$.

Lemma 2 (Splitting Property). *If* $\mathcal{P} \in \mathcal{PT}^{\Omega}_{OR}(s \twoheadrightarrow t)$ *then* $|\mathcal{P}|_{OR} > 0$ *and* $hd(s) \in \mathcal{F}_d$. *Moreover, if* $p \in dmd(s)$ *and* $\overline{x_q} = seq_{bv}(s, p)$, *then either*

(i) $hd(s|_p) = g \in \mathcal{F}_d$ *and there exist* $\lambda\overline{x_q}.\pi \in \mathcal{T}(\mathcal{F}_\perp, \mathcal{V})^*$, $\mathcal{P}_1 \in \mathcal{PT}^{\mathcal{R}_g}_{OR}(\lambda\overline{x_q}.(s|_p) \twoheadrightarrow \lambda\overline{x_q}.\pi)$ *and* $\mathcal{P}_2 \in \mathcal{PT}^{\Omega}_{OR}(s[\pi]_p \twoheadrightarrow t)$ *such that* $|\mathcal{P}_1|_{OR} + |\mathcal{P}_2|_{OR} = |\mathcal{P}|_{OR}$, *or*

(ii) $hd(s|_p) \in \mathcal{F}_c \cup \{\overline{x_q}\}$ *and* $\mathcal{P} \in \mathcal{PT}^{\Omega'}_{OR}(s \twoheadrightarrow t)$, *where* $\Omega' = \{(\pi \to r \Leftarrow C) \in \Omega \mid p \in Pos_s(\pi) \text{ and } hd(\pi|_p) = hd(s|_p)\}$.

2.3 Goals and Solutions

Finally, we give a precise definition for the class of *goals* (from a given COISS $\mathcal{R}$) and the set of *solutions* of a goal with which we are going to work.

Definition 9. *An* **atomic goal** *is one of the following:*

- **equation:** *multiset* $\{\!\{s, t\}\!\}$ *of total terms of the same type, written* $s ==^? \mathtt{t}$.
- **annotated equation:** *pair* $\langle s ==^? \mathtt{t}, \mathtt{u}\rangle$ *between an equation* $s ==^? \mathtt{t}$ *and a total fully extended linear pattern* u *of the same type as* s. *We write such an annotated equation as* $s ==^?_{\mathtt{u}} \mathtt{t}$. *Equations are symmetric:* $s ==^? \mathtt{t} \equiv \mathtt{t} ==^? \mathtt{s}$ *and* $s ==^?_{\mathtt{u}} \mathtt{t} \equiv \mathtt{t} ==^?_{\mathtt{u}} \mathtt{s}$.
- **suspension:** *pair* $\langle s, R\rangle \in Term(\mathcal{F}, \mathcal{V}) \times \mathcal{FV}$, *written* $s \rightarrowtail^? R$, *where* R *is a variable of the same type as* s.
- **production:** *ternary relation between a term* $\lambda\overline{x_k}.f(\overline{s_n})$ *with* $f \in \mathcal{F}_d$, *an* $\overline{x_k}$*-lifted ODT* $\mathcal{T}$ *for* f, *and a free variable* R *of the same type as* $\lambda\overline{x_k}.f(\overline{s_n})$, *written* $\lambda\overline{x_k}.\langle f(\overline{s_n}), \mathcal{T}\rangle \rightarrowtail^? R$.

or the distinguished symbol `fail`. *A* **goal** *is a multiset* $\{\!\{G_1, \ldots, G_n\}\!\}$ *of atomic goals* G_i.

In the sequel, we assume that w, w' denote either terms or expressions of the form $\lambda\overline{x_k}.\langle\pi, \mathcal{T}\rangle$, where $\mathcal{T}$ is an $\overline{x_k}$-lifted ODT for $hd(\pi)$. Then, $w \rightarrowtail^? R$ denotes either a suspension or a production. Similarly to other demand-driven or lazy narrowing calculi (see, e.g., [4] and [2]), we also need to define a suitable notion of *produced* and *demanded variable* to deal with a higher-order lazy evaluation.

Definition 10. R *is a* **produced variable** *in a goal* G *if* $\exists (w \rightarrowtail^? R) \in G$. H *is a* **strict variable** *in* G *if* $\exists (s ==^?_{\mathtt{u}} \mathtt{t}) \in \mathtt{G}$ *and* $H \in \mathcal{FV}(u)$. *We write* $\mathcal{PV}(G)$ *(resp.* $\mathcal{SV}(G)$*) for the set of produced variables (resp. strict variables) in* G. *The set* $\mathcal{DV}(G)$ *of* **demanded variables** *in* G *is defined inductively as follows:* $R \in \mathcal{DV}(G)$ *if* $\exists (w \rightarrowtail^? R) \in G$, *and either*

(a) $\exists\ (\lambda\overline{y_k}.\langle\pi', \underline{case}(\pi, p, \{\pi_i : \mathcal{T}_i\}_{1\le i\le m})\rangle \rightarrowtail^? R') \in G$ *with* $hd(\pi'|_p) = R$, *or*
(b) $\exists\ (s ==^?_{\mathtt{u}} \mathtt{t}) \in \mathtt{G}$ *with* $hd(s) = R$, *or*
(c) $\exists\ (\lambda\overline{y_k}.R(\overline{t_n}) \rightarrowtail^? R') \in G$ *and* $R' \in \mathcal{DV}(G)$.

The set $\mathcal{SDV}(G)$ *of* **strongly demanded variables** *is defined by strengthening condition* (b) *of* $\mathcal{DV}(G)$ *to*

(b') $\exists$ $(s ==^?_{\mathtt{u}} \mathtt{t}) \in \mathtt{G}$ *with* $hd(s) = R$ *and* $u{\downarrow_\eta} \notin \mathcal{FV}$.

Note that $\mathcal{SDV}(G) \subseteq \mathcal{DV}(G) \subseteq \mathcal{PV}(G)$. Additionally, any goal G is **admissible** if the following conditions (called *goal invariants*) hold:

1. If $(w \rightarrowtail^? R) \in G$ then R occurs only once in the rhs of a production or suspension,
2. $R \notin \mathcal{FV}(w)$ for all suspension or production of G,
3. If $(\lambda\overline{x_k}.\langle\pi', \mathcal{T}\rangle \rightarrowtail^? R) \in G$ then $R \in \mathcal{DV}(G)$, and either
   (i) $\mathcal{T} \equiv \underline{rule}(\pi, \{r_i \Leftarrow C_i\}_{1\le i\le m})$ and $\lambda\overline{x_k}.\pi$ matches $\lambda\overline{x_k}.\pi'$, or
   (ii) $\mathcal{T} \equiv \underline{case}(\pi, p, \{\pi_i : \mathcal{T}_i\}_{1\le i\le m})$ and $1^k.p \in dmd(\lambda\overline{x_k}.\pi')$,

and if $s ==^?_{\mathtt{u}} \mathtt{t} \in \mathtt{G}$ then

4. If $H \in \mathcal{FV}(u)$ then H occurs only once in G,
5. If $u{\downarrow_\eta} \notin \mathcal{FV}$ then $hd(u) \in \{hd(s), hd(t)\}$.

Definition 11. $\gamma \in Subst(\mathcal{F}_\perp, \mathcal{V})$ *is a* **solution** *of a goal* G *if* $\gamma\lceil_{\mathcal{FV}(G)\setminus\mathcal{PV}(G)} \in VSubst(\mathcal{F}_\perp, \mathcal{V})$, *and for each atomic goal* $G_i \in G$ *there exists a proof tree* $\mathcal{P}_i$ *such that*

(a) $\mathcal{P}_i \in \mathcal{PT}(s\gamma == \mathtt{t}\gamma)$ *if* $G_i \equiv s ==^? \mathtt{t}$.
(b) $\mathcal{P}_i \in \mathcal{PT}(s\gamma \twoheadrightarrow R\gamma)$ *if* $G_i \equiv s \rightarrowtail^? R$.
(c) $\mathcal{P}_i \in \mathcal{PT}^{u\gamma}_{J}(s\gamma == \mathtt{t}\gamma)$ *if* $G_i \equiv s ==^?_{\mathtt{u}} \mathtt{t}$.
(d) $\mathcal{P}_i \in \mathcal{PT}^{\mathcal{R}[\mathcal{T}]}_{OR}(\lambda\overline{x_k}.\pi\gamma \twoheadrightarrow R\gamma)$ *if* $G_i \equiv \lambda\overline{x_k}.\langle\pi, \mathcal{T}\rangle \rightarrowtail^? R$.

The proof tree $\mathcal{P}_i$ *is called a* **witness** *that* γ *is a solution of* G_i.

We write $Soln(G)$ for the set of solutions of a goal G, and $Wtn_\gamma(G_i)$ for the set of witnesses that γ is a solution of an atomic goal G_i. The next result is useful to prove properties of our demand-driven narrowing calculus and shows that GHRC semantics does not accept an undefined value for demanded variables.

Lemma 3 (Demand Lemma). *Let* $\gamma \in Soln(G)$. *Then,* $R\gamma \in \mathcal{T}(\mathcal{F}_\perp, \mathcal{V})^*$ *for all* $R \in \mathcal{SDV}(G)$.

Proof. Assume by contrary that there exists $R \in \mathcal{SDV}(G)$ with $hd(R\gamma) = \perp$. Then

1. there exists a (possibly empty) sequence of suspensions $\overline{s_q \twoheadrightarrow R_q}$ such that $R = R_0$ and $hd(s_i) = R_{i-1}$ for all $1 \le i \le q$, and
2. either (i) G contains $\lambda\overline{y_m}.\langle\pi', \underline{case}(\pi, p, \{\pi : \mathcal{T}_i\}_{1\le i\le m})\rangle \rightarrowtail^? X$ with $hd(\pi'|_p) = R_q$, or (ii) G contains a strict equation $s ==^?_{\mathtt{u}} \mathtt{t}$ with $hd(s) = R_q$ and $u = \lambda\overline{x_k}.a(\overline{H_n(\overline{x_k})})$ with $a \in \mathcal{F} \cup \{\overline{x_k}\}$.

From $\gamma \in Soln(G)$ and Lemma 1 results $hd(R_i\gamma) = \perp$ for all $i \le q$. If 2.(i) holds then $1^m.p \in dmd(\lambda\overline{y_m}.\pi'\gamma)$ and $\mathcal{R} \vdash_{OR} \lambda\overline{y_m}.\pi'\gamma \twoheadrightarrow X\gamma$. In this case, we get a contradiction with Lemma 2, because $1^m.p \in dmd(\lambda\overline{y_m}.\pi'\gamma)$ and $hd(\pi'\gamma|_p) = \perp$. If 2.(ii) holds then $\mathcal{R} \vdash s\gamma \twoheadrightarrow u\gamma$. Then, $hd(s\gamma){=}\perp$ because $hd(s){=}R_q$ and $hd(R_q\gamma){=}\perp$. Since $\perp \neq a{=}hd(u\gamma)$, we can not have $s\gamma \twoheadrightarrow u\gamma$, contradiction. □

3 A Higher-Order Demand-Driven Narrowing Calculus

HOLN^{DT} is a system of transformation rules designed to solve goals $\{\!\{s_1 ==^? \mathtt{t}_1, \ldots, s_n ==^? \mathtt{t}_n\}\!\}$, which we abbreviate by $\{\!\{\overline{s_n ==^? \mathtt{t}_n}\}\!\}$, where $s_i, t_i \in \mathcal{T}(\mathcal{F},\mathcal{V})$ for all $i \in \{1,\ldots,n\}$. It acts on *states* of the form $P \equiv \langle G \mid \mathcal{K}\rangle$, where G is a goal and $\mathcal{K}$ is a set of values. A state P is **admissible** if

(a_1) G is admissible,
(a_2) $\mathcal{K}$ is a set of total pattern terms, and
(a_3) for every $s ==^?_{\mathtt{u}} \mathtt{t} \in \mathtt{G}$ there exists a pattern $t' \in \mathcal{K}$ and a maximal position $p \in MPos(t')$ such that $t' \upharpoonright_p = u$.

We write `Adm` for the set of admissible states. The meaning of such a state is

$$[\![\langle G \mid \mathcal{K}\rangle]\!] = \{\gamma \in Soln(G) \mid \mathcal{K}\gamma \text{ is a set of values}\}.$$

We note that $[\![\langle \mathtt{fail} \mid \emptyset\rangle]\!] = [\![\langle G \mid \mathcal{K}\rangle]\!] = \emptyset$ whenever $\mathcal{K}$ is not a set of values. In the sequel, we denote the state $\langle \mathtt{fail} \mid \emptyset\rangle$ by `fail` and call it **failure state**. We identify with `fail` all pairs $\langle G \mid \mathcal{K}\rangle$ for which $\mathcal{K}$ is not a set of values. Solving a goal amounts to computing **refutations**, i.e., sequences of transformation steps.

Definition 12. *A* **HOLN^{DT}-refutation** *of a goal* $G = \{\!\{\overline{s_n ==^? \mathtt{t}_n}\}\!\}$ *is a maximal finite sequence of transformation steps*

$$\Pi : P_0 \equiv\langle G \mid \emptyset\rangle\equiv\langle G_0 \mid \mathcal{K}_0\rangle \Rightarrow_{\sigma_1} P_1\equiv\langle G_1 \mid \mathcal{K}_1\rangle \Rightarrow_{\sigma_2} \cdots \Rightarrow_{\sigma_m} P_m\equiv\langle G_m \mid \mathcal{K}_m\rangle$$

between states $P_0, P_1, \ldots, P_m$, such that $P_m \neq$ `fail` is a **final** *state, i.e., a non failure state which can not be transformed anymore. Each transformation step corresponds to an instance of some transformation rule of* HOLN^{DT}. *We abbreviate Π by $P_0 \Rightarrow^*_\sigma P_m$, where $\sigma = \sigma_1 \cdots \sigma_m$. Given such a goal G, the set of* **computed answers** *produced by* HOLN^{DT} *is*

$$\mathcal{A}(G) = \{\sigma\gamma\upharpoonright_{\mathcal{FV}(G)} \mid \langle G \mid \emptyset\rangle \Rightarrow^*_\sigma P \text{ is a HOLN}^{DT}\text{-refutation and } \gamma \in [\![P]\!]\}.$$

3.1 Design and Analysis Considerations

In the sequel, we will describe the HOLN^{DT} calculus and analyze its main properties. The general idea is to ensure the computation of solutions from goals which are correct with respect to GHRC's semantics, while using definitional trees in a similar way to [2,3] to ensure that all the narrowing steps performed during the computation are needed ones. Since the design considerations are quite involved and the analysis techniques quite complicated, we consider useful to precede our presentation with a brief outline of our design considerations and techniques.

Typical requirements in the design of such a calculus are **soundness**: every computed answer is a solution, i.e., $\mathcal{A}(G) \subseteq Soln(G)$, and **completeness**: for any $\gamma \in Soln(G)$ there exists $\gamma' \in \mathcal{A}(G)$ such that $\gamma' \leq \gamma\ [\mathcal{FV}(G)]$. Note that the completeness requirement demands the capability to compute a minimal complete set of solutions. It is easy to see that if HOLN^{DT} is complete then it suffices to enumerate minimal complete set of solutions of the final states.

Therefore, an important design issue is to guarantee that minimal complete sets of solutions are easy to read off for the final states. In the design of first-order lazy or demand-driven narrowing calculi, as for example [4] and [2], this is achieved by ensuring that final states have empty goal components; thus the minimal complete set of solutions of a final state consists of the empty substitution $\{\}$. Unfortunately, things are much more complicated in the higher-order case. This problem is inevitably related to the problem of unifying flex terms, which is in general intractable. We adopt an approach similar to Huèt's procedure of higher-order pre-unification: we refrain from solving atomic goals between flex terms as much as possible. As a consequence, our final states will be a class of states whose equations are only between flex terms. We will show that it is possible to guarantee that these final states are meaningful and that it is relatively easy to read off some of their solutions.

Of particular importance is the following additional design issue: the transformation rules of HOLN^{DT} take into account the structure of the witness trees for the solutions we aim to compute. For example, if we encounter an atomic goal $\lambda\overline{x_k}.f(\overline{s_n}) ==^?_{\mathtt{u}} \mathtt{t}$ with $f \in \mathcal{F}_d$, then we keep in mind that we are looking for a γ with a witness tree of the form $\frac{\mathcal{P}_1 \ \mathcal{P}_2}{\lambda\overline{x_k}.f(\overline{s_n})\gamma == \mathtt{t}\gamma}(\text{J})$, where $\mathcal{P}_1 \in Wtn_\gamma(\lambda\overline{x_k}.f(\overline{s_n}) \rightarrowtail^? u)$.

To ease the presentation of the goal transformation rules of HOLN^{DT}, we distinguish separately rules concerning the different components of an admissible goal: rules for (annotated) equations, rules for productions, rules for suspensions, and finally, rules for failure detection.

3.2 Transformation Rules for Equations

The goal transformation rules for (annotated) equations support an improved treatment of the strict equality $==^?$ as a built-in primitive symbol, along the lines of [4] and [2], rather than a defined function as in the case of [7]. We distinguish several cases according to the syntactic structure of their arguments.

(ann) **annotation**

$\langle\{\!\!\{s ==^? \mathtt{t}, \mathtt{E}\}\!\!\} \mid \mathcal{K}\rangle \Rightarrow \langle\{\!\!\{\mathtt{s} ==^?_{\mathtt{H}} \mathtt{t}, \mathtt{E}\}\!\!\} \mid \mathcal{K} \cup \{\mathtt{H}\}\rangle$ where H is a fresh variable of suitable type.

$(on)_1$ **rigid narrowing**

$\langle\{\!\!\{\lambda\overline{x_k}.f(\overline{s_n}) ==^?_{\mathtt{u}} \mathtt{t}, \mathtt{E}\}\!\!\} \mid \mathcal{K}\rangle \Rightarrow_{\{\}} \langle\{\!\!\{\lambda\overline{\mathtt{x_k}}.\langle \mathtt{f}(\overline{\mathtt{s_n}}), \mathcal{T}_{\mathtt{f}}^{\uparrow\overline{\mathtt{x_k}}}\rangle \rightarrowtail^? \mathtt{R}, \mathtt{R} ==^?_{\mathtt{u}} \mathtt{t}, \mathtt{E}\}\!\!\} \mid \mathcal{K}\rangle$

where $f \in \mathcal{F}_d$ and either $hd(t) \notin \mathcal{PV}$ or $u{\downarrow_\eta} \in \mathcal{FV}$.

$(ov)_1$ **flex narrowing**

$\langle\{\!\!\{\lambda\overline{x_k}.X(\overline{s_m}) ==^?_{\mathtt{u}} \mathtt{t}, \mathtt{E}\}\!\!\} \mid \mathcal{K}\rangle \Rightarrow_\sigma \langle\{\!\!\{\lambda\overline{x_k}.\langle X(\overline{s_m}), \mathcal{T}_f^{\uparrow\overline{x_k}}\rangle \rightarrowtail^? R, R ==^?_{\mathtt{u}} \mathtt{t}, \mathtt{E}\}\!\!\}\sigma \mid (\mathcal{K} \cup \{X\})\sigma\rangle$

where $u{\downarrow_\eta} \notin \mathcal{FV}$, $X \notin \mathcal{PV}$ and $\sigma = \{X \mapsto \lambda\overline{y_m}.f(\overline{X_n(\overline{y_m})})\}$ with $f \in \mathcal{F}_d$.

(sg) **strict guess**

$\langle\{\!\!\{\lambda\overline{x_k}.a(\overline{s_n}) ==^?_{\mathtt{H}} \mathtt{t}, \mathtt{E}\}\!\!\} \mid \mathcal{K}\rangle \Rightarrow_\sigma \langle\{\!\!\{\lambda\overline{\mathtt{x_k}}.\mathtt{a}(\overline{\mathtt{s_n}}) ==^?_{\mathtt{H}\sigma} \mathtt{t}, \mathtt{E} \mid \mathcal{K}\sigma\}\!\!\}\rangle$

where $a \in \mathcal{F} \cup \{\overline{x_k}\}$, and $\sigma = \{H \mapsto \lambda\overline{x_k}.a(\overline{H_n(\overline{x_k})})\}$.

(d) **decomposition**

$\langle\{\!\!\{\lambda\overline{x_k}.v(\overline{s_n}) ==^?_{\mathtt{u}} \lambda\overline{\mathtt{x_k}}.\mathtt{v}(\overline{\mathtt{t_n}}), \mathtt{E}\}\!\!\} \mid \mathcal{K}\rangle \Rightarrow_\sigma \langle\{\!\!\{\overline{\lambda\overline{\mathtt{x_k}}.\mathtt{s_n} ==^?_{\mathtt{H_n}} \lambda\overline{\mathtt{x_k}}.\mathtt{t_n}}, \mathtt{E}\}\!\!\} \mid \mathcal{K}\sigma\rangle$

where $v \in \{\overline{x_k}\} \cup \mathcal{F}$ and either

- $u \equiv H$ and $\sigma = \{H \mapsto \lambda\overline{x_k}.v(\overline{H_n(\overline{x_k})})\}$, or
- $u \equiv \lambda\overline{x_k}.v(\overline{H_n(\overline{x_k})})$ and $\sigma = \{\}$.

$(i)_1$ **imitation**

$\langle\{\!\!\{\lambda\overline{x_k}.X(\overline{s_p}) ==^?_{\mathtt{u}} \lambda\overline{\mathtt{x_k}}.\mathtt{f}(\overline{\mathtt{t_n}}), \mathtt{E}\}\!\!\} \mid \mathcal{K}\rangle \Rightarrow_\sigma \langle\{\!\!\{\overline{\lambda\overline{\mathtt{x_k}}.\mathtt{X_n}(\overline{\mathtt{s_p}}) ==^?_{\mathtt{H_n}} \lambda\overline{\mathtt{x_k}}.\mathtt{t_n}}, \mathtt{E}\}\!\!\}\sigma \mid (\mathcal{K} \cup \{\mathtt{X}\})\sigma\rangle$

where $X \notin \mathcal{PV}$ and either

- $u \equiv H$ and $\sigma = \{X \mapsto \lambda\overline{y_p}.f(\overline{X_n(\overline{y_p})}), H \mapsto \lambda\overline{x_k}.f(\overline{H_n(\overline{x_k})})\}$, or
- $u \equiv \lambda\overline{x_k}.f(\overline{H_n(\overline{x_k})})$ and $\sigma = \{X \mapsto \lambda\overline{y_p}.f(\overline{X_n(\overline{y_p})})\}$.

$(p)_1$ **projection**
$\langle \{\!\!\{ \lambda\overline{x_k}.X(\overline{s_p}) ==_{\mathtt{u}}^? \mathtt{t}, \mathtt{E} \}\!\!\} \mid \mathcal{K} \rangle \Rightarrow_\sigma \langle \{\!\!\{ \lambda\overline{\mathtt{x_k}}.\mathtt{X}(\overline{\mathtt{s_p}}) ==_{\mathtt{u}}^? \mathtt{t}, \mathtt{E} \}\!\!\} \sigma \mid (\mathcal{K} \cup \{\mathtt{X}\})\sigma \rangle$
where $X \notin \mathcal{PV}$, t is rigid, and $\sigma = \{X \mapsto \lambda\overline{y_p}.y_i(\overline{X_n(\overline{y_p})})\}$ is a valid projection binding.
(fs) **flex same**
$\langle \{\!\!\{ \lambda\overline{x_k}.X(\overline{y_p}) ==_{\mathtt{H}}^? \lambda\overline{\mathtt{x_k}}.\mathtt{X}(\overline{\mathtt{y'_p}}), \mathtt{E} \}\!\!\} \mid \mathcal{K} \rangle \Rightarrow_\sigma \langle \{\!\!\{ \mathtt{E} \}\!\!\} \sigma \mid (\mathcal{K} \cup \{\mathtt{X}\})\sigma \rangle$
where $X \notin \mathcal{PV}$, $\lambda\overline{x_k}.X(\overline{y_p})$ and $\lambda\overline{x_k}.X(\overline{y'_p})$ are patterns, $\sigma=\{X \mapsto \lambda\overline{y_p}.Z(\overline{z_q}), H \mapsto \lambda\overline{x_k}.Z(\overline{z_q})\}$, $\{\overline{z_q}\} = \{y_i \mid y_i = y'_i,\ 1 \le i \le n\}$.
(fd) **flex different**
$\langle \{\!\!\{ \lambda\overline{x_k}.X(\overline{y_p}) ==_{\mathtt{H}}^? \lambda\overline{\mathtt{x_k}}.\mathtt{Y}(\overline{\mathtt{y'_q}}), \mathtt{E} \}\!\!\} \mid \mathcal{K} \rangle \Rightarrow_\sigma \langle \{\!\!\{ \mathtt{E} \}\!\!\} \sigma \mid (\mathcal{K} \cup \{\mathtt{X}, \mathtt{Y}\})\sigma \rangle$
where $X, Y \notin \mathcal{PV}$, $\lambda\overline{x_k}.X(\overline{y_p})$ and $\lambda\overline{x_k}.Y(\overline{y'_q})$ are patterns, $X \neq Y$, $\sigma = \{X \mapsto \lambda\overline{y_p}.Z(\overline{z_r}), Y \mapsto \lambda\overline{y'_q}.Z(\overline{z_r}), H \mapsto \lambda\overline{x_k}.Z(\overline{z_r})\}$, and $\{\overline{z_r}\} = \{\overline{y_p}\} \cap \{\overline{y'_q}\}$.

3.3 Transformation Rules for Productions

The goal transformation rules for productions of the form $\lambda\overline{x_k}.\langle f(\overline{s_n}), \mathcal{T}\rangle \rightarrowtail^? R$ encode our higher-order demand-driven narrowing strategy, guided by the ODT $\mathcal{T}$ for the defined function symbol f, in a vein similar to the *needed narrowing strategy* of [7] and [2], and thanks to the *Splitting Property* given in Lemma 2.

(ev) **evaluation**
(1) $\langle \{\!\!\{ \lambda\overline{x_k}.\langle \pi', \underline{case}(\pi, p, \{\pi_i : \mathcal{T}_i\}_{1\le i\le m})\rangle \rightarrowtail^? R, E \}\!\!\} \mid \mathcal{K} \rangle \Rightarrow_{\{\}}$
$\langle \{\!\!\{ \lambda\overline{x_k}.\langle \pi', \mathcal{T}_i\rangle \rightarrowtail^? R, E \}\!\!\} \mid \mathcal{K} \rangle$ if $hd(\pi'|_p) = hd(\pi_i)$.
(2) $\langle \{\!\!\{ \lambda\overline{x_k}.\langle \pi', \underline{rule}(\pi, \{r_i \Leftarrow C_i\}_{1\le i\le m})\rangle \rightarrowtail^? R, E \}\!\!\} \mid \mathcal{K} \rangle \Rightarrow_{\{\}}$
$\langle \{\!\!\{ \overline{\lambda \overline{y_{k_q}}.s_q \rightarrowtail^? R_q}, C_i^?, \lambda\overline{x_k}.r_i \rightarrowtail^? R, E \}\!\!\} \mid \mathcal{K} \cup \{\overline{R_q}\} \rangle$
if $1 \le i \le m$, $matcher(\lambda\overline{x_k}.\pi', \lambda\overline{x_k}.\pi) = \{\overline{R_q \mapsto \lambda\overline{y_{k_q}}.s_q}\}$, and $\{\overline{R_q}\} = \mathcal{FV}(\lambda\overline{x_k}.\pi)$.
$(on)_2$ **rigid narrowing**
$\langle \{\!\!\{ \lambda\overline{x_k}.\langle \pi', \underline{case}(\pi, p, \{\pi_i : \mathcal{T}_i\}_{1\le i\le m})\rangle \rightarrowtail^? R, E \}\!\!\} \mid \mathcal{K} \rangle \Rightarrow_{\{\}}$
$\langle \{\!\!\{ \lambda\overline{x_q}.\langle \pi'|_p, \mathcal{T}_f^{\uparrow\overline{x_q}}\rangle \rightarrowtail^? R',$
$\lambda\overline{x_k}.\langle \pi'[R'(\overline{x_q})]_p, \underline{case}(\pi, p, \{\pi_i : \mathcal{T}_i\}_{1\le i\le m})\rangle \rightarrowtail^? R, E \}\!\!\} \mid \mathcal{K} \rangle$
if $\pi'|_p = f(\overline{t_n})$ with $f \in \mathcal{F}_d$, $\overline{x_q} = \mathcal{BV}(\lambda\overline{x_k}.\pi', 1^k.p)$.
$(ov)_2$ **flex narrowing**
$\langle \{\!\!\{ \lambda\overline{x_k}.\langle \pi', \underline{case}(\pi, p, \{\pi_i : \mathcal{T}_i\}_{1\le i\le m})\rangle \rightarrowtail^? R, E \}\!\!\} \mid \mathcal{K} \rangle \Rightarrow_\sigma$
$\langle \{\!\!\{ \lambda\overline{x_q}.\langle \pi'|_p, \mathcal{T}_f^{\uparrow\overline{x_q}}\rangle \rightarrowtail^? R',$
$\lambda\overline{x_k}.\langle \pi'[R'(\overline{x_q})]_p, \underline{case}(\pi, p, \{\pi_i : \mathcal{T}_i\}_{1\le i\le m})\rangle \rightarrowtail^? R, E \}\!\!\} \sigma \mid (\mathcal{K} \cup \{X\})\sigma \rangle$
if $\overline{x_q} = \mathcal{BV}(\lambda\overline{x_k}.\pi', 1^k.p)$, $hd(\pi'|_p) = X \notin \mathcal{PV}$, and $\sigma = \{X \mapsto \lambda\overline{y_r}.f(\overline{X_n(\overline{y_r})})\}$ for some $f \in \mathcal{F}_d$ of suitable type.
$(i)_2$ **imitation**
$\langle \{\!\!\{ \lambda\overline{x_k}.\langle \pi', \underline{case}(\pi, p, \{\pi_i : \mathcal{T}_i\}_{1\le i\le m})\rangle \rightarrowtail^? R, E \}\!\!\} \mid \mathcal{K} \rangle \Rightarrow_\sigma$
$\langle \{\!\!\{ \lambda\overline{x_k}.\langle \pi', \mathcal{T}_i\rangle \rightarrowtail^? R, E \}\!\!\} \sigma \mid (\mathcal{K} \cup \{X\})\sigma \rangle$
if $hd(\pi'|_p) = X \notin \mathcal{PV}$, $hd(\pi_i) = c \in \mathcal{F}_c$, and $\sigma = \{X \mapsto \lambda\overline{y_r}.c(\overline{X_n(\overline{y_r})})\}$.
$(p)_2$ **projection**
$\langle \{\!\!\{ \lambda\overline{x_k}.\langle \pi', \underline{case}(\pi, p, \{\pi_i : \mathcal{T}_i\}_{1\le i\le m})\rangle \rightarrowtail^? R, E \}\!\!\} \mid \mathcal{K} \rangle \Rightarrow_\sigma$
$\langle \{\!\!\{ \lambda\overline{x_k}.\langle \pi', \underline{case}(\pi, p, \{\pi_i : \mathcal{T}_i\}_{1\le i\le m})\rangle \rightarrowtail^? R, E \}\!\!\} \sigma \mid (\mathcal{K} \cup \{X\})\sigma \rangle$
if $hd(\pi'|_p) = X \notin \mathcal{PV}$ and $\sigma = \{X \mapsto \lambda\overline{z_r}.z_i(\overline{X_n(\overline{z_r})})\}$ is a valid projection binding for X.

3.4 Transformation Rules for Suspensions

The goal transformation rules concerning suspensions $s \rightarrowtail^? R$ are designed with the aim of modeling the behavior of lazy narrowing with *sharing*, as in other similar narrowing calculi [4,2,3], and thanks to the *Demand Lemma*.

(rm) **unnecessary suspension**
$\langle \{\!\!\{ t \rightarrowtail^? R, E \}\!\!\} \mid \mathcal{K} \rangle \Rightarrow_{\{\}} \langle \{\!\!\{ E \}\!\!\} \mid \mathcal{K} \rangle$ $(R \notin \mathcal{FV}(E))$
(rn) **rigid narrowing**
$\langle \{\!\!\{ \lambda\overline{x_k}.f(\overline{t_n}) \rightarrowtail^? R, E \}\!\!\} \mid \mathcal{K} \rangle \Rightarrow_{\{\}} \langle \{\!\!\{ \lambda\overline{x_k}.\langle f(\overline{t_n}), \mathcal{T}_f^{\uparrow\overline{x_k}}\rangle \rightarrowtail^? R, E \}\!\!\} \mid \mathcal{K} \rangle$ $(R \in \mathcal{DV})$
if $f \in \mathcal{F}_d$.

$(i)_3$ **imitation**
$\langle\{\!\{\lambda\overline{x_k}.f(\overline{s_n}) \rightarrowtail^? R, E\}\!\} \mid \mathcal{K}\rangle \Rightarrow_\sigma \langle\{\!\{\overline{\lambda\overline{x_k}.s_n \rightarrowtail^? R_n}, E\sigma\}\!\} \mid \mathcal{K}\sigma\rangle$ $(R \in \mathcal{DV})$
where $\sigma = \{R \mapsto \lambda\overline{x_k}.f(\overline{R_n(\overline{x_k})})\}$.

(rp) **rigid projection**
$\langle\{\!\{\lambda\overline{x_k}.x_i(\overline{t_n}) \rightarrowtail^? R, E\}\!\} \mid \mathcal{K}\rangle \Rightarrow_\sigma \langle\{\!\{\overline{\lambda\overline{x_k}.t_n \rightarrowtail^? R_n}, E\sigma\}\!\} \mid \mathcal{K}\sigma\rangle$ $(R \in \mathcal{DV})$
where $\sigma = \{R \mapsto \lambda\overline{x_k}.x_i(\overline{R_n(\overline{x_k})})\}$.

(fp) **flex projection**
$\langle\{\!\{\lambda\overline{x_k}.X(\overline{s_m}) \rightarrowtail^? R, E\}\!\}|\mathcal{K}\rangle \Rightarrow_\sigma \langle\{\!\{\lambda\overline{x_k}.X(\overline{s_m}) \rightarrowtail^? R, E\}\!\}\sigma|(\mathcal{K}\cup\{X\})\sigma\rangle$ $(R \in \mathcal{SDV})$
where $X \notin \mathcal{PV}$ and $\sigma = \{X \mapsto \lambda\overline{y_m}.y_i(\overline{X_n(\overline{y_m})})\}$.

(fg) **flex guess**
$\langle\{\!\{\lambda\overline{x_k}.X(\overline{s_m}) \rightarrowtail^? R, E\}\!\}|\mathcal{K}\rangle \Rightarrow_\sigma \langle\{\!\{\overline{\lambda\overline{x_k}.X(\overline{s_m}) \rightarrowtail^? R}, E\}\!\}\sigma|(\mathcal{K}\cup\{X\})\sigma\rangle$ $(R \in \mathcal{SDV})$
where $X \notin \mathcal{PV}$ and $\sigma = \{X \mapsto \lambda\overline{y_m}.g(\overline{X_n(\overline{y_m})}), R \mapsto \lambda\overline{x_k}.g(\overline{R_n(\overline{x_k})})\}$ with $g \in \mathcal{F}$.

3.5 Transformation Rules for Failure Detection

Failure rules are used for failure detection in the syntactic unification of annotated equations and in the case of symbol non-cover by an ODT in productions.

(f_1) **clash 1**
$\langle\{\!\{\lambda\overline{x_k}.v(\overline{s_n}) ==^?_{\mathtt{u}} \lambda\overline{\mathtt{x_k}}.\mathtt{v}'(\overline{\mathtt{t_m}}), \mathtt{E}\}\!\} \mid \mathcal{K}\rangle \Rightarrow_{\{\}} \mathtt{fail}$
if $v, v' \in \mathcal{F}_c \cup \{\overline{x_k}\}$ and either (i) $v \neq v'$ or (ii) $hd(u) \notin \mathcal{FV} \cup \{v, v'\}$.

(f_2) **clash 2**
$\langle\{\!\{\lambda\overline{x_k}.\langle\pi', \underline{case}(\pi, p, \{\pi_i : \mathcal{T}_i\}_{1\leq i\leq m})\rangle \rightarrowtail^? R, E\}\!\} \mid \mathcal{K}\rangle \Rightarrow_{\{\}} \mathtt{fail}$
if $hd(\pi'|_p) \notin \{hd(\pi_i) \mid 1 \leq i \leq m\} \cup \mathcal{F}_d \cup \mathcal{FV}$.

(f_3) **occur check**
$\langle\{\!\{\lambda\overline{x_k}.s ==^?_{\mathtt{u}} \lambda\overline{\mathtt{x_k}}.\mathtt{X}(\overline{\mathtt{y_n}}), \mathtt{E}\}\!\} \mid \mathcal{K}\rangle \Rightarrow_{\{\}} \mathtt{fail}$
if $X \notin \mathcal{PV}$, $\lambda\overline{x_k}.X(\overline{y_n})$ is a flex pattern, $hd(\lambda\overline{x_k}.s) \neq X$ and $(\lambda\overline{x_k}.s)|_p = X(\overline{z_n})$, where $\overline{z_n}$ is a sequence of distinct bound variables and $p \in Pos_s(\lambda\overline{x_k}.s)$.

Example 3. The classical higher-order function $foldr$ can be defined as

$$\begin{aligned} foldr(g, e, [\,]) &\to e \\ foldr(g, e, [x|xs]) &\to g(x, foldr(g, e, xs)) \end{aligned}$$

where the following result holds: if $f(e) = e'$ and $f(g(x, y)) = g'(x, f(y))$ then $f(foldr(g,\ e, xs)) = foldr(g', e', xs)$. Moreover, the following corollary can be easily obtained: if $f([\,]) = e'$ and $f([x|xs]) = g'(x,\ f(xs))$ then $f(xs) = foldr(g',$ $e', xs)$. As application, we can use HOLN^{DT} over the particular function $f \to \lambda xs.$ $pair(sum(xs), length(xs))$, where $pair$ is a data constructor, and

$$\begin{array}{lll} sum([\,]) \to 0 & length([\,]) \to 0 & fst(pair(x, y)) \to x \\ sum([x|xs]) \to x{+}sum(xs) & lenght([x|xs]) \to 1{+}length(xs) & snd(pair(x, y)) \to y \end{array}$$

to compute E' and G' s.t. $f([\,]) == E'$ and $\lambda x, xs.f([x|xs]) == \lambda x, xs.G'(x,$ $f(xs))$. We obtain the solutions $\{E' \mapsto pair(0, 0)\}$ and $\{G' \mapsto \lambda u, z.pair(u +$ $fst(z), 1 + snd(z))\}$. For example, we have the following HOLN^{DT}-refutation corresponding to $\{E' \mapsto pair(0, 0)\} \in \mathcal{A}(\{\!\{f([\,]) ==^? E'\}\!\})$:

$\langle\{\!\{f([\,]) ==^? \mathtt{E}'\}\!\} \mid \emptyset\rangle \Rightarrow (ann)$
$\langle\{\!\{f([\,]) ==^?_{\mathtt{H}} \mathtt{E}'\}\!\} \mid \{\mathtt{H}\}\rangle \Rightarrow_{\{\}} (on)_1$
$\langle\{\!\{\lambda xs.\langle f([\,]), \mathcal{T}_f\rangle \rightarrowtail^? R, R ==^?_{\mathtt{H}} \mathtt{E}'\}\!\} \mid \{\mathtt{H}\}\rangle \Rightarrow_{\{\}} (ev)(2)$
$\langle\{\!\{pair(sum([\,]), length([\,])) \rightarrowtail^? R, R ==^?_{\mathtt{H}} \mathtt{E}'\}\!\} \mid \{\mathtt{H}\}\rangle \Rightarrow_{\{R \mapsto pair(R_1, R_2)\}} (i)_3$
$\langle\{\!\{sum([\,]) \rightarrowtail^? R_1, length([\,]) \rightarrowtail^? R_2, pair(R_1, R_2) ==^?_{\mathtt{H}} \mathtt{E}'\}\!\} \mid \{\mathtt{H}\}\rangle \Rightarrow^2_{\{\}} (rn)$
$\langle\{\!\{\lambda x, xs.\langle sum([\,]), \mathcal{T}_{sum}\rangle \rightarrowtail^? R_1, \lambda x, xs.\langle length([\,]), \mathcal{T}_{length}\rangle \rightarrowtail^? R_2,$
$pair(R_1, R_2) ==^?_{\mathtt{H}} \mathtt{E}'\}\!\} \mid \{\mathtt{H}\}\rangle \Rightarrow^2_{\{\}} (ev)(1)$

$$\langle \{\!\{ \langle sum([\,]), \mathcal{T}_{sum([\,])} \rangle \rightarrowtail^{?} R_1, \langle length([\,]), \mathcal{T}_{length([\,])} \rangle \rightarrowtail^{?} R_2,$$
$$pair(R_1, R_2) ==^{?}_{\mathtt{H}} \mathtt{E}' \}\!\} \mid \{\mathtt{H}\} \rangle \Rightarrow^{2}_{\{\}} (ev)(2)$$
$$\langle \{\!\{ 0 \rightarrowtail^{?} R_1, 0 \rightarrowtail^{?} R_2, pair(R_1, R_2) ==^{?}_{\mathtt{H}} \mathtt{E}' \}\!\} \mid \{\mathtt{H}\} \rangle \Rightarrow^{2}_{\{R_1 \mapsto 0, R_2 \mapsto 0\}} (i)_3$$
$$\langle \{\!\{ pair(0,0) ==^{?}_{\mathtt{H}} \mathtt{E}' \}\!\} \mid \{\mathtt{H}\} \rangle \Rightarrow_{\{E' \mapsto pair(X,Y), H \mapsto pair(H_1,H_2)\}} (i)_1$$
$$\langle \{\!\{ X ==^{?}_{\mathtt{H_1}} \mathtt{0}, \mathtt{Y} ==^{?}_{\mathtt{H_2}} \mathtt{0} \}\!\} \mid \{\mathtt{pair(H_1,H_2)}, \mathtt{pair(X,Y)}\} \rangle \Rightarrow^{2}_{\{X \mapsto 0, Y \mapsto 0, H_1 \mapsto 0, H_2 \mapsto 0\}} (i)_1$$
$$\langle \{\!\{ \}\!\} \mid \{pair(0,0), pair(0,0), 0, 0\} \rangle.$$
□

4 Main Properties

The main properties of the calculus relate the solutions of a goal to the answers computed by HOLN^{DT}. First, we analyze how much local information about $Soln(G)$ is carried by $\mathcal{A}(G)$ to prove correctness of a single HOLN^{DT}-step.

Lemma 4 (Local Soundness). *If $P \in \mathtt{Adm}$ and $P \Rightarrow_\sigma P'$ is a HOLN^{DT}-step then $P' \in \mathtt{Adm}$ and $\{\sigma\gamma \mid \gamma \in [\![P']\!]\} \subseteq [\![P]\!]$. Moreover, if $P \in \mathtt{Adm}$ satisfies the preconditions of a transformation rule for failure detection, then $[\![P]\!] = \emptyset$.*

This property corresponds to "narrowing" the set of possible computed answers by each transformation step. Now, the *soundness* is quite easy to achieve from Lemma 4: we must check that each inference step in a derivation is locally sound.

Theorem 1 (Soundness). *Let $\Pi : \langle G \mid \emptyset \rangle \Rightarrow^{*}_{\sigma} P'$ be a HOLN^{DT}-derivation. Then, $\sigma\gamma \in Soln(G)$ whenever $\gamma \in [\![P']\!]$.*

Proof. Let $\gamma \in [\![P']\!]$. We prove by induction on the length of Π that $\sigma\gamma \in Soln(G)$. If $|\Pi| = 0$ then $\sigma = \{\}$ and $\sigma\gamma = \gamma \in [\![P']\!] = [\![\langle G \mid \emptyset \rangle]\!] = Soln(G)$. If $|\Pi| > 0$ then we can write $\Pi : \langle G \mid \emptyset \rangle \Rightarrow^{*}_{\sigma_1} P_1 \Rightarrow_{\sigma_2} P'$. By Lemma 4, we know that $\sigma_2\gamma \in [\![P_1]\!]$. We can now apply the IH to the shorter derivation $\langle G \mid \emptyset \rangle \Rightarrow^{*}_{\sigma_1} P$ and learn that $\sigma\gamma = \sigma_1\sigma_2\gamma \in [\![\langle G \mid \emptyset \rangle]\!] = Soln(G)$. □

Completeness is much more difficult to ensure: we must verify that *any* solution γ of a given goal G will be eventually *approximated*, i.e., that we will eventually reach a representation $S_{fin} = \langle G' \mid \mathcal{K}' \rangle$ of a computed answer γ' such that $\gamma' \leq \gamma\ [\mathcal{FV}(G)]$. This approximation process must take into account all the possible shapes of elementary goals, and make sure that *progress* can be made towards reaching S_{fin}. We achieve this by looking at the syntactic structures of atomic goals, the solution γ which we want to approximate, and the witness tree that γ is a solution of the given goal, and show how these grouped structures or triples (called *configurations* of a set of admissible configurations `Cfg`) can be looked up for computing a representation S_{fin} of an approximation of γ by means of a *well-founded ordering* $\succ$ over `Cfg`.

Lemma 5 (Progress). *There exists a poset $(\mathtt{Cfg}, \succ)$ with $\succ$ well-founded, and a surjection $\Im : \mathtt{Cfg} \rightarrow \mathtt{Adm}$, such that, if $P = \langle G \mid \mathcal{K} \rangle \in \mathtt{Adm}$ is a non-final state, W is a finite set of variables, and $\gamma \in [\![P]\!]$ with $Dom(\gamma) \subseteq \mathcal{V}$, then there exist $P' = \langle G' \mid \mathcal{K}' \rangle \in \mathtt{Adm}$, $\gamma' \in [\![P']\!]$, and a HOLN^{DT}-step $P \Rightarrow_\sigma P'$, with $\Im(P) \succ \Im(P')$ and $\gamma = \sigma\gamma'\ [W]$.*

We are ready now to state our completeness result by application of Lemma 5.

Theorem 2 (Strong Completeness). *Let* $G = \{\!\!\{\overline{s_n ==^? \mathtt{t_n}}\}\!\!\}$. *Then,* $\mathcal{A}(G) = \{\gamma\lceil_{\mathcal{FV}(G)} \mid \gamma \in Soln(G)\}$.

Proof. Since $\mathcal{A}(G) \subseteq Soln(G)$ by soundness (Theorem 1), we must only show that $Soln(G) \subseteq \mathcal{A}(G)$. Let $\gamma \in Soln(G)$, $P = \langle G \mid \emptyset \rangle$, and $W_0 = \mathcal{FV}(G) \cup Dom(\gamma)$. First, we prove that, for every given admissible state P, any finite set of variables W, and $\gamma \in [\![P]\!]$, there exists a HOLN^{DT}-refutation $\Phi : P \Rightarrow^*_\sigma P'$ such that $\gamma = \sigma\gamma'\ [W]$ for some $\gamma' \in [\![P']\!]$. The proof is by induction with respect to the well-founded ordering $\succ$ introduced in Lemma 5.

If P is final then we can choose $\Phi : P \Rightarrow^0_{\{\}} P$ and $\gamma' = \gamma$. Otherwise, we can apply Lemma 5 to determine $P_1 = \langle G_1 \mid \mathcal{K}_1 \rangle$, $\gamma_1 \in [\![P_1]\!]$, and a HOLN^{DT}-step $\varphi : P \Rightarrow_{\sigma_1} P_1$ with $\Im(P) \succ \Im(P_1)$ and $\gamma = \sigma_1\gamma_1\ [W]$. Let $W' = W \cup \mathcal{FV}(\{X\sigma_1 \mid X \in W\})$. By IH for $\Im(P_1)$, there exists a HOLN^{DT}-refutation $\Phi' : P_1 \Rightarrow^*_{\sigma'} P'$ such that $\gamma_1 = \sigma'\gamma'\lceil_{W'}$ for some $\gamma' \in [\![P']\!]$. Let $\sigma = \sigma_1\sigma'$ and Φ the HOLN^{DT}-refutation obtained by prepending φ to Φ'. Then, $\Phi : P \Rightarrow^*_\sigma P'$ and $\sigma\gamma'$ is a computed answer. Also, $\gamma\lceil_W = \sigma_1\gamma_1\lceil_W = \sigma_1\sigma'\gamma'\lceil_W = \sigma\gamma'\lceil_W$, and this concludes our preliminary proof. In particular, if $\gamma \in Soln(G)$ then $\gamma \in [\![P]\!]$ where $P = \langle G \mid \emptyset \rangle$. According to our preliminary result, there exists a HOLN^{DT}-refutation $\Phi : P \Rightarrow^*_\sigma P'$ such that $\gamma = \sigma\gamma'\ [\mathcal{FV}(G)]$ for some $\gamma' \in [\![P']\!]$. Thus, $\sigma\gamma'\lceil_{\mathcal{FV}(G)} \in \mathcal{A}(G)$, $\sigma\gamma'\lceil_{\mathcal{FV}(G)} = \gamma\lceil_{\mathcal{FV}(G)}$, and $\gamma \in \mathcal{A}(G)$. □

Our proof reveals that HOLN^{DT} is *strongly complete*, i.e., completeness does not depend on the choice of the selectable atomic goal in the current state.

5 Conclusion and Future Work

We have presented a generalization of the first-order Constructor-based ReWriting Logic CRWL [4] to the more expressive setting of the simply typed λ-calculus, in order to define a higher-order demand-driven narrowing calculus HOLN^{DT} for higher-order functional-logic programming. We have proved that HOLN^{DT} conserves the good properties of the needed narrowing strategy [7], while being sound and strongly complete w.r.t. our higher-order conditional rewriting logic. Higher-order overlapping definitional trees are used to efficiently control the narrowing strategy for answering joinability and reducibility queries, extending and generalizing the first-order case [2], which guarantee the usefulness of HOLN^{DT}.

Because of these results, we plan to implement the HOLN^{DT} calculus in *Mathematica* [6], a good framework for working with rewrite systems and narrowing. We hope that the implemented calculus serves as a functional-logic programming languages interpreter, allowing researchers in this field write higher-order functional-logic programs combined with powerful *Mathematica* rewrite rules.

References

1. Antoy, S.: Optimal non-deterministic functional logic computations. In: Hanus, M., Heering, J., Meinke, K. (eds.) ALP 1997 and HOA 1997. LNCS, vol. 1298, pp. 16–30. Springer, Heidelberg (1997)

2. del Vado Vírseda, R.: A demand-driven narrowing calculus with overlapping definitional trees. In: PPDP, pp. 253–263 (2003)
3. del Vado Vírseda, R.: Declarative constraint programming with definitional trees. In: FroCos, pp. 184–199 (2005)
4. González-Moreno, J.C., Hortalá-González, M.T., López-Fraguas, F.J., Rodríguez-Artalejo, M.: An approach to declarative programming based on a rewriting logic. J. Log. Program. 40(1), 47–87 (1999)
5. González-Moreno, J.C., Hortalá-González, M.T., Rodríguez-Artalejo, M.: A higher order rewriting logic for functional logic programming. In: ICLP, pp. 153–167 (1997)
6. Hamada, M., Ida, T.: Implementation of lazy narrowing calculi in mathematica. Technical report, RISC, Johannes Kepler University, Austria (1997)
7. Hanus, M., Prehofer, C.: Higher-order narrowing with definitional trees. J. Funct. Program. 9(1), 33–75 (1999)
8. Hindley, J.R., Seldin, J.P.: Introduction to Combinatorics and λ-Calculus. Cambridge University Press, Cambridge (1986)
9. Ida, T., Marin, M., Suzuki, T.: Higher-order lazy narrowing calculus: A solver for higher-order equations. In: Moreno-Díaz Jr., R., Buchberger, B., Freire, J.-L. (eds.) EUROCAST 2001. LNCS, vol. 2178, pp. 479–493. Springer, Heidelberg (2001)
10. Miller, D.: A logic programming language with lambda-abstraction, function variables, and simple unification. J. Log. Comput. 1(4), 497–536 (1991)

Distributed Time-Asynchronous Automata

Cătălin Dima[1] and Ruggero Lanotte[2]

[1] LACL, Université Paris 12, 61 av. du Général de Gaulle, 94010 Créteil Cedex, France
[2] Università dell'Insubria, Via Valleggio 11, 22100, Como, Italy

Abstract. We show that the class of distributed time-asynchronous automata is more expressive than timed automata, has a decidable emptiness problem, is closed under union, concatenation, star, shuffle and renaming, but not under intersection. The closure results are obtained by showing that distributed time-asynchronous automata are equivalent with a subclass of shuffle regular expressions and its related class of stopwatch automata.

1 Introduction

The theory of timed systems has reached a certain level of sofistication, proved by the various results in decidability for automata with dense timing [2,9,11], logical characterizations [8], regular expressions [4,7], monoidal characterizations [5]. However, as E. Asarin has noted in [3], the picture is still not that "nice" in the timed setting as it is in the untimed setting, and [3] states a number of challenges for enriching this picture, among which the first challenge is "to complete [...] a theory of timed systems and timed languages". The study of new classes of automata that have different expressive power than existing ones, though being decidable, can be a means to complete the timed languages picture.

We investigate here the class of *distributed time-asynchronous automata*, which are tuples of timed automata synchronized on input symbols and whose time-passage transitions are asynchronous (i.e. time is local to each automaton). Each automaton owns a set of clocks which only the owner can reset, but everyone may check the value of everyone's clocks. Synchronizations take place by jointly accepting an input symbol while testing global clock constraints (but note that we do not consider here distributed alphabets, in the sense of [13]). As we show, this class of automata has a decidable emptiness problem and are strictly more expressive than timed automata and incomparable with the rectangular automata of [9]. They are inspired from [10], being an intermediary step between the distributed timed automata and the interleaved timed automata of [10].

We investigate here the closure properties of this class, by comparing it with the class of *timed shuffle expressions*, which were suggested in [3] and studied in [7], where they were showed to be equivalent with stopwatch automata. Shuffle and stopwatches, as noted in [7], model preemptive scheduling, and their study would help understanding the benefits of using automata theory in solving scheduling problems [1].

C.B. Jones, Z. Liu, J. Woodcock (Eds.): ICTAC 2007, LNCS 4711, pp. 185–200, 2007.

Clearly, distributed time-asynchronous automata are strictly less expressive than stopwatch automata and timed shuffle expressions. However we may provide a subclass of shuffle expressions, called here *fair shuffle expressions* that are equivalent with distributed time-asynchronous automata. Fair shuffle expressions are only allowed to intersect with untimed regular expressions. This amounts to the fact that distributed timed automata are closed under union, concatenation, star, shuffle and renaming, but not under intersection. The equivalence result is proved by showing that our automata are equivalent with a subclass of stopwatch automata [9], called here *partitioned stopwatch automata* in which the set of stopwatches is partitioned into disjoint classes. Then, at each location, stopwatches in only one class are allowed to be active. The interesting fact about this equivalence is that global clock constraints suffice for simulating the centralized control in a partitioned stopwatch automaton – there is no need to be able to reset, in a component of a distributed time-asynchronous automaton, some clocks that are not owned by that component.

Finally, the result on nonclosure under intersection is proved by reducing the problem to checking that, when considering only *private clocksets*, that is, clock constraints in component i only refer to clocks owned by component i, then a certain language accepted by a (general) stopwatch automaton cannot be accepted by a distributed time-asynchronous automaton *modulo renaming*.

The paper goes on as follows: in the next section we introduce our class of distributed time-asynchronous automata and recall the definition of stopwatch automata. In the third section, we recall the timed shuffle expressions and introduce the fair shuffle expressions, then show the equivalence between distributed time-asynchronous automata, partitioned stopwatch automata and fair shuffle expressions. The fourth section shows the nonclosure under intersection of distributed time-asynchronous automata. We end with a section of conclusions.

2 Basic Notions

A *timed word*, also called *timed event sequence*, is a finite sequence of nonnegative numbers and symbols from Σ. For example, the sequence $1.2\,a\,1.3\,b$ denotes a behavior in which an *action* a occurs 1.2 time units after the beginning of the observation, and after another 1.3 time units action b occurs. The length $\ell(w)$ of a timed word w is the sum of all the reals in it, e.g. $\ell(1.2\,a\,1.3\,b) = 1.2+1.3 = 2.5$. *Timed (event) languages* are then sets of timed words.

Several operations on timed words will be used in this paper. The first is concatenation, which extends the classic concatenation of untimed words by considering that concatenation of two reals amounts to summation of the reals. Hence, $a\,1.3{\cdot}1.7\,b\,c\,0.4 = a(1.3+1.7)b = a\,3\,b\,c\,0.4$. The second operation on timed words is *shuffle*, which is formally defined as follows: for each $w_1, w_2 \in \mathsf{TW}(\Sigma)$, $w_1 \sqcup\!\sqcup w_2 = \{u_1v_1 \ldots u_nv_n \mid w_1 = u_1 \ldots u_n, w_2 = v_1 \ldots v_n\}$.

Concatenation and shuffle can be straightforwardly extended to languages, so, given $L_1, L_2 \subseteq \mathsf{TW}(\Sigma)$, we will denote $L_1 \cdot L_2 = \{w_1 \cdot w_2 \mid w_1 \in L_1, w_2 \in L_2\}$ and $L_1 \sqcup\!\sqcup L_2 = \bigcup \{w_1 \sqcup\!\sqcup w_2 \mid w_1 \in L_1, w_2 \in L_2\}$.

Another useful operation on timed languages is *renaming*: it replaces syntactically symbols with other symbols, while keeping durations the same. The renaming of $a \in \Sigma$ with $b \in \Sigma$ is denoted $[a/b]$. We also use *deletion*, which removes a symbol from a timed word, and consider it as a special case of renaming. The deletion of a symbol $a \in \Sigma$ is denoted $[a/\varepsilon]$. For example, $[a/c, b/\varepsilon](1.3\,a\,1.2\,b\,0.1\,a) = 1.3\,c\,1.3\,c$.

All our automata use nonnegative real-valued variables that are called *clocks* when used in timed automata, resp. *stopwatches* when used in stopwatch automata. The values of such variables may inhibit or allow taking some transition. Formally, transitions are enabled by *clock constraints* which are positive boolean combinations of elementary constraints of the type $x \in I$, with x being a (clock or stopwatch) variable and $I \subseteq \mathbb{R}_{\geq 0}$ an interval with bounds in $\mathbb{Z} \cup \{\infty\}$. The set of constraints with variables in a given set X is denoted $\mathsf{Constr}(X)$.

Given $v : X \to \mathbb{R}_{\geq 0}$ and $C \in \mathsf{Constr}(X)$, we denote as usual $v \models C$ if C holds when all occurrences of each $x \in X$ are replaced with $v(x)$. We also denote $v + t$ the valuation $(v + t) : X \to \mathbb{R}_{\geq 0}$ defined by $(v + t)(x) = v(x) + t$ for all $x \in X$. Further, for $Y \subseteq X$, we denote $v\big|_Y$ the valuation $v\big|_Y : Y \to \mathbb{R}_{\geq 0}$ defined by $v\big|_Y(x) = v(x)$ for all $x \in Y$.

A final notion to be employed is *clock* (or *stopwatch*) *reset*: given a valuation $v : X \to \mathbb{R}_{\geq 0}$ and a subset $Y \subseteq X$, we denote $v[Y := 0]$ the clock valuation defined by $v[Y := 0](x) = 0$ when $x \in Y$ and $v[Y := 0](x) = v(x)$ when $x \notin Y$.

2.1 Distributed Timed Automata

Definition 1. *A* ***distributed time-asynchronous automaton*** *is a tuple* $\mathcal{A} = (Q_1, \ldots, Q_n, \Sigma, X_1, \ldots, X_n, \delta_1, \ldots, \delta_n, q_1^0, \ldots, q_n^0, F_1, \ldots F_n)$ *where* Σ *is a finite set of* symbols, $X_1, \ldots, X_n$ *are* n *finite, pairwise-disjoint sets of* clocks, $Q_1, \ldots, Q_n$ *are* n *finite sets of* locations, $q_i^0 \in Q_i$ *are* initial locations, $F_i \subseteq Q_i$ *are subsets of* final *locations, and* $\delta_1, \ldots, \delta_n$ *are* transition relations, *with* $\delta_i \subseteq \{q \xrightarrow{C,a,Y} r \mid q, r \in Q_i, a \in \Sigma \cup \{\varepsilon\}, C \in \mathsf{Constr}(X), Y \subseteq X_i\}$.

A ***timed automaton*** *is a distributed time-asynchronous automaton with only one component.*

A ***distributed time-asynchronous automaton with private clocksets*** *is a distributed time-asynchronous automaton in which each component can test only clocks in* X_i*, i.e., for all* $1 \leq i \leq n$*, if* $q \xrightarrow{C,a,Y} q' \in \delta_i$ *then* $C \in \mathsf{Constr}(X_i)$.

We denote in the sequel $X = \bigcup_{1 \leq i \leq n} X_i$.

Intuitively, an distributed time-asynchronous automaton can make time-passage transitions in which clocks in different components evolve independently, and discrete transitions in which components may synchronize. Synchronizations take place by jointly accepting an input symbol while testing global clock constraints, and then reseting some clocks. This amounts to the fact that each component can see the value of every clock.

Formally, the semantics of a distributed time-asynchronous automaton is given as a *timed transition system* $\mathcal{T}(\mathcal{A}) = (\mathcal{Q}, \theta, \mathcal{Q}_0, \mathcal{Q}_f)$ where $\mathcal{Q} = Q_1 \times \ldots \times Q_n \times$

$\mathbb{R}^n_{\geq 0}$ represents the set of system states, $\mathcal{Q}_0 = \{(q_0^1, \ldots, q_0^n)\} \times \{\mathbf{0}_n\}$ is the initial state, $\mathcal{F} = F_1 \times \ldots \times F_n \times \mathbb{R}^n_{\geq 0}$ are the final states, while θ is the set of transitions:

$$\begin{aligned}\theta =& \big\{(q_1, \ldots, q_n, v) \xrightarrow{t} (q_1, \ldots, q_n, v') \mid \forall 1 \leq i \leq n, q_i \in Q_i \text{ and} \\ & \quad \exists t_i \in \mathbb{R}_{\geq 0} \text{ with } v'\big|_{X_i} = v\big|_{X_i} + t_i \text{ and } t = t_1 + \ldots + t_n\big\} \\ \cup& \big\{(q_1, \ldots, q_n, v) \xrightarrow{a} (q_1', \ldots, q_n', v') \mid \forall 1 \leq i \leq n \; \exists C_i \in \mathsf{Constr}(X) \text{ with } v \models C_i \\ & \quad \text{and } \exists Y_i \subseteq X_i \text{ with } q_i \xrightarrow{C_i, a, Y_i} q_i' \in \delta_i \text{ and } v' = v[Y_1 \cup \ldots \cup Y_n := 0]\big\} \\ \cup& \big\{(q_1, \ldots, q_n, v) \xrightarrow{\varepsilon} (q_1', \ldots, q_n', v') \mid \exists 1 \leq i \leq n \; \exists C_i \in \mathsf{Constr}(X), \text{ with } v \models C_i \\ & \quad \text{and } \exists Y_i \subseteq X_i \text{ with } q_i \xrightarrow{C_i, \varepsilon, Y_i} q_i' \in \delta_i, v' = v[Y_i := 0] \text{ and } \forall j \neq i, q_j' = q_j\big\}\end{aligned}$$

Informally, distributed time-asynchronous automata can make time passage transitions or discrete transitions. In time passage transitions, all components evolve independently one of the other, the local times being incremented independently, which will increment the global time with the sum of local increments. Discrete transitions are of two types: synchronizing transitions and asynchronous, silent transitions. In synchronizing transitions, each component checks the validity of a clock constraint and, upon validity, all agree on the same symbol $a \in \Sigma$ and reset some clocks while changing location. Only clocks "owned by" component i (i.e. $x \in X_i$) can be reset by component i, but any component may read clocks not owned by it. Finally, in silent transitions, a specified component checks for the validity of a clock constraint, then resets some clocks it owns and changes location "silently", i.e. on an ε-transition.

A *trajectory* in $\mathcal{A}$ is a sequence of transitions in θ, $\tau = \big((q_1^{j-1}, \ldots, q_n^{j-1}, v_{j-1}) \xrightarrow{\xi_j} (q_1^j, \ldots, q_n^j, v_j)\big)_{1 \leq j \leq m}$, where $\xi_j \in \Sigma \cup \{\epsilon\} \cup \mathbb{R}_{\geq 0}$ for all $1 \leq j \leq m$. Note that each trajectory starts in the initial state of $\mathcal{T}(\mathcal{A})$. The trajectory τ is *accepting* if it ends in $\mathcal{Q}_f$ and *does not end with a time passage transition.* The *timed word accepted by* τ is $\mathsf{acc}(\tau) = \xi_1 \ldots, \xi_m$. The *timed language accepted by* $\mathcal{A}$ is $L(\mathcal{A}) = \{acc(r) \mid r \text{ is accepted by } A\}$. An example of a distributed time-asynchronous automaton is given in Figure 1 below. Note that this language is not timed regular, that is, cannot be accepted by a timed automaton – see [7].

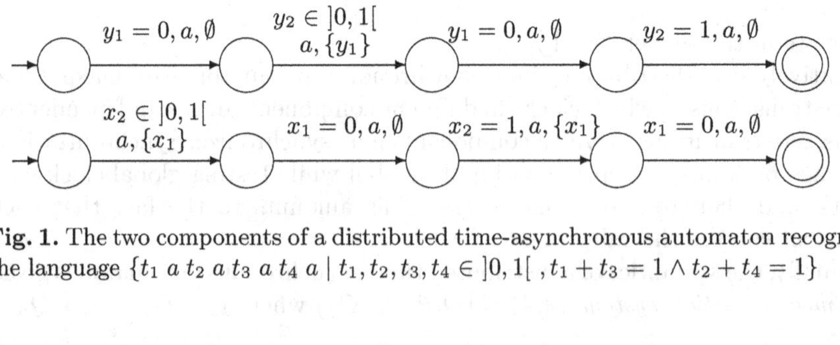

Fig. 1. The two components of a distributed time-asynchronous automaton recognizing the language $\{t_1 \; a \; t_2 \; a \; t_3 \; a \; t_4 \; a \mid t_1, t_2, t_3, t_4 \in]0, 1[\; , t_1 + t_3 = 1 \wedge t_2 + t_4 = 1\}$

2.2 Stopwatch Automata

Definition 2. *A* ***stopwatch automaton*** *is a tuple* $\mathcal{A} = (Q, \Sigma, X, \gamma, \delta, q_0, F)$ *where* Q *is a finite set of* locations, Σ *is a finite set of symbols and* X *is a finite set of* stopwatches, $\gamma : Q \to \mathcal{P}(X)$ *is a mapping assigning to each location the set of stopwatches that are* active *in that location,* $q_0 \in Q$ *is the* initial location, $F \subseteq Q$ *the set of* final locations, *and* δ *is a finite set of* transitions *with*

$$\delta \subseteq \{q \xrightarrow{C,a,Y} r \mid q, r \in Q, a \in \Sigma \cup \{\epsilon\}, C \in \mathsf{Constr}(X), Y \subseteq X)\}$$

A ***partitioned stopwatch automaton*** *is a stopwatch automaton in which*

$$\forall q, q' \in Q,\ \gamma(q) \neq \gamma(q') \Rightarrow\ \gamma(q) \cap \gamma(q') = \emptyset$$

Similarly to distributed time-asynchronous automata, we give the semantics of a stopwatch automaton as a timed transition system $\mathcal{T}(\mathcal{A}) = (\mathcal{Q}, \theta, \mathcal{Q}_0, \mathcal{Q}_f)$ where $\mathcal{Q} = Q \times \mathbb{R}^n_{\geq 0}$ is the set of *states*, $\mathcal{Q}_0 = \{(q_0, \mathbf{0}_n)\}$ is the (singleton) set of *initial states*, $\mathcal{Q}_f = Q_f \times \mathbb{R}^n_{\geq 0}$ is the set of *final states* and

$$\theta = \Big\{(q, v) \xrightarrow{t} (q, v') \mid t \in \mathbb{R}_{\geq 0}, v'\big|_{\gamma(q)} = v\big|_{\gamma(q)} + t, v'\big|_{X \setminus \gamma(q)} = v\big|_{X \setminus \gamma(q)}\Big\}$$
$$\cup \Big\{(q, v) \xrightarrow{a} (q', v') \mid a \in \Sigma \cup \{\varepsilon\},\ \exists (q, C, a, Y, q') \in \delta \text{ such that } v \models C \text{ and } v' = v[Y := 0]\Big\}$$

Informally, the automaton can make time passage transitions in which all stopwatches that are active in some location advance by τ, and discrete transitions, in which location changes. The discrete transitions are enabled when the current stopwatch valuation v satisfies the guard C of a certain transition $q \xrightarrow{C,a,X} q' \in \delta$, and when they are executed, the stopwatches in the reset component X are set to zero.

Formally, a *trajectory* in $\mathcal{T}(\mathcal{A})$ is a chain $\rho = \Big((q_{i-1}, v_{i-1}) \xrightarrow{\xi_i} (q_i, v_i)\Big)_{1 \leq i \leq k}$ of transitions from θ that starts in $\mathcal{Q}_0$. An *accepting trajectory* is a trajectory which ends in $\mathcal{Q}_f$ and does not end with a time passage transition. The accepting trajectory $\rho = \Big((q_{i-1}, v_{i-1}) \xrightarrow{\xi_i} (q_i, v_i)\Big)_{1 \leq i \leq k}$ *accepts* the timed word $\mathsf{acc}(\rho) = \xi_1 \xi_2 \ldots \xi_k$. The *language accepted by* $\mathcal{A}$ is then $L(\mathcal{A}) = \big\{\mathsf{acc}(\rho) \mid \rho \text{ is an accepting trajectory}\big\}$.

An example of a stopwatch automaton is given in Figure 2, and an example of a partitioned stopwatch automaton is given in Figure 3 below. Note that the timed language from Figure 1 is the same as for the automaton in Figure 3. Note also that the timed language in Figure 2 is not timed regular either.

Before ending this section, we state some useful properties of partitioned stopwatch automata.

Proposition 1. *For each partitioned stopwatch automaton* $\mathcal{A}$, *there exists an equivalent partitioned stopwatch automaton* $\mathcal{B}$ *satisfying the following properties:*

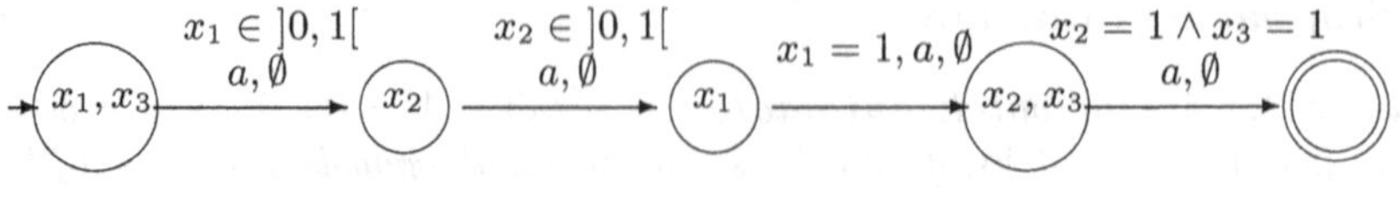

Fig. 2. A stopwatch automaton recognizing the language $\{t_1\ a\ t_2\ a\ t_3\ a\ t_4\ a \mid t_1, t_2, t_3, t_4 \in]0,1[\ , t_1 + t_3 = t_2 + t_4 = t_1 + t_4 = 1\}$

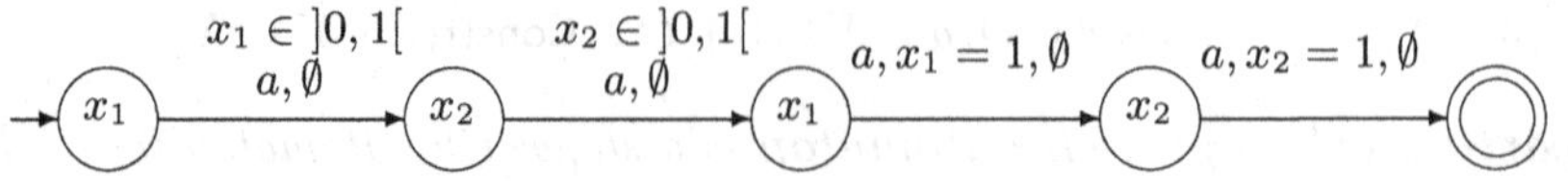

Fig. 3. A partitioned stopwatch automaton recognizing the language $\{t_1\ a\ t_2\ a\ t_3\ a\ t_4\ a \mid t_1, t_2, t_3, t_4 \in]0,1[\ , t_1 + t_3 = 1 \wedge t_2 + t_4 = 1\}$

1. *Between any two locations q, r there exists at most one transition, and there are no self-loops (i.e. no transitions $q \xrightarrow{C,a,Y} q$).*
2. *Exactly one of the following conditions is satisfied:*
   (a) *Either for each transition $q \xrightarrow{C,a,Y} r$, we have that $Y \subseteq \gamma(q)$ and $C \in \mathsf{Constr}(\gamma(q))$.*
   (b) *Or for each transition $q \xrightarrow{C,a,Y} r$, we have that $Y \subseteq \gamma(r)$ and $C \in \mathsf{Constr}(\gamma(r))$.*
3. *If $q \in Q$ is the target of a visible (i.e. non-ε) transition, then any transition leading to q is visible.*
4. *$\mathcal{A}$ must spend a non-zero amount of time in each location which is the source or the target of some ε-transition: there exists a stopwatch $\xi_i \in X_i$ which is reset when entering each location q with $\gamma(q) = X_i$. Moreover, on each transition $q \xrightarrow{C,\varepsilon,Y} q'$ or on each transition $r \xrightarrow{C,a,Y} r'$ in which r is the target of ε-transitions, then C contains also a constraint of the form $\xi_i \in I$ with $I \subseteq]0, \infty[$.*

These results rely on straightforward state-splitting constructions.

2.3 Decidability of the Reachability Problem for Partitioned Stopwatch Automata

A *zone* (see [12,6]) is a nonempty n-dimensional convex set of points characterized by a constraint of the form $C_Z = \bigwedge_{0 \leq i,j \leq n} x_i - x_j \in I_{ij}$, where $x_0 = 0$ and I_{ij} are non-negative intervals with integer bounds. In the sequel, we consider only zones that use variables from a set of stopwatches (or clocks) X.

An *M-region*, with $M \in \mathbb{R}_{\geq 0}$, is a zone R for which there exists $Y \subseteq X$ such that some constraint characterizing R can be put in the following format:

$$C_R = \bigwedge_{x \in Y} (x \in I_x) \wedge \bigwedge_{x,y \in Y, x \neq y} x - y \in I_{xy} \wedge \bigwedge_{x \in X \setminus Y} x \in]M, \infty[$$

where for each $x, y \in X, x \neq y$:

- Either $I_x = \{\alpha\}$ with $\alpha \in \mathbb{N}$, $\alpha \leq M$, or $I_x =]\alpha, \alpha+1[$ with $\alpha \in \mathbb{N}$, $\alpha \leq M-1$,
- Either $I_{xy} = \{\alpha\}$ with $\alpha \in \mathbb{N}$, $-M \leq \alpha \leq M$, or $I_x =]\alpha, \alpha+1[$ with $\alpha \in \mathbb{N}$, $-M \leq \alpha \leq M-1$,

We denote $\mathsf{Reg}_{\mathcal{A}}$ the set of regions for the automaton $\mathcal{A}$.

The following theorem adapts the well-known region construction of [2] for partitioned stopwatch automata:

Theorem 1. *The reachability problem for the class of partitioned stopwatch automata is decidable.*

Proof. Consider a partitioned stopwatch automaton $\mathcal{A} = (Q, \Sigma, X, \gamma, \delta, q_0, F)$ and denote $n = card\{\gamma(q) \mid q \in Q\}$ the number of partitions of the set of stopwatches X, and denote these partitions as $X_1, \ldots, X_n$. The *region automaton* corresponding to $\mathcal{A}$ will then be the following: $\mathcal{R}_{\mathcal{A}} = \big(Q \times \mathsf{Reg}^n_{\mathcal{A}}, \delta_{\mathcal{R}}, r_0, \mathcal{R}_f\big)$ where $r_0 = (q_0, \mathbf{0}_{X_1}, \ldots, \mathbf{0}_{X_n})$, $\mathcal{R}_f = \big\{(q, R_1, \ldots, R_n) \mid q \in Q_F\big\}$ and

$$\delta_{\mathcal{R}} = \big\{(q, R_1, \ldots, R_n) \to (q, R'_1, \ldots, R'_n) \mid \exists (q,v) \xrightarrow{\xi} (q',v') \in \theta, \xi \in \mathbb{R}_{\geq 0} \cup \Sigma \cup \{\varepsilon\} \\ \text{such that } \forall 1 \leq i \leq n,\ R_i, R'_i \in \mathsf{Reg}_{\mathcal{A}} \text{ and } v\big|_{X_i} \in R_i, v'\big|_{X_i} \in R'_i\big\}$$

It is easy to see that $L(\mathcal{A})$ is not empty if and only if $\mathcal{R}_{\mathcal{A}}$ has at least one reachable final configuration. □

3 Shuffle Regular Expressions

In this section we recall the notion of *timed shuffle expression* and its relationship with stopwatch autoamta. We then define the subclass of *fair shuffle expressions*, which will be proved to be equivalent with distributed time-asynchronous automata.

Definition 3. *The set of* ***timed shuffle expressions*** *over a set of symbols Σ is recursively defined as follows:*

$$E ::= a \mid \underline{\mathsf{t}} \mid \langle E \rangle_I \mid f(E) \mid E_1 \sqcup\!\sqcup E_2 \mid E_1 + E_2 \mid E_1 \wedge E_2 \mid (E)^*$$

where $a \in \Sigma \cup \{\epsilon\}$, $I \subseteq \mathbb{R}_{\geq 0}$ is an interval with integer and nonnegative bounds, or infinite bounds. and $f : \Sigma \to \Sigma \cup \{\epsilon\}$ is a renaming *function.*

A ***timed regular expression*** *is a timed shuffle expression constructed without the operator $\sqcup\!\sqcup$ and an* ***untimed shuffle expression*** *is a shuffled timed expression constructed without the operator $\langle \_ \rangle_I$.*

The *semantics* of a timed shuffle expression E is denoted $\|E\|$ and is given by the following rules:

$$\|a\| = \{a\} \qquad \|\underline{t}\| = \{t \mid t \in \mathbb{R}_{\geq 0}\}$$
$$\|E_1 + E_2\| = \|E_1\| \cup \|E_2\| \qquad \|E^*\| = \|E\|^*$$
$$\|E_1 \wedge E_2\| = \|E_1\| \cap \|E_2\| \qquad \|\langle E\rangle_I\| = \{w \in \|E\| \mid \ell(w) \in I\}$$
$$\|E_1 \cdot E_2\| = \|E_1\| \cdot \|E_2\| \qquad \|E_1 \sqcup\!\sqcup E_2\| = \|E_1\| \sqcup\!\sqcup \|E_2\|$$
$$\|f(E)\| = \{f(w) \mid w \in \|E\|\}$$

Theorem 2 ([4,7]). *Timed regular expressions are equivalent with timed automata and timed shuffle expressions are equivalent with stopwatch automata.*

The following expression is equivalent with the automaton in Figure 2:

$$[z_1/\varepsilon, z_2/\varepsilon, z_3/\varepsilon, z_4/\varepsilon]\Big(\big((\langle z_1\langle\underline{t}\rangle_{]0,1[}az_3\langle\underline{t}\rangle_{]0,1[}a\rangle_1) \sqcup\!\sqcup (\langle z_2\langle\underline{t}\rangle_{]0,1[}z_4\langle\underline{t}\rangle_{]0,1[}a\rangle_1)\big) \wedge \big(((z_2\underline{t}az_3\underline{t}a) \sqcup\!\sqcup (\langle z_1\underline{t}az_4\underline{t}a\rangle_1)\big)\Big)$$

Definition 4. *The set of* ***fair shuffle expressions*** *is the subset of timed shuffle expressions defined recursively as follows:*

$$F ::= U \mid f(F) \mid F_1 + F_2 \mid F \wedge T \mid (F)^* \mid F_1 \sqcup\!\sqcup F_2$$

where T is a timed expression, U is an untimed expression and $f : \Sigma \to \Sigma \cup \{\varepsilon\}$ is a renaming.

The following expression is a fair shuffle expression which is equivalent with the partitioned stopwatch automaton in Figure 3:

$$[z_1/\varepsilon, z_2/\varepsilon]\big((z_1\underline{t}az_2\underline{t}az_1\underline{t}az_2\underline{t}a) \wedge ((\langle z_1\langle\underline{t}\rangle_{]0,1[}az_1\underline{t}a\rangle_1) \sqcup\!\sqcup (\langle z_2\langle\underline{t}\rangle_{]0,1[}z_2\underline{t}a\rangle_1)\big)$$

3.1 Relations Between Partitioned Stopwatch Automata and Fair Shuffle Expressions

Theorem 3. *Partitioned stopwatch automata are equivalent with fair shuffle expressions, and the equivalence is effective.*

Proof. For the left-to-right inclusion, consider a partitioned stopwatch automaton $\mathcal{A} = (Q, \Sigma, X, \gamma, \delta, q_0, F)$. The set of states Q can be partitioned into $S_1, \ldots, S_n$ states such that $\gamma(q) = \gamma(q')$ iff $q, q' \in S_i$, for some i. By means of Proposition 1, we can assume that if $q \xrightarrow{C,a,Y} q' \in \delta$, then $Y \subseteq \gamma(q)$ and $C \in \mathsf{Constr}(\gamma(q))$.

The idea is to construct n timed automata $\mathcal{A}_1, \ldots, \mathcal{A}_n$ such that each $\mathcal{A}_i$ performs all the actions of $\mathcal{A}$ while letting time pass only in states from S_i. The languages of all $\mathcal{A}_i$ will be shuffled, and intersected with the language of an untimed automaton that will ensure proper interleaving. This proper interleaving is also ensured by considering distinct labeling for each transition and by introducing a new symbol ζ, to be performed instantaneously in each $\mathcal{A}_i$ before each step that simulates a step of $\mathcal{A}$. This is needed for keeping from mixing time elapses within $\mathcal{A}_i$ with time elapses within $\mathcal{A}_j$ when they are shuffled. This technique is a variation of the one used in [7]. Finally, each timed automaton will reference a new clock x_i which is needed for ensuring that time passage is 0 in each automaton $\mathcal{A}_i$ while passing through a state q with $\gamma(q) \neq X_i$.

Formally $\mathcal{A}_i = (Q \times \{1,2\}, \Sigma_i, X_i, \delta_i, q_0^i = (q_0, 1), F \times \{1,2\})$ with $\Sigma_i = \{\zeta\} \cup \{q \xrightarrow{C,a,Y} q' \mid q \xrightarrow{C,a,Y} q' \in \delta \text{ and } q \in S_i\}$, $X_i = \gamma(S_i) \cup \{x_i\}$ and:

$$\begin{aligned}\delta = &\left\{(q,1) \xrightarrow{x_i=0,\zeta,\emptyset} (q,2) \mid q \in Q\right\}\\ \cup &\left\{(q,2) \xrightarrow{C,(q,C,a,X,q'),Y\cup\{(x_i,0)\}} (r,1) \mid q \xrightarrow{C,a,Y} r \in \delta \text{ and } q \in S_i\right\}\\ \cup &\left\{(q,2) \xrightarrow{(x_i=0),\varepsilon,\{(x_i,0)\}} (r,1)) \mid q \xrightarrow{C,a,Y} r \in \delta \text{ and } q \notin S_i\right\}\end{aligned}$$

As a consequence of Theorem 2, we can construct timed expressions $T_1, \dots, T_n$ such that $\|T_i\| = L(\mathcal{A}_i)$ for all $1 \le i \le n$. Note that T_i expresses the accepting trajectories of $\mathcal{A}$ projected to states in S_i and with the introduction of the symbol ζ at the beginning of each step. More precisely, for any i,

$$\rho = (q_1, v_1) \xrightarrow{t_1} (q_1, \hat{v}_1) \xrightarrow{a_1} \dots (q_m, v_m) \xrightarrow{t_m} (q_m, \hat{v}_m) \dots \xrightarrow{a_m} (q_{m+1}, v_{m+1})$$

is an accepting trajectory of $\mathcal{A}$ iff, for any i, there exists $\zeta t'_1 a'_1 \zeta \cdot \dots \cdot \zeta t'_m a'_m \in \|T_i\|$ s.t. for all j, $t'_j = \begin{cases} t_j & \text{if } q_j \in S_i \\ 0 & \text{otherwise} \end{cases}$, $a_j = \begin{cases} (q_j, a_j, q_{j+1}) & \text{if } q_j \in S_i \\ \epsilon & \text{otherwise} \end{cases}$. Let then f be the renaming $f : \bigcup_{i \in [1,n]} \Sigma_i \to \Sigma$ defined by $f(q, C, a, Y, q') = a$ and $f(\zeta) = \epsilon$.

Observe that not all timed words specified by $T = f(T_1 \sqcup\!\sqcup \dots \sqcup\!\sqcup T_n)$ might be accepted by trajectories of $\mathcal{A}$ since the projected trajectories could be combined in a non-coherent way. Formally, from $\|T\|$ we must only keep the strings of the form $(q_0, C_1, a_1, Y_1, q_1)(q_1, C_2, a_2, Y_2, q_2) \dots$ of $(T_1 \sqcup\!\sqcup \dots \sqcup\!\sqcup T_n)$. But T might also contain strings of the form $(q_0, C_1, a_1, Y_1, r_1)(q_1, C_2, a_2, Y_2, r_2) \dots$ with $q_1 \neq r_1$.

Hence we need an extra expression that checks the right sequencing of states. Consider then the timed automaton $\mathcal{A}' = (Q \times \{1,2\}, \bigcup_{i \in [1,n]} \Sigma, \emptyset, \delta', (q_0, 1), F \times \{1,2\})$ in which:

$$\delta' = \left\{(q,1) \xrightarrow{\mathsf{true},\zeta,\emptyset} (q,2)) \mid q \in Q\right\} \cup \left\{(q,2) \xrightarrow{\mathsf{true},(q,C,a,Y,q'),\emptyset} (q',1) \mid (q,C,a,Y,q') \in \delta\right\}$$

Since $\mathcal{A}'$ has no clock constraint, we can construct an untimed expression ϑ such that $\|\vartheta\| = \mathcal{L}(\mathcal{A}')$. Finally, we have that $\mathcal{L}(\mathcal{A}) = ((\tau_1 \sqcup\!\sqcup \dots \sqcup\!\sqcup \tau_n) \wedge \vartheta)[f]$. This proves the left-to-right inclusion in Theorem 3.

For the right-to-left inclusion, we proceed by structural induction on the given regular expression T. The case when T is a timed regular expression is already covered by Theorem 2 while the cases of union, concatenation, star, shuffle and renaming can be treated exactly as in [7].

For the intersection case, suppose $T = T' \wedge U$, with T' a fair shuffle expression and U an untimed expression. Then, by induction, there exist $\mathcal{A}_1$ a partitioned stopwatch automaton and $\mathcal{A}_2$ a timed automaton such that $\mathcal{L}(\mathcal{A}_1) = \|T\|$ and $\mathcal{L}(\mathcal{A}_2) = \|E\|$. Let $\mathcal{A}_i = (Q_i, \Sigma, X_i, \gamma_i, \delta_i, q_0^i, F_i)$, for $i = 1, 2$.

Note that in U, between two symbols a, b we can have times equal to 0 (when ab is a subexpression of U) or all possible times (when $a\underline{t}b$ is a subexpression of U). Therefore, we can assume that $\mathcal{A}_2$ is such that $X_2 = \{x_q | q \in Q_2\}$ and each transition of $\mathcal{A}_2$ is of the form $q \xrightarrow{C,a,\{x_{q'}\}} q'$ with $C \in \{true, x_q = 0\}$. We then construct a partitioned stopwatch automaton $\mathcal{A} = (Q_1 \times Q_2, \Sigma, X_1 \cup X_2, \gamma, \delta, (q_0^1, q_0^2), F_1 \times F_2)$ in which $\gamma(q, q') = \gamma_1(q) \cup \{x_{q'}\}$ and

$$\delta = \{(q_1, q_2) \xrightarrow{C_1 \wedge C_2, a, Y_1 \cup Y_2} (q_1', q_2') \mid q_i \xrightarrow{C_i, a, Y_i} q_i' \in \delta_i, \ \ i = 1, 2\}$$

Note that the construction would not work with only one extra clock, since that clock would have to belong to each $\gamma(q)$, which would mean that the automaton $\mathcal{A}$ is not partitioned. □

Proposition 2. *The class of partitioned stopwatch automata is closed under union, renaming, shuffle, Kleene star but not under intersection.*

Proof. Closure under union, renaming, shuffle, Kleene star is obvious since fair shuffle expressions are.

For the proof of non-closure under intersection we rely on several results on distributed time-asynchronous automata from the following section. □

Theorem 4. *The classes of distributed time-asynchronous automata and partitioned stopwatch automata are equivalent.*

Proof. For the left-to-right inclusion, consider first a distributed time-asynchronous automaton $\mathcal{A} = (Q_1, \ldots, Q_n, \Sigma, X_1, \ldots, X_n, \delta_1, \ldots, \delta_n, q_1^0, \ldots, q_n^0, F_1, \ldots F_n)$.

The language $L(\mathcal{A})$ is then straightforwardly equal with the language of the partitioned stopwatch automaton $\mathcal{A}' = (Q, \Sigma, X, \gamma, \delta, q_0, F)$ in which:

- $Q = Q_1 \times \ldots \times Q_n \times \{1, \ldots, n\}$ where index j represents the sequential component for which the time elapses.
- The set of clocks is $X = \bigcup_{i \in [1,n]} X_i$ and γ is such that $\gamma(q_1, \ldots, q_n, j) = X_j$.
- δ is the following set of transitions:

$$\begin{aligned}\delta = \Big\{&(q_1, \ldots, q_n, j) \xrightarrow{C,a,Y} (q_1', \ldots, q_n', j) \mid \forall 1 \le i \le n \ \exists q_i \xrightarrow{C_i, a, Y_i} q_i' \in \delta_i \\ &\text{with } Y = \bigcup\nolimits_{i \in [1,n]} Y_i \text{ and } C = \bigwedge\nolimits_{1 \le i \le n} C_i\Big\} \\ \cup \Big\{&(q_1, \ldots, q_i, \ldots, q_n, j) \xrightarrow{C,\epsilon,Y} (q_1, \ldots, q_i', \ldots, q_n, j) \mid q_i \xrightarrow{C,\epsilon,Y} q_i' \in \delta_i\Big\} \\ \cup \Big\{&(q_1, \ldots, q_n, j) \xrightarrow{\mathsf{true},\epsilon,\emptyset} (q_1, \ldots, q_n, j+1)) \mid 1 \le j < n\Big\} \\ \cup \Big\{&(q_1, \ldots, q_n, n) \xrightarrow{\mathsf{true},\epsilon,\emptyset} (q_1, \ldots, q_n, 1)\Big\}\end{aligned}$$

- $q_0 = (q_0^1, \ldots, q_n^0)$ and $F = F_1 \times \ldots \times F_n \times \{1, \ldots, n\}$.

The reverse proof requires a slightly more involved construction, since this time we need to simulate some centralized control (the location of a partitioned stopwatch automaton) by a distributed control, via synchronous read of input and checking global constraints. The main problem here is posed by ε-transitions.

Consider then a partitioned stopwatch automaton $\mathcal{A} = (Q, \Sigma, X, \gamma, \delta, q_0, F)$. We will assume $\mathcal{A}$ satisfies conditions from Proposition 1. The main idea is to construct a distributed time-asynchronous automaton with n components, where $n = card\{\gamma(q) \mid q \in Q\}$ is the number of partitions of X. X_i will be (part of) the set of clocks that can be reset by component i. Each component will then basically behave like $\mathcal{A}$ but keeping from reseting *and* updating clocks that are not in X_i. A first (essential, but not sufficient) means of synchronization is the use of Σ as a common input alphabet.

Additionnaly, we will employ a second set of clocks $\overline{X}$ whose elements will be indexed by the set $Q \times \{1, \ldots, n\}$, which will be used to forbid local time to advance in component i, when it reaches a location q with $\gamma(q) \neq X_i$, that is, a component j that does not own the set of clocks X_i. Hence, each clock $x_{(q,i)}$ will be reset in each component $j \neq i$ when entering location q, and then tested for 0 when j leaves q.

But we need a supplimentary mechanism to ensure full synchronization in the presence of ε-transitions in the original automaton $\mathcal{A}$. This mecanisms employs an extra set of clocks $Z = \{z_{(q,r,i)} \mid 1 \leq i \leq n \text{ and } \exists q \xrightarrow{C,a,Y} r \in \delta\}$. Each clock $z_{(q,r,i)}$ will be reset in each component exactly when the (unique) transition between q and r is taken by the appropriate component.

The actual idea is that each component i *guesses* that the next transition is $q \to r$, by resetting the clock $z_{(q,r,i)}$; at the same time, it resets $x_{(q,i)}$. Immediately after (fact which can be checked by $x_{(q,i)} = 0$), each component checks that everybody has guessed the same transition, by checking that $\bigwedge_{1 \leq j \leq n} z_{(q,r,j)} = 0$. Here we rely on assumption 4 in Proposition 1, which ensures that $z_{(q,r,i)} \neq 0$ when $\mathcal{A}$ crosses a ε-transition different from that connecting q and r. The same reasoning will be employed when the transition between q and r is in Σ, as this will ensure the components that they all agree on the transition that links q to r, and do not employ some other transition that has the same input label.

Formally, the distributed time-asynchronous automaton that is equivalent with $\mathcal{A}$ is $\mathcal{B} = (Q_1, \ldots, Q_n, \Sigma, X'_1, \ldots, X'_n, \delta_1, \ldots, \delta_n, q_0^1, \ldots q_n^0, F_1, \ldots, F_n)$ where

1. $Q_i = (Q \cup (Q \times Q)) \times \{i\}$, $q_0^i = (q_0, i)$ and $F_i = F \times \{i\}$.
2. $X'_i = X_i \cup \{x_{(q,i)} \mid \gamma(q) \neq X_i\} \cup \{z_{(q,r,i)} \mid 1 \leq i \leq n\}$.
3. δ_i consists of transitions

$$\begin{aligned}
\delta = \big\{(q,i) \xrightarrow{C,a,Y} (q,r,i) \mid \gamma(q) = X_i \text{ and } \exists q \xrightarrow{C,a,Y'} r \in \delta, Y = \{x_{(q,i)}, z_{(q,r,i)}\}\big\} \\
\cup \big\{(q,i) \xrightarrow{C,a,Y} (q,r,i) \mid \gamma(q) \neq X_i \text{ and } \exists q \xrightarrow{C',a,Y'} r \in \delta, C = (x_{(q,i)} = 0) \\
\text{and } Y = \{x_{(q,i)}, z_{(q,r,i)}\}\big\} \\
\cup \big\{(q,r,i) \xrightarrow{C,a,Y} (r,i) \mid \gamma(q) = X_i \text{ and } \exists q \xrightarrow{C',a,Y'} r \in \delta, \\
C = C' \wedge (x_{(q,i)} = 0) \wedge \bigwedge_{1 \leq j \leq n} (z_{(q,r,j)} = 0) \text{ and } Y = Y'\big\} \\
\cup \big\{(q,r,i) \xrightarrow{C,a,Y} (r,i) \mid \gamma(q) \neq X_i \text{ and } \exists q \xrightarrow{C',a,Y'} r \in \delta, \\
C = C' \wedge (x_{(q,i)} = 0) \wedge \bigwedge_{1 \leq j \leq n} (z_{(q,r,j)} = 0) \text{ and } Y = \{x_{(r,i)}\}\big\}
\end{aligned}$$

Note first that, in any accepting trajectory, in locations of the type (q,r,i) time cannot pass since they are needed for synchronization purposes, which is achieved by resetting $z_{(q,r,i)}$ before entering that location, and then checking, when leaving (q,r,i), that $z_{(q,r,j)} = 0$ for all j.

We may then show that in any trajectory $\rho = \big((\overline{q}_1^{j-1}, \ldots, \overline{q}_n^{j-1}, v_{j-1}) \xrightarrow{\xi_j} (\overline{q}_1^j, \ldots, \overline{q}_n^j, v_j)\big)_{1 \leq j \leq m}$, each state $(\overline{q}_1^{j-1}, \ldots, \overline{q}_n^{j-1}, v_{j-1})$ has the following properties

1. There exists a (possibly empty) subset $Y_j \subseteq \{1, \ldots, n\}$ such that for each $i \in Y_j$ there exist $q, r \in Q$ such that $\overline{q}_i^{j-1} = (q,r,i)$.
2. If $Y_j = \emptyset$ then there exists $q \in Q$ such that for all $1 \leq i \leq n$, $\overline{q}_i^j = (q,i)$.
3. If $Y_j \neq \emptyset$ then and exactly one of the two following properties holds:
   (a) Either for all $1 \leq i \leq n, i \notin Y_j$, $\overline{q}_i^j = (q,i)$;
   (b) Or for all $1 \leq i \leq n, i \notin Y$, $\overline{q}_i^j = (r,i)$.

The correctness of this construction can then be proved by induction on the length of an accepting trajectory in $\mathcal{B}$, $\rho = \big((\overline{q}_1^{j-1}, \ldots, \overline{q}_n^{j-1}, v_{j-1}) \xrightarrow{\xi_j} (\overline{q}_1^j, \ldots, \overline{q}_n^j, v_j)\big)_{1 \leq j \leq m}$ by showing that there exists a corresponding accepting trajectory in $\mathcal{A}$, $\overline{\rho} = \big((r_{l-1}, u_{l-1}) \xrightarrow{\zeta_l} (r_j, u_l)\big)_{1 \leq l \leq p}$, which accepts the same timed word. The choice of r_j can be done as follows:

1. If $Y_j \neq \emptyset$ and hence $\overline{q}_i^j = (q,r,i)$ for all $i \in Y_j$, then we put $r_j = r$.
2. If $Y_j = \emptyset$ and hence $\overline{q}_i^j = (q,i)$ for some $q \in Q$ and all $1 \leq i \leq n$, then we put $r_j = q$.

□

4 Nonclosure Under Intersection of Partitioned Stopwatch Automata

In this subsection we prove the non-closure result from Proposition 2:

Proposition 3. *The class of languages accepted by distributed time-asynchronous automata is not closed under intersection.*

The proof of result relies on a series of additional properties, starting with the following:

Proposition 4. *For each distributed time-asynchronous automaton* $\mathcal{A} = (Q_1, \dots, Q_n, \Sigma, X_1, \dots, X_n, \delta_1, \dots, \delta_n, q_1^0, \dots, q_n^0, F_1, \dots F_n)$ *there exists a distributed time-asynchronous automaton with private clocksets* $\mathcal{B} = (\overline{Q}_1, \dots, \overline{Q}_n, \overline{\Sigma}, X_1, \dots, X_n, \overline{\delta}_1, \dots, \overline{\delta}_n, \overline{q}_1^0, \dots, \overline{q}_n^0, \overline{F}_1, \dots \overline{F}_n)$ *and a renaming* $f : \overline{\Sigma} \to \Sigma \cup \{\varepsilon\}$ *such that* $L(\mathcal{A}) = f\big(L(\mathcal{B})\big)$.

Moreover, if $\mathcal{A}$ *contains no* ε*-transition, then* f *contains no symbol deletion.*

Proof. The idea in the construction of $\mathcal{B}$ is to no longer have ε-transitions and thus have only synchronizing discrete transitions. Then, synchronization done by global constraints in $\mathcal{A}$ will be simulated by unique labels of the transitions.

If we recall that $Q = Q_1 \times \ldots \times Q_n$, $F = F_1 \times \ldots \times F_n$ and $q_0 = (q_0^1, \dots, q_0^n)$, then, formally, the components of $\mathcal{B}$ are:

- The set of locations is $\overline{Q}_i = Q \times \{i\}$, with $\overline{q}_0^i = (q_0, i)$ and $F_i = F \times \{i\}$.
- The set of inputs is

$$\begin{aligned}\overline{\Sigma} = &\big\{(tr_1, \dots, tr_n) \mid \forall 1 \le i \le n, tr_i = q \xrightarrow{C,a,Y} r \in \delta_i\big\} \\ &\cup \big\{q \xrightarrow{C,\varepsilon,Y} r \mid q \xrightarrow{C,\varepsilon,Y} r \in \delta_i \text{ for some } 1 \le i \le n\big\}\big\}\end{aligned}$$

- The i-th transition relation is:

$$\begin{aligned}\overline{\delta}_i = &\big\{(\overline{q}, i) \xrightarrow{\overline{C}_i, \xi, Y_i} (\overline{r}, i) \mid \overline{q} = (q_1, \dots, q_n), \overline{r} = (r_1, \dots, r_n), \\ &\quad \forall 1 \le j \le n,\ \exists tr_j = q_j \xrightarrow{C_j, a, Y_j} r_j \in \delta_j, \xi = (tr_1, \dots, tr_n), \overline{C}_i = C_i\big|_{X_i}\big\}\big\} \\ &\cup \big\{(\overline{q}, i) \xrightarrow{\overline{C}_i, \xi, \overline{Y}_i} (\overline{r}, i) \mid \overline{q} = (q_1, \dots, q_n), \overline{r} = (r_1, \dots, r_n), \text{ and } \exists j, \\ &\quad 1 \le j \le n \text{ for which } \exists tr_j = q_j \xrightarrow{C_j, \varepsilon, Y_j} r_j \in \delta_j \text{ such that } \xi = tr_j, \\ &\quad \overline{C}_i = C_j\big|_{X_i}, \overline{Y}_i = Y_j \cap X_i, \text{ and } \forall l \ne j, q_l = r_l\big\}\end{aligned}$$

For each constraint C, we have denoted here $C\big|_Y$ the sub-constraint of C which uses only clocks in Y. □

The following result is a generalization of Proposition 12 of [11] to the case of distributed time-asynchronous automata with private clocksets:

Lemma 1. *Given a distributed time-asynchronous automaton with private clockset* $\mathcal{A}$ *suppose that all timed words in* $L(\mathcal{A})$ *contain the same sequence of symbols,* $L(\mathcal{A}) = \{t_1 a_1 \dots t_n a_n t_{n+1} \mid t_i \in \mathbb{R}_{\ge 0}\}$, *for some* $a_1, \dots, a_n \in \Sigma$.

Then for each $t_1 a_1 \dots t_n a_n t_{n+1} \in L(\mathcal{A})$ *there exists some* $k \in \mathbb{N}$ *and* k *sequences of time points* $(t_i^j)_{1 \le i \le n+1}$ $(1 \le j \le k)$ *such that*

- $t_i = \sum_{1\leq j\leq k} t_i^j$ *for all* $1 \leq i \leq n+1$.
- *If, for each* $1 \leq j \leq k$, *we denote* $R_j \subseteq \mathbb{R}_{\geq 0}{}^{n+1}$ *the region to which belongs each* $(n+1)$*-dimensional point* v^j *defined by* $v_i^j = \sum_{1\leq l\leq i} t_l^j$ $(1 \leq i \leq n+1)$, *then for any other point* $u^j \in R$, *if we define* $s_i^j = u_i^j - u_{i-1}^j$ *(with* $u_0^j = 0$*), then*

$$(\sum_{1\leq j\leq k} s_1^j)a_1 \dots (\sum_{1\leq j\leq k} s_n^j)a_n(\sum_{1\leq j\leq k} s_{n+1}^j) \in L(\mathcal{A})$$

The last result that needed in the proof of Proposition 4 is the following:

Lemma 2 ([6]). *For any region* $R \subseteq \mathbb{R}_{\geq 0}^n$ *and subset of indices* $Y \subseteq \{1, \dots, n\}$, *if* $R\big|_Y$ *denotes the restriction (or projection) of* R *onto points whose coordinates belong to* Y, *then for any* $v \in R\big|_Y$, *there exist* $v' \in R$ *with* $v'\big|_Y = v$.

Proof (of Proposition 4). Consider the timed language

$$L = \{t_1at_2at_3at_4a \mid t_1, t_2, t_3, t_4 \in \,]0, 1[\,, t_1 + t_3 = t_2 + t_4 = t_1 + t_4 = 1\}$$

L is the intersection of the language of the distributed time-asynchronous automaton in Figure 1 with the language of the distributed time-asynchronous automaton in Figure 4, and is the language in Figure 2, hence is accepted by a stopwatch automaton.

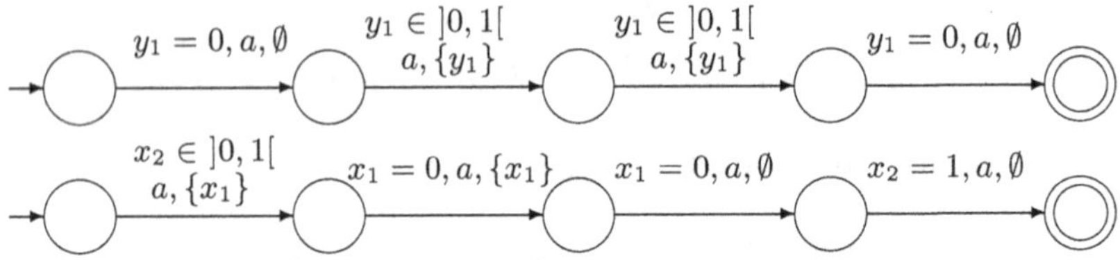

Fig. 4. The two components of a distributed time-asynchronous automaton recognizing the language $\{t_1\ a\ t_2\ a\ t_3\ a\ t_4\ a \mid t_1, t_2, t_3, t_4 \in \,]0, 1[\,, t_1 + t_4 = 1\}$

Suppose there exists a distributed time-asynchronous automaton with private clocks $\mathcal{A}$ and a renaming f such that $f(L(\mathcal{A})) = L$. In the sequel, we will present all elements of $L(\mathcal{A})$ in the form $t_1a_1(t_2 - t_1)a_2 \dots (t_n - t_{n-1})a_n$, for some $(t_1, \dots, t_n) \in \mathbb{R}_{\geq 0}{}^n$.

Take the timed word $w = 0.3\,a\,0.3\,a\,0.7\,a\,0.7\,a \in L$, hence there exists a timed word $w' \in L(\mathcal{A})$ with $f(w') = w$. Suppose $w' = t_1a_1(t_2 - t_1)a_2 \dots (t_n - t_{n-1})a_n$. Then, by Lemma 1, there exist k sequences of time points $(t_i^j)_{1\leq i\leq n}$ $(1 \leq j \leq k)$ such that $t_i = \sum_{1\leq j\leq k} t_i^j$, and regions $R_j \ni t_i^j$ which fulfill the properties in Lemma 1.

Consider now the renaming f and suppose that $f(a_l) = a$ for $l \in \mathcal{I} = \{i_1, i_2, i_3, i_4\}$ and $f(a_l) = \varepsilon$ otherwise. Hence,

$$\sum_{1\leq i\leq i_1} t_i = \sum_{i_1<i\leq i_2} t_i = 0.3 \qquad \sum_{i_2<i\leq i_3} t_i = \sum_{i_3<i\leq i_4} t_i = 0.7$$

By Lemma 2, if we consider the restriction of each region R_j to the set of indices $\mathcal{I}$, then for any $u^j \in R_j\big|_{\mathcal{I}}$ $(1 \leq j \leq k)$ there exists $v^j \in R_j$ with $u^j = v^j\big|_{\mathcal{I}}$, But this means that for any timed word

$$w_1 = \Big(\sum_{1\leq j\leq k} s_1^j\Big)a\Big(\sum_{1\leq j\leq k}(s_2^j - s_1^j)\Big)a\Big(\sum_{1\leq j\leq k}(s_3^j - s_2^j)\Big)a\Big(\sum_{1\leq j\leq k}(s_4^j - s_3^j)\Big)a$$

there exists a timed word $w_2 = \Big(\sum_{1\leq j\leq k} t_1^j\Big)a_1 \ldots \Big(\sum_{1\leq j\leq k}(t_n^j - t_{n-1}^j)\Big)a_n \in L(\mathcal{A})$ with $f(w_2) = w_1$ and $w_2 \in L(\mathcal{A})$, and hence $w_1 \in L$.

Therefore, we only need to consider what are the possible 4-dimensional regions R_j that may compose timed words in L of the form $t_1a(t_2 - t_1)a(t_3 - t_2)a(t_4 - t_3)a$, for which there exists s_l^j $(1 \leq j \leq k, 1 \leq l \leq 4)$ such that

- $\sum s_l^j = t_l$ and $(s_1^j, s_2^j, s_3^j, s_4^j) \in R_j$,
- And the same holds also for $t_1 = t_2 = 0.3$ and $t_3 = t_4 = 0.7$.

The first observation to make on R_j is that in its normal form C_{R_j}, the constraint for $s_l^j - s_{j-1}^j$ is of the form $s_l^j - s_{l-1}^j \in [l-1, l[$ $(1 \leq l \leq 4$, and we consider $s_0^j = 0)$. This follows since $s_l^j - s_{l-1}^j$ must belong to the same interval as the l-th time passage in w. For example, s_4^j must belong to the same unit length interval as 0.7.

We may then see that there exists only one region R_j whose constraint on s_1^j is not of the form $s_1^j = 0$. This follows by contradiction, since if we suppose that this holds for two indices j_1, j_2, that is, that $C_{R_{j_1}}$ and $C_{R_{j_2}}$ both contain $s_1^j \in]0,1[$, then, by lemma 2, we may construct s^{j_1}, s^{j_2} such that $s_1^{j_1} = s_1^{j_2} = 0.8$, which would mean that a timed word of the type $1.6\,a\,t_2\,a\,t_3\,a\,t_4a$ would have to be in L, which is obviously false.

This observation can be further generalized to all l and all constraints $s_l^j - s_{l-1}^j$. As a consequence, we only have to consider that $k \leq 4$. This gives only finitely many (actually only 4) cases to check, and all lead to the possibility to construct a timed word as in Lemma 2, but which is not in L. □

5 Conclusions

We have introduced the class of distributed time-asynchronous automata, that correspond to asynchronous compositions of timed automata, in which time is allowed to progress independently between components, and resynchronizations are done with the aid of global clock constraints and input symbols. We have proved that this class is equivalent with fair shuffle expressions, which are timed shuffle expressions which allow intersection only with untimed expressions. We have also proved nonclosure under intersection for distributed time-asynchronous automata.

An interesting question concerns the study of closure properties for distributed time-asynchronous automata with private clocksets.

References

1. Abdeddaïm, Y., Maler, O.: Preemptive job-shop scheduling using stopwatch automata. In: Katoen, J.-P., Stevens, P. (eds.) ETAPS 2002 and TACAS 2002. LNCS, vol. 2280, pp. 113–126. Springer, Heidelberg (2002)
2. Alur, R., Dill, D.: A theory of timed automata. Theoretical Computer Science 126, 183–235 (1994)
3. Asarin, E.: Challenges in timed languages. Bulletin of EATCS 83 (2004)
4. Asarin, E., Caspi, P., Maler, O.: Timed regular expressions. Journal of ACM 49, 172–206 (2002)
5. Bouyer, P., Petit, A., Thérien, D.: An algebraic approach to data languages and timed languages. Inf. Comput. 182(2), 137–162 (2003)
6. Dima, C.: Computing reachability relations in timed automata. In: Proceedings of LICS'02, pp. 177–186 (2002)
7. Dima, C.: Timed shuffle expressions. In: Abadi, M., de Alfaro, L. (eds.) CONCUR 2005. LNCS, vol. 3653, pp. 95–109. Springer, Heidelberg (2005)
8. Henzinger, T., Raskin, J.-F., Schobbens, P.-Y.: The regular real-time languages. In: Larsen, K.G., Skyum, S., Winskel, G. (eds.) ICALP 1998. LNCS, vol. 1443, pp. 580–591. Springer, Heidelberg (1998)
9. Henzinger, T.A., Kopke, P.W., Puri, A., Varaiya, P.: What's decidable about hybrid automata. J. Comput. Syst. Sci. 57, 94–124 (1998)
10. Krishnan, P.: Distributed timed automata. Electr. Notes Theor. Comput. Sci. 28 (1999)
11. Ouaknine, J., Worrell, J.: Revisiting digitization, robustness, and decidability for timed automata. In: Proceedings of LICS'03, pp. 198–207. IEEE Computer Society Press, Los Alamitos (2003)
12. Yovine, S.: Model-checking timed automata. In: Rozenberg, G. (ed.) Lectures on Embedded Systems. LNCS, vol. 1494, pp. 114–152. Springer, Heidelberg (1998)
13. Zielonka, W.: Notes on finite asynchronous automata. Informatique Théorique et Applications 21(2), 99–135 (1987)

Skolem Machines and Geometric Logic

John Fisher[1] and Marc Bezem[2]

[1] Department of Computer Science, California State Polytechnic University
Pomona, California, USA
jrfisher@csupomona.edu

[2] Department of Computer Science, University of Bergen
Bergen, Norway
bezem@ii.uib.no

Abstract. Inspired by the wonderful design and implementation of the Prolog language afforded by the Warren Abstract Machine (WAM), this paper describes an extended logical language which can compute larger realms of first-order logic, based upon theories for finitary *geometric logic*. The paper describes a *Geolog* language for expressing first-order geometric logic in tidy closed form, a mathematical *Skolem Machine* that computes the language, and an implementation prototype that intimately mimics the abstract machine, and which also reformulates *expensive bottom-up* inference into *efficient top-down* inference. There are promising *mathematical theorem proving applications* for geometric logic systems, collected on the website [5]. The emphasis of this paper is theory, abstract machine design and direct implementation of the abstract machine.

1 The *Geolog* Language

First-order geometric logic expresses general logic rules in a restricted and simplified form. Many kinds of reasoning problems, including those found in lattice theory, projective geometry and axiomatic abstract algebra, can be directly expressed in first-order geometric logic. This has led to the use of geometric logic for automated mathematical theorem proving. For example, the system Geo2006i by de Nivelle [10] is based on geometric logic and participated in CASC-J3 [14]. As a newcomer, it ended somewhere in the middle of the field (e.g., a 6-th place out of 11 in the category FOF). Clearly, the full potential of geometric logic for automated and interactive theorem proving has yet to be explored.

Geometric logic arose in algebraic geometry and includes infinite disjunctions and some higher-order logic; see [4]. In Categorical Logic first-order geometric logic is currently called coherent logic, see for example [7, Sect. D.1.1]. Although this article deals exclusively with first-order geometric logic we use the terminology 'geometric logic' to address the

C.B. Jones, Z. Liu, J. Woodcock (Eds.): ICTAC 2007, LNCS 4711, pp. 201–215, 2007.

logical forms of the input language, opening up for the possibility to add, for example, higher-order features to the language.

Geolog is a language for expressing first-order geometric logic in a format suitable for computations using an *abstract machine*. In the sequel *Geolog* rules will be used as machine instructions for an abstract machine that computes consequences for first-order geometric logic, and also *Geolog* rules will be used as input for the compiler/interpreter based on the abstract machine.

A *Geolog* rule has the general form

$$A_1, A_2, \ldots, A_m \Rightarrow C_1; C_2; \ldots; C_n \tag{1}$$

where the A_i are atomic expressions and each C_j is a conjunction of atomic expressions, $m, n \geq 1$. The left-hand side of a rule is called the *antecedent* of the rule (a conjunction) and the right-hand side is called the *consequent* (a disjunction). All atomic expressions can contain variables.

If $n = 1$ then there is a single consequent for the rule (1), and the rule is said to be *definite*. Otherwise the rule is a *splitting rule* that requires a case distinction (case of C_1, or case of C_2,..., or case of C_n).

The separate cases (disjuncts) C_j must each have a conjunctive form

$$B_1, B_2, \ldots, B_h \tag{2}$$

where the B_i are atomic expressions, and $h \geq 1$ varies with j. Any free variables occurring in (2) other than those which occurred free in the antecedent of the rule are taken to be existential variables and their scope is this particular disjunct (2). The variables occurring free in the antecedent are taken to be universal variables and their scope is the whole rule.

As an example, consider the *Geolog* rule, actually the last rule in Figure 1 below:

```
s(X,Y) => e(X,Y) ; domain(Z),r(X,Z),s(Z,Y) .
```

The variables `X,Y` are universally quantified and have scope covering the entire formula, whereas `Z` is existentially quantified and has scope covering the last disjunct in the consequent of rule. A fully quantified first-order logical formula representation of this *Geolog* rule would be

$$(\forall X)(\forall Y)[s(X,Y) \rightarrow e(X,Y) \vee (\exists Z)(r(X,Z) \wedge s(Z,Y))]$$

This existential quantification is the distinguishing feature which makes geometric logic more expressive than the conjunctive normal form (CNF) used in resolution logic [11]. In Section 2 we discuss the disadvantages of reducing geometric logic to CNF.

We now come to two special cases of rule forms in (1), the *true* antecedent and the *goal* or *false* consequents. Rules of the form

$$true \Rightarrow C_1; C_2; \ldots; C_n \tag{3}$$

are called *factuals.* Here '*true*' is a special constant term denoting the empty conjunction. Factuals are used to express initial information in *Geolog* theories.

Rules of the form

$$A_1, A_2, \ldots, A_m \Rightarrow goal \tag{4}$$

are called *goal* rules. Here '*goal*' is a special constant term. A goal rule expresses that its antecedent is sufficient (and relevant) for *goal*. Similarly, rules of the form

$$A_1, A_2, \ldots, A_m \Rightarrow false \tag{5}$$

are called *false* rules. Here '*false*' is a special constant term denoting the empty disjunction. A *false* rule expresses rejection of its antecedent.

The constant terms *true*, *goal* and *false* can only appear in *Geolog* rules as just described. All other predicate names, individual constants, and variable names are the responsibility of the *Geolog* programmer.

The definition of *Geolog* rules provided here is compatible with [2, Definition 1.1]. The main difference is that we allow function symbols.

A *Geolog theory* (or *program*) is a finite set of *Geolog* rules. A theory may have any number of factuals and any number of *goal* or *false* rules. The theories also serve as the instruction set for the abstract machine described in the next section, so the rules are also referred to as 'instructions'.

Figure 1 shows a *Geolog* theory for proving that confluence of a rewrite relation implies uniqueness of normal forms. This theory serves for an input to a Prolog reader that reads a geometric logic theory and uses it as the input for the goal interpreter. (The % symbol prefixes comments.)

The predicate `domain` is being used as a *domain (closure)* predicate in the theory of Figure 1. On the left of ⇒ in a rule, the intended meaning is 'belongs to the domain'. On the right of ⇒, `domain` can be used to introduce a new element to the domain, when the rule is actually used. For example, the first rule will add the fact `domain(a)` (`a` is in the domain) and then the seventh rule will add the fact `e(a,a)`. In the last two rules in Figure 1, `domain` is used to add newly generated elements to the domain.

To illustrate two different ways of using a domain closure predicate, consider the following rules.

```
true => domain(a), domain(b), domain(c).  %1 domain elements a,b,c
e(b,c) => goal.                           %2 the goal is to prove b=c
r(b,Z) => false.                          %3 for normal form b
r(c,Z) => false.                          %4 and normal form c
true => s(a,b),s(a,c).                    %5 both reducts of a
domain(X) => e(X,X).                      %6 reflexivity of e
e(X,Y) => e(Y,X).                         %7 symmetry of e
e(X,Y),e(Y,Z) => e(X,Z).                  %8 transitivity of e
e(X,Y) => s(X,Y).                         %9  s contains e
r(X,Y) => s(X,Y).                         %10 and r,
s(X,Y),s(Y,Z) => s(X,Z).                  %11 is transitive,
s(X,Y),s(X,Z) => domain(U),s(Y,U),s(Z,U). %12 satisfies diamond, and
s(X,Y) => e(X,Y);domain(Z),r(X,Z),s(Z,Y). %13 is included in e + r.s
```

Fig. 1. A *Geolog* theory expressing that confluence of a rewrite relation `r` implies uniqueness of normal forms

```
human(X) => human(Y), father(Y), parent(Y,X).
human(X) => human(father(X)), parent(father(X),X).
```

In these examples, `human` is being used as a domain closure predicate. Both rules express that all humans have a father who is a parent and that the father should be included in the human domain. If the antecedent is true (say with `X = bill`) then the first clause creates a new domain element, say `c`, puts it in the `human` relation, puts it in the `father` relation and puts the pair `(c,bill)` in the `parent` relation. The second clause adds `father(bill)` to the human domain and puts the pair `(father(bill),bill)` in the `parent` relation. Thus, one can use function symbols (like `father`) and also get partial domain closure. It is the responsibility of the *Geolog* programmer to choose the name and specify the particular rules for a domain closure predicate.

2 Skolem Machines

Finite sets of *Geolog* rules can serve as instruction sets for a mathematical tape machine, which we call a *Skolem Machine* or *SM* for short.

The logical formulas characterized by *Geolog* , and the bottom-up approach to reasoning with those logical formulas, finds its earliest (1920) precursor in a particular paper by Skolem [12]. A more recent (1988) precursor, without the existential quantification, is the system SATCHMO [9].

It may be argued that existential quantification is unnecessary, as it can be eliminated by introducing *Skolem functions*, another invention of the same Skolem. However, we wish to point out a few disadvantages of Skolem functions for formalizing and automating mathematics.

First, Skolem functions change the meaning of a formula. For example, a tautology like $p(X,Y) \rightarrow (\exists Z)p(X,Z)$ is turned into a non-tautology $p(X,Y) \rightarrow p(X, f(X,Y))$ or, slightly better, $p(X,Y) \rightarrow p(X, f(X))$. This is bad news for interactive theorem proving: your reasoning assistant works on a different problem than you do! How would you help it when it gets stuck? Even if you are so lucky that it finds a solution, you have either to believe this or to convert the solution back to the original problem.

Second, a Skolem function might not be aware of its own symmetry, such as in rule 12 in Figure 1, where the premiss is symmetric in `Y` and `Z`. Or of its own idempotency, in the same rule. This is bad news for automated theorem proving: many irrelevant Skolem terms are generated. A Skolem function, relevant or not, turns a finite set of constants into an infinite Herbrand universe. [1]

Skolem machines resemble multitape Turing machines and the two machine models actually have the same computational power, see [3]. The theory outlined in this section will influence implementations discussed later in this article. An SM has a finite instruction set, and this is the same as what was defined as a *Geolog* theory or program in the previous section.

An SM starts with one tape having `true` written on it, as shown in Figure 2.

```
-------------------------------------
 true
-------------------------------------
```

Fig. 2. Initialized tape

The basic operations of an SM use the *Geolog* rules in the instruction set to extend a tape (write logical terms at the end) and to create new tapes (for splitting rules).

The tapes are also called *states.* An SM with more than one tape is said to be in a *disjunctive* state, comprised of multiple separate simple states or tapes.

The basic purpose of a particular SM is to compute its instruction set and to halt when all of its tapes have `goal` or `false` written on them.

In order to motivate the general definitions for the workings of SM, let us work through a small example. To this end, consider the *Geolog* rulebase (SM instructions) in Figure 3.

[1] Note that newly generated witnesses for existential statements, do not have these disadvantages. These witnesses are called *Skolem constants* by some, but we would prefer to view them as eigenvariables in the elimination of existential quantification.

```
true => domain(X), p(X).                           % #1
p(X) => q(X) ; r(X) ; domain(Y), s(X,Y).           % #2
domain(X) => u(X).                                 % #3
u(X), q(X) => false.                               % #4
r(X) => goal.                                      % #5
s(X,Y) => goal.                                    % #6
```

Fig. 3. Sample instructions

The only instruction that applies to the initial tape is instruction #1. The antecedent of the rule matches `true` on the tape, so the tape can be *extended* using the consequent of the rule. In order to extend the tape using `domain(X),p(X)` a new instance for the existential variable `X` is first generated and then substituted, and the resulting terms are written on the tape, as shown in Figure 4.

```
--------------------------------------
 true domain(sk1) p(sk1)
--------------------------------------
```

Fig. 4. After applying rule #1

At this point in machine operation time either of the rules #2 or #3 can apply. The general definition of SM operation does not specify the order, but we will apply applicable rules in top-down order. So, applying instruction #2 we get tape *splitting*, as shown in Figure 5.

```
--------------------------------------
 true domain(sk1) p(sk1) q(sk1)
--------------------------------------
--------------------------------------
 true domain(sk1) p(sk1) r(sk1)
--------------------------------------
-----------------------------------------------
 true domain(sk1) p(sk1) domain(sk2) s(sk1,sk2)
-----------------------------------------------
```

Fig. 5. After applying rule #2

Each of the disjuncts in the consequent of rule #2 is used to extend the previous single tape. This requires that the previous tape be copied to two new tapes and then these tapes are extended.

Now, instruction #3 applies to all three tapes, even twice to the last tape, with result shown in Figure 6.

Instruction #4 now adds `false` to the top tape, shown in Figure 7.

```
-------------------------------------
true domain(sk1) p(sk1) q(sk1) u(sk1)
-------------------------------------

-------------------------------------
true domain(sk1) p(sk1) r(sk1) u(sk1)
-------------------------------------

-------------------------------------------------------------
true domain(sk1) p(sk1) domain(sk2) s(sk1,sk2) u(sk1) u(sk2)
-------------------------------------------------------------
```

Fig. 6. After applying rule #3 four times (!)

```
-------------------------------------------
true domain(sk1) p(sk1) q(sk1) u(sk1) false
-------------------------------------------

-------------------------------------
true domain(sk1) p(sk1) r(sk1) u(sk1)
-------------------------------------

-------------------------------------------------------------
true domain(sk1) p(sk1) domain(sk2) s(sk1,sk2) u(sk1) u(sk2)
-------------------------------------------------------------
```

Fig. 7. Goal tape, rule #4

Now instruction #5 applies to the second tape, and then instruction #6 applies to the third tape, shown in Figure 8.

```
-------------------------------------------
true domain(sk1) p(sk1) q(sk1) u(sk1) false
-------------------------------------------

------------------------------------------
true domain(sk1) p(sk1) r(sk1) u(sk1) goal
------------------------------------------

-----------------------------------------------------------------
true domain(sk1) p(sk1) domain(sk2) s(sk1,sk2)  u(sk1) u(sk2) goal
-----------------------------------------------------------------
```

Fig. 8. After applying rule #5 and then #6, HALTED

At this point the SM *halts* because each tape has either the term `goal` or the term `false` written on it.

The SM has effectively computed a proof that the *disjunction*

$$(\exists X)(u(X) \wedge q(X)) \vee (\exists X)r(X) \vee (\exists X)(\exists Y)s(X,Y)$$

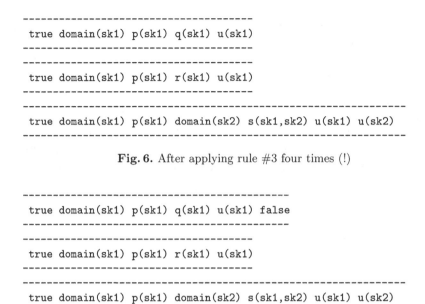

is a *logical* consequence of the *Geolog* theory consisting of the first three rules in Figure 3. This is so because every tape of the halted machine either has `q(sk1)` and `u(sk1)` written on it, or has `r(sk1)` written on it, or else has `s(sk1,sk2)` written on it. Note that the three disjuncts correspond to the *goal* and *false* rules in Figure 3. We will continue a discussion of this example (specifically, the role intended for the *false* rule) later in this section.

The *proof tree* displayed in Figure 9 was automatically drawn by the program whose implementation is described in the next section. The diagram displays the tapes generated by the SM in the form of a directed tree. Notice that the tree splits where the SM would have copied a tape.[2]

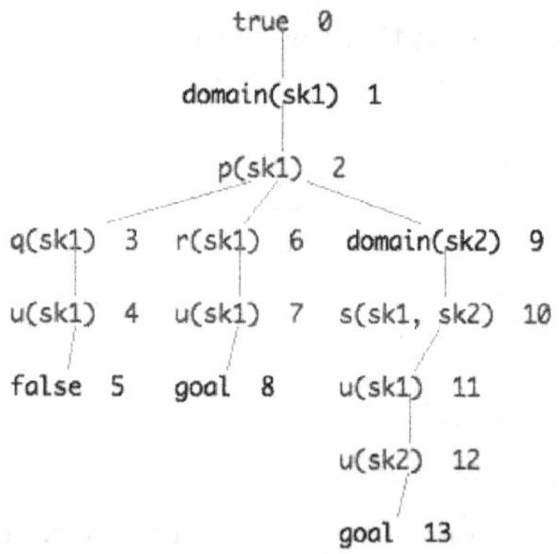

Fig. 9. Tree display

Here is the definition of SM operations, described in smaller steps.

- A *Geolog* rule $ANT \Rightarrow CONS$ is *applicable* to an SM tape T, provided that it is the case that all of the terms of ANT can be simultaneously matched against grounded terms written on T. (It may be that ANT can be matched against T in more than one way; for example, rule #3 and the third tape of Figure 5.)
- If the rule $ANT \Rightarrow CONS$ is applicable to tape T, then for some matching substitution σ apply σ to $CONS$ and then *expand* tape T using $\sigma(CONS)$.
- In order to *expand* tape T by $\sigma(CONS) = C_1; C_2; \ldots; C_k$ copy tape T making $k-1$ new tapes $T_2, T_3, \ldots, T_k$, and then *extend* T using C_1, extend T_2 using C_2, ..., and extend T_k using C_k. (No copying if $k = 1$.)
- In order to *extend* a tape T using a conjunction C, suppose that $X_1, \ldots, X_p$ are all of the free existential variables in C. Create new

[2] It is possible to describe an SM using trees rather than multiple tapes.

constants c_j, $1 \leq j \leq p$ and substitute c_j for X_j in C, obtaining C', and then write each of the terms of C' on tape T. (It is mandatory that the constant is new with repect to the theory and the tape, but different tapes may subsequently contain the same constant.)

Notice that only grounded terms ever appear on any SM tape. Thus the matching algorithm does not really need the full power of general term unification. Simple left-to-right term matching suffices.

Given an SM with tapes $T_1, \ldots, T_t$, $t \geq 0$, we say a particular tape T_i is *saturated* if no new instance of a rule can be applied to it. A tape is *halted* if it is either saturated or contains *goal* or contains *false* (any of which could occur at the same time). An SM is called *halted* if all its tapes are halted, it is *halted successfully* if it is halted with all tapes containing either *goal* or *false.* If a tape of an SM is saturated with neither *goal* nor *false* on it, then this tape actually constitutes a countermodel: all rules are satisfied, they are consistent (by absence of *false*) and yet the goal doesn't hold (by absence of *goal*).

Suppose that we write a *Geolog* theory in the form

$$T = A \cup G \cup F \tag{6}$$

where A is the *axioms*, G contains all of the affirming *goal* rules and F contains all of the rejecting *false* rules. It is intended that A contains all the rules of the theory other than the *goal* rules and the *false* rules and that A, G, and F are mutually disjoint sets.

The *Geolog query* Q for a *Geolog* theory $T = A \cup G \cup F$ is the disjunctive normal form $Q = C_1; C_2; \ldots; C_k$ consisting of all of the conjunctions C_i such that either C_i appears as antecedent of one of the *goal* rules (in G) or of one of the *false* rules (in F). As before, the free variables in Q are taken to be existential variables. The scope of a variable X appearing in a particular C_i (within Q) is restricted to C_i.

We say that a *Geolog* theory T *supports* its query Q if there is a successfully halted SM such that each C_i is satisfied on some tape.

Theorem 1. If theory T supports its query Q then Q is a logical consequence of the axioms of T. Here both T and Q are considered to be first-order logical formulas as described in the introductory section and in this section.

In our example from earlier in this section we demonstrated that the query `(u(X),q(X));r(Y);s(U,V)` is supported by the theory and therefore, according to Theorem 1,

$$(\exists X)(u(X) \wedge q(X)) \vee (\exists Y)r(Y) \vee (\exists U)(\exists V)s(U,V)$$

is a logical consequence of the axioms of the theory. The axioms are #1-3, and the query is given by #4-6.

In general, *false* and *goal* are interchangeable in *Geolog* rules, in so far the declarative semantics as expressed in Theorem 1 is concerned. Technically, *false*, being the empty disjunction, is a symbol which should be interpreted as logically false, in the same way as *true*, being the empty conjunction, is a symbol whose logical interpretation is intended as true. As part of the logical vocabulary, they have the same status as other connectives and quantifiers. In contrast, *goal* is an atom, a nullary predicate which could be interpreted as either true or as false.

In principle one could do with either only *goal*, or only *false*. If one doesn't use *false*, the theory is always consistent (all predicates can be taken to be true everywhere). If one doesn't use *goal*, the theory can be inconsistent. Although one could do with only one of *goal*, *false*, there can be pragmatic reasons to use both. The use of *goal* or *false* depends to a large extent on taste and tradition. For example, the query of a *Geolog* theory could be `r(b,X);r(c,Y);e(b,c)` where the first two are assumed never to be true. In that case `r(b,X) => false`, `r(c,Y) => false` and `e(b,c) => goal` are more clear than any other combination of conclusions `false` and `goal`. This is actually the choice made in the example in Figure 1. Another pragmatic ground for using *false* would be that some specific disjunct occurs in many different queries.

Theorem 1 is a *correctness* result for Skolem machine consequences: Skolem machines compute queries for *Geolog* theories and supported queries are logical consequences of the axioms of a theory. The issue of the *completeness* of SM computations, obviously depending on strategies for picking rules, is addressed in [6]. It is in general not decidable whether a *Geolog* theory supports its query. The *Geolog* programmer is mainly interested in designing theories that can be shown to support their intended queries, using some computational device, such as the implementation described in the next section.

The definitions for the SM operations allow for repeated use of an instruction for a working tape T. There is an obvious restriction that should be applied for efficiency reasons. Suppose the $ANT \Rightarrow CONS$ is an applicable rule for tape T, with matching substitution σ. We say that the disjunction $\sigma(CONS) = \sigma(C_1; C_2; \ldots; C_k)$ is *already satisfied* on T provided that at least one of the conjunctions C_i is satisfied, possibly with constant symbols substituted for the free existential variables. A closed conjuction C' is satisfied on T if all of the terms of C' are already written on T.

Theorem 2. If we expand tapes of Skolem machines using an applicable rule ANT $\Rightarrow$ CONS only if $\sigma(CONS)$ is not *already satisfied on the tape, exactly the same queries are supported.*

Another consequence of the restriction to applicable rules that are not already satisfied is that it may occur that a tape is saturated without containing *goal* or *false* and that a *counter model* will be discovered.

```
translate(+GeologRuleIn, -PrologRuleOut)
```

Fig. 10. The intended translation, *Geolog* rule to Prolog clause

3 Procedural Implementations

Implementations of Skolem machine operations using Prolog procedures can be very straightforward. Each of the *Geolog* rules in the instruction set is translated into a special kind of Prolog clause. The implementation that we illustrate is called the *Geometric Logic Abstract Machine* or GLAM for short. The reason for this name is that the clauses resemble the procedures of the *Warren Abstract Machine* (WAM), which is used as a basis for most of the efficient implementations of Prolog itself. In particular, each procedure tries to match bindings for variables in terms. For the GLAM procedures, however, the terms can be in different states (multiple tapes).

The Prolog translator is basically a one-line program that mimics the SM operations. The `translate` rule has the profile shown in Figure 10.

Figure 11 shows the full Prolog code for translating a *Geolog* rule. For example, consider *Geolog* rule #2 from the sample rulebase in the previous section, shown in Figure 12. First, any existential variables in the consequent are separated and flagged, as shown in Figure 13, and then the translated Prolog clause is displayed in Figure 14.

In the previous section the SM operations describing how to apply a *Geolog* rule to a tape were described. The code in Figure 11 mimics the steps defining how a SM applies instructions to tapes. The Prolog code implements the tape using a Prolog list, and terms are added to the beginning of the list (end of the tape).

Each of the `try` clauses describes how to *try* to extend a tape using the corresponding *Geolog* rule. The *Geolog* rules are translated into Prolog clauses in the order in which they appear in the *Geolog* instruction sequence. Figure 15 has an outline for all of the `try` clauses, showing the order in which they are asserted to memory (and compiled).

In the SWI-Prolog [15] implementation of the GLAM, after the *Geolog* rules are read from file and translated into Prolog clauses, the Prolog

```
%%%%%%%%%%%%%%%%%
%% Translator
%%%%%%%%%%%%%%%%%
translate((ANT => CONS) ,  % to the following Prolog clause ...
  (try((ANT => CONS),S) :-
      satisfy(ANT,S),
      \+satisfactual(CONS,S),
      cases(CONS,[F|R]),
      extend(F,S,FS),
      try(_,FS),              % try again
      continue(S,R) ) ) . % other cases, if any
```

Fig. 11. Translating *Geolog* rules to Prolog clauses

```
p(X) => q(X) ; r(X) ; domain(Y), s(X,Y).
```

Fig. 12. `+GeologRuleIn`, sample input term

clauses are asserted and then compiled into internal procedures for the underlying Prolog machine.

The remaining small amount of code for applying *Geolog* rules, expanding, and extending tapes (states) is given in the reference [5]. The Prolog interpreter has filename **`geoprolog.pl`**. The reference also provides a user guide and a number of examples.

The primary advantage of this approach is its excellent speed of execution. The implementation described here applies the *Geolog* instructions to the states (tapes) in a very strict top-down order: The first instruction that succeeds is applied to expand a tape or extend tapes, and then the interpreter goes all the way back to the first procedure (corresponding to the first *Geolog* instruction) in order to try other instructions. This is clear if one looks at the generated code, such as that in Figure 14, which is typical. This is a doggedly persistent top-down approach, which is very reminiscent of how Prolog itself works. And, this explains the speed! This can be a great source of efficiency, as it is for Prolog. The primary reference for the theoretical underpinnings for Prolog is [8], and relevant references for the machine model for the WAM are [1] and [13].

As it is for Prolog, the ordering of *Geolog* instructions becomes important for depth-first implementation of GLAM.

Now, in contrast, the advantage of breadth-first *Geolog* interpreters is that the order of the *Geolog* rules is not, in and of itself, a direct hindrance. Breadth-first interpreters for *Geolog* would typically apply all applicable rules to the current tapes (states) simultaneously. Such breadth-first interpreters can often deplete execution resources before halting, but they could *in principle* compute all consequences for a *Geolog* theory.

```
p(X) => q(X) ; r(X) ; Y^(domain(Y), s(X,Y)).
```

Fig. 13. `+GeologRuleIn`, flag existential variable

```
try((p(A)=>q(A);r(A);B^ (domain(B), s(A, B))), C) :-
        satisfy(p(A), C),
        \+satisfactual((q(A);r(A);B^ (domain(B), s(A, B))), C),
        cases((q(A);r(A);B^ (domain(B), s(A, B))), [E|H]),
        extend(E, C, F),
        try(_, F),
        continue(C, H).
```

Fig. 14. `-PrologRuleOut`, sample output term

As emphasized in [2], in case of depth-first, it is often best to sequence the instructions so that splitting rules and rules introducing existential quantifiers are placed *at the end* of the rulebase, such as. the rules 12 and 13 in Figure 1. Moving these rules higher up in the list is inhibitive for computing the query depth-first. In the presence of function symbols even more trivial examples can be given, such as the wrong order of the last two of the following rules:

```
true => p(a).
p(X) => p(f(X)). %alternatively: p(X) => succ(X,Y),p(Y).
p(X) => goal.
```

4 Conclusion and Future Research

Using an abstract machine to implement a language is a precise approach. We have advocated this approach for first-order geometric logic using the *Geolog* language. We have shown that the resulting machinery can be fruitfully put to work in automated reasoning in some areas of mathematics.

For extending this approach beyond the language restrictions imposed by geometric logic we envisage the integration of *Geolog* in more expressive logical frameworks. The role of *Geolog* is then to boost automation of the logical framework. For this purpose geometric logic could be a better choice than other candidates, such as resolution logic, since the existential quantification allows a more faithful representation of the problems to be delegated to *Geolog*. How to integrate and which particular strategies for computing *Geolog* queries, will be subjects of future research.

```
% START with initial state
try :- try(_,[true]).

% test for goal on tape (or \f )
try(_,S) :-
   member(goal,S), member(false,S),  !.

%%%%%%%%%%%%%%%%%%%%%%%%%%%%%%%%%%%%%%
%%% Translated Geolog clauses asserted
%%% here, in user-specified order.
%%%%%%%%%%%%%%%%%%%%%%%%%%%%%%%%%%%%%%

% last clause, must have stuck tape
try(_,S) :-
   write('counter_model('),
   write(S),
   writeln(').')
```

Fig. 15. Order for the translated Prolog clauses

References

1. Ait-Kaci, H.: Warrens's Abstract Machine, A Tutorial Reconstruction. School of Computing Science (February 18, 1999)
2. Bezem, M.A., Coquand, T.: Automating Coherent Logic. In: Sutcliffe, G., Voronkov, A. (eds.) LPAR 2005. LNCS (LNAI), vol. 3835, pp. 246–260. Springer, Heidelberg (2005)
3. Bezem, M.A.: On the Undecidability of Coherent Logic. In: Middeldorp, A., van Oostrom, V., van Raamsdonk, F., de Vrijer, R. (eds.) Processes, Terms and Cycles: Steps on the Road to Infinity. LNCS, vol. 3838, pp. 6–13. Springer, Heidelberg (2005)
4. Blass, A.: Topoi and computation. Bulletin of the EATCS 36, 57–65 (1998)
5. Fisher, J.R.: Geolog website, `www.csupomona.edu/~jrfisher/www/geolog/`
6. Fisher, J.R., Bezem, M.A.: Query Completeness of Skolem Machine Computations. In: Proceedings MCU'07 (to appear)
7. Johnstone, P.: Sketches of an Elephant: a topos theory compendium, vol. 2, Oxford Logic Guides 44, OUP (2002)
8. Lloyd, J.W.: Foundations of Logic Programming. revised edn. Springer, Berlin (1987)
9. Manthey, R., Bry, F.: SATCHMO: A Theorem Prover Implemented in Prolog. In: Lusk, E., Overbeek, R. (eds.) 9th International Conference on Automated Deduction. LNCS, vol. 310, pp. 415–434. Springer, Heidelberg (1988)
10. de Nivelle, H., Meng, J.: Geometric Resolution: A Proof Procedure Based on Finite Model Search. In: Furbach, U., Shankar, N. (eds.) IJCAR 2006. LNCS (LNAI), vol. 4130, pp. 303–317. Springer, Berlin (2006)
11. Robinson, J.A.: A Machine-Oriented Logic Based on the Resolution Principle. Journal of the ACM 12(1), 23–41 (1965)

12. Skolem, Th.: Logisch-kombinatorische Untersuchungen über die Erfüllbarkeit und Beweisbarkeit mathematischen Sätze nebst einem Theoreme über dichte Mengen, Skrifter I, vol. 4, pp. 1–36, Det Norske Videnskaps-Akademi (1920). Also in Jens Erik Fenstad, editor, Selected Works in Logic by Th. Skolem, pp. 103–136, Universitetsforlaget, Oslo (1970)
13. Warren, D.H.D.: An abstract Prolog instruction set. Technical Note 309, SRI International, Menlo Park, CA (October 1983)
14. Sutcliffe, G., Suttner, C.: The CADE ATP System Competition. Link available at: `www.cs.miami.edu/~tptp/CASC/`
15. Wielemaker, J.: SWI-Prolog Reference Manual. Link available at: `www.swi-prolog.org`

A Logical Calculus for Modelling Interferences

Christophe Fouqueré

LIPN – UMR7030
CNRS – Université Paris 13
99 av. J-B Clément, F–93430 Villetaneuse, France
cf@lipn.univ-paris13.fr

Abstract. A logic calculus is presented that is a conservative extension of linear logic. The motivation beneath this work concerns lazy evaluation, true concurrency and interferences in proof search. The calculus includes two new connectives to deal with multisequent structures and has the cut-elimination property. Extensions are proposed that give first results concerning our objectives.

1 Introduction

Linear Logic is a good framework for interpreting and computing over linear structures. Since Girard's seminal paper [1] that gives first insights (proof nets, phase and coherent spaces), a lot has been achieved among which normalization of proofs via focusing and polarization [2,3]. These last results seem to be intrinsically related to principles underlying cut elimination as it allows for investigating a reconstruction of logical structures as in Ludics [4]. Recent works done on concurrent modelling using such a framework seem promising [5,6]. However, non series-parallel situations are not taken into account.

We present a logic calculus (and variants) that is a conservative extension of linear logic. The motivation beneath this work is a careful study of lazy evaluation in logic programming. Since works of Andreoli [2], we know that full linear logic may be used as a logical programming language thanks to focalization and works have been done on lazy evaluation in this case [7]. However we show in Sect. 3 that cut elimination is false for a naive calculus taking laziness as a principle. A second motivation concerns the control of true concurrency and interferences in proof search. For instance, suppose the following problem to be modelled in logic programming. We have two 'packs' of actions: $f = \bigoplus f_n$ (resp. $g = \bigoplus g_n$) such that f_n (resp. g_n) transforms n occurences of a (resp. b) into n occurences of a and n occurences of b, where $n \geq 1$. We suppose at the initial state only one resource of each kind (hence one a and one b). We want to simulate exactly the two following situations:

(i) if the two actions are applied (whatever may be the order) then we have three possible results: 3 a and 2 b, 2 a and 3 b, 2 a and 2 b. The first (resp. second) result is obtained when action f (resp. g) is applied first followed by action g (resp. f). The third result occurs when the two actions are performed independently.

C.B. Jones, Z. Liu, J. Woodcock (Eds.): ICTAC 2007, LNCS 4711, pp. 216–230, 2007.

(ii) if the two actions are applied strictly concurrently, there is only one possible result: we get 2 a and 2 b.

This is not possible inside propositional classical or linear logic as it requires a control between proofs. For that purpose, we basically shift from a sequent view to a multisequent view. Moreover sharing of formulas occurences between such sequents is allowed. The reader should have in mind the following elements:

- logical operations are done on occurences of formulas that may be shared among different sequents,
- a sequent is a place grouping a bunch of occurences,
- each step of a proof transforms zero, one or two multisequents into one by means of an operation, either structural or logical (in this last case the operation is done on occurences of formula and entails the structure of the conclusion),
- equivalently, a multisequent may be defined as a set of places, a set of occurences of formulas and a function relating a place to a set of occurences.

In the following the two interpretations may be used. Shifting from sequents to multisequents gives place for a new structural operation that joins sequents (to be compared with the par operation that joins occurences in a sequent). In a first step we consider a "2-way" connective that "relates" two sequents in a multisequent. Its dual is denoted | and called cpar. We then consider the following extensions:

- add of a 'cloning' structural rule: this comes from the observation that interaction of a sequent by means of a cut elimination is behaviouraly equivalent to interaction with two sequents sharing exactly the same occurences. However this last observation is not provable without such a cloning rule.
- add exponential-like modalities (Sec. 4): standard modalities for linear logic are available. However as sharing is internal, it allows for adding modalities whose behaviour is the converse of the standard one.
- add a 3-way connective (Sec. 5): it relates three sequents in one shot. This is requested for a model of independence. It offers also a means to deal with non series-parallel structures as a 3-way connective is intrinsically a non-linear operation.

In Sect. 6, we end by some comments about a possible algebraic semantics.

2 Related Works

Modelling interferences has not yet been really investigated in logic. First of all, classical logic as well as modal logic do not take seriously into account the notion of resource, hence appear to be inadequate. Second, modelling (and controlling) interferences may seem contradictory in the framework of Linear Logic as the splitting mechanism seems at the heart of cut-elimination. However, current works done on concurrency are close. Following Girard's works on Ludics,

Curien, Faggian, Giamberardino [5,6] were able to formalize L-nets that quotient (abstract) proof trees w.r.t. commutation of tensors. This normalization goes further than the one given by Andreoli with focusing and polarization. However, non series-parallel situations cannot be taken into account in their denotational model. Works close to the research presented here include Bunched Implications [8] and Deep Inference [9]. But these two last frameworks seem to fail in keeping basic logical properties as focalization and polarization. The line of research that is undertaken here introduces a syntactic novelty by considering that occurences of formulae may be shared by different sequents. This sharing induces a strict synchronization between different computations (i.e. developments of proofs) and new connectives may be defined that internalize this mechanism.

3 A Multisequent Calculus

Besides the classical multiplicative and additive connectives of Linear Logic, we introduce two new connectives ctimes $\odot$ and cpar $|$ whose intended meaning is to model strict concurrency.

Definition 1. *The* formulas, *denoted $A, B, \ldots$, are built from atoms p, q, $\ldots$, $p^\perp$, $q^\perp$, $\ldots$, constants $\mathbf{1}$, $\perp$, $\mathbf{0}$, $\top$ and the following (linear) connectives:*

- *(parallel) multiplicative conjunction $\otimes$ (times) and disjunction $\parr$ (par),*
- *(concurrent) multiplicative conjunction $\odot$ (ctimes) and disjunction $|$ (cpar),*
- *additive conjunction $\oplus$ (plus) and disjunction $\&$ (with).*

Negation is defined by De Morgan rules:

$$
\begin{array}{ll}
(p)^\perp = p^\perp & (p^\perp)^\perp = p \\
(A \otimes B)^\perp = B^\perp \parr A^\perp & (A \parr B)^\perp = B^\perp \otimes A^\perp \\
(A \odot B)^\perp = B^\perp \mid A^\perp & (A \mid B)^\perp = B^\perp \odot A^\perp \\
(A \oplus B)^\perp = B^\perp \,\&\, A^\perp & (A \,\&\, B)^\perp = B^\perp \oplus A^\perp \\
\mathbf{1}^\perp = \perp \quad \mathbf{0}^\perp = \top & \perp^\perp = \mathbf{1} \quad \top^\perp = \mathbf{0}
\end{array}
$$

$$A \multimap B = A^\perp \parr B$$

3.1 Structures of Multisequents

Definition 2. *A* formula context *Γ has one of the two following forms:*

- *A formula A*
- *A finite multiset of formula contexts separated by commas $\Delta_1, \ldots, \Delta_n$. ',' is considered commutative and associative.*

Sequents *are of the form $\{\Gamma\}$, where Γ is a formula context. A* multisequent *is a finite multiset of sequents. Multisequents are denoted $\mathcal{S}, \mathcal{T}, \ldots$ If a multisequent is reduced to one sequent, '{' and '}' may be omitted. A multisequent may contain sequents that are not disjoint: an occurence of a formula may appear in different sequents. Such sequents are said to be* linked. *Superscripts are put if different occurences of the same formula occur. The* principal *formulas occurences of a (logical) rule are formulas from the hypotheses on which the rule applies. The* principal *sequents are sequents where the principal formulas occur.*

Example 1 (multisequents). $\{A, B\}\{C, D\}$: this multisequent involves four formulas and two (disjoint) sequents whereas $\{A, B\}\{B, C\}\{C, D\}$ involves three sequents and four occurences of formulas.

At first glance, rules given in sequent calculi may seem strange: Throughout the paper, contexts of a principal occurence are identified by a free subscript. For example, $\{\Gamma_i, A\}$ means a multiset of sequents (the domain of the free subscript i) where the *same* occurence A appears. Note that the domain of i cannot be empty. Sequents that remain unchanged by a rule are either replaced by dots or by a notation for a multisequent. If a proof involves different occurences of the same fomula (hence different contexts), these occurences are distinguished by a superscript:[1] remark this in the &-rule in Fig. 2.

3.2 A Naive (and Wrong) Attempt

Lazy logic programming relies mainly on a lazy splitting of contexts when considering the $\otimes$ rule. The standard $\otimes$ rule is the following one:

$$\frac{\{\Gamma, A\} \quad \{\Delta, B\}}{\{\Delta, \Gamma, A \otimes B\}}\ (\otimes)$$

In a bottom-up proof search, as it is the case in logic programming, applying this rule requires to know how to split the multiset Δ, Γ. A lazy way consists in delaying this separation. Let us note $|$ the connective $\otimes$ defined in a lazy way. Shifting to multisequents, this may be given by sharing the whole multiset Δ, Γ between the two sequents in the hypothesis (remember that occurences are shared between sequents if no superscript is present):

$$\frac{\{\Delta, \Gamma, A\}\{\Delta, \Gamma, B\}}{\{\Delta, \Gamma, A \mid B\}}\ (|)$$

We suppose further $\parr$ still dual to $|$: $(A \mid B)^\perp = B^\perp \parr A^\perp$. Following these guidelines, a system for a lazy Multiplicative Linear Logic (lazy MLL) is given in Fig. 1. However a counter-example to cut-elimination is easy to find:
$\{A^\perp, A \parr \perp\}$ and $\{A^\perp \mid 1, A \parr \perp\}\{A^\perp \mid 1, 1^1 \parr 1^2\}$ are provable.
But $\{A^\perp, A \parr \perp\}\{A^\perp, 1^1 \parr 1^2\}$ is not provable:

$$\dfrac{\dfrac{\dfrac{}{A^\perp, A}}{A^\perp, A, \perp}}{A^\perp, A \parr \perp} \quad \text{and} \quad \dfrac{\dfrac{\dfrac{\dfrac{}{\{A^\perp, A\}\{1^1\}\{1\}\{1^2\}}}{\{A^\perp, A\}\{A^\perp, 1^1, 1^2\}\{1, A\}\{1, 1^1, 1^2\}}}{\{A^\perp|1, A\}\{A^\perp|1, 1^1, 1^2\}}}{\dfrac{\{A^\perp|1, A, \perp\}\{A^\perp|1, 1^1, 1^2\}}{\{A^\perp|1, A \parr \perp\}\{A^\perp|1, 1^1 \parr 1^2\}}} \quad \text{but} \quad \dfrac{\dfrac{\dfrac{\dfrac{\dfrac{false}{\{1^1, 1^2\}}}{\{A^\perp, A\}\{1^1, 1^2\}}}{\{A^\perp, A\}\{A^\perp, 1^1, 1^2\}}}{\{A^\perp, A, \perp\}\{A^\perp, 1^1, 1^2\}}}{\{A^\perp, A \parr \perp\}\{A^\perp, 1^1 \parr 1^2\}}$$

[1] A context Γ with a supersript supposes the superscript for each formula of the context.

Structural rules

$$\frac{\ldots\{\Gamma_i, A\}\{\Delta\}\ldots}{\ldots\{\Gamma_i, A\}\{A, \Delta\}\ldots}\ (d) \qquad \frac{\mathcal{S}_1 \quad \mathcal{S}_2}{\mathcal{S}_1\mathcal{S}_2}\ (s) \qquad \frac{\ldots\{\Gamma, A, B, \Delta\}\ldots}{\ldots\{\Gamma, B, A, \Delta\}\ldots}\ (e)$$

Logical rules (in rules (1) and (*axiom*), the multisequent consists of only one sequent)

$$\frac{}{A, A^{\perp}}\ (axiom)$$

$$\frac{}{1}\ (1) \qquad \frac{\ldots\{\Gamma_i\}\ldots}{\ldots\{\Gamma_i, \perp\}\ldots}\ (\perp)$$

$$\frac{\ldots\{\Gamma_i, A, B\}\ldots}{\ldots\{\Gamma_i, A \parr B\}\ldots}\ (\parr) \qquad \frac{\ldots\{\Gamma_i, A\}\{\Gamma_i, B\}\ldots}{\ldots\{\Gamma_i, A \mid B\}\ldots}\ (\mid)$$

Cut rule

$$\frac{\ldots\{\Gamma_i, A\}\ldots \quad \ldots\{\Delta_j, A^{\perp}\}\ldots}{\ldots\{\Gamma_i, \Delta_j\}\ldots}\ (cut)$$

Fig. 1. Sequent calculus for a bad lazy MLL. $i, j \in \mathbb{N}^*$ in rules.

3.3 The Calculus CMALL

In order to circumvent the previous situation, lazyness is modelled by means of two specific connectives $\mid$ and $\odot$ besides the two multiplicative connectives $\parr$ and $\otimes$ of Linear Logic. The rules of the sequent calculus Concurrent Multiplicative Additive Linear Logic (CMALL) are given in Fig. 2. The system includes a cloning structural rule (c), however one may note that proofs of cut elimination, asynchrony, ... we give in the following are still true without this rule. Examples of instantiation of the rules are given below to help the reader recover standard situations.

Example 2 (Rule instantiation). (A, B, X, Y, Z are formulas)

$$\frac{\{X, A\}\{Y, A\} \quad \{Z, B\}}{\{X, Z, A \otimes B\}\{Y, Z, A \otimes B\}}\ (\otimes) \quad \frac{\{X\}\{X, A\}\{X, B\}}{\{X\}\{X, A \mid B\}}\ (\mid) \quad \frac{\{X\}\{X, A, B\}}{\{X\}\{X, A \parr B\}}\ (\parr)$$

It is easy to prove the following statements (multisequents may be given two-sided for easiness of reading):

– $A \otimes B \multimap A \mid B$ is provable:

$$\dfrac{\dfrac{\dfrac{\dfrac{\dfrac{\dfrac{}{\{A^{\perp}, A\}}\ ax \quad \dfrac{}{\{B^{\perp}, B\}}\ ax}{\{A^{\perp}, A\}\{B^{\perp}, B\}}\ s}{\{A^{\perp}, B^{\perp}, A\}\{B^{\perp}, B\}}\ d}{\{A^{\perp}, B^{\perp}, A\}\{A^{\perp}, B^{\perp}, B\}}\ d}{\{A^{\perp}, B^{\perp}, A|B\}}\ \mid}{\{A^{\perp} \parr B^{\perp}, A|B\}}\ \parr$$

- $|$ is asynchronous (lemma 2) whereas $\otimes$ is synchronous. Although $|$ does neither distribute over $⅋$, nor the converse. But $|$ does distribute over $\&$: $A \mid (B \,\&\, C) \dashv\vdash (A \mid B) \,\&\, (A \mid C)$ is provable

$$\dfrac{\dfrac{\dfrac{\dfrac{\dfrac{}{\{A^1,A^{\perp 1}\}} \quad \dfrac{}{\{B,B^{\perp 1}\}}}{\{A^1,(A^\perp\odot B^\perp)^1\} \quad \{B,(A^\perp\odot B^\perp)^1\}}}{\{A^1,(A^\perp\odot B^\perp)\oplus(A^\perp\odot C^\perp)^1\} \quad \{B,(A^\perp\odot B^\perp)\oplus(A^\perp\odot C^\perp)^1\}} \quad \dfrac{\dfrac{\dfrac{}{\{A^2,A^{\perp 2}\}} \quad \dfrac{}{\{C,C^{\perp 2}\}}}{\{A^2,(A^\perp\odot C^\perp)^2\} \quad \{C,(A^\perp\odot C^\perp)^2\}}}{\{A^2,(A^\perp\odot B^\perp)\oplus(A^\perp\odot C^\perp)^2\} \quad \{C,(A^\perp\odot B^\perp)\oplus(A^\perp\odot C^\perp)^2\}}}{\{A,(A^\perp\odot B^\perp)\oplus(A^\perp\odot C^\perp)\} \quad \{B\&C,(A^\perp\odot B^\perp)\oplus(A^\perp\odot C^\perp)\}}}{\{A|(B\&C),(A^\perp\odot B^\perp)\oplus(A^\perp\odot C^\perp)\}}$$

$$\dfrac{\dfrac{\dfrac{\dfrac{}{\{A,A^{\perp 1}\}} \quad \dfrac{\dfrac{}{\{B,B^{\perp 1}\}}}{\{B,(B^\perp\oplus C^\perp)^1\}}}{\{A,[A^\perp\odot(B^\perp\oplus C^\perp)]^1\} \quad \{B,[A^\perp\odot(B^\perp\oplus C^\perp)]^1\}}}{\{A|B,[A^\perp\odot(B^\perp\oplus C^\perp)]^1\}} \quad \dfrac{\dfrac{\dfrac{}{\{A,A^{\perp 2}\}} \quad \dfrac{\dfrac{}{\{C,C^{\perp 2}\}}}{\{C,(B^\perp\oplus C^\perp)^2\}}}{\{A,[A^\perp\odot(B^\perp\oplus C^\perp)]^2\} \quad \{C,[A^\perp\odot(B^\perp\oplus C^\perp)]^2\}}}{\{A|C,[A^\perp\odot(B^\perp\oplus C^\perp)]^2\}}}{\{(A|B)\&(A|C),A^\perp\odot(B^\perp\oplus C^\perp)\}}$$

- $\otimes \not\equiv |$ Remark that $\{\mathbf{1}, \perp \otimes \perp\}$ is not provable, but $\{\mathbf{1}, \perp \mid \perp\}$ is provable (the two $\perp$ are indexed to distinguish them, however these two denote the same constant; note also that there is only one occurence of $\mathbf{1}$ throughout the proof):

$$\dfrac{\dfrac{\dfrac{\dfrac{\overline{\mathbf{1}}\ \mathbf{1}}{\{\mathbf{1}\}\{\mathbf{1}\}}\ w}{\{\mathbf{1}\}\{\mathbf{1},\perp^2\}}\ \perp}{\{\mathbf{1},\perp^1\}\{\mathbf{1},\perp^2\}}\ \perp}{\mathbf{1},\perp^1|\perp^2}\ |$$

Proposition 1. *The system enjoys cut-elimination: if $\mathcal{S}$ is a provable multisequent, then there exists at least one cut-free proof of $\mathcal{S}$.*

The proof of cut-elimination (proofs may be found in [10]) relies mainly on a reconstruction of proofs in case the two last rules concern the cut formulas, and on the three following lemmas that allow the commutation of rules. The standard definition of the height of a proof is generalized: the height of the proof of a multisequent is the maximum of the heights of each partial proof.

Lemma 1 (Separability). *Let $\mathcal{S}$ and $\mathcal{T}$ be disjoint multisequents (i.e. there is no occurence of formulas shared by $\mathcal{S}$ and $\mathcal{T}$), the multisequent $\mathcal{S}\mathcal{T}$ is provable iff $\mathcal{S}$ is provable and $\mathcal{T}$ is provable.*

Lemma 2 (Asynchrony). *The connectives $⅋, \&, |$ are asynchronous: let R be an inference rule of one of these connectives (denoted $\circ$ below), let $\mathcal{S}$ be a provable sequent of proof*

$$\dfrac{\dfrac{\mathcal{T}}{\dots\{A\circ B,\Gamma\}\dots}\ R \text{ on } A\circ B}{\genfrac{}{}{0pt}{}{\vdots}{\dots\ \vdots\ \dots}}$$
$$\dfrac{}{\dots\{A\circ B,\Gamma\}\dots}$$

then there exists a proof of the same height of $\mathcal{S}$ with R as the last rule.

Lemma 3 (Synchrony of the cut rule). *The cut rule is synchronous, i.e. let a proof of $\mathcal{S}$ be of the form in the left hand side (R is a rule), then one can build a proof of the same height of $\mathcal{S}$ of the form in the right hand side:*

$$\dfrac{\dfrac{\mathcal{U}[A]}{\mathcal{W}_1[A]}\,R \quad \mathcal{V}[A^\perp]}{\mathcal{S}}\,cut \qquad\qquad \dfrac{\dfrac{\mathcal{U}[A] \quad \mathcal{V}[A^\perp]}{\mathcal{W}_2}\,cut}{\mathcal{S}}\,R$$

Structural rules

$$\frac{\ldots\{\Delta\}\ldots}{\ldots\{\Delta\}\{\Delta\}\ldots}\,(c) \qquad \frac{\ldots\{\Gamma_i, A\}\{\Delta\}\ldots}{\ldots\{\Gamma_i, A\}\{A, \Delta\}\ldots}\,(d) \qquad \frac{\mathcal{S}_1 \quad \mathcal{S}_2}{\mathcal{S}_1\mathcal{S}_2}\,(s)$$

Logical rules (in rules (1) and (*axiom*), the multisequent consists of only one sequent)

$$\frac{}{A, A^\perp}\,(axiom)$$

$$\frac{}{1}\,(1) \qquad \frac{\ldots\{\Gamma_i\}\ldots}{\ldots\{\Gamma_i, \bot\}\ldots}\,(\bot)$$

$$\frac{\ldots}{\ldots\{\Gamma_i, \top\}\ldots}\,(\top) \qquad \text{no rule for } 0$$

$$\frac{\ldots\{\Gamma_i, A\}\ldots \quad \ldots\{\Delta_j, B\}\ldots}{\ldots\{\Delta_j, \Gamma_i, A \otimes B\}\ldots}\,(\otimes) \qquad \frac{\ldots\{\Gamma_i, A, B\}\ldots}{\ldots\{\Gamma_i, A \parr B\}\ldots}\,(\parr)$$

$$\frac{\ldots\{\Gamma_i, A\}\ldots \quad \ldots\{\Delta_j, B\}\ldots}{\ldots\{\Gamma_i, A \odot B\}\{\Delta_j, A \odot B\}\ldots}\,(\odot) \qquad \frac{\ldots\{\Gamma_i, A\}\{\Gamma_i, B\}\ldots}{\ldots\{\Gamma_i, A \mid B\}\ldots}\,(\mid)$$

$$\frac{\ldots\{\Gamma_i, A\}\ldots}{\ldots\{\Gamma_i, A \oplus B\}\ldots}\,(\oplus_1) \quad \frac{\ldots\{\Gamma_i, B\}\ldots}{\ldots\{\Gamma_i, A \oplus B\}\ldots}\,(\oplus_2) \quad \frac{\mathcal{S}^1\{\Gamma_i^1, A\} \quad \mathcal{S}^2\{\Gamma_i^2, B\}}{\mathcal{S}\{\Gamma_i, A \,\&\, B\}}\,(\&)$$

Cut rule

$$\frac{\ldots\{\Gamma_i, A\}\ldots \quad \ldots\{\Delta_j, A^\perp\}\ldots}{\ldots\{\Gamma_i, \Delta_j\}\ldots}\,(cut)$$

Fig. 2. Sequent calculus for CMALL

4 Shared and Unshared Modalities

Modalities may be added to the system in the spirit of exponentials in Soft Linear Logic [11]. They are written as upperscripts on formulas: A^s and A^u. The sharing $.^s$ modality (resp. the unsharing $.^u$) is reminiscent of the why-not ? (resp. the of-course !). Rules are completed with the ones given below:

$$\frac{\ldots\{\Gamma_i^j, \Delta_j\}\ldots}{\ldots\{\Gamma_i, \Delta_j^s\}\ldots}\,(.^s) \qquad \frac{\ldots\{\Gamma_i, A\}\ldots}{\ldots\{\Gamma_i^s, A^u\}\ldots}\,(.^u)$$

Proposition 2. *Cut-elimination for CMALL with modalities is valid.*

Example 3. (Rule instantiation)

$$\frac{\{X^1,A\}\{Y^1,A\}\{X^2,B\}\{Y^2,B\}}{\{X,A^s\}\{Y,A^s\}\{X,B^s\}\{Y,B^s\}}\,(.^s) \qquad\qquad \frac{\{X,A\}\{Y,A\}}{\{X^s,A^u\}\{Y^s,A^u\}}\,(.^u)$$

The sharing modality enjoys the following property: $A \multimap A^s \mid A^s$ is provable

$$\dfrac{\dfrac{\dfrac{}{A^{\perp 1},A^1}\,\text{ax} \qquad \dfrac{}{A^{\perp 2},A^2}\,\text{ax}}{\{A^{\perp},A^s\}\{A^{\perp},A^s\}}\,.^s}{A^{\perp},A^s|A^s}\,|$$

The previous example shows that a unique resource A may be used for two different actions: let us suppose a system has one resource A, and a set of processes each needing one resource A, may we run them together ? The answer is yes if two conditions are satisfied: (i) each process accepts to share its needed resource with others, (ii) the processes run concurrently. We formalize each process $\mathcal{P}_i$ as $A^s \multimap\!\!\odot\, R_i$ where $A \multimap\!\!\odot\, B = A^{\perp} \mid B$ (R_i is the formula modelling the result of $\mathcal{P}_i$): this answers condition (i). Concurrence between processes is denoted as $\mathcal{P}_1 \odot \ldots \odot \mathcal{P}_n$. We have then the following provable and non-provable two-sided sequents ($1 \leq i \leq n$):

$$A, \mathcal{P}_i \vdash R_i$$

$$A, \mathcal{P}_1 \odot \ldots \odot \mathcal{P}_n \vdash R_1 \odot \ldots \odot R_n$$

$$A, \mathcal{P}_1 \otimes \cdots \otimes \mathcal{P}_n \nvdash R_1 \otimes \cdots \otimes R_n$$

The fact that the third sequent is not provable is obvious (even if each process is modelled $A \multimap R_i$!). We just give the proofs for the two others (we set $n = 2$ in the second proof for sake of clarity).

$$\dfrac{\dfrac{}{R_i^{\perp},R_i}\,\text{ax} \qquad \dfrac{\dfrac{}{A^{\perp},A}\,\text{ax}}{A^{\perp},A^s}\,(.^s)}{A^{\perp},A^s \otimes R_i^{\perp},R_i}\,\otimes$$

$$\dfrac{\dfrac{\dfrac{\dfrac{\dfrac{\dfrac{\dfrac{\dfrac{\dfrac{\dfrac{\dfrac{}{\{A^{\perp 1},A^1\}}\,\text{ax} \qquad \dfrac{}{\{A^{\perp 2},A^2\}}\,\text{ax}}{\{A^{\perp 1},A^1\}\{A^{\perp 2},A^2\}}\,s}{\{A^{\perp},A^{s1}\}\{A^{\perp},A^{s2}\}}\,(.^s) \qquad \dfrac{\dfrac{}{\{R_1^{\perp},R_1\}}\,\text{ax} \qquad \dfrac{}{\{R_1^{\perp},R_1\}}\,\text{ax}}{\{R_1^{\perp},R_1 \odot R_2\}\{R_2^{\perp},R_1 \odot R_2\}}\,\odot}{\{A^{\perp},A^{s1}\}\{R_1^{\perp},R_1 \odot R_2\}\{A^{\perp},A^{s2}\}\{R_2^{\perp},R_1 \odot R_2\}}\,s}{\{A^{\perp},A^{s1}\}\{R_1^{\perp},R_1 \odot R_2\}\{A^{\perp},A^{s2}\}\{A^{\perp},R_2^{\perp},R_1 \odot R_2\}}\,d}{\{A^{\perp},A^{s1}\}\{R_1^{\perp},R_1 \odot R_2\}\{A^{\perp},A^{s2},R_1 \odot R_2\}\{A^{\perp},R_2^{\perp},R_1 \odot R_2\}}\,d}{\{A^{\perp},A^{s1},R_1 \odot R_2\}\{R_1^{\perp},R_1 \odot R_2\}\{A^{\perp},A^{s2},R_1 \odot R_2\}\{A^{\perp},R_2^{\perp},R_1 \odot R_2\}}\,d}{\{A^{\perp},A^{s1},R_1 \odot R_2\}\{A^{\perp},R_1^{\perp},R_1 \odot R_2\}\{A^{\perp},A^{s2},R_1 \odot R_2\}\{A^{\perp},R_2^{\perp},R_1 \odot R_2\}}\,d}{\{A^{\perp},A^{s1},R_1 \odot R_2\}\{A^{\perp},R_1^{\perp},R_1 \odot R_2\}\{A^{\perp},A^s|R_2^{\perp},R_1 \odot R_2\}}\,|}{\{A^{\perp},A^s|R_1^{\perp},R_1 \odot R_2\}\{A^{\perp},A^s|R_2^{\perp},R_1 \odot R_2\}}\,|}{A^{\perp},(A^s|R_1^{\perp})|(A^s|R_2^{\perp}),R_1 \odot R_2}\,|$$

5 Managing Interferences

Connectives $|$ and $\odot$ as defined in Sect. 3 cannot deal with interference. In fact, the calculus is designed having lazy logic programming in mind: the context is not immediately split with the $\odot$ rule but a splitting should occur when applying $|$ rules. However, even if a splitting property should be valid, there is no need to have it explicitly for one of the connectives. In fact, interference may be introduced by considering triples instead of pairs of hypotheses in the rule introducing $|$. We then modify the calculus given for CMALL by changing the rules for connectives $\odot$ and $|$ (we call this calculus I-CLL):

$$\frac{...\{\Gamma_i,A\}... \quad ...\{\Delta_j,B\}...}{...\{\Gamma_i,A\odot B\}\{\Gamma_i,\Delta_j,A\odot B\}\{\Delta_j,A\odot B\}...}\ (\odot) \qquad \frac{...\{\Gamma_i,A\}\{\Gamma_i,A,B\}\{\Gamma_i,B\}...}{...\{\Gamma_i,A|B\}...}\ (|)$$

It is easy to prove that $|$ is asynchronous and $\odot$ is synchronous, and also that cut-elimination is valid. Note that the calculus CMALL can be simulated by I-CLL (in order to distinguish the two connectives we note $||$ connective cpar defined in CMALL and $|$ the connective defined in I-CLL):

Proposition 3. *If $\mathcal{S}[A \mid\mid B]$ is provable in CMALL then $\mathcal{S}[A \mid B]$ is provable in I-CLL.*

Proof. The following partial proof shows that one can use a proof with $||$ to build a proof with $|$. Remind that these connectives are asynchronous.

$$\cfrac{\cfrac{\cfrac{...\{\Gamma_i,A\}\{\Gamma_i,B\}...}{...\{\Gamma_i,A\}\{\Gamma_i,A\}\{\Gamma_i,B\}...}\ w}{...\{\Gamma_i,A\}\{\Gamma_i,A,B\}\{\Gamma_i,B\}...}\ d}{...\{\Gamma_i,A|B\}...}\ |$$

This allows us to recover previous properties: $A \otimes B \multimap A \mid B$ and $\otimes \not\equiv \ |$. We are now able to model independent actions:

Example 4. Suppose we have two 'packs' of actions: $f = \bigoplus f_n$ (resp. $g = \bigoplus g_n$) such that f_n (resp. g_n) transforms n occurences of a (resp. b) into n occurences of a and n occurences of b, where $n \geq 1$. Suppose also that we have only one resource of each kind (hence one a and one b). We want to simulate the two following situations:

(i) if the two actions are applied (whatever may be the order) then we have three possible results: 3 a and 2 b, 2 a and 3 b, 2 a and 2 b. The first (resp. second) result is obtained when action f (resp. g) is applied first followed by action g (resp. f). The third result occurs when the two actions are performed simultaneously.
(ii) if the two actions are applied concurrently, there is only one possible result: we get 2 a and 2 b.

As proofs are one-sided (and on the right), we take the negation of propositional variables to get more readable proofs. Let us formalize f_1 as $a^\perp \multimap 0 \odot ((a^\perp \otimes b^\perp)$ &

$(\bot \mid (a^\perp \otimes b^\perp)))$ and g_1 as $b^\perp \multimap 0 \odot ((a^\perp \otimes b^\perp) \mathbin{\&} (\bot \mid (a^\perp \otimes b^\perp)))$. These formalizations are straightforwardly generalized to f_n and g_n.

We consider the following aliases: $X \equiv \top \mid Y$ and $Y \equiv (a \parr b) \oplus (1 \odot (a \parr b))$. Hence $f^\perp \equiv a^\perp \otimes X$ and $g^\perp \equiv b^\perp \otimes X$. Notice that we omit $\oplus$ rules in proofs to shorten them and recall that when two occurences of the same formula appear, these occurences are indexed.

(i) application of f and g is formalized as $f \otimes g$:

$$\dfrac{\dfrac{\{a^\perp,a\} \qquad \dfrac{\dfrac{\dfrac{\dfrac{\begin{matrix}\{2a,3b\}\\ \vdots \\ \{b,a,b,g^\perp\}\end{matrix}}{\{b,Y,g^\perp\}}\parr}{\{b,\top,g^\perp\}\{b,\top,Y,g^\perp\}\{b,Y,g^\perp\}}\top}{\{b,\top,g^\perp\}\{b,\top,Y,g^\perp\}\{b,Y,g^\perp\}}d}{\{b,X,g^\perp\}}\mid}{\{a,b,f^\perp,g^\perp\}}\otimes}{\{a,b,f^\perp \parr g^\perp\}}\parr$$

The other results are obtained by swapping f and g or by using g only on one b in the last step of the previous proof.

(ii) concurrent application of f and g is formalized as $f \odot g$.

$$\dfrac{\dfrac{\dfrac{\dfrac{\overline{\{a^\perp,a\}}\,ax \qquad \dfrac{\dfrac{\dfrac{\dfrac{\dfrac{\dfrac{\overline{1}\,1 \quad \dfrac{\begin{matrix}\{2a,2b\}\\ \vdots \\ \{a,b,X_2\}\{X_2\}\end{matrix}}{\{a\parr b,X_2\}\{X_2\}}\parr}{\{Y\}\{Y,X_2\}\{Y,X_2\}\{X_2\}}\odot}{\{\top\}\{\top\}\{Y\}\{\top,X_2\}\{Y,X_2\}\{Y,X_2\}\{X_2\}}\top}{\{\top\}\{\top\}\{Y\}\{\top,X_2\}\{\top,Y,X_2\}\{Y,X_2\}\{X_2\}}d}{\{\top\}\{\top,Y\}\{Y\}\{\top,X_2\}\{\top,Y,X_2\}\{Y,X_2\}\{X_2\}}d}{\{X_1\}\{X_1,X_2\}\{X_2\}}\mid \qquad \overline{\{b^\perp,b\}}\,ax}{\{X_1\}\{X_1,b,g^\perp\}\{b,g^\perp\}}\otimes}{\{a,f^\perp\}\{a,b^\perp,f^\perp,g^\perp\}\{b,g^\perp\}}\otimes}{\{a,b,f^\perp\}\{a,b,f^\perp,g^\perp\}\{b,g^\perp\}}d}{\{a,b,f^\perp\}\{a,b,f^\perp,g^\perp\}\{a,b,g^\perp\}}d}{\{a,b,f^\perp \mid g^\perp\}}\mid$$

Note that the sequent $\{a, b, f^\perp \mid g^\perp\}$ is not provable when using $\{2a, 3b\}$ as hypothesis.

6 Comments About a Phase Semantics

In this section, a phase semantics is proposed for Linear Logic. It is built as a kind of Fock space on top of a free commutative monoid. Comultiplication is used to model the splitting process. We conjecture that it may give a phase semantics for our calculus. Let $(M, \star, 1)$ be a free commutative, associative monoid with neutral element 1. Elements range as $x, y, \ldots$. The product will be denoted as a concatenation: $xy \triangleq x \star y$. We consider the following notations and definitions:

- $\mathcal{M}$ is the set of multisets of M. These multisets are denoted additively: $x_1 + \cdots + x_n \triangleq \{x_1, \ldots, x_n\}$. M is considered as a subset of $\mathcal{M}$ by identifying a singleton and its element. The empty set may be denoted 0.
- $\mathcal{M}^{\times_n}$ is the closure under $+$ of the cartesian product of n copies of $\mathcal{M}$ (and $\times$ distributes over $+$). Elements range as $a, b, \ldots$. Elements of the cartesian product of M are called *simple*. a_i is the ith part of the simple element a.
- $\mathcal{M}^{\circ_n}$ is the closure under $+$ of the symmetric cartesian product, i.e. $\mathcal{M}^{\circ_n} = \mathcal{M}^{\times_n}/\mathfrak{S}_n$ where $\mathfrak{S}_n$ is the group of permutations on n elements. The symmetric product is denoted $\circ$.
- $\mathcal{M}^{\circ_0} = \mathcal{M}^{\times_0} = \{\emptyset\}$.
- $\texttt{Fock}(M) = \bigcup_{n \geq 0} \mathcal{M}^{\circ_n}$. Elements of $\texttt{Fock}(M)$ range as $f, g, \ldots$
- Let $\Delta : \mathcal{M} \to \mathcal{M}^{\times_2}$ be such that (shuffle coproduct on $\mathcal{M}$):

$$\begin{array}{ll} \forall x \in M, & \Delta(x) = \sum_{x_{(1)} x_{(2)} = x} x_{(1)} \times x_{(2)} \\ \forall a_1, a_2 \in \mathcal{M}, & \Delta(a_1 + a_2) = \Delta(a_1) + \Delta(a_2) \end{array}$$

  We use the Sweedler notation: sums are over all possible decompositions.
- $\Delta_{n-1} : \mathcal{M} \to \mathcal{M}^{\times_n}$ $(n \geq 1)$ is recursively defined:
  - $\Delta_0(a) = a$
  - $\Delta_1(a) = \Delta(a)$
  - $\Delta_{n+1}(a) = (\Delta \times id^n) \circ \Delta_n(a)$ (here $\circ$ refers to composition and $id^n \triangleq id \times \cdots \times id$ (n times))
- We extend Δ_n as a morphism on $(\texttt{Fock}(M), \circ, +)$:
  - $\Delta_n(f + g) = \Delta_n(f) + \Delta_n(g)$
  - $\Delta_n(f \circ g) = \Delta_n(f) \circ \Delta_n(g)$

Proposition 4

- *Δ is coassociative and cocommutative.*
- $\forall n \geq 0, i \in [0, n]$, $\Delta_{n+1} = (id^i \times \Delta \times id^{n-i}) \circ \Delta_n$ *(n-coassociativity).*
- $\forall n \geq 0, i, j \in [1, n+1]$, $c_{i,j} \circ \Delta_n = \Delta_n$ *(n-cocommutativity)* *where* $c_{i,j}(a_1 \times \cdots \times a_i \times \cdots \times a_j \times \cdots \times a_{n+1}) = a_1 \times \cdots \times a_j \times \cdots \times a_i \times \cdots \times a_{n+1}$.

Proofs are obtained by direct computations and induction on n. We finally extend $\star$ to get a product on $\texttt{Fock}(M)$:

Definition 3. *Let $f \in \mathcal{M}^{\circ_m}, g \in \mathcal{M}^{\circ_n}$, f and g simple elements,*

$$f \star g \triangleq \sum \circ_{i,j} f_{i(j)} g_{j(i)}$$

where $i \in [1, m]$ and $j \in [1, n]$. $\star$ is extended by linearity to the Fock space.

Proposition 5. $\star$ *enjoys the following properties:*

- $\star$ *is well defined on* $\texttt{Fock}(M)$ *and is commutative, associative.*
- $\forall u \in M, \forall n \geq 0, i \in [0,n], \Delta_{n+1}(u) = \sum \Delta_i(u_{(1)}) \circ \Delta_{n-i}(u_{(2)})$
- $u \star (f \circ g) = \sum (u_{(1)} \star f) \circ (u_{(2)} \star g)$

Proof. Notations are the following ones:

$$\begin{cases} f &= f_1 \circ \cdots \circ f_m \\ f_i &= f_{i(1)} \cdots f_{i(n)} \end{cases} \qquad \begin{cases} g &= g_1 \circ \cdots \circ g_n \\ g_j &= g_{j(1)} \cdots g_{j(m)} \end{cases}$$

where f_i and g_j are elements of M. Then

$$f \star g = \sum f_{1(1)}g_{1(1)} \circ \cdots \circ f_{1(n)}g_{n(1)} \circ f_{2(1)}g_{1(2)} \circ \cdots \circ f_{m(n)}g_{n(m)}$$

- the definition does not depend on the chosen representatives: permuting f_i with f_j replaces in the sum the term $f_{i(k)}g_{k(i)}$ by $f_{j(k)}g_{k(i)}$ and $f_{j(l)}g_{l(j)}$ by $f_{i(l)}g_{l(j)}$. However, the sum being computed over all decompositions of g_k and g_l, and invariant over permutations, the global sum remains the same. Finally, the product $\star$ is commutative as $\star$ is commutative on M.
- Note that $f \star g$ is the symmetric of $\Delta_n(f) \cdot \Delta_m(g)$ where $\cdot$ is the dot product (here on $\mathcal{M}^{\circ_{mn}}$).
- The dot product is associative (because $\star$ is associative on M), so is the $\star$ product.
- the two last propositions are proven by induction and direct computation.

We add to $\mathcal{M}$ an element $\mathbf{1}$ and extend Δ in the following way: $\Delta(\mathbf{1}) = \mathbf{1} \times \mathbf{1}$. Note that $\mathbf{1}$ is neutral w.r.t. $\star$. $(\texttt{Fock}(M), \star, \circ, \mathbf{1})$ is called a *distribution* space. A model of Linear Logic may be obtained by defining as usual an order relation and by interpreting formulas of Linear Logic as facts. We use the following notations: $f, g \in \texttt{Fock}(M)$, $F, G \subset \texttt{Fock}(M)$. Elements of the dual are denoted with a prime: $f' \in F^{\perp}$. A, B denote facts, i.e. subsets of $\texttt{Fock}(M)$ closed by biorthogonal: $A = A^{\perp\perp}$. We give the following definitions:

Definition 4

- $\geq$ *is the least partial order relation on* $\texttt{Fock}(M)$ *satisfying* $(\forall f, g, h \in \texttt{Fock}(M))$*:*
  ($\geq_1$) $f \leq g$ *then* $f \star h \leq g \star h$
  ($\geq_2$) $f \leq f + g$
- $\perp\!\!\!\perp$ *is a subset of* $\texttt{Fock}(M)$ *satisfying:*
  ($\perp\!\!\!\perp_1$) *it is the smallest ideal for* $\geq$*:* $f \in \perp\!\!\!\perp$ *and* $f \leq g$ *then* $g \in \perp\!\!\!\perp$
  ($\perp\!\!\!\perp_2$) *it contains a subset* $\perp \subset M$
  ($\perp\!\!\!\perp_3$) $f, g \in \perp\!\!\!\perp$ *iff* $f \circ g \in \perp\!\!\!\perp$
- $f^{\perp} = \{g \in \texttt{Fock}(M) / f \star g \in \perp\!\!\!\perp\}$
- $F^{\perp} = \bigcap_{f \in F} f^{\perp}$
- $F \star G = \{f \star g / f \in F, g \in G\}$
- $F \circ G = \{f \circ g / f \in F, g \in G\}$

Lemma 4

$$f < g \text{ then } \exists h \neq 0, \text{ such that } g = f + h$$

Proof. We proceed by induction on $p = m + n$: $f \in \mathcal{M}^{\circ m}$ and $g \in \mathcal{M}^{\circ n}$.

- The property is true for $p = m = n = 0$ ($f = g = 0$ is the only possibility).
- Let $p \geq 1$ and the property true for all $p' < p$. We consider the various cases implying $f < g$.
  ($\geq_1$) $\exists f_1, g_1, h_1$ such that $f = f_1 \star h_1$, $g = g_1 \star h_1$ and $f_1 < g_1$. Hence by induction (inductive construction of the partial order on $\mathcal{M}$ or induction on p), $\exists h_2 \neq 0$ such that $g_1 = f_1 + h_2$. Then $g = g_1 \star h_1 = (f_1 + h_2) \star h_1 = f_1 \star h_1 + h_2 \star h_1 = f + h_2 \star h_1$.
  ($\geq_2$) $g = f + h$: the case is obvious.
  transitivity $f_1 < f_2$ and $f_2 < f_3$. Then $\exists h_1 \neq 0$ such that $f_2 = f_1 + h_1$ and $\exists h_2 \neq 0$ such that $f_3 = f_2 + h_2$.Thus $f_3 = (f_1 + h_1) + h_2 = f_1 + (h_1 + h_2)$.

Lemma 5

$$f \in \perp\!\!\!\perp \text{ iff } \exists (g_i)_{i \in I}, I \text{ finite non-empty}, g_i \in \perp\!\!\!\perp, g_i \in M \text{ such that } f = \bigcirc_i g_i + h$$

Proof. One direction results from ($\perp\!\!\!\perp_3$), ($\geq_2$). Suppose $f \in \perp\!\!\!\perp$. We prove the other result by induction on n such that $f \in \mathcal{M}^{\circ n}$.

- $n = 1$ We can suppose that $f = \sum_{j \in J} f_j$ and $f_j \in M$. We proceed by induction on the cardinality of J. Either $f \in M$ and we are finished, or (definition of the order relation $\geq$) $\exists g \in \mathcal{M}, g \in \perp\!\!\!\perp, g \neq f$ such that $g < f$, hence $\exists h$ and $f = g + h$ (situation ($\perp\!\!\!\perp_3$) does not occur). We finish by using the property on g.
- Suppose the property true till $n - 1$, $n > 0$. Either situation ($\perp\!\!\!\perp_1$) occurs and $\exists g \in \mathcal{M}, g \in \perp\!\!\!\perp, g \neq f$ such that $g < f$ and we conclude with Lemma 4, or situation ($\perp\!\!\!\perp_3$) occurs and $\exists f_1, f_2$ and $f = f_1 \circ f_2$ and $f_1, f_2 \in \perp\!\!\!\perp$ and induction on n applies.

Note that Lemma 5 shows in fact that the splitting of the context may be "anticipated" in terms of phase semantics (one element of a sum has a "good" property). Then the following property shows that the two sets of connectives coincide:

Proposition 6. $(A \star B)^{\perp\perp} = (A^{\perp} \circ B^{\perp})^{\perp}$ *(i.e.* $\otimes$ *and* $|$ *are equivalent) when* A *and* B *are facts.*

Proof. – $A^{\perp} \circ B^{\perp} \subset (A \star B)^{\perp}$: with the definition given,

$$\begin{aligned}(A^{\perp} \circ B^{\perp}) \star A \star B &= ((A^{\perp} \star A) \circ B^{\perp} + A^{\perp} \circ (B^{\perp} \star A)) \star B \\ &= (A^{\perp} \star A) \circ (B^{\perp} \star B) + (A^{\perp} \star A \star B) \circ B^{\perp} \\ &\quad + (A^{\perp} \star B) \circ (B^{\perp} \star A) + A^{\perp} \circ (B^{\perp} \star A \star B)\end{aligned}$$

and $(A^{\perp} \star A) \circ (B^{\perp} \star B) \subset \perp$ hence the result follows.

- $(A \star B)^\perp \subset (A^\perp \circ B^\perp)^{\perp\perp}$:
  - let $u \in (A^\perp \circ B^\perp)^\perp$, then $\forall a' \in A^\perp, b' \in B^\perp$, $u \star (a' \circ b') \in \perp$.
  - Furthermore $u \star (a' \circ b') = \sum (u_{(1)} \star a') \circ (u_{(2)} \star b')$ (Lemma 5).
  - Then by Lemma 5, there exist $u_{(1)}$ and $u_{(2)}$ such that $u = u_{(1)} \star u_{(2)}$, and $(u_{(1)} \star a') \circ (u_{(2)} \star b') \in \perp$.
  - Hence $u_{(1)} \star a' \in \perp$ and $u_{(2)} \star b' \in \perp$, i.e. $u_{(1)} \in a'^\perp$ and $u_{(2)} \in b'^\perp$, then $u = u_{(1)} \star u_{(2)} \in a'^\perp \star b'^\perp$.
  - Then $u \in \bigcap_{a',b'} a'^\perp \star b'^\perp = \bigcap_{a'} a'^\perp \star \bigcap_{b'} b'^\perp$.
  - Furthermore $A^\perp = \bigcup_{a'} \{a'\}$, then $A = A^{\perp\perp} = \bigcap_{a'} a'^\perp$, idem for B.
  - Then $u \in A \star B$.

Definition 5. *A* phase structure $(P, \mathcal{V})$ *is given by a phase space P and a valuation that associates a fact $\mathcal{V}(p)$ to each proposition symbol p. The interpretation $\mathcal{V}(A)$ of a formula A is defined in a standard way:*

$$\mathcal{V}(A^\perp) = \mathcal{V}(A)^\perp$$

$$\begin{array}{ll} \mathcal{V}(\perp) = \mathbf{1} & \mathcal{V}(\mathbf{1}) = \perp \\ \mathcal{V}(A \otimes B) = \mathcal{V}(A) \otimes \mathcal{V}(B) & \mathcal{V}(A \parr B) = \mathcal{V}(A) \parr \mathcal{V}(B) \\ \mathcal{V}(A \odot B) = \mathcal{V}(A) \odot \mathcal{V}(B) & \mathcal{V}(A \mid B) = \mathcal{V}(A) \mid \mathcal{V}(B) \\ \mathcal{V}(A \oplus B) = \mathcal{V}(A) \oplus \mathcal{V}(B) & \mathcal{V}(A \,\&\, B) = \mathcal{V}(A) \,\&\, \mathcal{V}(B) \end{array}$$

The interpretation of sequents is defined in the following way: let $\mathcal{S}$ be a multisequent, $\mathcal{S}$ may be defined as a triple $(I, \mathcal{O}, p)$ where $I \subset \mathbb{N}$ is finite, $\mathcal{O}$ is a finite multiset of occurrences of formulas, p is a function from I to the powerset of $\mathcal{O}$ (i.e. $p(i)$ gives the set of occurrences present in the ith sequent of $\mathcal{S}$). Define $n(A,i) = \#\{j \leq i / A \in p(j)\}$. Then

$$\mathcal{V}(\mathcal{S}) = \{\sum \bigcirc_{i \in I} \bigstar_{\substack{X \in p(i) \\ x' \in \mathcal{V}(X^\perp)}} x'_{(n(X,i))}\}^{\perp\perp}$$

where the sum is over all tuples $(x'_{(1)}, \ldots, x'_{(n(X,|I|))})$ for all $X^\perp$, i.e. $x' \in \mathcal{V}(X^\perp)$ and $\Delta_{n(X,|I|)}(x') = \sum_{x' = x'_{(1)} \star \cdots \star x'_{(n(X,|I|))}} x'_{(1)} \circ \cdots \circ x'_{(n(X,|I|))}$.

Note that the valuation $\mathcal{V}$ is well defined as Δ_n is associative for all n, and operations $\circ, \star$ are associative and commutative.

Definition 6. *Let A be a formula, A is* valid for $\mathcal{V}$ *iff $\mathcal{V}(A) \subset \perp\!\!\!\perp$. A multisequent $\mathcal{S}$ is* valid *iff $\mathcal{V}(\mathcal{S}) \subset \perp\!\!\!\perp$ for all phase structure $(P, \mathcal{V})$.*

Theorem 1. *If a multisequent is provable in Linear Logic, then it is valid.*

The proof is done, as usual, by induction on the structure of a proof.

Even if the phase semantics as described here has lost part of its significance w.r.t. CMALL because of Lemma 5, we conjecture that this algebraic framework may give fruitful insights to the understanding of calculi over multisequents.

7 Conclusion

An original logic calculus (with variants) is presented that is a conservative extension of Linear Logic, at the theoretical level, and at the language level. The motivation beneath this work concerns lazy evaluation, true concurrency and interferences in proof search. We show that cut elimination is false if one considers a naive approach. The calculus CMALL adds two new connectives to deal with multisequent structures. It has the cut-elimination property. Extensions are proposed that give first results concerning our objectives. A proposal is made concerning an algebraic semantics where formulas shared among different sequents could be denoted as elements in a Fock-like space. Among lines of future research, one may cite also the search for a proofnet-like syntax: the intuitive way consists of authorizing multitrips instead of a single trip as in proofnets (for example if a path traverses a cpar node then two trips are fired, and the dual node joins two trips that arrive).

References

1. Girard, J.Y.: Linear logic. Theoretical Computer Science 50, 1–102 (1987)
2. Andreoli, J.M.: Logic programming with focusing proofs in linear logic. Journal of Logic and Computation 2(3), 297–347 (1992)
3. Laurent, O.: Syntax vs. semantics: a polarized approach. Theoretical Computer Science 343(1–2), 177–206 (2005)
4. Girard, J.Y.: Locus solum. Mathematical Structures in Computer Science 11, 301–506 (2001)
5. Curien, P.L., Faggian, C.: L-nets, strategies and proof-nets. In: Ong, L. (ed.) CSL 2005. LNCS, vol. 3634, pp. 167–183. Springer, Heidelberg (2005)
6. Giamberardino, P.D., Faggian, C.: Jump from parallel to sequential proofs: Multiplicatives. In: Ésik, Z. (ed.) CSL 2006. LNCS, vol. 4207, pp. 319–333. Springer, Heidelberg (2006)
7. Cervesato, I., Hodas, J.S., Pfenning, F.: Efficient resource management for linear logic proof search. In: Herre, H., Dyckhoff, R., Schroeder-Heister, P. (eds.) ELP 1996. LNCS, vol. 1050, pp. 67–81. Springer, Heidelberg (1996)
8. O'Hearn, P.W., Pym, D.J.: The logic of bunched implications. Bulletin of Symbolic Logic 5(2), 215–244 (1999)
9. Guglielmi, A.: A system of interaction and structure. ACM Transactions on Computational Logic 8(1) (2007)
10. Fouqueré, C.: A Sequent Calculus for Modelling Interferences. Technical report, LIPN, Université Paris 13 (2007), `http://hal.archives-ouvertes.fr/hal-00156386/en/`
11. Lafont, Y.: Soft linear logic and polynomial time. Theoretical Computer Science 318(1-2), 163–180 (2004)

Reflection and Preservation of Properties in Coalgebraic (bi)Simulations*

Ignacio Fábregas, Miguel Palomino, and David de Frutos Escrig

Departamento de Sistemas Informáticos y Computación, UCM
fabregas@fdi.ucm.es, {miguelpt, defrutos}@sip.ucm.es

Abstract. Our objective is to extend the standard results of preservation and reflection of properties by bisimulations to the coalgebraic setting, as well as to study under what conditions these results hold for simulations. The notion of bisimulation is the classical one, while for simulations we use that proposed by Hughes and Jacobs. As for properties, we start by using a generalization of linear temporal logic to arbitrary coalgebras suggested by Jacobs, and then an extension by Kurtz which includes atomic propositions too.

1 Introduction

To reason about computational systems it is customary to mathematically formalize them by means of state-based structures such as labelled transitions systems or Kripke structures. This is a fruitful approach since it allows to study the properties of a system by relating it to some other, possibly better-known system, by means of simulations and bisimulations (see e.g., [15,14,12,3]).

The range of structures used to formalize computational systems is quite wide. In this context, coalgebras have emerged with a unifying aim [18]. A coalgebra is simply a function $c : X \longrightarrow FX$, where X is the set of states and FX is some expression on X (a functor) that describes the possible outcomes of a transition from a given state. Choosing different expressions for F one can obtain coalgebras that correspond to transition systems, Kripke structures, ...

Coalgebras can also be related by means of (bi)simulations. Our goal in this paper is to prove that, like their concrete instantiations, (bi)simulations between arbitrary coalgebras preserve some interesting properties. A first step in this direction consists in choosing an appropriate notion for both bisimulation and simulation, as well as a logic in which to express these properties.

Bisimulations were originally introduced by Aczel and Mendler [1], who showed that the general definition coincided with the standard ones when particularized; it is an established notion. Simulations, on the other hand, were defined by Hughes and Jacobs [8] and lack such canonicity. Their notion of simulation depends on the use of orders that allow (perhaps too) much flexibility in what it can be considered as a simulation; in order to show that simulations preserve properties, we

* Research supported by the Spanish projects DESAFIOS TIN2006-15660-C02-01, WEST TIN2006-15578-C02-01 and PROMESAS S-0505/TIC/0407.

C.B. Jones, Z. Liu, J. Woodcock (Eds.): ICTAC 2007, LNCS 4711, pp. 231–245, 2007.

will have to impose certain restrictions on such orders. As for the logic used for the properties, there is likewise no canonical choice at the moment. Jacobs proposes a temporal logic (see [9]) that generalizes linear temporal logic (LTL), though without atomic propositions; a clever insight of Pattinson [17] provides us with a way to endow Jacobs' logic with atomic propositions.

Since our original motivation was the generalization of the results about simulations and preservation of LTL properties, we will focus on Jacobs' logic and its extension with atomic propositions. Actually, modal logic seems to be the right logic to express properties of coalgebras and several proposals have been made in this direction, among them those in [10,13,17], which are invariant under behavioral equivalence. The reason for studying preservation/reflection of properties by bisimulations here is twofold: on the one hand, some of the operators in Jacobs' logic do not seem to fall under the framework of those general proposals; on the other hand, some of the ideas and insights developed for that study are needed when tackling simulations. As far as we know, reflection of properties by simulations in coalgebras has not been considered before in the literature.

2 Preliminaries

In this section we summarize definitions and concepts from [8,11,9], and introduce the notation we are going to use.

Given a category $\mathbb{C}$ and an endofunctor F in $\mathbb{C}$, an F-coalgebra, or just a coalgebra, consists of an object $X \in \mathbb{C}$ together with a morphism $c : X \longrightarrow FX$. We often call X the state space and c the transition or coalgebra structure.

Example 1. We show how two well-known structures can be seen as coalgebras:

- Labelled transition systems are coalgebras for the functor $F = \mathcal{P}(id)^A$, where A is the set of labels.
- Kripke structures are coalgebras for the functor $F = \mathcal{P}(AP) \times \mathcal{P}(id)$, where AP is a set of atomic propositions.

It is well-known that an arbitrary endofunctor F on **Sets** can be lifted to a functor in the category **Rel** of relations, that is, $\mathrm{Rel}(F) : \mathbf{Rel} \longrightarrow \mathbf{Rel}$. Given a relation $R \subseteq X \times Y$, its lifting is defined by

$$\mathrm{Rel}(F)(R) = \{\langle u, v\rangle \in FX_1 \times FX_2 \mid \exists w \in F(R).\, F(r_1)(w) = u, F(r_2)(w) = v\}\ ,$$

where $r_i : R \longrightarrow X_i$ are the projection morphisms.

A predicate P of a coalgebra $c : X \longrightarrow FX$ is just a subset of the state space. Also, a predicate $P \subseteq X$ can be lifted to a functor structure using the relation lifting:

$$\mathrm{Pred}(F)(P) = \coprod_{\pi_1}(\mathrm{Rel}(F)(\coprod_\delta(P))) = \coprod_{\pi_2}(\mathrm{Rel}(F)(\coprod_\delta(P))),$$

where $\delta = \langle id, id\rangle$ and $\coprod_f(X)$ is the image of X under f, so $\coprod_{\delta_x}(P) = \{(x, x) \mid x \in P\}$, $\coprod_{\pi_1}(R) = \{x_1 \mid \exists x_2.x_1 R x_2\}$ is the domain of the relation R, and $\coprod_{\pi_2}(R) = \{x_2 \mid \exists x_1.x_1 R x_2\}$ is its codomain.

The class of polynomial endofunctors is defined as the least class of endofunctors on **Sets** such that it contains the identity and constant functors, and is closed under product, coproduct, constant exponentiation, powerset and finite sequences. For polynomial endofunctors, $\mathrm{Rel}(F)$ and $\mathrm{Pred}(F)$ can be defined by induction on the structure of F. For further details on these definitions see [9]; we will introduce some of those when needed. For example, for the cases of labelled transition systems and Kripke structures we have:

$$\mathrm{Rel}(\mathcal{P}(id)^A)(R) = \{(f,g) \mid \forall a \in A. (f(a), g(a)) \in \{(U,V) \mid \forall u \in U. \exists v \in V. uRv \wedge \forall v \in V. \exists u \in U. uRv\}\}$$

$$\mathrm{Pred}(\mathcal{P}(id)^A)(P) = \{f \mid \forall a \in A. f(a) \in \{U \mid \forall u \in U. Pu\}\}$$

$$\begin{aligned}\mathrm{Rel}(\mathcal{P}(AP) \times \mathcal{P}(id))(R) = \; & \{((u_1,u_2),(v_1,v_2)) \mid (u_1 = v_1. u_1, v_1 \in \mathcal{P}(AP)) \wedge \\ & (u_2, v_2) \in \{(U,V) \mid \forall u \in U. \exists v \in V. uRv \wedge \\ & \forall v \in V. \exists u \in U. uRv\}\}\end{aligned}$$

$$\mathrm{Pred}(\mathcal{P}(AP) \times \mathcal{P}(id))(P) = \{(u,v) \mid (u \subseteq \mathcal{P}(AP)) \wedge (v \in \{U \mid \forall u \in U. Pu)\}$$

A bisimulation for coalgebras $c : X \longrightarrow FX$ and $d : Y \longrightarrow FY$ is a relation $R \subseteq X \times Y$ which is "closed under c and d":

$$\text{if } (x,y) \in R \text{ then } (c(x), d(y)) \in \mathrm{Rel}(F)(R).$$

In the same way, an invariant for a coalgebra $c : X \longrightarrow FX$ is a predicate $P \subseteq X$ such that it is "closed under c", that is, if $x \in P$ then $c(x) \in \mathrm{Pred}(F)(P)$.

We will use the definition of simulation introduced by Hughes and Jacobs in [8] which uses an order $\sqsubseteq$ for functors F that makes the following diagram commute

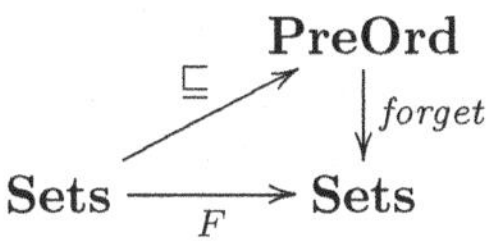

Given an order $\sqsubseteq$ on F, a simulation for the coalgebras $c : X \longrightarrow FX$ and $d : Y \longrightarrow FY$ is a relation $R \subseteq X \times Y$ such that

$$\text{if } (x,y) \in R \text{ then } (c(x), d(y)) \in \mathrm{Rel}(F)_{\sqsubseteq}(R),$$

where $\mathrm{Rel}(F)_{\sqsubseteq}(R)$ is defined as

$$\mathrm{Rel}(F)_{\sqsubseteq}(R) = \{(u,v) \mid \exists w \in F(R). u \sqsubseteq Fr_1(w) \wedge Fr_2(w) \sqsubseteq v\}.$$

To express properties we will use a generalization of LTL proposed by Jacobs (see [9]) that applies to arbitrary coalgebras, whose formulas are given by the following BNF expression:

$$\varphi = P \subseteq X \mid \neg\varphi \mid \varphi \vee \varphi \mid \varphi \wedge \varphi \mid \varphi \Rightarrow \varphi \mid \bigcirc\varphi \mid \Diamond\varphi \mid \Box\varphi \mid \varphi\, \mathcal{U}\, \varphi$$

$\bigcirc$ is the *nexttime* operator and its semantics (abusing notation) is defined as $\bigcirc P = c^{-1}(\mathrm{Pred}(F)(P)) = \{x \in X \mid c(x) \in \mathrm{Pred}(F)(P)\}$; $\Box$ is the *henceforth* operator defined as $\Box P$ if exists an invariant for c, such that $Q \subseteq P$ with $x \in Q$ or, equivalently by means of the greatest fixed point ν, $\Box P = \nu S.(P \wedge \bigcirc S)$; $\Diamond$ is the *eventually* operator defined as $\Diamond P = \neg\Box\neg P$; and $\mathcal{U}$ is the *until* operator defined as $P\,\mathcal{U}\,Q = \mu S.(Q \vee (P \wedge \neg \bigcirc \neg S))$, where μ is the least fixed point.

We denote the set of states in X that satisfies φ as $[\![\varphi]\!]_X$. That is, if $P \subseteq X$ is a predicate, then $[\![P]\!]_X = P$; if $\alpha \in \{\neg, \bigcirc, \Box, \Diamond\}$ then $[\![\alpha\varphi]\!]_X = \alpha[\![\varphi]\!]_X$, and if $\beta \in \{\wedge, \vee, \Rightarrow, \mathcal{U}\}$ then $[\![\varphi_1\beta\varphi_2]\!]_X = [\![\varphi_1]\!]_X\beta[\![\varphi_2]\!]_X$. We will usually omit the reference to the set X when it is clear from the context. We say that an element x satisfies a formula φ, and we denote it by $c, x \models \varphi$, when $x \in [\![\varphi]\!]$. Again, we will usually omit the reference to the coalgebra c.

3 Reflection and Preservation in Bisimulations

These definitions of reflection and preservation are slightly more involved than for classical LTL because the logic proposed by Jacobs does not use atomic propositions, but predicates (subsets of the set of states). Later, we will see how atomic propositions can be introduced in the logic.

Given a predicate P on X and a binary relation $R \subseteq X \times Y$, we will say that an element $y \in Y$ is in the direct image of P, and we will denote it by $y \in RP$, if there exists $x \in X$ with $x \in P$ and xRy. The inverse image of R is just the direct image for the relation R^{-1}.

Definition 1. *Given two formulas φ on X and ψ on Y, built over predicates $P_1, \ldots P_n$ and $Q_1, \ldots Q_n$, respectively, and a binary relation $R \subseteq X \times Y$, we define the image of φ as a formula φ^* on Y, obtained by substituting in φ RP_i for P_i. Likewise, we build ψ^{-1}, the inverse of ψ, substituting $R^{-1}Q_i$ for Q_i in ψ.*

Remark 1. It is important to notice that φ^* coincides with φ^{-1} when we consider R^{-1} instead of R. Analogously, φ^{-1} is just φ^* when we consider R^{-1} instead of R.

Now we can define when a relation preserves or reflects properties.

Definition 2. *Let $R \subseteq X \times Y$ be a binary relation and a and b elements such that aRb. We say that R* preserves *the property φ on X if, whenever $a \models \varphi$, $b \models \varphi^*$. We say that R* reflects *the property φ on Y if $b \models \varphi$ implies $a \models \varphi^{-1}$.*

Let us first state a couple of technical lemmas whose proofs appear in [6].

Lemma 1. *Let F be a polynomial functor, $R \subseteq X \times Y$ a bisimulation between coalgebras $c : X \longrightarrow FX$ and $d : Y \longrightarrow FY$, $P \subseteq Y$, $Q \subseteq X$ and xRy. If $d(y) \in \mathrm{Pred}(F)(P)$, then $c(x) \in \mathrm{Pred}(F)(R^{-1}P)$; and if $c(x) \in \mathrm{Pred}(F)(Q)$, then $d(y) \in \mathrm{Pred}(F)(RQ)$.*

Another auxiliary lemma we need to prove the main result of this section is the following:

Lemma 2. *The direct and inverse images of an invariant are also invariants.*

Proof. Let R be a bisimulation between $c : X \longrightarrow FX$ and $d : Y \longrightarrow FY$. Let us suppose that $P \subseteq X$ is an invariant and let us prove that so is RP; that is, for all $y \in RP$ it must be the case that $d(y) \in \text{Pred}(F)(RP)$. If $y \in RP$, then there exists $x \in P$ such that xRy. Since P is an invariant, we also have $c(x) \in \text{Pred}(F)(P)$ and by Lemma 1 we get $d(y) \in \text{Pred}(F)(RP)$.

On the other hand, since R^{-1} is also a bisimulation, the inverse image of an invariant is an invariant too. □

At this point it is interesting to recall that our objective is to prove that bisimulations preserve and reflect properties of a temporal logic, that is, if we have xRy and $y \models \varphi$ then we must also have $x \models \varphi^{-1}$; and, analogously, if $x \models \varphi$ then $y \models \varphi^*$. We will show this result for all temporal operators except for the negation; it is well-known that negation is reflected and preserved by standard bisimulations, but not here because of the lack of atomic propositions in the coalgebraic temporal logic.

To prove the result for the rest of temporal operators, we will see that if $y \in [\![\varphi]\!]$ then we also have $x \in R^{-1}[\![\varphi]\!]$ and, analogously, if $x \in [\![\varphi]\!]$ then $y \in R[\![\varphi]\!]$. Ideally, we would like to have both $R^{-1}[\![\varphi]\!] = [\![\varphi^{-1}]\!]$ and $R[\![\varphi]\!] = [\![\varphi^*]\!]$ but, in general, only the inclusion $\subseteq$ is true. Fortunately this is enough to prove our propositions, since the temporal operators are all monotonic except for the negation. In fact, here is where the problem with negation appears.

Lemma 3 ([6]). *Let R be a bisimulation between coalgebras $c : X \longrightarrow FX$ and $d : Y \longrightarrow FY$. For all temporal formulas φ and ψ which do not contain the negation operator, it follows that*

$$R^{-1}[\![\varphi]\!]_Y \subseteq [\![\varphi^{-1}]\!]_X \quad \textit{and} \quad R[\![\psi]\!]_X \subseteq [\![\psi^*]\!]_Y .$$

Finally we can show that bisimulations reflect and preserve properties given by any temporal operator except for the negation.

Proposition 1. *Let ψ be a formula over a set Y which does not use the* negation *operator and let R be a bisimulation between coalgebras $c : X \longrightarrow FX$ and $d : Y \longrightarrow FY$. Then the property ψ is reflected by R.*

Proof. The result is proved by structural induction over the formula ψ using the first half of Lemmas 1 and 3, and Lemma 2. See [6] for further details. □

Preservation of properties is a consequence of the reflection of properties together with the fact that if R is a bisimulation then R^{-1} is also a bisimulation. We have thus proved the following theorem.

Theorem 1. *Let ψ and φ be formulas over sets Y and X, respectively, which do not use the* negation *operator and let R be a bisimulation between coalgebras $c : X \longrightarrow FX$ and $d : Y \longrightarrow FY$. Then ψ is reflected by R and φ is preserved by R.*

4 Reflection and Preservation in Simulations

In [3,16] it is proved not only that bisimulations reflect and preserve properties but also that simulations reflect them: it turns out that this result does not generalize straightforwardly to the coalgebraic setting.

The main problem that we have found concerning this is that the coalgebraic definition of simulation uses an arbitrary functorial order $\sqsubseteq$, and in general reflection of properties will not hold for all orders.

Let us show a counterexample that will convince us that simulations may not reflect properties without restricting the orders. Let us take $F = \mathcal{P}(id)$, $X = \{x_1, x_2\}$, $Y = \{y_1, y_2\}$ and the coalgebras c and d defined as $c(x_1) = \{x_1, x_2\}$, $c(x_2) = \{x_2\}$, $d(y_1) = y_2$ and $d(y_2) = y_2$. We define $u \sqsubseteq v$ whenever $v \subseteq u$ and consider the formula $\varphi = \bigcirc P$, where $P = \{y_2\}$, and the simulation $R = \{(x_1, y_2)\}$. It is immediate to check that R is a simulation and $y_2 \in [\![\varphi]\!]$, but $x_1 \notin [\![\varphi^{-1}]\!]$.

- $y_2 \in [\![\varphi]\!]$. Indeed, since $d(y_2) = y_2$ then $y_2 \in [\![\varphi]\!] = \bigcirc P$ is equivalent to $y_2 \in P = \{y_2\}$, which is trivially true.
- $x_1 \notin [\![\varphi^{-1}]\!]$. By definition, $\varphi^{-1} = \bigcirc R^{-1} P = \bigcirc\{x_1\}$. Since $c(x_1) = \{x_1, x_2\}$, it is enough to see that $x_2 \notin \{x_1\}$, which is also true.

As a consequence, we will need to restrict the functorial orders that are involved in the definition of simulation. In a first approach we will impose an extra requirement that the order must fulfill, and later we will not only restrict the orders but also the functors that are involved.

4.1 Restricting the Orders

The idea is that we are going to require an extra property for each pair of elements which are related by the order. In particular, we are particularly interested in the following property (which is defined in [8]):

Definition 3. *Given a functor F : **Sets** $\longrightarrow$ **Sets**, we say that an order $\sqsubseteq$ associated to it is "down-closed" whenever $a \sqsubseteq b$, with $a, b \in FX$, implies that*

$$b \in \mathrm{Pred}(F)(P) \implies a \in \mathrm{Pred}(F)(P), \quad \textit{for all predicates } P \subseteq X\,.$$

We can show some examples of down-closed orders:

Example 2. 1. Kripke structures are defined by the functor $F = \mathcal{P}(AP) \times \mathcal{P}(id)$, so a down-closed order must fulfill that if $(u, v) \sqsubseteq (u', v')$, then $(u', v') \in \mathrm{Pred}(F)(P)$ implies $(u, v) \in \mathrm{Pred}(F)(P)$; that is, by definition of $\mathrm{Pred}(\mathcal{P}(AP) \times \mathcal{P}(id))$, $u, u' \subseteq \mathcal{P}(AP)$ and, if $v' \in \mathrm{Pred}(\mathcal{P}(id))(P) = \{U \mid \forall u \in U.\, u \in P\}$ then $v \in \mathrm{Pred}(\mathcal{P}(id))(P)$. In other words, for all $b \in v$ and $b' \in v'$, if $b' \in P$ then $b \in P$. Therefore, what is needed in this case is that the set of successors v of the smaller pair is contained in the set of successors v' of the bigger pair, that is, if $(u, v) \sqsubseteq (u', v')$ then $v \subseteq v'$.

2. Labelled transition systems are defined by the functor $F = \mathcal{P}(id)^A$, so the order must fulfill the following: if $u \sqsubseteq v$ then $\forall a \in A.\ u(a) \subseteq u'(a)$.

Those examples show that there are not many down-closed orders, but it does not seem clear how to further extend this class in such a way that we could still prove the reflection of properties by simulations. Unfortunately, even under this restriction we can only prove reflection (or preservation) of formulas that only use the operators $\vee$, $\wedge$, $\bigcirc$ and $\Box$.

To convince us of this fact, we present a counterexample with operator $\Diamond$. Let $X = \{x_1, x_2\}$, $Y = \{y_1, y_2\}$ and the functor $F = \mathcal{P}(id)$. We consider the following down-closed order: $u \sqsubseteq v$ if $u \subseteq v$. We also define the coalgebras $c : X \longrightarrow FX$ and $d : Y \longrightarrow FY$ as $c(x_1) = \{x_1\}$, $c(x_2) = \{x_2\}$, $d(y_1) = \{y_1, y_2\}$ and $d(y_2) = \{y_2\}$. Obviously $R = \{(x_1, y_1)\}$ is a simulation since $c(x_1) = \{x_1\} \sqsubseteq \{x_1\}$ and $\{y_1\} \sqsubseteq \{y_1, y_2\} = d(y_1)$ and, also, $\{x_1\}\mathrm{Rel}(F)(R)\{y_1\}$. We have $y_1 \in \Diamond\{y_2\}$, since we can reach y_2 from y_1, but $x_1 \notin \Diamond R^{-1}\{y_2\} = \Diamond\emptyset$. Indeed, $x_1 \notin \Diamond\emptyset$ is equivalent to $x_1 \in \Box\neg\emptyset$ and this is true since $\{x_1\}$ is an invariant such that $x_1 \in \{x_1\}$, with $\{x_1\} \subseteq \neg\emptyset$.

In order to prove reflection of properties that only use the operators $\vee$, $\wedge$, $\bigcirc$ and $\Box$, we will need a previous elementary result involving binary relations.

Proposition 2. *Let $R \subseteq X \times Y$ be a binary relation and $P \subseteq Y$ a predicate. Let us suppose that $u\mathrm{Rel}(F)(R)v$; then, if $v \in \mathrm{Pred}(F)(P)$ it is also true that $u \in \mathrm{Pred}(F)(R^{-1}P)$.*

Proof. Once again the proof will proceed by structural induction on the functor F. See [6] for further details. □

We will also need a subtle adaptation of Lemmas 2 and 3 from the framework of bisimulations to the framework of simulations. In particular, we can adapt Lemma 2 to prove that if Q is an invariant and R a simulation, $R^{-1}Q$ is still an invariant, whereas the first half of Lemma 3 will also be true in the framework of simulations for formulas that only use the operators $\vee$, $\wedge$, $\bigcirc$ and $\Box$.

Lemma 4. *Let R be a simulation between coalgebras $c : X \longrightarrow FX$ and $d : Y \longrightarrow FY$, with a down-closed order, and let $Q \subseteq Y$ be an invariant. Then $R^{-1}Q$ is also an invariant.*

Proof. We are going to show that for all $x \in R^{-1}Q$ we have $c(x) \in \mathrm{Pred}(F)(R^{-1}Q)$. Let us take an arbitrary $x \in R^{-1}Q$; then, by definition there exists $y \in Q$ such that xRy and, since Q is an invariant, $d(y) \in \mathrm{Pred}(F)(Q)$. On the other hand, since R is a simulation, $c(x) \sqsubseteq u\mathrm{Rel}(F)(R)v \sqsubseteq d(y)$. Henceforth, since we are working with a down-closed order and $d(y) \in \mathrm{Pred}(F)(Q)$, then $v \in \mathrm{Pred}(F)(Q)$. Also, by Proposition 2 we have $u \in \mathrm{Pred}(F)(R^{-1}Q)$ and, using again that the order is down-closed, it follows that $c(x) \in \mathrm{Pred}(F)(R^{-1}Q)$. □

Lemma 5 ([6]). *Let R be a simulation between coalgebras $c : X \longrightarrow FX$ and $d : Y \longrightarrow FY$, with a down-closed order. If φ is a temporal formula constructed only with operators $\vee$, $\wedge$, $\bigcirc$ and $\Box$, then*

$$R^{-1}[\![\varphi]\!]_Y \subseteq [\![\varphi^{-1}]\!]_X\,.$$

Now we can state the corresponding theorem:

Theorem 2 ([6]). *Let R be a simulation between coalgebras $c : X \longrightarrow FX$ and $d : Y \longrightarrow FY$ with a down-closed order. If φ is a temporal formula constructed only with operators $\vee$, $\wedge$, $\bigcirc$ and $\Box$, then the property φ is reflected by the simulation.*

Instead of considering down-closed orders, we could have imposed the converse implication, that is, those orders that satisfy that if $a \in \text{Pred}(F)(P)$ then $b \in \text{Pred}(F)(P)$.

Definition 4. *Given a functor F : **Sets** $\longrightarrow$ **Sets** we say that an order $\sqsubseteq$ is* up-closed *if whenever $a \sqsubseteq b$ then*

$$a \in \text{Pred}(F)(P) \implies b \in \text{Pred}(F)(P), \quad \textit{for all predicates } P\,.$$

Obviously up-closed is symmetrical to down-closed, that is, it is equivalent to taking $\sqsubseteq^{op}$ instead of $\sqsubseteq$ in Definition 3. So, for example, in the case of Kripke structures an up-closed order would satisfy $(u, v) \sqsubseteq (u', v')$ if $v' \subseteq v$.

The interesting thing about up-closed orders is that they allow us to prove *preservation* of properties; again, this result will hold only for formulas constructed with the operators $\vee$, $\wedge$, $\bigcirc$ and $\Box$. We need the following auxiliary result whose proof is analogous to the case of down-closed orders. Since if R is a simulation for the order $\sqsubseteq$, then R^{-1} is a simulation for the oposite order $\sqsubseteq^{op}$, we can apply Theorem 2 to get the following (see [6] for more details):

Theorem 3. *Let R be a simulation between coalgebras $c : X \longrightarrow FX$ and $d : Y \longrightarrow FY$ carrying an up-closed order. If φ is a temporal formula constructed only with the operators $\vee$, $\wedge$, $\bigcirc$ and $\Box$, then R preserves the property φ.*

4.2 Restricting the Class of Functors

As we have just seen, it is not enough to restrict ourselves to down-closed (or up-closed) orders to get a valid result for all properties. What we want is a necessary and sufficient condition over functorial orders that implies reflection (or preservation) of properties by simulations. So far we have not found such a condition, but we have a sufficient one for simulations to reflect properties (and, in fact, also so that they preserve properties).

Recalling the structure of lemmas and propositions used to prove reflection and preservation of properties by bisimulations, we notice that the key ingredient was Lemma 1. With this lemma we were able to prove directly preservation of invariants (Lemma 2) and the relation between R^{-1} (respectively R) of a formula and the inverse of a formula (respectively direct image of a formula). Also, Lemma 1 was essential to prove directly reflection and preservation of formulas built with the *nexttime* operator and the rest of temporal operators.

In the previous section the problem we faced was that either the second half of Lemma 1 (for down-closed orders) or the first half of Lemma 1 (for up-closed orders) held, but not both simultaneously. As a consequence, the results for the operators *eventually* and *until* did not hold. So, if we were capable of finding a subclass of functors and orders such that they fulfill results analogous to Lemma 1 then, translating those proofs, we would get reflection and preservation of arbitrary properties.

We are going to define a subclass of functors and orders in the way that Hughes and Jacobs did in [8] for the subclass **Poly**.

Definition 5. *The class* **Order** *is the least class of functors closed under the following operations:*

1. *For every preorder* $(A, \leq)$*, the constant functor* $X \mapsto A$ *with the order given by* $\sqsubseteq_X = \leq_A$.
2. *The identity functor with equality order.*
3. *Given two polynomial functors* F_1 *and* F_2 *with orders* $\sqsubseteq^1$ *and* $\sqsubseteq^2$*, the product functor* $F_1 \times F_2$ *with order* $\sqsubseteq_X$ *given by*
$$(u, v) \sqsubseteq_X (u', v') \quad \text{if} \quad u \sqsubseteq^1 u' \quad \text{and} \quad v \sqsubseteq^2 v' \,.$$
4. *Given the polynomial functor* F *with order* $\sqsubseteq^F$ *and the set* A*, the functor* F^A *with order* $\sqsubseteq_X$ *given by*
$$u \sqsubseteq_X v \text{ if } u(a) \sqsubseteq^F v(a) \text{ for all } a \in A.$$
5. *Given two polynomial functors* F_1 *and* F_2 *with orders* $\sqsubseteq^1$ *and* $\sqsubseteq^2$*, the coproduct functor* $F_1 + F_2$ *with order* $\sqsubseteq_X$ *given by*
$$\begin{aligned} u \sqsubseteq_X v \text{ if } u &= \kappa_1(u_0) \text{ and } v = \kappa_1(v_0) \text{ with } u_0 \sqsubseteq^1 v_0 \\ \text{or } u &= \kappa_2(u_0) \text{ and } v = \kappa_2(v_0) \text{ with } u_0 \sqsubseteq^2 v_0 \,. \end{aligned}$$
6. *Given the polynomial functor* F *with order* $\sqsubseteq^F$*, the powerset functor* $\mathcal{P}(F)$ *with order* $\sqsubseteq_X$ *given by*
$$\begin{aligned} u \sqsubseteq_X v \quad \text{if} \quad & \forall a \in u\ \exists b \in v \quad \text{such that} \quad a \sqsubseteq^F b \\ \text{and also } & \forall b \in v\ \exists a \in u \quad \text{such that} \quad a \sqsubseteq^F b \,. \end{aligned}$$

For example the usual order for Kripke structures is not in the class **Order**. Besides, in the definition of **Poly** in [8] the authors did not consider the powerset functor but we do, although we are not using the *usual* order for this functor.

At first, to obtain that simulations not only reflect but also preserve properties may seem a little surprising. If we think about the elements in the subclass **Order** we notice that we have restricted the orders to equality-like orders, that is, almost all possible orders in **Order** are the equality. However, since the class **Order** is very similar to the class **Poly**, it has the same good properties shown in [8] (like the stablility of the orders and functors).

Example 3. 1. If we consider the functor $\mathcal{P}(id)$, then the order $\sqsubseteq$ defined in Definition 5 says that $u \sqsubseteq v$ if and only if for each $a \in u$ there exists $b \in v$ such that $a = b$, and if for each $b \in v$ there exists $a \in u$ such that $a = b$. This means that $\sqsubseteq$ is the identity relation. As an immediate consequence for transition systems the only possible **Order** simulations are bisimulations.

2. If we consider the functor $A \times id$ where A has a preorder $\leq_A$ different from the identity, the order $\sqsubseteq$ from Definition 5 is the following: $(u, v) \sqsubseteq (u', v')$ iff $v = v'$ and $u \leq_A u'$. So, if $\leq_A$ is not the identity, neither is $\sqsubseteq$. For example, let us take $X = \{x_1, x_2, x_3\}$, $Y = \{y_1, y_2\}$, $AP = \{p_1, p_2, p_3\}$ and consider the functor $F = \mathcal{P}(id) \times \mathcal{P}(AP)$ and the coalgebras $c : X \longrightarrow FX$ and $d : Y \longrightarrow FY$ defined by $c(x_1) = (\{x_2, x_3\}, \{p_1\})$, $c(x_2) = (\{x_3\}, \{p_2\})$, $c(x_3) = (\{x_2\}, \{p_3\})$, $d(y_1) = (\{y_2\}, \{p_2\})$ and $d(y_2) = (\{y_2\}, \{p_1\})$. Obviously there is no bisimulation between x_1 and y_1 since this atomic propositions are not the same, but taking the order $\sqsubseteq$ defined as $(u, v) \sqsubseteq (u', v')$ iff $u = u'$ (that is, taking as the preorder $\leq_{AP}$ the total relation) we have that there exists a simulation R in **Order** between x_1 and y_1.

Lemma 6 ([6]). *Let $R \subseteq X \times Y$ be a simulation between coalgebras $c : X \longrightarrow FX$ and $d : Y \longrightarrow FY$, such that the functor F is in the class* **Order**. *Let us also suppose that $P \subseteq Y$ and xRy; then, if $d(y) \in \mathrm{Pred}(F)(P)$ we have $c(x) \in \mathrm{Pred}(F)(R^{-1}P)$.*

In a similar way we have the corresponding lemma involving direct predicates.

Lemma 7. *Let $R \subseteq X \times Y$ be a simulation between coalgebras $c : X \longrightarrow FX$ and $d : Y \longrightarrow FY$, such that the functor F is in* **Order**. *Let us suppose also that $P \subseteq X$ and xRy. Then, if $c(x) \in \mathrm{Pred}(F)(P)$, $d(y) \in \mathrm{Pred}(F)(RP)$.*

Now we can conclude that under these hypothesis simulations reflect and preserve properties, simultaneously! This fact is a straightforward result from Lemmas 6 and 7.

Theorem 4. *Let R be a simulation between coalgebras $c : X \longrightarrow FX$ and $d : Y \longrightarrow FY$, with F a polynomial functor in the class* **Order**. *Then, the simulation R reflects and preserves properties.*

5 Including Atomic Propositions

A consequence of the fact that the logic proposed by Jacobs does not introduce atomic propositions was the need of giving non-standard definitions of reflection and preservation of properties. Kurz, in his work [13] includes atomic propositions in a temporal logic for coalgebras by means of natural transformations.

Definition 6. *Given a set AP of atomic propositions, the formulas of the temporal logic associated to a coalgebra $c : X \longrightarrow FX$ are given by the BNF expression:*

$$\varphi = p \mid \neg\varphi \mid \varphi \vee \varphi \mid \varphi \wedge \varphi \mid \varphi \Rightarrow \varphi \mid \bigcirc\varphi \mid \Diamond\varphi \mid \Box\varphi \mid \varphi\, \mathcal{U}\, \varphi$$

where $p \in AP$ is an atomic proposition.

Kurz also defines when a state x satisfies an atomic proposition p, that is, he defines the semantics of an atomic proposition.

Definition 7. *Let F : **Sets** $\longrightarrow$ **Sets** be a functor and AP a set of atomic propositions. Let $\nu : F \Rightarrow \mathcal{P}(AP)$ be a natural transformation and $c : X \longrightarrow FX$ a coalgebra. We say that x satisfies an atomic proposition $p \in AP$, and denote it $x \models p$, when $p \in (\nu_X \circ c)(x)$. This way $[\![p]\!] = \{x \mid p \in (\nu_X \circ c)(x)\}$.*

Notice that in fact this defines not only a semantics but a family of possible semantics that depends on the natural transformation. For example, we can define a natural transformation for the functor for Kripke structures in this way:

$$\begin{array}{rcl} \nu_X : \mathcal{P}(AP) \times \mathcal{P}(X) & \longrightarrow & \mathcal{P}(AP) \\ (P, Q) & \longmapsto & P \end{array}$$

With ν_X we have characterized the standard semantics of LTL for Kripke structures. Analogously, we could define the following interpretation: $\nu'_X(P, Q) = \mathcal{P}(AP) \setminus P$.

Introducing in our temporal logic the semantics of the atomic propositions, we can prove the following theorem involving bisimulations:

Theorem 5. *Let R be a bisimulation between coalgebras $c : X \longrightarrow FX$ and $d : Y \longrightarrow FY$. Let φ be a temporal formula; then, the following is true for all $x \in X$ and $y \in Y$ such that xRy:*

$$x \in [\![\varphi]\!]_X \quad \Longleftrightarrow \quad y \in [\![\varphi]\!]_Y\,.$$

Here we have captured in the same theorem the classical ideas of reflection and preservation of properties: we have some property in the lefthand side of a bisimulation if and only if we have the property in its righthand side. In this case the theorem is true also for the negation operator thanks to the atomic propositions. Intuitively, this is because now we have an "if and only if" theorem, whereas in Theorem 1 we needed to reason separately for each implication using monotonicity, and negation lacks it. Also notice that even though we could think that in Theorem 1 our predicates played the role of atomic propositions, there are some essential differences: first, predicates are not independent of each other, unlike atomic propositions, and secondly, while atomic propositions stay the same predicates vary with each set of states.

Proof. Once again the proof will proceed by structural induction on the formula φ. We only show some of the cases (the complete proof can be found in [6]).

1. Let $\varphi = p$ where p is an arbitrary atomic proposition. This way we have the following diagram, for ν an arbitrary natural trasformation:

$$\begin{array}{ccccc} X & \xleftarrow{\pi_1} & R & \xrightarrow{\pi_2} & Y \\ {\scriptstyle c}\downarrow & & \downarrow{\scriptstyle [c,d]} & & \downarrow{\scriptstyle d} \\ FX & \xleftarrow{F\pi_1} & FR & \xrightarrow{F\pi_2} & FY \\ {\scriptstyle \nu_X}\downarrow & & \downarrow{\scriptstyle \nu_R} & & \downarrow{\scriptstyle \nu_Y} \\ \mathcal{P}(AP) & \xleftarrow{id} & \mathcal{P}(AP) & \xrightarrow{id} & \mathcal{P}(AP) \end{array}$$

This diagram is commutative. Indeed, since R is a bisimulation the upper side commutes, while the lower side commutes because ν is a natural transformation.
So, $x \in [\![\varphi]\!]_X$ means by definition that $p \in (\nu_X \circ c)(x)$. Since the diagram commutes then $p \in (\nu_R \circ [c,d])(x,y) \Leftrightarrow p \in (\nu_Y \circ d)(y)$, that is, $y \in [\![\varphi]\!]_Y$.

2. Let us suppose $\varphi = \neg\varphi_0$. In this case we must show that $x \in \neg[\![\varphi_0]\!]_X$ if and only if $y \in \neg[\![\varphi_0]\!]_Y$, that is, we must see that $x \notin [\![\varphi_0]\!]_X$ if and only if $y \notin [\![\varphi_0]\!]_Y$. By induction hypothesis we have $x \in [\![\varphi_0]\!]_X$ if and only if $y \in [\![\varphi_0]\!]_Y$.
3. Let us suppose now that $\varphi = \bigcirc\varphi_0$. We must prove that $x \in \bigcirc[\![\varphi_0]\!]_X$ is equivalent to $y \in \bigcirc[\![\varphi_0]\!]_Y$, that is, $c(x) \in \mathrm{Pred}(F)([\![\varphi_0]\!]_X)$ is equivalent to $d(y) \in \mathrm{Pred}(F)([\![\varphi_0]\!]_Y)$. The latter will be proved by structural induction on the functor F. As an example we show the case of $F = G^A$. Let us prove only one implication since the other one is almost identical. We have

$$\mathrm{Pred}(F)([\![\varphi_0]\!]_X) = \{f \mid \forall a \in A.\ f(a) \in \mathrm{Pred}(G)([\![\varphi_0]\!]_X)\}\,.$$

Once again, as we have shown in other proofs, we define for each $a \in A$ and each F-coalgebra $c : X \longrightarrow F(X)$ a G-coalgebra, $c^a : X \longrightarrow G(X)$ where for each $x \in X$ we have $c^a(x) = c(x)(a)$. In this way, we have xRy and $c^a(x) = c(x)(a) \in \mathrm{Pred}(G)([\![\varphi_0]\!]_X)$. By induction hypothesis we have that $d^a(y) \in \mathrm{Pred}(G)([\![\varphi_0]\!]_Y)$. Since this is a valid argument for all $a \in A$, we obtain $d(y) \in \mathrm{Pred}(F)([\![\varphi_0]\!]_Y)$.
4. $\varphi = \Box\varphi_0$. Assuming that $x \in [\![\varphi]\!]_X$ we get that there exists

$$Q \subseteq X \text{ an invariant for } c \text{ with } Q \subseteq [\![\varphi_0]\!]_X \text{ and } x \in Q.$$

Now, RQ is a invariant for d and, also, such that $RQ \subseteq [\![\varphi_0]\!]_Y$ with $y \in RQ$. Indeed, if $x \in Q$ then $y \in RQ$ and if $b \in RQ$ there must exists some $a \in Q \subseteq [\![\varphi_0]\!]_X$ such that aRb. So, by induction hypothesis we get that $b \in [\![\varphi_0]\!]_Y$
On the other hand, if $y \in [\![\varphi]\!]_Y$ there must exists some invariant T on Y, such that $T \subseteq [\![\varphi_0]\!]_Y$ with $y \in T$, hence for proving $x \in [\![\varphi]\!]_X$ it is enough to consider the invariant $R^{-1}T$. □

To obtain a similar result for simulations, we will need again to restrict the class of functors and orders as we did in Sections 4.1 and 4.2. In particular we are interested in the following antimonotonicity property: if $u \sqsubseteq u'$ then $\nu(u') \subseteq \nu(u)$.

Definition 8. *Let F : **Sets** $\longrightarrow$ **Sets** be a functor, AP a set of atomic propositions and $\nu : F \Rightarrow \mathcal{P}(AP)$ a natural transformation. We say that $\sqsubseteq$ is a down-natural ν-order if, whenever $u \sqsubseteq u'$ then $\nu(u') \subseteq \nu(u)$.*

Obviously this definition depends on the natural transformation that we consider in each case. For example, for Kripke structures we have the following natural transformation: $\nu_X((A_X, B_X)) = A_X \subseteq AP$. To obtain a down-natural ν-order the following must hold: $(u,v) \sqsubseteq (u',v')$ then $\nu((u',v')) \subseteq \nu((u,v))$, that is, it will be enough to require $(u,v) \sqsubseteq (u',v')$ iff $u' \subseteq u$.

This way, if we combine the down-closed and the down-natural orders we get:

$$\text{If} \quad (u,v) \sqsubseteq (u',v') \quad \text{then} \quad u' \subseteq u \text{ and } v \subseteq v' \, .$$

This characterization is not as restrictive as one could think. Indeed, if we recall the definition of functorial order we had:

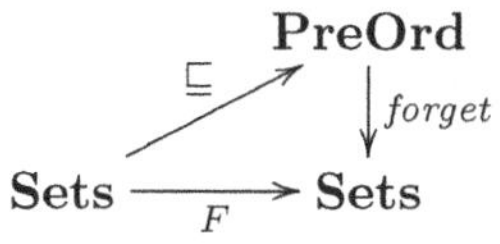

This diagram means that the functor F and the order $\sqsubseteq$ almost have the same structure and indeed, we could use a natural transformation between $\sqsubseteq$ and $\mathcal{P}(AP)$ in Definition 7 instead of a natural transformation between F and $\mathcal{P}(AP)$, that is, $\nu : \sqsubseteq \Rightarrow \mathcal{P}(AP)$. Considering ν in this way, an immediate consequence is that if we take as order in $\mathcal{P}(AP)$ the relation $\supseteq$ (as is done in [16]), then $u \sqsubseteq v$ implies $\nu(u) \sqsubseteq \nu(v)$.

We can tackle the proof of reflection of properties (with atomic propositions) by simulations as we did in Section 4.1, imposing to the order not only to be down-natural but also down-closed. But, if we do that we will find the same difficulties we faced in Section 4.1 (that is, we would not be able to prove reflection of formulas built with the operators *until* and *eventually*). Therefore, we must restrict the class of functors and orders, as we did with the class **Order** in Section 4.2, but imposing also that the orders must be down-natural.

Definition 9. *The class* **Down-Natural ν-Order** *is the subclass of* **Order** *where all orders are down-natural.*

Notice that we are defining a different class for each natural transformation ν. Under this condition we state the corresponding theorem involving simulations and the reflection of properties (with atomic propositions); for the proof see [6].

Theorem 6. *Let R be a simulation between coalgebras $c : X \longrightarrow FX$ and $d : Y \longrightarrow FY$ on the same polynomial functor F from* **Sets** *to* **Sets** *belonging to the class* **Down-Natural ν-Order** *and let φ be a temporal formula. Then, for each $x \in X$ and $y \in Y$ such that xRy:*

$$y \in [\![\varphi]\!]_Y \quad \Longrightarrow \quad x \in [\![\varphi]\!]_X \, .$$

We showed above that simulations for functors in the class **Order** reflected and preserved all kinds of properties. Instead, now we can only prove one implication, that corresponding to the reflection of properties. This is so because down-natural ν-orders have a natural direction.

Exactly in the same way as we did with down-natural ν-orders, we can define the corresponding class of up-natural ν-orders:

Definition 10. *Let $F : \mathbf{Sets} \longrightarrow \mathbf{Sets}$ be a functor, AP a set of atomic propositions and $\nu : F \Rightarrow \mathcal{P}(AP)$ a natural transformation. We say that $\sqsubseteq$ is an up-natural ν-order if $u \sqsubseteq u'$ implies $\nu(u) \subseteq \nu(u')$.*

As we did for down-natural ν-orders, we define a subclass of **Order**:

Definition 11. *The class* **Up-Natural ν-Order** *is the subclass of* **Order** *where all orders are up-natural.*

Theorem 7. *Let R be a simulation between coalgebras $c : X \longrightarrow FX$ and $d : Y \longrightarrow FY$ on the same polynomial functor F in the class* **Up-Natural ν-Order***, and let φ be a temporal formula. Then, for all $x \in X$ and $y \in Y$ such that xRy:*

$$x \in [\![\varphi]\!]_X \quad \Longrightarrow \quad y \in [\![\varphi]\!]_Y .$$

6 Conclusions

The main goal of this paper was to study under what assumptions coalgebraic simulations reflect properties. In our way towards the proof of this result, we were also able to prove reflection and preservation of properties by coalgebraic bisimulations. For expressing the properties we used Jacobs' temporal logic [9], later extended with atomic propositions using the idea presented in [13].

That coalgebraic bisimulations reflect and preserve properties expressed in modal logic is a well-known topic (e.g, [10,13,17]), but not so the corresponding results for simulations. The main difficulty is that Hughes and Jacobs' notion of simulation is defined by means of an arbitrary functorial order which bestows them with a high degree of freedom. We have dealt with this by restricting the class of functorial orders (although even so we are not able of obtaining a general result) and by restricting also the class of allowed functors.

In order to get more general results on the subject, an interesting path that we intend to explore is the search for a canonical notion of simulation. This definition would provide us, not only with a "natural" way to understand simulations but, hopefully, would also give rise to "natural" general results about reflection of properties.

Another promising direction of research is the study of reflection and preservation of properties in probabilistic systems, following our results of [4] in combination with the ideas presented in [7,5,2].

Acknowledgement

The authors would like to thank the anonymous referees for their comments and suggestions.

References

1. Aczel, P., Mendler, N.P.: A final coalgebra theorem. In: Dybjer, P., Pitts, A.M., Pitt, D.H., Poigné, A., Rydeheard, D.E. (eds.) Category Theory and Computer Science. LNCS, vol. 389, pp. 357–365. Springer, Heidelberg (1989)
2. Bartels, F., Sokolova, A., de Vink, E.P.: A hierarchy of probabilistic system types. Theor. Comput. Sci. 327(1-2), 3–22 (2004)
3. Clarke, E.M., Grumberg, O., Peled, D.A.: Model Checking. MIT Press, Cambridge (1999)
4. de Frutos Escrig, D., Palomino, M., Fábregas, I.: Multiset bisimulation as a common framework for ordinary and probabilistic bisimulations (submitted)
5. de Vink, E.P., Rutten, J.J.M.M.: Bisimulation for probabilistic transition systems: a coalgebraic approach. In: Degano, P., Gorrieri, R., Marchetti-Spaccamela, A. (eds.) ICALP 1997. LNCS, vol. 1256, pp. 4460–4470. Springer, Heidelberg (1997)
6. Fábregas, I., Palomino, M., de Frutos Escrig, D.: Reflection and preservation of properties in coalgebraic (bi)simulations (extended) (2007), `http://maude.sip.ucm.es/~miguelpt/`
7. Hasuo, I.: Generic forward and backward simulations. In: Baier, C., Hermanns, H. (eds.) CONCUR 2006. LNCS, vol. 4137, pp. 406–420. Springer, Heidelberg (2006)
8. Hughes, J., Jacobs, B.: Simulations in coalgebra. Theor. Comput. Sci. 327(1-2), 71–108 (2004)
9. Jacobs, B.: Introduction to Coalgebra. Towards Mathematics of States and Observations. Book in preparation. Draft available in the web, `http://www.cs.ru.nl/B.Jacobs/CLG/JacobsCoalgebraIntro.pdf`
10. Jacobs, B.: *Categorical Logic and Type Theory.* Studies in Logic and the Foundations of Mathematics, vol. 141. North-Holland, Amsterdam (1999)
11. Jacobs, B., Rutten, J.J.M.M.: A tutorial on (co)algebras and (co)induction. Bulletin of the European Association for Theoretical Computer Science 62, 222–259 (1997)
12. Kesten, Y., Pnueli, A.: Control and data abstraction: The cornerstones of practical formal verification. International Journal on Software Tools for Technology Transfer 4(2), 328–342 (2000)
13. Kurz, A.: Logics for coalgebras and applications to computer science. PhD thesis, Universität München (2000)
14. Loiseaux, C., Graf, S., Sifakis, J., Bouajjani, A., Bensalem, S.: Property preserving abstractions for the verification of concurrent systems. Formal Methods in System Design 6, 1–36 (1995)
15. Milner, R.: Communication and Concurrency. Prentice-Hall, Englewood Cliffs (1989)
16. Palomino, M.: Reflexión, abstracción y simulación en la lógica de reescritura. PhD thesis, Universidad Complutense de Madrid, Spain (March 2005)
17. Pattinson, D.: Expressivity Results in the Modal Logic of Coalgebras. PhD thesis, Universität München (2001)
18. Rutten, J.J.M.M.: Universal coalgebra: a theory of systems. Theor. Comput. Sci. 249(1), 3–80 (2000)

Controlling Process Modularity in Mobile Computing

Takashi Kitamura and Huimin Lin

Institute of Software, Chinese Academy of Sciences
{takashi,lhm}@ios.ac.cn

Abstract. A variant of π-calculus which can flexibly and dynamically control process modularity is presented. The calculus is equipped with a two level structure to represent process distribution and mobility over flat locations. It provides a suitable model for modular programming in concurrent and mobile computing. Several bisimulation relations are discussed, and a notion of bisimulation-preorder is proposed to reflect some aspects of mobile distributed computing such as interaction costs.

Keywords: Mobile computing, process modularity, bisimulation-preorder, interaction-costs.

1 Introduction

Several variants of the π-calculus have been proposed to describe specific aspects in mobile distributed computing [1,2,3,4,10,12,14,16]. These calculi extend the π-calculus with explicit notions of process distribution and mobility. Though developed for different purposes, they possess some basic features in common: they are normally equipped with a two-level location structure to represent process distributions over flat locations, and a primitive for process migration.

The device for process migration among locations in these calculus is quite simple. Modulo syntactical differences, process mobility in these calculi is implemented by a specific action **go** l where l is a location name. By performing this action a process can move from its current location to location l. If we denote a process P located at a location m by $m[P]$, then $m[\mathbf{go}\ l.P] \rightarrow l[P]$. Furthermore, the structural congruence rule $m[P \mid Q] \equiv m[P] \mid m[Q]$, for splitting and joining co-located processes, is commonly taken in these calculi. As a consequence, one has $m[\mathbf{go}\ l.P \mid Q] \rightarrow l[P] \mid m[Q]$, but not $m[\mathbf{go}\ l.P \mid Q] \rightarrow l[P \mid Q]$. That is, the *unit of movement* is a single thread of computing syntactically following the **go** operator.

Such a design of process mobility primitives may bring some simplicity, e.g., the semantic theory is simple. However, in many occasions one would like to have more flexible controls over process movements. Especially in describing highly mobile distributed systems, e.g., ubiquitous computing systems, such that mobility happens anytime and anywhere or that a system is deployed on several computers over networks and the structure of deployment evolves dynamically,

C.B. Jones, Z. Liu, J. Woodcock (Eds.): ICTAC 2007, LNCS 4711, pp. 246–259, 2007.

it is desirable to determine process movement units *dynamically*, at run time, rather than *statically* by syntactical scoping. Let us call the way process mobility units is determined *process modularity*.

To illustrate why dynamic process modularity is desired, consider a *packet* process which acts as a carrier taking a resource from location l to destination d. The functionality of such a system can be specified by the following transition

$$l[Packet] \parallel l[R] \rightarrow^* d[Packet] \parallel d[R]$$

(we use $\parallel$ for the *distributed parallel composition operator*, and reserve $|$ as the *local parallel composition operator*). Since the mission of *Packet* is to take resource R to location d, as the first approximation it could be implemented as $Packet = \textbf{go}\ d.Packet'$. However, as we have just observed, if the structural congruence rule $m[P \mid Q] \equiv m[P] \mid m[Q]$ is assumed then we will have $l[Packet] \parallel l[R] \rightarrow d[Packet'] \parallel l[R]$, *i.e.* *Packet* cannot take R to d.

To facilitate the description of such functionalities, in designing our calculus we do not assume the structural congruence rule $m[P|Q] \equiv m[P] \mid m[Q]$. Instead, we let

$$m[\textbf{go}\ l.P \mid R] \rightarrow l[P \mid Q],$$

i.e. the unit of movement is the entire distributed process enclosing the **go** operator. In order to be able to control process modularity dynamically, we provide two primitives **merge** and **split**, with the semantics

$$m[\textbf{merge}.P] \parallel m[Q] \rightarrow m[P \mid Q]$$

and

$$m[\textbf{split}.P \mid Q] \rightarrow m[P] \parallel m[Q],$$

respectively.

With these operators *Packet* can be implemented as

$$Packet = \overline{start}.ready.\textbf{go}\ d.\overline{arrive}.Packet'.$$

And the resource R, who wishes to use the carrier service , is

$$R = start.\textbf{merge}.\overline{ready}.arrive.\textbf{split}.R'.$$

The system and a trace of the computation are as follows;

$$\begin{array}{l} l[Packet] \parallel l[R] \\ \rightarrow l[ready.\textbf{go}\ d.\overline{arrive}.Packet'] \parallel l[\textbf{merge}.\overline{ready}.arrive.\textbf{split}.R'] \\ \rightarrow l[ready.\textbf{go}\ d.\overline{arrive}.Packet' \mid \overline{ready}.arrive.\textbf{split}.R'] \\ \rightarrow l[\textbf{go}\ d.\overline{arrive}.Packet' \mid arrive.\textbf{split}.R'] \\ \rightarrow d[\overline{arrive}.Packet' \mid arrive.\textbf{split}.R'] \\ \rightarrow d[Packet' \mid \textbf{split}.R'] \\ \rightarrow d[Packet'] \parallel d[R']. \end{array}$$

In this implementation, *Packet* first send a signal to notify R that the service is starting. It then waits till R is ready. Upon receiving the start signal, R joins with *Packet*, to allow the carrier to take it to the destination d, and tells *Packet* that it is ready to go. After arriving at d, R separates itself from *Packet* by performing the **split** action. A refined version of the packet process system, where the packet takes a resource to its destination through repeatedly routed among several locations, can be found in Section 3.

The highlight of the process description given above is a dynamic evolution of process modularity. First packet *Packet* and resource R **merge** into a single module at the original location l (so that they can move together); Then, after arriving at the destination location d, they split into two module, so that *Packet* can go back to l leaving R at d alone. This feature makes the calculus a suitable model for mobile systems with dynamic process modularity, for example, a mobile distributed system in which process modules are dynamically deployed on computers among network. And more generally, it provides a suitable model for modular programming in concurrent and mobile computing.

We present an operational semantics for the calculus and discuss two kinds of bisimilarity, reflecting different aspects of mobile distributed computing. First, we consider the usual notion of bisimilarity which does not take locations into account. Then we propose a refinement notion of bisimilarity which is location-aware, in the sense that two bisimilar processes can not only mimic each other's communication behaviours but also locations. For the location-aware bisimilarity, we further discuss a preorder relation on bisimilar processes which reflects *interaction costs*, namely process P is *costlier-than* Q, if P is bisimilar to Q and it costs more for P to exhibit the same behaviour as Q.

Related work. Our calculus is a variant of the π-calculus extended with a two-level structure to represent process distribution and mobility among flat locations, which is in common with the calculi proposed by many others [1, 2, 3, 10, 12, 14, 16]. The dynamic control on process modularity is influenced by Mobile Ambients (MA) [5]. And the Seal-calculus [15] and Mobile Resources [8] are variants of MA equipped with communication channels as in π-calculus. But in these calculi locations are organized into a hierarchical structure, while in our calculus locations are flat. Also the Distributed Join-calculus (the DJoin calculus) [7] and the M-calculus [13] are extended variants of the Join-calculus [6] with explicit notion of locations to model distributed computing, but these calculi do not consider the idea of dynamic control on process modularity.

2 The Calculus

2.1 Syntax

Assume an infinite set $\mathcal{N}_c$ of channel names, ranged over $a, b, c, \cdots$, and an infinite set $\mathcal{N}_l$ of location names, ranged over $l, m, n, \cdots$. We denote the union of $\mathcal{N}_c$ and $\mathcal{N}_l$ as $\mathcal{N}$, ranged over by $x, y \cdots$. The syntax of the language is given in Definition 1.

Definition 1

$$\begin{array}{ll}\alpha & ::= \bar{a}\langle x\rangle \mid a(x) \mid \textbf{\textit{go}}\ l \mid \textbf{\textit{merge}} \mid \textbf{\textit{split}} \mid \tau \\ P,Q & ::= 0 \mid \alpha.P \mid [x=y]P \mid [x\neq y]P \mid P+Q \mid P|Q \mid (\nu a)P \mid A(x_1,\cdots,x_n) \\ M,N & ::= m[P] \mid M||N \mid (\nu a)M \mid X(x_1,\cdots,x_n)\end{array}$$

The set of local processes is denoted by $\mathcal{P}$, whose elements are ranged over by $P, Q, R, \cdots$. Local processes can be considered as a collection of threads of computation that run at a single location, and hence may be called *threads.* Threads are constructed by inaction 0, action prefix $\alpha.P$, match $[x = y]$, mismatch $[x \neq y]$ nondeterministic choice $+$, parallel composition $|$, channel name restriction $(\nu a)P$, and recursively defined processes. A defining equation A of arity n is of the form $A(x_1, \cdots, x_n) \stackrel{def}{=} P$ where the x_i are pairwise distinct.

Action prefix is of five kinds: an output action $\bar{a}\langle x\rangle$, an input action $a(x)$, a silent action τ, and joining and splitting actions **merge** and **split**. The set of *actions* is denoted by Act, ranged by $\alpha, \beta, \cdots$. When defining operational semantics we shall use *bound output actions* of the form $\bar{a}\langle \nu x\rangle$. The set of free names and bound names of an action α are defined thus: if α is an input action $a(x)$ or a bound output action $\bar{a}\langle \nu x\rangle$ then $bn(\alpha) = \{x\}$ and $fn(\alpha) = \{a\}$; for all other actions $bn(\alpha) = \emptyset$ and $fn(\alpha)$ is the set of the names occurring in α.

The set of distributed processes are denoted by $\mathcal{M}$, whose elements are ranged over by $M, N, \cdots$. Distributed processes are also called *agents.* Agents are constructed by located threads $m[P]$, distributed parallel composition $||$, channel name restriction $(\nu a)M$, and recursively defined agents. A defining equation X of arity n is of the form $X(x_1, \cdots, x_n) \stackrel{def}{=} M$ where the x_i are pairwise distinct.

In each one of the forms $a(x).P$, $(\nu a)P$ and $(\nu a)M$, the occurrences of x and a are binding. These lead to the notions of bound and free names as usual. We use $bn(P)/bn(M)$ and $fn(P)/fn(M)$ to denote the sets of bound and free names of P and M, respectively. We also write $n(P)/n(M)$ for the set of names of P/M, i.e., $n(P) = bn(P) \cup fn(P)$ and $n(M) = bn(M) \cup fn(M)$. In defining equations of $A(x_1, \cdots, x_n) \stackrel{def}{=} P$ and $X(x_1, \cdots, x_n) \stackrel{def}{=} M$, we assume that $fn(P) \subseteq \{x_1, \cdots, x_n\}$ and $fn(M) \subseteq \{x_1, \cdots, x_n\}$. In some examples, we shall elide the parameters of defining equations when they are unimportant or can be inferred from context.

Substitutions, ranged over by σ are partial mapping from $\mathcal{N}$ to $\mathcal{N}$. We write $\{x/y\}$ for the substitution that maps y to x. Substitutions are post-fixing and bind tighter that any operators in the language. We shall use $\equiv_\alpha$ for α-equivalence.

2.2 Structural Congruence

Structural congruence is defined for threads and agents.

Definition 2. *(Structural congruence) Structural congruence for threads and agents, $\equiv$, are defined respectively as the smallest congruence satisfying the following rules:*

- *Structural congruence for threads*

1. $P \equiv Q$ *if* $P \equiv_\alpha Q$
2. $P|0 \equiv P$, $P|Q \equiv Q|P$, $P|(Q|R) \equiv (P|Q)|R$
3. $P + 0 \equiv P$, $P + Q \equiv Q + P$, $P + (Q + R) \equiv (P + Q) + R$
4. $(\nu a)0 \equiv 0$, $(\nu a)(P + Q) \equiv P + (\nu a)Q$ *if* $a \notin fn(P)$, $(\nu a)(P|Q) \equiv P|(\nu a)Q$ *if* $a \notin fn(P)$
5. $A(y) \equiv P\{y/x\}$ *if* $A(x) = P$

- *Structural congruence for agents*

1. $M \equiv N$ *if* $M \equiv_\alpha N$
2. $m[P] \equiv m[Q]$ *if* $P \equiv_l Q$
3. $M||N \equiv N||M$, $M||(N||L) \equiv (M||N)||L$
4. $m[(\nu a)P] \equiv (\nu a)m[P]$, $(\nu a)(M||N) \equiv M||(\nu a)N$ *if* $a \notin fn(M)$, $(\nu a)(\nu b)M \equiv (\nu b)(\nu a)M$
5. $X(y) \equiv M\{y/x\}$ *if* $X(x) = M$

The rules of structural congruence for threads are in the usual way. The second rule of structural congruence for agents, i.e., $m[P] \equiv m[Q]$ if $P \equiv_l Q$, means that agents, acquired by locating structural congruent threads at a same location, are structural congruent. The first rule in 4 of structural congruence for agents, i.e., $m[(\nu a)P] \equiv (\nu a)m[P]$, means that restrictions at top level of threads can be pulled out to the distributed level, where notice that $a \neq m$ since restrictions are only on channel names in the calculus. The other rules of structural congruence for agents are straightforward.

2.3 Operational Semantics

The operational semantics is given in terms of an enriched variant of the usual labelled transition systems.

Let the set of *locations* be defined as $Loc = \mathcal{N}_l \cup \{null\}$, ranged by $h, i, \cdots$. *Null* is used in cases where concrete location names are of no interest.

A labelled transition system is a tuple: $(S, Act, Loc, \rightarrow)$, where S is a set of *states* and $\rightarrow \in S \times Act \times Loc \times S$ a *located transition*. We write $M \xrightarrow[h]{\alpha} M'$ to mean $(M, \alpha, h, M') \in \rightarrow$, meaning agent M can evolve into M' by performing *action* α at *location* h.

Definition 3. *The transition relations are defined by the rules in Table 1.*

We omit the location label *null* in transitions. For example, $M \xrightarrow{\tau} M'$ means $M \xrightarrow[null]{\tau} M'$.

The STRUCT rule makes explicit our intuition that structurally congruent processes are deemed to have the same behaviours. This simplifies the definition of the operational semantics. For example, rules for locally restricted processes of the form $m[(\nu a)P]$ are not needed, because transitions of such processes can be inferred using structurally congruent to pull out restrictions outside location names:

$$\cfrac{\cfrac{m[P] \xrightarrow[m]{\alpha} m'[P'], \quad a \notin n(\alpha)}{(\nu a)m[P] \xrightarrow[m]{\alpha} (\nu a)m'[P'], \quad m \neq x \wedge m' \neq a}\ \text{D-RES}}{m[(\nu a)P] \xrightarrow[m]{\alpha} m'[(\nu a)P']}\ \text{STRUCT}$$

Table 1. Transition rules

$$\textbf{ACT:}\ \frac{\alpha \neq a(x)}{\alpha.P \xrightarrow{\alpha} P} \qquad \textbf{INP:}\ \frac{-}{a(x).P \xrightarrow{ay} P\{y/x\}} \qquad \textbf{SUM:}\ \frac{P \xrightarrow{\alpha} P'}{P+Q \xrightarrow{\alpha} P'}$$

$$\textbf{MATCH:}\ \frac{P \xrightarrow{\alpha} P'}{[x=x]P \xrightarrow{\alpha} P'} \qquad \textbf{MISMATCH:}\ \frac{P \xrightarrow{\alpha} P',\ x \neq y}{[x \neq y]P \xrightarrow{\alpha} P'}$$

$$\textbf{L-COM:}\ \frac{P \xrightarrow{\bar{a}\langle x\rangle} P',\ Q \xrightarrow{a(x)} Q'}{P \mid Q \xrightarrow{\tau} P' \mid Q'} \qquad \textbf{L-PAR:}\ \frac{P \xrightarrow{\alpha} P',\ bn(\alpha) \cap fn(Q) = \emptyset,\ \alpha \neq \textbf{split}}{P \mid Q \xrightarrow{\alpha} P' \mid Q}$$

$$\textbf{LACT:}\ \frac{P \xrightarrow{\alpha} P',\ \ \alpha \neq \tau, \textbf{go}\ l}{m[P] \xrightarrow[m]{\alpha} m[P']} \qquad \textbf{LTAU:}\ \frac{P \xrightarrow{\tau} P'}{m[P] \xrightarrow{\tau} m[P']} \qquad \textbf{GO:}\ \frac{P \xrightarrow{\textbf{go}\ l} P'}{m[P] \xrightarrow{\tau} l[P']}$$

$$\textbf{SPLIT:}\ \frac{m[P] \xrightarrow[m]{\textbf{split}} m[P']}{m[P \mid Q] \xrightarrow{\tau} m[P'] \parallel m[Q]} \qquad \textbf{MERGE:}\ \frac{m[P] \xrightarrow[m]{\textbf{merge}} m[P']}{m[P] \parallel m[Q] \xrightarrow{\tau} m[P' \mid Q]}$$

$$\textbf{D-PAR:}\ \frac{M \xrightarrow[h]{\alpha} M',\ bn(\alpha) \cap fn(N) = \emptyset,\ \alpha \neq \textbf{merge}}{M \parallel N \xrightarrow[h]{\alpha} M' \parallel N}$$

$$\textbf{D-COM:}\ \frac{M \xrightarrow[h]{\bar{a}\langle x\rangle} M',\ N \xrightarrow[i]{ax} N'}{M \parallel N \xrightarrow{\tau} M' \parallel N'} \qquad \textbf{RES:}\ \frac{M \xrightarrow[h]{\alpha} M',\ \ x \notin n(\alpha)}{(\nu a)M \xrightarrow[h]{\alpha} (\nu a)M'}$$

$$\textbf{OPEN:}\ \frac{M \xrightarrow[h]{\bar{a}\langle b\rangle} M',\ \ a \neq b}{(\nu b)M \xrightarrow[h]{\bar{a}\langle\nu b\rangle} M'} \qquad \textbf{STRUCT:}\ \frac{M \equiv N,\ M \xrightarrow[h]{\alpha} M',\ M' \equiv N'}{N \xrightarrow[h]{\alpha} N'}$$

Also rules for communication involving bound output actions are elided since such an interactions can be inferred using STRUCT and RES, by pulling outside the restrictions in both interacting agents (possibly after α-conversion) using structural congruence rule. In a similar way, the transition rule for process identifiers is unnecessary since they are defined through structural congruence rules $A(y) \equiv P\{y/x\}$ if $A(x) = P$ and $X(y) \equiv M\{y/x\}$ if $X(x) = M$. (see [11])

ACT, INP, SUM, MATCH, MISMATCH, L-COM and L-PAR define the behaviours of local processes in the usual way. Note that ACT does not handle input action since we separately consider it in INP (in the early style of semantics). LACT and LTAU lift local transitions to the distributed level. We consider LACT and LTAU separately, because we do not assign locations to internal interactions between local processes. GO is the rule for process mobility. SPLIT and MERGE respectively define the behaviours of merging and splitting process modularities. D-PAR, D-COM, RES and OPEN specify the behaviours of distributed processes. As D-COM shows, communication between processes at different locations, *i.e.*, distributed communication, is admitted in this calculus.

3 Descriptive Examples

3.1 Routed Packet

We implement the system of *Routed packet* whose concept is explained in Introduction. This example mainly shows the aspect of dynamic control on process modularities of the calculus.

$$\begin{aligned}
Packet &= call(l,d).\mathbf{go}\ l.\overline{start}.ready.P(l,d)\\
P(l,d) &= if\ l = d\ then\ \overline{arrive}.Packet\\
&\quad\ else\ \overline{route}\langle d\rangle.next(n).\mathbf{go}\ n.P(n,d)\\
R &= \overline{call}\langle l,d\rangle.start.\mathbf{merge}.\overline{ready}.arrive.\mathbf{split}.R'\\
Sys &= m[Packet] \parallel l[R]
\end{aligned}$$

Packet is a routed packet which carries process R to its destination. The implementation of *Packet* is based on a program of routed forwarding in [10]. The resource process R calls the service *Packet*, passing its current location name l and the destination location name d to the service. Upon receiving the call, *Packet* moves to l, to allow R to use the service. It then signals the start of the service, and waits till R is ready. R makes itself on board by executing a **merge** action, and tells *Packet* that it is ready for departure. When R finds itself has arrived at d, it separates from the carrier by performing **split**. The *Packet* process relies on a routing mechanism to find the way to d. This is modeled by the output action $\overline{route}\langle d\rangle$ (asking the routing mechanism how to get to d) and the input action $next(n)$ (receiving the next hop information from the routing mechanism).

3.2 Follow-Me Application

"Follow-me application" is a case study by Cambridge University's Sentient Computing project and is a special case of context aware applications [9]. The basic concept of follow-me application is that applications are deployed at computers around a user, and they must follow the user as she moves, in order to support ubiquitous and personalized services. Figure 1 shows the basic concept of the "follow-me application". The figure depicts that when the user moves from location l to m, the application deployed at location l follows the user moving to m.

As we can see, a characteristic feature of the follow-me application is that the timing of process mobility is highly dynamic. The application program's movements depend on the user's which are arbitrary, sudden and unpredictable. Hence the application system on the one hand must provide services to the user, and on the other hand must be ready to move at any moment to follow the user.

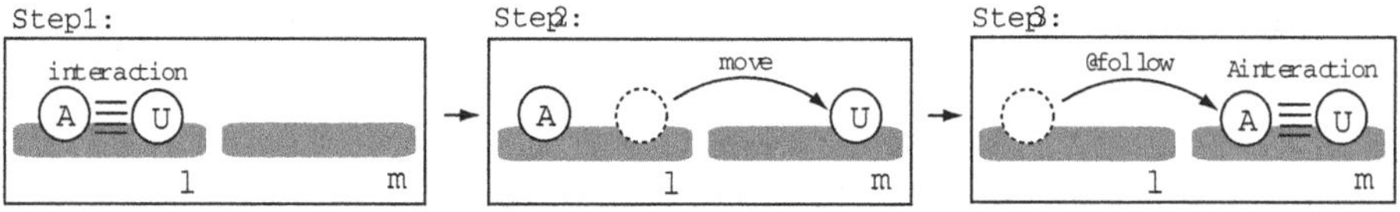

Fig. 1. Basic concept of follow-me application

The design of process mobility of our calculus enables to describe such a highly mobile system, where mobility is anytime and anywhere. The monitor program *FmMon* can be implemented easily as $FmMon = l[FM]$, where

$$FM = fm(x).\mathbf{go}\ x.FM + \overline{mon}.FM$$

Assume that user's behaviour is as follows:

$$User = l[\overline{enter}.mon.mon.mon.\mathbf{go}\ m.\overline{fm}\langle m\rangle.mon.mon.mon.\overline{exit}.0].$$

The user is initially located at l and her activities are monitored by the monitor there. When the user moves to location m she notifies the application via the *fm* channel. Upon receiving the notification, the application follows the user's moving to m, then keeps monitoring the user at the new location. The monitor system Sys_{FmM} and its trace are as follows;

$$\begin{aligned}
&Sys_{FmM} = (\nu fm, mon)(FmMon \parallel User) \\
&\xrightarrow[l]{\overline{enter}} \xrightarrow{\tau} \xrightarrow{\tau} \xrightarrow{\tau} (\nu fm, mon)(l[FM] \parallel m[\overline{fm}\langle m\rangle.User']) \\
&\xrightarrow{\tau} \xrightarrow{\tau} (\nu fm, mon)(m[FM] \parallel m[User'']) \\
&\xrightarrow{\tau} \xrightarrow{\tau} \xrightarrow{\tau} \xrightarrow[m]{\overline{exit}} (\nu fm, mon)(m[FM] \parallel m[0])
\end{aligned}$$

This example demonstrates that the process mobility mechanism in our calculus enables direct and simple descriptions for highly mobile systems where process mobility is anytime and anywhere as in ubiquitous computing.

On the other hand, in our view, the design of process mobility in the calculi [1, 2, 3, 10, 12, 14, 16] may require an intricate scheme to describe such a highly mobile system as follow-me application. With the design of process mobility in these calculi [1, 2, 3, 10, 12, 14, 16], process modularity is specified as a single thread of computing syntactically following the **go** operator, hence process ready to move, e.g., $l[\mathbf{go}\ m.P]$, is blocked by **go** operator and hence it can not do anything but move[1]. Due to this, the timing of process mobility is not flexibly specified with the design. Although this problem is partly due to the way how the implementation is designed, its root may lie on the design of process mobility in these calculi itself.

[1] This scheme may be reminiscent of *serialization* in programming languages such as Java.

4 Bisimulations

Consider a DNS (Domain name system) implemented as follows

$$DNS = nslookup(dn, a).\bar{a}\langle resolve(dn)\rangle.0 \mid DNS.$$

The process *DNS* receives, along port *nslookup*, a request to resolve a domain name *dn* together with a returning channel name *a*, and send back the the resolved name *resolve*(*dn*) via *a*. Suppose the service is deployed at two locations l and m. The two systems, $l[DNS]$ and $m[DNS]$, though at different locations, provide the same service, namely resolving domain names.

The standard notion of bisimulation, which takes into account only communication behaviours, identifies the two DNS services. This is appropriate, as we are only interested in the functional aspects of these two processes.

But in some occasions it is also plausible to distinguish processes which have the same communication behaviour exhibited at different locations. Recall that, in our calculus, processes are explicitly distributed over locations, and the location awareness is reflected in the transition systems used to provide operational semantics for processes.

In this section we shall consider two kind (weak) bisimulation relations, one ignoring location information and the other is location-aware. The later is called *location-conscious bisimulation*, or *LC-bisimulation* for short, which equates processes that can mimic each other's communication behaviours *as well as* the operating locations of observable transitions.

Weak transitions are defined in the usual way: (1) $\Longrightarrow$ stands for $(\xrightarrow{\tau})^*$; (2) $\xRightarrow{\tau}$ stands for $(\xrightarrow{\tau})^+$; (3) $\underset{h}{\xRightarrow{\alpha}}$ stands for $\Longrightarrow \underset{h}{\xrightarrow{\alpha}} \Longrightarrow$ if $\alpha \neq \tau$, and $\xRightarrow{\tau}$ if $\alpha = \tau$; (4) $\underset{h}{\xRightarrow{\hat{\alpha}}}$ stands for $\underset{h}{\xRightarrow{\alpha}}$ if $\alpha \neq \tau$, and $\Longrightarrow$ if $\alpha = \tau$.

We start with ground weak bisimilarity and LC-bisimilarity.

Definition 4

1. *A ground weak bisimulation is a symmetric binary relation $\mathcal{S} \subseteq \mathcal{M} \times \mathcal{M}$, satisfying the following; $(M, N) \in \mathcal{S}$ then $\forall \alpha \in Act$ and $\forall h \in Loc$*
   - $M \underset{h}{\xrightarrow{\alpha}} M' \wedge bn(\alpha) \notin fn(M, N)$ *implies* $\exists N', h' : N \underset{h'}{\xRightarrow{\hat{\alpha}}} N' \wedge (M', N') \in \mathcal{S}$.

   M and N are ground weak bisimilar, written $M \dot{\approx} N$, if $(M, N) \in \mathcal{S}$ for some ground weak bisimulation.
2. *A ground weak LC-bisimulation is a symmetric binary relation $\mathcal{S} \subseteq \mathcal{M} \times \mathcal{M}$, satisfying the following; $(M, N) \in \mathcal{S}$ then $\forall \alpha \in Act$ and $\forall h \in Loc$,*
   - $M \underset{h}{\xrightarrow{\alpha}} M' \wedge bn(\alpha) \notin fn(M, N)$ *implies* $\exists N' : N \underset{h}{\xRightarrow{\hat{\alpha}}} N' \wedge (M', N') \in \mathcal{S}$.

   M and N are ground weak LC-bisimilar, written $M \dot{\approx}_l N$, if $(M, N) \in \mathcal{S}$ for some ground weak LC-bisimulation.

In the definition of $\dot{\approx}$ the location information of the two processes under consideration is ignored. On the other hand, $\dot{\approx}_l$ refines $\dot{\approx}$ in that it takes into account not only observable transitions but also the locations where these transitions happen. Note that the locations of invisible transitions are ignored in both equivalences.

Proposition 1. *(1) $\dot{\approx}$ and $\dot{\approx}_l$ are equivalence relations. (2) $\dot{\approx}$ includes $\dot{\approx}_l$.*

As usual, the notions of weak bisimilarity $\approx$ and weak LC-bisimilarity $\approx_l$ are defined by closing up $\dot{\approx}$ and $\dot{\approx}_l$, respectively, with respect to substitutions.

Definition 5. *1. $M \approx N$ if and only if $M\sigma \dot{\approx} N\sigma$ for any σ.*
2. $M \approx_l N$ if and only if $M\sigma \dot{\approx}_l N\sigma$ for any σ.

As expected, in our calculus, summation does not preserve $\approx$, but interestingly it is preserved by all other operators. For $\approx_l$, besides summation, parallel compositions at distributed level do not preserve $\approx_l$, i.e. $M \approx_l N \not\Rightarrow M||L \approx_l N||L$. For example, although $m[a.0] \mid\mid m[b.0] \approx_l m[a.0 \mid b.0]$, we do not have $m[a.0] \mid\mid m[b.0] \mid\mid m[\textbf{merge.go}\ l.0] \approx_l m[a.0 \mid b.0] \mid\mid m[\textbf{merge.go}\ l.0]$, because

$$m[a.0] \mid\mid m[b.0] \mid\mid m[\textbf{merge.go}\ l.0] \stackrel{\tau}{\longrightarrow} l[a.0] \mid\mid m[b.0]$$
$$m[a.0 \mid b.0] \mid\mid m[\textbf{merge.go}\ l.0] \stackrel{\tau}{\longrightarrow} l[a.0 \mid b.0]$$

and $l[a.0] \mid\mid m[b.0] \not\approx_l l[a.0 \mid b.0]$.

Theorem 1. *(1) $\approx$ is preserved by all operators at distributed level. (2) $\approx_l$ is preserved by name restriction at distributed level. (3) $\approx$ and $\approx_l$ are preserved by all local operators except summation.*

5 A Bisimulation-Based Preorder

Consider another implementation of the monitor system in Section 3.2:

$$Sys_M = (\nu mon)(l[Mon] \mid\mid l[User])$$
$$l[Mon] = l[\overline{mon}.Mon],$$
$$l[User] = l[\overline{enter}.mon.mon.mon.\textbf{go}\ m.mon.mon.mon.\overline{exit}.0]$$

Sys$_M$ is similar to Sys$_{FmM}$ in Section 3.2: both specify a monitor program which monitors an user moving between locations. In fact $Sys_{FmM} \approx_l Sys_M$. But the two systems are implemented differently. In Sys$_M$, the monitor program *Mon* resides in location l, never trying to follow the user's move, and monitors the user by remote communications only, while the monitor program *FmM* in Sys$_{FmM}$ follows the user's move by process migration and locally communicates with the user.

In any practical mobile computing environment, it is reasonable to assume that local communications, remote communications and process migrations may incur different costs. Thus, although the systems mentioned above implement the same functionality, there is a good reason to compare them in terms of interaction costs.

In the following, we consider a bisimulation-based ordering relation w.r.t. interaction costs, which we may call *costlier-than* relation, such that it relates processes with identical behaviours but and requiring different interaction costs.

5.1 LTS with Interaction Costs

To define the *costlier-than* relation, first we slightly modify the transition rules in section 2 which involve the invisible action τ.

Invisible transitions arise from four kinds of interactions: communication, process merge, process split and process mobility. Consequently we tag the label τ with four indices: τ_c, τ_g, τ_m and τ_s, which respectively represent the internal actions resulting from communication, merge, split and process mobility.

Next the set of locations *Loc* is enriched, so that the sources and destinations of remote communications and process migrations can be remembered. The *enriched locations*, denoted by *ELoc* and ranged over λ, are given by the following rule:

$$\lambda ::= h \mid l \cdot m \qquad \textit{where } l, m \in \mathcal{N} \textit{ and } h \in \mathcal{N} \cup \textit{null}$$

Thus locations are either *single locations*, h, or *composed locations*, $l \cdot m$. Composed locations are used for remote communication or process migration, both of which involves two locations l and m.

The modified transition rules are as follows:

Table 2. Modified transition rules

$$\textbf{LTAU:}\ \frac{P \xrightarrow{\tau} P'}{m[P] \xrightarrow[m]{\tau_c} m[P']} \qquad \textbf{GO:}\ \frac{P \xrightarrow{\textbf{go } l} P'}{m[P] \xrightarrow[m\cdot l]{\tau_g} l[P']}$$

$$\textbf{SPLIT}_1\text{:}\ \frac{m[P] \xrightarrow[m]{\textbf{split}} m[P']}{m[P \mid Q] \xrightarrow[m]{\tau_s} m[P'] \parallel m[Q]} \qquad \textbf{MERGE}_1\text{:}\ \frac{m[P] \xrightarrow[m]{\textbf{merge}} m[P']}{m[P] \parallel m[Q] \xrightarrow[m]{\tau_m} m[P' \mid Q]}$$

$$\textbf{D-COM}_1\text{:}\ \frac{M \xrightarrow[l]{\bar{a}\langle x\rangle} M',\ N \xrightarrow[m]{ax} N'}{M \parallel N \xrightarrow[l\cdot m]{\tau_c} M' \parallel N'}$$

The bisimulation-based preorder will be parameterized on a *cost domain* and a *cost function*. A cost domain $(D, \sqsubseteq, +)$ is a set D equipped with a total order relation $\sqsubseteq$ and a binary function $+$ over D. A cost function $f :: T_\tau \mapsto D$, where $T_\tau = \{(s, \alpha, \lambda, s') \in T \mid \alpha = \tau\}$, maps each τ-transition to an element of D. We shall write $s \xrightarrow[\lambda]{\tau}{}_c s'$ to mean denote $s \xrightarrow[\lambda]{\tau} s'$ such that $f(\xrightarrow[\lambda]{\tau}) = c$.

5.2 Bisimulation Preorder w.r.t Costs

We proceed to formalize bisimulation preorder w.r.t. interaction costs. Weak transitions with the notion of costs are defined as follows; (1) $\Longrightarrow_c \triangleq \xrightarrow[\lambda_1]{\tau}{}_{c_1} \cdots \xrightarrow[\lambda_n]{\tau}{}_{c_n}$ for some $n \geq 0$ and $c = \sum_{i=0}^{n} c_i$; (2) $\overset{\alpha}{\underset{\lambda}{\Longrightarrow}}{}_c \triangleq \Longrightarrow_{c_1} \xrightarrow[\lambda]{\alpha}{}_{c_2} \Longrightarrow_{c_3}$ and $c = c_1 + c_2 + c_3$; (3) $\overset{\hat{\alpha}}{\underset{\lambda}{\Longrightarrow}}{}_c \triangleq \overset{\alpha}{\underset{\lambda}{\Longrightarrow}}{}_c$ if $\alpha \neq \tau$ and $\Longrightarrow_c$ if $\alpha = \tau$. Note that in (1) location labels are not attached to a sequence of τ-transitions, $\Longrightarrow_c$, though they are attached to a single τ-transition, $\xrightarrow[\lambda_1]{\tau}_{c_1}$. This is because location labels for a τ-transition is not for observing the location where the action occurs, but for measuring the cost. Costs for a sequence of τ-transition is acquired by accumulating the cost on each τ-transition. Hence location labels for a sequence of τ-transitions are not required and hence omitted.

The *costlier-than* relations are defined as refinements of weak bisimulation and LC-bisimulation. That is, we define two notions of costlier-than relation, *bisim-and-costlier-than* and *LC-bisim-and-costlier-than* refining $\approx$ and $\approx_l$, respectively.

Definition 6

1. *A binary relation $\mathcal{S} \subseteq \mathcal{M} \times \mathcal{M}$ is a bisim-and-costlier-than relation, if, whenever $(M, N) \in \mathcal{S}$, for all $\alpha \in Act$, λ and $c \in D$,*
   (a) $M \overset{\alpha}{\underset{\lambda}{\Longrightarrow}}_c M' \wedge bn(\alpha) \notin fn(M, N)$ implies $\exists N', \lambda', c' : N \overset{\hat{\alpha}}{\underset{\lambda'}{\Longrightarrow}}_{c'} N' \wedge (M', N') \in \mathcal{S} \wedge c' \leq c$;
   (b) v.v. with $c \leq c'$.
   M is bisim-and-costlier-than N, written $M \gtrsim N$, if $(M, N) \in \mathcal{S}$ for some bisim-and-costlier-than relation $\mathcal{S}$.
2. *A binary relation $\mathcal{S} \subseteq \mathcal{M} \times \mathcal{M}$ is a LC-bisim-and-costlier-than relation, if, whenever $(M, N) \in \mathcal{S}$, for all $\alpha \in Act$, λ and $c \in D$,*
   (a) $M \overset{\alpha}{\underset{\lambda}{\Longrightarrow}}_c M' \wedge \alpha \neq \tau \wedge bn(\alpha) \notin fn(M, N)$ implies $\exists N', c' : N \overset{\hat{\alpha}}{\underset{\lambda}{\Longrightarrow}}_{c'} N' \wedge (M', N') \in \mathcal{S} \wedge c' \leq c$;
   (b) v.v. with $c \leq c'$;
   (c) $M \overset{\tau}{\underset{\lambda}{\Longrightarrow}}_c M'$ implies $\exists N', d : N \Longrightarrow_{c'} N' \wedge (M', N') \in \mathcal{S} \wedge c' \leq c$;
   (d) v.v. with $c \leq c'$.
   M is LC-bisim-and-costlier-than N, written $M \gtrsim_l N$, if $(M, N) \in \mathcal{S}$ for some LC-bisim-and-costlier-than relation $\mathcal{S}$. □

The bisim-and-costlier-than relation refines weak bisimulation in a straightforward manner, by additionally taking onto account of costs. In the definition of LC-bisim-and-costlier-than relation, τ-transitions and non-τ-transitions are considered separately. This is because we assume location-awareness only in the case of non-τ-transitions, the location information is ignored for τ-transitions but are used for non-τ-transitions.

Proposition 2. *1. $\gtrsim$ and $\gtrsim_l$ are preorder relations.*
2. $\gtrsim$ and $\gtrsim_l$ are included by $\approx$ and $\approx_l$, respectively.

5.3 Example of Modeling Analysis

We demonstrate an example of modeling analysis with the two systems Sys_M and Sys_{FmM}, using the costlier-than relation proposed above. Assume in the setting that the cost function assigns costs as follows;

$$f(\xrightarrow[m\cdot m]{\tau_c}) = 1,$$
$$f(\xrightarrow[l\cdot m]{\tau_c}) = f(\xrightarrow[m\cdot l]{\tau_c}) = 6,$$
$$f(\xrightarrow[l\cdot m]{\tau_g}) = f(\xrightarrow[m\cdot l]{\tau_g}) = 8.$$

Then the traces of these systems with costs are as follows;

$$\begin{array}{l}
Sys_{FmM} = (\nu fm, mon)(l[FM] \parallel l[User]) \\
\xrightarrow[l]{\overline{enter}} \xrightarrow[l\cdot l]{\tau_c}_1 \xrightarrow[l\cdot l]{\tau_c}_1 \xrightarrow[l\cdot l]{\tau_c}_1 \\
(\nu fm, mon)(l[FmMon] \parallel l[\mathbf{go}\ m.\overline{fm}\langle m\rangle.User]) \\
\xrightarrow[l\cdot m]{\tau_g}_8 \xrightarrow[m\cdot l]{\tau_c}_6 \xrightarrow[l\cdot m]{\tau_g}_8 \\
(\nu fm, mon)(m[FmMon] \parallel m[User]) \\
\xrightarrow[m\cdot m]{\tau_c}_1 \xrightarrow[m\cdot m]{\tau_c}_1 \xrightarrow[m\cdot m]{\tau_c}_1 \xrightarrow[m]{\overline{exit}} \\
(\nu fm, mon)(m[FmMon] \parallel m[0])
\end{array}$$

$$\begin{array}{l}
Sys_M = (\nu mon)(l[Mon] \parallel l[User]) \\
\xrightarrow[l]{\overline{enter}} \xrightarrow[l\cdot l]{\tau_c}_1 \xrightarrow[l\cdot l]{\tau_c}_1 \xrightarrow[l\cdot l]{\tau_c}_1 \\
(\nu mon)(l[Mon] \parallel l[\mathbf{go}\ m.User]) \\
\xrightarrow[l\cdot m]{\tau_g}_8 \\
(\nu mon)(l[Mon] \parallel m[User]) \\
\xrightarrow[l\cdot m]{\tau_c}_6 \xrightarrow[l\cdot m]{\tau_c}_6 \xrightarrow[l\cdot m]{\tau_c}_6 \xrightarrow[m]{\overline{exit}} \\
(\nu mon)(l[Mon] \parallel m[0])
\end{array}$$

In this setting we have $Sys_M \gtrapprox_l Sys_{FmM}$.

6 Conclusion and Future Work

We have presented a variant of π-calculus that can flexibly specify *process modularity* and dynamically control it. It brings a simple and suitable model for modular programming in distributed mobile computing. Two notions of bisimilarities, location-unaware and location-aware, are discussed. Furthermore, two bisimulation-based preorders are introduced to reflect interaction costs. To our best knowledge, this is the first bisimulation-based preorder taking interaction costs into consideration.

As future work, we would like to consider axiomatization for the bisimulation relations proposed in this calculus. Also we are interested in the expressive power of the subset of the calculus whose operators consist of only **go**, **split** and **merge**. Another avenue of research is to design a spatial logic for the calculus. The calculus bears a spatial structure constituted of locations and link connectivity, which may be considered as a hybrid of π-calculus and Mobile Ambient. Thus it is interesting to investigate spatial properties in this framework.

References

1. Amadio, R., Boudol, G., Lousshaine, C.: The receptive distributed π-calculus. In: ACM Transactions on Programming Languages and Systems (TOPLAS), ACM Press, New York (2003)
2. Amadio, R.M.: An asynchronous model of locality, failure, and process mobility. In: Garlan, D., Le Métayer, D. (eds.) COORDINATION 1997. LNCS, vol. 1282, Springer, Heidelberg (1997)
3. Amadio, R.M.: On modelling mobility. Theoretical Computer Science 240(1) (2000)

4. Boudol, G., Castellani, I., Germain, F., Lacoste, M.: Models of distribution and mobility: state of the art, MIKADO Global Computing Project, IST-2001-32222, Deliverable D1.1.1 (2002)
5. Cardelli, L., Gordon, A.D.: Mobile ambients. In: Nivat, M. (ed.) ETAPS 1998 and FOSSACS 1998. LNCS, vol. 1378, Springer, Heidelberg (1998)
6. Fournet, C., Gonthier, G.: The reflexive cham and the join-calculus. In: Conference Record of the ACM Symposium on Principles of Programming Languages, ACM Press, New York (1996)
7. Fournet, C., Gonthier, G., Lévy, J.-J., Maranget, L., Rémy, D.: A calculus of mobile agents. In: Sassone, V., Montanari, U. (eds.) CONCUR 1996. LNCS, vol. 1119, pp. 406–421. Springer, Heidelberg (1996)
8. Godskesen, J., Hildebrandt, T., Sassone, V.: A calculus of mobile resources. In: Brim, L., Jančar, P., Křetínský, M., Kucera, A. (eds.) CONCUR 2002. LNCS, vol. 2421, Springer, Heidelberg (2002)
9. Harter, A., Hopper, A., Steggles, P., Ward, A., Webster, P.: The anatomy of a context-aware application. Mobile Computing and Networking (1999)
10. Hennessy, M., Riely, J.: Resource access control in systems of mobile agents. Information and Computation 173, 82–120 (2002)
11. Parrow, J.: Handbook of Process Algebra. Elsevier, Amsterdam (2001) (chapter An introduction to the π-calculus)
12. Ravara, A., Matos, A., Vasconcelos, V., Lopes, L.: A lexically scoped distributed π-calculus. Technical report, Di/fcul tr, DIFCUL, Department of Computer Science, University of Lisbon (2002)
13. Schmitt, A., Stefani, J.B.: The m-calculus: A higher-order distributed process calculus. Technical report, RR-4361, INRIA (2002)
14. Sewell, P., Wojciechowski, P., Pierce, B.: Location-independent communication for mobile agents: A two-level architecture. In: Bal, H.E., Cardelli, L., Belkhouche, B. (eds.) ICCL 1998. LNCS, vol. 1686, Springer, Heidelberg (1999)
15. Vitek, J., Castagna, G.: Seal: A framework for secure mobile computations. In: Bal, H.E., Cardelli, L., Belkhouche, B. (eds.) Internet Programming Languages. LNCS, vol. 1686, Springer, Heidelberg (1999)
16. Wojciechowski, P., Sewell, P.: Nomadic pict: Language and infrastructure design for mobile agents. In: Proceedings of ASA/MA '99, First International Symposium on Agent Systems and Applications/Third International Symposium on Mobile Agents (1999)

Failures: Their Definition, Modelling and Analysis

Brian Randell and Maciej Koutny

School of Computing Science, Newcastle University
Newcastle upon Tyne, NE1 7RU, United Kingdom
{brian.randell,maciej.koutny}@ncl.ac.uk

Abstract. This paper introduces the concept of a 'structured occurrence net', which as its name indicates is based on that of an 'occurrence net', a well-established formalism for an abstract record that represents causality and concurrency information concerning a single execution of a system. Structured occurrence nets consist of multiple occurrence nets, associated together by means of various types of relationship, and are intended for recording either the actual behaviour of complex systems as they interact and evolve, or evidence that is being gathered and analyzed concerning their alleged past behaviour. We provide a formal basis for the new formalism and show how it can be used to gain better understanding of complex fault-error-failure chains (i) among co-existing interacting systems, (ii) between systems and their sub-systems, and (iii) involving systems that are controlling, supporting, creating or modifying other systems. We then go on to discuss how, perhaps using extended versions of existing tools, structured occurrence nets could form a basis for improved techniques of system failure prevention and analysis.

Keywords: failures, errors, faults, dependability, judgement, occurrence nets, abstraction, formal analysis.

1 Introduction

The concept of a failure of a system is central both to system dependability and to system security, two closely associated and indeed somewhat overlapping research domains. Specifically, particular types of failures (e.g., producing wrong results, ceasing to operate, revealing secret information, causing loss of life, etc.) relate to, indeed enable the definition of, what can be regarded as different attributes of dependability/security: respectively reliability, availability, confidentiality, safety, etc. The paper by Avizienis et al. [1] provides an extended (informal) discussion of the basic concepts and terminology of dependability and security, and contains a detailed taxonomy of dependability and security terms. Our aims in this present paper are: (i) to improve our understanding — in part by formalising — of the concept of failure (and error and fault) as given by [1]; (ii) to reduce (in fact by uniting the apparently different concepts of 'system' and 'state') the number of base concepts, i.e., concepts that the paper uses without explicit definition; and (iii) to initiate an investigation of possible improved techniques of system failure prevention and analysis.

Complex real systems, made *up* of other systems, and made *by* other systems (e.g., of hardware, software and people) evidently fail from time to time, and reducing the

C.B. Jones, Z. Liu, J. Woodcock (Eds.): ICTAC 2007, LNCS 4711, pp. 260–274, 2007.

frequency and severity of their failures is a major challenge — common to both the dependability and the security communities. Indeed, a dependable/secure system can be regarded as *one whose (dependability/security) failures are not unacceptably frequent or severe* (from some given viewpoint).

We will return shortly to the issue of viewpoint. But first let us quote the definitions of three basic and subtly-distinct concepts, termed 'failure', 'fault' and 'error' in [1]:

> 'A system *failure* occurs when the delivered service deviates from fulfilling the system function, the latter being what the system is *aimed at*. An *error* is that part of the system state which is *liable to lead to subsequent failure*: an error affecting the service is an indication that a failure occurs or has occurred. The *adjudged or hypothesised cause* of an error is a *fault*.'

Note that errors do not necessarily lead to failures — such occurrences may be avoided by chance or design. Similarly, failures in a component system do not necessarily constitute faults to the surrounding system — this depends on how the surrounding system is relying on the component. These three concepts (respectively an event, a state, and a cause) are evidently distinct, and so need to be distinguished, whatever names are chosen to denote them. The above quotation makes it clear that judgement can be involved in identifying error causes, i.e., faults. However it is also the case that identifying failures and errors involves judgement (not necessarily simple adherence to some pre-existing specification) — a critical point that we will return to shortly.

A failure can be judged to have occurred when an error 'passes through' the system-user interface and affects the service delivered by the system — a system being composed of components which are themselves systems. This failure may be significant, and thus constitute a fault, to the enclosing system.

Thus the manifestation of failures, faults and errors follows a 'fundamental chain': . . . → failure → fault → error → failure → fault → . . ., i.e., . . . → event → cause → state → event → cause → . . .. It is critical to note that this chain can flow from one system to: (i) another system that it is interacting with; (ii) a system which it is part of; and (iii) a system which it creates or sustains.

Typically, a failure will be judged to be due to multiple co-incident faults, e.g., the activity of a hacker exploiting a bug left by a programmer. Identifying failures (and hence errors and faults), even understanding the concepts, is difficult. There can be uncertainties about system boundaries, the very complexity of the systems (and of any specifications) is often a major difficulty, the determination of possible causes or consequences of failure can be a very subtle and iterative process, and any provisions for preventing faults from causing failures may themselves be fallible. Attempting to enumerate a system's possible failures beforehand is normally impracticable. Instead, one can appeal to the notion of a 'judgemental system'.

The 'environment' of a system is the wider system that it affects (by its correct functioning, and by its failures), and is affected by. What constitutes correct (failure-free) functioning *might* be implied by a system specification — assuming that this exists, and is complete, accurate and agreed. (Often the specification is part of the problem!) However, in principle a third system, a *judgemental system*, is involved in determining whether any particular activity (or inactivity) of a system in a given environment constitutes or would constitute — *from its viewpoint* — a *failure*. Note that the judgemental

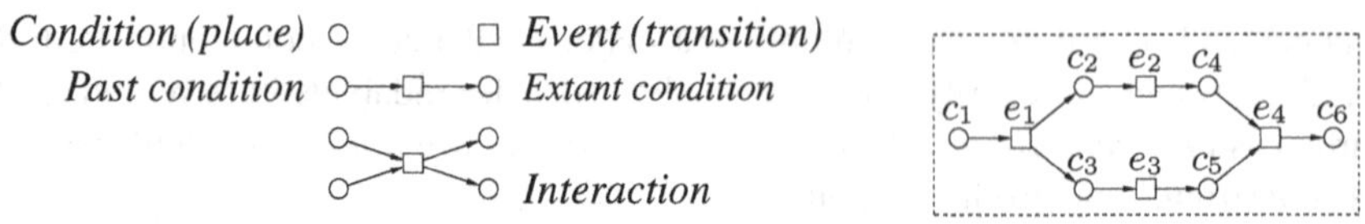

Fig. 1. Basic notation (left) and an occurrence net (right)

system and the environmental system might be one and the same, and the judgement might be instant or delayed. The judgemental system might itself fail — as judged by some further system — and different judges, or the same judge at different times, might come to different judgements.

The term 'Judgemental System' is deliberately broad — it covers from on-line failure detector circuits, via someone equipped with a system specification, to the retrospective activities of a court of enquiry (just as the term 'system' is meant to range from simple hardware devices to complex computer-based systems, composed of hardware, software and people). Thus the judging activity may be clear-cut and automatic, or essentially subjective — though even in the latter case a degree of predictability is essential, otherwise the system designers' task would be impossible. The judgement is an action by a system, and so can in principle fail either positively or negatively. This possibility is allowed for in the legal system, hence the concept of a hierarchy of crown courts, appeal courts, supreme courts, etc.

In this paper we describe a means of modelling the activity of systems — operational computing systems, the systems of people and computers that created them or are adapting them, the systems that are passing judgements on them, etc. The formalism that we use in this paper is based on that of *occurrence nets* [2,6,18] and our extensions of such nets [13]. We introduce this formalism not just in order to clarify such concepts as fault-error-failure chains, and the role of judgemental systems, but also because the occurrence net formalism is well-supported by tools for system validation and synthesis [7,8,9], tools which we believe could be significantly enhanced by being extended so as to take advantage of the concept that we introduce in Sections 3-6 of this paper of "structured occurrence nets". (Section 7 sketches the ways in which we envisage exploiting such enhanced tools.)

As can be seen in Fig. 1, occurrence nets are directed acyclic graphs that portray the (alleged) past and present state of affairs, in terms of places (i.e., conditions, represented by circles), transitions (i.e., events, represented by squares) and arrows (each from a place to a transition, or from a transition to a place, representing (alleged) causality). For simple nets, an actual graphical representation suffices — and will be used here using the notation shown in Fig. 1. (In the case of complex nets, these might be better represented in some linguistic or tabular form.) We will also take advantage of our belated realization that the concepts of 'system' and 'state' are not separate, but just a question of abstraction, so that (different related) occurrence nets can represent both systems and their states using the same symbol — a 'place'. In fact in this paper we introduce and define, and discuss the utility of, several types of relationship, and term a set of related occurrence nets a *structured occurrence net* (or *SON*). These types of relationship differ depending on the specific means and objectives of a particular investigation. However, there are some fundamental constraints that any structured occurrence net ought to satisfy. Crucially, we will require that the structures we admit *avoid cycles* in systems' temporal behaviour as these contradict the accepted view on the way physical systems could possibly behave.

Note: it is easy to understand how occurrence nets could be 'generated' by executing Petri nets representing computing systems, but they could in fact be used to record the execution of any (potentially asynchronous) process, hardware or software, indeed human, no matter what notation or language might be used to define it. (It is worth noting that various other graphical notations similar to occurrence nets can be found in both the hardware and the software design worlds, e.g., strand spaces [19], signal diagrams [14] and message sequence charts [15].)

2 Occurrence Nets

In this section, we present the basic model of an occurrence net, which is standard within Petri net theory [2,6,18]. Later on, we will extend it to express more intricate features of our approach to the modelling of complex behaviours. In a nutshell, an occurrence net is an abstract record of a single execution of some computing system (though they can be used to portray behaviours of quite general systems, e.g., ones that include people) in which only information about causality and concurrency between events and visited local states is represented.

Definition 1 (occurrence net). *An* occurrence net *is a triple* $\mathcal{ON} = (C, E, F)$ *where:* $C \neq \varnothing$ *and* E *are finite disjoint sets of respectively* conditions *and* events *(collectively, conditions and events are the* nodes *of* $\mathcal{ON}$*); and* $F \subseteq (C \times E) \cup (E \times C)$ *is a* flow relation *satisfying the following: (i) for every* $c \in C$ *there is at most one* e *such that* $(e, c) \in F$*, and at most one* f *such that* $(c, f) \in F$*; (ii) for every* $e \in E$ *there is* c *such that* $(c, e) \in F$*, and* d *such that* $(e, d) \in F$*; and (iii)* $\mathcal{ON}$ *forms an acyclic graph (in other words, the transitive closure of the relation* F*, denoted by* F^+*, is irreflexive).*

In the above definition — aimed at capturing the essence of a computation history — E represents the events which have actually been executed and C represents conditions (or holding of local states) enabling their executions. Here we will discuss computation histories as though they have actually occurred; however, the term will also be used of 'histories' that *might* have occurred, or that might occur in the future, given the existence of an appropriate system. Now we introduce few useful notations:

- For each condition or event x we use $pre(x)$ and $post(x)$ to denote the set of all elements y such that $(y, x) \in F$ and $(x, y) \in F$, respectively. In other words, $pre()$ and $post()$ correspond to the incoming and outgoing arcs, respectively.
- Two distinct nodes of $\mathcal{ON}$, x and y, are *causally related* if $(x, y) \in F^+$ or $(y, x) \in F^+$; otherwise they are *concurrent*.
- During the execution captured by the occurrence net, the system has passed through a series of (global) states, and the concurrency relation in $\mathcal{ON}$ provides full information about all such potential states. A *cut* is a maximal (w.r.t. set inclusion) set of conditions $Cut \subseteq C$ which are mutually concurrent.

- Let $Cut^{init}_{\mathcal{ON}}$ and $Cut^{fin}_{\mathcal{ION}}$ be the sets of all conditions c such that $pre(c) = \varnothing$ and $post(c) = \varnothing$, respectively. These two sets are cuts; the former corresponds to the initial state of the history represented by $\mathcal{ON}$, and the latter to its final state.

For the occurrence net depicted in Fig. 1, we have $C = \{c_1, \ldots\}$ and $E = \{e_1, \ldots\}$. Moreover, $Cut^{init}_{\mathcal{ON}} = \{c_1\}$ and $Cut^{fin}_{\mathcal{ION}} = \{c_6\}$, and the other four cuts are $\{c_2, c_3\}$, $\{c_2, c_5\}$, $\{c_4, c_3\}$ and $\{c_4, c_5\}$. An occurrence net is usually derived from a single execution history of the system. However, since it only records essential (causal) orderings, it also conveys information about other potential executions.

Definition 2 (sequential execution). *A* sequential execution *of the occurrence net $\mathcal{ON}$ is $D_0\, e_1\, D_1 \ldots e_n\, D_n$, where each D_i is a set of conditions and each e_i is an event, such that $D_0 = Cut^{init}_{\mathcal{ON}}$ and, for every $i \leq n$, $pre(e_i) \subseteq D_{i-1}$ and $D_i = (D_{i-1} \setminus pre(e_i)) \cup post(e_i)$. We will call $e_1 \ldots e_n$ a* firing sequence *of $\mathcal{ON}$.*

For the occurrence net in Fig. 1, $\{c_1\}\, e_1\, \{c_2, c_3\}\, e_2\, \{c_4, c_3\}\, e_3\, \{c_4, c_5\}\, e_4\, \{c_6\}$ is a possible execution. Thus an execution starts in the initial global state, and each successive event transforms a current global state into another one according to the set of conditions in its vicinity. Basically, all conditions (local states) which made possible its execution cease to hold, and new conditions (local states) created by the event begin to hold. It follows that $\mathcal{ON}$ is sound in the sense of obeying some natural temporal properties as well as testifying to the fact that $\mathcal{ON}$ does not contain redundant parts. We also have a complete characterisation of global states reachable from the default initial one — these are all the cuts of $\mathcal{ON}$. Hence we can verify state properties of the computations captured by $\mathcal{ON}$ by running a model checker which inspects all the cuts. Such a model checker could be based on a SAT-solver, e.g., as in [9], or integer programming, e.g., as in [7].

Theorem 1 ([2]). *Given an execution as in Def. 2, each D_i is a cut of $\mathcal{ON}$, and no event occurs more than once. Moreover, each cut of $\mathcal{ON}$ can be reached from the initial cut through some execution, and each event of $\mathcal{ON}$ is involved in at least one execution.*

An alternative, more concurrent, notion of execution considers that in a single computational move, a set of events (called a *step*) rather than a single event is executed. A *step execution* of $\mathcal{ON}$ is a sequence $D_0\, G_1\, D_1 \ldots G_n\, D_n$, where each D_i is a set of conditions and each G_i is a set of events, such that $D_0 = Cut^{init}_{\mathcal{ON}}$ and, for every $i \leq n$, we have $pre(G_i) \subseteq D_{i-1}$ and $D_i = (D_{i-1} \setminus pre(G_i)) \cup post(G_i)$. For the net in Fig. 1, $\{c_1\}\, \{e_1\}\, \{c_2, c_3\}\, \{e_2, e_3\}\, \{c_4, c_5\}\, \{e_4\}\, \{c_6\}$ is a possible step execution. For the basic model of occurrence nets, the sequential and step executions are broadly speaking equivalent; in particular, Theorem 1 holds also for step executions. However, for extended notions of occurrence nets, which we discussed in [10], sequential and step executions may, e.g., admit different sets of reachable global states.

3 Structuring Occurrence Nets

We now outline two simple ways of structuring occurrence nets. The first one captures *system interaction*, i.e., a situation in which two or more systems (in other words, a

(a) 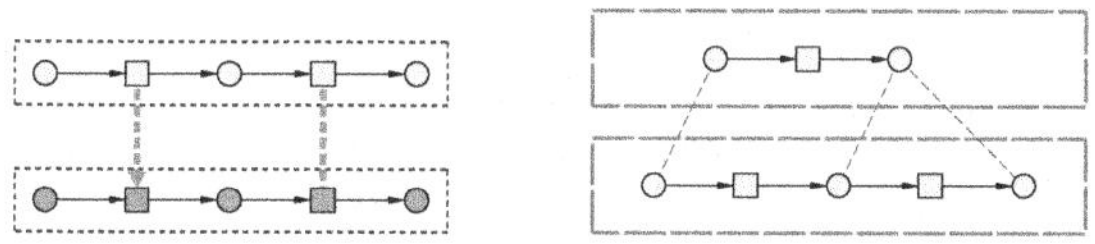 (b)

Fig. 2. System interaction (a), and simple abstraction (b)

compound system) proceed concurrently and (occasionally) interact with each other. As shown in Fig. 2(a), the systems — in this case two — or more precisely the actions of two systems, are represented by occurrence nets. We will follow a convention that conditions and events of different systems are recognised by shading them differently. There are some obvious rules about legal such colourings (e.g., that they partition the nodes into disjoint sets the members of each of which are connected; in this case, linearly but in general any occurrence net might be used).

We have two types of interactions to relate events of separate systems, represented by thick dashed arcs (relation κ in the next definition) and edges (relation σ in the next definition). The former relation means that one event is a causal predecessor of another event (i.e., information flow was unidirectional), while the latter means that two events have been executed synchronously (i.e., information flow was bidirectional).

Definition 3 (interaction ON). *An* interaction occurrence net *is defined to be a tuple* $\mathcal{ION} = (\mathcal{ON}_1, \ldots, \mathcal{ON}_k, \kappa, \sigma)$*, where each* $\mathcal{ON}_i = (C_i, E_i, F_i)$ *is an occurrence net,*[1] *and* $\kappa, \sigma \subseteq \bigcup_{i \neq j} E_i \times E_j$ *are two relations (*σ *being symmetric) such that the relation* $Prec_{\mathcal{ION}} = \mathbf{F}|_{\mathbf{C}\times\mathbf{C}} \cup (\mathbf{F} \circ (\kappa \cup \sigma) \circ \mathbf{F})$ *is acyclic.*
In the above, as well as later on, we denote $\mathbf{C} = \bigcup_i C_i$, $\mathbf{F} = \bigcup_i F_i$ *and* $\mathbf{E} = \bigcup_i E_i$.

Intuitively, if $(e, f) \in \kappa$ then e cannot happen after f, and if $(e, f) \in \sigma$ then e and f must happen synchronously. For an interaction occurrence net as in Def. 3, cuts and step executions need to be re-defined. A *cut* of $\mathcal{ION}$ is a maximal (w.r.t. set inclusion) set of conditions $Cut \subseteq \mathbf{C}$ such that $(Cut \times Cut) \cap Prec^{+}_{\mathcal{ION}} = \varnothing$. The initial cut of $\mathcal{ION}$, $Cut^{init}_{\mathcal{ION}}$, is the union of the initial cuts of all the $\mathcal{ON}_i$'s.

Definition 4 (step execution of ION). *A* step execution *of the interaction occurrence net* $\mathcal{ION}$ *is a sequence* $D_0\, G_1\, D_1 \ldots G_n\, D_n$*, where each* $D_i \subseteq \mathbf{C}$ *is a set of conditions and each* $G_i \subseteq \mathbf{E}$ *is a set of events, such that* $G_0 = Cut^{init}_{\mathcal{ION}}$ *and, for every* $i \leq n$*:*

- $pre(G_i) \subseteq D_{i-1}$ *and* $D_i = (D_{i-1} \setminus pre(G_i)) \cup post(G_i)$*;*
- $(e, f) \in \kappa \wedge f \in G_i$ *implies* $e \in \bigcup_{j \leq i} G_j$*; and* $(e, f) \in \sigma \wedge f \in G_i$ *implies* $e \in G_i$*.*

We can re-establish the basic behavioural characteristics of occurrence nets (proofs of these, and other new results formulated later on, are provided in [13]). Moreover, there is a consistency between the individual and interactive views of computation.

Theorem 2. *Given a step execution as in Def. 4, each* D_i *is a cut of* $\mathcal{ION}$*, and no event occurs more than once. Moreover, each cut of* $\mathcal{ION}$ *can be reached from the initial cut through some step execution, and each event of* $\mathcal{ION}$ *is involved in at least one step execution of* $\mathcal{ION}$*. Finally, for* $m \leq k$ *and* $i, j \leq n$*, we have:*

[1] In this, and other similar definitions, different occurrence nets have *disjoint* sets of nodes.

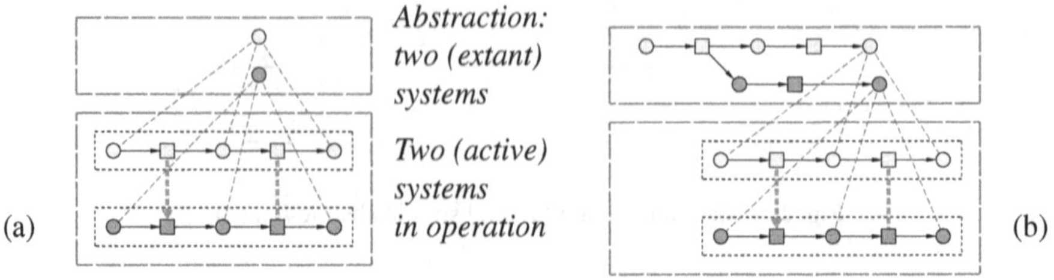

Fig. 3. Behavioural abstraction (a), and system creation (b)

- $D_0 \cap C_m \;\; G_1 \cap E_m \;\; D_1 \cap C_m \; \ldots \; G_n \cap E_m \;\; D_n \cap C_m$ *is a step execution of* $\mathcal{ON}_m$.
- $e \in G_i$, $f \in G_j$ *and* $(e, f) \in \kappa$ *(or* $(e, f) \in \sigma$*) imply* $i \leq j$ *(resp.* $i = j$*).*

Note, however, that it may happen that a cut of an individual occurrence net $\mathcal{ON}_i$ may no longer be reachable through any step execution of the composite system $\mathcal{ION}$.

Structures like that shown in Fig. 2(a) capture interactions between different systems but give no information about the evolution of individual systems. This orthogonal view is illustrated in Fig. 2(b), where we have a two-level view of a system's history. The two levels are delineated by dashed boxes, whereas (as before) dotted boxes will delineate occurrence nets when there are multiple occurrence nets within a level.

A possible interpretation of Fig. 2(b) is that the upper level provides a high-level view of system which went through two successive versions which are represented by two conditions of the upper occurrence net (the event in the middle represents a version update). The lower occurrence net captures the behaviour of the system during the same period. Fig. 2(b) also shows the 'abstracts' relation working across the two levels of description. The relation connects conditions in the lower part with those in the upper part which abstract them. We omit a formal definition of the two-level occurrence net as it is a special case of the construct introduced later in Def. 6.

4 Evolutional Abstractions

As already indicated in Fig. 2(b), any condition can be viewed either as a state (of some system), or as a (sub)system itself that presumably has its own states and events — just which is simply a matter of viewpoint. Moreover, as indicated in Fig. 2(a), behaviours of different systems can interact with each other. In general, it is possible to have sets of related occurrence nets, some showing what has happened in terms of systems and their evolution, the other showing the behaviours of these systems. In fact, the former can be viewed as the *behavioural abstraction* of the latter. What comes now is a combination of the structuring mechanisms that were illustrated in Fig. 2(a) and 2(b).

Fig. 3(a) shows a simple example, involving the interacting activities of two systems (note that the same shading is used for the higher- and lower-level view of each system). This picture gives no information about the evolution of the two systems — some such additional information is portrayed in the following figures. Moreover, the upper part of the picture does not provide any information about the interactions between the two systems (basically, all it says is that 'there are two systems').

More interesting is Fig. 4(a) which shows the history of an online modification of two systems, i.e., one in which the modified systems carry on from the states that had been reached by the original systems — a possibility that is easy to imagine, though often difficult to achieve dependably, especially with software systems. In this case, the 'abstracts' relation is non-trivial as it identifies those parts of the behaviours which are pre- and post-modification ones. Another type of system modification is shown in Fig. 4(b). It again shows that the two systems have each suffered some sort of modification, i.e., have evolved, once — the 'abstracts' relations between the two levels show which state sequences are associated with the systems before they were modified, and which with the modified systems. Note that in this case the behaviour of each system is represented by two disjoint occurrence nets. Thus the standard theory does not work as desired as it would consider these two parts as concurrent whereas, in fact, one is meant to precede the other. In the proposed structured view the upper part provides the necessary information for the desired sequencing of the occurrence nets. The last motivating example in this section, Fig. 3(b), shows some of the earlier history of the two systems in Fig. 3(a), i.e., that one system has spawned the other system, and after that both systems went through some independent further evolutions.

Note that additional information could have been portrayed in the figures by showing relations, from the earlier versions of the two systems, to parts of the occurrence nets which recorded the behaviour that occurred when these earlier versions were active — but to avoid undue graphical complexity no attempt is made to show that here (it may happen that no records of the prior behaviour of the two systems are available).

We will now formalise the 'evolutional abstractions' outlined above. After an auxiliary definition, we introduce the notion of an occurrence net corresponding to a record of modification, creation, etc., of some compound system.

An *interval* of $\mathcal{ON} = (C, E, F)$ is a non-empty set of conditions $int = \{c_1, \ldots, c_m\}$ such that there are $e_1, \ldots, e_{m-1}$ satisfying $(c_i, e_i) \in F$ and $(e_i, c_{i+1}) \in F$, for every $i \leq m - 1$. Intuitively, int captures successive stages in the *evolution* of some system.

Definition 5 (evolutional ON). *An* evolutional *occurrence net is* $\mathcal{EON} = (\mathcal{ON}, \ell)$, *where* $\mathcal{ON} = (C, E, F)$ *is an occurrence net and* $\ell : C \to \{1, \ldots, N\}$ $(N \geq 1)$. *Moreover, the inverse image* $\ell^{-1}(i) = \{c \in C \mid \ell(c) = i\}$ *is an interval, for* $i \leq N$.

The next definition combines together the above ideas about structuring behaviours.

Definition 6 (evolutional SON). *An* evolutional structured occurrence net *is a tuple* $\mathcal{ESON}=(\mathcal{EON}, \mathcal{ION}, \alpha)$, *where* $\mathcal{EON}$ *and* $\mathcal{ION}$ *are as in Def. 5 and 3, respectively, and* $\alpha : \mathbf{C} \to C$ *is a mapping such that:*

- $\ell(\alpha(\mathbf{C})) = \{1, \ldots, N\}$, *and* $\alpha(C_i) \cap \alpha(C_j) \neq \varnothing$ *implies* $i = j$, *for all* $i, j \leq k$;
- $\alpha(C_i)$ *is an interval and* $|\ell(\alpha(C_i))|=1$, *for all* $i \leq k$;
- *for every* $i \leq k$ *and every condition* $c \in C$ *with* $\alpha^{-1}(c) \subseteq C_i$, *the sets* Min_c *and* Max_c *of, respectively, all minimal and maximal elements of* $\alpha^{-1}(c)$ *w.r.t. the flow relation* F_i *are cuts of* $\mathcal{ON}_i$;
- *for every* $i \leq N$ *and all conditions* $b, c, d \in \mathbf{C}$ *such that* $\ell(\alpha(b))=\ell(\alpha(d))=i$, *if* $(\alpha(b), \alpha(c)) \in F^+$ *and* $(\alpha(c), \alpha(d)) \in F^+$, *then we have* $\ell(\alpha(c))=i$;
- $Prec_{\mathcal{ESON}} = Prec_{\mathcal{ION}} \cup Prec$ *is an acyclic relation, where* $Prec$ *is the union of sets* $Max_c \times Min_d$, *for all* $e \in E$ *and* $(c, d) \in pre(e) \times post(e)$.

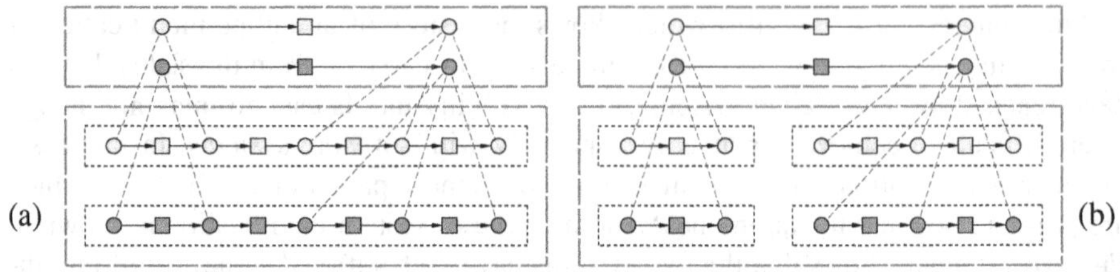

Fig. 4. System modifications

Intuitively, $Prec_{\mathcal{ION}}$ captures causalities resulting from intra-level interactions between behaviours, whereas *Prec* reflects the succession of evolutions the system had undergone during the history captured by $\mathcal{ESON}$.

We now introduce cuts and step executions for the evolutional structured occurrence net in Def. 6. A *cut* of $\mathcal{ESON}$ is a maximal (w.r.t. set inclusion) set of conditions $Cut \subseteq C \cup \mathbf{C}$ such that $(Cut \times Cut) \cap (Prec^{+}_{\mathcal{ESON}} \cup F^{+}) = \varnothing$ and, moreover, $\alpha(Cut \cap \mathbf{C}) = Cut \cap C$. (Taking into account F^{+} means that only a single version of a system can be active at any time.) The initial cut of $\mathcal{ESON}$ is the union, $Cut^{init}_{\mathcal{ESON}}$, of the initial cut of $\mathcal{ON}$ and the initial cuts of all the $\mathcal{ON}_i$'s such that $\alpha(Cut^{init}_{\mathcal{ON}_i}) \cap Cut^{init}_{\mathcal{ON}} \neq \varnothing$.

Definition 7 (step execution of SON). *A* step execution *of the evolutional structured occurrence net $\mathcal{ESON}$ is a sequence $D_0\, G_1\, D_1 \ldots G_n\, D_n$, where each $D_i \subseteq C \cup \mathbf{C}$ is a set of conditions and each $G_i \subseteq E \cup \mathbf{E}$ is a set of events, such that $G_0 = Cut^{init}_{\mathcal{ESON}}$ and, for every $i \leq n$, we have the following (below $Min = \bigcup_{c \in post(E \cap G_i)} Min_c$ and $Max = \bigcup_{c \in pre(E \cap G_i)} Max_c$):*

- $pre(G_i) \cup Max \subseteq D_{i-1}$ *and* $post(Max) \subseteq G_i$;
- $D_i = (D_{i-1} \setminus (pre(G_i) \cup Max)) \cup post(G_i) \cup Min$;
- $(e, f) \in \kappa \wedge f \in G_i$ *implies* $e \in \bigcup_{j \leq i} G_j$; *and* $(e, f) \in \sigma \wedge f \in G_i$ *implies* $e \in G_i$.

Theorem 3. *Given a step execution as in Def. 7, each D_i is a cut of $\mathcal{ESON}$, and no event occurs more than once. Moreover, each cut of $\mathcal{ESON}$ can be reached from the initial cut through some step execution, and each event of $\mathcal{ESON}$ is involved in at least one step execution of $\mathcal{ESON}$.*

We next establish a consistency between the individual and interactive views of computation, intertwined with the record of evolutions of the systems involved.

Theorem 4. *Given a step execution as in Def. 7, for every $m \leq k$, we have that the sequence $D_0 \cap C_m \;\; G_1 \cap E_m \;\; D_1 \cap C_m \; \ldots \; G_n \cap E_m \;\; D_n \cap C_m$ is either a sequence of empty steps, or a step execution of the occurrence net $\mathcal{ON}_m$ possibly preceded and/or followed by a sequence of empty sets (in the former case, the first non-empty set is the initial cut of $\mathcal{ON}_m$, and in the latter the final one). Moreover, the following sequence $D_0 \cap \mathbf{C} \;\; G_1 \cap \mathbf{E} \;\; D_1 \cap \mathbf{C} \; \ldots \; G_n \cap \mathbf{E} \;\; D_n \cap \mathbf{C}$ is a step execution of $\mathcal{ON}$.*

A version of Theorem 2 also holds, and using such results one can attempt to model check state based properties of evolving systems by inspecting all cuts of $\mathcal{ESON}$.

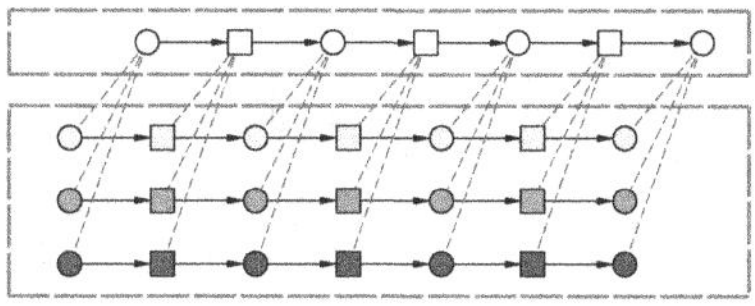
(a)

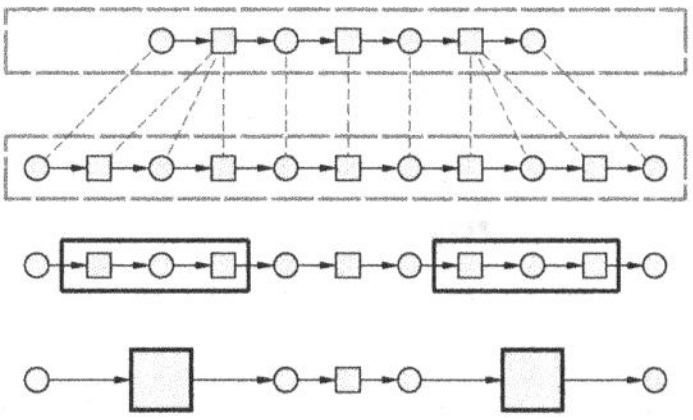
(b)
(c)
(d)

Fig. 5. System composition (a), and system abbreviation (b,c,d)

5 Spatial and Temporal Abstractions

Another type of abstraction, that we will call *composition abstraction*, is based on the relation 'contains / is component of'. Fig. 5(a) shows the behaviour of a system and of its three component systems, and how its behaviour is related to that of its components. (This figure does not represent the matter of *how*, or indeed whether, the component systems are enabled to interact, i.e., what design is used, or what connectors are involved.) Having identified such a set of interacting systems, and hence the *containing* system which they make up, then each member of this set has the other members as its *environment*.

Definition 8 (spatial abstraction SON). *A* spatial abstraction structured occurrence net *is a tuple* $\mathcal{SASON} = (\mathcal{ON}, \mathcal{ION}, \vartheta, \epsilon)$*, where* $\mathcal{ON}$ *and* $\mathcal{ION}$ *are as in Def. 1 and 3,* $\vartheta : C \to 2^{\mathbf{C}}$ *and* $\epsilon : \mathbf{E} \to E$*, and, moreover, the following hold (below* $\vartheta(H) = \bigcup_{c \in H} \vartheta(c)$*, for every* $H \subseteq C$*):*

- $\vartheta(C) = \mathbf{C}$ *and* $\epsilon(\mathbf{E}) = E$*; if Cut is a cut of* $\mathcal{ON}$ *and* $c, d \in Cut$*, then* $\vartheta(Cut)$ *is a cut of* $\mathcal{ION}$ *and* $\vartheta(c) \cap \vartheta(d) = \varnothing$*;*
- *for every event* $e \in \mathbf{E}$*,* $pre(e) \subseteq \vartheta(pre(\epsilon(e)))$ *and* $post(e) \subseteq \vartheta(post(\epsilon(e)))$*;*
- $Prec_{\mathcal{SASON}} = Prec_{\mathcal{ION}} \cup Prec'$ *is a acyclic, where* $Prec'$ *is the union of relations* $(\vartheta(pre(e)) \setminus \vartheta(post(e))) \times \epsilon^{-1}(e)$ *and* $\epsilon^{-1}(e) \times (\vartheta(post(e)) \setminus \vartheta(pre(e)))$*, for* $e \in E$*.*

One can define the cuts and step executions for $\mathcal{SASON}$ similarly as it has been done in Section 4 for $\mathcal{ESON}$, and then obtain results similar in essence and applicability to those formulated for $\mathcal{ESON}$. The above is in effect a *spatial* abstraction — one can also have a *temporal* abstraction, through the 'abbreviation' relation, i.e., an *abbreviation abstraction*, as shown in Fig. 5(b).

When one 'abbreviates' parts of an occurrence net one is in effect defining atomic actions, i.e., actions that appear to be instantaneous to their environment. The rules that enable one to make such abbreviations are non-trivial when multiple concurrent activities are shown in the net. These are best illustrated by an alternative representation for an occurrence net together with its abbreviations, namely a structured occurrence net in which each abbreviated section (or 'atomic' activity) of the net is shown surrounded by an enclosing 'event box'. Fig. 5(c) shows this alternative representation of Fig. 5(b), the top part of which can readily be recreated by 'collapsing' Fig. 5(c)'s occurrence net, i.e., by replacing the enclosed sections by simple event symbols, as shown in Fig. 5(d).

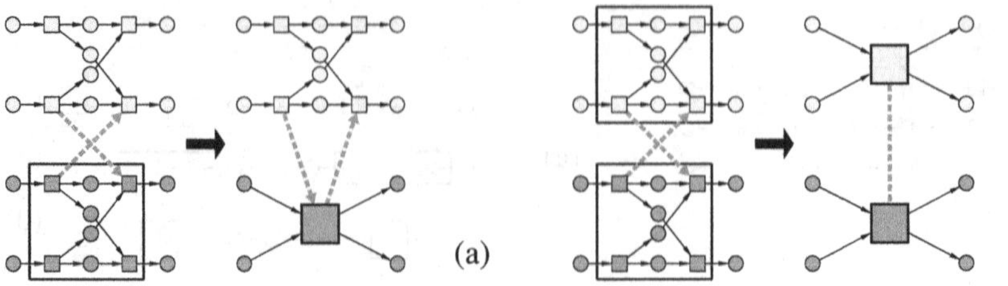

Fig. 6. Two valid collapsings

This net collapsing operation is much trickier with occurrence nets that represent asynchronous activity since there is a need to avoid introducing cycles into what is meant to be an acyclic directed graph. (Hence the need, on occasion, to use synchronous system interactions.) This is the main subject of [3] and is illustrated in Fig. 6.

A *block* of an occurrence net $\mathcal{ON} = (C, E, F)$ is a non-empty set $Bl \subset C \cup E$ of nodes where both the maximal and minimal (w.r.t. F) elements are events, and for all nodes $x, y \in Bl$, $(x, z) \in F^+$ and $(z, y) \in F^+$ imply $z \in Bl$. Thus in a block there are no 'gaps' between the nodes it comprises.

Definition 9 (temporal abstraction SON). *A* temporal abstraction structured occurrence net *is* $\mathcal{TASON} = (\mathcal{ION}, \mathcal{ION}', \xi)$ *where* $\mathcal{ION}$ *is as in Def. 3,* $\mathcal{ION}' = (\mathcal{ON}'_1, \ldots, \mathcal{ON}'_k, \kappa', \sigma')$ *is an interaction occurrence net with* $\mathcal{ON}'_i = (C'_i, E'_i, F'_i)$ *(for* $i \leq k$*), and* $\xi : \mathbf{C}' \cup \mathbf{E}' \to \mathbf{C} \cup \mathbf{E}$*; and, moreover, the following are satisfied, for every* $i \leq k$ *(below* $\mathbf{C}' = \bigcup_i C'_i$*,* $\mathbf{F}' = \bigcup_i F'_i$ *and* $\mathbf{E}' = \bigcup_i E'_i$*):*

- $\xi(C'_i \cup E'_i) = C_i \cup E_i$, $\xi^{-1}(C_i) \subseteq C'_i$ *and* $\xi(E'_i) = E_i$*;*
- $\xi^{-1}(e)$ *is a block of* $\mathcal{ON}'_i$*, for every* $e \in E_i$*; and* $|\xi^{-1}(c)| = 1$*, for every* $c \in C_i$*;*
- $F_i = \{(x, y) \mid (\xi^{-1}(x) \times \xi^{-1}(y)) \cap F'_i \neq \varnothing\}$*;*
- $\kappa = \{(e, f) \mid (\xi^{-1}(e) \times \xi^{-1}(f)) \cap \kappa' \neq \varnothing\}$*; and*
- $\sigma = \{(e, f) \mid (\xi^{-1}(e) \times \xi^{-1}(f)) \cap \sigma' \neq \varnothing\} \cup$
  $\{(e, f) \mid (((\xi^{-1}(e) \times \xi^{-1}(f)) \cap \kappa' \neq \varnothing) \wedge ((\xi^{-1}(f) \times \xi^{-1}(e)) \cap \kappa' \neq \varnothing))\}$.

A practical way in which temporal abstraction might be used is to analyse the behaviour at the higher level of abstraction, which can be done more efficiently, and after finding a problem mapping it to a corresponding behaviour at the lower level (and possibly continuing the analysis there). To give a flavour of the kind of result which would provide an underpinning for this approach, we have the following.

Theorem 5. *Let* $\mathcal{TASON}$ *be a temporal abstraction structured occurrence net as in Def. 9, and* $D_0 \{e_1\} D_1 \ldots \{e_n\} D_n$ *be a step execution of* $\mathcal{ION}$*. Let* $i \leq k$ *and* $f_1 \ldots f_q$ *be the subsequence of* $e_1 \ldots e_n$ *comprising the events in* E_i*. For every* $j \leq q$*, let* $e_{j1} \ldots e_{jm_j}$ *be a firing sequence of* $\mathcal{ON}'_i$ *involving exactly the events of* $\xi^{-1}(f_j)$ *starting from* $pre(f_j)$ *(which is possible). Then* $e_{11} \ldots e_{1m_1} \cdots e_{n1} \ldots e_{qm_q}$ *is a firing sequence of* $\mathcal{ON}'_i$*.*

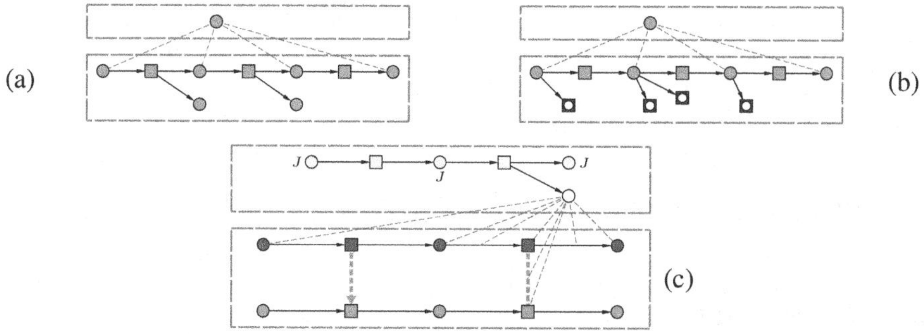

Fig. 7. State retention (a), what did not occur (b), and post-hoc judgement (c) involving a judgemental system (upper part) and an active system (lower part)

6 Dependability

To allow for the possibility of failure a system might, e.g., make use of 'recovery points'. Such recovery points can be recorded in states that take no further (direct) part in the system's ongoing (normal) behavior, as shown in Fig. 7(a). The notion of a 'failure' event involves, in principle, three systems — the given (possibly failing) system, its environment, and a judging system. This judging system may interact directly and immediately with the given system, in which case it is part of the system's environment, e.g., in VLSI an on-chip facility [12]; another example, in a very different world, is a football referee! Alternatively the judging system may also be deployed after the fact using an occurrence net that represents how the failing event occurred. Such an occurrence net is also something that can for example be recorded in a retained state, e.g., that of the judgment system. Fig. 7(c) is an attempt to portray this. It deliberately represents a situation in which a judgement system has obtained and retained only incomplete evidence of the systems' states and events and even the causal relationships between conditions and events.

In practice, judgement is likely to involve consideration not just of what (allegedly) happened but also what could have and should have happened, perhaps based on a system design or specification. An extended occurrence net notation that is used to represent such matters is the 'barb' (introduced in [11]), namely an event that could have occurred, given the condition(s) that existed, but which did not — see Fig. 7(b), where the barbs are represented by a distinctive kind of boxes.

Retracing the 'fault-error-failure' chain, after a judgment has been made that a particular event needs to be regarded as a failure involves following causal arrows *in either direction* within a given occurrence net, and following relations so as to move from one occurrence net to another. Thus one could retrace (i) the source and / or consequence of an interaction between systems, (ii) from a system to some guilty component(s), (iii) from a component to the system(s) built from it, or (iv) from a given system to the system(s) that created or modified it, or to the system(s) that should have allowed it to continue to exist. All this tracing activity can be undertaken by some tracing system (perhaps a part of the judgement system) using whatever evidence is available (e.g., a retained occurrence net which is alleged to record what happened). This tracing system (just like a judgment system) can of course itself fail (in the eyes of some other judgment system)! The actual implementation of such tracing in situations of ongoing activity, and of potential further failures, e.g., such as interfering with witnesses and the jury (in a judicial context), involves problems such as those addressed by the *chase protocols* [17].

7 Utilising Structured Occurrence Nets

One can envisage a given judge, having identified some system event as a failure, analysing a structured occurrence net, i.e., a set of related occurrence nets (dealing with the various abstractions of the various relevant systems), in an attempt to identify (i) the fault(s) that should be blamed for the failure, and / or (ii) the erroneous states that could and should be corrected or compensated for. Unless we assume that the occurrence nets are recorded correctly and completely as an automated by-product of system activity, in undertaking such a task it may well prove appropriate during such an analysis to correct or add to the occurrence nets, both individually and as a set, based on additional evidence or assumptions about what occurred.

Different judges (even different automated judgement systems) could of course, even if they identify the same failure event, come to different decisions regarding what actually happened and in determining the related faults and errors — possibly because they use different additional information (e.g., assumptions and information relating to system designs and specifications) to augment the information provided by the occurrence nets themselves. The result of such analyses could be thought of as involving the marking-up of the set of occurrence nets so as to indicate a four-way classification of all their places, namely as 'Erroneous', 'Correct', 'Undecided', and 'Not considered'.

As indicated earlier, the production of such a classification is likely to involve repeated partial traversals of the occurrence nets, following causal arrows backwards within a given occurrence net in a search for causes and forwards in a search for consequences. In addition it will involve following relations so as to move from one occurrence net to another. Two simplistic examples of this are: (i) the recognition that a given system's behaviour had, after a period of correct operation, started to exhibit a succession of faults, might lead to investigating the related occurrence net representing the system's evolution to determine if it had suffered a modification at the relevant time, and (ii) evidence of the non-occurrence of an expected event might be found to be due to a failure of an infrastructural system, such as a power supply. (Due to the page limit we omitted here a discussion, included in [13], of an abstraction relation which can be used to model the 'supports' relationship between hardware and the software processes that are running on it, and indeed between the electricity source and the hardware that it powers.)

This way of describing the failure analysis task using occurrence nets might be regarded as essentially metaphorical, i.e., essentially just as a way of describing (semi)-formally what is often currently done by expert investigators in the aftermath of a major system failure. However, at the other extreme one can imagine attempting to automate the recording and analysis of actual occurrence nets — indeed one could argue that this is likely to be a necessary function of any complex system that really merited the currently fashionable appellations 'self-healing' and 'autonomic'. The more likely, and practical, possibility — one that we plan to investigate — is the provision of computer assistance for the tasks of representing, checking the legality of, and performing analyses of, structured occurrence nets. This is because the task of analysing and / or deriving the scenarios depicted by structured occurrence nets will, in real life, be too complex to be undertaken as a simple paper and pencil exercise. The main reason is that the systems we primarily aim at are (highly) concurrent and so their behaviour suffers from the so-called 'state explosion problem'. In a nutshell, even the most basic problems are then of non-polynomial complexity and so perhaps the only way to deal with them is to use highly optimised automated tools. This work could build on earlier work at Newcastle [7,9] on the *unfoldings* of Petri nets introduced in [16], and also benefit, e.g., from recent work at Rennes [4] on the diagnosis of executions of concurrent systems.

A quite different use of such sets of related occurrence nets might in fact prove feasible. This would be to use them as a way of modelling complex system behaviour *prior* to system deployment, so as to facilitate the use of some form of automated model-checking in order to verify at least some aspects of the design of the system(s). Alternatively such automated model-checking might be used to assist analysis of the records of actual failures of complex systems. Such work could take good advantage of recent work at Newcastle on the model-checking of designs, originally expressed in the pi-calculus, work which involves the automated generation and analysis of occurrence nets [8]. For the integration of different formalisms, solvers and quantitative tools one could follow an approach adopted in modelling tools like Möbius [5].

There is in principle yet another avenue that could be explored, namely that of using structured occurrence nets which have been shown to exhibit desirable behaviour, including automated tolerance and / or diagnosis of faults, as an aid to designing systems that are guaranteed to exhibit such behaviour when deployed. We have in fact, with colleagues, already shown that it is possible to synthesize asynchronous VLSI sub-systems via the use of formal representations based on occurrence nets [9], but such designs are much less complex than those that we have had in mind while developing the concept of structured occurrence nets.

8 Concluding Remarks

A major aim of the present paper has been to introduce, and motivate the study of, the concept that we term structured occurrence nets, a concept that we claim could serve as a basis for possible improved techniques of failure prevention and analysis of complex evolving systems. This is because the various types of abstractions that the concept of a structured occurrence nets make use of are all ones that we suggest could facilitate the task of understanding complex systems and their failures, and that of the analysis of the cause(s) of such failures. These abstractions would in most cases be a natural consequence of the way the system(s) have been conceived and perceived, rather than abstractions that have to be generated after the fact, during analysis.

As mentioned earlier, we are working on the report [13] expanding on the results formulated in this paper, and containing a sketch of a structured representation of the various activities and mistakes which led up to the tragic Ladbroke Grove Train Crash [20]. (In this example sketch separate related occurrence nets are used for each of the trains that collided, for the train maintenance and inspection activities, and for the signalling system design effort. In doing so, we make use of such SON relationships as interaction, abstraction and system modification.)

Acknowledgements. We would like to thank the referees for their helpful comments. This research was supported by the EC IST grants RESIST and RODIN.

References

1. Avizienis, A., Laprie, J.-C., Randell, B., Landwehr, C.: Basic Concepts and Taxonomy of Dependable and Secure Computing. IEEE Trans. on Dep. and Sec. Comp. 1, 11–33 (2004)
2. Best, E., Devillers, R.: Sequential and Concurrent Behaviour in Petri Net Theory. TCS 55, 87–136 (1988)
3. Best, E., Randell, B.: A Formal Model of Atomicity in Asynchronous Systems. ACTA 16, 93–124 (1981)
4. Chatain, T., Jard, C.: Symbolic Diagnosis of Partially Observable Concurrent Systems. In: de Frutos-Escrig, D., Núñez, M. (eds.) FORTE 2004. LNCS, vol. 3235, Springer, Heidelberg (2004)
5. Clark, G., Courtney, T., Daly, D., Deavours, D., Derisavi, S., Doyle, J.M., Sanders, W.H., Webster, P.: The Möbius Modeling Tool. In: PNPM'01, pp. 241–250. IEEE Computer Society, Los Alamitos (2001)
6. Holt, A.W., Shapiro, R.M., Saint, H., Marshall, S.: Information System Theory Project RADC-TR-68-305 US Air Force, Rome Air Development Center (1968)
7. Khomenko, V., Koutny, M.: Verification of Bounded Petri Nets Using Integer Programming. Formal Methods in System Design 30, 143–176 (2007)
8. Khomenko, V., Koutny, M., Niaouris, A.: Applying Petri Net Unfoldings for Verification of Mobile Systems CS-TR 953 Newcastle University (2006)
9. Khomenko, V., Koutny, M., Yakovlev, A.: Logic Synthesis for Asynchronous Circuits Based on STG Unfoldings and Incremental SAT. Fundamenta Informaticae 70, 49–73 (2006)
10. Kleijn, H.C.M., Koutny, M.: Process Semantics of General Inhibitor Nets. INFCOM 190, 18–69 (2004)
11. Kleijn, J., Koutny, M., Rozenberg, G.: Towards a Petri Net Semantics for Membrane Systems. In: Freund, R., Păun, G., Rozenberg, G., Salomaa, A. (eds.) WMC 2005. LNCS, vol. 3850, Springer, Heidelberg (2006)
12. Koppad, D., Sokolov, D., Bystrov, A., Yakovlev, A.: Online Testing by Protocol Decomposition. In: IOLTS'06, pp. 263–268. IEEE CS Press, Los Alamitos (2006)
13. Koutny, M., Randell, B.: Understanding Failures (in preparation)
14. Lenk, S.: Extended Timing Diagrams as a Specification Language. In: European Design Automation, pp. 28–33. IEEE Computer Society Press, Los Alamitos (1994)
15. Mauw, S.: The Formalization of Message Sequence Charts. Computer Networks and ISDN Systems 28, 1643–1657 (1996)
16. McMillan, K.L.: A Technique of State Space Search Based on Unfoldings. Formal Methods in System Design 6, 45–65 (1995)
17. Merlin, P.M., Randell, B.: State Restoration in Distributed Systems. In: FTCS-8, pp. 129–134. IEEE Computer Society Press, Los Alamitos (1978)
18. Rozenberg, G., Engelfriet, J.: Elementary Net Systems. In: Reisig, W., Rozenberg, G. (eds.) Lectures on Petri Nets I: Basic Models. LNCS, vol. 1491, pp. 12–121. Springer, Heidelberg (1998)
19. Thayer, F.J., Herzog, J.C., Guttman, J.D.: Strand Spaces: Proving Security Protocols Correct. Journal of Computer Security 7, 191–230 (1999)
20. `http://www.rail-reg.gov.uk/upload/pdf/incident-ladbrokegrove-ladbroke-optim.pdf`

C⌚WS: A Timed Service-Oriented Calculus*

Alessandro Lapadula, Rosario Pugliese, and Francesco Tiezzi

Dipartimento di Sistemi e Informatica Università degli Studi di Firenze
{lapadula,pugliese,tiezzi}@dsi.unifi.it

Abstract. COWS (*Calculus for Orchestration of Web Services*) is a foundational language for Service Oriented Computing that combines in an original way a number of ingredients borrowed from well-known process calculi, e.g. asynchronous communication, polyadic synchronization, pattern matching, protection, delimited receiving and killing activities, while resulting different from any of them. In this paper, we extend COWS with timed orchestration constructs, this way we obtain a language capable of completely formalizing the semantics of WS-BPEL, the 'de facto' standard language for orchestration of web services. We present the semantics of the extended language and illustrate its peculiarities and expressiveness by means of several examples.

1 Introduction

Service-Oriented Computing (SOC) is an emerging computing paradigm that uses loosely coupled 'services' to support the development of interoperable, evolvable systems and applications, and exploits the pervasiveness of the Internet technologies. Services are computational entities made available on a network as autonomous, platform-independent resources that can be described, published, discovered, and dynamically assembled, as the basic blocks for building applications. Companies like IBM, Microsoft and Sun have invested a lot of efforts to promote their deployment on Web Services, that are one of the present more successful instantiation of the SOC paradigm.

Many research efforts are currently addressed to define clean semantic models and rigorous methodological foundations for SOC applications. A main line of research aims at developing process calculi-like formalisms that provides in a distilled form the paradigm at the heart of SOC (see, e.g., [2,3,4,5,9,10,12,13,16]). Most of these formalisms, however, do not model the different aspects of currently available SOC technologies in their completeness. One such aspect is represented by *timed activities* that are frequently exploited in service orchestration and are typically used for handling timeouts. For example, in WS-BPEL [21], timeouts turn out to be essential for dealing with service transactions or with message losses. Thus, a service process could wait a callback message for a certain amount of time after which, if no callback has been received, it invokes another operation or throws a fault. However, only a few process calculi for SOC deal with timed activities. In particular, [12,13] introduce webπ, a timed extension of the π-calculus tailored to study 'web transactions'. [8,9] present a timed calculus based on a more general notion of time, and an approach to verify WS-BPEL

* This work has been supported by the EU project SENSORIA, IST-2 005-016004.

C.B. Jones, Z. Liu, J. Woodcock (Eds.): ICTAC 2007, LNCS 4711, pp. 275–290, 2007.

specifications with compensation/fault constructs. [11] proposes a general purpose task orchestration language that manages timeouts as signals returned by dedicated services after some specified time intervals. Furthermore, all these formalisms, do not take into account such fundamental aspects of SOC as service instantiation and correlation.

To meet the demands arising from modelling SOC middlewares and applications, in [15] we have introduced COWS (*Calculus for Orchestration of Web Services*), a new modelling language that takes its origin from linguistic formalisms with opposite objectives, namely from WS-BPEL, the 'de facto' standard language for orchestration of web services, and from well-known process calculi, that represent a cornerstone of current foundational research on specification and analysis of concurrent and mobile systems. In [14] we show that COWS can model different and typical aspects of (web) services technologies, such as, e.g., multiple start activities, receive conflicts, routing of correlated messages, service instances and interactions among them. In this paper, since it is not known to what extent timed computation can be reduced to untimed forms of computation [22], we extend COWS with timed activities. Specifically, we introduce a WS-BPEL-like *wait* activity, that causes execution of the invoking service to be suspended until the time interval specified as an argument has elapsed, and permit using it to choose among alternative behaviours, alike the WS-BPEL *pick activity*. This way, the resulting language, that we call C⊕WS (*timed* COWS), can faithfully capture also the semantics of WS-BPEL timed constructs.

For modelling time and timeouts, we draw again our inspiration from the rich literature on timed process calculi (see, e.g., [7,20] for a survey). Thus, in C⊕WS, basic actions are *durationless*, i.e. instantaneous, and the passing of time is modelled by using explicit actions, like in TCCS [18]. Moreover, actions execution is *lazy*, i.e. can be delayed arbitrary long in favour of passing of time, like in lTCCS [19]. Finally, since many distributed systems offer only weak guarantees on the upper bound of inter-location clock drift [1], passing of time is modelled synchronously for services deployed on a same 'service engine', and asynchronously otherwise.

The rest of the paper is organized as follows. The syntax of C⊕WS is presented in Section 2, while its operational semantics is introduced in Section 3. Section 4 presents an extension that makes it explicit the notion of service engine and of deployment of services on engines. Section 5 illustrates three example applications of our framework and Section 6 concludes the paper. We refer the interested reader to [14] for further motivations on the design of COWS and C⊕WS, for many examples illustrating their peculiarities and expressiveness, for comparisons with other process-based and orchestration formalisms, and for the presentation of a variant of the wait activity, that suspends the invoking service until the absolute time reaches its argument value.

2 C⊕WS Syntax

The syntax of C⊕WS, given in Table 1, is parameterized by three countable and pairwise disjoint sets: the set of *(killer) labels* (ranged over by $k, k', \ldots$), the set of *values* (ranged over by v, v', ...), and the set of 'write once' *variables* (ranged over by x, y, ...). The set of values is left unspecified; however, we assume that it includes the set of *names*, ranged over by $n, m, \ldots$, mainly used to represent partners and operations, and a

Table 1. C◷WS syntax

s ::=		(services)	g ::=		(input-guarded choice)
	$\mathbf{kill}(k)$	(kill)		$\mathbf{0}$	(nil)
|	$u \bullet u'!\bar{e}$	(invoke)	|	$p \bullet o?\bar{w}.s$	(request processing)
|	g	(input-guarded choice)	|	◷$_e.s$	(wait)
|	$s \mid s$	(parallel composition)	|	$g + g$	(choice)
|	$\{\!|s|\!\}$	(protection)			
|	$[d]\,s$	(delimitation)			
|	$*\,s$	(replication)			

set of positive numbers (ranged over by $\delta, \delta', \ldots$), used to represent *time intervals*. The language is also parameterized by a set of *expressions*, ranged over by e, whose exact syntax is deliberately omitted; we just assume that expressions contain, at least, values and variables. Notably, killer labels are *not* (communicable) values. Notationally, we prefer letters $p, p', \ldots$ when we want to stress the use of a name as a *partner*, $o, o', \ldots$ when we want to stress the use of a name as an *operation*. We will use w to range over values and variables, u to range over names and variables, and d to range over killer labels, names and variables. Notation $\bar{\cdot}$ stands for tuples of objects, e.g. $\bar{x}$ is a shortening for the tuple of variables $\langle x_1, \ldots, x_n \rangle$ (with $n \geq 0$). We assume that variables in the same tuple are pairwise distinct. All notations shall extend to tuples component-wise.

Partner names and operation names can be combined to designate *communication endpoints*, written $p \bullet o$, and can be communicated, but dynamically received names can only be used for service invocation (as in the Lπ [17]). Indeed, communication endpoints of receive activities are identified statically because their syntax only allows using names and not variables. *Services* are structured activities built from basic activities, i.e. the empty activity $\mathbf{0}$, the kill activity $\mathbf{kill}(\_)$, the invoke activity $\_ \bullet \_!\_$, the receive activity $\_ \bullet \_?\_$ and the wait activity ◷$_\_$, by means of prefixing $\_.\_$, choice $\_ + \_$, parallel composition $\_ \mid \_$, protection $\{\!|\_|\!\}$, delimitation $[\_]\,\_$ and replication $*\,\_$. The major difference with COWS is that the choice construct can be guarded both by receive activities and by wait activities. In particular, the *wait activity* ◷$_e$ specifies the time interval, whose value is given by evaluation of e, the executing service has to wait for. We adopt the following conventions about the operators precedence: monadic operators bind more tightly than parallel composition, and prefixing more tightly than choice. We shall omit trailing occurrences of $\mathbf{0}$, writing e.g. $p \bullet o?\bar{w}$ instead of $p \bullet o?\bar{w}.\mathbf{0}$, and use $[d_1, \ldots, d_n]\,s$ in place of $[d_1] \ldots [d_n]\,s$.

The only *binding* construct is delimitation: $[d]\,s$ binds d in the scope s. In fact, to enable concurrent threads within each service instance to share (part of) the state, receive activities in C◷WS bind neither names nor variables, which is different from most process calculi. Instead, the range of application of the substitutions generated by a communication is regulated by the delimitation operator, that additionally permits to generate fresh names (as the restriction operator of the π-calculus) and to delimit the field of action of kill activities. Thus, the occurrence of a name/variable/label is *free* if it is not under the scope of a delimitation for it. We denote by $\mathrm{fk}(t)$ the set of killer labels that occur free in t, and by $\mathrm{fd}(t)$ that of free names/variables/killer labels in t. Two terms

Table 2. C⊕WS structural congruence (excerpt of laws)

$*\mathbf{0} \equiv \mathbf{0}$	$*\, s \equiv s \mid *\, s$	$\{\!\|\mathbf{0}\|\!\} \equiv \mathbf{0}$
$\{\!\|\, \{\!\|s\|\!\}\, \|\!\} \equiv \{\!\|s\|\!\}$	$\{\!\|[d]\, s\|\!\} \equiv [d]\, \{\!\|s\|\!\}$	$[d]\, \mathbf{0} \equiv \mathbf{0}$
$[d_1]\,[d_2]\, s \equiv [d_2]\,[d_1]\, s$	$s_1 \mid [d]\, s_2 \equiv [d]\,(s_1 \mid s_2)$	if $d \notin \mathrm{fd}(s_1) \cup \mathrm{fk}(s_2)$

are *alpha-equivalent* if one can be obtained from the other by consistently renaming bound names/variables/labels. As usual, we identify terms up to alpha-equivalence.

3 C⊕WS Operational Semantics

The operational semantics of C⊕WS is defined over an enriched set of services that also includes those auxiliary services where the argument of wait activities can also be 0. Moreover, the semantics is defined only for *closed* services, i.e. services without free variables/labels (similarly to many real compilers, we consider terms with free variables/labels as programming errors), but of course the rules also involve non-closed services. Formally, the semantics is given in terms of a structural congruence and of a labelled transition relation. We assume that evaluation of expressions and execution of basic activities, except for $\oplus_e$, are instantaneous (i.e. do not consume time units) and that time elapses between them.

The structural congruence ≡ identifies syntactically different services that intuitively represent the same service. It is defined as the least congruence relation induced by a given set of equational laws. We explicitly show in Table 2 the laws for replication, protection and delimitation, while omit the (standard) laws for the other operators stating that parallel composition is commutative, associative and has **0** as identity element, and that guarded choice enjoys the same properties and, additionally, is idempotent. All the presented laws are straightforward. In particular, commutativity of consecutive delimitations implies that the order among the d_i in $[\langle d_1, \ldots, d_n \rangle]\, s$ is irrelevant, thus in the sequel we may use the simpler notation $[d_1, \ldots, d_n]\, s$. Notably, the last law can be used to extend the scope of names (like a similar law in the π-calculus), thus enabling communication of restricted names, except when the argument d of the delimitation is a free killer label of s_2 (this avoids involving s_1 in the effect of a kill activity inside s_2).

To define the labelled transition relation, we need a few auxiliary functions. First, we exploit a function $[\![\_]\!]$ for evaluating *closed* expressions (i.e. expressions without variables): it takes a closed expression and returns a value. However, $[\![\_]\!]$ cannot be explicitly defined because the exact syntax of expressions is deliberately not specified.

Then, through the rules in Table 3, we define the partial function $\mathcal{M}(\_,\_)$ that permits performing *pattern-matching* on semi-structured data thus determining if a receive and an invoke over the same endpoint can synchronize. The rules state that two tuples match if they have the same number of fields and corresponding fields have matching values/variables. Variables match any value, and two values match only if they are identical. When tuples $\bar{w}$ and $\bar{v}$ do match, $\mathcal{M}(\bar{w}, \bar{v})$ returns a substitution for the variables in $\bar{w}$; otherwise, it is undefined. *Substitutions* (ranged over by σ) are functions mapping variables to values and are written as collections of pairs of the form $x \mapsto v$. Application

Table 3. Matching rules

$$\mathcal{M}(x,v)=\{x\mapsto v\} \qquad \mathcal{M}(v,v)=\emptyset \qquad \frac{\mathcal{M}(w_1,v_1)=\sigma_1 \qquad \mathcal{M}(\bar{w}_2,\bar{v}_2)=\sigma_2}{\mathcal{M}((w_1,\bar{w}_2),(v_1,\bar{v}_2))=\sigma_1\uplus\sigma_2}$$

Table 4. Is there an active $\mathbf{kill}(k)$? / Are there conflicting receives along $p\bullet o$ matching $\bar{v}$?

$$\mathbf{kill}(k)\downarrow_{kill} \qquad \frac{s\downarrow_{kill}\ \vee\ s'\downarrow_{kill}}{s\mid s'\downarrow_{kill}} \qquad \frac{s\downarrow_{kill}}{\{\!|s|\!\}\downarrow_{kill}} \qquad \frac{s\downarrow_{kill}}{[d]\,s\downarrow_{kill}} \qquad \frac{s\downarrow_{kill}}{*\,s\downarrow_{kill}}$$

$$\frac{|\mathcal{M}(\bar{w},\bar{v})|<\ell}{p\bullet o?\bar{w}.s\downarrow^{\ell}_{p\bullet o,\bar{v}}} \qquad \frac{s\downarrow^{\ell}_{p\bullet o,\bar{v}} \qquad d\notin\{p,o\}}{[d]\,s\downarrow^{\ell}_{p\bullet o,\bar{v}}} \qquad \frac{s\downarrow^{\ell}_{p\bullet o,\bar{v}}}{\{\!|s|\!\}\downarrow^{\ell}_{p\bullet o,\bar{v}}}$$

$$\frac{g\downarrow^{\ell}_{p\bullet o,\bar{v}}\ \vee\ g'\downarrow^{\ell}_{p\bullet o,\bar{v}}}{g+g'\downarrow^{\ell}_{p\bullet o,\bar{v}}} \qquad \frac{s\downarrow^{\ell}_{p\bullet o,\bar{v}}\ \vee\ s'\downarrow^{\ell}_{p\bullet o,\bar{v}}}{s\mid s'\downarrow^{\ell}_{p\bullet o,\bar{v}}} \qquad \frac{s\downarrow^{\ell}_{p\bullet o,\bar{v}}}{*\,s\downarrow^{\ell}_{p\bullet o,\bar{v}}}$$

of substitution σ to s, written $s\cdot\sigma$, has the effect of replacing every free occurrence of x in s with v, for each $x\mapsto v\in\sigma$, by possibly using alpha conversion for avoiding v to be captured by name delimitations within s. We use $|\sigma|$ to denote the number of pairs in σ and $\sigma_1\uplus\sigma_2$ to denote the union of σ_1 and σ_2 when they have disjoint domains.

We also define a function, named *halt*(_), that takes a service s as an argument and returns the service obtained by only retaining the protected activities inside s. *halt*(_) is defined inductively on the syntax of services. The most significant case is $halt(\{\!|s|\!\})=\{\!|s|\!\}$. In the other cases, *halt*(_) returns $\mathbf{0}$, except for parallel composition, delimitation and replication operators, for which it acts as an homomorphism.

$$halt(\mathbf{kill}(k)) = halt(u_1\bullet u_2!\bar{e}) = halt(g) = \mathbf{0} \qquad halt(s_1\mid s_2)=halt(s_1)\mid halt(s_2)$$

$$halt(\{\!|s|\!\})=\{\!|s|\!\} \qquad halt([d]\,s)=[d]\,halt(s) \qquad halt(*\,s)=*\,halt(s)$$

Finally, in Table 4, we inductively define two predicates: $s\downarrow_{kill}$ checks if s can immediately perform a kill activity; $s\downarrow^{\ell}_{p\bullet o,\bar{v}}$, with ℓ natural number, checks existence of potential communication conflicts, i.e. the ability of s of performing a receive activity matching $\bar{v}$ over the endpoint $p\bullet o$ that generates a substitution with fewer pairs than ℓ.

The labelled transition relation $\xrightarrow{\hat{\alpha}}$ is the least relation over services induced by the rules in Table 5, where label $\hat{\alpha}$ is generated by the following grammar:

$$\begin{aligned}\hat{\alpha} &::= \alpha \mid \delta\\ \alpha &::= \dagger k \mid (p\bullet o)\lhd\bar{v} \mid (p\bullet o)\rhd\bar{w} \mid p\bullet o\lfloor\sigma\rfloor\,\bar{w}\,\bar{v} \mid \dagger\end{aligned}$$

In the sequel, we use $d(\alpha)$ to denote the set of names, variables and killer labels occurring in α, except for $\alpha=p\bullet o\lfloor\sigma\rfloor\,\bar{w}\,\bar{v}$ for which we let $d(p\bullet o\lfloor\sigma\rfloor\,\bar{w}\,\bar{v})=d(\sigma)$, where

Table 5. C⊕WS operational semantics

$$\mathbf{kill}(k) \xrightarrow{\dagger k} \mathbf{0}\ (kill) \qquad\qquad p \bullet o ? \bar{w}.s \xrightarrow{(p \bullet o) \rhd \bar{w}} s\ (rec)$$

$$\frac{[\![\bar{e}]\!] = \bar{v}}{p \bullet o ! \bar{e} \xrightarrow{(p \bullet o) \lhd \bar{v}} \mathbf{0}}\ (inv) \qquad\qquad \frac{g_1 \xrightarrow{\alpha} s}{g_1 + g_2 \xrightarrow{\alpha} s}\ (choice)$$

$$\frac{s \xrightarrow{p \bullet o \lfloor \sigma \uplus \{x \mapsto v'\} \rfloor\, \bar{w}\, \bar{v}} s'}{[x]\, s \xrightarrow{p \bullet o \lfloor \sigma \rfloor\, \bar{w}\, \bar{v}} s' \cdot \{x \mapsto v'\}}\ (del_{sub}) \qquad\qquad \frac{s \xrightarrow{\dagger k} s'}{[k]\, s \xrightarrow{\dagger} [k]\, s'}\ (del_{kill})$$

$$\frac{s \xrightarrow{\alpha} s' \quad d \notin d(\alpha) \quad s \downarrow_{kill} \Rightarrow \alpha = \dagger, \dagger k}{[d]\, s \xrightarrow{\alpha} [d]\, s'}\ (del_{pass}) \qquad\qquad \frac{s \xrightarrow{\alpha} s'}{\{\!|s|\!\} \xrightarrow{\alpha} \{\!|s'|\!\}}\ (prot)$$

$$\frac{s_1 \xrightarrow{(p \bullet o) \rhd \bar{w}} s_1' \qquad s_2 \xrightarrow{(p \bullet o) \lhd \bar{v}} s_2' \qquad \mathcal{M}(\bar{w}, \bar{v}) = \sigma \qquad \neg(s_1 \mid s_2 \downarrow^{|\sigma|}_{p \bullet o, \bar{v}})}{s_1 \mid s_2 \xrightarrow{p \bullet o \lfloor \sigma \rfloor\, \bar{w}\, \bar{v}} s_1' \mid s_2'}\ (com)$$

$$\frac{s_1 \xrightarrow{p \bullet o \lfloor \sigma \rfloor\, \bar{w}\, \bar{v}} s_1' \qquad \neg(s_2 \downarrow^{|\mathcal{M}(\bar{w}, \bar{v})|}_{p \bullet o, \bar{v}})}{s_1 \mid s_2 \xrightarrow{p \bullet o \lfloor \sigma \rfloor\, \bar{w}\, \bar{v}} s_1' \mid s_2}\ (par_{conf}) \qquad\qquad \frac{s_1 \xrightarrow{\dagger k} s_1'}{s_1 \mid s_2 \xrightarrow{\dagger k} s_1' \mid halt(s_2)}\ (par_{kill})$$

$$\frac{s_1 \xrightarrow{\alpha} s_1' \qquad \alpha \neq (p \bullet o \lfloor \sigma \rfloor\, \bar{w}\, \bar{v}), \dagger k}{s_1 \mid s_2 \xrightarrow{\alpha} s_1' \mid s_2}\ (par_{pass}) \qquad\qquad \frac{s \equiv s_1 \quad s_1 \xrightarrow{\alpha} s_2 \quad s_2 \equiv s'}{s \xrightarrow{\alpha} s'}\ (cong)$$

$$\mathbf{0} \xrightarrow{\delta} \mathbf{0}\ (nil_{elaps}) \qquad * s \xrightarrow{\delta} * s\ (repl) \qquad u \bullet u' ! \bar{e} \xrightarrow{\delta} u \bullet u' ! \bar{e}\ (inv_{elaps})$$

$$\frac{s \xrightarrow{\delta} s'}{\{\!|s|\!\} \xrightarrow{\delta} \{\!|s'|\!\}}\ (prot_{elaps}) \qquad \frac{s \xrightarrow{\delta} s'}{[d]\, s \xrightarrow{\delta} [d]\, s'}\ (scope_{elaps}) \qquad p \bullet o ? \bar{w}.s \xrightarrow{\delta} p \bullet o ? \bar{w}.s\ (rec_{elaps})$$

$$\oplus_0.s \xrightarrow{\dagger} s\ (wait_{tout}) \qquad \frac{[\![e]\!] \neq \delta'}{\oplus_e.s \xrightarrow{\delta} \oplus_e.s}\ (wait_{err}) \qquad \frac{\delta \leqslant [\![e]\!]}{\oplus_e.s \xrightarrow{\delta} \oplus_{[\![e - \delta]\!]}.s}\ (wait_{elaps})$$

$$\frac{g_1 \xrightarrow{\delta} g_1' \qquad g_2 \xrightarrow{\delta} g_2'}{g_1 + g_2 \xrightarrow{\delta} g_1' + g_2'}\ (pick) \qquad\qquad \frac{s_1 \xrightarrow{\delta} s_1' \qquad s_2 \xrightarrow{\delta} s_2'}{s_1 \mid s_2 \xrightarrow{\delta} s_1' \mid s_2'}\ (par_{sync})$$

$d(\{x \mapsto v\}) = \{x, v\}$ and $d(\sigma_1 \uplus \sigma_2) = d(\sigma_1) \cup d(\sigma_2)$. The meaning of labels is as follows. $\hat{\alpha}$ denotes taking place of *computational activities* α or *time elapsing* δ (recall that δ is a time interval). $\dagger k$ denotes execution of a request for terminating a term from within the delimitation $[k]$. $(p \bullet o) \lhd \bar{v}$ and $(p \bullet o) \rhd \bar{w}$ denote execution of invoke and receive activities over the endpoint $p \bullet o$, respectively. $p \bullet o \lfloor \sigma \rfloor \bar{w}\,\bar{v}$ (if $\sigma \neq \emptyset$) denotes execution of a communication over $p \bullet o$ with receive parameters $\bar{w}$, matching values $\bar{v}$ and substitution σ to be still applied. $\dagger$ and $p \bullet o \lfloor \emptyset \rfloor \bar{w}\,\bar{v}$ denote taking place of timeout/forced termination or communication (without pending substitutions), respectively. A *computation* from a closed service s_0 is a sequence of connected transitions of the form

$$s_0 \xrightarrow{\hat{\alpha}_1} s_1 \xrightarrow{\hat{\alpha}_2} s_2 \xrightarrow{\hat{\alpha}_3} s_3 \ldots$$

where, for each i, $\hat{\alpha}_i$ can be δ, $\dagger$ or $p \bullet o \lfloor \emptyset \rfloor \bar{w}\,\bar{v}$ (for some $p, o, \bar{w}$ and $\bar{v}$).

The rules in the upper part of Table 5 model computational activities, those in the lower part model time passing. We prefer to keep separate the two sets of rules to make it evident that C⊕WS is a 'conservative' extension of COWS (indeed, the rules in the upper part are exactly those of COWS). We now comment on salient points. Activity **kill**(k) forces termination of all unprotected parallel activities (rules *(kill)* and *(par$_{kill}$)*) inside an enclosing $[k]$, that stops the killing effect by turning the transition label $\dagger k$ into $\dagger$ (rule *(del$_{kill}$)*). Existence of such delimitation is ensured by the assumption that the semantics is only defined for closed services. Sensitive code can be protected from killing by putting it into a protection $\{\!|\_|\!\}$; this way, $\{\!|s|\!\}$ behaves like s (rule *(prot)*). Similarly, $[d]\,s$ behaves like s, except when the transition label α contains d or when a kill activity is active in s and α does not correspond to a kill activity or a timeout (rule *(del$_{pass}$)*): in such cases the transition should be derived by using rules *(del$_{sub}$)* or *(del$_{kill}$)*. In other words, kill activities are executed *eagerly*. A service invocation can proceed only if the expressions in the argument can be evaluated (rule *(inv)*). A receive activity offers an invocable operation along a given partner name (rule *(rec)*). The execution of a receive permits to take a decision between alternative behaviours (rule *(choice)*). Communication can take place when two parallel services perform matching receive and invoke activities (rule *(com)*). Communication generates a substitution that is recorded in the transition label (for subsequent application), rather than a silent transition as in most process calculi. If more then one matching is possible, the receive that needs fewer substitutions is selected to progress (rules *(com)* and *(par$_{conf}$)*). This mechanism permits to correlate different service communications thus implicitly creating interaction sessions and can be exploited to model the precedence of a service instance over the corresponding service specification when both can process the same request. When the delimitation of a variable x argument of a receive is encountered, i.e. the whole scope of the variable is determined, the delimitation is removed and the substitution for x is applied to the term (rule *(del$_{sub}$)*). Variable x disappears from the term and cannot be reassigned a value. Execution of parallel services is interleaved (rule *(par$_{pass}$)*), but when a kill activity or a communication is performed. Indeed, the former must trigger termination of all parallel services (according to rule *(par$_{kill}$)*), while the latter must ensure that the receive activity with greater priority progresses (rules *(com)* and *(par$_{conf}$)*). Rule *(cong)* states that structurally congruent services have the same transitions.

Time can elapse while waiting on invoke/receive activities, rules *(inv$_{elaps}$)* and *(rec$_{elaps}$)*. When time elapses, but the timeout is still not expired, the argument of wait activities ⊕ is updated (rule *(wait$_{elaps}$)*). Time elapsing cannot make a choice within a pick activity (rule *(pick)*), while the occurrence of a timeout can. This is signalled by label $\dagger$ (thus, it is a computation step), that is generated by rule *(wait$_{tout}$)* and used by rule *(choice)* to discard the alternative branches. Time elapses synchronously for all services running in parallel: this is modelled by rule *(par$_{sync}$)* and the remaining rules for the empty activity *(nil$_{elaps}$)*, the wait activity *(wait$_{err}$)*, replication *(repl)*, protection *(prot$_{elaps}$)* and delimitation *(scope$_{elaps}$)*. Furthermore, rule *(wait$_{err}$)* enables time passing for the wait activity also when the expression e used as an argument does not return a positive number; in this case the argument of the wait is left unchanged. Notably, in agreement with its eager semantics, the kill activity does not allow time to pass.

We end this section with a simple example aimed at clarifying some peculiarities of our formalism and at specifying *timeouts* as described in [11,22]. Consider the service:

$$[x,y,k]\,(\,p\bullet o_1?\langle x\rangle.(\,p\bullet o_2?\langle x,y\rangle + \circleddash_{10}.\mathbf{kill}(k)\,)\mid \{\!|p'\bullet o_3!\langle x\rangle|\!\}\mid p'\bullet o_4!\langle x,y\rangle\,)$$
$$\mid\ [n]\,p\bullet o_1!\langle n\rangle$$

Communication of private names is standard and exploits scope extension as in the π-calculus. Notably, receive and invoke activities can interact only if both are within the scopes of the delimitations that bind the variables argument of the receive. Thus, in the example, to enable communication of the private name n, besides its scope, we must extend the scope of variable x, as in the following computation:

$$
\begin{array}{ll}
[n,x]\,(\,[y,k]\,(\,p\bullet o_1?\langle x\rangle.(\,p\bullet o_2?\langle x,y\rangle + \circleddash_{10}.\mathbf{kill}(k)\,) & \\
\qquad\qquad \mid \{\!|p'\bullet o_3!\langle x\rangle|\!\}\mid p'\bullet o_4!\langle x,y\rangle\,) & \xrightarrow{p\bullet o_1\,\lfloor\emptyset\rfloor\,\langle x\rangle\,\langle n\rangle} \\
\qquad \mid p\bullet o_1!\langle n\rangle\,) & \\
[n,y,k]\,(\,(\,p\bullet o_2?\langle n,y\rangle + \circleddash_{10}.\mathbf{kill}(k)\,)\mid \{\!|p'\bullet o_3!\langle n\rangle|\!\}\mid p'\bullet o_4!\langle n,y\rangle\,) & \xrightarrow{6} \\
[n,y,k]\,(\,(\,p\bullet o_2?\langle n,y\rangle + \circleddash_{4}.\mathbf{kill}(k)\,)\mid \{\!|p'\bullet o_3!\langle n\rangle|\!\}\mid p'\bullet o_4!\langle n,y\rangle\,) & \xrightarrow{4} \\
[n,y,k]\,(\,(\,p\bullet o_2?\langle n,y\rangle + \circleddash_{0}.\mathbf{kill}(k)\,)\mid \{\!|p'\bullet o_3!\langle n\rangle|\!\}\mid p'\bullet o_4!\langle n,y\rangle\,) & \xrightarrow{\dagger} \\
[n,y,k]\,(\,\mathbf{kill}(k)\mid \{\!|p'\bullet o_3!\langle n\rangle|\!\}\mid p'\bullet o_4!\langle n,y\rangle\,) & \xrightarrow{\dagger} \\
[n]\,\{\!|p'\bullet o_3!\langle n\rangle|\!\} &
\end{array}
$$

When the communication takes place, a timer starts and the substitution $\{x \mapsto n\}$ is applied to all terms delimited by $[x]$, not only to the continuation of the service performing the receive. Then, the time elapses until the timeout expires, this way the receive along $p\bullet o_2$ is discarded. Finally, the kill activity removes the unprotected invoke activity.

4 Service Deployment

In the language presented so far, time passes synchronously for all services in parallel, thus we can think of as all services run on a same service *engine*. As a consequence, the services share the same clock and can be tightly coupled. Instead, existing SOC systems are loosely coupled because they are usually deployed on top of distributed systems that offer only weak guarantees on the upper bound of inter-location clock drift. Consider for example a scenario including a customer service and a service provider composed of two subservices – one used as an interface to interact with external services, the other being an internal service that performs queries in a database – sharing a tuple of variables, operations, ... The scenario could be modelled by the term

$$customer \mid [\bar{d}_{shared}]\,(\,provider\_interface \mid provider\_internal\_service\,)$$

The customer and the provider service are loosely coupled and can be deployed on different engines, while the provider subservices are tightly coupled and must be colocated. To emphasize these aspects, we introduce explicitly the notions of service engine and of *deployment* of services on engines and we will write the previous term as follows:

$$\{\, customer \,\} \mid \{\, [\bar{d}_{shared}]\,(\, provider\_interface \mid provider\_internal\_service \,)\,\}$$

Formally, we extend the language syntax with the syntactic category of (*service*) *engines* (alike the 'machines' of [12]) defined as follows:

$$\mathbb{E} \;::=\; 0 \;\mid\; \{s\} \;\mid\; [n]\,\mathbb{E} \;\mid\; \mathbb{E} \mid \mathbb{E}$$

Each engine $\{s\}$ has its own clock (whose value does not matter and, hence, is not made explicit), that is not synchronized with the clock of other parallel engines (namely, time progresses asynchronously among different engines). Besides, (private) names can be shared among engines, while variables and killer labels cannot. In the sequel, we will only consider *well-formed* engine compositions, i.e. engine compositions where partners used in communication endpoints of receive activities within different service engines are pairwise distinct. The underlying rationale is that each service has its own partner names and that the service and all its instances run within the same engine.

To define the semantics, we first extend the structural congruence of Section 3 with the abelian monoid laws for engines parallel composition and with the following laws:

$$\{s\} \equiv \{s'\} \quad \text{if } s \equiv s' \qquad \{\mathbf{0}\} \equiv 0 \qquad \{[n]\, s\} \equiv [n]\,\{s\} \qquad [n]\,0 \equiv 0$$
$$[n]\,[m]\,\mathbb{E} \equiv [m]\,[n]\,\mathbb{E} \qquad \mathbb{E} \mid [n]\,\mathbb{F} \equiv [n]\,(\mathbb{E} \mid \mathbb{F}) \quad \text{if } n \notin \text{fd}(\mathbb{E})$$

The first law lifts to engines the structural congruence defined on services, the second law transforms an engine with empty activities into an empty engine, while the third law permits to extrude a private name outside an engine. The remaining laws are standard.

Secondly, we define a reduction relation $\longrightarrow$ among engines through the rules shown in Table 6. Rule *(loc)* models occurrence of a computation step within an engine, while rule *(res)* deals with private names. Rule *(cong$_E$)* says that structurally congruent engines have the same behaviour, while rule *(par$_{async}$)* says that time elapses asynchronously between different engines (indeed, $\mathbb{F}$ and, then, the clocks of its engines remain unchanged after the transition). Rule *(com$_E$)*, where fv($\bar{w}$) are the free variables of $\bar{w}$, enables interaction between services executing within different engines. It combines the effects of rules *(del$_{sub}$)* and *(com)* in Table 5. Indeed, since the delimitations $[\bar{x}]$ for the input variables are singled out, the communication effect can be immediately applied to the continuation s'_2 of the service performing the receive. The last premise ensures that, in case of multiple start activities, the message is routed to the correlated service instance rather than triggering a new instantiation.

Notably, computations from a given parallel composition of engines are sequences of (connected) reductions. Communication can take place *intra-engine*, by means of rule *(com)*, or *inter-engine*, by means of rule *(com$_E$)*. In both cases, since we are only considering well-formed compositions of engines, checks for receive conflicts are confined to services running within a single engine, the one performing the receive, differently from the language without explicit engines, where checks involve the whole composition of services. Notice that, to communicate a private name between engines, first

Table 6. Operational semantics of C⊕WS plus engines (additional rules)

$$\frac{s \xrightarrow{\hat{\alpha}} s' \qquad \hat{\alpha} \in \{\delta, \dagger, p \bullet o \lfloor \emptyset \rfloor \bar{w}\, \bar{v}\}}{\{s\} \rightarrow \{s'\}}\ (loc) \qquad \frac{\mathbb{E} \rightarrow \mathbb{E}'}{[n]\,\mathbb{E} \rightarrow [n]\,\mathbb{E}'}\ (res)$$

$$\frac{\mathbb{E} \equiv \mathbb{E}' \qquad \mathbb{E}' \rightarrow \mathbb{F}' \qquad \mathbb{F}' \equiv \mathbb{F}}{\mathbb{E} \rightarrow \mathbb{F}}\ (cong_E) \qquad \frac{\mathbb{E} \rightarrow \mathbb{E}'}{\mathbb{E} \mid \mathbb{F} \rightarrow \mathbb{E}' \mid \mathbb{F}}\ (par_{async})$$

$$\frac{s_1 \xrightarrow{(p \bullet o) \lhd \bar{v}} s_1' \qquad s_2 \xrightarrow{(p \bullet o) \rhd \bar{w}} s_2' \qquad \mathcal{M}(\bar{w}, \bar{v}) = \sigma \qquad \mathrm{fv}(\bar{w}) = \bar{x} \qquad \neg(s_2 \downarrow^{|\sigma|}_{p \bullet o, \bar{v}})}{\{s_1\} \mid \{[\bar{x}]\, s_2\} \rightarrow \{s_1'\} \mid \{s_2' \cdot \sigma\}}\ (com_E)$$

it is necessary to exploit the structural congruence for extruding the name outside the sending engine and to extend its scope to the receiving engine, then the communication can take place, by applying rules *(com$_E$)*, *(res)* and *(cong$_E$)*.

5 Examples

In this section, we illustrate three applications of our framework. The first one is an example of a web service inspired by the well-known game *Rock/Paper/Scissors*, while the remaining ones are use-cases inspired by [6]. In the sequel, we will write $Z \triangleq W$ to assign a symbolic name Z to the term W. We will use $\hat{n}$ to stand for the endpoint $n_p \bullet n_o$ and, sometimes, we will write $\hat{n}$ for the tuple $\langle n_p, n_o \rangle$ and rely on the context to resolve any ambiguity. For the sake of readability, in the examples we will use assignment and conditional choice constructs. They can be thought of as 'macros' corresponding to the following C⊕WS encodings

$$\langle\!\langle [w = e].s \rangle\!\rangle = [\hat{m}]\,(\hat{m}!\langle e \rangle \mid \hat{m}?\langle w \rangle.\langle\!\langle s \rangle\!\rangle)$$

$$\langle\!\langle \mathbf{if}\ (e)\ \mathbf{then}\ \{s_1\}\ \mathbf{else}\ \{s_2\} \rangle\!\rangle = [\hat{m}]\,(\hat{m}!\langle e \rangle \mid (\hat{m}?\langle \mathbf{true} \rangle.\langle\!\langle s_1 \rangle\!\rangle + \hat{m}?\langle \mathbf{false} \rangle.\langle\!\langle s_2 \rangle\!\rangle))$$

where $\hat{m}$ is fresh, and **true** and **false** are the values that can result from evaluation of e.

Rock/Paper/Scissors service. Consider the following service:

$$\begin{array}{rl} rps \triangleq & *\,[x_{champ\_res}, x_{chall\_res}, x_{id}, x_{thr\_1}, x_{thr\_2}, x_{win}, k] \\ & \quad ((\,p_{champ} \bullet o_{throw}?\langle x_{champ\_res}, x_{id}, x_{thr\_1} \rangle. \\ & \qquad (\,p_{chall} \bullet o_{throw}?\langle x_{chall\_res}, x_{id}, x_{thr\_2} \rangle. \\ & \qquad\qquad (\,x_{champ\_res} \bullet o_{win}!\langle x_{id}, x_{win} \rangle \mid x_{chall\_res} \bullet o_{win}!\langle x_{id}, x_{win} \rangle\,) \\ & \qquad\quad + \oplus_{30}\,.\,(\,\{\!|x_{champ\_res} \bullet o_{win}!\langle x_{id}, x_{champ\_res} \rangle|\!\} \mid \mathbf{kill}(k)\,)\,) \\ & \quad + \ p_{chall} \bullet o_{throw}?\langle x_{chall\_res}, x_{id}, x_{thr\_2} \rangle. \\ & \qquad (\,p_{champ} \bullet o_{throw}?\langle x_{champ\_res}, x_{id}, x_{thr\_1} \rangle. \\ & \qquad\qquad (\,x_{champ\_res} \bullet o_{win}!\langle x_{id}, x_{win} \rangle \mid x_{chall\_res} \bullet o_{win}!\langle x_{id}, x_{win} \rangle\,) \\ & \qquad\quad + \oplus_{30}\,.\,(\,\{\!|x_{chall\_res} \bullet o_{win}!\langle x_{id}, x_{chall\_res} \rangle|\!\} \mid \mathbf{kill}(k)\,)\,)\,) \\ & \quad \mid Assign\,) \end{array}$$

The task of service rps is to collect two throws, stored in x_{thr_1} and x_{thr_2}, from two different participants, the current champion and the challenger, assign the winner to x_{win} and then send the result back to the two players. The service receives throws from the players via two distinct endpoints, characterized by operation o_{throw} and partners p_{champ} and p_{chall}. The service is of kind 'request-response' and is able to serve challenges coming from any pairs of participants. The players are required to provide the partner names, stored in x_{champ_res} and x_{chall_res}, which they will use to receive the result. A challenge is uniquely identified by a challenge-id, here stored in x_{id}, that the partners need to provide when sending their throws. Partner throws arrive randomly. Thus, when a throw is processed, for instance the challenging one, it must be checked if a service instance with the same challenge-id already exists or not. An instance of service rps, that is created because of the reception of the first throw of a challenge, waits the reception of the corresponding second throw for at most 30 time units. If this throw arrives within the deadline, the instance behaves as usual. Otherwise, when the timeout expires, the instance declares the sender of the first throw as the winner of the challenge and terminates. We assume that $Assign$ implements the rules of the game and thus, by comparing x_{thr_1} and x_{thr_2}, assigns the winner of the match by producing the assignment $[x_{win} = x_{champ\_res}]$ or $[x_{win} = x_{chall\_res}]$. Thus, we have

$$\begin{aligned} Assign \triangleq\ & \mathbf{if}\ (x_{thr\_1} == \text{"}rock\text{"}\ \&\ x_{thr\_2} == \text{"}scissors\text{"}) \\ & \quad \mathbf{then}\ \{\ [x_{win} = x_{champ\_res}]\ \} \\ & \quad \mathbf{else}\ \{\ \mathbf{if}\ (x_{thr\_1} == \text{"}rock\text{"}\ \&\ x_{thr\_2} == \text{"}paper\text{"}) \\ & \qquad \mathbf{then}\ \{\ [x_{win} = x_{chall\_res}]\ \} \\ & \qquad \mathbf{else}\ \{\ \ldots\ \}\ \} \end{aligned}$$

A partner may simultaneously play multiple challenges by using different challenge identifiers as a means to correlate messages received from the server. E.g., the partner

$$\begin{aligned} & (p_{chall} \bullet o_{throw}!\langle p'_{chall}, 0, \text{"}rock\text{"}\rangle \mid [x]\, p'_{chall} \bullet o_{win}?\langle 0, x\rangle.s_0) \\ & \mid (p_{chall} \bullet o_{throw}!\langle p'_{chall}, 1, \text{"}paper\text{"}\rangle \mid [y]\, p'_{chall} \bullet o_{win}?\langle 1, y\rangle.s_1) \end{aligned}$$

is guaranteed that the returned results will be correctly delivered to the corresponding continuations.

Let us now consider the following match of rock/paper/scissors identified by the correlation value 0:

$$\begin{aligned} s \triangleq\ & rps \mid p_{champ} \bullet o_{throw}!\langle p'_{champ}, 0, \text{"}rock\text{"}\rangle \mid [x]\, p'_{champ} \bullet o_{win}?\langle 0, x\rangle.s_{champ} \\ & \mid p_{chall} \bullet o_{throw}!\langle p'_{chall}, 0, \text{"}scissors\text{"}\rangle \mid [y]\, p'_{chall} \bullet o_{win}?\langle 0, y\rangle.s_{chall} \end{aligned}$$

where p'_{champ} and p'_{chall} denote the players' partner names.

Figure 1 shows a customized UML sequence diagram depicting a possible run of the above scenario. The champion and a challenger participate to the match, play their throws (i.e. "*rock*" and "*scissors*"), wait for the resulting winner, and (possibly) use this result in their continuation processes (i.e. s_{champ} and s_{chall}). Here is a computation produced by selecting the champion's throw:

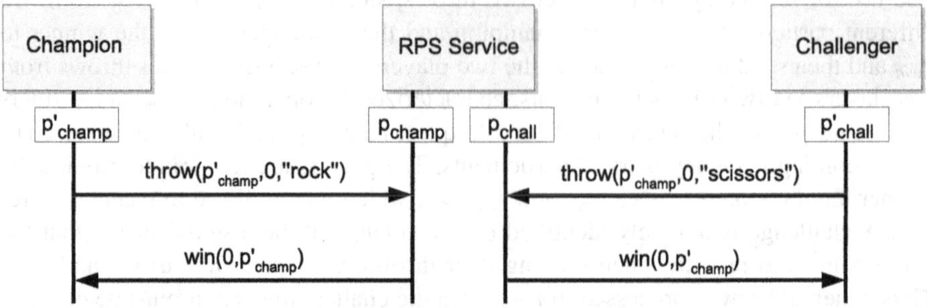

Fig. 1. Graphical representation of the Rock/Paper/Scissors service scenario

$$
\begin{array}{l}
s \xrightarrow{p_{champ} \bullet o_{throw} \lfloor \emptyset \rfloor \langle x_{champ\_res}, x_{id}, x_{thr\_1} \rangle \langle p'_{champ}, 0, \text{“}rock\text{”} \rangle} \\
rps \mid [x_{chall\_res}, x_{thr\_2}, x_{win}, k] \\
\quad ((p_{chall} \bullet o_{throw} ? \langle x_{chall\_res}, 0, x_{thr\_2} \rangle . \\
\qquad (p'_{champ} \bullet o_{win} ! \langle 0, x_{win} \rangle \mid x_{chall\_res} \bullet o_{win} ! \langle 0, x_{win} \rangle) \\
\qquad + \oplus_{30} . (\{\!| p'_{champ} \bullet o_{win} ! \langle 0, p'_{champ} \rangle |\!\} \mid \mathbf{kill}(k))) \\
\quad \mid Assign \cdot \{ x_{champ\_res} \mapsto p'_{champ}, x_{id} \mapsto 0, x_{thr\_1} \mapsto \text{“}rock\text{”} \}) \\
\mid [x]\, p'_{champ} \bullet o_{win} ? \langle 0, x \rangle . s_{champ} \\
\mid p_{chall} \bullet o_{throw} ! \langle p'_{chall}, 0, \text{“}scissors\text{”} \rangle \mid [y]\, p'_{chall} \bullet o_{win} ? \langle 0, y \rangle . s_{chall} \quad \triangleq \quad s'
\end{array}
$$

In case the challenger's throw is not consumed within the deadline, the timeout expires:

$$
\begin{array}{l}
s' \xrightarrow{30} \xrightarrow{\dagger} \\
rps \mid [x_{chall\_res}, x_{thr\_2}, x_{win}, k] \\
\quad (\{\!| p'_{champ} \bullet o_{win} ! \langle 0, p'_{champ} \rangle |\!\} \mid \mathbf{kill}(k) \\
\quad \mid Assign \cdot \{ x_{champ\_res} \mapsto p'_{champ}, x_{id} \mapsto 0, x_{thr\_1} \mapsto \text{“}rock\text{”} \}) \\
\mid [x]\, p'_{champ} \bullet o_{win} ? \langle 0, x \rangle . s_{champ} \\
\mid p_{chall} \bullet o_{throw} ! \langle p'_{chall}, 0, \text{“}scissors\text{”} \rangle \mid [y]\, p'_{chall} \bullet o_{win} ? \langle 0, y \rangle . s_{chall}
\end{array}
$$

Then, the kill activity terminates the instance and the champion is declared to be the winner. Instead, if the challenger's throw is consumed by the existing instance within the deadline, the service evolves as follows:

$$
\begin{array}{l}
s' \xrightarrow{5} \xrightarrow{p_{chall} \bullet o_{throw} \lfloor \emptyset \rfloor \langle x_{chall\_res}, 0, x_{thr\_2} \rangle \langle p'_{chall}, 0, \text{“}scissors\text{”} \rangle} \\
rps \mid [x_{win}] (p'_{champ} \bullet o_{win} ! \langle 0, x_{win} \rangle \mid p'_{chall} \bullet o_{win} ! \langle 0, x_{win} \rangle \\
\qquad \mid Assign \cdot \{ x_{champ\_res} \mapsto p'_{champ}, x_{id} \mapsto 0, x_{thr\_1} \mapsto \text{“}rock\text{”}, \\
\qquad\qquad x_{chall\_res} \mapsto p'_{chall}, x_{thr\_2} \mapsto \text{“}scissors\text{”} \}) \\
\mid [x]\, p'_{champ} \bullet o_{win} ? \langle 0, x \rangle . s_{champ} \\
\mid [y]\, p'_{chall} \bullet o_{win} ? \langle 0, y \rangle . s_{chall}
\end{array}
$$

In the computation above, rules *(com)* and *(par$_{conf}$)* allow only the existing instance to evolve (thus, creation of a new conflicting instance is avoided). Once *Assign* determines that p_{champ} won, the substitutive effects of communication transforms the system as follows:

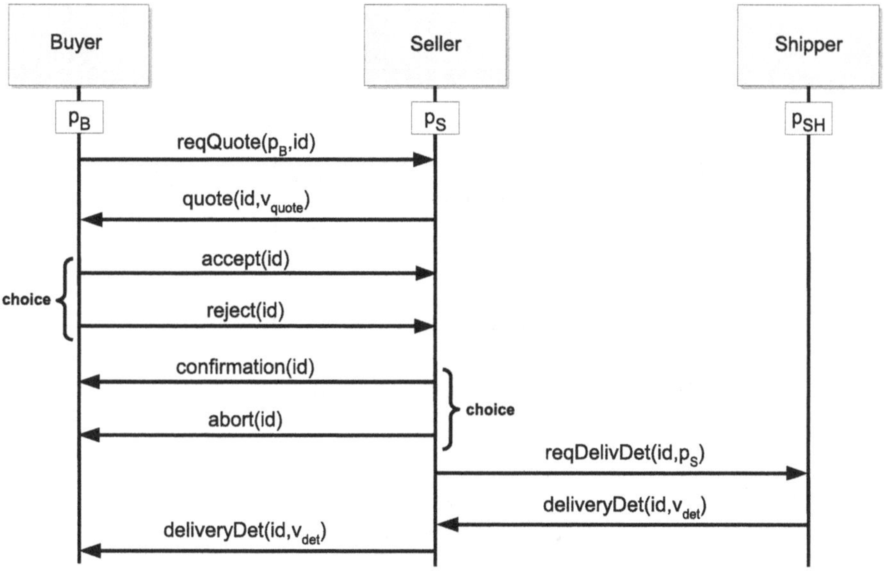

Fig. 2. Graphical representation of the Buyer/Seller/Shipper protocol

$$
\begin{aligned}
s'' \triangleq\ & rps \mid p'_{champ} \bullet o_{win}!\langle 0, p_{champ}\rangle \mid p'_{chall} \bullet o_{win}!\langle 0, p_{champ}\rangle \\
& \mid [x]\, p'_{champ} \bullet o_{win}?\langle 0, x\rangle.s_{champ} \\
& \mid [y]\, p'_{chall} \bullet o_{win}?\langle 0, y\rangle.s_{chall}
\end{aligned}
$$

At the end, the name of the resulting winner is sent to both participants as shown by the following computation:

$$
\begin{aligned}
s'' & \xrightarrow{p'_{champ} \bullet o_{win} \lfloor \emptyset \rfloor \langle 0,x\rangle \langle 0,p_{champ}\rangle} \xrightarrow{p'_{chall} \bullet o_{win} \lfloor \emptyset \rfloor \langle 0,y\rangle \langle 0,p_{champ}\rangle} \\
& rps \mid s_{champ} \cdot \{x \mapsto p_{champ}\} \mid s_{chall} \cdot \{y \mapsto p_{champ}\}
\end{aligned}
$$

A Buyer/Seller/Shipper protocol. We illustrate a simple business protocol for purchasing a fixed good. The protocol, graphically represented in Figure 2, involves a buyer, a seller and a shipper. Firstly, *Buyer* asks *Seller* to offer a quote, then, after the *Seller*'s reply, *Buyer* answers with either an acceptance or a rejection message (it sends the latter when the quote is bigger than a certain amount). In case of acceptance, *Seller* sends a confirmation to *Buyer* and asks *Shipper* to provide delivery details. Finally, *Seller* forwards the received delivery information to *Buyer*. Moreover, after *Seller* presents a quote, if *Buyer* does not reply in 30 time units, then *Seller* will abort the transaction. In the end, the whole system is

$$
\{Buyer\} \mid \{Seller\} \mid \{Shipper\}
$$

where

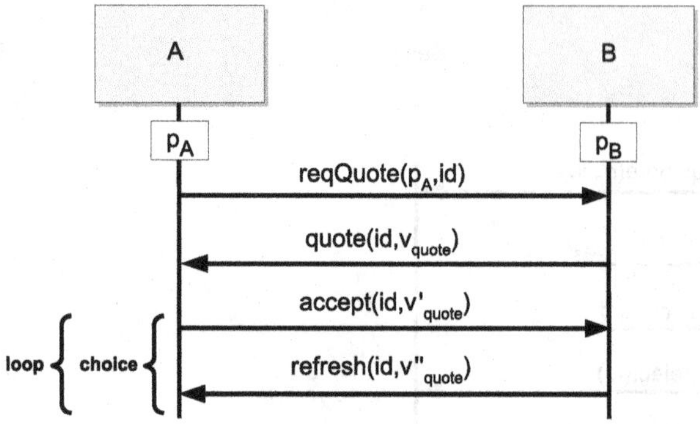

Fig. 3. Graphical representation of the Investment Bank interaction pattern

$$
\begin{aligned}
Buyer \triangleq [id]\,(\, & p_S \bullet o_{reqQuote}!\langle p_B, id\rangle \\
\mid\ & [x_{quote}]\ p_B \bullet o_{quote}?\langle id, x_{quote}\rangle\,. \\
& \quad [k]\,(\,\mathbf{if}\ (x_{quote} \leq 1000) \\
& \qquad \mathbf{then}\ \{\ p_S \bullet o_{accept}!\langle id\rangle \\
& \qquad\qquad \mid p_B \bullet o_{confirmation}?\langle id\rangle\,. \\
& \qquad\qquad\ [x_{det}]\ p_B \bullet o_{deliveryDet}?\langle id, x_{det}\rangle\ \} \\
& \qquad \mathbf{else}\ \{\ p_S \bullet o_{reject}!\langle id\rangle\ \} \\
& \quad \mid p_B \bullet o_{abort}?\langle id\rangle\,.\,\mathbf{kill}(k)\,)\,)
\end{aligned}
$$

$$
\begin{aligned}
Seller \triangleq * \,[x_B, x_{id}]\ & p_S \bullet o_{reqQuote}?\langle x_B, x_{id}\rangle\,. \\
& (\,x_B \bullet o_{quote}!\langle x_{id}, v_{quote}\rangle \\
& \ \mid p_S \bullet o_{accept}?\langle x_{id}\rangle\,. \\
& \qquad (\,x_B \bullet o_{confirmation}!\langle x_{id}\rangle \\
& \qquad\ \mid p_{SH} \bullet o_{reqDelivDet}!\langle x_{id}, p_S\rangle \\
& \qquad\ \mid [x_{det}]\ p_S \bullet o_{deliveryDet}?\langle x_{id}, x_{det}\rangle\,. \\
& \qquad\qquad x_B \bullet o_{deliveryDet}!\langle x_{id}, x_{det}\rangle\,) \\
& \quad + p_S \bullet o_{reject}?\langle x_{id}\rangle \\
& \quad + \oplus_{30}\,.\,x_B \bullet o_{abort}!\langle x_{id}\rangle\,)
\end{aligned}
$$

$$
\begin{aligned}
Shipper \triangleq * \,[x_{id}, x_S]\ & p_{SH} \bullet o_{reqDelivDet}?\langle x_{id}, x_S\rangle\,. \\
& [x_{det}]\ [x_{det} = computeDelivDet(x_S)]\,.\,x_S \bullet o_{deliveryDet}!\langle x_{id}, x_{det}\rangle
\end{aligned}
$$

Function *computeDelivDet*(_) computes the delivery details associated to a seller. Notably, if *Buyer* receives an *abort* message from *Seller*, then it immediately halts its other activities, by means of the killing activity.

Investment Bank interaction pattern. We describe a typical interaction pattern in Investment Bank and other businesses, graphically represented in Figure 3. We consider two participants, *A* and *B*. *A* starts by requiring a quote to *B*, that answers with an initial quote. Then, *B* enters a loop, sending a new quote every 5 time units until *A* accepts a quote. Of course, in order to receive new quotes, also *A* cycles until it sends the quote acceptance message to *B*. Services *A* and *B* are modelled as follows:

$$
\begin{aligned}
A \triangleq\ & p_B \bullet o_{reqQuote}!\langle p_A, id\rangle \\
& \mid [x_{quote}]\, p_A \bullet o_{quote}?\langle id, x_{quote}\rangle\,. \\
& \qquad [\hat{n}]\,(\,\hat{n}!\langle x_{quote}\rangle \\
& \qquad\quad \mid *\,[x]\,\hat{n}?\langle x\rangle\,. \\
& \qquad\qquad [x_{new}]\,(\,\circleddash_{rand()} \cdot p_B \bullet o_{accept}!\langle id, x\rangle \\
& \qquad\qquad\qquad + \ p_A \bullet o_{refresh}?\langle id, x_{new}\rangle\,.\,\hat{n}!\langle x_{new}\rangle\,)\,)
\end{aligned}
$$

$$
\begin{aligned}
B \triangleq\ & *\,[x_A, x_{id}]\ p_B \bullet o_{reqQuote}?\langle x_A, x_{id}\rangle\,. \\
& \quad (\,x_A \bullet o_{quote}!\langle x_{id}, v_{quote}\rangle \\
& \quad \mid [\hat{n}]\,(\,\hat{n}!\langle v_{quote}\rangle \\
& \qquad \mid *\,[x]\,\hat{n}?\langle x\rangle\,. \\
& \qquad\quad [x_{quote}]\,(\,p_B \bullet o_{accept}?\langle x_{id}, x_{quote}\rangle \\
& \qquad\qquad + \circleddash_5\,.\,(\,x_A \bullet o_{refresh}!\langle x_{id}, newQuote(x)\rangle \\
& \qquad\qquad\qquad \mid \hat{n}!\langle newQuote(x)\rangle\,)\,)\,)\,)
\end{aligned}
$$

Function $newQuote(\_)$, given the last quote sent from B to A, computes and returns a new quote. Notably, in both services, the iterative behaviour is modelled by means of a private endpoint (i.e. $\hat{n}$) and the replication operator. At each iteration, A waits a randomly chosen period of time, whose value is returned by function $rand()$, before replying to B. If this time interval is longer than 5 time units, a receive on operation $o_{refresh}$ triggers a new iteration.

Now, consider the system $A \mid B$. If the participant A does not accept the current quote in 5 time units, then a new quote is produced by the participant B, because its timeout has certainly expired. Instead, if we consider the system $\{A\} \mid \{B\}$, the clock of B can be slower than that of A, thus the production of a new quote is not ensured.

6 Concluding Remarks

We have introduced C⌚WS, a formalism for specifying and combining services, while modelling their dynamic behaviour. We have first considered a language where all services are implicitly allocated on a same engine. Then, we have presented an extension with explicit notions of service engine and of deployment of services on engines.

We plan to continue our programme to lay rigorous methodological foundations for specification and validation of SOC middlewares and applications. We are currently working on formalizing the semantics of WS-BPEL through labelled transition systems. We intend then to prove that this semantics and that defined by translation in COWS do agree. Of course, the extension presented in this paper will be essential to faithfully capture the semantics of WS-BPEL timed constructs. As a further work, we want to develop type systems and behavioural equivalences capable of dealing also with time aspects. Pragmatically, they could provide a means to express and guarantee time-based QoS properties of services (such as, e.g., time to reply to service requests), that should be published in service contracts.

Acknowledgements. We thank the anonymous referees for their useful comments.

References

1. Berger, M.: Basic theory of reduction congruence for two timed asynchronous pi-calculi. In: Gardner, P., Yoshida, N. (eds.) CONCUR 2004. LNCS, vol. 3170, pp. 115–130. Springer, Heidelberg (2004)

2. Bocchi, L., Laneve, C., Zavattaro, G.: A calculus for long-running transactions. In: Najm, E., Nestmann, U., Stevens, P. (eds.) FMOODS 2003. LNCS, vol. 2884, pp. 124–138. Springer, Heidelberg (2003)
3. Boreale, M., Bruni, R., Caires, L., De Nicola, R., Lanese, I., Loreti, M., Martins, F., Montanari, U., Ravara, A., Sangiorgi, D., Vasconcelos, V.T., Zavattaro, G.: SCC: a Service Centered Calculus. In: Bravetti, M., Núñez, M., Zavattaro, G. (eds.) WS-FM 2006. LNCS, vol. 4184, pp. 38–57. Springer, Heidelberg (2006)
4. Butler, M.J., Hoare, C.A.R., Ferreira, C.: A trace semantics for long-running transactions. In: Abdallah, A.E., Jones, C.B., Sanders, J.W. (eds.) CSP 2004. LNCS, vol. 3525, pp. 133–150. Springer, Heidelberg (2005)
5. Carbone, M., Honda, K., Yoshida, N.: Structured communication-centred programming for web services. In: De Nicola, R. (ed.) ESOP 2007. LNCS, vol. 4421, pp. 2–17. Springer, Heidelberg (2007)
6. Carbone, M., Honda, K., Yoshida, N., Milner, R., Brown, G., Ross-Talbot, S.: A theoretical basis of communication-centred concurrent programming. Technical report, W3C (2006)
7. Corradini, F., D'Ortenzio, D., Inverardi, P.: On the relationships among four timed process algebras. Fundam. Inform. 38(4), 377–395 (1999)
8. Geguang, P., Huibiao, Z., Zongyan, Q., Shuling, W., Xiangpeng, Z., Jifeng, H.: Theoretical foundations of scope-based compensable flow language for web service. In: Gorrieri, R., Wehrheim, H. (eds.) FMOODS 2006. LNCS, vol. 4037, pp. 251–266. Springer, Heidelberg (2006)
9. Geguang, P., Xiangpeng, Z., Shuling, W., Zongyan, Q.: Towards the semantics and verification of bpel4ws. In: WLFM 2005, Elsevier, Amsterdam (2005)
10. Guidi, C., Lucchi, R., Gorrieri, R., Busi, N., Zavattaro, G.: SOCK: a calculus for service oriented computing. In: Dan, A., Lamersdorf, W. (eds.) ICSOC 2006. LNCS, vol. 4294, pp. 327–338. Springer, Heidelberg (2006)
11. Kitchin, D., Cook, W.R., Misra, J.: A language for task orchestration and its semantic properties. In: Baier, C., Hermanns, H. (eds.) CONCUR 2006. LNCS, vol. 4137, pp. 477–491. Springer, Heidelberg (2006)
12. Laneve, C., Zavattaro, G.: Foundations of web transactions. In: Sassone, V. (ed.) FOSSACS 2005. LNCS, vol. 3441, pp. 282–298. Springer, Heidelberg (2005)
13. Laneve, C., Zavattaro, G.: web-pi at work. In: De Nicola, R., Sangiorgi, D. (eds.) TGC 2005. LNCS, vol. 3705, pp. 182–194. Springer, Heidelberg (2005)
14. Lapadula, A., Pugliese, R., Tiezzi, F.: A Calculus for Orchestration of Web Services (full version). Technical report, Dipartimento di Sistemi e Informatica, Univ. Firenze (2006), `http://rap.dsi.unifi.it/cows`
15. Lapadula, A., Pugliese, R., Tiezzi, F.: A Calculus for Orchestration of Web Services. In: ESOP. LNCS, vol. 4421, pp. 33–47. Springer, Heidelberg (2007)
16. Mazzara, M., Lucchi, R.: A pi-calculus based semantics for WS-BPEL. Journal of Logic and Algebraic Programming 70(1), 96–118 (2006)
17. Merro, M., Sangiorgi, D.: On asynchrony in name-passing calculi. Mathematical Structures in Computer Science 14(5), 715–767 (2004)
18. Moller, F., Tofts, C.: A temporal calculus of communicating systems. In: Baeten, J.C.M., Klop, J.W. (eds.) CONCUR 1990. LNCS, vol. 458, pp. 401–415. Springer, Heidelberg (1990)
19. Moller, F., Tofts, C.: Relating processes with respect to speed. In: Groote, J.F., Baeten, J.C.M. (eds.) CONCUR 1991. LNCS, vol. 527, pp. 424–438. Springer, Heidelberg (1991)
20. Nicollin, X., Sifakis, J.: An overview and synthesis on timed process algebras. In: Larsen, K.G., Skou, A. (eds.) CAV 1991. LNCS, vol. 575, pp. 376–398. Springer, Heidelberg (1992)
21. OASIS: Web Services Business Process Execution Language Version 2.0. Technical report, WS-BPEL TC OASIS (August 2006), `http://www.oasis-open.org/`
22. van Glabbeek, R.J.: On specifying timeouts. ENTCS 162, 173–175 (2006)

Regular Linear Temporal Logic*

Martin Leucker[1] and César Sánchez[2,3]

[1] Institut für Informatik
TU München, Germany
[2] Computer Science Department
Stanford University, Stanford, USA
[3] Computer Engineering Department
University of California, Santa Cruz, USA

Abstract. We present regular linear temporal logic (RLTL), a logic that generalizes linear temporal logic with the ability to use regular expressions arbitrarily as sub-expressions. Every LTL operator can be defined as a context in regular linear temporal logic. This implies that there is a (linear) translation from LTL to RLTL.

Unlike LTL, regular linear temporal logic can define all ω-regular languages, while still keeping the satisfiability problem in PSPACE. Unlike the extended temporal logics ETL_*, RLTL is defined with an algebraic signature. In contrast to the linear time μ-calculus, RLTL does not depend on fix-points in its syntax.

1 Introduction

We present *regular linear temporal logic* (RLTL), a formalism to express properties of infinite traces by conveniently *fusing* regular-expressions and linear-temporal logic. Moreover, we show that the satisfiability and equivalence of RLTL expressions are PSPACE-complete problems.

The linear temporal logic (LTL) [19,16] is a modal logic over a linear frame, whose formulas express properties of infinite traces using two modalities: *next-time* and *until*. LTL is a widely accepted formalism for the specification and verification of concurrent and reactive systems. However, Wolper [26] showed that LTL cannot express all ω-regular properties (the properties expressible by finite-state automata on infinite words, known as Büchi automata [4]). In particular, it cannot express the property "p holds at every other moment". In spite of being a useful specification language, this lack of expressivity seems to surface in practice [20] and it has been pointed out (see for example [3]) that regular-expressions are sometimes very convenient in addition to LTL, in formal specifications. Actually, in the industry standard specification language PSL, arbitrary mixtures of regular expressions and LTL are allowed [1].

* Part of this work was done during the first author's stay at Stanford University and was supported by ARO DAAD190310197. The second author has been supported in part by NSF grants CCR-01-21403, CCR-02-20134, CCR-02-09237, CNS-0411363, and CCF-0430102, and by NAVY/ONR contract N00014-03-1-0939.

C.B. Jones, Z. Liu, J. Woodcock (Eds.): ICTAC 2007, LNCS 4711, pp. 291–305, 2007.

To solve the expressivity problem, Wolper introduced the so called extended temporal logic ETL where new operators are defined as right linear grammars, and language composition is used to compose operators. ETL was later extended [25] to different kinds of automata. The main drawback of the extended temporal logics is that, in order to obtain the full expressivity, an infinite number of operators is needed.

An alternative approach consists on adapting the modal μ-calculus [5,12] to the linear setting, which gives rise to the linear time μ-calculus, denoted as νTL [2]. Here, the full expressivity is obtained by allowing the use of fix point operators. It can be argued that this formalism is not algebraic either since one needs to specify recursive equations to describe temporal properties. Moreover, the only modality is the *nexttime*. Even though every ground regular expression can be translated into a νTL expression (see [14]), the concatenation operator cannot be directly represented in νTL, i.e., there is no context of νTL that captures concatenation. On the other hand, extending νTL with concatenation (the so-called fix point logic with chop FLC [18,15]) allows expressing non-regular languages. This extra expressive power comes at the price of undecidable satisfiability and equivalence problems. A more restricted extension of νTL allowing only left concatenation with regular expressions is possible along the lines presented here, but this is out of the scope of this paper.

There have also been dynamic logics that try to merge regular expressions (for the program part) and LTL (for the action part), for example, Regular Process Logic [7]. However, it makes the satisfiability problem non-elementary by allowing arbitrary combinations of negations and regular operators. Dynamic linear-temporal logic DLTL [8] keeps the satisfiability problem in PSPACE, but restricts the use of regular expressions only as a generalization of the until operator. While the generalized until present in DLTL and the power operators present in RLTL are complementary (in the sense that none can be defined in terms of each other), the power operators are more suitable for extensions that can handle past, as discussed in Section 5.

An arbitrary mixture of (sequentially extended) regular expressions and LTL is possible in PSL [1,6]. However, decision procedures for satisfiability etc. and their complexities are still an area of active research (for full PSL). Thus, RLTL can be understood as subset of PSL for which an efficient satisfiability procedure (PSPACE) is available.

The logic that we present here is a generalization of linear temporal logic and ω-regular expressions, based on the following observation. It is common for different formalisms to find the following three components in the (recursive) definition of operators:

1. *attempt*: an expression that captures the first try to satisfy the enclosing expression.
2. *obligation*: an expression that must be satisfied, if the attempt fails, to continue trying the enclosing expression. If both the attempt and the obligation fail, the sequence is not matched.

3. *delay*: an expression that describes when the enclosing expression must be started again.

For example, the binary Kleene-star z^*y matches a string s if either y (the attempt) matches s, or if after z (the delay), the whole expression z^*y matches the remaining suffix. In this case, no obligation is specified, so it is implicitly assumed to hold. Formally, the following equivalence holds $z^*y = y + z\,;z^*y$, or more explicitly

$$z^*y = y \; + \; (\Gamma^* \;\mid\; z\,;z^*y),$$

where $x \mid y$ denotes the intersection operator present in (semi-)extended regular expressions [22]. Consider also the linear temporal logic expression $x\,\mathcal{U}\,y$. An ω-sequence satisfies this expression if either y does (the attempt) or else, if x does (the obligation) and in the next step (the delay), the whole formula $x\,\mathcal{U}\,y$ holds. Formally,

$$x\,\mathcal{U}\,y = y \vee (x \wedge \bigcirc(x\,\mathcal{U}\,y)).$$

In Section 2 we will formalize this intuition by introducing a general operator that can be specialized for temporal logic and regular-expression constructs.

The rest of this document is structured as follows. Section 2 defines regular linear-temporal logic. Section 3 shows how to translate LTL and ω-regular expressions into RLTL. Section 4 shows, via a translation to alternating Büchi automata, that the logic defines only ω-regular languages, and that the satisfiability and equivalence problems are in PSPACE. Finally, Section 5 presents some concluding remarks.

2 Regular Linear Temporal Logic

We define in this section *regular linear temporal logic*, in two stages. First, we introduce a variation of regular expressions over finite words, and then—using these—we define regular linear temporal logic to describe languages over infinite words. Each formalism is defined as an algebraic signature, by giving meanings to the operators. We use Σ_{RE} for the operators in the language of regular expressions, Σ_{TL} for the signature of the language for infinite words, and Σ as a short hand for $\Sigma_{\mathrm{RE}} \cup \Sigma_{\mathrm{TL}}$.

We begin by fixing a finite set of propositions *Prop*, and from it the alphabet $\Gamma = 2^{Prop}$ of input actions (observable properties of individual states). As usual, Γ^* denotes the finite sequences of words over Γ, Γ^ω stands for the set of infinite words, and Γ^∞ is $\Gamma^* \cup \Gamma^\omega$. Given a word w, we use $pos(w)$ to denote the set of positions of w: if $w \in \Gamma^\omega$ then $pos(w)$ is $\{1,\ldots\} = \omega$; if $w \in \Gamma^*$ then $pos(w) = \{1,\ldots,|w|\}$, where $|w|$ denotes the length of w as usual. We use $w[i]$ to denote the letter from Γ at position i of w. We use *Pos* to denote the set of positions of words in Γ^ω, i.e., *Pos* is an alias of ω.

2.1 Regular Expressions

We first introduce a variation of regular expressions that can define regular languages that do not contain the empty word. Basic expressions are boolean combinations of elements from $\mathbb{B}(Prop)$ that identify the elements of Γ, including **true** for *Prop* and **false** for $\emptyset$.

Syntax. The language of the regular expressions for finite words is the smallest set closed under:

$$\alpha ::= \alpha + \alpha \;\big|\; \alpha \,;\, \alpha \;\big|\; \alpha^{*}\alpha \;\big|\; p \tag{1}$$

where p ranges over basic expressions. The operators $+$, ; and $*$ define the standard union, concatenation and binary Kleene-star[1]. The signature of regular expressions is then

$$\Sigma_{\mathrm{RE}} = \{\mathbb{B}(Prop)^{0},\ +^{2},\ ;^{2},\ *^{2}\}$$

where the superindices indicate the arity of the operators. The set of regular expressions RE is the set of all ground expressions over this signature. Note that this signature contains no variables or fix-point quantifiers.

Semantics. To ease the definition of RLTL for infinite languages, we define regular expressions as accepting *segments* of an infinite word. Given an infinite word w and two positions i and j, the tuple (w, i, j) is called a segment of the word w. Similarly, (w, i) is called a *pointed word.* The semantics of regular expressions is described by defining a relation $\models_{\mathrm{RE}}$ that relates expressions with their sets of segments, that is $\models_{\mathrm{RE}} \subseteq (\Gamma^{\omega} \times Pos \times Pos) \times \mathrm{RE}$. The semantics is defined inductively as follows. Given a proposition $p \in Prop$, expressions x, y, and z, and a word w,

- $(w, i, j) \models_{\mathrm{RE}} p$ whenever $w[i]$ satisfies p and $j = i + 1$.
- $(w, i, j) \models_{\mathrm{RE}} x + y$ whenever either $(w, i, j) \models_{\mathrm{RE}} x$ or $(w, i, j) \models_{\mathrm{RE}} y$, or both.
- $(w, i, j) \models_{\mathrm{RE}} x \,;\, y$ whenever for some $k \in pos(w)$, $(w, i, k) \models_{\mathrm{RE}} x$ and $(w, k, j) \models_{\mathrm{RE}} y$.
- $(w, i, j) \models_{\mathrm{RE}} x^{*}y$ whenever either $(w, i, j) \models_{\mathrm{RE}} y$, or for some sequence $(i_0 = i, i_1, \ldots i_m)$ $(w, i_k, i_{k+1}) \models_{\mathrm{RE}} x$ and $(w, i_m, j) \models_{\mathrm{RE}} y$.

The semantical style used above, more conventional for temporal logics, is equivalent to the more classical of associating a language over finite words to a given expression: for $v \in \Gamma^{*}$, $v \in \mathcal{L}(x)$ whenever for some $w \in \Gamma^{\omega}$, $(vw, 1, |v|) \models_{\mathrm{RE}} x$. In this manner the definition of $*$ is equivalent to the conventional definition, that is, both describe the same language:

$$\mathcal{L}(x^{*}y) = \mathcal{L}(\sum_{i \geq 0} x^{i} \,;\, y)$$

where $x^{i} \,;\, y$ is defined inductively as $x^{0}; y = y$ and $x^{i+1} = x \,;\, x^{i}$, as usual. Since p satisfies that if $(w, i, j) \models_{\mathrm{RE}} p$ then $j > i$, it follows the empty word is not in

[1] Stephen C. Kleene himself in [11] introduced the $*$ operator as a binary operator. Our choice of a binary $*$ is determined by our key decision of defining languages that do not contain the empty word. An alternative is to introduce a unary x^{+} operator.

$\mathcal{L}(p)$, and also that $\mathcal{L}(x + y)$ and $\mathcal{L}(x \; ; \; y)$ cannot contain the empty word. It also follows that x^*y cannot contain the empty word: if v is in $\mathcal{L}(z^*y)$ then v is in $\mathcal{L}(z^k y)$ for some k.

Moreover, every regular language over finite words (that does not contain the empty word) can be defined, since x^+ is equivalent to x^*x.

2.2 Regular Linear Temporal Logic over Infinite Words

RLTL is built from regular expressions by using intersection, concatenation of a finite and an infinite expression, and two ternary operators, called the *power* operators. As we will see, the power operators generalize both the LTL constructs and the ω-operator.

Syntax. The set of RLTL expressions is the smallest set closed under:

$$\phi ::= \phi \vee \phi \;\big|\; \phi \wedge \phi \;\big|\; \alpha \,;\, \phi \;\big|\; \alpha^{\phi}\phi \;\big|\; \alpha_{\phi}\phi \;\big|\; \widehat{\alpha} \qquad (2)$$

where α ranges over regular expressions RE. The symbols $\vee$ and $\wedge$ stand for the conventional union and intersection of languages (i.e., conjunction and disjunction in logics and $+$ and $|$ in semi-extended ω-regular expressions). The symbol ; stands for the conventional concatenation of an expression over finite words and an expression over infinite words.

The operators $\alpha^{\phi}\phi$, called the power operator, and its dual $\alpha_{\phi}\phi$ allow simple recursive definitions, including the Kleene-star (x^{ω} for infinite words) and the various operators in linear temporal logic. Finally, $\widehat{\alpha}$ denotes the suffix closure (arbitrary extension of a set of finite words to infinite words). The signature of RLTL is then:

$$\Sigma_{\mathrm{TL}} = \{\vee^2,\ \wedge^2,\ ;^2,\ (\cdot^{\cdot}\cdot)^3\ ,\ (\cdot_{\cdot}\cdot)^3,\ \widehat{\cdot}^1\}$$

where the superindices again indicate the arity of the operators. Even though the symbol ; is overloaded we consider the signatures to be disjoined. The operators $\vee$ and $\wedge$ require two expressions in the language of Σ_{TL}, while $(\cdot^{\cdot}\cdot)$, $(\cdot_{\cdot}\cdot)$ and $\widehat{\cdot}$ require the first argument to be an expression in the language of Σ_{RE} and the rest in Σ_{TL}. The set of regular linear temporal logic expressions RLTL is the set of all ground expressions over this signature. Note again that this signature contains no variable or fix-point quantifier.

Semantics. The semantics of an RLTL expression is defined as a binary relation $\models$ between pointed words and expressions, that is $\models \subseteq (\Gamma^{\omega} \times Pos) \times RLTL$. This relation is defined inductively as follows. Given RLTL expressions x and y and regular expression z:

- $(w, i) \models x \vee y$ whenever either $(w, i) \models x$ or $(w, i) \models y$, or both.
- $(w, i) \models x \wedge y$ whenever both $(w, i) \models x$ and $(w, i) \models y$.
- $(w, i) \models z \,;\, y$ whenever for some $k \in pos(w)$, $(w, i, k) \models_{\mathrm{RE}} z$ and $(w, k) \models y$.
- $(w, i) \models z^x y$ whenever $(w, i) \models y$ or for some sequence $(i_0 = i, i_1, \ldots i_m)$ $(w, i_k, i_{k+1}) \models_{\mathrm{RE}} z$ and $(w, i_k) \models x$, and $(w, i_m) \models y$.

– $(w,i) \models z_x y$ whenever one of:
(i) $(w,i) \models y$ and $(w,i) \models x$
(ii) for some sequence $(i_0 = i, i_1, \ldots i_m)$
$(w, i_k, i_{k+1}) \models_{\mathrm{RE}} z$ and $(w, i_k) \models y$ and $(w, i_m) \models x$
(iii) for some infinite sequence $(i_0 = i, i_1, \ldots)$
$(w, i_k, i_{k+1}) \models_{\mathrm{RE}} z$ and $(w, i_k) \models y$

– $(w,i) \models \hat{z}$ whenever for some $k \in pos(w)$, $(w,i,k) \models_{\mathrm{RE}} z$.

The semantics of $z^x y$ establish that either the obligation y is satisfied at the point i of evaluation, or there is a sequence of delays—as determined by z—after which y holds, and x holds after each individual delay. The semantics of $z_x y$ establish that y must hold initially and after each delay—as determined by z— and that x determines when the repetition of the delay can stop (if it stops at all).

As with regular expressions, languages can also be associated with RLTL expressions in the standard form: a word $w \in \Gamma^\omega$ is in the language of an expression x, denoted by $w \in \mathcal{L}(x)$, whenever $(w,1) \models x$. The following lemmas hold immediately from the definitions:

Lemma 1. *For every RLTL expressions x and y and* RE *expression z:*

– *The expression $z^x y$ is equivalent to $y \vee (x \wedge z\,;\, z^x y)$.*
– *The expression $z_x y$ is equivalent to $y \wedge (x \vee z\,;\, z_x y)$.*

Lemma 2. *If L_x is the language of x, L_y is the language of y and L_z the language of z, then*

– *The language of $z^x y$ is the least fix-point solution of the equation:*

$$X = L_y \cup (L_x \cap L_z; X)$$

– *The language of $z_x y$ is the greatest fix-point solution of the equation:*

$$X = L_y \cap (L_x \cup L_z; X)$$

where ; is the standard language concatenation.

Thus, although the semantics of the power operators is not defined using fix point equations, it can be characterized by such equations, similar as the until operator in LTL.

We finish this section by justifying the need of the operator $\widehat{\alpha}$ in RLTL. It is clear, directly from the semantics, that the operators $\wedge$, $\vee$ and ; will not define infinite languages (or equivalently pointed models) unless their arguments do. By Lemma 1, the same holds for the power and dual power operators. The expression $\widehat{x}$ serves as a *pump* of the finite models (segments) of x to any continuation. An alternative would have been to include a universal expression ($\top$ in the next section) from which $\widehat{x} = x\,;\,\top$. Similarly, $\top = \widehat{true}$, so both alternatives are equivalent.

In the sequel, the *size* of an RLTL formula is defined as the total number of its symbols.

3 Translating LTL and Regular Expressions into RLTL

We will use $\top$ and $\bot$ as syntactic sugar for $\widehat{\mathbf{true}}$ and $\widehat{\mathbf{false}}$ (resp). In particular, observe that $(w, i) \models \top$ and $(w, i) \not\models \bot$ for every pointed word (w, i). We first introduce some equivalences of RLTL, very simple to prove, that will assist in our definitions:

$$\begin{array}{ll} x \vee y = y \vee x & x \wedge y = y \wedge x \\ \top \vee x = \top & \top \wedge x = x \\ \bot \vee x = x & \bot \wedge x = \bot \end{array}$$

3.1 Translating ω-Regular Expressions

First, we show how to translate ω-regular expressions into regular linear temporal logic. An ω-regular expression is of the form:

$$\sum_i x_i \,;\, (y_i)^\omega$$

for a finite family of regular expressions x_i and y_i. Note that when a more conventional definition of regular expressions is used (one that allows the definition of languages containing the empty word), one must explicitly require that y_i does not posses the empty word property, which is not needed in our definition. Also, the case of x_i possessing the empty word property (in the classical definition), can be handled easily since for every y_i the following equivalence holds: $y_i^\omega = y_i \,;(y_i^\omega)$. Then every expression of the form $x_i \,;(y_i)^\omega$ can be translated into $(x_i \,; y_i) \,; (y_i^\omega)$, for which the finite prefix does not accept the empty word and it is in the variation of regular expressions introduced here.

Lemma 3. *Given a regular expression z, the regular linear temporal logic expression $z_\bot\top$ is equivalent to z^ω.*

Proof. As no pointed word (w, i) satisfies $\bot$, the only relevant case in the semantics of the dual power operator for $z_\bot\top$ is that there is an infinite sequence of points $(i_1, i_2, \ldots)$ for which $(w, i_k, i_{k+1}) \models z$. Therefore $w \in \mathcal{L}(z^\omega)$. □

It follows that the ω-regular expression $\sum_i x_i \,; (y_i)^\omega$ is equivalent to the RLTL expression $\bigvee_i x_i \,; (y_{i\bot}\top)$. This immediately implies:

Corollary 1. *The following are true for regular linear temporal logic:*
- *RLTL can express every ω-regular language.*
- *The set of operators $\{\vee, ;,$ dual power$\}$ is complete.*

Observe that no alternation of the power operators is needed to obtain expressive completeness (or in terms of Lemma 2 no alternation of fix points is necessary). This result is analogous to the linear μ-calculus [14], where the alternation hierarchy collapses at level 0 (in terms of expressiveness).

3.2 Translating LTL

We consider the following definition of LTL:

$$\psi ::= p \mid \psi \vee \psi \mid \psi \wedge \psi \mid \bigcirc\psi \mid \Box\psi \mid \Diamond\psi \mid \psi\,\mathcal{U}\,\psi \mid \psi\,\mathcal{R}\,\psi$$

which allows to express every linear temporal logic property in negation normal form. Note that $\Box\psi$ and $\Diamond\psi$ are just added for convenience.

The semantics of LTL expressions are defined, similarly to RLTL, by defining a binary relation $\models_{\mathrm{LTL}}$ between pointed words and LTL expressions: $\models_{\mathrm{LTL}} \subseteq (\Gamma^\omega \times Pos) \times LTL$. The semantics is defined inductively. The basic expressions and boolean operators are mapped as conventionally. Let x and y be arbitrary LTL expressions. The semantics of the temporal operators is:

- $(w, i) \models_{\mathrm{LTL}} \Diamond x$ whenever $(w, j) \models_{\mathrm{LTL}} x$ for some $j \geq i$.
- $(w, i) \models_{\mathrm{LTL}} \Box x$ whenever $(w, j) \models_{\mathrm{LTL}} x$ for all $j \geq i$.
- $(w, i) \models_{\mathrm{LTL}} \bigcirc x$ whenever $(w, i + 1) \models_{\mathrm{LTL}} x$.
- $(w, i) \models_{\mathrm{LTL}} x\,\mathcal{U}\,y$ whenever $(w, j) \models_{\mathrm{LTL}} y$ for some $j \geq i$, and $(w, k) \models_{\mathrm{LTL}} x$ for all $i \leq k < j$.
- $(w, i) \models_{\mathrm{LTL}} x\,\mathcal{R}\,y$ whenever $(w, j) \models_{\mathrm{LTL}} y$ for all $j \geq i$, or for some j, $(w, j) \models_{\mathrm{LTL}} x$ and for all k within $i \leq k < j$, $(w, j) \models_{\mathrm{LTL}} y$.

Consider the following procedure, that translates an LTL expression ψ into an RLTL expression $\tau(\psi)$:

- $\tau(p) = \widehat{p}$, $\tau(x \wedge y) = \tau(x) \wedge \tau(y)$, $\tau(x \vee y) = \tau(x) \vee \tau(y)$,
- $\tau(\bigcirc x) = \mathbf{true}\,;\tau(x)$,
- $\tau(\Box x) = \mathbf{true}_{\perp}\tau(x)$,
- $\tau(\Diamond x) = \mathbf{true}^{\top}\tau(x)$,
- $\tau(x\,\mathcal{U}\,y) = \mathbf{true}^{\tau(x)}\tau(y)$,
- $\tau(x\,\mathcal{R}\,y) = \mathbf{true}_{\tau(x)}\tau(y)$.

Theorem 1. *Every LTL expression defines the same language as its RLTL translation.*

Proof. The proof proceeds by structural induction. For the basic expression, the boolean operators and $\bigcirc$ the result holds directly from the definitions. We show here the equivalence for $\mathcal{U}$ (the rest follow similarly). It is well known that $x\,\mathcal{U}\,y$ is the least fix point solution of the equation $X \equiv y \vee (x \wedge \bigcirc(x\,\mathcal{U}\,y))$, which is by Lemma 2 the semantics of $\mathbf{true}^{\tau(x)}\tau(y)$. $\Box$

Our translation maps every LTL operator into an equivalent RLTL context (with the same number of *holes*). Consequently, this translation only involves a linear blow-up in the size of the original formula. Since checking satisfiability of linear temporal logic is PSPACE-hard [21] this translation immediately gives a lower bound on the complexity of RLTL.

Proposition 1. *The problems of satisfiability and equivalence for regular linear temporal logic are PSPACE-hard.*

4 Translating RLTL into Alternating Automata

We now show that every RLTL formula can be translated with a linear blow-up into an alternating automaton accepting precisely its models.

4.1 Preliminaries

Let us, however, first recall the definitions of (nondeterministic) automata operating on finite words and alternating Büchi automata operating on infinite words.

A *nondeterministic finite automaton* (NFA) is a tuple $\mathcal{A} : \langle \Gamma, Q, q_0, \partial, F\rangle$ where Γ is the alphabet, Q a finite set of *states*, $q_0 \in Q$ the *initial state*, $\partial : Q \times \Gamma \to 2^Q$ the *transition function*, and $F \subseteq Q$ is the set of *final states*. An NFA operates on finite words: A *run* of $\mathcal{A}$ on a word $w = a_1 \ldots a_n \in \Gamma^*$ is a sequence of states and actions $\rho = q_0 a_1 q_1 \ldots q_n$, where q_0 is the initial state of $\mathcal{A}$ and for all $i \in \{1, \ldots n\}$, we have $q_{i+1} \in \partial(q_i, a_i)$. The run is called *accepting* if $q_n \in F$. The *language* of $\mathcal{A}$, denoted by $\mathcal{L}(\mathcal{A})$, is the set of words $w \in \Gamma^*$ for which an accepting run exists.

For a finite set $\mathcal{X}$ of variables, let $\mathcal{B}^+(\mathcal{X})$ be the set of *positive Boolean formulas* over $\mathcal{X}$, i.e., the smallest set such that $\mathcal{X} \subseteq \mathcal{B}^+(\mathcal{X})$, $\mathbf{true}, \mathbf{false} \in \mathcal{B}^+(\mathcal{X})$, and $\phi, \psi \in \mathcal{B}^+(\mathcal{X})$ implies $\phi \wedge \psi \in \mathcal{B}^+(\mathcal{X})$ and $\phi \vee \psi \in \mathcal{B}^+(\mathcal{X})$. We say that a set $Y \subseteq \mathcal{X}$ *satisfies* (or is a *model* of) a formula $\phi \in \mathcal{B}^+(\mathcal{X})$ iff ϕ evaluates to **true** when the variables in Y are assigned to **true** and the members of $\mathcal{X} \backslash Y$ are assigned to **false**. A model is called *minimal* if none of its proper subsets is a model. For example, $\{q_1, q_3\}$ as well as $\{q_2, q_3\}$ are minimal models of the formula $(q_1 \vee q_2) \wedge q_3$.

An *alternating Büchi automaton* (ABA) is a tuple $\mathcal{A} : \langle \Gamma, Q, q_0, \partial, F\rangle$ where Γ, Q, and F are as for NFAs. The transition function ∂, however, yields a positive boolean combination of successor states: $\partial : Q \times \Gamma \to \mathcal{B}^+(Q)$. Furthermore, an ABA operates on infinite words: A *run* over an infinite word $w = a_0 a_1 \ldots \in \Gamma^\omega$ is a Q-labeled directed acyclic graph (V, E) such that there exist labellings $l : V \to Q$ and $h : V \to \mathbb{N}$ which satisfy the following properties:

- there is a single $v_0 \in V$ with $h(v_0) = 0$. Moreover, $l(v_0) = q_0$.
- for every $(v, v') \in E$, $h(v') = h(v) + 1$.
- for every $v' \in V$ with $h(v') \geq 1$, $\{v \in V \mid (v, v') \in E\} \neq \varnothing$,
- for every $v, v' \in V$, $v \neq v'$, $l(v) = l(v')$ implies $h(v) \neq h(v')$, and
- for every $v \in V$, $\{l(v') \mid (v, v') \in E\}$ is a minimal model of $\partial(l(v), a_{h(v)})$.

A run (V, E) is *accepting* if every maximal finite path ends in a node $v \in V$ with $\partial(l(v), a_{h(v)}) = \mathbf{true}$ and every maximal infinite path, wrt. the labeling l, visits at least one final state infinitely often. The language $\mathcal{L}(\mathcal{A})$ of an automaton $\mathcal{A}$ is determined by all strings for which an accepting run of $\mathcal{A}$ exists. We also consider *alternating co-Büchi automaton* (AcBA), defined exactly as ABA, except that the accepting condition establishes that all final states are visited only finitely many times in accepting paths.

We measure the *size* of an NFA, ABA and AcBA in terms of its number of states.

An ABA is *weak* (WABA), if there exists a partition of Q into disjoints sets Q_i, such that for each set Q_i either $Q_i \subseteq F$ or $Q_i \cap F = \emptyset$, and, there is a partial order $\leq$ on the collection of the Q_i's such that for every $q \in Q_i$ and $q' \in Q_j$ for which q' occurs in $\delta(q, a)$, for some $a \in \Gamma$, we have $Q_j \leq Q_i$.

It was shown in [13] that every AcBA can be translated into a WABA with a quadratic blow-up. Furthermore, it was shown in [17] that for an ABA accepting L, we get an AcBA accepting the complement of L, when dualizing the transition function (switching $\wedge$ with $\vee$ and **true** with **false**) and turning the acceptance condition into a co-Büchi acceptance condition. This gives

Proposition 2. *For every ABA $\mathcal{A}$ with n states, there is an ABA $\bar{\mathcal{A}}$ with at most n^2 states accepting the complement of $\mathcal{A}$'s language.*

4.2 Translation

We are now ready to formulate the main theorem of this section:

Theorem 2. *For every $\phi \in RLTL$, there is an ABA $\mathcal{A}_\phi$ accepting precisely the ω-words satisfying ϕ. Moreover, the size of $\mathcal{A}_\phi$ is linear in the size of ϕ.*

Corollary 2. *Checking satisfiability of an RLTL formula is PSPACE-complete.*

Proof. By Proposition 1, satisfiability of an RLTL formula is PSPACE-hard. Given $\phi \in RLTL$, we can construct $\mathcal{A}_\phi$ according to Theorem 2, and check $\mathcal{A}_\phi$ for emptiness, which can be done in PSPACE [24].

As usual, we call two formulas of *RLTL equivalent* iff their sets of models coincide.

Lemma 4. *Checking equivalence of two RLTL formulas is PSPACE-complete.*

Proof. By Proposition 1, equivalence of two RLTL formulas ϕ and ψ is PSPACE-hard.

The formulas ϕ and ψ are equivalent iff both $(\neg\phi \wedge \psi)$ and $(\phi \wedge \neg\psi)$ are unsatisfiable. Even though complementation is not present in RLTL, we can use automata constructions to perform these two tests. The construction of Theorem 2 gives ABA $\mathcal{A}_\phi$ and $\mathcal{A}_\psi$ polynomial in the size of the formula. By Proposition 2, we can complement an ABA with an at most quadratic blow-up. ABAs in turn can be combined with $\wedge$. The check for emptiness of the resulting alternating automata can be done in PSPACE [24]. □

In the remainder of this section, we present the construction of $\mathcal{A}_\phi$ for $\phi \in RLTL$, hereby proving Theorem 2. The procedure works bottom-up the parse tree of ϕ. Recall that every regular expression α can be translated into an equivalent NFA [9].

Now, consider alternating Büchi automata for x and y, $\mathcal{A}_x : \langle \Gamma, Q^x, q_o^x, \partial^x, F^x \rangle$ and $\mathcal{A}_y : \langle \Gamma, Q^y, q_o^y, \partial^y, F^y \rangle$, and a non-deterministic automaton (over finite words) for z: $\mathcal{A}_z : \langle \Gamma, Q^z, q_o^z, \partial^z, F^z \rangle$. Without loss of generality, we assume that their state spaces are disjoint. We consider the different operators of RLTL:

Disjunction. The automaton for $x \vee y$ is:

$$\mathcal{A}_{x \vee y} \;:\; \langle \Gamma, Q^x \cup Q^y, q_0, \partial, F^x \cup F^y \rangle$$

where q_0 is a fresh new state. The transition function is defined as

$$\partial(q, a) = \begin{cases} \partial^x(q, a) & \text{if } q \in Q^x \\ \partial^y(q, a) & \text{if } q \in Q^y \end{cases}$$
$$\partial(q_0, a) = \partial^x(q_0^x, a) \vee \partial^y(q_0^y, a).$$

Thus, from the fresh initial state q_0, $\mathcal{A}_{x \vee y}$ chooses non-deterministically one of the successor states of $\mathcal{A}_x$'s or $\mathcal{A}_y$'s initial state. Clearly, the accepted language is the union.

Conjunction. The automaton for $x \wedge y$ is:

$$\mathcal{A}_{x \wedge y} \;:\; \langle \Gamma, Q^x \cup Q^y, q_0, \partial, F^x \cup F^y \rangle$$

where q_0 is again a fresh new state. The transition function is defined as before except

$$\partial(q_0, a) = \partial^x(q_0^x, a) \wedge \partial^y(q_0^y, a).$$

Hence, from the fresh initial state q_0, $\mathcal{A}_{x \wedge y}$ follows both $\mathcal{A}_x$'s and $\mathcal{A}_y$'s initial state. Clearly, the accepted language is the intersection.

Suffix extensions. The automaton for $\widehat{z}$ is:

$$\mathcal{A}_{\widehat{z}} \;:\; \langle \Gamma, Q^z \cup \{q_{tt}\}, q_0^z, \partial, \{q_{tt}\} \rangle$$

where q_{tt} is a fresh new state and ∂ is defined, for $q \in Q^z$ as:

$$\partial(q, a) = \begin{cases} \bigvee\{\partial^z(q, a)\} & \text{if } q \notin F^z \\ \bigvee\{\partial^z(q, a)\} \vee \{q_{tt}\} & \text{if } q \in F^z \end{cases}$$

and $\partial(q_{tt}, a) = q_{tt}$. Thus, from a final state, which signals that the prefix of the infinite word read so far matches the regular expression, the automaton may non-deterministically choose to accept the remainder of the word.

Concatenation. The automaton for $z\,;x$ is:

$$\mathcal{A}_{z;x} \;:\; \langle \Gamma, Q^z \cup Q^x, q_0^z, \partial, F^x \rangle$$

where ∂ is defined, for $q \in Q^z$ as:

$$\partial(q, a) = \begin{cases} \bigvee\{\partial^z(q, a)\} & \text{if } \partial^z(q, a) \cap F^z = \emptyset \\ \bigvee\{\partial^z(q, a)\} \vee q_0^x & \text{if } \partial^z(q, a) \cap F^z \neq \emptyset \end{cases}$$

and, for $q \in Q^x$ as $\partial(q, a) = \partial^x(q, a)$. Recall that $\mathcal{A}_z$ is a nondeterministic automaton. Whenever $\mathcal{A}_z$ can non-deterministically choose a successor that is a final state, it can also switch to $\mathcal{A}_x$. Thus, the accepted language is indeed the concatenation.

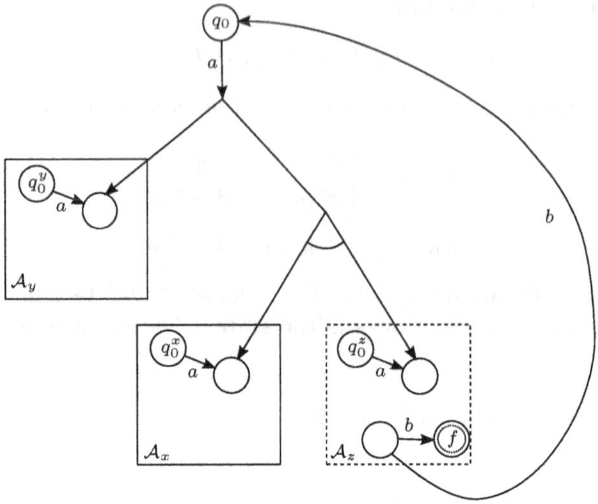

Fig. 1. Construction for the power operator

Power. The automaton for $z^x y$ is:

$$\mathcal{A}_{z^x y} \; : \; \langle \Gamma, Q^z \cup Q^x \cup Q^y \cup \{q_0\}, q_0, \partial, F^x \cup F^y \rangle$$

where ∂ is defined as follows. The successor for a of the initial state is:

$$\partial(q_0, a) = \partial^y(q_0^y, a) \vee (\partial^x(q_0^x, a) \wedge \bigvee\{\partial^z(q_0^z, a)\})$$

The successor of Q^x and Q^y are defined as in $\mathcal{A}_x$ and $\mathcal{A}_y$, i.e., $\partial^x(q, a)$ for $q \in Q^x$, $\partial^y(q, a)$ for $q \in Q^y$. For $q \in Q_z$

$$\partial(q, a) = \begin{cases} \bigvee\{\partial^z(q, a)\} & \text{if } \partial^z(q, a) \cap F^z = \emptyset \\ \bigvee\{\partial^z(q, a)\} \vee q_0 & \text{if } \partial^z(q, a) \cap F^z \neq \emptyset \end{cases}$$

The construction, depicted in Fig. 1, follows precisely the equivalence $z^x y \equiv y \vee (x \wedge z; z^x y)$ established in Lemma 1 and the construction for disjunction, conjunction, and concatenation.

Dual power. The automaton for $z_x y$ is:

$$\mathcal{A}_{z^x y} \; : \; \langle \Gamma, Q^z \cup Q^x \cup Q^y \cup \{q_0\}, q_0, \partial, F^x \cup F^y \cup \{q_0\} \rangle$$

where ∂ is defined exactly as before except for the successor for a of the initial state:

$$\partial(q_0, a) = \partial^y(q_0^y, a) \wedge (\partial^x(q_0^x, a) \vee \bigvee\{\partial^z(q_0^z, a)\})$$

Note, however, the state q_0 is now accepting, since the evaluation is allowed to loop in z for ever, restarting a copy of y at each repetition of z.

Complexity. Recall that a regular expression can linearly be translated into a corresponding NFA [9,10]. Examining the construction given above, we see that each operator adds at most one extra state. Thus, the overall number of states of the resulting automaton is linear with respect to the size of the formula.

The above construction for the concatenation operator relies heavily on the fact that the automaton $\mathcal{A}_z$ for a regular expression is nondeterministic. If RLTL were based on extended regular expressions, which offer boolean combinations of regular expressions (including negation), there would be no hope to get a PSPACE satisfiability procedure, as checking emptiness for extended regular expressions is already of non-elementary complexity [22]. On the same line, semi-extended regular expressions (that add *conjunction* to regular expressions) and input-synchronizing automata as introduced by Yamamoto [27] do neither give a PSPACE algorithm.

5 Conclusion and Discussion

In this paper, we introduced RLTL, a temporal logic that allows to express all ω-regular properties. It allows a smooth combination of LTL-formulas and regular expressions. Besides positive boolean combinations, only two *power* operators are introduced, which generalize LTL's *until* as well as the $*/\omega$-operator found in ω-regular expressions. In contrast to LTL, RLTL allows to define arbitrary ω-regular properties, while keeping LTL's complexity of satisfiability (PSPACE). In contrast to νTL, RLTL refrains the user to deal with fix point formulas.

Technically, RLTL can be considered as a sublogic of linear fix point logic with chop (LFLC). As satisfiability for LFLC is undecidable, RLTL spots an interesting subset of LFLC. Moreover, practically, the techniques developed for LFLC [18,15] should be usable for RLTL as well.

The careful reader has probably observed that complementation has not been included in RLTL, even though doing so does not immediately turn the decision problems non-elementary (regular-expressions would be built completely before complementation is applied). The reason is that complementation for ABA (using the translation from AcBA to WABA to obtain an ABA) involves a quadratic blow-up, and the resulting ABA for a given formula obtained at the end of the inductive construction will no-longer have a polynomial size in all cases.

A different accepting condition can be used, for example a parity condition, giving a linear size parity automaton at the end of the translation (using possibly a linear number of colors). One way to attack the emptiness problem of parity automata is then to translate the automaton into a *weak* alternating parity automaton, whose emptiness problem is well known to be in PSPACE. However, the best procedure known generates a weak automaton of size $O(n^k)$, for n states and k ranks). The use of weak parity automata directly in the construction is precluded by the dual power operator $z_x y$, since one seems to be forced to express that the initial state q_0 must be visited infinitely often.

Recent developments [23] seem to indicate that the emptiness problem for alternating parity automata is in PSPACE, by a direct algorithm. This result would allow the introduction of negation in RLTL freely with no penalty in the complexity class of the algorithms.

Nevertheless, as the resulting alternating Büchi automaton for a given RLTL formula can be complemented with an at most quadratic blow-up, we can easily get an exponentially bigger nondeterministic Büchi automaton accepting the formula's refutations, so that automata-based model checking of RLTL specifications can be carried out as usual (for LTL).

Clearly, since ETL, νTL, DLTL, and RLTL are all expressively complete wrt. ω-regular languages, for every ground formula in one logic defining some ω-regular language, there is an equivalent ground formula in any of the other logics defining the same language. From that perspective, all logics are equally expressive. However, ETL, and νTL offer, for example, no translation of the sequencing operator ; respecting a given context and DLTL does not allow to formulate a corresponding ω-operator. Thus, RLTL's unique feature is that every LTL operator and the operators in regular expressions can be translated into an equivalent RLTL context (with the same number of *holes*). This allows a linear, *inductive* translation of LTL properties or regular expressions.

The closest approach to RLTL is DLTL, though it is motivated in the context of dynamic logic. Similarly as RLTL, DLTL implicitly follows similar concepts as *attempt*, *obligation*, and *delay* by enriching the until operator. However, the obligation must be met in every "intermediate" position between the current and the one where the attempt holds. In RLTL, however, a sequence of delays has to be considered and the obligation has to hold only when the delay begins. The choice taken in RLTL has a huge advantage: It is straightforward to extend RLTL with past operators, by changing the *direction* of delay expressions. Extending DLTL to handle past seems to be much more cumbersome. However, this addition is left for future work.

References

1. IEEE P1850 - Standard for PSL - Property Specification Language (September 2005)
2. Barringer, H., Kuiper, R., Pnueli, A.: A really abstract concurrent model and its temporal logic. In: POPL'86. Procs. of the 13th Annual ACM Symp. on Principles of Programming Languages, pp. 173–183. ACM Press, New York (1986)
3. Beer, I., Ben-David, S., Eisner, C., Fisman, D., Gringauze, A., Rodeh, Y.: The temporal logic Sugar. In: Berry, G., Comon, H., Finkel, A. (eds.) CAV 2001. LNCS, vol. 2102, pp. 363–367. Springer, Heidelberg (2001)
4. Büchi, J.R.: On a decision method in restricted second order arithmetic. In: Proc. of the Int'l Congress on Logic Methodology and Philosophy of Science, pp. 1–12. Stanford University Press (1962)
5. Emerson, E.A., Clarke, E.M.: Characterizing correctness properties of parallel programs using fixpoints. In: de Bakker, J.W., van Leeuwen, J. (eds.) Automata, Languages and Programming. LNCS, vol. 85, pp. 169–181. Springer, Heidelberg (1980)
6. Fisman, D., Eisner, C., Havlicek, J.: Formal syntax and Semantics of PSL: Appendix B of Accellera Property Language Reference Manual, Version 1.1 (March 2004)
7. Harel, D., Peleg, D.: Process logic with regular formulas. Theoretical Computer Science 38, 307–322 (1985)

8. Henriksen, J.G., Thiagarajan, P.S.: Dynamic linear time temporal logic. Annals of Pure and Applied Logic 96(1–3), 187–207 (1999)
9. Hopcroft, J.E., Ullman, J.D.: Introduction to automata theory, languages and computation. Addison-Wesley, Reading (1979)
10. Hromkovic, J., Seibert, S., Wilke, T.: Translating regular expressions into small ϵ-free nondeterministic finite automata. In: Reischuk, R., Morvan, M. (eds.) STACS 97. LNCS, vol. 1200, pp. 55–66. Springer, Heidelberg (1997)
11. Kleene, S.C.: Representation of events in nerve nets and finite automata. In: Shannon, C.E., McCarthy, J. (eds.) Automata Studies, vol. 34, pp. 3–41. Princeton University Press, Princeton, New Jersey (1956)
12. Kozen, D.: Results on the propositional μ-calculus. In: Nielsen, M., Schmidt, E.M. (eds.) Automata, Languages, and Programming. LNCS, vol. 140, pp. 348–359. Springer, Heidelberg (1982)
13. Kupferman, O., Vardi, M.Y.: Weak alternating automata are not that weak. In: ISTCS'97. Proc. of the Fifth Israel Symposium on Theory of Computing and Systems, pp. 147–158. IEEE Computer Society Press, Los Alamitos (1997)
14. Lange, M.: Weak automata for the linear time μ-calculus. In: Cousot, R. (ed.) VMCAI 2005. LNCS, vol. 3385, pp. 267–281. Springer, Heidelberg (2005)
15. Lange, M., Stirling, C.: Model checking fixed point logic with chop. In: Nielsen, M., Engberg, U. (eds.) ETAPS 2002 and FOSSACS 2002. LNCS, vol. 2303, Springer, Heidelberg (2002)
16. Manna, Z., Pnueli, A.: Temporal Verification of Reactive Systems. Springer, Heidelberg (1995)
17. Muller, D.E., Schupp, P.E.: Altenating automata on infinite trees. Theoretical Computer Science 54, 267–276 (1987)
18. Müller-Olm, M.: A modal fixpoint logic with chop. In: Meinel, C., Tison, S. (eds.) STACS 99. LNCS, vol. 1563, pp. 510–520. Springer, Heidelberg (1999)
19. Pnueli, A.: The temporal logic of programs. In: FOCS'77. Proc. of the 18th IEEE Symposium on Foundations of Computer Science, pp. 46–67. IEEE Computer Society Press, Los Alamitos (1977)
20. Pnueli, A.: Applications of temporal logic to the specification and verification of reactive systems – a survey of current trends. In: Rozenberg, G., de Bakker, J.W., de Roever, W.-P. (eds.) Current Trends in Concurrency. LNCS, vol. 224, pp. 510–584. Springer, Heidelberg (1986)
21. Sistla, A.P., Clarke, E.M.: The complexity of propositional linear termporal logics. Journal of the ACM 32(3), 733–749 (1985)
22. Stockmeyer, L.J.: The Complexity of Decision Problems in Automata Theory and Logic. PhD thesis, Department of Electrical Engineering, MIT, Boston, Massachusetts (1974)
23. Vardi, M.Y.: Personal communication
24. Vardi, M.Y.: An automata-theoretic approach to linear temporal logic. In: Moller, F., Birtwistle, G. (eds.) Logics for Concurrency. LNCS, vol. 1043, pp. 238–266. Springer, Heidelberg (1996)
25. Vardi, M.Y., Wolper, P.: Reasoning about infinite computations. Information and Computation 115, 1–37 (1994)
26. Wolper, P.: Temporal logic can be more expressive. Information and Control 56, 72–99 (1983)
27. Yamamoto, H.: On the power of input-synchronized alternating finite automata. In: Du, D.-Z., Eades, P., Sharma, A.K., Lin, X., Estivill-Castro, V. (eds.) COCOON 2000. LNCS, vol. 1858, p. 457. Springer, Heidelberg (2000)

Algebraic Semantics for Compensable Transactions*

Jing Li, Huibiao Zhu, and Jifeng He

Software Engineering Institute, East China Normal University
Shanghai, China, 200062
{jli, hbzhu, jifeng}@ sei.ecnu.edu.cn

Abstract. This paper presents the algebraic semantics of a novel transactional language *t*-calculus. This language focuses on modeling long running transactions in terms of compensable transactions, showing how the compensations can be orchestrated to ensure atomicity. The typical operators of sequential and parallel compositions are redefined so that the corresponding compensations will be activated in a suitable order whenever some failure occurs in later stage. In addition, we investigate more transactional operators, such as speculative choice, exception handling, alternative forwarding and programmable compensation. The wise use of these constructs is rather helpful to set up a flexible and effective business process. We present a clear algebraic semantics for *t*-calculus and derive its operational semantics mechanically based on a given derivation strategy. This work provides a foundation for optimization and implementation of this language.

1 Introduction

Business transactions need to deal with failures that arise at any stage of execution and this is both difficult and critical. Since business transactions usually require long periods of time to complete, it is infeasible and unreasonable to block resources so long. Additionally, in the context of web services, the activities involved in a transaction possibly belong to different organizations, so there is no control to lock resources of the other parties. Particularly, the business transaction usually involves communications with external agents. In this case, the external agent should also take some actions while aborting a transaction, which makes the pure roll-back technique no longer adequate. For instance, the cancelation of a flight ticket should be accompanied by an extra payment. In order to recover from failure, a weaker notion of atomicity based on the concept of compensation was introduced [1] so as to make an overall long-lived transaction still execute as a unit. A compensation is some ad-hoc activity declared by application developers so as to remove partial effects in a semantic manner. If a long-running transaction fails in the middle, appropriate compensations are activated to compensate for completed parts of this transaction.

* Supported by National Basic Research Program of China (No. 2005CB321904) and Shanghai STCSM Project (No. 06JC14058).

C.B. Jones, Z. Liu, J. Woodcock (Eds.): ICTAC 2007, LNCS 4711, pp. 306–321, 2007.

A transaction equipped with a compensation is referred as a compensable transaction, whose effect can be semantically removed by its compensating actions. The transactional language t-calculus was introduced by Li et al [2] to model business flow in terms of compensable transactions. t-calculus provides a framework to combine smaller compensable transactions into a larger one, thus gradually setting up a long running business transaction which has compensation as its main error recovery technique. The typical operators of sequential and parallel compositions are redefined so that compensations will be activated in a suitable order whenever some failure occurs later. In addition, more transactional operators, such as speculative choice, exception handling, alternative forwarding and programmable compensation, are studied to orchestrate compensations in a different way. The plentiful operators facilitate the developers to design a distributive system with high responsiveness to environment and strong capability for dealing with failures.

Algebraic semantics is useful for studying program properties which are elegantly expressed as equational laws. These laws are well suited to support program transformation and optimization. In this paper, we explore the algebraic semantics for t-calculus based on normal forms, where each compensable transaction can be re-written as a kind of head normal form. This approach provides a computable method for justifying kinds of properties for compensable transactions. In addition, we consider the derivation of operational semantics from algebraic semantics for t-calculus by proposing a related derivation strategy. This work builds a certain kind of linking theory between two different semantic models, which are strongly advocated by Unifying Theories of Programming [3].

2 Transactional Calculus

The transactional language t-calculus is intended to describe the behavior of top-level transactions but not low-level computations. Transactions are modeled in terms of atomic activities they can engage in and a number of operators are introduced to support compensable transactions. An atomic activity is such an activity where no errors can take place in the middle of execution, the atomicity of which is guaranteed by the underlying system. We use an infinite set Σ of names to represent atomic activities ranged over by $A, B, \ldots$. Moreover, we consider two other special activities: the empty activity 0 always completes but has no effect; the error activity $\Diamond$ always leads to a failure. The syntax of this transactional calculus is summarized as follows.

$$\begin{aligned} BT &::= A \div B \mid A \div 0 \mid A \div \Diamond \mid \mathit{Skip} \mid \mathit{Abort} \mid \mathit{Fail} \\ S, T &::= BT \mid S; T \mid S \| T \mid S \mathbin{[\,]} T \mid S \sqcap T \mid S \otimes T \mid \\ &\qquad S \unrhd T \mid S \rhd T \mid S \rightsquigarrow T \mid S \circledast T \\ P &::= \{T\} \end{aligned}$$

Basically, a compensable transaction consists of two parts: a forward flow and a compensating flow. In case of failure, compensation will be activated to compensate its forward flow. The basic way to construct a compensable transaction is through a transactional pair $A \div B$, where A is the forward flow and B is its compensation. The compensation B is responsible for undoing the effect of A and should be installed on the successful completion of A for possibly later use. Especially, $A \div 0$ denotes that the forward flow A is associated with an empty compensation. In other words, the effect made by A does not need to be removed when error occurs. Besides, not every activity can be semantically undone, so sometimes the application designer cannot find a suitable compensation. In this case, we use $A \div \Diamond$ to denote that the forward flow A is associated with an unacceptable compensation which always encounters a failure.

Moreover, there are three variations for basic transactions. *Skip* stands for a successfully completed transaction without anything really done. *Abort* means a certain error has taken place and all installed compensations should be activated to recover from this failure. *Fail* indicates an error too. However, it has no chance to enable compensations and causes an exception instead.

The sequential and parallel operators are redefined for composing compensable transactions. For sequential composition, the compensations are installed in a reverse order as opposed to their forward flow. As for parallel composition, both forward flow and compensating flow are arranged in parallel. It is worth noting that, in parallel composition, if one branch fails, the whole transaction is regarded as fail too. Thus, the other branch does not need to continue but terminates early by stoping executing the non-performed activities and enabling its compensation immediately. This mechanism is called *forced termination* which is used to avoid unnecessary executions. For example,

$$(A_1 \div B_1; A_2 \div B_2) \,\|\, Abort$$

the right branch can only fail, this failure may occur before A_1 starts, after A_1 completes or even when A_2 finishes. The left part cannot predict the time when its sibling encounters a failure, so it must support forced termination in any stage of execution. Suppose a failure takes place after A_1 completes, then the latter transaction is not performed at all and the installed compensation B_1 is run to compensate for the effect of A_1.

Apart from external choice $S \,[]\, T$ and internal choice $S \sqcap T$, we study another useful construct of choice $S \otimes T$ called *speculative choice*. For speculative choice, two branches are arranged to run in parallel. The choice is delayed when one branch has succeeded. That is, the successfully completed one is chosen while another one should be compensated. This operator provides a way for developers to design two or more threads to finish one task. If one thread is failed, the others are still active trying to achieve the same target. This construct is quite useful to improve the responsiveness to the environment. Especially, if one branch has completed successfully, the other one is forced to terminate. For instance,

$$(A_1 \div B_1; A_2 \div B_2) \otimes (A_3 \div B_3; A_4 \div B_4)$$

suppose A_4 completes after A_1 finishes, then the left branch is forced to terminate by inhibiting the execution of A_2. Besides, B_1 is run to compensate for the effect of A_1, and B_4, B_3 have been installed for possibly later activation.

Compensation is proposed to compensate for its forward flow so as to remove any partial effect. However, a partial compensation which fails in the middle will lead to inconsistency. In order to deal with partial compensations, two kinds of exception handling are introduced. For *backward handling* $S \trianglerighteq T$, the backward

$$OrderTran = \{ProcOrder\}$$
$$ProcOrder = (AccOrder \div RefOrder; FulOrder) \unrhd (GetIndem \div 0)$$
$$FulOrder = PrepOrder \,||\, UpdCredit \,||\, BookShip$$
$$PrepOrder = (PackOrder \div UnpackOrder) \sqcap (PackOrder \div \Diamond)$$
$$UpdCredit = CheckCredit \div 0; (Abort \sqcap DeductMoney \div RefundMoney)$$
$$BookShip = (RequestSA \div 0; (Abort \sqcap BookSA \div QuitSA)) \rightsquigarrow (BookSB \div QuitSB)$$

Fig. 1. Transaction for order fulfillment

handler T aims to supply the lack for the partial compensation so as to result in a perfect transactional abort. With regard to *forward handling* $S \rhd T$, the forward handler T tries to go forward again from a specific point. If the forward handler succeeds, the whole transaction is considered successful too.

When a sub-transaction aborts, all previously committed sub-transactions should be aborted. However, it would be quite costly when aborting a long running transaction. Instead, it is more satisfactory if we can restart the aborted sub-transaction in an alternative way without aborting the other siblings. Based on this consideration, a new construct $S \rightsquigarrow T$ called *alternative forwarding* is introduced to achieve this goal. T is the alternative which is triggered on the abortion of S so as to re-fulfil the same goal.

So far, compensations can only be accumulated through its sub-transactions. However, in some situations, compensations need to be programmed according to application-specific requirements. Thus, it is better to provide a way for developers to define a novel compensation instead of the original one. In the construct of programmable compensation $S \circledast T$, T is the newly programmed compensation for S and it is installed only when S has completed successfully. For instance:

$$(A_1 \div B_1; A_2 \div B_2; A_3 \div B_3) \circledast (T_1 \rightsquigarrow T_2)$$

the original compensation B_3, B_2, B_1 is replaced by $T_1 \rightsquigarrow T_2$. It is worth noting that the compensation itself is also treated as a compensable transaction.

Our target is to set up a long running transaction in terms of compensable transactions. The transactional block $\{T\}$ represents a complete business transaction by enclosing a compensable transaction T. An example of a transaction for processing customer orders is presented in Figure 1. At first, the seller accepts an order request compensated by refusing the order. Afterwards, three sub-tasks begin to process in parallel. According to distinct features of goods, some kind of goods damage easily. For solid goods, the activity *PackOrder* is compensated by *UnpackOrder*. For fragile ones, the special construct $PackOrder \div \Diamond$ denotes that simple unpacking is not enough. In this case, the seller would ask for extra indemnities *GetIndem* from the client which is transacted within an exception handler. The choice is made internally based on which kind of goods the client orders. The credit update is performed concurrently since this task normally succeeds. Once the credit checking fails, the signal of abort will cause all the finished activities to be compensated. Assume that this seller has only two shippers to contact with. Shipper A is cheaper but hard to book whereas shipper B is more expensive but always available. For saving money, shipper A is preferred and shipper B is booked only when shipper A is unavailable.

3 Algebraic Semantics

In this section, our main objective is to explore equivalence for compensable transactions using an algebraic theory. Our approach for this is to identify a *normal form* which has a highly restricted syntax.

3.1 Head Normal Form

A transaction advances one step by performing an activity. We express this one-step behavior as $h \to T$ called a *guarded transaction*. The guard h is an activity of the following ones:

- atomic activity which always succeed, denoted by $A, B, \ldots \in \Sigma$.
- error activity which indicates an error, denoted by $\lozenge$ and $\overline{\lozenge}$.
- ready activity which denotes a tendency to succeed, denoted by $\sharp$.
- forced activity which leads to forced termination, denoted by $\Lsh$.

In the above, $\lozenge$ denotes a failure occurring during the forward flow, while $\overline{\lozenge}$ stands for a failure arising during the compensating flow. The forced activity $\Lsh$ is not given explicitly within a transaction. It is used to indicate that the environment has the chance to terminate a compensable transaction forcibly.

During the course of executing a compensable transaction, we need to introduce some assistant constructs to describe the *intermediate running objects*:

- $S \upharpoonright T$ denotes the non-performed forward flow is S and the compensation T has already been installed.
- $\overleftarrow{T}$ denotes the compensation T has been activated automatically on failure.
- $\overleftrightarrow{T}$ denotes the compensation T has been activated by forced termination.
- $S \setminus\!\!\setminus T$ denotes two parallel transactions are executing, in which at most one branch is in the forward flow.

Besides, a compensable transaction may end in five states:

- $\boxdot \backslash T$ (success) represents the transaction has successfully completed with a compensation T installed.
- $\boxtimes$ (abort) represents the transaction has been successfully compensated due to a failure during its forward flow.
- $\overline{\boxtimes}$ (forced abort) represents the transaction has been forced to terminate and it has been compensated successfully.
- $\circledast$ (fail) represents some failure occurs during the forward flow but the compensation fails to amend partial execution.
- $\overline{\circledast}$ (forced fail) represents the transaction has been forced to terminate but its compensation fails halfway.

We call the five transactions above as *terminated transactions*. The normal form introduced here is called *head normal form* (hnf), we formally define a transaction to be in hnf if:

– it is in $\{\boxdot\backslash T, \boxtimes, \overline{\boxtimes}, \boxast, \overline{\boxast}\}$, or
– it has the form $[]_{i\leq N}\, h_i \rightarrow T_i$ where each T_i is in hnf, or
– it has the form $\sqcap_{j\leq M} T_j$ where each T_j is in hnf.

From the above definition, the first item says that any terminated transaction is a kind of hnf. As for the second item, $[]_{i\leq N} T_i$ is a shorthand for $T_1 \,[]\, T_2 \,[]\, \ldots \,[]\, T_{N-1} \,[]\, T_N$ in which each branch T_i must be a guarded transaction in the form of $h \rightarrow T$ where T is in hnf too. We call this construct as *guarded choice*. If we allow $N = 1$, then a guarded transaction is a degenerate form of guarded choice. The internal choice $\sqcap_{j\leq M} T_j$ is an abbreviation for $T_1 \sqcap T_2 \sqcap \ldots \sqcap T_{M-1} \sqcap T_M$ which is intended to make a nondeterministic choice between a set of transactions. Particularly, each branch T_j can be a nondeterministic choice too.

The normal form has some elegant laws. Both $[]$ and $\sqcap$ satisfy associativity ($[]$-asso,$\sqcap$-asso), commutativity ($[]$-comm,$\sqcap$-comm) and idempotency ($[]$-idem,$\sqcap$-idem). In addition, $[]$ distributes through $\sqcap$ ($[]$-dist). Any pair of head normal forms are semantically equal if and only if one can be rewritten into the other by using these laws. Especially, while judging whether $\boxdot\backslash T_1$ is equivalent to $\boxdot\backslash T_2$, we need to further compare their installed compensations based on their own normal forms.

3.2 Algebraic Laws for Compensable Transactions

Now we transform a compensable transaction into a head normal form and investigate its relevant properties. We use $\mathcal{HF}(T)$ to represent its head normal form for a transaction T. For basic transactions, the transformation is direct and easy. For composite ones, we first suppose its components have already been in hnf, then define its transformation according to its semantics as designed. Particularly, if T is already in hnf, then $\mathcal{HF}(T) = T$, e.g. $\mathcal{HF}(\overline{\boxtimes}) = \overline{\boxtimes}$.

Basic Transactions. A transactional pair either starts by performing its forward flow or can be initially prevented from performing by force.

$$
\begin{aligned}
\mathcal{HF}(A \div B) &= \Lsh \rightarrow \overline{\boxtimes} \,[]\, A \rightarrow \mathcal{HF}(\mathit{Skip} \uparrow (B \div 0)) \\
\mathcal{HF}(A \div 0) &= \Lsh \rightarrow \overline{\boxtimes} \,[]\, A \rightarrow \mathcal{HF}(\mathit{Skip}) \\
\mathcal{HF}(A \div \Diamond) &= \Lsh \rightarrow \overline{\boxtimes} \,[]\, A \rightarrow \mathcal{HF}(\mathit{Skip} \uparrow \mathit{Abort})
\end{aligned}
$$

From the above definition, we see that after the forward behavior A finishes, we mark the remaining flow as *Skip* which actually does nothing and install its corresponding compensation. The compensation itself is regarded as a compensable transaction too, so we make use of $B \div 0$ instead of a simple activity B. In addition, no compensation is installed due to an empty compensation for $A \div 0$, and *Abort* is installed to denote an unacceptable compensation for $A \div \Diamond$.

As for *Skip*, it comes to successful completion instantly with an empty compensation installed. Both *Abort* and *Fail* indicate a failure but lead to different states. Moreover, all of them can be terminated by force initially.

$$
\begin{aligned}
\mathcal{HF}(\mathit{Skip}) &= \Lsh \rightarrow \overline{\boxtimes} \,[]\, \sharp \rightarrow \boxdot\backslash \mathit{Skip} \\
\mathcal{HF}(\mathit{Abort}) &= \Lsh \rightarrow \overline{\boxtimes} \,[]\, \Diamond \rightarrow \boxtimes \\
\mathcal{HF}(\mathit{Fail}) &= \Lsh \rightarrow \overline{\boxtimes} \,[]\, \Diamond \rightarrow \boxast
\end{aligned}
$$

Sequential Composition. If the first transaction is an internal choice, this composition is in this form too:

$$\frac{\mathcal{HF}(S) = \sqcap_{j \le M} \mathcal{HF}(S_j)}{\mathcal{HF}(S;T) = \sqcap_{j \le M} \mathcal{HF}(S_j;T)}$$

The following expression tells that any guarded activity except $\sharp$ is moved forward out of the sequential composition. Especially, the ready activity $\sharp$ is hidden for the successor decides how the composition terminates:

$$\frac{\mathcal{HF}(S) = [\!]_{i \le N}\, h_i \to \mathcal{HF}(S_i) \;[\!]\; \sharp \to \mathcal{HF}(S'),\ \forall h_i \neq \sharp}{\mathcal{HF}(S;T) = [\!]_{i \le N}\, h_i \to \mathcal{HF}(S_i;T) \;[\!]\; \mathcal{HF}(S';T)}$$

If the first transaction S terminates unsuccessfully, so does the whole transaction. Otherwise, the overall transaction is denoted as $T \uparrow S'$:

$$\frac{\mathcal{HF}(S) = S',\ S' \in \{\boxtimes, \overline{\boxtimes}, \boxast, \overline{\boxast}\}}{\mathcal{HF}(S;T) = S'} \qquad \frac{\mathcal{HF}(S) = \boxdot \backslash S'}{\mathcal{HF}(S;T) = \mathcal{HF}(T \uparrow S')}$$

Now, we define the semantics for the assistant construct $S \uparrow T$. When $\mathcal{HF}(S)$ is a kind of choice, each branch is associated with the fore-installed compensation:

$$\frac{\mathcal{HF}(S) = \sqcap_{j \le M} \mathcal{HF}(S_j)}{\mathcal{HF}(S \uparrow T) = \sqcap_{j \le M} \mathcal{HF}(S_j \uparrow T)} \qquad \frac{\mathcal{HF}(S) = [\!]_{i \le N}\, h_i \to \mathcal{HF}(S_i)}{\mathcal{HF}(S \uparrow T) = [\!]_{i \le N}\, h_i \to \mathcal{HF}(S_i \uparrow T)}$$

When S terminates successfully then its installed compensation S' is composed in front of the existing compensation T, which ensures that the compensations are accumulated in the reverse order to their original operational sequence:

$$\frac{\mathcal{HF}(S) = \boxdot \backslash S'}{\mathcal{HF}(S \uparrow T) = \boxdot \backslash (S';T)}$$

If S is failed to compensate, the installed compensation T is simply discarded and the whole transaction fails too. If S is aborted on failure or by force, the already installed compensation T will run to compensate for the completed part:

$$\frac{\mathcal{HF}(S) = S',\ S' \in \{\boxast, \overline{\boxast}\}}{\mathcal{HF}(S \uparrow T) = S'} \qquad \frac{\mathcal{HF}(S) = \boxtimes}{\mathcal{HF}(S \uparrow T) = \mathcal{HF}(\overleftarrow{T})} \qquad \frac{\mathcal{HF}(S) = \overline{\boxtimes}}{\mathcal{HF}(S \uparrow T) = \mathcal{HF}(\overleftrightarrow{T})}$$

As for $\overleftarrow{T}$, the forced activity $\Lsh$ is not allowed to happen since there is no reason to prevent compensation from undoing partial effects. Besides, the ready activity $\sharp$ in the compensating flow is not a signal of success, so we eliminate this activity here. In addition, a failure arising during the compensating flow will lead to fail immediately Further, we rename $\Diamond$ by $\overline{\Diamond}$ to explicitly denote an error occurring within a compensation:

$$\frac{\mathcal{HF}(T) = \sqcap_j \mathcal{HF}(T_j)}{\mathcal{HF}(\overleftarrow{T}) = \sqcap_j \mathcal{HF}(\overleftarrow{T_j})} \quad \frac{\mathcal{HF}(T) = [\!]_i\, k_i \to \mathcal{HF}(T_i) \;[\!]\; \Lsh\!\to S \;[\!]\; \sharp \to \mathcal{HF}(S_1) [\!] \Diamond \to \mathcal{HF}(S_2)}{\mathcal{HF}(\leftarrow\! T) = [\!]_i\, k_i \!\to\! \mathcal{HF}(\overleftarrow{T_i}) \;[\!]\; \mathcal{HF}(\overleftarrow{S_1}) \;[\!]\; \overline{\Diamond} \to \boxast}$$

For simplicity, we list all kinds of guards in the above expression. In fact, some guards cannot appear simultaneously. In t-calculus, the construct like $Skip \;[\!]\; T$ is not allowed, then a guarded choice with a guard $\sharp$ can only have this form: $\Lsh\!\to S \;[\!]\; \sharp \to T$. Since the forced activity in a compensating flow is inhibited, the resulted transaction is still in the head normal form.

A successful compensation means the partial forward flow is successfully compensated for. In this case, the compensation installed for compensation is ignored since it is no longer used. When the compensation aborts or fails, the partial effect is not removed completely and the whole transaction leads to fail instantly:

$$\frac{\mathcal{HF}(T) = \boxdot \backslash T'}{\mathcal{HF}(\overleftarrow{T}) = \boxtimes} \qquad \frac{\mathcal{HF}(T) = T', T' \in \{\boxtimes, \boxast\}}{\mathcal{HF}(\overleftarrow{T}) = \boxast}$$

Terminating a compensation by force is not allowed, so these is no need to consider the case that $\mathcal{HF}(T)$ is $\overline{\boxtimes}$ or $\overline{\boxast}$. The only difference between $\overleftrightarrow{T}$ and $\overleftarrow{T}$ shows below, where the ended transaction is a forced one, either $\overline{\boxtimes}$ or $\overline{\boxast}$.

$$\frac{\mathcal{HF}(T) = \boxdot \backslash T'}{\mathcal{HF}(\overleftrightarrow{T}) = \overline{\boxtimes}} \qquad \frac{\mathcal{HF}(T) = T', \ T' \in \{\boxtimes, \boxast\}}{\mathcal{HF}(\overleftrightarrow{T}) = \overline{\boxast}}$$

Sequential composition is associative and has $Skip$ as its left unit, $Abort, Fail$ as its left zeros.

Theorem 3.1 (Sequence)

(1) $Abort; T = Abort$ (2) $Fail; T = Fail$
(3) $Skip; T = T$ (4) $(T_1; T_2); T_3 = T_1; (T_2; T_3)$

We give the proof of (1) by computing the head normal forms of both sides according to the above definitions. The proofs for others may be tedious but techniques are similar.

$$\begin{aligned} \mathcal{HF}(Abort; T) &= \Lsh \rightarrow \mathcal{HF}(\overline{\boxtimes}; T) \mathbin{[\,]} \Diamond \rightarrow \mathcal{HF}(\boxtimes; T) \\ &= \Lsh \rightarrow \overline{\boxtimes} \mathbin{[\,]} \Diamond \rightarrow \boxtimes \\ &= \mathcal{HF}(Abort) \end{aligned}$$

Parallel Composition. With regard to the parallel composition, if at least one branch is in an internal choice, the whole transaction is in this form too:

$$\frac{\mathcal{HF}(S) = \sqcap_{j \le M} \mathcal{HF}(S_j), \ \mathcal{HF}(T) = \sqcap_{i \le N} \mathcal{HF}(T_i), \ M + N > 2}{\mathcal{HF}(S \,\|\, T) = \sqcap_{j \le M, i \le N} \mathcal{HF}(S_j \,\|\, T_i)}$$

If one branch has encountered some error, the other branch is forced to compensate instead of keeping on performing. Two errors from different branches just produce one error from the viewpoint of the environment. Terminating a whole transaction by force means both branches are willing to yield to this forced termination. Besides, when both branches are ready to succeed, the overall composition is ready too. Firstly, we redefine a parallel operator among the three activities $\{\Diamond, \Lsh, \sharp\}$ to describe how they synchronize in a parallel composition.

$$\Diamond \,\|\, \Lsh = \Diamond \qquad \Lsh \,\|\, \Diamond = \Diamond \qquad \Diamond \,\|\, \Diamond = \Diamond \qquad \Lsh \,\|\, \Lsh = \Lsh \qquad \sharp \,\|\, \sharp = \sharp$$

In the following, we suppose $k_i, l_j \in \Sigma \cup \{\overline{\Diamond}\}$ and $f_i, g_j \in \{\Diamond, \Lsh, \sharp\}$. For atomic activities, each parallel branch goes forward independently. As for other three activities, we only choose these pairs (f_i, g_j) which have a synchronization, i.e.,

Table 1. Conjunctions between terminated transactions

&	$\boxtimes$	$\boxast$	$\overline{\boxtimes}$	$\overline{\boxast}$
$\boxtimes$	$\boxtimes$			
$\boxast$	$\boxast$	$\boxast$		
$\overline{\boxtimes}$	$\boxtimes$	$\boxast$	$\overline{\boxtimes}$	
$\overline{\boxast}$	$\boxast$	$\boxast$	$\overline{\boxast}$	$\overline{\boxast}$

*	$\boxtimes$	$\boxast$	$\overline{\boxtimes}$	$\overline{\boxast}$
$\boxtimes$	$\boxtimes$			
$\boxast$	$\boxast$	$\boxast$		
$\overline{\boxtimes}$	$\overline{\boxtimes}$	$\boxast$	$\overline{\boxtimes}$	
$\overline{\boxast}$	$\overline{\boxast}$	$\boxast$	$\overline{\boxast}$	$\overline{\boxast}$

the value of $f_i \,\|\, g_j$ is defined. For instance, the pair $(\Diamond, \sharp)$ is not chosen to form a guard since $\Diamond \,\|\, \sharp$ is undefined:

$$\frac{\mathcal{HF}(S) = (\Box_i\, k_i \rightarrow \mathcal{HF}(S_i)) \;\Box\; (\Box_i\, f_i \rightarrow \mathcal{HF}(S_i')),\quad \mathcal{HF}(T) = (\Box_j\, l_j \rightarrow \mathcal{HF}(T_j)) \;\Box\; (\Box_j\, g_j \rightarrow \mathcal{HF}(T_j'))}{\mathcal{HF}(S \,\|\, T) = (\Box_i\, k_i \rightarrow \mathcal{HF}(S_i \,\|\, T)) \;\Box\; (\Box_j\, l_j \rightarrow \mathcal{HF}(S \,\|\, T_j)) \;\Box\; (\Box_{i,j}\, f_i \,\|\, g_j \rightarrow \mathcal{HF}(S_i' \,\|\, T_j'))}$$

Only when both branches succeed, the whole composition is successful and the installed compensations for two branches are constructed in parallel:

$$\frac{\mathcal{HF}(S) = \boxdot\backslash S',\ \mathcal{HF}(T) = \boxdot\backslash T'}{\mathcal{HF}(S \,\|\, T) = \boxdot\backslash(S' \,\|\, T')}$$

If one branch leads to abort or fail, the other one is forced to terminate. Thus, we need not to consider the case that one branch succeeds but another one not. In this case, the terminal state of the parallel composition is defined as follows:

$$\frac{\mathcal{HF}(S) = S',\ \mathcal{HF}(T) = T',\ \{S', T'\} \subset \{\boxtimes, \overline{\boxtimes}, \boxast, \overline{\boxast}\}}{\mathcal{HF}(S \,\|\, T) = S' \& T'}$$

The commutative operator & is defined in Table 1. It says that if one branch is failed (i.e., it ends in $\boxast$), the whole composition actually fails in spite of the state of the other branch. Besides, when both branches are forced to terminate, the whole transaction is terminated by force too.

Parallel composition is commutative, associative and has *Skip* as its unit.

Theorem 3.2 (Parallel)

$$(1)\ S \,\|\, T = T \,\|\, S \qquad (2)\ Skip \,\|\, T = T \qquad (3)\ (T_1 \,\|\, T_2) \,\|\, T_3 = T_1 \,\|\, (T_2 \,\|\, T_3)$$

Choice. For external choice, the whole composition is a guarded choice. Especially, if one branch has the form of $\sqcap_i T_i$, we move $\sqcap$ out of the outside by using the law $\Box$-dist and the whole composition is guaranteed in hnf. As for internal choice, which branch is chosen is unpredictable:

$$\mathcal{HF}(S \;\Box\; T) = \mathcal{HF}(S) \;\Box\; \mathcal{HF}(T) \qquad \mathcal{HF}(S \sqcap T) = \mathcal{HF}(S) \sqcap \mathcal{HF}(T)$$

With regard to speculative choice, it resolves the internal choice at first:

$$\frac{\mathcal{HF}(S) = \sqcap_{j \le M} \mathcal{HF}(S_j),\ \mathcal{HF}(T) = \sqcap_{i \le N} \mathcal{HF}(T_i),\ M + N > 2}{\mathcal{HF}(S \otimes T) = \sqcap_{j \le M, i \le N} \mathcal{HF}(S_j \otimes T_i)}$$

In speculative choice, two branches are performing in parallel and the decision of choice is delayed until one branch succeeds. Then, when one branch shows the tendency to succeed, the other one is forced to terminate. In this case, the developer should guarantee that the forcibly terminated branch cannot fail but always abort. Otherwise, the successful branch should also be compensated due to an inconsistent state. Here we enforce the requirement that any branch in a speculative choice cannot fail so that the whole composition always ensures a positive response to the environment. Same as parallel composition, both branches should be willing to yield to a forced termination. Consequently, the two events $\sharp$ and $\Lsh$ must synchronize in some way. We redefine the operator $\otimes$ among the two activities to describe how they interact within a speculative choice.

$$\sharp \otimes \Lsh = \sharp \qquad \Lsh \otimes \sharp = \sharp \qquad \Lsh \otimes \Lsh = \Lsh$$

In the following expression, we suppose $k_i, l_j \in \Sigma \cup \{\overline{\Diamond}\}$ and $f_i, g_j \in \{\Lsh, \sharp\}$. Each branch goes forward independently while performing an atomic activity. Any pair (f_i, g_j) which has a synchronization will be chosen to form a guard. Especially, the pair $(\sharp, \sharp)$ cannot be selected as $\sharp \otimes \sharp$ is undefined. Besides, the error activity $\Diamond$ from one branch is unseen by the environment, since the other branch still has the chance to fulfil the same business goal:

$$\frac{\begin{array}{c}\mathcal{HF}(S) = ([\!]_i\, k_i \rightarrow \mathcal{HF}(S_i))\ [\!]\ ([\!]_i\, f_i \rightarrow \mathcal{HF}(S_i'))\ [\!]\ (\Diamond \rightarrow \mathcal{HF}(S')),\\ \mathcal{HF}(T) = ([\!]_j\, l_j \rightarrow \mathcal{HF}(T_j))\ [\!]\ ([\!]_j\, g_j \rightarrow \mathcal{HF}(T_j'))\ [\!]\ (\Diamond \rightarrow \mathcal{HF}(T'))\end{array}}{\begin{array}{l}\mathcal{HF}(S \otimes T) = ([\!]_i\, k_i \rightarrow \mathcal{HF}(S_i \otimes T))\ [\!]\ ([\!]_j\, l_j \rightarrow \mathcal{HF}(S \otimes T_j))\\ \qquad\qquad [\!]\ ([\!]_{i,j}\, f_i \otimes g_j \rightarrow \mathcal{HF}(S_i' \backslash\!\backslash T_j'))\ [\!]\ \mathcal{HF}(S' \backslash\!\backslash T)\ [\!]\ \mathcal{HF}(S \backslash\!\backslash T')\end{array}}$$

Notice that, after one of the three guards $\{\Diamond, \Lsh, \sharp\}$ emerges, at least one branch has started its compensating flow. So we introduce the intermediate construct $S \backslash\!\backslash T$ to describe this kind of business flow, which reflects how speculative choice works when at most one branch moves forward. Likewise, this new construct will first resolve the nondeterministic choice. However, it does not have synchronous execution of any activities.

$$\frac{\mathcal{HF}(S) = \sqcap_{j \le M} \mathcal{HF}(S_j),\ \mathcal{HF}(T) = \sqcap_{i \le N} \mathcal{HF}(T_i),\ M + N > 2}{\mathcal{HF}(S \backslash\!\backslash T) = \sqcap_{j \le M, i \le N} \mathcal{HF}(S_j \backslash\!\backslash T_i)}$$

$$\frac{\mathcal{HF}(S) = [\!]_{i \le M}\, h_i \rightarrow \mathcal{HF}(S_i),\ \mathcal{HF}(T) = [\!]_{j \le N}\, l_j \rightarrow \mathcal{HF}(T_j)}{\mathcal{HF}(S \backslash\!\backslash T) = ([\!]_{i \le M}\, h_i \rightarrow \mathcal{HF}(S_i \backslash\!\backslash T))\ [\!]\ ([\!]_{j \le N}\, l_j \rightarrow \mathcal{HF}(S \backslash\!\backslash T_j))}$$

When one branch succeeds, the whole composition is regarded as success. Moreover, the compensation installed for the successful branch is preserved:

$$\frac{\mathcal{HF}(S) = \boxdot \backslash S',\ \mathcal{HF}(T) = T' \in \{\boxtimes, \overline{\boxtimes}\}}{\mathcal{HF}(S \backslash\!\backslash T) = \boxdot \backslash S'} \qquad \frac{\mathcal{HF}(S) = S' \in \{\boxtimes, \overline{\boxtimes}\},\ \mathcal{HF}(T) = \boxdot \backslash T'}{\mathcal{HF}(S \backslash\!\backslash T) = \boxdot \backslash T'}$$

Both branches may terminate abnormally (i.e., aborts or fails), and the result of the whole transaction is defined as follows:

$$\frac{\mathcal{HF}(S) = S',\ \mathcal{HF}(T) = T',\ \{S', T'\} \subset \{\boxtimes, \overline{\boxtimes}, \boxast, \overline{\boxast}\}}{\mathcal{HF}(S \,\|\, T) = S' * T'}$$

The commutative operator $*$ is defined in Table 1. In speculative choice, when one branch has aborted, the whole composition still has the chance to succeed if another branch terminates successfully. Thus, when one branch is aborted on failure (i.e., it ends in $\boxtimes$) and the other is forcibly terminated (i.e., it either ends in $\overline{\boxtimes}$ or $\overline{\boxast}$), the whole transaction is considered as forced termination. This point reflects the difference between the two operators $*$ and $\&$.

Speculative choice is commutative, associative and has *Abort* as its unit.

Theorem 3.3 (Speculative Choice)

$$(1)\ S \otimes T = T \otimes S \qquad (2)\ \mathit{Abort} \otimes T = T \qquad (3)\ (T_1 \otimes T_2) \otimes T_3 = T_1 \otimes (T_2 \otimes T_3)$$

Exception Handling. Firstly, we focus on the backward handling $S \trianglerighteq T$. The handler T keeps invariant while the first transaction S does not terminate:

$$\frac{\mathcal{HF}(S) = \sqcap_{j \le M} \mathcal{HF}(S_j)}{\mathcal{HF}(S \trianglerighteq T) = \sqcap_{j \le M} \mathcal{HF}(S_j \trianglerighteq T)} \qquad \frac{\mathcal{HF}(S) = \|_{i \le N}\, h_i \rightarrow \mathcal{HF}(S_i)}{\mathcal{HF}(S \trianglerighteq T) = \|_{i \le N}\, h_i \rightarrow \mathcal{HF}(S_i \trianglerighteq T)}$$

When the first transaction fails either automatically or forcibly, the backward hander is activated to do the untouched compensation so as to remove all partial effects:

$$\frac{\mathcal{HF}(S) = \boxast}{\mathcal{HF}(S \trianglerighteq T) = \mathcal{HF}(\overleftarrow{T})} \qquad \frac{\mathcal{HF}(S) = \overline{\boxast}}{\mathcal{HF}(S \trianglerighteq T) = \mathcal{HF}(\overleftrightarrow{T})}$$

If the first transaction succeeds or aborts, the handler is simply abandoned:

$$\frac{\mathcal{HF}(S) = \boxdot \backslash S'}{\mathcal{HF}(S \trianglerighteq T) = \boxdot \backslash S'} \qquad \frac{\mathcal{HF}(S) = S',\ S' \in \{\boxtimes, \overline{\boxtimes}\}}{\mathcal{HF}(S \trianglerighteq T) = S'}$$

Regarding the forward handling $S \rhd T$, the error activity $\Diamond$ occurring within the first transaction S is unobservable by the environment, for the forward handler T may recover from this error and terminate successfully at last:

$$\frac{\mathcal{HF}(S) = \sqcap_j \mathcal{HF}(S_j)}{\mathcal{HF}(S \rhd T) = \sqcap_j \mathcal{HF}(S_j \rhd T)} \qquad \frac{\mathcal{HF}(S) = \|_i\, h_i \rightarrow \mathcal{HF}(S_i) \ \| \ \Diamond \rightarrow \mathcal{HF}(S'),\ \forall h_i \neq \Diamond}{\mathcal{HF}(S \rhd T) = \|_i\, h_i \rightarrow \mathcal{HF}(S_i \rhd T) \ \| \ \mathcal{HF}(S' \rhd T)}$$

Different from backward handling, the forward handler T is enabled only when S fails on failure not by force. In particular, if S tends to abort, the activity $\Diamond$ should take place in advance so as to notify its parallel siblings if they exist:

$$\frac{\mathcal{HF}(S) = \boxast}{\mathcal{HF}(S \rhd T) = \mathcal{HF}(T)} \qquad \frac{\mathcal{HF}(S) = S',\ S' \in \{\boxdot \backslash S'', \overline{\boxtimes}, \overline{\boxast}\}}{\mathcal{HF}(S \rhd T) = S'} \qquad \frac{\mathcal{HF}(S) = \boxtimes}{\mathcal{HF}(S \rhd T) = \Diamond \rightarrow \boxtimes}$$

Exception handling has *Skip* and *Abort* as its left zeros. Below, we use $\odot$ to stand for $\trianglerighteq$ or $\rhd$. Property (3) says that the handler just monitors the area which may raise failures, provided that S_1 does not fail. The last three properties distinguish backward handling from forward handling. The difference is backward handler inhibits the latter execution while the forward handler does not. Besides, forward handling is associative whereas backward handling is not.

Theorem 3.4 (Exception Handling)

$$\begin{array}{ll} (1)\ \mathit{Skip} \odot T = \mathit{Skip} & (2)\ \mathit{Abort} \odot T = \mathit{Abort} \\ (3)\ (S_1; S_2) \odot T = S_1; (S_2 \odot T) & (4)\ (\mathit{Fail} \trianglerighteq S); T = \mathit{Fail} \trianglerighteq S \\ (5)\ (\mathit{Fail} \rhd S); T = \mathit{Fail} \rhd (S; T) & (6)\ (T_1 \rhd T_2) \rhd T_3 = T_1 \rhd (T_2 \rhd T_3) \end{array}$$

Alternative Forwarding. In the construct of $S \rightsquigarrow T$, when S encounters a failure, this failure is unobservable as its alternative T may possibly remedy this error. Anyway, its algebraic semantics is quite similar to forward handling:

$$\frac{\mathcal{HF}(S) = \sqcap_j \mathcal{HF}(S_j)}{\mathcal{HF}(S \rightsquigarrow T) = \sqcap_j \mathcal{HF}(S_j \rightsquigarrow T)} \quad \frac{\mathcal{HF}(S) = [\!]_i\, h_i \rightarrow \mathcal{HF}(S_i) \,[\!]\, \Diamond \rightarrow \mathcal{HF}(S'),\, \forall h_i \neq \Diamond}{\mathcal{HF}(S \rightsquigarrow T) = [\!]_i\, h_i \rightarrow \mathcal{HF}(S_i \rightsquigarrow T) \,[\!]\, \mathcal{HF}(S' \rightsquigarrow T)}$$

Analogously, the alternative T is activated only when S aborts on failure. If S tends to fail, the error activity $\Diamond$ should take place in advance so as to notify its parallel siblings if they exist:

$$\frac{\mathcal{HF}(S) = \boxtimes}{\mathcal{HF}(S \rightsquigarrow T) = \mathcal{HF}(T)} \quad \frac{\mathcal{HF}(S) = S',\, S' \in \{\boxdot \backslash S'', \overline{\boxtimes}, \overline{\boxast}\}}{\mathcal{HF}(S \rightsquigarrow T) = S'} \quad \frac{\mathcal{HF}(S) = \boxast}{\mathcal{HF}(S \rightsquigarrow T) = \Diamond \rightarrow \boxast}$$

Alternative forwarding is associative and has $Skip$ and $Fail$ as its left zeros.

Theorem 3.5 (Alternative Forwarding)

(1) $Skip \rightsquigarrow T = Skip$ (2) $Fail \rightsquigarrow T = Fail$ (3) $(T_1 \rightsquigarrow T_2) \rightsquigarrow T_3 = T_1 \rightsquigarrow (T_2 \rightsquigarrow T_3)$

Programmable Compensation. The newly programmed compensation T is simply attached for possibly later installation while S does not terminate:

$$\frac{\mathcal{HF}(S) = \sqcap_{j \le M} \mathcal{HF}(S_j)}{\mathcal{HF}(S \ast T) = \sqcap_{j \le M} \mathcal{HF}(S_j \ast T)} \quad \frac{\mathcal{HF}(S) = [\!]_{i \le N}\, h_i \rightarrow \mathcal{HF}(S_i)}{\mathcal{HF}(S \ast T) = [\!]_{i \le N}\, h_i \rightarrow \mathcal{HF}(S_i \ast T)}$$

When the first transaction S terminates successfully, the original compensation is thrown away and the new compensation T is installed instead. If the first transaction aborts or fails, the whole transaction terminates abnormally without any compensation installed:

$$\frac{\mathcal{HF}(S) = \boxdot \backslash S'}{\mathcal{HF}(S \ast T) = \boxdot \backslash T} \quad \frac{\mathcal{HF}(S) = S',\, S' \in \{\boxtimes, \overline{\boxtimes}, \boxast, \overline{\boxast}\}}{\mathcal{HF}(S \ast T) = S'}$$

Programmable compensation has $Abort$ and $Fail$ as its left zeros, and several other interesting properties shown below.

Theorem 3.6 (Programmable Compensation)

$(1) Abort \ast T = Abort$ $(2) Fail \ast T = Fail$
$(3) (T_1 \ast T_2) \ast T_3 = T_1 \ast T_3$ $(4) T_1 \ast (T_2 \ast T_3) = T_1 \ast T_2$
$(5) (T_1 \odot T_2) \ast T_3 = (T_1 \ast T_3) \odot (T_2 \ast T_3)$ $(6) (T_1 \rightsquigarrow T_2) \ast T_3 = (T_1 \ast T_3) \rightsquigarrow (T_2 \ast T_3)$
$(7) (T_1 \ast T_1'); (T_2 \ast T_2') = (T_1; T_2) \ast (T_2'; T_1')$ $(8) (T_1 \ast T_1') \parallel (T_2 \ast T_2') = (T_1 \parallel T_2) \ast (T_1' \parallel T_2')$

Properties (3) says that the new compensation always replaces the older one, while (4) tells that compensations produced by compensations make no effect. Programmable compensation distributes right through exception handling and alternative forwarding respectively, shown as (5) and (6). In addition, assuming T_1, T_2 terminate successfully without raising errors or encountering forced termination, the properties (7),(8) show the installation order of compensations according to the sequential or parallel compositions.

Transactional Block. A transactional block $\{T\}$ stands for a complete business transaction. It masks forced termination in the forward flow:

$$\frac{\mathcal{HF}(T) = \sqcap_{j \le M} \mathcal{HF}(T_j)}{\mathcal{HF}(\{T\}) = \sqcap_{j \le M} \mathcal{HF}(\{T_j\})} \qquad \frac{\mathcal{HF}(T) = [\!]_{i \le N}\, h_i \to \mathcal{HF}(T_i) \;[\!]\; \daleth \to \mathcal{HF}(T'), \forall h_i \ne \daleth}{\mathcal{HF}(\{T\}) = [\!]_{i \le N}\, h_i \to \mathcal{HF}(\{T_i\})}$$

It discards the installed compensation when the inner compensable transaction T succeeds. Otherwise, it terminates unsuccessfully like T does:

$$\frac{\mathcal{HF}(T) = \boxdot \backslash T'}{\mathcal{HF}(\{T\}) = \boxdot \backslash Skip} \qquad \frac{\mathcal{HF}(T) = T', T' \in \{\boxtimes, \boxast\}}{\mathcal{HF}(\{T\}) = T'}$$

Notice that the inner transaction cannot be terminated by force, since the forced activity $\daleth$ has been forbidden to occur.

4 Correspondence with Operational Semantics

The traditional way of defining an operational semantics is to provide a set of individual transition steps directly. In contrast to the standard style, this section derives the operational semantics from the given algebraic semantics. This work helps to relate two different semantical models for a particular language, which guarantees the consistency between different theories to some extent.

The operational semantics for t-calculus describes the behavior of compensable transactions in terms of transition rules using the approach of Plotkin [4]:

$$T \xrightarrow{\alpha} T'$$

It says that the transaction T turns to T' by performing an event α. Here, $\alpha \in \Sigma \cup \{\Diamond, \overline{\Diamond}, \sharp, \daleth, \tau\} \cup \Delta$, where τ denotes a silent or internal event and Δ is a set of five terminated events $\{\checkmark, !, \dagger, \overline{!}, \overline{\dagger}\}$. $\checkmark$ stands for successful completion (success), ! for successful compensation after a failure (abort), $\dagger$ for partial compensation after a failure (fail). $\overline{!}$ for successful compensation by forced termination (forced abort), and $\overline{\dagger}$ for partial compensation by forced termination (forced fail). These terminated events correspond to the terminated transactions respectively.

Especially, when a compensable transaction performs $\checkmark$, it converts to another transaction representing its installed compensation. However, when a compensable transaction performs some other terminal events, it turns to a dormant transaction denoted as $Null$ which has no further transition rules. In order to derive the operational semantics from the fore-mentioned algebraic semantics, we propose a derivation strategy based on normal forms.

Definition 4.1 (Derivation Strategy)

(1) If $\mathcal{HF}(T) = \boxdot \backslash T'$, then $T \xrightarrow{\checkmark} T'$
(2) If $\mathcal{HF}(T) = \boxtimes$, then $T \xrightarrow{!} Null$
(3) If $\mathcal{HF}(T) = \overline{\boxtimes}$, then $T \xrightarrow{\overline{!}} Null$
(4) If $\mathcal{HF}(T) = \boxast$, then $T \xrightarrow{\dagger} Null$
(5) If $\mathcal{HF}(T) = \overline{\boxast}$, then $T \xrightarrow{\overline{\dagger}} Null$
(6) If $\mathcal{HF}(T) = [\!]_{i \le N}\, h_i \to \mathcal{HF}(T_i)$, then $T \xrightarrow{h_i} T_i$
(7) If $\mathcal{HF}(T) = \sqcap_{j \le M} \mathcal{HF}(T_j)$, then $T \xrightarrow{\tau} T_j$
(8) If $\mathcal{HF}(T) = \mathcal{HF}(S)$, then $T \xrightarrow{\tau} S$

The last item says that if two syntactically different transactions have the same normal forms, the transition label is a silent event τ which denotes an underlying transformation on syntactic structures. Based on the fore-defined algebraic semantics and the given derivation strategy, deriving a complete operational semantic model for t-calculus is direct and apparent. For demonstration, we simply list some transition rules for several compensable transactions. With regard to basic transactions, their operational semantics is easy to obtain:

$$A \div B \xrightarrow{\Lsh} \overline{\boxtimes} \qquad A \div B \xrightarrow{A} Skip \uparrow (B \div 0)$$
$$Abort \xrightarrow{\Lsh} \overline{\boxtimes} \qquad Abort \xrightarrow{\Diamond} \boxtimes$$

As for composite transactions, here we investigate the operational semantics for alternative forwarding which is derived from its algebraic semantics.

$$\frac{S \xrightarrow{a} S',\ a \in \Sigma \cup \{\overline{\Diamond}, \sharp, \Lsh, \tau\}}{S \rightsquigarrow T \xrightarrow{a} S' \rightsquigarrow T} \qquad \frac{S \xrightarrow{\Diamond} S'}{S \rightsquigarrow T \xrightarrow{\tau} S' \rightsquigarrow T} \qquad \frac{S \xrightarrow{\checkmark} S'}{S \rightsquigarrow T \xrightarrow{\checkmark} S'}$$

$$\frac{S \xrightarrow{!} Null}{S \rightsquigarrow T \xrightarrow{\tau} T} \qquad \frac{S \xrightarrow{\dagger} Null}{S \rightsquigarrow T \xrightarrow{\Diamond} \circledast} \qquad \frac{S \xrightarrow{\nu} Null,\ \nu \in \{\overline{!}, \overline{\dagger}\}}{S \rightsquigarrow T \xrightarrow{\nu} Null}$$

5 Related Work

Most languages proposed for web services composition (e.g., WSFL, XLANG, BPEL4WS and WSCDL) have the corresponding constructs to deal with long running transactions. Nevertheless, these proposals do not provide a formal semantics, whose informal descriptions easily lead to ambiguous understanding. In our previous works [5,6,7,8,9], we have offered a theoretical foundation for the two representative proposals: BPEL and WSCDL. Especially, the transactional mechanisms adopted by these languages are carefully studied and formalized.

Recently, some researchers have devised new process calculi from scratch for modeling long-running transactions based on the concept of compensation. The representatives of this kind are StAC [10,11], cCSP [12,13] and Sagas calculi [14]. StAC is a language taking inspiration from process algebras like CCS and CSP, together equipped with exception and compensation handling mechanisms. It provides two explicit operators (reverse and accept) for activating or discarding installed compensations respectively, which inhibits a clean compositional semantics and makes the reasoning more difficult. Considering this, cCSP is then designed as a subset of StAC, which supports automatic compensating and leads to a neater compositional semantics. As for Sagas calculi, it provides a richer set of operators to model robust business transactions. Particularly, in terms of parallel composition, Sagas calculi gives a different explanation from cCSP. A detailed comparison can be found in [15].

Our work has been inspired by Sagas Calculi and cCSP. We have introduced several transactional operators recommended by Sagas calculi into our transactional language. Different from Sagas Calculi and cCSP, we treat compensations as compensable transactions too, through which we provide a uniform manner to manage the forward flow and compensating flow. In addition, properties for compensable transactions are not given by assumption but guaranteed to be justified by the pre-defined algebraic semantics.

6 Conclusion

The transactional language *t*-calculus aims to precisely model long-running business flow in terms of compensable transactions. In order to take care of interrupt handling among concurrent flows, the technique of forced termination is introduced to handle this kind of requirement. By working with an algebraic semantics, we provide a clear meaning for kinds of transactional operators. Since each compensable transaction can be expressed as a kind of head normal form, it is easy for us to justify a set of equational properties for compensable transactions by computing the respective normal forms for both sides. Further, we have established a correspondence between the algebraic semantics and operational semantics for this transactional language. Thus, the operational model does not need to set up from scratch but directly from the algebraic model based on a proposed derivation strategy. This work provides a basis for optimization and implementation of a transactional language with compensations.

References

1. Garcia-Molina, H., Salem, K.: Sagas. In: Proc. of ACM SIGMOD'87, pp. 249–259. ACM Press, New York (1987)
2. Li, J., Zhu, H., Pu, G., He, J.: Looking into compensable transactions. In: SEW-31, IEEE Computer Society Press, Los Alamitos (to appear, 2007)
3. Hoare, C.A.R., He, J.: Unifying Theories of Programming. Prentice-Hall, Englewood Cliffs (1998)
4. Plotkin, G.D.: A structural approach to operational semantics. Technical report, Aarhus University (1981)
5. Pu, G., Zhu, H., Qiu, Z., Wang, S., Zhao, X., He, J.: Theoretical foundations of scope-based compensable flow languange for web service. In: Gorrieri, R., Wehrheim, H. (eds.) FMOODS 2006. LNCS, vol. 4037, pp. 251–266. Springer, Heidelberg (2006)
6. Zhu, H., Pu, G., He, J.: A detational approach to scope-based compensable flow language for web services. In: Proc. of ASIAN'06 (2006)
7. He, J., Zhu, H., Pu, G.: A model for BPEL-like languages. Frontiers of Computer Science in China (2006)
8. Li, J., He, J., Pu, G., Zhu, H.: Towards the semantics for web service choreography description language. In: Liu, Z., He, J. (eds.) ICFEM 2006. LNCS, vol. 4260, pp. 246–263. Springer, Heidelberg (2006)
9. Li, J., He, J., Zhu, H., Pu, G.: Modeling and verifying web services choreography using process algebra. In: SEW-31, IEEE Computer Society Press, Los Alamitos (to appear, 2007)
10. Butler, M., Ferreira, C.: A process compensation language. In: Grieskamp, W., Santen, T., Stoddart, B. (eds.) IFM 2000. LNCS, vol. 1945, pp. 61–76. Springer, Heidelberg (2000)

11. Butler, M., Ferreira, C.: An operational semantics for StAC, a language for modelling long-running business transactions. In: De Nicola, R., Ferrari, G.L., Meredith, G. (eds.) COORDINATION 2004. LNCS, vol. 2949, pp. 87–104. Springer, Heidelberg (2004)
12. Butler, M., Hoare, T., Ferreira, C.: A trace semantics for long-running transaction. In: Abdallah, A.E., Jones, C.B., Sanders, J.W. (eds.) CSP 2004. LNCS, vol. 3525, pp. 133–150. Springer, Heidelberg (2005)
13. Butler, M., Ripon, S.: Executable semantics for compensating CSP. In: Bravetti, M., Kloul, L., Zavattaro, G. (eds.) Formal Techniques for Computer Systems and Business Processes. LNCS, vol. 3670, pp. 243–256. Springer, Heidelberg (2005)
14. Bruni, R., Melgratti, H., Montanari, U.: Theoretical foundations for compensations in flow composition languages. In: POPL'05, pp. 209–220. ACM Press, New York (2005)
15. Bruni, R., Butler, M., Ferreira, C., Hoare, T., Melgratti, H., Montanari, U.: Comparing two approaches to compensable flow composition. In: Abadi, M., de Alfaro, L. (eds.) CONCUR 2005. LNCS, vol. 3653, pp. 383–397. Springer, Heidelberg (2005)

Axiomatizing Extended Temporal Logic Fragments Via Instantiation*

Wanwei Liu, Ji Wang, Wei Dong, and Huowang Chen

National Laboratory of Parallel and Distributed Processing, China
{wwliu,wj,wdong,hwchen}@nudt.edu.cn

Abstract. ETLs are temporal logics employing ω-automata as temporal connectives. This paper presents sound and complete axiom systems for ETL_l, ETL_f, and ETL_r, respectively. Axioms and rules reflecting temporal behaviors of looping, finite and repeating automaton connectives are provided. Moreover, by encoding temporal operators into automaton connectives and instantiating the axioms and rules relating to automaton connectives, one may derive axiom systems for given ETL fragments.

1 Introduction

Temporal logics have been frequently used as property specification languages in verification of reactive and concurrent systems. In the broad sense, temporal logics can be categorized into linear time ones and branching time ones. As indicated by Vardi [Var01], temporal logics in linear framework have several advantages — such as can be more naturally expressed and have a better compositionality.

There are two major ways to make temporal logics in linear framework to be as expressive as ω-regular languages. One possible approach is to employ second order qualifiers or fixpoint operators, like QPTL, [PVW87], linear μ-calculus [BB87] and S1S; the other approach is to enrich the temporal connectives, as done in ETL (Extended Temporal Logic, cf. [Wol83,WVS83,VW94]).

The temporal logics achieved by the second approach have an infinite family of temporal operators. In fact, a spectrum of temporal logics will be obtained by incorporating different temporal connectives, and each of them can be viewed as a fragment (sub logic) of ETL. These fragments provide the rich choices to make a proper tradeoff between the expressiveness and complexity in defining property specifications.

Axiomatization might lead people into better understanding of the logics. In this paper, we present three axiom systems, namely $\mathscr{L}$,$\mathscr{F}$,$\mathscr{R}$, respectively for ETL_l, ETL_f and ETL_r.

* This research is supported by the National Natural Science Foundation of China under Grant No.60233020, 90612009, 60673118; the National High-Tech Research and Development Plan of China under Grant No.2006AA01Z178, 2006AA01Z429; the National Grand Fundamental Research 973 Program of China under Grant No.2005CB321802; Program for New Century Excellent Talents in University under Grant No.NCET-04-0996.

C.B. Jones, Z. Liu, J. Woodcock (Eds.): ICTAC 2007, LNCS 4711, pp. 322–336, 2007.

Though ETLs are known to have clear automaton decision procedures (cf. [VW94,Pit00]), we reveal an important feature of ETL axiom systems: one may derive a sound and complete axiom system for a given ETL fragment from them.

Axiomatizations of other temporal logics having the same expressive power to ω-regular languages, e.g. linear μ-calculus [Kai97], QPTL [KP95,FR03], usually give the characterization of second order operators. In comparison, ETL axiom systems involve axioms and rules reflecting behaviors of temporal connectives. We believe that using explicit temporal connectives might yield a more intuitive way for doing specification.

Related work. The earliest axiomatization for ETL can be dated back to Wolper's graceful axiom system for temporal logic that uses ω-grammar as operators [Wol83]. ω-grammar operators can be roughly viewed as looping acceptance automaton connectives. In this paper, axioms corresponding to ω-regular operators that using finite or repeating conditions are also considered. Kaivola [Kai98] presented a sound and complete deductive system for extended computation tree logic. This logic is acquired form CTL* by adding μ operator to the pure path formulas. Therefore the axioms and rules are specialized for the fixed point operator and path qualifiers.

2 Automata on ω-Words and Extended Temporal Logic

Given a finite alphabet Σ, an *ω-word* over Σ is an infinite sequence $w_0w_1\cdots$, where $w_i \in \Sigma$ for each $i \in \mathbb{N}$.

A *(nondeterministic) automaton on ω-words* is a tuple $\mathcal{A} = \langle \Sigma, Q, \delta, Q_0, F\rangle$ where: Σ is a finite *alphabet*; Q is a finite set of *states*; $\delta : Q \times \Sigma \to 2^Q$ is the *transition function*; $Q_0 \subseteq Q$ is a set of *initial states*; $F \subseteq Q$ is a set of *final states.*

A *run* (resp. *infinite run*) of $\mathcal{A}$ over an ω-word $w_0w_1\dots$ is an infinite (resp. finite) sequence $\sigma = s_0s_1\dots$, (resp. $\sigma = s_0s_1\dots s_k$) where $s_0 \in S_0$, and $s_{i+1} \in \delta(s_i, w_i)$.

Different types of automata can be defined depending on the acceptance conditions. For *looping acceptance automata*, any run is accepting. For *finite acceptance automata*, a finite run $\sigma = s_0s_1\dots s_k$ is accepting iff $s_k \in F$. For *repeating acceptance automata* (Büchi automata), a run $\sigma = s_0s_1\dots$ is accepting iff there are infinitely many i's such that $s_i \in F$.

An ω-word is *accepted* by $\mathcal{A}$ if there is an accepting run (when the acceptance condition is looping or repeating) or an accepting finite run (when the acceptance condition is finite) of $\mathcal{A}$ over it. We denote by $\mathcal{L}(\mathcal{A})$ the set of ω-words accepted by $\mathcal{A}$.

Fix a set of atomic propositions AP, formulas of ETL (Extended Temporal Logic) can be defined as follows.

- $\top$, $\bot$ and each $p \in AP$ are formulas.
- If φ is a formula then both $\neg\varphi$ and $\bigcirc\varphi$ are formulas.

- If φ_1 and φ_2 are formulas then both $\varphi_1 \wedge \varphi_2$ and $\varphi_1 \vee \varphi_2$ are formulas.
- If $\mathcal{A}$ is an automaton with the alphabet $\Sigma = \{a_1, \ldots, a_n\}$ and $\varphi_1, \ldots, \varphi_n$ are formulas, then $\mathcal{A}(\varphi_1, \ldots, \varphi_n)$ is also a formula.

$\top, \bot$, propositions and their negations are said to be *literals*.

Remark 1. ETLs using automaton connectives with finite, looping and repeating acceptance conditions are named ETL_f, ETL_l and ETL_r, respectively. Vardi and Wolper's original definition does not involve the *nexttime* operator $\bigcirc$. We explicitly demand it because tableaux can be defined succinctly with this operator, and this does not change the essence of the logic.

A *structure* π is an ω-word over the alphabet 2^{AP}. Let $\pi(i)$ be the i-th letter of π, then *satisfaction* of a formula φ at position i of a structure π, denoted $(\pi, i) \models \varphi$, is defined inductively as follows.

- $(\pi, i) \models \top$, for any structure π and i; $(\pi, i) \not\models \bot$, for any structure π and i.
- For each $p \in AP$, $(\pi, i) \models p$ iff $p \in \pi(i)$.
- $(\pi, i) \models \neg\varphi$ iff $(\pi, i) \not\models \varphi$; $(\pi, i) \models \bigcirc\varphi$ iff $(\pi, i+1) \models \varphi$.
- $(\pi, i) \models \varphi_1 \wedge \varphi_2$ iff both $(\pi, i) \models \varphi_1$ and $(\pi, i) \models \varphi_2$; $(\pi, i) \models \varphi_1 \vee \varphi_2$ iff either $(\pi, i) \models \varphi_1$ or $(\pi, i) \models \varphi_2$.
- Let $\mathcal{A} = \langle\{a_1, \ldots, a_n\}, Q, \delta, Q_0, F\rangle$, $(\pi, i) \models \mathcal{A}(\varphi_1, \ldots, \varphi_n)$ iff when the acceptance type of $\mathcal{A}$ is looping or repeating (resp. finite), we require an accepting run (resp. finite accepting run) of $\mathcal{A}$ over an ω-word w, such that for any $j \in \mathbb{N}$ (resp. $0 \leq j \leq m$), if the j-th letter of w is a_k then $(\pi, i + j) \models \varphi_k$.

$(\pi, 0) \models \varphi$ is abbreviated as $\pi \models \varphi$. A formula φ is *satisfiable* if there exists a structure π such that $\pi \models \varphi$. A formula φ is *valid* iff $\pi \models \varphi$ holds for any structure π.

Assume that $\mathcal{A} = \langle\Sigma, Q, \delta, Q_0, F\rangle$ and $q \in Q$, we use $\mathcal{A}^q$ to denote the automaton $(Q, \Sigma, \delta, \{q\}, F)$, which has the same acceptance condition as $\mathcal{A}$.

We now impose an additional constraint on the automaton connectives occurring in formulas: *each automaton connective should have a unique initial state.* Therefore, each connective should be of the form $\mathcal{A}^q$. This would not lose any expressiveness, because $\mathcal{A}(\varphi_1, \ldots, \varphi_n) \leftrightarrow \bigvee_{q \in Q_0} \mathcal{A}^q(\varphi_1, \ldots, \varphi_n)$ holds in all kinds of ETLs.

Theorem 1. *[VW94] Expressiveness of* ETL_l, ETL_f *and* ETL_r *are all equal to* ω*-regular languages.*

3 Axiomatization of ETL_l

3.1 ETL_l Tableau Rules

Given an ETL_l formula φ, a *tableau* of φ is a tuple $\langle\mathcal{T}, \rho, \Gamma_0\rangle$. Where: $\mathcal{T}$ is a finite set of *nodes*, and each node is a finite set of ETL_l formulas. $\rho \subseteq \mathcal{T} \times \mathcal{T}$ is the *transition relation*, and $\langle\Gamma, \Gamma'\rangle \in \rho$ only if Γ' is obtained from Γ by applying a tableau rule (tableau rules are shown in Figure 1). $\Gamma_0 = \{\varphi\}$ is the *initial node*.

$$\text{(and)}\ \frac{\Gamma \cup \{\varphi_1 \wedge \varphi_2\}}{\Gamma \cup \{\varphi_1, \varphi_2\}} \qquad \text{(or)}\ \frac{\Gamma \cup \{\varphi_1 \vee \varphi_2\}}{\Gamma \cup \{\varphi_1\},\ \Gamma \cup \{\varphi_2\}} \qquad \text{(neg-neg)}\ \frac{\Gamma \cup \{\neg\neg\varphi\}}{\Gamma \cup \{\varphi\}}$$

$$\text{(neg-and)}\ \frac{\Gamma \cup \{\neg(\varphi_1 \wedge \varphi_2)\}}{\Gamma \cup \{\neg\varphi_1 \vee \neg\varphi_2\}} \qquad \text{(neg-or)}\ \frac{\Gamma \cup \{\neg(\varphi_1 \vee \varphi_2)\}}{\Gamma \cup \{\neg\varphi_1 \wedge \neg\varphi_2\}} \qquad \text{(neg-next)}\ \frac{\Gamma \cup \{\neg\bigcirc\varphi\}}{\Gamma \cup \{\bigcirc\neg\varphi\}}$$

$$\text{(pos-exp)}\ \frac{\Gamma \cup \{\mathcal{A}^{q_i}(\varphi_1, \ldots, \varphi_n)\}}{\Gamma \cup \{\bigvee_{a_k \in \Sigma} \bigvee_{q_j \in \delta(q_i, a_k)} (\varphi_k \wedge \bigcirc\mathcal{A}^{q_j}(\varphi_1, \ldots, \varphi_n))\}}$$

$$\text{(neg-exp)}\ \frac{\Gamma \cup \{\neg\mathcal{A}^{q_i}(\varphi_1, \ldots, \varphi_n)\}}{\Gamma \cup \{\bigwedge_{a_k \in \Sigma} \bigwedge_{q_j \in \delta(q_i, a_k)} (\neg\varphi_k \vee (\varphi_k \wedge \bigcirc\neg\mathcal{A}^{q_j}(\varphi_1, \ldots, \varphi_n)))\}}$$

$$\text{(modal)}\ \frac{\{\varphi_1, \ldots, \varphi_n, \bigcirc\psi_1, \ldots, \bigcirc\psi_m\}}{\{\psi_1, \ldots, \psi_m\}} \qquad \text{each } \varphi_i \text{ is a literal}$$

Fig. 1. Tableau rules for ETL_l

Remark 2. The rule (neg-exp) is not exactly the dual of (pos-exp). Instead, we explicitly require that $\bigcirc\neg\mathcal{A}^{q_j}(\varphi_1, \ldots, \varphi_n))$ accompanied with φ_k, which is useful in proving some theorems (e.g. Theorem 3).

Nodes in a tableau are pairwise different, and hence a tableau has only finitely many nodes.

In a tableau $\langle \mathcal{T}, \rho, \Gamma_0 \rangle$, if $\langle \Gamma, \Gamma' \rangle \in \rho$, then we say Γ' is a *successor* of Γ and Γ a *predecessor* of Γ'. When Γ' is a successor of Γ, the formula $\varphi \in \Gamma$ to which we apply tableau rule to obtain Γ' is said to be the *reducing formula.*

Nodes being of the form $\{\varphi_1, \ldots, \varphi_n, \bigcirc\psi_1, \ldots, \bigcirc\psi_m\}$ are called *modal nodes,* where either $m \neq 0$ or $n \neq 0$ and each φ_i is a literal. Others are said to be *non-modal nodes.* Clearly, the only tableau rule that can be applied to a modal node is (modal). A modal node has exactly one successor. The initial state and successors of modal nodes are said to be *state nodes.* Note that if $m = 0$, its successor should be the node $\emptyset$. $\emptyset$ is not a modal node and it has no successor.

A *path* in a tableau is a finite or infinite node sequence $\Gamma_1\Gamma_2\cdots$, where Γ_{i+1} is a successor of Γ_i. A path is *complete* if: 1) the first node is the initial node; and 2) the path is either an infinite one or ending with $\emptyset$.

A *loop* is a finite path whose first node and last node are the same one. It is easy to prove the following lemma.

Lemma 1. *Each loop in a tableau contains at least one modal node.*

To capture the internal structure of a tableau, we need the notion *trace*— a trace in the tableau $\langle \mathcal{T}, \rho, \Gamma_0 \rangle$ is a finite or infinite formula sequence $\phi_0\phi_1\ldots$. Where: 1) Each ϕ_i belongs to a node in $\mathcal{T}$. 2) If $\phi_i \in \Gamma$ and $\phi_{i+1} \in \Gamma'$ then $\langle \Gamma, \Gamma' \rangle \in \rho$. Moreover, if ϕ_i is the reducing formula of Γ w.r.t. Γ', then ϕ_{i+1} is the formula obtained from ϕ_i by applying the corresponding rule; otherwise, $\phi_{i+1} = \phi_i$.

Each trace τ determines a unique path P, and we say that τ *belongs to* P.

Nodes containing $\bot$, $\neg\top$ or complementary pairs (such as ϕ and $\neg\phi$) are immediately removed. Consequently, nodes (except for the node $\emptyset$) that have no successors are also removed. This process is called *local consistency filtering*.

A tableau meets *local consistency* if the initial node is not removed after the recursive process of local consistency filtering.

A tableau meets *global consistency* if it has a complete path P such that no formula of the form $\neg\mathcal{A}^{q_i}(\varphi_1, \ldots, \varphi_n)$ appears infinitely often in any trace belonging to P.

A tableau meeting both local consistency and global consistency is said to be a *consistent* tableau. For the tableau approach, we have the following theorem.

Theorem 2. *An* ETL$_l$ φ *is satisfiable iff it has a consist tableau.*

3.2 The Axiom System for ETL$_l$

The ETL$_l$ axiom system, namely $\mathscr{L}$, is shown in Figure 2. Here, $\varphi \to \psi$ is the abbreviation of $\neg\varphi \vee \psi$, and $\varphi \leftrightarrow \psi$ is $(\varphi \to \psi) \wedge (\psi \to \varphi)$. The axiom (P) involves all tautology instances such as $\top \leftrightarrow \neg\bot$, $\neg\neg\varphi \to \varphi$, etc. For the aim of simplicity, we use $\bigwedge\Gamma$ as the abbreviation of $\bigwedge_{\phi\in\Gamma}\phi$ from now on, and define that $\bigwedge\emptyset = \top$, $\bigvee\emptyset = \bot$.

Axioms

1. (P) All tautology instances
2. (N) $\neg\bigcirc\varphi \leftrightarrow \bigcirc\neg\varphi$
3. (K) $\bigcirc(\varphi_1 \to \varphi_2) \leftrightarrow (\bigcirc\varphi_1 \to \bigcirc\varphi_2)$
4. (Exp) $\mathcal{A}^{q_i}(\varphi_1, \ldots, \varphi_n) \leftrightarrow \bigvee_{a_k\in\Sigma}(\bigvee_{q_j\in\delta(q_i,a_k)}(\varphi_k \wedge \bigcirc\mathcal{A}^{q_j}(\varphi_1, \ldots, \varphi_n)))$ (where $\mathcal{A} = \langle Q, \Sigma, \delta, Q_0, F\rangle$)

Rules

1. (MP) If $\varphi_1 \to \varphi_2$ and φ_1 then φ_2
2. (XGen) If φ then $\bigcirc\varphi$
3. (Loop) If $\bigwedge_{1\le i\le m}(\psi_i \to \bigvee_{1\le k\le n}(\bigvee_{q_j\in\delta(q_i,a_k)}(\varphi_k \wedge \bigcirc\psi_j)))$ then $\psi_i \to \mathcal{A}^{q_i}(\varphi_1, \ldots, \varphi_n)$ for all $1 \le i \le m$ (where $\mathcal{A} = \langle\{a_1, \ldots, a_n\}, \{q_1, \ldots, q_m\}, \delta, Q_0, F\rangle$)

Fig. 2. The axiom system $\mathscr{L}$

Clear to see that each axiom is valid and each rule preserves validity. Thus, the system is sound.

Lemma 2 (Reasoning property of tableaux). *Given a tableau* $\langle\mathcal{T}, \rho, \Gamma_0\rangle$, *then every node* $\Gamma \in \mathcal{T}$ *satisfies the* reasoning property. *i.e.*

$$\begin{cases} \bigwedge\Gamma \to \bigvee_{\langle\Gamma,\Gamma'\rangle\in\rho}\bigwedge\Gamma', & \text{when } \Gamma \text{ is not a modal node} \\ \bigwedge\Gamma \to \bigcirc\bigwedge\Gamma', & \text{when } \Gamma \text{ is a modal node and } \Gamma' \text{ is its successor} \end{cases}.$$

According to the tableau rules, Lemma 2 can be easily proven.

Theorem 3. *If an* ETL_l *formula* φ *is not satisfiable, then* $\vdash_{\mathscr{L}} \neg\varphi$.

Proof. Let $\langle \mathcal{T}, \rho, \Gamma_0 \rangle$ be an arbitrary tableau of φ. Since φ is not satisfiable, according to Theorem 2, this tableau must not be a consistent one. We show how to obtain a deductive sequence of $\neg\varphi$ from this tableau.

I) If the tableau does not meet local consistency, we can construct the deductive sequence of $\neg\varphi$ with the consistency filtering process.

- A node Γ involving $\bot$ or $\neg\top$ or complementary pairs is removed immediately. $\neg\bigwedge\Gamma$ can be proven by the axiom (P).
- Suppose Γ' is successor of a non-modal node Γ. If $\neg\bigwedge\Gamma'$ is proved, then $\bigwedge\Gamma \to \bigvee_{\langle\Gamma,\Gamma''\rangle\in\rho, \Gamma''\neq\Gamma'} \bigwedge\Gamma''$ is also proved by the reasoning property and classical propositional logic. This implies that the remaining tableau having Γ' removed still fulfils reasoning property.
- For a non-modal node Γ, if all its successors are removed, inductively, we have $\vdash_{\mathscr{L}} \bigwedge\Gamma'$ for each successor Γ' of Γ. According to the reasoning property, $\bigwedge_{\langle\Gamma,\Gamma'\rangle\in\rho} \neg\bigwedge\Gamma' \to \neg\bigwedge\Gamma$ holds. Hence we can infer $\neg\bigwedge\Gamma$ by (MP).
- Suppose that Γ a modal node, and Γ' is its unique successor. If Γ' is removed, inductively, i.e. $\vdash_{\mathscr{L}} \neg\bigwedge\Gamma'$, then we have $\vdash_{\mathscr{L}} \bigcirc\neg\bigwedge\Gamma'$ by (XGen), and subsequently, we have $\vdash_{\mathscr{L}} \neg\bigcirc\bigwedge\Gamma'$ by (N) and (MP). According to the reasoning property $\neg\bigcirc\bigwedge\Gamma' \to \neg\bigwedge\Gamma$. Therefore, $\neg\bigwedge\Gamma$ is inferred.

Since the initial node $\Gamma_0 = \{\varphi\}$ is also removed, we will eventually get the deductive sequence of $\neg\varphi$.

II) If the tableau meets local consistency, then the node $\emptyset$ must not exist in the tableau [1]. Therefore, each complete path has to be infinite.

Let P be an arbitrary infinite path. Since the tableau is connected, one can find a complete path in the tableau whose suffix is P. Since the tableau does not meet global consistency, there must exist an infinite trace τ belonging to P such that some formula $\neg\mathcal{A}^{q_i}(\varphi_1, \ldots, \varphi_n)$ appears in τ infinitely often.

For a node Γ in P, τ takes a formula in Γ at each visit to Γ, (notice that τ may take different formulas at different visit to Γ). We denote by $\Gamma_{[\tau]}$ the set of formulas that τ ever takes in all his visiting to Γ. Since P is infinite, then it contains loops. By Lemma 1, P involves modal nodes, and hence involves state nodes. Suppose that $\mathcal{A} = \langle \{a_1, \ldots, a_n\}, \{q_1, \ldots, q_m\}, \delta, Q_0, F \rangle$, then for any $1 \leq k \leq m$, let $\mathcal{D}_k = \{\Gamma \mid \Gamma \text{ is a state node in } P \text{ and } \neg\mathcal{A}^{q_k}(\varphi_1, \ldots, \varphi_n) \in \Gamma_{[\tau]}\}$, and let $\psi_k = \bigvee_{\Gamma\in\mathcal{D}_k} \bigwedge\Gamma$. It is easy to prove there is at least one $\mathcal{D}_k$, such that $\mathcal{D}_k \neq \emptyset$.

By the reasoning property of tableau and the tableau rule (neg-exp), $\psi_k \to \bigvee_{1\leq l\leq n}(\bigvee_{q_j\in\delta(q_k,a_l)}(\varphi_l \wedge \bigcirc\psi_j))$ is inferred for all $1 \leq k \leq m$. Therefore, we have $\psi_k \to \mathcal{A}^{q_k}(\varphi_1, \ldots, \varphi_n)$ according to the (Loop).

On the other hand, we have $\psi_k \to \neg\mathcal{A}^{q_k}(\varphi_1, \ldots, \varphi_n)$ because $\neg\mathcal{A}^{q_k}(\varphi_1, \ldots, \varphi_n)$ appears in each state node belonging to $\mathcal{D}_k$.

[1] Otherwise, we can find a complete path ending with $\emptyset$. Since this path is finite, no infinite trace is involved. Then the tableau meets global consistency by definition.

Therefore, for all $1 \leq k \leq m$, $\neg\psi_k$ can be proven. It implies that for each state node $\Gamma \in \mathcal{D}_k$, $\neg \bigwedge \Gamma$ can be proven. Thus, at least one node can be removed. Consequently, remove components those are unreachable from the initial state, and remove nodes that now having no successors as in I).

Clearly, the reasoning property still holds by the remaining tableau, and the remaining tableau is still a one that does not meets global consistency. Repeat this way, we can go on with removing other nodes, until the initial node $\Gamma_0 = \{\varphi\}$ is removed, and then $\neg\varphi$ is proven. □

Subsequently, if φ is a valid ETL_l formula, then $\neg\varphi$ is not satisfiable. Thus, $\neg\neg\varphi$ can be proven, and then φ is proven.

4 Axiomatization of $\mathbf{ETL}_f$ and $\mathbf{ETL}_r$

4.1 Axiomatization of $\mathbf{ETL}_f$

Tableau rules of ETL_f are similar to that of ETL_l, except that the rules (pos-exp) and (neg-exp) are replaced by four new rules (pos-exp$_1$), (pos-exp$_2$), (neg-exp$_1$) and (neg-exp$_2$), as shown in Figure 3.

Assume that the finite acceptance automaton $\mathcal{A} = \langle \Sigma, Q, \delta, Q_0, F \rangle$

$$\text{(pos-exp}_1\text{)}\quad \frac{\Gamma \cup \{\mathcal{A}^{q_i}(\varphi_1, \cdots, \varphi_n)\}}{\Gamma \cup \{\bigvee_{a_k \in \Sigma} \bigvee_{q_j \in \delta(q_i, a_k)} (\varphi_k \wedge \bigcirc \mathcal{A}^{q_j}(\varphi_1, \cdots, \varphi_n))\}} \quad q_i \notin F$$

$$\text{(pos-exp}_2\text{)}\quad \frac{\Gamma \cup \{\mathcal{A}^{q_i}(\varphi_1, \cdots, \varphi_n)\}}{\Gamma \cup \{\top\}} \quad q_i \in F$$

$$\text{(neg-exp}_1\text{)}\quad \frac{\Gamma \cup \{\neg\mathcal{A}^{q_i}(\varphi_1, \cdots, \varphi_n)\}}{\Gamma \cup \{\bigwedge_{a_k \in \Sigma} \bigwedge_{q_j \in \delta(q_i, a_k)} (\neg\varphi_k \vee \bigcirc \neg\mathcal{A}^{q_j}(\varphi_1, \cdots, \varphi_n))\}} \quad q_i \notin F$$

$$\text{(neg-exp}_2\text{)}\quad \frac{\Gamma \cup \{\neg\mathcal{A}^{q_i}(\varphi_1, \cdots, \varphi_n)\}}{\Gamma \cup \{\bot\}} \quad q_i \in F$$

Fig. 3. Tableau rules (pos-exp$_1$), (pos-exp$_2$), (neg-exp$_1$) and (neg-exp$_2$)

For ETL_f tableaux, the notion of *local consistency* is the same as for ETL_l tableaux. An ETL_f tableau meets *global consistency* if there is a complete path P in the tableau, and no formula of the form $\mathcal{A}^q(\varphi_1, \cdots, \varphi_n)$ appears infinitely often in any trace belonging to P.

Analogously, we may show an ETL_f is satisfiable iff it has a consistent tableau.

The axiom system for ETL_f, namely $\mathscr{F}$, is shown in Figure 4.

Theorem 4. *If an* ETL_f *formula* φ *is not satisfiable, then* $\vdash_{\mathscr{F}} \neg\varphi$.

The proof is almost identical to Theorem 3. We firstly construct a tableau for φ, then this tableau must be inconsistent. If the tableau does not meet local

Axioms

1. (P), 2. (N), 3.(K), same as the corresponding axioms in $\mathscr{L}$.
4. (Exp) $\mathcal{A}^{q_i}(\varphi_1,\ldots,\varphi_n) \leftrightarrow \bigvee_{a_k\in\Sigma}(\bigvee_{q_j\in\delta(q_i,a_k)}(\varphi_k \wedge \bigcirc\mathcal{A}^{q_j}(\varphi_1,\ldots,\varphi_n)))$
(where $\mathcal{A} = \langle\{q_1,\ldots,q_m\},\Sigma,\delta,Q_0,F\rangle$, and $q_i \notin F$)
5. (Acc) $\mathcal{A}^{q_i}(\varphi_1,\cdots,\varphi_n)$ (where q_i is a final state of $\mathcal{A}$)

Rules

1. (MP), 2.(XGen), same as corresponding rules in $\mathscr{L}$.
3. (Fin) If $\bigwedge_{1\le i\le m, q_i\notin F}(\psi_i \to \bigwedge_{1\le k\le n}(\varphi_k \to \bigcirc\bigvee_{q_j\in\delta(q_i,a_k)}\psi_j))$
and $\bigwedge_{1\le i\le m, q_i\notin F}(\psi_i \to \bigwedge_{\delta(q_i,a_k)\in F}\neg\varphi_k)$
then $\psi_i \to \neg\mathcal{A}^{q_i}(\varphi_1,\ldots,\varphi_n)$ for all $1\le i\le m$ such that $q_i\notin F$
(where $\mathcal{A} = \langle\{a_1,\ldots,a_n\},\{q_1,\ldots,q_m\},\delta,Q_0,F\rangle$)

Fig. 4. The axiom system $\mathscr{F}$

consistency, $\neg\varphi$ can be proven accompanied with the consistency filtering. If this tableau does not meet global consistency, for an arbitrary infinite path P, there is a trace τ having infinitely many occurrences of some $\mathcal{A}^{q_i}(\varphi_1,\ldots,\varphi_n)$. Assume that $\mathcal{A} = \langle\{a_1,\ldots,a_n\},\{q_1,\ldots,q_m\},\delta,Q_0,F\rangle$, for every $1\le k\le m$, we now let $\mathcal{D}_k = \{\Gamma \mid \Gamma$ is a state node in P and $\mathcal{A}^{q_k}(\varphi_1,\ldots,\varphi_n)\in\Gamma_{[\tau]}\}$ and $\psi_k = \bigvee_{\Gamma\in\mathcal{D}_k}\bigwedge(\Gamma\backslash\{\mathcal{A}^{q_k}(\varphi_1,\ldots,\varphi_n)\})$.

By rule (Fin), we have $\psi_k \to \neg\mathcal{A}^{q_k}(\varphi_1,\ldots,\varphi_n)$ for all $1\le k\le m$. It implies that for any $\Gamma\in\mathcal{D}_k$, $\bigwedge\Gamma \to \neg\mathcal{A}^{q_k}(\varphi_1,\ldots,\varphi_n)$ can be proven. On the other hand, $\bigwedge\Gamma \to \mathcal{A}^{q_k}(\varphi_1,\ldots,\varphi_n)$ holds because $\mathcal{A}^{q_k}(\varphi_1,\ldots,\varphi_n)$ belongs to Γ. Hence, at least one state node is removed. And, repeat this way to remove other nodes.

Therefore, if an ETL$_f$ φ is not satisfiable, then $\neg\varphi$ can be proven in $\mathscr{F}$. Consequently, all valid ETL$_f$ formulas can be proven in $\mathscr{F}$.

4.2 Axiomatization of ETL$_r$

ETL$_r$ has a wider application in practice. For example, the *ForSpec Language Logic* (cf. [AFF$^+$02,AFF$^+$05]) and IBM's *Sugar*. Tableau rules for ETL$_r$ are exactly the same as those for ETL$_l$. The definition of *global consistency* is modified as follows.

There is a complete path P in the tableau and each trace τ belonging to P satisfies:

- *Positive eventuality*: if a formula $\mathcal{A}^{q_i}(\varphi_1,\ldots,\varphi_n)$ appears infinitely often in τ, then there is a $\mathcal{A}^{q_f}(\varphi_1,\ldots,\varphi_n)$ appears infinitely often in τ, where q_f is a final state of $\mathcal{A}$.
- *Negative eventuality*: if a formula $\neg\mathcal{A}^{q_i}(\varphi_1,\ldots,\varphi_n)$ appears infinitely often in τ, then for each final state q_f of $\mathcal{A}$, the formula $\mathcal{A}^{q_f}(\varphi_1,\ldots,\varphi_n)$ does not appear infinitely often in τ.

As in ETL$_l$ and ETL$_f$, we can show that an ETL$_r$ formula is satisfiable iff it has a consistent tableau.

The axiom system for ETL_r is $\mathscr{R} = (\mathscr{L}\backslash\{(\text{Loop})\})\cup\{(\text{Sim}), (\text{Rep}), (\text{R-Loop})\}$. The axiom (Sim), rules (Rep) and (R-Loop) are depicted in Figure 5.

(Sim) $\mathcal{A}_1^{q_1}(\varphi_1,\ldots,\varphi_n) \to \mathcal{A}_2^{q_2}(\varphi_1,\ldots,\varphi_n)$
(where $\mathcal{A}_1$ and $\mathcal{A}_2$ have the same alphabet and $\mathcal{L}(\mathcal{A}_1^{q_1}) \subseteq \mathcal{L}(\mathcal{A}_2^{q_2})$)

(Rep) If $\bigwedge_{1\le t\le m}(\psi_t \to \bigwedge_{1\le k\le n}(\varphi_k \to \bigcirc \bigvee_{q_r\in\delta(q_t,a_k)} \psi_r))$ and
$\bigwedge_{q_f\in F}(\bigwedge_{q_u\in I_{\mathcal{A}}(q_s)}(\psi_u \to \bigwedge_{q_f\in\delta(q_u,a_k)} \neg\varphi_k)$
$\vee \bigwedge_{q_v\in I_{\mathcal{A}}(q_f)}(\psi_v \to \bigwedge_{q_f\in\delta(q_v,a_k)} \neg\varphi_k))$
then $\psi_s \to \neg\mathcal{A}^{q_s}(\varphi_1,\ldots,\varphi_n)$
(where $\mathcal{A} = \langle\{a_1,\ldots,a_n\},\{q_1,\ldots,q_m\},\delta,Q_0,F\rangle$, and $1\le s\le m$,
$I_{\mathcal{A}}(q_i)$ is the states that can be reached from q_i in $\mathcal{A}$, including q_i itself)

(R-Loop) If $\bigwedge_{1\le i\le m}(\psi_i \to \bigvee_{1\le k\le n}(\bigvee_{q_j\in\delta(q_i,a_k)}(\varphi_k \wedge \bigcirc\psi_j)))$
then $\psi_i \to \mathcal{A}^{q_i}(\varphi_1,\ldots,\varphi_n)$ for all $1\le i\le m$
(where $\mathcal{A} = \langle\{a_1,\ldots,a_n\},\{q_1,\ldots,q_m\},\delta,Q_0,\{q_1,\ldots,q_m\}\rangle$)

Fig. 5. The axiom (Sim) and rule (Rep), (R-Loop) of $\mathscr{R}$

Theorem 5. *If an* ETL_r *formula* φ *is not satisfiable, then* $\vdash_{\mathscr{R}} \neg\varphi$.

This proof is a combination of those for $\mathscr{L}$ and $\mathscr{F}$, we here just describe the proof sketch.

Given an unsatisfiable ETL_r formula φ, one can construct an arbitrary tableau for it, and this tableau must not be consistent. If the tableau does not meet the local consistency, $\neg\varphi$ can be easily proven with the consistency filtering process. When the global consistency is not satisfied, then each infinite path P must involve a trace τ, which violates either positive eventuality or negative eventuality. If the trace does not meet positive eventuality, then use the rule (Rep) to remove state nodes involved in the path — just like what we done in proving the completeness of $\mathscr{F}$. When the trace does not meet negative eventuality, we use both (Sim) and (R-loop) to remove such nodes. Repeat this, we can remove other nodes. Once the initial node is removed, then $\neg\varphi$ is proven.

5 Axiomatizing Fragments of Extended Temporal Logic

5.1 The Instantiating Axiomatization Approach

For ETLs, one can get their *fragments* (sub logics) by restricting the temporal connectives to a special subset (but at least the operator "nexttime" should be reserved). The original ETL is said to be the *base logics* of that fragment.

For an n-ary temporal operator K in an ETL fragment, if the automaton $\mathcal{A}_{\mathsf{K}}^{q}$ fulfills that $\mathsf{K}(\varphi_1,\ldots,\varphi_n)$ and $\mathcal{A}_{\mathsf{K}}^{q}(\varphi_1,\ldots,\varphi_n)$ are logically equivalent for all $\varphi_1,\ldots,\varphi_n$, then we say $\mathcal{A}_{\mathsf{K}}^{q}$ is an *automaton encoding* of K.

For example, consider the logic LTL, besides the nexttime operator, it has another operator "until" (U). Let the finite acceptance automaton $\mathcal{A}_{\mathsf{U}} = \langle\{a_1,a_2\}, \{q_1,q_2\}, \delta_{\mathsf{U}}, \{q_1\}, \{q_2\}\rangle$, where $\delta_{\mathsf{U}}(q_1,a_1) = \{q_1\}, \delta_{\mathsf{U}}(q_1,a_2) = \{q_2\}$ and $\delta_{\mathsf{U}}(q_2,a_1) = \delta_{\mathsf{U}}(q_2,a_2) = \emptyset$. Clearly, $\varphi_1\mathsf{U}\varphi_2$ is exactly $\mathcal{A}_{\mathsf{U}}^{q_1}(\varphi_1,\varphi_2)$ and hence LTL can be viewed as a fragment of ETL_f, and $\mathcal{A}_{\mathsf{U}}^{q_1}$ is an automaton encoding of U in ETL_f.

In the ETL axiom systems, there exist axioms like (Exp) etc, and rules like (Loop) etc., we call them "*automaton-related axioms/rules*". For ETL fragments, we can instantiate the automaton-related axioms and/or rules for the special operators. — i.e. using the automaton encodings as concrete connectives, one can get an instanced version of each automaton-related axiom or rule. The resulted axioms and rules are called *instanced axioms* and *instanced rules*. The new axiom system we obtained is called *instanced axiom systems* for the fragment.

E.g., for LTL, $\mathcal{A}_{\mathsf{U}}^{q_2}(\varphi_1,\varphi_2)$ is directly replaced by $\top$ according to (Acc). The instance axiom (Exp) for U is

$$\varphi_1\mathsf{U}\varphi_2 \leftrightarrow (\varphi_1 \wedge \bigcirc(\varphi_1\mathsf{U}\varphi_2)) \vee \varphi_2.$$

The instanced rule (Fin) for U is

$$\begin{array}{rl}\text{If} & \psi_1 \to ((\varphi_1 \to \bigcirc\psi_1) \wedge (\varphi_2 \to \bigcirc\psi_2)) \text{ and } \psi_1 \to \neg\varphi_2 \\ \text{then} & \psi_1 \to \neg(\varphi_1\mathsf{U}\varphi_2)\end{array},$$

and since the second premise is $\psi_1 \to \neg\varphi_2$, in practice, we usually let the first premise be $\psi_1 \to (\varphi_1 \to \bigcirc\psi_1)$.

The axioms (P),(N),(K), and instanced (Exp), together with rules (MP), (XGen) and instanced (Fin) formalize a new reasoning system [2] for LTL.

This axiom system is a sound and complete one for LTL. To show this, we compare it with the LTL axiom system presented by Lange and Stirling [LS01].

Lange and Stirling's system has seven axioms and three rules, and involves two operators U and R. The relation between these two operators can be described as: $\varphi_1\mathsf{R}\varphi_2 \leftrightarrow \neg(\neg\varphi_1\mathsf{U}\neg\varphi_2)$. Thus, by replacing each occurrence of $\varphi_1\mathsf{R}\varphi_2$ with $\neg(\neg\varphi_1\mathsf{U}\neg\varphi_2)$, Lange and Stirling's axiom system is given in Figure 6.

We now show that all the axioms and rules in Lange and Stirling's system can be inferred by our instanced axiom system. Axiom 2 and axiom 3 can be proven by instanced (Exp), (P) and (MP), axioms 5 and 6 can be proven by (K) and (MP). The only interesting thing here is to obtain the rule (Rel).

Let $\phi = \varphi_2 \wedge (\varphi_1 \vee \bigcirc\neg(\neg(\varphi_1 \vee \psi)\mathsf{U}\neg(\varphi_2 \vee \psi)))$, then the premiss becomes $\psi \to \phi$. It is straightforward to show that $\phi \to \neg\neg\varphi_2$ and

$$\phi \to (\neg\varphi_1 \to \bigcirc\neg(\neg(\varphi_1 \vee \psi)\mathsf{U}\neg(\varphi_2 \vee \psi))) \qquad (*)$$

[2] Instanced (Acc) has already been used to eliminate the connective of $\mathcal{A}_{\mathsf{U}}^{q_2}$, and its instance axiom $\top$ is merged to (P).

Axioms

1. (P), 4. (N), 7. definition of R, given as above.
2. $\varphi_1 \mathsf{U} \varphi_2 \to \varphi_2 \vee (\varphi_1 \wedge \bigcirc(\varphi_1 \mathsf{U} \varphi_2))$.
3. $\neg(\neg\varphi_1 \mathsf{U} \neg\varphi_2) \to \varphi_2 \wedge (\varphi_1 \vee \bigcirc\neg(\neg\varphi_1 \mathsf{U} \neg\varphi_2))$.
5. $\bigcirc(\varphi_1 \wedge \varphi_2) \to \bigcirc\varphi_1 \wedge \bigcirc\varphi_2$.
6. $\bigcirc(\varphi_1 \to \varphi_2) \to (\bigcirc\varphi_1 \to \bigcirc\varphi_2)$.

Rules

1. (MP), 2.(XGen).
3. (Rel) If $\psi \to (\varphi_2 \wedge (\varphi_1 \vee \bigcirc\neg(\neg(\varphi_1 \vee \psi)\mathsf{U}\neg(\varphi_2 \vee \psi))))$ then $\psi \to \neg(\neg\varphi_1 \mathsf{U} \neg\varphi_2)$

Fig. 6. Lange and Stirling's axiom system for LTL

By instanced (Exp), $\neg(\neg(\varphi_1 \vee \psi)\mathsf{U}\neg(\varphi_2 \vee \psi)) \leftrightarrow (\varphi_2 \vee \psi) \wedge ((\varphi_1 \vee \psi) \vee \bigcirc\neg(\neg(\varphi_1 \vee \psi)\mathsf{U}\neg(\varphi_2 \vee \psi)))$ holds. Notice that $(\varphi_2 \vee \psi) \wedge ((\varphi_1 \vee \psi) \vee \bigcirc\neg(\neg(\varphi_1 \vee \psi)\mathsf{U}\neg(\varphi_2 \vee \psi))) \leftrightarrow \psi \vee \phi$, and $\psi \to \phi$ is the premiss, thus

$$\neg(\neg(\varphi_1 \vee \psi)\mathsf{U}\neg(\varphi_2 \vee \psi)) \to \phi \qquad (**)$$

Then, $\phi \to (\neg\varphi_1 \to \bigcirc\phi)$ is proven by (*) and (**). Because $\phi \to \neg\neg\varphi_2$ and $\phi \to (\neg\varphi_1 \to \bigcirc\phi)$, according to the instanced (Fin), we have $\phi \to \neg(\neg\varphi_1 \mathsf{U} \neg\varphi_2)$, and hence $\psi \to \neg(\neg\varphi_1 \mathsf{U} \neg\varphi_2)$ then the rule (Rel) is proven.

We now summarize the approach of instantiating axiomatization for ETL fragments.

1. Firstly, choose a proper ETL as the base logic.
2. Encode the temporal operators with corresponding automaton connectives.
3. Obtain the instanced axiom system by instantiating corresponding automaton-related axioms and deductive rules.

For the instantiating axiomatization approach, we have the following theorem.

Theorem 6. *Given a fragment of* ETL_l *(resp.* ETL_f, ETL_r *), the corresponding instanced axiom system of* $\mathscr{L}$ *(resp.* $\mathscr{F}$, $\mathscr{R}$*) is a sound and complete axiom system for the fragment.*

Proof. For the given ETL fragment, without loss of generality, assume that it is a fragment of ETL_l. After encoding its temporal operators to (looping acceptance) automata, one can give an axiom system of this logic by instantiating the axiom (Exp) and rule (Loop).

Soundness of the resulted system is trivially held, because each instance of automaton-related axioms and rules preserves validity. To prove completeness of the instanced axiom system, we also need to build tableaux for the formulas.

Since each operator in the fragment has an automaton encoding, tableau rules for base logic still suit the fragment. It is no wonder that formulas those cannot be satisfied do not have consistent tableaux — otherwise, they have consistent tableaux in the base logic, which violates the conclusion of Theorem 2.

Given a formula φ that cannot be satisfied, we create a tableau of it. It is easy to show that the"reasoning property" still holds. If the tableau does not meet local consistency, $\neg\varphi$ can be easily proven with the local filtering process. Otherwise, if the tableau does not meet global consistency, we can find a infinite path P, and an infinite trace τ belonging to P and contains infinitely many occurrences of some $\neg\mathcal{A}^{q_i}(\varphi_1,\ldots,\varphi_n)$ where $\mathcal{A}^{q_i}$ is the automaton encoding for some operator in the fragment.

Assume that $\mathcal{A}$ has the state set $\{q_1,\ldots,q_m\}$, then for each $1 \le k \le m$, still let $\mathcal{D}_k = \{\Gamma \mid \Gamma \text{ is a state node of } P \text{ and } \neg\mathcal{A}^{q_k}(\varphi_1,\ldots,\varphi_n) \in \Gamma_{[\tau]}\}$ and $\psi_k = \bigvee_{\Gamma\in\mathcal{D}_k}\bigwedge\Gamma$. There exists some $1 \le k \le m$, such that $\mathcal{D}_k \neq \emptyset$.

According to the reasoning property and the tableau rule (neg-exp), we have $\psi_k \to \bigvee_{1\le i\le n}\bigvee_{q_j\in\delta(q_k,a_i)}(\varphi_i \wedge \bigcirc\psi_j)$ for each $1 \le k \le m$. Since each $\mathcal{A}^{q_k}$ is an automaton encoding of some operator in the fragment, we can now apply the instanced (Loop). Therefore, we have $\psi_k \to \mathcal{A}^{q_k}(\varphi_1,\ldots,\varphi_n)$, and hence $\bigwedge\Gamma \to \mathcal{A}^{q_k}(\varphi_1,\ldots,\varphi_n)$ for each $\Gamma \in \mathcal{D}_k$.

On the other hand, for every $\Gamma \in \mathcal{D}_k$, $\bigwedge\Gamma \to \neg\mathcal{A}^{q_k}(\varphi_1,\ldots,\varphi_n)$ can be proven because $\neg\mathcal{A}^{q_k}(\varphi_1,\ldots,\varphi_n) \in \Gamma$. Thus, at least one node can be removed. Consequently, remove components those are unreachable from the initial state, and remove nodes that now having no successors. Repeat this process to eliminate other nodes.

From this, we can see that the proof for the fragment almost performs an identical routine of that for the base logic, but with temporal operators restricted to a special set. It is same to prove that in the case of the logic is a fragment of ETL_f or ETL_r. □

5.2 Further Examples and Discussions

In the previous subsection, we have given an approach namely "instantiating axiomatization" to produce axiom system for ETL. It should be pointed out that for a given temporal logic, the axiom system we obtain is highly sensitive to the base logic and automaton encodings we choose.

For example, LTL can also be viewed as a fragment of ETL_l. To do this, we consider LTL to be the ETL_l fragment equipped with the operators $\bigcirc$ and "*release*" (R).

Let the looping acceptance automaton $\mathcal{A}_{\mathsf{R}} = \langle\{a_1,a_2,a_3\},\{q_1,q_2\},\delta_{\mathsf{R}},\{q_1\},\emptyset\rangle$, where $\delta_{\mathsf{R}}(q_1,a_1) = \{q_1\}$, $\delta_{\mathsf{R}}(q_1,a_2) = \{q_2\}$, $\delta_{\mathsf{R}}(q_2,a_3) = \{q_2\}$, $\delta_{\mathsf{R}}(q_1,a_3) = \delta_{\mathsf{R}}(q_2,a_1) = \delta_{\mathsf{R}}(q_2,a_2) = \emptyset$.

Clearly, $\varphi_1\mathsf{R}\varphi_2 = \mathcal{A}_{\mathsf{R}}^{q_1}(\varphi_2,\varphi_1\wedge\varphi_2,\top)$, and we can prove $\neg\mathcal{A}_{\mathsf{R}}^{q_2}(\varphi_2,\varphi_1\wedge\varphi_2,\top) \to \mathcal{A}_{\mathsf{R}}^{q_2}(\varphi_2,\varphi_1\wedge\varphi_2,\top)$ in $\mathscr{L}$. Hence, $\mathcal{A}_{\mathsf{R}}^{q_2}(\varphi_2,\varphi_1\wedge\varphi_2,\top)$ can be directly replaced by $\top$. Now, the instanced axiom (Exp) becomes

$$\varphi_1\mathsf{R}\varphi_2 \leftrightarrow (\varphi_2 \wedge \bigcirc(\varphi_1\mathsf{R}\varphi_2)) \vee (\varphi_1 \wedge \varphi_2),$$

and the instance rule (Loop) becomes

$$\text{If} \quad (\psi_1 \to (\varphi_2 \wedge \bigcirc\psi_1 \vee (\varphi_1 \wedge \varphi_2) \wedge \bigcirc\psi_2)) \wedge (\psi_2 \to \bigcirc\psi_2)$$
$$\text{then } \psi_1 \to \varphi_1 \mathsf{R} \varphi_2.$$

For the instanced (Loop), the trivial conclusion $\psi_2 \to \top$ is omitted.

Once the base logic is decided, it is also important to choose proper operators. For example, when we decide to derive an LTL axiom system underlying the base logic ETL_r, things become complex. For doing this, we suggest to use G, W and $\bigcirc$ as LTL temporal operators [3]. The reason why we choose G and W as additional operators is that we can give them repeating automaton encodings that all the states are final states this fulfills the requirement of (R-Loop)'s premise.

In detail, $\mathcal{A}_\mathsf{W} = \langle\{a_1, a_2, a_3\}, \{q_1, q_2\}, \delta_\mathsf{W}, \{q_1\}, \{q_1, q_2\}\rangle$ and $\mathcal{A}_\mathsf{G} = \langle\{q_1\}, \{a_1\}, \delta_\mathsf{G}, \{q_1\}, \{q_1\}\rangle$, where $\delta_\mathsf{W}(q_1, a_1) = \{q_1\}$, $\delta_\mathsf{W}(q_1, a_2) = \{q_2\}$, $\delta_\mathsf{W}(q_2, a_3) = \{q_2\}$, $\delta_\mathsf{W}(q_1, a_3) = \delta_\mathsf{W}(q_2, a_1) = \delta_\mathsf{W}(q_2, a_2) = \emptyset$ and $\delta_\mathsf{G}(q_1, a_1) = \{q_1\}$. It is easy to proof that $\mathsf{G}\varphi \leftrightarrow \mathcal{A}_\mathsf{G}^{q_1}\varphi$, $\varphi_1 \mathsf{W} \varphi_2 \leftrightarrow \mathcal{A}_\mathsf{W}^{q_1}(\varphi_1, \varphi_2, \top)$. and $\mathcal{A}_\mathsf{W}^{q_2}(\varphi_1, \varphi_2, \top) \leftrightarrow \top$.

(Sim) derives no instanced rules because $\mathcal{A}_\mathsf{W}$ and $\mathcal{A}_\mathsf{G}$ do not share the same alphabet. Instanced axioms (Exp) for G and W are respectively $\mathsf{G}\varphi \leftrightarrow \varphi \wedge \bigcirc\mathsf{G}\varphi$ and $\varphi_1 \mathsf{W} \varphi_2 \leftrightarrow (\varphi_1 \wedge \bigcirc(\varphi_1 \mathsf{W} \varphi_2)) \vee \varphi_2$. Instanced rules of (Rep) and (R-Loop) for G can be respectively described as

$$(\text{Rep }) \quad \begin{array}{l} \text{If} \quad \psi \to (\varphi \to \bigcirc\psi) \\ \text{and } \psi \to \neg\varphi \\ \text{then } \psi \to \neg\mathsf{G}\varphi \end{array} \qquad (\text{R-Loop}) \quad \begin{array}{l} \text{If} \quad \psi \to (\varphi \wedge \bigcirc\psi) \\ \text{then } \psi \to \mathsf{G}\varphi \end{array}.$$

Instanced (Rep) for G can be reduced to have only one premise $\psi \to \neg\varphi$. Instanced rules of (Rep) and (R-Loop) for W can be respectively described as

$$(\text{Rep}) \quad \begin{array}{l} \text{If} \quad (\psi \to \neg\varphi_1) \wedge (\psi \to \neg\varphi_2) \\ \text{then } \psi \to \neg(\varphi_1 \mathsf{W} \varphi_2) \end{array} \qquad (\text{R-Loop}) \quad \begin{array}{l} \text{If} \quad \psi \to (\varphi_1 \wedge \bigcirc\psi) \vee \varphi_2 \\ \text{then } \psi \to \varphi_1 \mathsf{W} \varphi_2 \end{array}.$$

Please note that the premiss of instanced (Rep) for W has been reduced.

As the final example, we show how to axiomatize temporal logics involving infinitely many temporal connectives. Consider such a logic: it involves the next-time operator and all the connectives like P^k ($k \in \mathbb{N}$), where $(\pi, i) \models \mathsf{P}^k\varphi$ if and only if $(\pi, i + k \times j) \models \varphi$ for all $j \in \mathbb{N}$. For example, $\mathsf{P}^2 p$ means "p holds at least in all even moments". To get its axiom system, we consider this logic to be a fragment of ETL_l.

For each $k \geq 1$, we create a loop acceptance automaton $\mathcal{A}_k = \langle\{a, b\}, \{q_1, \ldots, q_k\}, \delta_k, \{q_1\}, \emptyset\rangle$, where:

$$\delta_k(q_i, a) = \begin{cases} \{q_1\} , & \text{if } i = 1 \\ \emptyset , & \text{otherwise} \end{cases} \quad \text{and} \quad \delta_k(q_i, b) = \begin{cases} \emptyset , & \text{if } i = 1 \\ q_{i+1} , & \text{if } 1 < i < k \\ q_1 , & \text{if } i = k \end{cases}.$$

Clearly, $\mathsf{P}^k\varphi = \mathcal{A}_k^{q_0}(\varphi, \top)$. According to (Exp), we have $\mathcal{A}_k^{q_i}(\varphi, \top) \leftrightarrow \bigcirc\mathcal{A}_k^{q_{i+1}}(\varphi, \top)$ for all $1 \leq i < k$, and $\mathcal{A}_k^{q_{k-1}}(\varphi, \top) \leftrightarrow \bigcirc\mathsf{P}^k\varphi$. Thus, we combine previous axioms and let

[3] Here, G is the "*global*" operator, and W is the "*weak until*" operator. The relation among W, G and U can be described as: $\varphi_1 \mathsf{W} \varphi_2 \leftrightarrow ((\varphi_1 \mathsf{U} \varphi_2) \vee \mathsf{G}\varphi_1)$, or $\varphi_1 \mathsf{U} \varphi_2 \leftrightarrow ((\varphi_1 \mathsf{W} \varphi_2) \wedge \neg\mathsf{G}\neg\varphi_2)$.

$$\mathsf{P}^k\varphi \leftrightarrow \varphi \wedge \bigcirc^k \mathsf{P}^k\varphi \qquad (k \in \mathbb{N})$$

to be the final form of instanced (Exp), where $\bigcirc^k$ is the abbreviation of k successive $\bigcirc$ operators. Similarly, one can give the instanced rule (Loop) as

$$\text{If} \quad \psi \to \varphi \wedge \bigcirc^k \psi \quad \text{then} \quad \psi \to \mathsf{P}^k\varphi \qquad k \in \mathbb{N}.$$

In comparison, when choosing ETL_f as the base logic, to produce the axiom system for this logic might make things complex.

6 Concluding Remarks

In this paper, we first present three complete axiom systems for ETL_l, ETL_f and ETL_r, respectively, and then present the axiomatizing approach by instantiation.

The axioms and rules for ETLs we provided are orthogonal. Each axiom system includes automaton-related axiom and rules, these characterize the essential properties of looping, finite and repeating temporal connectives, respectively. The utilities (K), (N) and (XGen) give a description of the nexttime operator.

We discussed three kinds of acceptance conditions of automaton connectives, and we believe that these are rich enough [KMM04] to produce axiom systems for various ETL fragments.

These deductive systems for ETLs are flexible. It is easy to rewrite them into ETL using alternating automaton connectives. To do this, just modify the automaton-related axioms and rules into the alternating version.

One of the further work is the axiomatization of ETLs equipped with "past operators" — i.e. Extended Temporal Logics employing two-way automata as connectives [KPV01]. In such systems, new axioms and rules reflecting "backward" and "stuttering" behaviors might be provided.

References

AFF+02. Armoni, R., Fix, L., Flaisher, A., Gerth, R., Ginsburg, B., Kanza, T., Landver, A., Mador-Haim, S., Singerman, E., Tiemeyer, A., Vardi, M.Y., Zbar, Y.: The forspec temporal logic: A new temporal property-specification language. In: Katoen, J.-P., Stevens, P. (eds.) ETAPS 2002 and TACAS 2002. LNCS, vol. 2280, pp. 211–296. Springer, Heidelberg (2002)

AFF+05. Armoni, R., Fix, L., Fraer, R., Huddleston, S., Piterman, N., Vardi, M.Y.: Sat-based induction for temporal safety properties. Electr. Notes Theor. Comput. Sci. 119(2), 3–16 (2005)

BB87. Banieqbal, B., Barringer, H.: Temporal logic with fixed points. In: Banieqbal, B., Pnueli, A., Barringer, H. (eds.) Temporal Logic in Specification. LNCS, vol. 398, pp. 62–74. Springer, Heidelberg (1989)

FR03. French, T., Reynolds, M.: A sound and complete proof system for QPTL. In: Proceedings of 4th Advances in Modal Logic, pp. 127–148. King's College Publications (2003)

Kai97. Kaivola, R.: Using Automata to Characterise Fixed Point Temporal Logics. PhD thesis, University of Edinburgh (1997)

Kai98. Kaivola, R.: Axiomatising extended computation tree logic. Theoretical Computer Science 190(1), 41–60 (1998)

KMM04. Kupferman, O., Morgenstern, G., Murano, A.: Typeness for ω-regular automata. In: Wang, F. (ed.) ATVA 2004. LNCS, vol. 3299, pp. 324–333. Springer, Heidelberg (2004)

KP95. Kesten, Y., Pnueli, A.: A complete proof systems for QPTL. In: Logic in Computer Science, pp. 2–12 (1995)

KPV01. Kupferman, O., Piterman, N., Vardi, M.Y.: Extended temporal logic revisited. In: Larsen, K.G., Nielsen, M. (eds.) CONCUR 2001. LNCS, vol. 2154, pp. 519–535. Springer, Heidelberg (2001)

LS01. Lange, M., Stirling, C.: Focus games for satisfiability and completeness of temporal logic. In: LICS'01. Proceedings of the 16th Annual IEEE Symposium on Logic in Computer Science, Boston, MA, USA, IEEE Computer Society Press, Los Alamitos (2001)

Pit00. Piterman, N.: Extending temporal logic with ω-automata. Thesis for the M.Sc Degree, School of the Weizmann Institute of Science (August 2000)

PVW87. Prasad, S.A., Vardi, M.Y., Wolper, P.: The complementation problem for Büchi automata with applications to temporal logic. Theoretical Computer Science 49, 217–237 (1987)

Var01. Vardi, M.Y.: Branching vs. linear time: Final showdown. In: Margaria, T., Yi, W. (eds.) ETAPS 2001 and TACAS 2001. LNCS, vol. 2031, pp. 1–22. Springer, Heidelberg (2001)

VW94. Vardi, M.Y., Wolper, P.: Reasoning about infinite computations. Information and Computation 115(1), 1–37 (1994)

Wol83. Wolper, P.: Temporal logic can be more expressive. Information and Control 56(1–2), 72–99 (1983)

WVS83. Wolper, P., Vardi, M.Y., Sistla, A.P.: Reasoning about infinite computation paths. In: Proc. 24th IEEE Symposium on Foundations of Computer Science, Tucson, pp. 185–194. IEEE Computer Society Press, Los Alamitos (1983)

Deciding Weak Bisimilarity of Normed Context-Free Processes Using Tableau*

Xinxin Liu[1] and Haiyan Chen[1,2]

[1] State Key Laboratory Computer Science, Institute of Software, Chinese Academy of Sciences, Beijing, 100080, China
[2] Graduate School of the Chinese Academy of Sciences, Beijing, 100039, China
{xinxin,chy}@ios.ac.cn

Abstract. Deciding strong and weak bisimilarity of context-free processes are challenging because of the infinite nature of the state space of such processes. Deciding weak bisimilarity is harder since the usual decomposition property which holds for strong bisimilarity fails. Hirshfeld proposed the notion of bisimulation tree to prove that weak bisimulation is decidable for totally normed BPA and BPP processes. Suggested by his idea of decomposition, in this paper we present a tableau method for deciding weak bisimilarity of totally normed context-free processes. Compared with Hirshfeld's bisimulation tree method, our method is more intuitive and more direct.

1 Introduction

There have been a lot of efforts on the study of decidability and complexity of verification problems for infinite-state systems [1,2,3]. In [4] Baeten, Bergstra, and Klop proved the remarkable result that bisimulation equivalence is decidable for irredundant context-free grammars (without the empty production). Within process calculus theory these grammars correspond to normed processes defined by a finite family of guarded recursion equations in the signature of BPA(Basic Process Algebra) [4]. In general these processes have infinite state space. The decidability result has later been extended to the class of all (not necessarily normed)BPA processes in [5,6]. J.Srba keeps an updated record of results on this subject [7].

Most of the results on infinite state system are concerning strong bisimilarity. For weak bisimilarity, much less is known. Semidecidability of weak bisimilarity for BPP has been shown in [8]. Hirshfeld proved a decomposition property for a generalized weak bisimilarity of totally normed context-free processes, and with this directly obtained decidability of bisimilarity of totally normed BPA in [9]. This decidability result is also a consequence of a more elaborate theorem proved by Stirling in [10].

* Supported by the National Natural Science Foundation of China under Grant Nos. 60673045, 60496321.

C.B. Jones, Z. Liu, J. Woodcock (Eds.): ICTAC 2007, LNCS 4711, pp. 337–350, 2007.

Our work is inspired by Hirshfeld's idea of decomposition for a generalized weak bisimilarity. By refining Hirshfeld's notion of weak bisimulation up to, we obtain an equivalence relation which enables us to devise a tableau method for deciding weak bisimilarity of totally normed context-free processes. In [11], Hüttel and Stirling proposed a tableau decision procedure for deciding strong bisimilarity of normed context-free processes. Later in [12], Hüttel adapted the tableau method and proved the decidability of branching bisimulation of totally normed context-free processes. As Hüttel pointed out in [12], the key for tableau method to work is a nice decomposition property which holds for strong bisimulation and branching bisimulation, but fails for weak bisimulation. Our work in some sense is to propose a version of weak bisimulation equivalence for which certain decomposition property (Proposition 6) makes the tableau method work correctly.

The paper is organized as follows. In section 2 we review some important concepts about BPA processes and weak bisimulation. In section 3 we describe relative weak bisimulation equivalence which is the key for the tableau method. In section 4 we present the tableau decision method and show the sound and completeness result. Section 5 contains conclusion and suggestions for further work.

2 BPA Processes

Following [9], here we present BPA processes as states in a sequential labeled rewrite system.

Definition 1. *A sequential labeled rewrite system is a tuple* $\langle \mathcal{V}, \Sigma_\tau, \Delta \rangle$ *where*

1. $\mathcal{V}$ *is a finite set of variables; the elements of* $\mathcal{V}^*$*, finite strings on* $\mathcal{V}$*, are referred to as states.*
2. Σ_τ *is a finite set of labels, containing a special label* τ*.*
3. $\Delta \subseteq \mathcal{V} \times \Sigma_\tau \times \mathcal{V}^*$ *is a finite set of rewrite rules.*

We use X, Y, Z to range over elements of $\mathcal{V}$; a, b, c to range over elements of Σ; α, β, γ to range over elements of $\mathcal{V}^*$, and write $\alpha\beta$ for the concatenation of α and β. The operational semantics of the processes (states) can be simply given by a labeled transition system $(\mathcal{V}^*, \Sigma_\tau, \longrightarrow)$ where $\longrightarrow \subseteq \mathcal{V}^* \times \Sigma_\tau \times \mathcal{V}^*$ is defined as follows:

$$\longrightarrow = \{(X\beta, a, \alpha\beta) | (X, a, \alpha) \in \Delta,\ \beta \in \mathcal{V}^*\}.$$

As usual we write $\alpha \xrightarrow{a} \beta$ for $(\alpha, a, \beta) \in \longrightarrow$, and write $\alpha \overset{\epsilon}{\Longrightarrow} \beta$ or simply $\alpha \Longrightarrow \beta$ for $\alpha(\xrightarrow{\tau})^*\beta$, and write $\alpha \overset{a}{\Longrightarrow} \beta$ for $\alpha \overset{\epsilon}{\Longrightarrow}\xrightarrow{a}\overset{\epsilon}{\Longrightarrow} \beta$. We say α is terminating, written $\alpha \Downarrow$, if $\alpha(\xrightarrow{\tau})^*\epsilon$ where ϵ is the empty string.

Here is an example adapted from [11]. Consider the labeled rewrite system $\langle \mathcal{V}, \Sigma_\tau, \Delta \rangle$, where

$$\mathcal{V} = \{X, Y\},\ \Sigma_\tau = \{a, c, \tau\},$$

$$\Delta = \{(X, a, \epsilon),\ (X, \tau, XY),\ (Y, c, \epsilon)\}.$$

Clearly the state space generated from X (i.e. the set of states reachable from X by performing transitions) consists of strings of the forms $X, XY, \cdots, XY^n, \cdots$ and $\epsilon, Y, \cdots, Y^n, \cdots$. Obviously the number of such states are infinite, even under quotient of weak bisimulation equivalence.

Let $\hat{}: \Sigma_\tau \longrightarrow \Sigma_\tau^*$ be the function such that $\hat{a} = a$ when $a \neq \tau$ and $\hat{\tau} = \epsilon$, the following general definition of weak bisimulation on $\mathcal{V}^*$ is standard.

Definition 2. *A binary relation $R \subseteq \mathcal{V}^* \times \mathcal{V}^*$ is a weak bisimulation if for all $(\alpha, \beta) \in R$ the following hold:*

1. *$\alpha \Downarrow$ if and only if $\beta \Downarrow$;*
2. *whenever $\alpha \xrightarrow{a} \alpha'$, then $\beta \xRightarrow{\hat{a}} \beta'$ for some β' with $(\alpha', \beta') \in R$;*
3. *whenever $\beta \xrightarrow{a} \beta'$, then $\alpha \xRightarrow{\hat{a}} \alpha'$ for some α' with $(\alpha', \beta') \in R$.*

Two states α and β are said to be weak bisimulation equivalent, written $\alpha \approx \beta$, if there is a weak bisimulation R such that $(\alpha, \beta) \in R$.

It is standard to prove that $\approx$ is an equivalence relation between processes. Moreover the following proposition shows that it is a congruence with respect to string composition on $\mathcal{V}^*$.

Proposition 1. *If $\alpha \approx \beta$ and $\alpha' \approx \beta'$ then $\alpha\alpha' \approx \beta\beta'$.*

Proof. We construct a binary relation $R = \{(\alpha\alpha', \beta\beta') | \alpha \approx \beta,\ \alpha' \approx \beta'\}$. We will show that R is a weak bisimulation, i.e. R satisfies the clause 1. 2. and 3. of Definition 2. Suppose $(\alpha\alpha', \beta\beta') \in R$ with $\alpha \approx \beta$, $\alpha' \approx \beta'$. If $\alpha\alpha' \Downarrow$ then $\alpha \Downarrow$ and $\alpha' \Downarrow$, since $\alpha \approx \beta$ and $\alpha' \approx \beta'$, $\alpha \Downarrow$ iff $\beta \Downarrow$ and $\alpha' \Downarrow$ iff $\beta' \Downarrow$, so $\beta\beta' \Downarrow$; in the same way we can prove that $\beta\beta' \Downarrow$ implies $\alpha\alpha' \Downarrow$, thus clause 1 of Definition 2 is satisfied. For clause 2. suppose $\alpha\alpha' \xrightarrow{a} \alpha''$, we discuss by two cases: if $\alpha \neq \epsilon$ and $\alpha \xrightarrow{a} \alpha_1$, then $\alpha'' \equiv \alpha_1\alpha'$, since $\alpha \approx \beta$, $\exists \beta_1 . \beta \xRightarrow{\hat{a}} \beta_1$ with $\alpha_1 \approx \beta_1$, then $\beta\beta' \xRightarrow{\hat{a}} \beta_1\beta'$ with $(\alpha_1\alpha', \beta_1\beta') \in R$, clause 2. of Definition 2 is satisfied; if $\alpha = \epsilon$, then $\alpha\alpha' = \alpha'$ and $\beta \Downarrow$ (since $\alpha \approx \beta$, now $\alpha \Downarrow$), in this case $\alpha\alpha' \xrightarrow{a} \alpha''$, then $\alpha' \xrightarrow{a} \alpha''$, since $\alpha' \approx \beta'$, $\exists \beta'' . \beta' \xRightarrow{\hat{a}} \beta''$ *with* $(\alpha'', \beta'') \in R$, so $\beta\beta' \Longrightarrow \beta' \xRightarrow{\hat{a}} \beta''$ with $(\alpha'', \beta'') \in R$, thus clause 2 of Definition 2 is satisfied. For clause 3. the situation is similar to clause 2. □

Note that in general clause 1. of Definition 2 is necessary. Otherwise any $X \in \mathcal{V}$ which has no transitions will be equated with ϵ, and as a consequence Proposition 1 would fail.

3 Relative Weak Bisimulation Equivalence

In this section we propose a notion of weak bisimulation relative to a binary relation on states. This notion is a refinement of Hirshfeld's notion of "bisimulation up to" introduced in [9]. For the induced new equivalence, we then study its decomposition properties, its relationship to $\approx$. This provides a foundation for the tableau decision method discussed in the next section.

The following definition settles some notations and terminologies.

Definition 3. *A state α is said to be* normed *if there exists a finite sequence of transitions from α to ϵ, and un-normed otherwise. The weak norm of a normed α is the length of the shortest transition sequence of the form $\alpha \stackrel{a_1}{\Longrightarrow} \ldots \stackrel{a_n}{\Longrightarrow} \epsilon$, where each $a_i \neq \tau$ and $\stackrel{a_i}{\Longrightarrow}$ is counted as 1. We denote by $||\alpha||$ the weak norm of α. Also, we follow the convention that $||\alpha|| = \infty$ for unnormed α, and $\infty > n$ for any number n. A state is totally normed if it is a state of a system $\langle \mathcal{V}, \Sigma_\tau, \Delta \rangle$ where for every variable $X \in \mathcal{V}$, $0 < ||X|| < \infty$.*

Note that $||X|| < \infty$ is the same as saying that X is normed, while $||X|| > 0$ implies that X cannot terminate silently.

It is obvious that weak norm is additive: $||\alpha\beta|| = ||\alpha|| + ||\beta||$. Moreover, weak norm is respected by $\approx$.

For a binary relation Γ on states, we write $\stackrel{\Gamma}{=}$ for the equivalence relation generated by the following four rules:

$$ref: \ \alpha \stackrel{\Gamma}{=} \alpha \qquad\qquad axiom: \alpha \stackrel{\Gamma}{=} \beta((\alpha, \beta) \in \Gamma)$$

$$tran: \frac{\alpha \stackrel{\Gamma}{=} \beta, \ \beta \stackrel{\Gamma}{=} \gamma}{\alpha \stackrel{\Gamma}{=} \gamma} \qquad symm: \frac{\alpha \stackrel{\Gamma}{=} \beta}{\beta \stackrel{\Gamma}{=} \alpha}$$

i.e. $\stackrel{\Gamma}{=}$ is the smallest reflexive, symmetry, and transitive binary relation containing Γ. Clearly if Γ is finite then so is $\stackrel{\Gamma}{=}$, and in this case it is decidable whether $\alpha \stackrel{\Gamma}{=} \beta$.

Definition 4. *Let $R, \Gamma \subseteq \mathcal{V}^* \times \mathcal{V}^*$. R is a weak bisimulation w.r.t Γ if for all $(\alpha, \beta) \in R$, then either $||\alpha|| = ||\beta|| \leq 1$ and $\alpha \stackrel{\Gamma}{=} \beta$, or $||\alpha|| > 1$ and $||\beta|| > 1$ and the following hold:*

1. whenever $\alpha \stackrel{a}{\longrightarrow} \alpha'$, then $\beta \stackrel{\hat{a}}{\Longrightarrow} \beta'$ for some β' such that $(\alpha', \beta') \in R$,
2. whenever $\beta \stackrel{a}{\longrightarrow} \beta'$, then $\alpha \stackrel{\hat{a}}{\Longrightarrow} \alpha'$ for some α' such that $(\alpha', \beta') \in R$.

For $\alpha, \beta \in \mathcal{V}^*$ and $\Gamma \subseteq \mathcal{V}^* \times \mathcal{V}^*$, we say that α is weak bisimilar to β w.r.t. Γ, written $\alpha \approx_\Gamma \beta$, if there is $R \subseteq \mathcal{V}^* \times \mathcal{V}^*$ such that R is a weak bisimulation w.r.t Γ and $(\alpha, \beta) \in R$.

This is a typical co-inductive definition for $\approx_\Gamma$. With such definition, the following properties of $\approx_\Gamma$ are expected and have standard proofs which are omitted here.

Proposition 2. *Let $\Gamma \subseteq \mathcal{V}^* \times \mathcal{V}^*$, then*

1. $\approx_\Gamma$ is the largest weak bisimulation w.r.t Γ;
2. $\approx_\Gamma$ is an equivalence, i.e. it is reflexive, symmetric, and transitive.

Remark: Our definition differs from Hirshfeld's bisimulation up to as follows. First, bisimulation up to is defined through a series of approximation while $\approx_\Gamma$

is defined using maximum fixed-point approach. Second, in our definition we use the weak norms of α, β *as pre-conditions to determine when "bisimulation clauses" 1 and 2 are required to hold when are not, moreover in the case clauses 1 and 2 are not required to hold we then require* $\alpha \stackrel{\Gamma}{=} \beta$ *instead of simply* $(\alpha, \beta) \in \Gamma$. *As a result* $\approx_\Gamma$ *is an equivalence relation, an important property which is necessary for the tableau method to work correctly. Bisimulation up to is not an equivalence relation in general.*

Next we define some special kinds of Γ which have useful properties.

Definition 5. *Let* $\Gamma \subseteq \mathcal{V}^* \times \mathcal{V}^*$. *We say* Γ *is uniform if* $||\alpha|| = ||\beta|| = 1$ *for all* $(\alpha, \beta) \in \Gamma$. *We say* Γ *is sound if for all* $(\alpha, \beta) \in \Gamma$ *the following hold:*

1. *whenever* $\alpha \stackrel{a}{\longrightarrow} \alpha'$ *then* $\beta \stackrel{\hat{a}}{\Longrightarrow} \beta'$ *for some* β' *with* $\alpha' \approx_\Gamma \beta'$;
2. *whenever* $\beta \stackrel{a}{\longrightarrow} \beta'$ *then* $\alpha \stackrel{\hat{a}}{\Longrightarrow} \alpha'$ *for some* α' *with* $\alpha' \approx_\Gamma \beta'$.

Proposition 3. *Let* $\Gamma \subseteq \mathcal{V}^* \times \mathcal{V}^*$ *be uniform. Then* $\stackrel{\Gamma}{=}$ *respects weak norms, i.e. if* $\alpha \stackrel{\Gamma}{=} \beta$ *then either both* α, β *are un-normed, or both are normed and* $||\alpha|| = ||\beta||$. *Moreover* $\approx_\Gamma$ *also respects weak norms.*

Proof. It is obvious that $\stackrel{\Gamma}{=}$ respects weak norms.

Let α be normed and $\alpha \approx_\Gamma \beta$. We prove that β is also normed and $||\alpha|| = ||\beta||$ by induction on the weak norm of α. By Definition 4 either $||\alpha|| = ||\beta|| \leq 1$ and $\alpha \stackrel{\Gamma}{=} \beta$, or $||\alpha|| > 1$, $||\beta|| > 1$ and clauses 1.2. hold. In the first case since $\alpha \stackrel{\Gamma}{=} \beta$ and $\stackrel{\Gamma}{=}$ respects weak norms, so $||\alpha|| = ||\beta||$. If $||\alpha|| > 1$, suppose $\alpha \stackrel{\tau^i}{\longrightarrow} \alpha_1 \stackrel{a}{\longrightarrow} \alpha'$ with $a \neq \tau$ and $||\alpha|| = ||\alpha'|| + 1$, then $\alpha \approx_\Gamma \beta$ implies that $\beta \stackrel{a}{\Longrightarrow} \beta'$ for some β' with $\alpha' \approx_\Gamma \beta'$. Now since $||\alpha'|| < ||\alpha||$, by the induction hypothesis β' is normed and $||\alpha'|| = ||\beta'||$, thus β is normed and $||\beta|| \leq ||\alpha||$. Now we can apply the same reasoning with α, β switching places we obtain $||\alpha|| \leq ||\beta||$, thus $||\alpha|| = ||\beta||$. □

The following easy to prove lemma shows an important property of sound Γ.

Lemma 1. *Let* $\Gamma \subseteq \mathcal{V}^* \times \mathcal{V}^*$ *be sound. If* $\alpha \stackrel{\Gamma}{=} \beta$ *then the following hold:*

1. *whenever* $\alpha \stackrel{a}{\longrightarrow} \alpha'$ *then* $\beta \stackrel{\hat{a}}{\Longrightarrow} \beta'$ *for some* β' *with* $\alpha' \approx_\Gamma \beta'$;
2. *whenever* $\beta \stackrel{a}{\longrightarrow} \beta'$ *then* $\alpha \stackrel{\hat{a}}{\Longrightarrow} \alpha'$ *for some* α' *with* $\alpha' \approx_\Gamma \beta'$.

Lemma 2. *If* $\Gamma \subseteq \mathcal{V}^* \times \mathcal{V}^*$ *is both uniform and sound then* $\approx_\Gamma$ *is a weak bisimulation.*

Proof. Let $\alpha \approx_\Gamma \beta$, we will show that clauses 1. 2. and 3. of Definition 2 are satisfied. By Proposition 3 in this case $\approx_\Gamma$ respects weak norms, thus $\alpha \Downarrow$ iff $||\alpha|| = 0$ iff $||\beta|| = 0$ iff $\beta \Downarrow$, clause 1. of Definition 2 is satisfied. For clause 2. and clause 3. since $\approx_\Gamma$ respects weak norms we only need to consider the following two cases. If $||\alpha|| > 1$ and $||\beta|| > 1$, then since $\approx_\Gamma$ is a weak bisimulation w.r.t Γ, $\alpha \approx_\Gamma \beta$ implies clause 2. and clause 3. If $||\alpha|| = ||\beta|| \leq 1$, then $\alpha \approx_\Gamma \beta$ implies $\alpha \stackrel{\Gamma}{=} \beta$, and clause 2. and 3. are satisfied by Lemma 1. □

Proposition 4. *Let $\alpha, \beta, \gamma \in \mathcal{V}^*$, $\Gamma \subseteq \mathcal{V}^* \times \mathcal{V}^*$. If $\alpha \approx_\Gamma \beta$ then $\gamma\alpha \approx_\Gamma \gamma\beta$.*

Proof. It is easy to check that $\{(\gamma\alpha, \gamma\beta) \mid \gamma \in \mathcal{V}^*, \alpha \approx_\Gamma \beta\}$ is a weak bisimulation w.r.t. Γ. □

Lemma 3. *Let $\Gamma \subseteq \mathcal{V}^* \times \mathcal{V}^*$, $\alpha_1, \alpha_2, \beta_1, \beta_2 \in \mathcal{V}^*$ with α_1, β_1 normed and $||\alpha_1|| \geq ||\beta_1||$. If $\alpha_1\alpha_2 \approx_\Gamma \beta_1\beta_2$ and $||\beta_1\beta_2|| > 1$ then there exists $\delta \in \mathcal{V}^*$ such that $\delta\alpha_2 \approx_\Gamma \beta_2$.*

Proof. By induction on $||\beta_1||$. If $||\beta_1|| = 0$, let $\beta_1 \stackrel{\epsilon}{\Longrightarrow} \epsilon$, then $\beta_1\beta_2 \stackrel{\epsilon}{\Longrightarrow} \beta_2$, and since $\alpha_1\alpha_2 \approx_\Gamma \beta_1\beta_2$, there exists $\alpha' \in \mathcal{V}^*$ such that $\alpha_1\alpha_2 \stackrel{\epsilon}{\Longrightarrow} \alpha'$ and $\alpha' \approx_\Gamma \beta_2$. Since in this case $||\alpha_1|| > 0$, it must be that $\alpha_1 \stackrel{\epsilon}{\Longrightarrow} \delta$ and $\alpha' = \delta\alpha_2$ for some $\delta \in \mathcal{V}^*$, thus we proved the case for $||\beta_1|| = 0$. If $||\beta_1|| > 0$, let $\beta_1 \stackrel{a}{\Longrightarrow} \beta'$ be a weak norm reducing transition sequence, then $\beta_1\beta_2 \stackrel{a}{\Longrightarrow} \beta'\beta_2$ and since $\alpha_1\alpha_2 \approx_\Gamma \beta_1\beta_2$, there exists $\alpha' \in \mathcal{V}^*$ such that $\alpha_1\alpha_2 \stackrel{a}{\Longrightarrow} \alpha'$ and $\alpha' \approx_\Gamma \beta'\beta_2$. Since in this case $||\alpha_1|| > 1$, it must be that $\alpha_1 \stackrel{a}{\Longrightarrow} \alpha''$ and $\alpha' = \alpha''\alpha_2$ for some $\alpha'' \in \mathcal{V}^*$. Now $\alpha''\alpha_2 \approx_\Gamma \beta'\beta_2$, $||\beta'|| < ||\beta_1||$, and $||\alpha''||$ at most reduce $||\alpha_1||$ by 1 thus still $||\alpha''|| > ||\beta'||$, by the induction hypothesis there exists $\delta \in \mathcal{V}^*$ such that $\delta\alpha_2 \approx_\Gamma \beta_2$. □

4 The Tableau Method for Totally Normed BPA

From now on, we restrict our attention to totally normed BPA processes, i.e. processes of a sequential labeled rewrite system $\langle \mathcal{V}, \Sigma_\tau, \Delta \rangle$ where $\infty > ||X|| > 0$ for all $X \in \mathcal{V}$. And throughout the rest of the paper, we assume that all the processes considered are totally normed unless stated otherwise.

We show that for totally normed processes the following are decidable:

1. whether $\alpha \approx_\Gamma \beta$, where $\Gamma \subseteq \mathcal{V}^* \times \mathcal{V}^*$ is uniform;
2. whether $\alpha \approx \beta$.

We first show that 1 above is decidable. Then we show 2 is also decidable by showing a reduction to 1.

First we list the following obvious properties of such processes.

Proposition 5. *In a totally normed process system $\langle \mathcal{V}, \Sigma_\tau, \Delta \rangle$,*

1. *for a fixed n, there are only finitely many $\alpha \in \mathcal{V}^*$ such that $||\alpha|| = n$;*
2. *if $\Gamma \subseteq \mathcal{V}^* \times \mathcal{V}^*$ is uniform then Γ is finite;*
3. *there are only finitely many $\Gamma \subseteq \mathcal{V}^* \times \mathcal{V}^*$ which are uniform.*

In the following, we devise a tableau decision method to decide whether $\alpha \approx_\Gamma \beta$. The rules of the tableau system are built around equations of the form $\alpha =_\Gamma \beta$, where $\alpha, \beta \in \mathcal{V}^*$, $\Gamma \subseteq \mathcal{V}^* \times \mathcal{V}^*$ is uniform. Each rule has the form

$$\text{name} \quad \frac{\alpha =_\Gamma \beta}{\alpha_1 =_{\Gamma_1} \beta_1 \ldots \alpha_n =_{\Gamma_n} \beta_n} \quad \text{side condition.}$$

The premise of a rule represents the goal to be achieved while the consequents are the subgoals. There are three rules altogether. One rule for reducing the weak norms of the states in the goal, one rule for aligning the states so that rule reduc can be applied, and one rule for unfolding. We now explain the three rules in turn.

4.1 Reducing Weak Norms

The following proposition states an important decomposition property of weak bisimulation with respect to Γ. With this property, we introduce the first rule of our tableau method which can be used to reduce the weak norms of the states in the goal.

Proposition 6. *Let $\alpha, \beta \in \mathcal{V}^*$ with $||\alpha|| = ||\beta|| > 1$, $X \in \mathcal{V}$, $\Gamma \subseteq \mathcal{V}^* \times \mathcal{V}^*$ be uniform. Then $\alpha X \approx_\Gamma \beta X$ if and only if there exists $\Gamma' \subseteq \mathcal{V}^* \times \mathcal{V}^*$ such that Γ' is uniform and $\alpha \approx_{\Gamma'} \beta$ and $\alpha' X \approx_\Gamma \beta' X$ for all $(\alpha', \beta') \in \Gamma'$.*

Proof. For the "if" direction, let $R = \{(\alpha' X, \beta' X) \mid \alpha' \approx_{\Gamma'} \beta'\}$, it is not difficult to check that $R \cup \approx_\Gamma$ is a weak bisimulation w.r.t. Γ. Also, obviously $(\alpha X, \beta X) \in R$, thus $(\alpha X, \beta X) \in R \cup \approx_\Gamma$, and so $\alpha X \approx_\Gamma \beta X$.

For the "only if" direction, let

$$\Gamma' = \{(\alpha', \beta') \mid ||\alpha'|| = ||\beta'|| = 1, \alpha' X \approx_\Gamma \beta' X\},$$
$$R = \{(\alpha', \beta') \mid \alpha' X \approx_\Gamma \beta' X\}.$$

Obviously Γ' is uniform and $\alpha' X \approx_\Gamma \beta' X$ for all $(\alpha', \beta') \in \Gamma'$. Also it is easy to check that R is a weak bisimulation w.r.t. Γ' and $(\alpha, \beta) \in R$. □

This proposition guarantees the soundness and backwards soundness of the following rule:

$$\text{reduc}\ \frac{\alpha X =_\Gamma \beta X}{\alpha =_{\Gamma'} \beta \quad \{\alpha' X =_\Gamma \beta' X \mid (\alpha', \beta') \in \Gamma'\}} \qquad ||\alpha|| = ||\beta|| > 1$$

Note that the states in the subgoals all have smaller weak norms than the states in the original goal. Also note that, by 3. of Proposition 5, there are only finitely many possible choices for Γ'. This means there are only finitely many different ways to apply this rule.

4.2 Aligning the States

The next rule can be used to align the states in the goal so that rule reduc can be applied to the subgoals. The rule is based on the following observation.

Proposition 7. *Let $\alpha_1, \beta_1, \alpha, \beta \in \mathcal{V}^*$ with $||\alpha_1|| \geq ||\beta_1|| > 1$. Then $\alpha_1 \alpha \approx_\Gamma \beta_1 \beta$ if and only if there exists $\delta \in \mathcal{V}^*$ such that $\delta \alpha \approx_\Gamma \beta$ and $\alpha_1 \alpha \approx_\Gamma \beta_1 \delta \alpha$ and $||\delta|| = ||\alpha_1|| - ||\beta_1||$.*

Proof. For the "if" direction, suppose $\alpha_1\alpha \approx_\Gamma \beta_1\delta\alpha$ and $\delta\alpha \approx_\Gamma \beta$. Then by Proposition 4 $\beta_1\delta\alpha \approx_\Gamma \beta_1\beta$. Then since $\approx_\Gamma$ is an equivalence, by transitivity we obtain $\alpha_1\alpha \approx_\Gamma \beta_1\beta$.

For the "only if" direction, suppose $\alpha_1\alpha \approx_\Gamma \beta_1\beta$. Since $||\alpha_1|| \geq ||\beta_1||$, by Lemma 3 there exists $\delta \in \mathcal{V}^*$ with $\delta\alpha \approx_\Gamma \beta$. Then by Proposition 4 $\beta_1\delta\alpha \approx_\Gamma \beta_1\beta$, and again since $\approx_\Gamma$ is an equivalence, by transitivity $\alpha_1\alpha \approx_\Gamma \beta_1\delta\alpha$. By Proposition 3 $\approx_\Gamma$ respects weak norms, thus $||\alpha_1|| + ||\alpha|| = ||\beta_1|| + ||\delta|| + ||\alpha||$, and $||\delta|| = ||\alpha_1|| - ||\beta_1||$. □

This proposition guarantees the soundness and backwards soundness of the following rule:

$$\text{align}\ \frac{\alpha_1\alpha =_\Gamma \beta_1\beta}{\alpha_1\delta\beta =_\Gamma \beta_1\beta \quad \alpha =_\Gamma \delta\beta} \qquad ||\delta|| = ||\beta_1|| - ||\alpha_1||, ||\alpha_1|| > 1$$

Note that by 1. of Proposition 5 there are only finitely many possible choices for δ. Thus there are only finitely many ways to apply each rule.

Discussion. In fact we can refine the rule by imposing more strict restrictions on δ. To do so, for $\alpha, \beta \in \mathcal{V}^*$ with $||\alpha|| \geq ||\beta||$, we first define the set $D(\alpha,\beta)$ inductively defined the weak norm of β as follows: if $||\beta|| = 0$ then $D(\alpha,\beta) = \{\alpha\}$, otherwise

$$D(\alpha,\beta) = \cup\{D(\alpha',\beta') \mid \exists a \in \Sigma.\alpha \stackrel{a}{\Longrightarrow} \alpha', \beta \stackrel{a}{\Longrightarrow} \beta', ||\alpha'|| < ||\alpha||, ||\beta'|| < ||\beta||, ||\alpha'|| \geq ||\beta'||\}.$$

Note that in the above formula the weak norm of α' (β') is exactly one less than that of α (β). With this in mind it is not difficult to see that $D(\alpha,\beta)$ is finite and can be easily computed. Then instead of requiring $||\delta|| = ||\beta_1|| - ||\alpha_1||$ in the side condition of rule align, we can require $\delta \in D(\beta_1, \alpha_1)$, and the refined rule remains both sound and backwards sound. With the new restriction, we only need to consider fewer choices for δ.

4.3 Unfolding by Matching the Transitions

Definition 6. *Let $(\alpha,\beta) \in \mathcal{V}^* \times \mathcal{V}^*$. A binary relation $M \subseteq \mathcal{V}^* \times \mathcal{V}^*$ is a match for (α,β) if the following hold:*

1. *whenever $\alpha \stackrel{a}{\longrightarrow} \alpha'$ then $\beta \stackrel{\hat{a}}{\Longrightarrow} \beta'$ for some $(\alpha',\beta') \in M$;*
2. *whenever $\beta \stackrel{a}{\longrightarrow} \beta'$ then $\alpha \stackrel{\hat{a}}{\Longrightarrow} \alpha'$ for some $(\alpha',\beta') \in M$;*
3. *whenever $(\alpha',\beta') \in M$ then $||\alpha'|| = ||\beta'||$ and either $\alpha \stackrel{a}{\longrightarrow} \alpha'$ or $\beta \stackrel{a}{\longrightarrow} \beta'$ for some $a \in \Sigma$.*

It is easy to see that for a given $(\alpha,\beta) \in \mathcal{V}^* \times \mathcal{V}^*$, there are finitely many possible $M \subseteq \mathcal{V}^* \times \mathcal{V}^*$ which satisfies 3. above and moreover each of them must be finite. And for such M it is not difficult to see that it is decidable whether M is a match for (α,β).

The last rule can be used to obtain subgoals by matching transitions, and it is based on the following observation.

Proposition 8. *Let $\alpha, \beta \in \mathcal{V}^*$ with $||\alpha|| = ||\beta|| > 1$. Then $\alpha \approx_\Gamma \beta$ if and only if there exists a match M for (α, β) such that $\alpha' \approx_\Gamma \beta'$ for all $(\alpha', \beta') \in M$.*

Proof. Obvious from Definition 4. □

This proposition guarantees the soundness and backwards soundness of the following rule:

$$\textsf{unfold}\ \frac{\alpha =_\Gamma \beta}{\{\alpha' =_\Gamma \beta' \mid (\alpha', \beta') \in M\}} \qquad ||\alpha|| = ||\beta|| > 1, M \text{ is a match for } (\alpha, \beta)$$

As pointed out above there are finitely many matches for a given (α, β), so there are finitely many ways to apply this rule on (α, β).

4.4 Constructing Tableaux

We determine whether $\alpha \approx_\Gamma \beta$ by constructing a tableau with root $\alpha =_\Gamma \beta$ using the three rules introduced above. A tableau is a finite tree with nodes labeled by equations of the form $\alpha =_\Gamma \beta$, where $\alpha, \beta \in \mathcal{V}^*$, $\Gamma \subseteq \mathcal{V}^* \times \mathcal{V}^*$ is uniform.

Moreover if $\alpha =_\Gamma \beta$ labels a non-leaf node, then the following are satisfied:

1. $||\alpha|| = ||\beta||$;
2. its sons are labeled by $\alpha_1 =_{\Gamma_1} \beta_1 \ldots \alpha_n =_{\Gamma_n} \beta_n$ obtained by applying rule reduc or align or unfold to $\alpha =_\Gamma \beta$, in that priority order;
3. no other non-leaf node is labeled by $\alpha =_\Gamma \beta$.

A tableau is a successful tableau if the labels of all its leaves have either of the following forms:

1. $\alpha =_\Gamma \beta$ where there is a non-leaf node also labeled $\alpha =_\Gamma \beta$;
2. $\alpha =_\Gamma \beta$ where $\alpha \stackrel{\Gamma}{=} \beta$.

Note that as we pointed out earlier that for finite Γ (by 2. of Proposition 5 this must be the case), whether $\alpha \stackrel{\Gamma}{=} \beta$ is decidable.

4.5 Decidability, Soundness, and Completeness

Theorem 1. *For $\alpha, \beta \in \mathcal{V}^*$, and uniform $\Gamma \subseteq \mathcal{V}^* \times \mathcal{V}^*$, there are finitely many tableaux with root $\alpha =_\Gamma \beta$, and all of them can be effectively enumerated.*

Proof. Note that the only rule in which the weak norms of states in the subgoals can be greater than that in the original goal is rule unfold, and the priority rule mentioned above determines that this rule can only be applied when all two other rules are not applicable, and it is easy to see that this can only happen when both states in the goal contains no more than 2 letters. This fact implies that each state in the nodes of a tableau with root $\alpha \approx_\Gamma \beta$ has bounded weak norms. Then by 1. and 3. of Proposition 5 there are bounded number of different labels in such a tableau. And since no two non-leaf nodes are labeled the same, a tableau with root $\alpha \approx_\Gamma \beta$ can only have bounded number of non-leaf nodes, thus the number of tableaux with root $\alpha \approx_\Gamma \beta$ must be finite.

There are finitely many (exactly 3) rules to apply on each node, and each rule with finitely many different ways to apply, thus there is a way to enumerate all different tableaux with a root $\alpha \approx_\Gamma \beta$. □

This theorem gives us a decision procedure for the problem whether there is a successful tableau with root $\alpha =_\Gamma \beta$, since we just need to enumerate all tableaux with root $\alpha =_\Gamma \beta$, and then test if each of them are successful (this test is also decidable as mentioned earlier).

Definition 7. *A sound tableau is a tableau such that if $\alpha =_\Gamma \beta$ is a label in it then $\alpha \approx_\Gamma \beta$.*

Theorem 2. *A successful tableau is a sound tableau.*

Proof. Let T be a successful tableau. We define $W = \{(\alpha, \Gamma, \beta) \mid \alpha, \beta \in \mathcal{V}^*, \Gamma \subseteq \mathcal{V}^* \times \mathcal{V}^* \text{ is uniform}\}$ to be the smallest set of triples satisfies the following:

1. if $\alpha \stackrel{\Gamma}{=} \beta$ then $(\alpha, \Gamma, \beta) \in W$;
2. if there is a node in T labeled with $\alpha =_\Gamma \beta$ and on which rule unfold is applied then $(\alpha, \Gamma, \beta) \in W$;
3. if $(\alpha, \Gamma, \alpha') \in W$, $(\gamma\alpha', \Gamma, \beta) \in W$, and $||\gamma|| > 1$, then $(\gamma\alpha, \Gamma, \beta) \in W$;
4. if $(\alpha, \Gamma', \beta) \in W$, $||\alpha|| = ||\beta|| > 1$, and moreover $(\alpha', \beta') \in \Gamma'$ implies $(\alpha' X, \Gamma, \beta' X) \in W$, then $(\alpha X, \Gamma, \beta X) \in W$.

We will prove the following properties about W:

A. If $\alpha =_\Gamma \beta$ labels a node in T then $(\alpha, \Gamma, \beta) \in W$.

B. If $(\alpha, \Gamma, \beta) \in W$, then either $||\alpha|| = ||\beta|| \leq 1$ and $\alpha \stackrel{\Gamma}{=} \beta$, or $||\alpha|| > 1$ and $||\beta|| > 1$ and moreover the following hold:
   (a) if $\alpha \xrightarrow{a} \alpha'$ then $\beta \stackrel{\hat{a}}{\Longrightarrow} \beta'$ for some β' such that $(\alpha', \Gamma, \beta') \in W$;
   (b) if $\beta \xrightarrow{a} \beta'$ then $\alpha \stackrel{\hat{a}}{\Longrightarrow} \alpha'$ for some α' such that $(\alpha', \Gamma, \beta') \in W$.

Clearly property B. implies that for every uniform Γ,

$$B_\Gamma = \{(\alpha, \beta) \mid (\alpha, \Gamma, \beta) \in W\}$$

is a weak bisimulation w.r.t. Γ. Then together with property A. it implies that T is a sound tableau.

We prove A. by induction on $n = ||\alpha|| = ||\beta||$. If $\alpha =_\Gamma \beta$ is a label of an non-leaf node, there are three cases according to which rule is applied on this node. If unfold is applied, then by rule 2. of the construction of W clearly $(\alpha, \Gamma, \beta) \in W$. If reduc is applied, in this case $\alpha =_\Gamma \beta$ is of the form $\alpha_1 X =_\Gamma \beta_1 X$, and the node has sons labeled by $\alpha_1 =_{\Gamma'} \beta_1$ and $\alpha' X =_\Gamma \beta' X$ for every $(\alpha', \beta') \in \Gamma'$. Clearly α_1, β_1 and $\alpha' X, \beta' X$ for every $(\alpha', \beta') \in \Gamma'$ have shorter weak norms than α and β, then by the induction hypothesis $(\alpha_1, \Gamma', \beta_1) \in W$ and $(\alpha' X, \Gamma, \beta' X) \in W$ for every $(\alpha', \beta') \in \Gamma'$. Then by rule 4. in the construction of W, $(\alpha, \Gamma, \beta) \in W$. If align is applied, in this case $\alpha =_\Gamma \beta$ is of the form $\alpha_1\alpha_2 =_\Gamma \beta_1\beta_2$ and the two sons have labels $\alpha_1\delta\beta_2 =_\Gamma \beta_1\beta_2$ and $\alpha_2 =_\Gamma \delta\beta_2$ where $||\delta|| = ||\beta_1|| - ||\alpha_1||$. According to the priority of the applicability of the rules in 4.4 reduc must be applied on $\alpha_1\delta\beta_2 =_\Gamma \beta_1\beta_2$, then by what we have just proved $(\alpha_1\delta\beta_2, \Gamma, \beta_1\beta_2) \in W$. Also $\alpha_2, \delta\beta_2$ have weak norms shorter than that of α and β, by the induction hypothesis $(\alpha_2, \Gamma, \delta\beta_2) \in W$. Then by rule 3. of the construction of W, $(\alpha, \Gamma, \beta) \in W$. If $\alpha =_\Gamma \beta$ is a label of a leaf node, then since T is a successful tableau either there is a non-leaf node also labeled by $\alpha =_\Gamma \beta$ and in this case we have proved that $(\alpha, \Gamma, \beta) \in W$, or $\alpha \stackrel{\Gamma}{=} \beta$ must hold and in this case by rule 1. in the construction of W we also have $(\alpha, \Gamma, \beta) \in W$.

We prove B. by induction on the four rules define W. Suppose $(\alpha, \Gamma, \beta) \in W$, there are the following cases.

Case of rule 1. i.e. $\alpha \stackrel{\Gamma}{=} \beta$. We have two subcases here. The first is $||\alpha|| = ||\beta|| \leq 1$, then B. holds obviously. The second is $||\alpha|| = ||\beta|| > 1$, then it must be that $\alpha = \beta$ and B. also holds.

Case of rule 2. i.e. there exists M which is a match for (α, β) such that $\alpha' =_\Gamma \beta'$ is a label of T for all $(\alpha', \beta') \in M$. Then by A. it holds that $(\alpha', \Gamma, \beta') \in W$ for all $(\alpha', \beta') \in M$, then by definition of a match, clearly B. holds.

Case of rule 3. i.e. there exist $(\alpha_1, \Gamma, \alpha_2) \in W$ and $(\gamma\alpha_2, \Gamma, \beta) \in W$ where $||\gamma|| > 1$ and $\alpha = \gamma\alpha_1$. If $\gamma\alpha_1 \stackrel{a}{\longrightarrow} \gamma''$, we have to match this by looking for a β' such that $\beta \stackrel{\hat{a}}{\Longrightarrow} \beta'$ and $(\gamma'', \Gamma, \beta') \in W$. Since $||\gamma|| > 1$, it must be that $\gamma \stackrel{a}{\longrightarrow} \gamma'$ and $\gamma'' = \gamma'\alpha_1$ for some γ', thus $\gamma\alpha_2 \stackrel{a}{\longrightarrow} \gamma'\alpha_2$. Now $(\gamma\alpha_2, \Gamma, \beta) \in W$, by the induction hypothesis there exists $\beta' \in \mathcal{V}^*$ such that $\beta \stackrel{\hat{a}}{\Longrightarrow} \beta'$ and $(\gamma'\alpha_2, \Gamma, \beta') \in W$. Since $(\alpha_1, \Gamma, \alpha_2) \in W$, by rule 2 we have $(\gamma'\alpha_1, \Gamma, \beta') \in W$ that is $(\gamma'', \Gamma, \beta') \in W$. For another direction, let $\beta \stackrel{a}{\longrightarrow} \beta'$, since $(\gamma\alpha_2, \Gamma, \beta) \in W$, by the induction hypothesis there exists γ'' such that $\gamma\alpha_2 \stackrel{\hat{a}}{\Longrightarrow} \gamma''$ and $(\gamma'', \Gamma, \beta') \in W$. Since $||\gamma|| > 1$, it must be that $\gamma'' = \gamma'\alpha'$, and $\gamma \stackrel{\hat{a}}{\Longrightarrow} \gamma'$, thus $\gamma\alpha_1 \stackrel{\hat{a}}{\Longrightarrow} \gamma'\alpha_1$. Again because $(\alpha_1, \Gamma, \alpha_2) \in W$, by rule 2 we have $(\gamma'\alpha_1, \Gamma, \beta') \in W$.

Case of rule 4. i.e. $\alpha = \alpha_0 X$ and $\beta = \beta_0 X$ for some α_0, β_0, X with $||\alpha_0|| = ||\beta_0|| > 1$, and $(\alpha_0, \Gamma', \beta_0) \in W$, and moreover $(\alpha', \beta') \in \Gamma'$ implies $(\alpha' X, \Gamma, \beta' X) \in W$. Let $\alpha_0 X \stackrel{a}{\longrightarrow} \alpha''$. Since $||\alpha_0|| > 1$, it must be that $\alpha'' = \alpha_0' X$ and $\alpha_0 \stackrel{a}{\longrightarrow} \alpha_0'$. Since $(\alpha_0, \Gamma', \beta_0) \in W$, by the induction hypothesis there exists $\beta_0' \in \mathcal{V}^*$ such that $\beta_0 \stackrel{\hat{a}}{\Longrightarrow} \beta_0'$ and $(\alpha_0', \Gamma', \beta_0') \in W$. Now $\beta_0 X \stackrel{\hat{a}}{\Longrightarrow} \beta_0' X$, and $(\alpha_0' X, \Gamma, \beta_0' X) \in W$ by rule 4. The another direction can be proved in a similar way. □

This theorem means that the decision procedure for existence of successful tableau with root $\alpha =_\Gamma \beta$ is sound for $\alpha \approx_\Gamma \beta$.

Theorem 3. *Let $\alpha, \beta \in \mathcal{V}^*$, and $\Gamma \subseteq \mathcal{V}^* \times \mathcal{V}^*$ be uniform. If $\alpha \approx_\Gamma \beta$ then there is a successful tableau with root $\alpha =_\Gamma \beta$.*

Proof. By using Propositions 6, 7, and 8 we can prove the following basic fact: if a sound tableau T is not successful, then we can construct another sound tableau T' which has the same root as T and which has one more non-leaf node than T.

Repeatedly using this basic fact, we can construct a sequence of sound tableaux $T_0, \ldots, T_n, \ldots$ such that T_0 is just the single leaf node $\alpha =_\Gamma \beta$. However since there are only finitely many tableaux with root $\alpha =_\Gamma \beta$, this sequence must end, and obviously the last tableau in the sequence is a successful tableau with root $\alpha =_\Gamma \beta$. □

This theorem means that the decision procedure for existence of successful tableau with root $\alpha =_\Gamma \beta$ is complete for $\alpha \approx_\Gamma \beta$.

At last, the following theorem shows how to use the decidability of $\approx_\Gamma$ to solve the decidability of $\approx$.

Theorem 4. *Let $\alpha, \beta \in \mathcal{V}^*$ be totally normed. Then $\alpha \approx \beta$ if and only if there exists a sound and uniform $\Gamma \subseteq \mathcal{V}^* \times \mathcal{V}^*$ such that $\alpha \approx_\Gamma \beta$.*

Proof. The if direction follows from Lemma 2. For the only if direction, let $\Gamma = \{(\alpha', \beta') \mid ||\alpha'|| = ||\beta'|| = 1, \alpha' \approx \beta'\}$. It is easy to check that Γ is both uniform and sound, and $\approx$ is a weak bisimulation with respect to Γ. Thus we found a sound and uniform Γ such that $\alpha \approx_\Gamma \beta$. □

Thus to decide whether $\alpha \approx \beta$, we just need to enumerate all uniform Γ, and then check

1. if Γ is sound;
2. if $\alpha \approx_\Gamma \beta$ holds.

We have already shown that 2. is decidable. The following easy to prove theorem gives a decision procedure for 1. Thus for totally normed $\alpha, \beta \in \mathcal{V}^*$, whether $\alpha \approx \beta$ is decidable.

Theorem 5. *Let $\Gamma \subseteq \mathcal{V}^* \times \mathcal{V}^*$ be uniform. Then Γ is sound if and only if for all $(\alpha, \beta) \in \Gamma$, there is a match M for (α, β) such that $\alpha' \approx_\Gamma \beta'$ for all $(\alpha', \beta') \in M$.*

4.6 Complexity of the Tableau System

The complexity of the tableau system can be measured in terms of the longest path of a tableau. Let us examine the structure of a path of a tableau. A node is called an unfold node if the rule unfold is applied on it. A segment of a path is called a basic segment if non of the nodes in the segment is an unfold node. It is clear that each path of a tableau consists of several basic segments separated by a number of unfold nodes. Note that the unfold nodes on a path of a tableau must be pairwise distinct, and by the discussion in the proof of Theorem 1 the two states in an unfold node each contains no more than 2 variables. Thus the number of unfold nodes in a path must be bounded by $O(v^4)$, where v is the size of $\mathcal{V}$. Thus if there is a bound M for the length of any basic segment, then the longest path of a tableau is bounded by $O(v^4 M)$. Now we define a set $S = \{\alpha | \alpha \stackrel{a}{\longrightarrow} \beta, length(\alpha) \leq 2\}$ and $M = max\{||\beta|| | \alpha \stackrel{a}{\longrightarrow} \beta, \alpha \in S\}$. It is easy to see that M is the largest weak norm of any node following an unfold node. Since rule reduc and align decrease norms, a basic segment is bounded by M.

5 Conclusion

In this paper we introduced the notion of weak bisimulation with respect to an uniform equivalence relation, and proposed a tableau decision method to decide whether a pair of totally normed context-free processes are weak bisimilar w.r.t. an uniform equivalence relation. Since weak bisimulation w.r.t. an equivalence relation subsumes weak bisimulation as a special case, we obtain a tableau decision procedure for weak bisimilarity of totally normed context-free processes. The tableau decision procedure is intuitively more appealing than the decidability proofs by Stirling [10] and Hirshfeld [9]. Recent results by Richard Mayr show that the problem is EXPTIME-hard for (general) BPA and even for normed BPA [13].

For future work we are interested to see if this tableau method can be extended to instances where the restriction of totally normedness can be relaxed.

References

1. Moller, F.: Infinite results. In: Sassone, V., Montanari, U. (eds.) CONCUR 1996. LNCS, vol. 1119, pp. 195–216. Springer, Heidelberg (1996)
2. Esparza, J.: Decidability of model checking for infinite-state concurrent systems. Acta Informatica 97(34), 85–107 (1997)
3. burkart, O., Esparza, J.: More infinite results. Electronic Notes in Theoretical computer Science 5 (1997)
4. Baeten, J.C.M., Bergstra, J.A., Klop, J.W.: Decidability of bisimulation equivalence for processes generating context-free languages. Journal of the Association for Computing Machinery 93(40), 653–682 (1993)
5. Christensen, S., Hüttel, H., Stirling, C.: Bisimulation equivalence is decidable for all context-free processes. Information and Computation 95(121), 143–148 (1995)
6. Burkart, O., Caucal, D., Steffen, B.: An elementary bisimulation decision procedure for arbitrary context-free processes. In: Hájek, P., Wiedermann, J. (eds.) MFCS 1995. LNCS, vol. 969, pp. 423–433. Springer, Heidelberg (1995)
7. Srba, J.: Roadmap of Infinite Results. In: Current Trends in Theoretical Computer Science, The Challenge of the New Century. Formal Models and Semantics, vol. 2, pp. 337–350. World Scientific Publishing Co., Singapore (2004)
8. Esparza, J.: Petri nets,commutative context-free grammars, and basic parallel processes. In: Reichel, H. (ed.) FCT 1995. LNCS, vol. 965, pp. 221–232. Springer, Heidelberg (1995)
9. Hirshfeld, Y.: Bisimulation trees and the decidability of weak bisimulations. In: INFINITY'96. Proceedings of the 1st International Workshop on Verification of Infinite State Systems, Germany, vol. 5 (1996)
10. Stirling, C.: Decidability of bisimulation equivalence for normed pushdown processes. In: Sassone, V., Montanari, U. (eds.) CONCUR 1996. LNCS, vol. 1119, pp. 217–232. Springer, Heidelberg (1996)
11. Hüttel, H., Stirling, C.: Actions speak louder than words. Proving bisimilarity for context-free processes. In: LICS 91. Proceedings of 6th Annual symposium on Logic in Computer Science, Amsterdam, pp. 376–386 (1991)
12. Hans, H.: Silence is golden: Branching bisimilarity is decidable for context-free processes. In: Larsen, K.G., Skou, A. (eds.) CAV 1991. LNCS, vol. 575, pp. 2–12. Springer, Heidelberg (1992)

13. Mayr, R.: Weak bisimulation and regularity of BPA is EXPTIME-hard. In: EXPRESS'03. Proceedings of the 10th International Workshop on Expressiveness in Concurrency, France, pp. 143–160 (2003)
14. Milner, R.: A Calculus of Communication Systems. LNCS, vol. 92. Springer, Heidelberg (1980)
15. Milner, R.: Communication and Concurrency. Prentice-Hall International, Englewood Cliffs (1989)
16. Bergstra, J.A., Klop, J.W.: Process theory based on bisimulation semantics. In: Proceedings of REX Workshop, Amsterdam, The Netherlands, pp. 50–122 (1988)
17. Caucal, D.: Graphes canoniques de graphes algébriques. Informatique théorique et Applications(RAIRO) 90-24(4), 339–352 (1990)
18. Hirshfeld, Y., Jerrum, M., Moller, F.: Bisimulation equivalence is decidable for normed process algebra. In: Wiedermann, J., van Emde Boas, P., Nielsen, M. (eds.) ICALP 1999. LNCS, vol. 1644, pp. 412–421. Springer, Heidelberg (1999)

Linear Context Free Languages

Roussanka Loukanova

Computational Linguistics
Dept. of Linguistics and Philology
Uppsala University
rloukano@stp.lingfil.uu.se

Abstract. In this paper, I present the class of linear context free languages (LCFLs) with a class of non-deterministic one-way two-head (read only) automata, called non-deterministic linear automata (NLA). At the begining of the work of an NLA, the reading heads are installed under the opposite ends of the given input string. Then, each head can move in one direction only, the left head from left to right, while the right head from right to left. I give formal definitions of two non-deterministic versions of the linear automata, without and with ε-transitions, and their corresponding computations. Deterministic linear automata model unambiguous structural analysers, while the class of the languages recognized by them does not coincide with the class of deterministic linear languages recognized by deterministic push-down machines. I compare the linear automata with other models of LCFLs. In particular, I consider a subclass of unambiguous linear context-free languages and define corresponding linear automata serving as efficient parsing tools for them, in deterministic and non-deterministic variants.

1 Introduction

Various automata models have been proposed for the class of linear context-free languages (LCFLs) and some of its subclasses. For overviews, see, for example, Hopcroft and Ullman [7], Salomaa [11], Rosenberg and Salomaa [10], and Autebert, Berstel and Boasson [6]. In particular, Amar and Putzolu, in [2] and [3], studied automata realization of the even LCFLs; Ibarra [8] described the power properties of the class of the two-way multi-head automata; Rosenberg [9] gave 2-tape finite automata characterization of LCFLs; Andrei and Kudlek [4] introduced a parsing algorithm for a subclass of LCFLs.

This paper[1] introduces a class of non-deterministic linear automata (NLA) recognizing the class of LCFLs. I will give a formal presentation of the NLA and some of their properties with some suggestions for potential applications. Intuitively, an NLA has: a tape in the cells of which an input string over a given input alphabet is written; a control unit that can be in any of a given finite number of states; a subset of states designated as the final states; a set of work instructions defined by a transition function; and two reading heads. An NLA is

[1] I am grateful to anonymous readers of this paper for their valuable feedback.

C.B. Jones, Z. Liu, J. Woodcock (Eds.): ICTAC 2007, LNCS 4711, pp. 351–365, 2007.

similar to a finite state automaton except that the work of an NLA is distributed among two heads. At start, the heads are installed correspondingly under the leftmost and rightmost end characters of the input. Each head can move in one direction only: the left head advances cell-by-cell from the leftmost beginning of the string in the right direction, while the right head proceeds similarly in the opposite direction. At each move (i.e., at each discrete step), depending on the state of the control and the symbol scanned by either of the heads, the control chooses non-deterministically one of the heads as being active, goes non-deterministically into a set of new states and moves the active head one cell forward in its direction. The automaton halts when no further move is defined by its transition function, or right after all characters of the input have been read. The input string is recognized just in case when all of its characters have been read and the control is in a final state.

Rosenberg [9] represents a correspondence between LCFLs and sets of ordered pairs of strings $\langle x, y\rangle$. For each LCFL L, there is a two-tape one-way automaton A, such that a string $\alpha \in L$ iff there is a pair of strings $\langle x, y\rangle$ such that $\alpha = xy^{-1}$, where y^{-1} is the reversal of y, and $\langle x, y\rangle$ brings the automaton to an accepting state by placing x on the first tape and y on the second. Rosenberg's model is an important characterization of the LCFLs and their properties, which implies various theoretical results. While being equivalent to Rosenberg's model (Rosenberg [9]) with respect to the recognized class of languages, NLA have distinctive computational features. Firstly, NLA define analyses of the input strings without splitting them. Secondly, the sequences of computations over input strings associate corresponding analyses to them in a direct mode which represents their structure.

NLA computations model natural processes and structures in deterministic and non-deterministic variants. An NLA is a direct computational model of symmetrically dependent patterns which are symbolically encoded with strings and computation steps of the NLA over strings. Note that the modelled patterns are not necessarily symmetric. They may have symmetrically dependent branches, as for example, in a pattern $A_1 \ldots A_k B_k \ldots B_1$, where A_i and B_i $(i \geq 1)$ represent branches that are dependent on each other.

The class of NLA gives possibilities for efficient parsing and pattern recognition. For example, a subclass of NLA, presented in this paper, realizes a parsing algorithm defined by Andrei and Kudlek [4].

2 Non-deterministic Linear Automata (NLA)

2.1 The Basic Definitions of NLA

Definition 1. *A nondeterministic linear automaton (NLA) is a tuple* $M = \langle Q, \Sigma, \delta, q_0, L, R, F\rangle$, *where*

1. $Q \neq \emptyset$ *is a nonempty finite set; the elements of* Q *are called the states of* M*;*
2. Σ *is a finite set called the input alphabet of* M*;*
3. $q_0 \in Q$ *is a distinguished state called the initial state of* M*;*
4. $L, R \notin Q \cup \Sigma$, $L \neq R$*;* L *and* R *are interpreted as markers for the left and right reading heads, correspondingly;*

5. *$F \subseteq Q$; the elements of F are called the final states of M;*
6. *$\delta : Q \times \Sigma \longrightarrow \mathcal{P}(Q \times \{L, R\})$ is the transition function of M.*

Let $M = \langle Q, \Sigma, \delta, q_0, L, R, F\rangle$ be an NLA. In a more detailed informal way, the work of M can be described as follows. Each input to the sequences of calculations performed by M is a string $\alpha \in \Sigma^*$ given to M by having it written on the tape in the usual way, the successive characters in successive cells. At the beginning of the work, the control is in its initial state q_0, the left reading head is installed under the first character of α, while the right head is under the last character of α. At each step of the work, exactly one of the two heads is advanced in its direction to the next cell — the left head to right, the right head to left. At the beginning of each step, both heads are scanning their position cells. The move is determined non-deterministically by the current state of the control and the character scanned by the head that is selected to be moved. On completion of a step, the control can non-deterministically enter multiple states. After some moves, both heads can get positioned under one and the same cell. Depending on the transition function of M, either of the heads can read the character in that cell and get advanced into its direction. At that moment, the heads cross each other and M halts. The work can end before such move, if no transition is defined. Formally, the successive moves, i.e., all possible sequences of calculations of M on any given string $\alpha \in \Sigma^*$ are determined by the transition function δ. The following cases are possible:

1. Let $q \in Q$ and $a \in \Sigma$. Assume that the control of M is in the state q and both heads are scanning the character a in the same or different tape cells. Let, for some $p_1, \ldots, p_k, q_1, \ldots, q_l \in Q$,

$$\delta(q, a) = \{(p_1, L), \ldots, (p_k, L), (q_1, R), \ldots, (q_l, R)\} \tag{1}$$

   (a) If $k, l \geq 1$, M selects non-deterministically either of the two heads to be the active one. If the left head has been selected, it reads its character a and advances in the right direction, while the control enters non-deterministically the states $p_1, \ldots, p_k$. The right head stays at its place during any such move. Or, non-deterministically, M can select the right head as being the one that reads the a in its square and moves in the left direction. The control enters the states $q_1, \ldots, q_l$ in a non-deterministic mode.
   (b) If $k = 0$ ($l = 0$) and $l \geq 1$ ($k \geq 1$), the left (right) head stays under its a without reading it (at least, as long as the control is in the state q), while the other head reads its a and moves in its direction by entering non-deterministically the states $q_1, \ldots, q_l$ ($p_1, \ldots, p_k$).
   (c) If $k = 0$ and $l = 0$, M halts without being able to read a.
2. Let $q \in Q$, $a, b \in \Sigma$ and $a \neq b$. Assume that the control of M is in the state q and the left head is scanning a, while the right head is under the other symbol b. Let for some $p_1, \ldots, p_k, q_1, \ldots, q_l \in Q$

$$\delta(q, a) = \{(p_1, L), \ldots, (p_k, L), (q_1, R), \ldots, (q_l, R)\} \tag{2}$$

And let for some $r_1, \ldots, r_m, s_1, \ldots, s_n \in Q$

$$\delta(q, b) = \{(r_1, L), \ldots, (r_m, L), (s_1, R), \ldots, (s_n, R)\} \tag{3}$$

(a) If $k \geq 1$, the left head can be selected non-deterministically to be active during the current move. In such case, the control enters non-deterministically the states $p_1, \ldots, p_k$, determined by (2).
(b) If $n \geq 1$, the right head can be selected non-deterministically as the active one for the current move. In such case, the control enters non-deterministically the states $s_1, \ldots, s_n$, determined by (3).
(c) If $k = 0$ and $n = 0$, M halts without being able to read.

We say that a square is read-off iff it has been scanned by one of the heads which then moves into its direction. We require that each square is read at most once either by the left or the right head. This means that after the heads exchange their sides, e.g. when the left head has just moved to the right hand side of the right head (or the vice versa) the NLA M halts its work.

M behaves non-deterministically (disjunctively) in two different aspects. At first, one non-deterministic branch of computations can be followed by choosing either of the heads to be moved according to the transition function. Second, after the choice of the active head has been made, the control can be simultaneously, i.e., non-deterministically, in more than one state.

2.2 NLA's Configurations and Sequences of Computations. Some Examples

Let $M = \langle Q, \Sigma, \delta, q_0, L, R, F\rangle$ be an NLA. The successive moves and stages of the work of an NLA M are formalized by the notion of a configuration and the traditional binary relation $\vdash$ between configurations.

Definition 2. *A configuration of M is an ordered pair $\langle q, \alpha_1 X \alpha_2 Y \alpha_3\rangle$, where $q \in Q$, $\alpha_1, \alpha_2, \alpha_3 \in \Sigma^*$, and $X, Y \in \{L, R\}$ are such that either:*

1. *$X = L$, $Y = R$, and $\alpha_2 \neq \varepsilon$; or*
2. *$X = L$, $Y = R$, and $\alpha_1 = \alpha_2 = \alpha_3 = \varepsilon$; or*
3. *$X = R$, $Y = L$, $\alpha_2 = \varepsilon$, and $\alpha_1\alpha_3 \neq \varepsilon$.*

An initial configuration *is any configuration $\langle q_0, L\omega R\rangle$, where q_0 is the initial state of M and $\omega \in \Sigma^*$. An* accepting configuration *is any configuration $\langle q, \alpha_1 RL \alpha_2\rangle$, where $q \in F$ and $\alpha_1, \alpha_2 \in \Sigma^*$ ($\alpha_1\alpha_2 \neq \varepsilon$), or $\langle q, LR\rangle$ where $q \in F$ (the later is possible only if $q = q_0 \in F$).*

A configuration $\langle q, \alpha_1 X \alpha_2 Y \alpha_3\rangle$ represents an instantaneous description of the work of an automaton M after a finite number of steps. The string $\alpha_1\alpha_2\alpha_3$ is the input written on the tape and it has to be either recognized or rejected by M. The markers $X, Y \in \{L, R\}$ represent the left and right reading heads, respectively. The above three kinds of configurations of M are interpreted in the following way:

1. $\langle q, \alpha_1 L \alpha_2 R \alpha_3 \rangle$, where $q \in Q$, $\alpha_1, \alpha_2, \alpha_3 \in \Sigma^*$ and $\alpha_2 \neq \varepsilon$. The control of M is in the state q, the left head is scanning the first character of α_2, while the right head is scanning the last character of α_2. The strings α_1 and α_3 have already been read by the left and right head, respectively. The string α_2 is pending to be read. In the case when $\alpha_2 \in \Sigma$, both heads are scanning the same square filled up with the symbol α_2, and either one of them may read it in the next move if $\delta(q, \alpha_2)$ is appropriately defined. After one of the heads has read α_2, the entire string $\alpha_1\alpha_2\alpha_3$ has been read and M halts.
2. $\langle q, LR \rangle$ where $q \in Q$. The tape is empty and both heads are scanning its first square which is blank. By the formal definitions of a configuration (Definition 2) and of the moves of M (Definition 3) any configuration of the kind $\langle q, \alpha_1 LR \alpha_3 \rangle$ is unreachable unless $q = q_0$ and $\alpha_1\alpha_3 = \varepsilon$.
3. $\langle q, \alpha_1 RL \alpha_3 \rangle$, where $q \in Q$, $\alpha_1, \alpha_3 \in \Sigma^*$ and $\alpha_1\alpha_3 \neq \varepsilon$
   (a) $\alpha_1 = \alpha_1' a$ and $\alpha_3 = b\alpha_3'$ for some $\alpha_1', \alpha_3' \in \Sigma^*$ and $a, b \in \Sigma$. The interpretation of the configuration $\langle q, \alpha_1' aRLb\alpha_3' \rangle$ is as follows. The string $\alpha_1' a$ has been read-off by the left head which after scanning and reading-off the last character a of α_1 has moved under the next right hand side square which is filled up by b. The string $b\alpha_3'$ has been read-off by the right head which after scanning and reading-off the leftmost symbol b of α_3 has moved to its left hand side, i.e. under a. The two heads have just crossed and exchanged their positions. Since all input characters have been read-off and any square can be read-off at most once, M halts.
   (b) $\alpha_3 = \varepsilon$ and $\alpha_1 = \alpha_1' a$ for some $a \in \Sigma$. In this case, the configuration is $\langle q, \alpha_1' aRL \rangle$. The input string has been read-off only by the left head during its moves to right, while the right head has not done any move at all.
   (c) $\alpha_1 = \varepsilon$ and $\alpha_3 = b\alpha_3' \neq \varepsilon$. Similarly to the previous case, the configuration is $\langle q, RL\alpha_3 \rangle$, where the string α_3 has been read-off by the right head with moves in the left direction.
   Notice that if $X = R$, $Y = L$, $\alpha_1 = \alpha_1 = \alpha_3 = \varepsilon$, then $\langle q, \alpha_1 X \alpha_2 Y \alpha_3 \rangle = \langle q, RL \rangle$. In this case, the "configuration" is unreachable by M, because according to Definition 1, a NLA, does not allow any ε-transitions.

Next, we define the traditional computation steps $\vdash_M$ and $\vdash_M^*$ of M. If Φ and Ψ are some configurations, then $\Phi \vdash_M \Psi$ is interpreted as an immediate (one-step) move of M from the configuration Φ to the configuration Ψ, while $\Phi \vdash_M^* \Psi$ is a sequence of successive moves from Φ to Ψ. Formally:

Definition 3. *The binary relation $\vdash_M$ between configurations of M, called an* immediate move *(or* transition*) of M, is defined as follows. For any two configurations Φ and Ψ of M, $\Phi \vdash_M \Psi$ iff there are some $p, q \in Q$, $a \in \Sigma$ and $\alpha_1, \alpha_2, \alpha_3 \in \Sigma^*$, such that one of the following conditions is fulfilled:*

1. $(q, L) \in \delta(p, a)$, $\alpha_2 \neq \varepsilon$, $\Phi = \langle p, \alpha_1 La\alpha_2 R\alpha_3 \rangle$ and $\Psi = \langle \alpha_1 aL\alpha_2 R\alpha_3 \rangle$, i.e., $\langle p, \alpha_1 La\alpha_2 R\alpha_3 \rangle \vdash_M \langle q, \alpha_1 aL\alpha_2 R\alpha_3 \rangle$;

2. $(q, L) \in \delta(p, a)$, $\alpha_2 = \varepsilon$, $\Phi = \langle p, \alpha_1 L a R \alpha_3 \rangle$ *and* $\Psi = \langle q, \alpha_1 a R L \alpha_3 \rangle$, *i.e.*, $\langle p, \alpha_1 L a R \alpha_3 \rangle \vdash_M \langle q, \alpha_1 a R L \alpha_3 \rangle$;
   (The left head has just moved to right and is scanning the leftmost character of α_3, *while the right head is under the square containing* a. *No further transitions are possible because all characters have been read-off.)*
3. $(q, R) \in \delta(p, a)$, $\alpha_2 \neq \varepsilon$, $\Phi = \langle p, \alpha_1 L \alpha_2 a R \alpha_3 \rangle$ *and* $\Psi = \langle q, \alpha_1 L \alpha_2 R a \alpha_3 \rangle$, *i.e.*, $\langle p, \alpha_1 L \alpha_2 a R \alpha_3 \rangle \vdash_M \langle q, \alpha_1 L \alpha_2 R a \alpha_3 \rangle$;
4. $(q, R) \in \delta(p, a)$, $\alpha_2 = \varepsilon$, $\Phi = \langle p, \alpha_1 L a R \alpha_3 \rangle$ *and* $\Psi = \langle q, \alpha_1 R L a \alpha_3 \rangle$, *i.e.*, $\langle p, \alpha_1 L a R \alpha_3 \rangle \vdash_M \langle q, \alpha_1 R L a \alpha_3 \rangle$.

If Φ *and* Ψ *are two configurations such that* $\Phi \vdash_M \Psi$, *we say that* M *has done an immediate move (or an immediate transition step) from* Φ *to* Ψ.

Let $\vdash_M^*$ be the binary relation between configurations of M, which is the transitive and reflexive closure of $\vdash_M$. In case that $\Phi \vdash_M^* \Psi$, we say that there is a transition of M from the configuration Φ to the configuration Ψ. We also say that M has done a sequence of (successive) moves from Φ to Ψ.

Definition 4. *The* language $L(M)$ accepted *(i.e.,* recognized*) by* M *is the set*

$$L(M) = \{\omega : \omega \in \Sigma^*, \langle q_0, L\omega R \rangle \vdash_M^* \Psi, \text{ where } \Psi \text{ is an accepting configuration}\}.$$

Corollary 1. *The* language $L(M)$ accepted *by* M *is the set*

$$L(M) = \{\omega : \omega \in \Sigma^* \text{ and } \langle q_0, L\omega R \rangle \vdash_M^* \langle q, \alpha_1 R L \alpha_2 \rangle \text{ for some } q \in F \text{ and } \alpha_1, \alpha_2 \in \Sigma^* \text{ such that } \omega = \alpha_1 \alpha_2\} \cup \Gamma, \text{ where}$$

$$\Gamma = \begin{cases} \varepsilon, & \text{if } q_0 \in F; \\ \emptyset, & \text{otherwise.} \end{cases}$$

Proof. By the definition of the relation $\vdash_M^*$, the definition of an accepting configuration (Definition 2) and Definition 4. □

Lemma 1. *Let* $M = \langle Q, \Sigma, \delta, q_0, L, R, F \rangle$ *be an NLA. For every* $p, q \in Q$ *and every* $\omega, \alpha_1, \alpha_2, \alpha_3, \beta_1, \beta_2 \in \Sigma^*$ *such that* $\omega = \alpha_1 \alpha_2 \alpha_3$, *it is true that*

$$\langle p, L\omega R \rangle \vdash_M^* \langle q, \alpha_1 L \alpha_2 R \alpha_3 \rangle$$

if and only if

$$\langle p, \beta_1 L \omega R \beta_2 \rangle \vdash_M^* \langle q, \beta_1 \alpha_1 L \alpha_2 R \alpha_3 \beta_2 \rangle.$$

Proof. The proof can be easily carried on by induction on the length of $\vdash_M^*$. □

The following are examples of languages recognized by NLA:

Example 1. $L = \{a^n b^n c^m : n, m \in \mathbb{N}, n, m \geq 1\}$.

Example 2. $L = \{a^n b^m : n, m \in \mathbb{N}, n \geq m \geq 1\}$.

Example 3. Let Σ be an alphabet and let $k \in \mathbb{N}$, $k \geq 1$, $m_1, \ldots, m_k \in \mathbb{N}$, $n_1, \ldots, n_k \in \mathbb{N}$, $a_1, \ldots, a_k \in \Sigma$ and $b_1, \ldots, b_k \in \Sigma$.

1. $L_1 = \{a_1^{x_1} \ldots a_k^{x_k} b_k^{m_k x_k + n_k} \ldots b_1^{m_1 x_1 + n_1} : x_1, \ldots, x_k \in \mathbb{N}\}$;
2. $L_2 = \{a_1^{m_1 x_1 + n_1} \ldots a_k^{m_k x_k + n_k} b_k^{x_k} \ldots b_1^{x_1} : x_1, \ldots, x_k \in \mathbb{N}\}$.

Example 4. A more interesting class of NLA, with potential applications in symmetric dependences, are those recognizing the following LCFLs:

Let $k \in \mathbb{N}$, $k \geq 1$, $m_1, \ldots, m_k, n_1, \ldots, n_k \in \mathbb{N}$, $a_1, \ldots, a_k, b_1, \ldots, b_k \in \Sigma$, and let $f_1, \ldots, f_k, g_1, \ldots, g_k$, be given functions such that, for every $i \in \{1, \ldots, k\}$, either $f_i(x_i) = x_i$ and $g_i(x_i) = m_i x_k + n_i$ or $g_i(x_i) = x_i$ and $f_i(x_i) = m_i x_k + n_i$.

$$L = \{a_1^{f_1(x_1)} \ldots a_k^{f_k(x_k)} b_k^{g_k(x_k)} \ldots b_1^{g_1(x_1)} : x_1, \ldots, x_k \in \mathbb{N}\}.$$

Example 5. Let $L_1, \ldots, L_k$ be languages recognized by NLA, i.e., for every $i = 1, \ldots, k$, there is an NLA M_i such that $L_i = L(M_i)$, and let

$$L = \{\alpha_1 \ldots \alpha_k \beta_k \ldots \beta_1 : \alpha_i \beta_i \in L_i \text{ for } i = 1, \ldots, k\}$$

Then $L = L(M)$ for an NLA M.

3 NLA and Linear Context Free Grammars

Definition 5. *A* linear context free grammar, *or in brief, a* linear grammar, *is a context free grammar $G = \langle N, \Sigma, S, P \rangle$ (in the Chomsky hierarchy), the rules of which are of the form $A \to \alpha B$, $A \to B\alpha$ or $A \to \alpha$, where $A, B \in N$ and $\alpha \in \Sigma^*$.*

Definition 6. *A linear grammar G is in a standard form if all of its rules are of the form $A \to aB$, $A \to Ba$ or $A \to a$, where $A, B \in N$ and $a \in \Sigma$; and also in case when G contains the rule $S \to \varepsilon$, where S is the initial nonterminal of G and S does not occur in the right hand side of any rule. If a linear grammar G is in a standard form, we say that G is a standard linear grammar.*

Theorem 1. *(*An well known result*) For each linear grammar G there is an equivalent linear grammar G' in a standard form, i.e., such that $L(G) = L(G')$.*

Construction of NLA from Linear Grammar: Let $G = \langle N, \Sigma, S, P \rangle$ be a standard linear grammar such that $L = L(G)$. Let R, L and q_f be new pairwise different symbols such that $R, L, q_f \notin N \cup \Sigma$. Consider the NLA $M = \langle N \cup \{q_f\}, \Sigma, \delta, S, R, L, F \rangle$, where $N \cup \{q_f\}$ is the set of the states of M, and the initial symbol S of G is the initial state of M. The set of the final states of M is:

$$F = \begin{cases} \{q_f, S\}, \text{ if } \varepsilon \in L; \\ \{q_f\}, \quad \text{otherwise.} \end{cases} \tag{4}$$

The transition function δ is defined as follows. For every $A \in N$, $a \in \Sigma$ and $X \in \{L, R\}$,

$$\begin{aligned}\delta(A, a) = &\{(B, L) : B \in N \text{ and } A \to aB \in P\} \cup \\ &\{(B, R) : B \in N \text{ and } A \to Ba \in P\} \cup \\ &\{(q_f, L) : A \to a \in P\}\end{aligned} \tag{5}$$

Lemma 2. *Let $G = \langle N, \Sigma, S, P\rangle$ be a standard linear grammar. Let M be the NLA constructed as above. Then for all $A \in N$ and $\omega \in \Sigma^*$ such that $\omega \neq \varepsilon$:*

$$\begin{aligned}&\textit{if } A \Rightarrow^*_{\mathrm{G}} \omega \ \textit{ then } \ \langle A, L\omega R\rangle \vdash^*_M \langle q_f, \alpha_1 RL\alpha_2\rangle \\ &\qquad\qquad \textit{for some } \alpha_1, \alpha_2 \in \Sigma^* \textit{ such that } \omega = \alpha_1\alpha_2.\end{aligned} \tag{6}$$

Proof. Using induction on i, we prove that for all $i \geq 1$:

$$\begin{aligned}&\text{if } A \Rightarrow^i_{\mathrm{G}} \omega, \text{ then } \ \langle A, L\omega R\rangle \vdash^*_M \langle q_f, \alpha_1 RL\alpha_2\rangle \\ &\qquad\qquad \text{for some } \alpha_1, \alpha_2 \in \Sigma^* \text{ such that } \omega = \alpha_1\alpha_2.\end{aligned} \tag{7}$$

Basis. Let $A \Rightarrow_{\mathrm{G}} \omega$. Since G is in a standard form, then $A \to a \in P$ for some $a \in \Sigma$ such that $\omega = a$. Hence, $(q_f, L) \in \delta(A, a)$, and $\langle A, LaR\rangle \vdash_M \langle q_f, aRL\rangle$.

Induction Step. Assume that the claim is true for some $i \geq 1$. Let $A \Rightarrow^{i+1}_{\mathrm{G}} \omega$.

Case 1. There is an $a \in \Sigma$ such that the derivation $A \Rightarrow^{i+1}_{\mathrm{G}} \omega$ is of the form: $A \Rightarrow_{\mathrm{G}} aB \Rightarrow^i_{\mathrm{G}} \omega$. Then $A \to aB \in P$ and $\omega = a\omega_1$ for some $\omega_1 \in \Sigma^+$ such that $B \Rightarrow^i_{\mathrm{G}} \omega_1$. Hence, $(B, L) \in \delta(A, a)$, and by the induction hypothesis:

$$\langle B, L\omega_1 R\rangle \vdash^*_M \langle q_f, \alpha_1 RL\alpha_2\rangle \text{ for some } \alpha_1, \alpha_2 \in \Sigma^* \text{ such that } \omega_1 = \alpha_1\alpha_2. \tag{8}$$

Then $\omega = a\omega_1 = a\alpha_1\alpha_2$. By $(B, L) \in \delta(A, a)$ and the definition of the relation $\vdash_M$, and then, by (8) and Lemma 1, respectively, it follows that:

$$\langle A, L\omega R\rangle = \langle A, La\omega_1 R\rangle \vdash_M \langle B, aL\omega_1 R\rangle \vdash^i_M \langle q_f, a\alpha_1 RL\alpha_2\rangle.$$

Case 2. There is an $a \in \Sigma$ such that the derivation $A \Rightarrow^{i+1}_{\mathrm{G}} \omega$ is of the form: $A \Rightarrow_{\mathrm{G}} Ba \Rightarrow^i_{\mathrm{G}} \omega$. The proof is similar to the Case 1. □

Lemma 3. *Let $G = \langle N, \Sigma, S, P\rangle$ be a standard linear grammar. Let M be the NLA constructed as above. Then for all $A \in N$ and $\omega \in \Sigma^*$ such that $\omega \neq \varepsilon$:*

$$\begin{aligned}&\textit{if } \langle A, L\omega R\rangle \vdash^*_M \langle q_f, \alpha_1 RL\alpha_2\rangle \ \textit{for some } \alpha_1, \alpha_2 \in \Sigma^* \\ &\qquad\qquad\qquad\qquad \textit{such that } \omega = \alpha_1\alpha_2, \\ &\textit{then } A \Rightarrow^*_{\mathrm{G}} \omega.\end{aligned} \tag{9}$$

Proof. Using induction on i, we prove that for all $i \geq 1$:

$$\begin{aligned}&\text{if } \langle A, L\omega R\rangle \vdash^i_M \langle q_f, \alpha_1 RL\alpha_2\rangle \ \text{for some } \alpha_1, \alpha_2 \in \Sigma^* \\ &\qquad\qquad\qquad\qquad \text{such that } \omega = \alpha_1\alpha_2, \\ &\text{then } A \Rightarrow^*_{\mathrm{G}} \omega.\end{aligned} \tag{10}$$

Basis. Let $\langle A, L\omega R\rangle \vdash_M \langle q_f, \alpha_1 RL\alpha_2\rangle$ for some $\alpha_1, \alpha_2 \in \Sigma^*$ ($\omega = \alpha_1\alpha_2$). Then, there is $a \in \Sigma$ such that $\omega = a$, $\alpha_1 = a$, $\alpha_2 = \varepsilon$ and $(q_f, L) \in \delta(A, a)$. Hence, $A \to a \in P$, and $A \Rightarrow_G a$.

Induction Step. Assume that the claim is true for some $i \geq 1$. Let

$$\langle A, L\omega R\rangle \vdash_M^{i+1} \langle q_f, \alpha_1 RL\alpha_2\rangle, \text{ where } \omega = \alpha_1\alpha_2. \tag{11}$$

Case 1. There are some $a \in \Sigma$, $\omega_1 \in \Sigma^*$, and $B \in N$ such that $\omega = a\omega_1$ and the sequence of the transitions (11) is:

$$\langle A, L\omega R\rangle = \langle A, La\omega_1 R\rangle \vdash_M \langle B, aL\omega_1 R\rangle \vdash_M^i \langle q_f, \alpha_1 RL\alpha_2\rangle \tag{12}$$

Then $\alpha_1 = a\alpha_1'$ for some $\alpha_1' \in \Sigma^*$ such that $\omega_1 = \alpha_1'\alpha_2$ and $\langle B, aL\omega_1 R\rangle \vdash_M^i \langle q_f, a\alpha_1' RL\alpha_2\rangle$. By Lemma 1, $\langle B, L\omega_1 R\rangle \vdash_M^i \langle q_f, \alpha_1' RL\alpha_2\rangle$. Therefore, by the induction hypothesis, $B \Rightarrow_G^* \alpha_1'\alpha_2 = \omega_1$. The first transition in (12) is possible only if $(B, L) \in \delta(A, a)$. By the definition of the transition function δ, it follows that $A \to aB \in P$. Therefore,

$$A \Rightarrow_G aB \Rightarrow_G^* a\omega_1 = \omega.$$

Case 2. There are some $a \in \Sigma$, $\omega_1 \in \Sigma^*$ and $B \in N$ such that $\omega = \omega_1 a$ and the sequence (11) of the transitions is: $\langle A, L\omega_1 aR\rangle \vdash_M \langle B, L\omega_1 Ra\rangle \vdash_M^i \langle q_f, \alpha_1 RL\alpha_2\rangle$. The proof is similar to the one for the Case 1. □

Lemma 4. *Let $G = \langle N, \Sigma, S, P\rangle$ be a standard linear grammar. Let M be the NLA constructed as above. Then for all $A \in N$ and $\omega \in \Sigma^*$ such that $\omega \neq \varepsilon$:*

$$A \Rightarrow_G^* \omega \;\textit{ iff }\; \langle A, L\omega R\rangle \vdash_M^* \langle q_f, \alpha_1 RL\alpha_2\rangle$$
$$\textit{for some } \alpha_1, \alpha_2 \in \Sigma^* \textit{ such that } \omega = \alpha_1\alpha_2. \tag{13}$$

Proof. Follows from Lemma 2 and Lemma 3. □

Theorem 2. *If L is a linear language, then $L = L(M)$ for some NLA M.*

Proof. Let L be a linear language, then there is a standard linear grammar that generates it. Let $G = \langle N, \Sigma, S, P\rangle$ be such standard linear grammar, i.e., $L = L(G)$. Let M be the NLA constructed as above from G. Let $\omega \in \Sigma^*$.

Case 1. If $\omega = \varepsilon$, then by the construction of M,

$$\varepsilon \in L = L(G) \;\text{ iff }\; S \in F \;\text{ iff }\; \varepsilon \in L(M). \tag{14}$$

Case 2. If $\omega \neq \varepsilon$, then, by Lemma 4,

$$S \Rightarrow_G^* \omega \;\text{ iff }\; \langle S, L\omega R\rangle \vdash_M^* \langle q_f, \alpha_1 RL\alpha_2\rangle$$
$$\text{for some } \alpha_1, \alpha_2 \in \Sigma^* \text{ such that } \omega = \alpha_1\alpha_2. \tag{15}$$

By (14) and (15), it follows that for all $\omega \in \Sigma^*$, $\omega \in L(G)$ iff $\omega \in L(M)$. Therefore, $L(G) = L(M)$. □

Construction of Linear Grammar from NLA: Consider an NLA $M = \langle Q, \Sigma, \delta, q_0, R, L, F\rangle$. Construct the grammar $G = \langle N, \Sigma, S, P\rangle$, where $N = Q$, $S = q_0$, and the set of rules P is:

$$\begin{aligned} P = \{q \to ap :\ & p, q \in Q, \text{ and } (p, L) \in \delta(q, a)\} \cup \\ \{q \to a\ \ :\ & q \in Q, p \in F \text{ and } (p, L) \in \delta(q, a)\} \cup \\ \{q \to pa :\ & p, q \in Q, \text{ and } (p, R) \in \delta(q, a)\} \cup \\ \{q \to a\ \ :\ & q \in Q, p \in F \text{ and } (p, R) \in \delta(q, a)\} \cup P' \end{aligned} \tag{16}$$

where $P' = \{q_0 \to \varepsilon\}$, if $q_0 \in F$, otherwise $P' = \emptyset$.

Lemma 5. *Let $M = \langle Q, \Sigma, \delta, q_0, R, L, F\rangle$ be an NLA, and G be the grammar constructed as above by (16). Then for all $q \in Q$ and $\omega \in \Sigma^*$ such that $\omega \neq \varepsilon$:*

$$\begin{aligned} &\textit{if } \langle q, L\omega R\rangle \vdash^*_M \langle p, \alpha_1 RL\alpha_2\rangle, \textit{ for some } p \in F \textit{ and } \alpha_1, \alpha_2 \in \Sigma^*, \\ &\qquad\qquad\qquad\qquad\qquad\qquad\quad \textit{such that } \omega = \alpha_1\alpha_2, \\ &\textit{then } q \Rightarrow^*_{\mathrm{G}} \omega. \end{aligned} \tag{17}$$

Proof. (outline) Using induction on i, $i \geq 1$, we prove that for all $q \in Q$ and $\omega \in \Sigma^*$ such that $\omega \neq \varepsilon$:

$$\begin{aligned} &\text{if } \langle q, L\omega R\rangle \vdash^i_M \langle p, \alpha_1 RL\alpha_2\rangle, \text{ for some } p \in F \text{ and } \alpha_1, \alpha_2 \in \Sigma^*, \\ &\qquad\qquad\qquad\qquad\qquad\qquad\quad \text{such that } \omega = \alpha_1\alpha_2, \\ &\text{then } q \Rightarrow^*_{\mathrm{G}} \omega. \end{aligned} \tag{18}$$

The statement (17) follows from (18). □

Lemma 6. *Let $M = \langle Q, \Sigma, \delta, q_0, R, L, F\rangle$ be an NLA, and G be the grammar constructed as above by (16). Then for all $q \in Q$ and $\omega \in \Sigma^*$ such that $\omega \neq \varepsilon$:*

$$\begin{aligned} &\textit{if } q \Rightarrow^*_{\mathrm{G}} \omega, \textit{then } \langle q, L\omega R\rangle \vdash^*_M \langle p, \alpha_1 RL\alpha_2\rangle, \\ &\qquad\qquad\qquad \textit{for some } p \in F \textit{ and } \alpha_1, \alpha_2 \in \Sigma^* \ (\omega = \alpha_1\alpha_2) \end{aligned} \tag{19}$$

Proof. (outline) By induction on i, $i \geq 1$, we prove that for all $q \in Q$ and $\omega \in \Sigma^*$ such that $\omega \neq \varepsilon$:

$$\begin{aligned} &\text{if } q \Rightarrow^i_{\mathrm{G}} \omega, \text{then } \langle q, L\omega R\rangle \vdash^*_M \langle p, \alpha_1 RL\alpha_2\rangle, \\ &\qquad\qquad\qquad \text{for some } p \in F \text{ and } \alpha_1, \alpha_2 \in \Sigma^* \ (\omega = \alpha_1\alpha_2) \end{aligned} \tag{20}$$

Then, (19) follows from (20). □

Lemma 7. *Let $M = \langle Q, \Sigma, \delta, q_0, R, L, F\rangle$ be an NLA, and G be the grammar constructed as above by (16). Then for all $q \in Q$ and $\omega \in \Sigma^*$ such that $\omega \neq \varepsilon$:*

$$\begin{aligned} &q \Rightarrow^*_{\mathrm{G}} \omega \textit{ iff } \langle q, L\omega R\rangle \vdash^*_M \langle p, \alpha_1 RL\alpha_2\rangle, \\ &\qquad\qquad \textit{for some } p \in F \textit{ and } \alpha_1, \alpha_2 \in \Sigma^* \ (\omega = \alpha_1\alpha_2) \end{aligned} \tag{21}$$

Proof. The statement follows from Lemma 5 and Lemma 6. □

Theorem 3. *If L is such that $L = L(M)$ for some NLA, then there is a linear grammar G (in a standard form) such that $L = L(G)$.*

Proof. Let $L = L(M)$, where $M = \langle Q, \Sigma, \delta, q_0, L, R, F\rangle$ is an NLA. Let G be the grammar constructed as above by (16). Let $\omega \in \Sigma^*$.

Case 1. If $\omega = \varepsilon$, then by the construction of G,

$$\varepsilon \in L(G) \text{ iff } q_0 \in F \text{ iff } \varepsilon \in L = L(M). \tag{22}$$

Case 2. If $\omega \neq \varepsilon$, then, by Lemma 7,

$$\begin{array}{l} q_0 \Rightarrow_{\mathrm{G}}^{*} \omega \text{ iff } \langle q_0, L\omega R\rangle \vdash_M^{*} \langle p, \alpha_1 R L \alpha_2\rangle \\ \qquad\qquad \text{for some } p \in F \text{ and } \alpha_1, \alpha_2 \in \Sigma^* \ (\omega = \alpha_1\alpha_2) \end{array} \tag{23}$$

By (22) and (23), it follows that for all $\omega \in \Sigma^*$, $\omega \in L(G)$ iff $\omega \in L(M)$. Therefore, $L = L(G) = L(M)$. □

Definition 7. *A NLA $M = \langle Q, \Sigma, \delta, q_0, L, R, F\rangle$ is called a deterministic linear finite automaton (DLA), if all values of δ have at most one element.*

There are linear languages that are recognised by deterministic push down automata, but for which there is no DLA. An example of such a language is $L_1 = \{a^n cb^n,\ a^n b^{2n} : n \in \mathbb{N},\ n \geq 1\}$. And vice versa, there are non-deterministic context-free languages (i.e., such that are not recognizable by any deterministic push down automata), that can be recognized by DLA. An example of such language is $L_2 = \{a^n b^n c,\ a^n b^{2n} : n \in \mathbb{N}, n \geq 1\}$.

4 NLA with ε-Transitions

In this section, I will generalize the class of the NLA by permitting ε-transitions, i.e., moves from one to another state without reading input symbols and without advancing any of the reading heads. This generalization does not add to the power of the NLA, but the construction of the class $LA(m, n)$ of automata given in the following section is significantly simplified by permitting ε-transitions.

Definition 8. *A nondeterministic linear automaton (NLA) which allows ε-transitions is a tuple $M = \langle Q, \Sigma, \delta, q_0, L, R, F\rangle$, where*

1. *$Q \neq \emptyset$ is the set of the states of M;*
2. *Σ is a finite set, that is the input alphabet of M;*
3. *$q_0 \in Q$ is the initial state of M;*
4. *$L, R \notin Q \cup \Sigma$, $L \neq R$; L and R are the markers for the left and right reading heads, correspondingly;*
5. *$F \subseteq Q$ is the set of the final states of M;*
6. *$\delta : Q \times \Sigma \cup \{\varepsilon\} \longrightarrow \mathcal{P}(Q \times \{L, R, \varepsilon\})$ is the transition function of M.*

Note that infinite ε-loops are possible and can be algorithmically detected and removed. An algorithms for this will be included in the complete version of the paper.

Theorem 4. *For each NLA, M with ε-transitions, there is an NLA M' without ε-transitions recognizing the same language, i.e., such that $L(M) = L(M')$.*

Proof. The intuition behind the formal proof is that, at first, all chains of successive ε-transitions are calculated. Then each chain of successive ε-transitions starting from a state q and ending in a state p is replaced by non-ε-transitions in all possible (non-deterministic) ways: for each $a \in \Sigma$, we add all elements of the set $\delta(p, a)$ to the set of the elements of $\delta(q, a)$. □

5 A Class of Unambiguous Linear Languages and Linear Automata

Andrei and Kudlek [4] consider a subclass of linear languages generated by a subclass $LLin(m, n)$ of linear grammars that resemble the class of $LL(k)$ grammars (see Aho and Ullman [1] and Hopcroft and Ullman [7]). They also define a class of bidirectional parsers corresponding to $LLin(m, n)$ that, intuitively, "look ahead" the next m terminal symbols and the "look back" to the previous n terminals to determine uniquely the grammar rule that has to be used. The class of $LLin(m, n)$ grammars is useful because it designate an unambiguous subclass of linear languages the membership problem for which can be solved by a linear time complexity algorithm. In this section, I will introduce some of the definitions (in slightly modified versions of those in Andrei and Kudlek [4]) of the class of $LLin(m, n)$ languages and then I wil define a class of linear automata, $LA_{(m,n)}$ that recognizes the same class $LLin(m, n)$ of languages. The linear automata $LA_{(m,n)}$ are an automata version of the bidirectional parsers of Andrei and Kudlek [4].

Definition 9. *Let $\mathcal{A}$ be an alphabet, $k, n, m \in \mathbb{N}$ and $w = w_1 \ldots w_k \in \mathcal{A}^*$, where $w_1, \ldots, w_k \in \mathcal{A}$. Then*

$$^{(m)}w = \begin{cases} w_1 \ldots w_m, & \text{if } m \leq k \\ w, & \text{otherwise.} \end{cases} \qquad w^{(n)} = \begin{cases} w_{k-n+1} \ldots w_k, & \text{if } n \leq k \\ w, & \text{otherwise.} \end{cases}$$

Definition 10. *Let $G = \langle N, \Sigma, S, P \rangle$ be a linear grammar and let $n, m \in \mathbb{N}$. The grammar G is said to be $LLin(m, n)$ if for every pair of derivations*

$$A \Longrightarrow \alpha_1 \Longrightarrow^* x \quad \text{and} \quad A \Longrightarrow \alpha_2 \Longrightarrow^* y$$

where $x, y \in \Sigma^*$, $A \in N$ and $\alpha_1, \alpha_2 \in (N \cup \Sigma)^*$, the equalities of the m leftmost and n rightmost characters of x and y, respectively, i.e. $^{(m)}x = {}^{(m)}y$ and $x^{(n)} = y^{(n)}$, imply that $\alpha_1 = \alpha_2$ (i.e., the rule that is applied, $A \to \alpha$, is uniquely determined by looking at the first m and last n symbols of the generated string).

The class of all languages L such that for some $m, n \in \mathbb{N}$ there is a $LLin(m, n)$ grammar G for which $L = L(G)$ is denoted by $\mathcal{LL}in(m, n)$. There are linear languages that are not in $\mathcal{LL}in(m, n)$ for any $m, n \in \mathbb{N}$. For example, $L_1 = \{a^n cb^n, a^n b^{2n} : n \geq 1\}$ is such language. Also, every $LLin(m, n)$ grammar is unambiguous, but there are unambiguous linear languages that are not $\mathcal{LL}in(m, n)$ (see Andrei and Kudlek [4]).

Definition 11. *Let $G = \langle N, \Sigma, S, P\rangle$ be an $LLin(m,n)$ grammar for some $n, m \in \mathbb{N}$ and $\gamma \in (N \cup \Sigma)^*$. Let $\# \notin N \cup \Sigma$. The set $first_m{-}last_n(\gamma)$ is the union of the folowing sets:*

1. $\{(u,v) : u,v,x \in \Sigma^*,\ |u| = m,\ |v| = n,\ |uxv| \geq max\{m,n\},\ \gamma \Longrightarrow_G^* uxv\}$
2. $\{(\#xv, v) : v, x \in \Sigma^*,\ |xv| < m,\ |v| = n,\ \gamma \Longrightarrow_G^* xv\}$
3. $\{(u, ux\#) : u, x \in \Sigma^*,\ |ux| < n,\ |u| = m,\ \gamma \Longrightarrow_G^* ux\}$
4. $\{(\#x, x\#) : x \in \Sigma^*,\ |x| < m,\ |x| < n,\ \gamma \Longrightarrow_G^* x\}$

Construction of $LA_{(m,n)}$: Let $G = \langle N, \Sigma, S, P\rangle$ be an $LLin(m,n)$ grammar for some $n, m \in \mathbb{N}$. Let $\# \notin N \cup \Sigma$. We construct an NLA automaton $LA_{(m,n)}(G) = \langle Q, \Sigma, \delta, q_0, L, R, F\rangle$ as follows:

1. $Q = \{[\#\alpha, \beta\#, \gamma] : \alpha, \beta \in \Sigma^*, |\alpha| \leq m, |\beta| \leq n,\ \gamma \in (N \cup \Sigma)^*,$ and either $\gamma \in N$ or $A \to \gamma \in P$ for some $A \in N\}$ (not all states are reachable);
2. $q_0 = [\#, \#, S]$ is the initial state;
3. $F = \{[\#, \#, \varepsilon]\}$ is the set of a single final state;
4. the transition function δ is defined as follows
   (a) for every $A \in N$:
   $\delta([\#, \#, A], \varepsilon) = \{([\#, \#, \gamma], \varepsilon) : A \to \gamma \in P\}$
   (b) for every $\alpha_0 \in \Sigma^*$, $\alpha \in \Sigma^* \cup \#\Sigma^*$, $\beta \in \Sigma^* \cup \Sigma^*\#$, $a \in \Sigma$ and $\gamma \in (N \cup \Sigma)^*$ such that $A \to \gamma \in P$, for some $A \in N$, $(\alpha, \beta) \in first_m{-}last_n(\gamma)$ and $\alpha_0 a$ (or $\#\alpha_0 a$) is a prefix of α :
   include $([\#\alpha_0 a, \#, \gamma], L)$ in $\delta([\#\alpha_0, \#, \gamma], a)$;
   (c) for every $\beta_0, \alpha, \beta \in \Sigma^*$, $a \in \Sigma$ and $\gamma \in (N \cup \Sigma)^*$ such that $A \to \gamma \in P$ for some $A \in N$ and $(\alpha, \beta) \in first_m{-}last_n(\gamma)$ and $a\beta_0$ (or $a\beta_0\#$) is a sufix of β:
   include $([\#\alpha, a\beta_0\#, \gamma], R)$ in $\delta([\#\alpha, \beta_0\#, \gamma], a)$;
   (d) for every $X \in N \cup \{\varepsilon\}$, and $\alpha_1, \alpha_2, \beta_1, \beta_2 \in \Sigma^*$
   $\delta([\#\alpha_1\alpha_2, \beta_2\beta_1\#, \alpha_1 X \beta_1], \varepsilon) = ([\#\alpha_2, \beta_2\#, X], \varepsilon)$;
   (e) for every $X \in N \cup \{\varepsilon\}$, and $\alpha_1, \alpha_2, \beta \in \Sigma^*$
   $\delta([\#\alpha_1\alpha_2, \beta\#, \alpha_1 X], \varepsilon) = ([\#\alpha_2, \beta\#, X], \varepsilon)$;
   (f) for every $X \in N \cup \{\varepsilon\}$, and $\alpha, \beta_1, \beta_2 \in \Sigma^*$
   $\delta([\#\alpha, \beta_2\beta_1\#, X\beta_1], \varepsilon) = ([\#\alpha, \beta_2\#, X], \varepsilon)$.

We denote the class of all linear automata $LA_{(m,n)}(G)$ constructed as above with $LA_{(m,n)}$, i.e., for any $m, n \in \mathbb{N}$

$$LA_{(m,n)} = \{LA_{(m,n)}(G) : G \in LLin(m,n)\}.$$

Lemma 8. *Let $G = \langle N, \Sigma, S, P\rangle$ be an $LLin(m,n)$ grammar for some $n, m \in \mathbb{N}$ and let $LA_{(m,n)}(G) = \langle Q, \Sigma, \delta, q_0, L, R, F\rangle$ be an automaton constructed as above. Then, for every $\alpha_1, \alpha_2, u \in \Sigma^*$, $X \in N$, and $A \in N$:*

1. *If* $\langle [\#, \#, A], L\alpha_1 u \alpha_2 R\rangle \vdash_{LA_{(m,n)}(G)}^* \langle [\#, \#, X], \alpha_1 L u R \alpha_2\rangle$ *then* $A \Longrightarrow_G^* \alpha_1 X \alpha_2$

2. *If* $\alpha_1\alpha_2 \neq \varepsilon$ *and* $\langle[\#,\#,A], L\alpha_1\alpha_2 R\rangle \vdash^*_{LA_{(m,n)}(G)} \langle[\#,\#,\varepsilon], \alpha_1 RL\alpha_2\rangle$ *then* $A \Longrightarrow^*_G \alpha_1\alpha_2$

Proof. The proof of (1) is carried on by induction on the number of moves made by $LA_{(m,n)}(G)$. □

Lemma 9. *Let* $G = \langle N, \Sigma, S, P\rangle$ *be an* $LLin(m,n)$ *grammar for some* $n, m \in \mathbb{N}$ *and let* $LA_{(m,n)}(G) = \langle Q, \Sigma, \delta, q_0, L, R, F\rangle$ *be an automaton constructed as above. Then, for every* $\alpha_1, \alpha_2, u \in \Sigma^*$, $X \in N$, *and* $A \in N$:

1. *If* $A \Longrightarrow^*_G \alpha_1 X \alpha_2$ *then* $\langle[\#,\#,A], L\alpha_1 u\alpha_2 R\rangle \vdash^*_{LA_{(m,n)}(G)} \langle[\#,\#,X], \alpha_1 LuR\alpha_2\rangle$
2. *If* $\alpha_1\alpha_2 \neq \varepsilon$ *and* $A \Longrightarrow^*_G \alpha_1\alpha_2$ *then* $\langle[\#,\#,A], L\alpha_1\alpha_2 R\rangle \vdash^*_{LA_{(m,n)}(G)} \langle[\#,\#,\varepsilon], \alpha_1 RL\alpha_2\rangle$

Proof. The proof of (1) is carried on by induction on the length of the derivation in G. □

Theorem 5. *Let* $G = \langle N, \Sigma, S, P\rangle$ *be an* $LLin(m,n)$ *grammar for some* $n, m \in \mathbb{N}$ *and let* $LA_{(m,n)}(G) = \langle Q, \Sigma, \delta, q_0, L, R, F\rangle$ *be constructed as above. Then, for every* $\alpha_1\alpha_2 \in \Sigma^*$

$$\langle[\#,\#,S], L\alpha_1\alpha_2 R\rangle \vdash^*_{LA_{(m,n)}(G)} \langle[\#,\#,\varepsilon], \alpha_1 RL\alpha_2\rangle \text{ iff } S \Longrightarrow^*_G \alpha_1\alpha_2$$

Proof. Follows from the items (2) of Lemma 8 and Lemma 9. □

6 Conclusions

The class of NLA is of further interest from theoretic and application perspectives. Various operations, such as union, homomorphism and concatenation over NLA can be defined and studied for applications in modeling natural processes. The class of the NLA (LCFLs) are not necessarily closed under such operations. The result of such an operation can be an automaton which is not an NLA, but is a composition of components that are modeled by NLA. The NLA components of such "combined" abstract devices represent symmetrically dependent patterns and processes. For example, a set of such dependences can be modelled by a finite union of concatenations of NLA. In particular, $L = \bigcup_{i=1}^{n}(\Pi_{j=1}^{m_i} L_{i,j})$, where each $L_{i,j}$ ($i = 1, \ldots, n$; $j = 1, \ldots, m_i$) is a LCFL representing symmetric dependences. L can be represented with a set of context-free rules such as $A_i \longrightarrow A_{i,1} \ldots A_{i,m_i}$, where each $A_{i,j}$ is the initial symbol of the corresponding LCFL $L_{i,j}$. Research on such operators, their closure properties, algorithms and applications are subject of further work.

NLA have potential applications in natural language processing for morphology analysis, shallow parsing and part of speech tagging. They have also potential applications in neuroscience, including neurolinguistics and bioinformatics for modeling "mirror" patterns and dependences on processes in symmetric branches, for example, symmetric or paralleled neural paths governed by a common originator. In particular, this is a plausible model of language cognitive faculty on morphological interrelations between sounds, lexical units, co-occurrence restrictions, meanings, which are beyond the capacity of finite-state automata, but do not need full context free power.

References

1. Aho, A.V., Ullman, J.D.: Theory of Parsing, Translation and Compiling, Parsing, vol. 1. Prentice Hall, Englewood Cliffs (1972)
2. Amar, V., Putzolu, G.: On a Family of Linear Grammars. Information and Control 7, 283–291 (1964)
3. Amar, V., Putzolu, G.: Generalizations of Regular Events. Information and Control 8(1), 56–63 (1965)
4. Andrei, S., Kudlek, M.: Linear Bidirectional Parsing for a Subclass of Linear Languages. FBI-Bericht 215/98, p. 22 (1998)
5. Andrei, S., Kudlek, M.: Bidirectional Parsing for Linear Languages. In: Thomas, W. (ed.) Preproceedings of DLT'99. Aachener Informatik-Berichte 99-5, pp. 331–344 (1999)
6. Autebert, J.-M., Berstel, J., Boasson, L.: Context-free languages and pushdown automata. In: Rozenberg, R., Salomaa, A. (eds.) Handbook of Formal Languages, ch. 3, vol. 1, Springer, Heidelberg (1997)
7. Hopcroft, J.E., Ullman, J.D.: Introduction To Automata Theory, Languages, And Computation, 1st edn. Addison-Wesley, Reading (1979)
8. Ibarra, O.H.: On Two-way Multihead Automata. J. Comput. Syst. Sci. 7(1), 28–36 (1973)
9. Rosenberg, A.L.: A machine realization of the linear context-free languages. Information and Control 10(2), 175–188 (1967)
10. Grzegorz, R., Salomaa, A.: Handbook of Formal Languages, vol. 1-3. Springer, Heidelberg (1997)
11. Salomaa, A.: Formal Languages. Academic Press. New York (1973). Revised edition in the series "Computer Science Classics" Academic Press (1987)

FM for FMS: Lessons Learned While Applying Formal Methods to the Study of Flexible Manufacturing Systems

Andrea Matta[1], Matteo Rossi[2], Paola Spoletini[2], Dino Mandrioli[2], Quirico Semeraro[1], and Tullio Tolio[1]

[1] Dipartimento di Meccanica, Politecnico di Milano
{andrea.matta,quirico.semeraro,tullio.tolio}@polimi.it
[2] Dipartimento di Elettronica e Informazione, Politecnico di Milano
{rossi,spoletini,mandrioli}@elet.polimi.it

Abstract. In the past few years two research groups of Politecnico di Milano, whose activities were centered on Formal Methods for the production of critical software and on industrial manufacturing systems, respectively, have carried out a joint research project that, among other things, aimed at introducing the use of formal methods in the design and analysis phases of industrial production systems (and especially of so-called Flexible Manufacturing Systems, FMSs) as a complementary tool to the ones used in the current practice of the field. This paper reports on the challenges that the research groups faced during the project, and on the lessons that have been learned in the process.

Keywords: Experience, Formal Methods, Production Systems, Temporal Logics, Finite-State Models, System Design, Formal Verification.

1 Introduction

The authors of this paper belong to two different research groups of the school of engineering at Politecnico di Milano. One group is a software engineering (SwE) group who has been active in the development and application of formal methods (FMs) for critical software; the other group is an industrial engineering (IE) group whose research addresses the problems related to Flexible Manufacturing Systems (FMSs), i.e., industrial production systems composed of computer numerically controlled machining centers (workstations) that are capable of producing different kinds of products in different ratios and volumes, depending on the needs of the firm (hence, flexibility).

During some brainstorming the two groups realized that they had in common not only typical engineering problems and quality goals such as reliability, flexibility, maintainability, but also fundamental design principles such as abstraction, hierarchical development, and even some notion of object-oriented approach to the design and documentation. The next step suggested that some techniques originally developed within the software engineering world –those under the "hat" of formal methods in particular– could nicely complement common

C.B. Jones, Z. Liu, J. Woodcock (Eds.): ICTAC 2007, LNCS 4711, pp. 366–380, 2007.

practices in the development of FMSs. This led to the launching of a pilot project to validate this idea.

A case study was defined based on previous experience of the IE group. Much cooperative work was devoted to a mutual exchange of knowledge between the two groups so as to state a common "language": the SwE group had to understand the essential features of FMSs, whereas the IE group augmented its knowledge of notations and models such as UML, logic-based specification, abstract state machines, still maintaining each subgroup precise and distinguished competences and responsibilities. Starting from the original documentation and knowledge supplied by the IE people we developed a specification, design and verification of the FMS case study by applying innovative techniques imported from the FM community (logic-based specification and verification through model-checking in particular). The pilot project showed that the FM-based approach yielded a deeper understanding of the finer points of the system (e.g. it uncovered "holes" in the specification), an improved system reliability (through verification of desired properties), and other typical engineering qualities. Also, several guidelines for further improvements were derived. Let us point out that, for a number of reasons, which include the material costs that such an endeavor would entail, realizing the designed FMS down to acquiring the physical devices and deploying them was not one of the goals of the research project within which this work was carried out. Nevertheless, we are confident that the qualitative lessons we learned throughout this work are very general, and would only be confirmed by a project that included also the implementation phase and a quantitative evaluation of the benefits.

This paper reports on our experience on joining interdisciplinary expertise, rooted however on a strong common engineering background, with the goal of advancing the state of the art of designing FMSs by exploiting techniques imported from the FM community. It is organized as follows: Section 2 presents the features that are in common between software engineering and production systems development, and lists some works that are across the two fields; Section 3 briefly reviews the state of the art of production systems development, which motivated the research, and the project's goal; Section 4 describes the major phases through which the research activity was carried out; Section 5 presents the lessons we learned while carrying out the research; finally, Section 6 draws some conclusions, and outlines future developments for the current research.

2 Background

The research was carried out in close collaboration by two research groups: the Formal Methods/Software Engineering group at the Department of Electronics and Computer Science, and the group of Industrial Engineering at the Department of Mechanical Engineering. The two groups had never worked together, but nonetheless it was soon realized that, in addition to some shared technical background, there was, most notably, a common "frame of mind" when it came to problems, problem representation and problem analysis. It became clear from the beginning of the collaboration that Software Engineering and Industrial Engineering share a significant set of goals, which entail also a common set of problems and difficulties to overcome.

Software systems and production systems are both complex agglomerate of components interacting with each other according to some (possibly user-defined) logic. They are *modular* in nature, and their components are designed to be *reusable* (they should not be re-developed for each new instance of system). In addition, both software and production systems are often required to be *flexible* and *reconfigurable* to adapt to different situations (different configurations, different products to be produced, different production targets, etc.). Also, both software and production systems can have aspects of *criticality*: a widely-studied class of software applications is the one of the so-called safety-critical systems, where a malfunction (for example due to a software bug) can cause catastrophic consequences (including, possibly, loss of human lives); production systems are critical more from an economic point of view, in that the wrong design might result in loss of millions (of euros/dollars) due for example to lack of production capacity or, at the opposite end, to excess of production capacity (with corresponding waste of highly expensive resources such as production machines).

As a consequence of their characteristics, both kinds of systems must be designed with great care and through a rigorous process, which should facilitate the use of precise and sound analysis techniques for the evaluation of the system design well before its implementation. More precisely, in both cases one would like to be able to guarantee that deadlines are met (for example, that a certain amount of items is produced in a day), and that results and goals are achieved.

However, the similarities between software and production systems are not limited to the above abstract features, but have also a technical counterpart: in both fields the UML notation is employed in the early phases of development to model the system being designed. As a matter of fact, while UML was born in the SwE community for the development of software systems, in recent years its use has spread also to different engineering areas, including the design of production systems [1]. The use of the UML notation in both software and industrial engineering reinforces the above perception that the two fields have many points in common: they share not only problems, but also approaches to solve them, such as the Object-Oriented one incarnated in the UML. In addition, the shared use of UML highlights a common attitude towards modeling, and constitutes a first step towards the adoption of a common set of concepts and terminology (even if, as Section 4 points out, it can also hide subtle differences).

While software and industrial engineers share both a similar attitude towards modeling and, to a certain extent, the same modeling languages (albeit limited to the semi-formal variety of modeling), traditionally they have used different approaches when it comes to precise, mathematical (i.e. formal) modeling for design and analysis purposes. In fact, the standard practice in the early phases (i.e. before implementation) of the development of production systems employs mostly statistical/probabilistic models; these are usually based on Markov chains and Queuing theory to carry out an analytic study of the system and are typically combined with a heavy use of (statistical) numerical discrete events simulation tools for the analysis of the performance of the system under different configurations and loads [2]. In SwE practice, instead, models focus mostly on the logic aspects of the application (whether conditions will or will not occur, what course of action must be taken in each case, etc.), rather than on the statistical ones (e.g. how often a certain condition occurs). In addition, what is simulation for production systems becomes testing for software applications.

To conclude this Section, it is clear that the development of software applications (especially critical ones) and that of production systems share many traits. This is evidenced also by a number of previous works, in which modeling and –to a lesser extent– verification techniques (mostly based on Petri Nets) originally developed by the computer science community have been applied to the production systems domain [3,4,5,6]. However, we feel that such techniques could and should also be tightly integrated in the design process of manufacturing systems, as a complementary and synergic approach to the existing ones [7].

3 Project Motivation and Aim

This Section presents the goals of our research project. To put these goals in better perspective, we first briefly describe the main features and components of FMSs; then, we outline the techniques used in the current practice for the design and analysis of FMSs; finally, we state the goals of the project.

3.1 Flexible Manufacturing Systems

FMSs are production systems composed of computer numerically controlled (CNC) machining centers that generally process prismatic metal components. A process cycle defining all the technological information (e.g. type of operations, tools, feed movements, working speeds, etc.) is available for each product so that the system has the whole knowledge for transforming *raw parts*, the state in which a piece enters into the system, into *finished parts*, the state in which a piece has completed the process cycle. The main components of an FMS are described below.

CNC machines (also called working stations, WS for short) perform the operations on raw parts. A machining operation consists in the removal of material from the raw parts with a tool, which is mounted on the *spindle* of the machine. The machines are CNC in that their movements during the machining operations are controlled by a local computer. Machines can differ, in addition to other minor technical characteristics, in their size, power, speed, and number of controlled axes.

Pallets are the hardware standard physical interfaces between the system components (e.g. WSs) and the parts that are to be machined. Parts are clamped on pallets by means of automated fixtures providing them stability during the machining operation. Usually, but not always, fixtures are dedicated to products; also, more than one part is tipically mounted on a pallet. Parts to

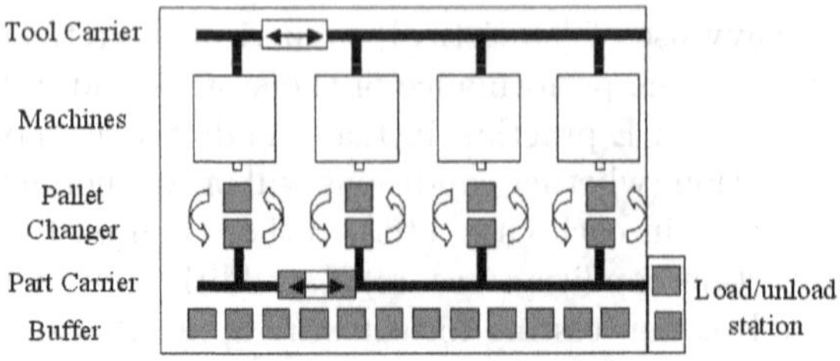

Fig. 1. An example of FMS

be machined must first be clamped on pallets before they can be worked on by a WS. A pallet is an expensive resource (its cost is generally between 10 and 50 keuro), so only a limited number of them is available in an FMS.

The **load/unload (L/U) station** executes the operations of 1) clamping raw parts onto pallets (and thus allowing them to enter the system), and 2) removing finished parts from pallets after their process cycle has been completed by the WSs of the system. L/U stations can be manned, i.e. an operator accomplishes the task, or unmanned, i.e. the operation is done by a gantry robot. After finished parts are dismounted from a pallet, the latter can be used anew to insert other parts into the system.

The **part handling sub-system** is the set of devices that move parts (and pallets) through the system. In practice, a number of different mechanical devices can be used to transport pallets/parts: automated guided vehicles, carriers, conveyors, etc.

Tools perform the cutting operations on raw parts. Since tools are expensive resources their number is limited and, as a consequence, they are moved through the system only when requested by WSs. Tools wear out with use and have to be reconditioned from time to time in order to be usable again.

The **tool handling sub-system** is the set of devices that move tools through the system. The automated transport of tools among WSs is not always present in FMSs due to management difficulties encountered in practice. However, when this solution is adopted, the most frequently adopted device to transport tools consists of a carrier moving on tracks.

The **central part buffer** is the place where pallets wait for the availability of system resources (i.e. machines, carriers, load/unload stations).

The **central tool buffer** is the place where tools can be stored when they are not used.

The **supervisor** is the software that controls resources at system level by assigning pallets to machines and L/U stations and by scheduling tool and pallet transports.

The **tool room** is the place where tools are reconditioned.

Figure 1 shows an example of an FMS with four WSs and one L/U station.

Let us now briefly describe the flow of parts through an FMS. In general, at the L/U station more than one part is loaded onto a pallet. The type and the number of parts on a pallet depend on the products to be manufactured and on the system components (e.g. the WSs). If the load/unload operation is executed manually by human operators (i.e. the L/U station is manned), then its duration can be considered a random variable according to some estimated distribution; otherwise, if the L/U station is unmanned, then deterministic load/unload times can be assumed. After parts are loaded onto pallets, the supervisor decides, for each pallet, the path that it will follow in the FMS to complete the process cycle of all its parts. In order to complete the process cycle, a pallet must visit at least one WS; if all WSs are busy, pallets wait in the central buffer. Each machine has at least two pallet positions: the first one is the *pallet working position*, which is used when the pallet is machined by the tool; the other positions, which are known as *pallet waiting positions*, are instead used to decouple the WS from the part handling sub-system. Indeed, a pallet in a waiting position waits either for the machine to complete working on the pallet that is in the working position, or for the carrier to become available for a transport if the pallet has already been worked. For example, in the FMS of Figure 1 every WS has exactly one waiting position in addition to the working one. To move a pallet from a waiting position to the working position (and vice versa), every WS is provided with a *pallet changer*; a pallet changer is an automatic device, so the movement between different positions can be considered deterministic since there is no source of variability in the operation. After the pallet has been blocked in the working position and the tools necessary for the operations are available to the machine, the processing operations can be executed. Processing times of machines can be reasonably assumed deterministic. In fact, the trajectory of the tool during the cutting of material is computer numerically controlled and therefore the sources of variability are negligible.

The architecture of FMSs has expanded to different sectors with different technologies (e.g. plastic deformation, lathes, assembly machines, etc.) with high benefits in terms of increase of performance and business.

3.2 Current Practice in the Design of FMSs

The goal of the design of an FMS is to determine the "right" system configuration that permits to attain the desired production targets. The system "configuration" is a mixture of physical and logical settings that affect many different aspects of the system; some of the most relevant settings are: the number of copies of each kind of tool; the number of instances of each kind of pallet; the rules used by the supervisor to manage resources (to decide for example to which WS a pallet entering the system is to be sent, or which tool request must be satisfied first); the rules through which WSs manage process cycles (e.g. what operations to execute first, or the order in which tools are requested), etc.

As mentioned in Section 2, the design of production systems is a difficult task; as a consequence, it is often decomposed into several hierarchical sub-problems, which differ in the level of detail of the analysis and in the tools adopted to select, assess and test alternative configurations. In addition, the levels for design and analysis are difficult to establish and depend on the type of production system, the importance of the decision, and the available budget [2].

To solve the design problem outlined above, a number of tools for selecting and managing the equipment, assessing the system performance and testing alternative solutions are used in the current practice. Such tools rely on models for the evaluation of the performance of the different system configurations, and on optimization techniques to identify the configuration that best matches the production targets and the company's goals. As customary with any kind of model, a performance evaluation model should be accurate, complete, easy to use and cheap; however, there is usually a trade-off between these features, so that greater accuracy and completeness entail higher costs and time. The techniques that are most used in practice for the design and analysis of production systems are *analytical methods* and *discrete events simulation*.

Analytical methods (mostly based on Markov chains and Queuing theory) represent the most relevant behavior of complex systems through a limited number of variables that are (often implicitly) related through dynamic equations. However, analytical methods often require to introduce restrictive assumptions to simplify the mathematical treatment of the model, thus reducing the applicability of the technique. In this regard, a classic example is the memoryless property of Markovian models, which does not fit well with the phenomena of mechanical wear of machines and tools. On the other hand, analytical methods generally perform fast and the provided results have average accuracy.

A simulation model, instead, can represent a complex manufacturing system in all its details. Quite naturally, this translates to higher costs in terms of both development time for the simulation code and computational time to run the experiments. Thus, the level of adequacy of a simulation model is decided by the user coherently with the objectives and the budget of the analysis. The accuracy of performance measures estimated by simulation greatly depends on the completeness of the model and on the length of simulation experiments.

The choice of the most appropriate performance evaluation method depends on the level of the analysis. A widespread approach [8] consists of using analytical methods for an initial selection of good configuration candidates and then refining the choice among the selected candidates by performing simulation experiments. This two-step approach benefits from the speed of analytical methods in the initial phase (which eliminates distinctively poor configurations), while at the same time exploiting the higher detail of simulation models in the second phase to search for the best candidate. However, as explained in the next Section, both analytical methods and simulation (used alone or in combination) are inadequate to answer a number of important design questions. Hence, important benefits can be gained if new, innovative techniques that are able to address these deficiencies were used in *conjunction* (not as substitutes) with the classic ones in the design process of production systems.

3.3 FMs for FMSs

Despite their large adoption in the design and analysis phases of production systems, analytical methods and simulation are not enough to check if the system under design meets its requirements. Systems may be required to avoid deadlock, to guarantee certain resource utilizations thresholds, to use some preferred system paths, etc. Analytical methods model the system dynamics by means of feasible states and random transitions among the system states, but they only provide aggregate statistics on the system behavior. Indeed these methods can provide probabilities about the occurrence of one or more events in a given time period, but very seldom they can be used to determine whether an event will *certainly* happen or not (e.g. the production of a lot in a time period, the unavailability of transporters under heavy system loading conditions, a deadlock, etc.). The main difficulties arising when using analytical methods to check the system being designed lie in the intractability of the underlying mathematical models and in the restrictive assumptions that limit their scope of application.

Simulation for production systems is akin to testing for software applications: it can be used to check several different paths in order to unearth incorrect system behaviors and to check some properties; however, in the vast majority of cases simulation cannot guarantee the global correctness of the system configuration, as one or more unexplored paths, out of the infinite possible ones, may invalidate the conclusions of the analyst. For instance, deadlocks are often encountered in practice when the production system is physically tested after its deployment; in this case the supervisor, i.e. the software controlling the system equipment and flows, must be changed in order to overcome these unforeseen design problems.

The ultimate aim of our research project was to apply formal methods from the computer science domain to FMS design, in order to overcome the limitations of the techniques currently used outlined above. More precisely, the goal was twofold: on one hand, to build formal models of FMS components (and of whole systems), for the purpose of gaining better insight into their dynamics and their interactions; on the other hand, to apply formal verification techniques to such models, in order to check the kinds of requirements that cannot be analyzed with classic tools such as analytical methods and simulation.

The next Section outlines the various phases of the research project, and the issues and problems that arose while carrying them out.

4 Project Phases

The project went through three major phases: one devoted to familiarizing the researchers involved in the project with the core issues of each field; one in which a first formalization of FMS components was given in terms of the TRIO [9] logic language; and one dedicated to the elaboration of a finite-state model of a real-life FMS, on which model checking-based formal verification was carried out. While the three phases are presented here in sequential order, they were not actually carried out in a waterfall-like manner. For example, the task of familiarizing researchers with the different concepts involved from the production systems and the software engineering domains was not confined temporally to the first months of the project, but was carried out throughout. This (and other) issue(s) will be analyzed in greater depth in the next Section.

The first, essential task that needed to be carried out consisted in establishing a common ground of terms and concepts that was shared by the researchers involved, in order to facilitate the interaction. As mentioned in Section 2, a common language, which constituted the basis for the first exchange of ideas, already existed in the form of the UML. In fact, the IE research group had already developed a UML model of a generic FMS [10] in an autonomous manner, without input from the SwE group. The UML description, which consists of class and sequence diagrams, gives a semi-formal view of the core elements of an FMS (parts, pallets, tools, WSs, rules, etc.) and their main features and roles; this allowed the SwE group to get a first, fairly complete idea of the elements involved (and related terms and definitions), and was the first step towards the creation of a "vocabulary" of concepts that was shared by the two groups. Let us remark that creating a common vocabulary did not simply mean that the researchers of the SwE group had to learn what a "pallet" is, or what a WS does. Subtler challenges hid in apparently common concepts such as "verification", which in IE is used as a synonym for "validation". As a matter of fact, validation is a central concept in IE, and refers to the issue of ensuring that the system model matches the behavior of the studied production system up to a certain error, which is *a priori* defined (the validation activity is often carried out in IE through a statistical analysis). Instead, the term "verification" in formal methods is mostly used in the sense of "checking if a desired property descends from a model" [11][1].

Establishing a common base of terms was only part of the initial work that had to be carried out before delving into the formalization/verification stages of the project. Another crucial aspect was sharing and understanding the skills of the two groups, and the issues and problem areas of each domain. This was important for finding the modeling and analysis techniques that best fit the kinds of systems at hand, and for deciding which features and properties were the most interesting to be analyzed. For example, at the beginning it was not apparent that some resources, pallets in particular, are in fact scarce in production systems, and considering their number as unbounded could have relevant consequences on the significance of the analyses carried out; such information came to the surface only after lengthy discussions among the two groups, and was used in the later stages of the work.

In the second stage of the work, a logic-based model of some of the components of an FMS was built [7,12]. The model is written in the TRIO [9] logic language, and was developed by the SwE group from the initial UML description provided by the IE group. A detailed description of the TRIO model is outside the scope of the present experience report. Let us simply point out that TRIO is a very expressive temporal logic, which is capable of representing a wide range of

[1] Such difference in the use of the term "verification" is perhaps not surprising, if one considers that even in the SwE community there is often disagreement on what V&V exactly refers to.

properties, especially those defining the dynamic constraints on the system (e.g. timing constraints, or the semantics of the rules used to manage the system). The TRIO model was very useful in a number of ways: it allowed the SwE group to get a first grasp of the key elements of an FMS, to gather some initial ideas on them, and to experiment with them at a very high level. In addition, it helped focus the research on the parts of the system that the production system experts deemed the most relevant to analyze; in fact, it was decided early on that the research should focus on studying the effects on production of different management rules for tools and pallets –rather than, for example, checking timeliness properties for the transport network.

The experimentation with the TRIO model, which included carrying out the verification of some simple properties through theorem proving techniques [7] evidenced a number of relevant features of FMSs. Among these, an important one is the finiteness of the cardinal elements of the system; for example, the number of WSs in an FMS is usually limited to a small number, rarely more than five; in addition, the number of management rules that are implemented in an FMS is typically small (one or two to decide in which order tools should be requested/the requests should be satisfied, one or two to decide how to assign pallets to WSs, etc.), even though they can be chosen from a fairly large (albeit finite) set. In addition, it became apparent that to represent the features of interest of FMSs a discrete time model was sufficient: most temporal quantities (operation duration, transportation delays, etc.) are deterministic and with precise (integer) values, whereas a continuous-time model (which would allow to temporally separate between nearly-simultaneous events) is in this case not necessary, as the number of events that can occur in the system is finite and well-defined (hence, they can be easily separated even if they occur in the same discrete instant). Therefore, for the verification phase it was decided to employ model checking techniques [13], which fit very well the main characteristics of FMSs. Let us remark that the TRIO language does not impose a specific temporal model [14] and TRIO formulas can be interpreted over temporal domains that can be either discrete or dense. In fact, the initial FMS TRIO model did not mandate a specific temporal domain (even if the first analyses based on this model were carried out using the PVS-based TRIO tool [15], which uses continuous time).

In the last few years, techniques to model check TRIO specifications interpreted over a discrete time domain have been developed [16]. However, the SPIN-based prototype TRIO model checker was not fully operational at the time of the project; hence, it was decided that, to carry out formal verification on FMSs, developing a model directly in Promela [17], the modeling language of the SPIN model checker was the best solution. Then, in the third stage of the project, a finite state, discrete-time Promela model of part of a real-life FMS was developed and verified for some interesting properties through the SPIN model checker [18] (a detailed account of the Promela model and the verifications carried out is outside the scope of this report). While the TRIO model is at a very general and high level of detail (for example, it does not include a representation of the process cycle that products undergo), the Promela one is much more detailed and less general, as it represents a very specific FMS, with a given set of WSs, tools, pallets, and products to be machined. In addition, it includes a model of the *part programs* that are executed by the WSs (where a part program contains the information concerning the set of operations that must be carried out on a certain pallet). The Promela model was developed in close collaboration by the two groups participating in the research; more precisely, while the SwE group actually built the model, the IE group gave continuous input on it, to make sure that it matched real-life FMSs, and as a form of model validation.

To conclude this Section, let us remark that the "vocabulary building" phase was in fact spread throughout the project, and was not limited to the first months, prior to the development of the different models. For example, the existence of only a limited, and usually not large number of pallets in an FMS – a fact that was obvious (hence in no need to be explained) to the IE researchers, but not at all so to the SwE ones – is a feature that emerged in the later stages, during the development of the Promela model. In fact, building and verifying the models helped disseminate the various concepts among the groups, and was a means for familiarizing the researchers from both groups with the key issues and techniques of each field.

5 Lessons Learned

We can derive several lessons from our experience. Some of them confirm fairly well established –but neither universally accepted nor practiced– beliefs on best practices to apply in complex systems development; others may drive future enhancements both in industrial practices and in research. We are confident that they can be exploited within industrial environments too, although our experience has been carried out by a purely academic team, which, nevertheless, could count on a long-standing experience of cooperation with industrial environments.

The first fundamental lesson confirms the fact that [19] in most cases *system* engineering is mostly the integration of heterogeneous components that are developed on the basis of different technologies and cultures. Thus, at least in its high phases, system engineering cannot be carried out in isolation by the specialists of different fields. Stated in this way, such a "lesson" may sound fairly obvious; in our opinion, however, far less obvious are its consequences on working group organization and even on engineering education.

As we emphasized in Section 4, in our experience much effort has been devoted to –continuously– enrich and update the "shared knowledge" of the group, still maintaining a clear distinction in roles, special skills, and responsibilities. On the one hand this was fostered by an already strong common background on basic engineering disciplines: IE people were already provided with some programming skills and with a rudimentary knowledge of UML; SwE people had some knowledge of basic mechanical engineering, not only in terms of essential physics' laws but also in terms of elementary mechanical devices. On the other hand the "fine tuning" of the necessary "groups' common language" still uncovered important "holes" in the knowledge of each others' culture which, if remained hidden, could severely undermine the whole project.

A pleasant side remark is that not only *problems and goals* are often the same in different engineering fields (e.g. reusability, flexibility, and other qualities both of the products and of the processes) but also techniques and methods to approach the solution of such problems can quite profitably be mutually "imported" from each other's cultures: in our case the initial common knowledge consisting of basic models such as mathematical equations, Markov chains, and of the UML notation evolved to include more sophisticated formal methods such as TRIO and model checking.

At the other side of the coin it was also confirmed that in general engineers (not only IEs, but often even SwEs) are more familiar with operational formalisms such as state-based abstract machines than with descriptive formalisms such as logic-based languages. This is unfortunate since it hinders reasoning at a high level of abstraction about the properties of the system under construction.

In our opinion these lessons should have a strong impact in the whole setting of engineering education. Whereas the keyword "interdisciplinarity" is often invoked when talking about education [20], its interpretation in actual and proposed engineering curricula is quite far from building a real *shared engineering culture*. For instance [21] and others [19,22] properly recommend that a SW engineer has a robust knowledge of non-engineering disciplines such as financial, human, and social sciences (which are all the more important when Software Engineering moves towards *System* Engineering [23]), but, by contrast, very little attention is devoted to engineering fields other than SwE: a very shallow knowledge of elementary physics is often all that is recommended and offered in SwE curricula. On the other hand most curricula in fields of engineering other than computing see the knowledge in computer science as simple "service", consisting of a little programming, use of productivity tools and access to Internet, hiding to their students that computing is based on a deep and long-standing *culture*, whose roots date back several millennia. We believe that the present tendency to overspecialize curricula in the various engineering disciplines may have in the long term negative consequences and should be contrasted.

Moving to more technical issues, our experience confirmed once more the usefulness of applying FMs to produce artifacts of better quality and more robust. In fact, the effort of stating and verifying system properties in a formally rigorous way, with the help of automatic tools, helped uncovering subtle errors and obtaining improvements that were not possible when adopting more traditional methods. For instance, during the formal verification (through model checking) of the configuration of a test FMS, we realized that the tool management rules did not guarantee the desired performance. In fact, since the rules were incomplete, they did not sufficiently constrain the tool reservation mechanism. Hence an additional rule was added to the specification of the FMS configuration.

More generally, through model checking we were able to (formally) analyze properties and characteristics of the test FMS that could not have been checked through statistical approaches; for instance, we have proved that, in the test FMS, which is composed of 4 WSs working on 5 different kinds of pallets, no WS has *ever* to wait for tool number 2 for more than 100 seconds.

Once more, we emphasize the benefits of applying FMs *per se*, where by FM we intend here any technique that exploits the rigor and precision of mathematics; again, methods produced by different cultures such as statistical and probabilistic methods, simulation based on differential or difference equations, theorem proving, model-checking etc. should not be used in isolation, but integrated to exploit their complementarities.

On the other hand the choice –and possibly the tailoring– of the appropriate method for the problem at hand is often far from obvious and standardized: in some sense such a choice is itself the result of a spiral process, which aims at selecting and tuning the FMs and tools that are best suited for a specific goal on the basis of early experiences through continuous refinements. For instance, in our project, realizing the finiteness of the essential features of a FMS and discretizing the time domain led to prefer model-checking techniques over more general but less automatic verification approaches such as theorem proving.

Furthermore several abstraction techniques can be applied to master and mitigate the typical combinatorial explosion problem of exhaustive verification (for example, we were able to exploit the physical and logical symmetry of some system configurations to considerably reduce in those cases the state space to be searched).

6 Conclusions and Future Work

We reported on our experience on "importing" formal models, methods, and tools typical of the SwE community into the design of FMSs. The cooperation between the two groups belonging to the respective engineering communities confirmed that not only problems and goals are similar, if not exactly the same, in different engineering fields, but also much mutual benefit can be achieved by complementing and integrating approaches and techniques of the different communities. This requires a strong common cultural background so that interaction and cooperation within the team can be effective and productive in a short time. Of course, a fine tuning in terms of knowledge exchange between the groups' members and a tailoring of models, techniques and tools to the peculiarities of the application field has been and will be necessary in similar endeavors.

Our pilot experience soundly confirmed the expected benefits in the overall quality and productivity of the FMS design process; it also suggested a few guidelines for further exploitation of our approach.

First, in this initial experience our attention has been focused on the modeling and verification techniques that appeared to be more "ready to use", i.e., whose technical features and supporting tools seemed to produce immediate benefits. For instance, model checking has been selected as the principal approach to verify properties, such as the absence of deadlock and the maximum time to complete the machining (i.e. the execution of the part program) of a pallet, that are not easily checkable by more traditional techniques. It is likely, however, that the obtained benefits can be further enhanced by deepening and fine tuning existing techniques (e.g. employing abstraction techniques for model checking, other than symmetry, that are especially tailored to suit the specific features of FMS[2]); by including more techniques –whether traditional, such as numerical simulation, or innovative, such as theorem proving– that have not been fully explored yet; and by better integrating them (and their related tools) with one another.

Second, the transition between the various phases of the process often involved a sharp change in the adopted (semi)formalism, leaving the full responsibility of guaranteeing the consistency among the various deliverables to the human actors. The state of the art, however, is rapidly evolving towards integrated environments that support a seamless transition among the various process phases. For instance, during this project a new version of TRIO, ArchiTRIO, has been defined which supports a smooth transition from requirements specification to architectural design, down to the lower implementation phases and verification. Its integration with verification tools both based on theorem proving and on model checking is also on the way [24]. ArchiTRIO is also fully compatible with the UML notation, and allows users to enrich it with a "desired and appropriate amount of formalism" [25], so that it can be adopted with little effort by practitioners who are familiar with the UML standard. A revised version of the system presented in this paper based on ArchiTRIO will be developed.

Finally, and fairly obviously, we plan to enrich our experience with more, and more complex projects, possibly in cooperation with industrial colleagues.

Acknowledgements

Work supported by the MIUR FIRB project: "Software frameworks and technologies for the development and maintenance of open-source distributed simulation code, oriented to the manufacturing field." Contract code: RBNE013SWE.

References

1. Bruccoleri, M., La Diega, S.N., Perrone, G.: Object-oriented approach for flexible manufacturing control systems analysis and design using the Unified Modeling Language. Int. Journal of Flexible Manufacturing Systems 15(3), 195–216 (2003)
2. Matta, A., Semeraro, Q., Tolio, T.: A framework for long term capacity decisions in advanced manufacturing systems. In: Matta, A., Semeraro, Q. (eds.) Design of Advanced Manufacturing Systems, Springer, Heidelberg (2005)
3. Zhou, M., Venkatesh, K.: Modeling, Simulation, and Control of Flexible Manufacturing Systems: A Petri Net Approach. World Scientific, Singapore (1999)
4. Wang, J., Deng, Y.: Incremental modeling and verification of flexible manufacturing systems. Journal of Intelligent Manufacturing 10(6), 485–502 (1999)
5. Hatono, I., Yamagata, K., Tamura, H.: Modeling and online scheduling of flexible manufacturing systems using stochastic petri nets. IEEE Transactions on Software Engineering 17(2), 126–132 (1991)

[2] Model checking techniques and tools, which are of the "push button" kind, lend themselves to being used by sufficiently-trained application domain experts, without help –at least in this phase– from the formal method experts.

6. Flake, S., Mueller, W., Pape, U., Ruf, J.: Specification and formal verification of temporal properties of production automation systems. In: Ehrig, H., Damm, W., Desel, J., Große-Rhode, M., Reif, W., Schnieder, E., Westkämper, E. (eds.) INT 2004. LNCS, vol. 3147, pp. 206–226. Springer, Heidelberg (2004)
7. Matta, A., Furia, C., Rossi, M.: Semi-formal and formal models applied to flexible manufacturing systems. In: Aykanat, C., Dayar, T., Körpeoğlu, İ. (eds.) ISCIS 2004. LNCS, vol. 3280, pp. 718–728. Springer, Heidelberg (2004)
8. Starr, P.J.: Integration of simulation and analytical submodels for supporting manufacturing decisions. Int. J. of Production Research 29, 1733–1746 (1991)
9. Ciapessoni, E., Coen-Porisini, A., Crivelli, E., Mandrioli, D., Mirandola, P., Morzenti, A.: From formal models to formally-based methods: an industrial experience. ACM Trans. on Software Engineering and Methodology 8(1), 79–113 (1999)
10. Matta, A., Tolio, T., Tomasella, M., Zanchi, P.: A detailed uml model for general flexible manufacturing systems. In: Proc. of ICME '04, pp. 113–118 (2004)
11. Ghezzi, C., Jazayeri, M., Mandrioli, D.: Fundamentals of Software Engineering, 2nd edn. Prentice-Hall, Englewood Cliffs (2001)
12. Leone, F.: Specifica e analisi di un flexible manufacturing system. Elaborato di laurea, Politecnico di Milano (in Italian) (2005)
13. Clarke, E., Grunberg, O., Peled, D.: Model Checking. MIT Press, Cambridge (2000)
14. Morzenti, A., Mandrioli, D., Ghezzi, C.: A model parametric real-time logic. ACM Transactions on Programming Languages and Systems 14(4), 521–573 (1992)
15. Gargantini, A., Morzenti, A.: Automated deductive requirement analysis of critical systems. ACM Trans. on Software Eng. and Methodology 10(3), 255–307 (2001)
16. Morzenti, A., Pradella, M., San Pietro, P., Spoletini, P.: Model-checking trio specifications in SPIN. In: Araki, K., Gnesi, S., Mandrioli, D. (eds.) FME 2003. LNCS, vol. 2805, pp. 542–561. Springer, Heidelberg (2003)
17. Holzmann, G.: The SPIN Model Checker, Primer and Reference Manual. Addison-Wesley, Reading (2003)
18. Spoletini, P., Tomasella, M., Matta, A., Rossi, M.: Formal verification in analysis and design of production systems. In: Proc. of ICME '06, pp. 367–372 (2006)
19. Ghezzi, C., Mandrioli, D.: The challenges of software engineering education. In: Inverardi, P., Jazayeri, M. (eds.) ICSE 2005. LNCS, vol. 4309, pp. 115–127. Springer, Heidelberg (2006)
20. Knight, J.C., Leveson, N.G.: Software and higher education. Communications of the ACM 49(1), 160 (2006)
21. Bourque, P., Dupuis, R. (eds.): Guide to the Software Engineering Book of Knowledge. IEEE Computer Society Press, Los Alamitos (2004)
22. Lethbridge, T., LeBlanc, R., Sobel, A.K., Hilburn, T., Diaz-Herrera, J.: SE2004: Recommendations for undergraduate software engineering curricula. IEEE Software 23(6), 19–25 (2006)
23. International Council on Systems Engineering (INCOSE): Guide to the systems engineering body of knowledge – G2SEBoK, online at `http://g2sebok.incose.org`
24. Furia, C.A., Rossi, M., Strunk, E.A., Mandrioli, D., Knight, J.C.: Raising formal methods to the requirements level. Technical Report TR 2006.64, Politecnico di Milano (2006)
25. Pradella, M., Rossi, M., Mandrioli, D.: ArchiTRIO: A UML-compatible language for architectural description and its formal semantics. In: Wang, F. (ed.) FORTE 2005. LNCS, vol. 3731, pp. 381–395. Springer, Heidelberg (2005)

On Equality Predicates in Algebraic Specification Languages

Nakamura Masaki and Futatsugi Kokichi

School of Information Science, Japan Advanced Institute of Science and Technology

Abstract. The execution of OBJ algebraic specification languages is based on the term rewriting system (TRS), which is an efficient theory to perform equational reasoning. We focus on the equality predicate implemented in OBJ languages. The equality predicate is used to test the equality of given terms by TRS. Unfortunately, it is well known that the current execution engine of OBJ languages with the equality predicate is not sound. To solve this problem, we define a modular term rewriting system (MTRS), which is suitable for the module system of OBJ languages, and propose a new equality predicate based on MTRS.

1 Introduction

We propose a new equality predicate for algebraic specification languages that support a module system and a rewrite engine. The principals of the module system for algebraic specifications were first realized in the Clear language [7] and have been inherited by OBJ languages [9,12,3,5,2]. The theory of the CafeOBJ module system updates the original concepts of Clear or other OBJ languages to a more sophisticated situation [8], which helps describe the specifications of a large and complex system by using several types of module imports, built-in modules and the loose and tight denotation for each module. The execution of OBJ languages is based on the term rewriting system (TRS) [14,15], which is a useful notion for realizing equational reasoning, the most basic building block of the verification of OBJ specifications. Using a rewriting engine based on TRS, we obtain a powerful semi-automatic verification system. Although OBJ languages support a sophisticated module system for specification description, the specification verification, however, does not benefit greatly from the module system. Actually, in the current implementation of CafeOBJ, the rewrite engine treats all equations equally. OBJ languages support the equality predicate, which is a special operation symbol used to test the equality of terms. However, the use of the equality predicate in a specification makes its verification unsound [11].

We present an example of CafeOBJ modules to show that the current equality predicate is problematic. The following specification `Z` denotes the set of integers. The constant operator `0` stands for 0, and the unary operators `s` and `p` are the successor and predecessor functions. The equations mean that the successor of the predecessor, and the predecessor of the successor, of an integer is the integer itself, where `X` is a variable that denotes an arbitrary integer.

C.B. Jones, Z. Liu, J. Woodcock (Eds.): ICTAC 2007, LNCS 4711, pp. 381–395, 2007.

```
mod! Z{ [Zero < Int]
  op 0 : -> Zero
  ops s p : Int -> Int
  eq s(p(X:Int)) = X .
  eq p(s(X:Int)) = X .}
```

The equality predicate `_==_` is used for checking the equality of terms, for example, `s(p(X)) == p(s(X))` means the predecessor of the successor is equivalent to the successor of the predecessor for any integer. The equational reasoning with the CafeOBJ system is performed as follows: the system first reduces the both sides of the equation, and returns `true` if the results are the same, and otherwise returns `false`. Here, terms are reduced according to the equations in the specification where the equations are regarded as left-to-right oriented rewrite rules. For the above equation, the both sides are reduced into `X`, and the CafeOBJ system returns `true`. The equality predicate has a problem when being inside the specification. The following specification tt ZERO specifies the predicate that tests whether an integer is zero or not.

```
mod! ZERO{ pr(Z)
  op zero : Int -> Bool
  eq zero(X:Int) = (X == 0) .}
```

The equation in the specification defines the predicate `zero(X)` as the result of `X == 0`. We next try to prove the equation `zero(s(X)) == false`. The left-hand side is reduced into `false` as follows: `zero(s(X))` $\rightarrow$ `s(X) == 0` $\rightarrow$ `false`, and the CafeOBJ system returns `true` for the above equation, however, it is not true in the case of `X` $=$ `p(0)`. Thus, the current CafeOBJ system is unsound if the equality predicate is used inside a specification. In the following sections, we discuss the reason for the unsoundness problem. We propose a term rewriting system based on the module system, called the modular term rewriting system (MTRS), and define a new equality predicate by using the MTRS to solve the unsoundness problem.

In the next section, we briefly introduce CafeOBJ algebraic specification language. We focus on the module system. In Section 3, we propose a modular equational proof system (MEPS) for the module system of the CafeOBJ specification language. In Section 4, we propose MTRS. In Section 5, we discuss the problems of the existing equality predicate and propose a new equality predicate. In Section 6, we discuss applications of our research, and we present conclusions in Section 7.

2 Preliminaries

We introduce OBJ algebraic specification languages [8,9,12,13,16] with the notations and definitions from CafeOBJ [8]. To simplify the discussion, we treat only a subset of CafeOBJ, which does not include, for example, conditional equations, parameterized modules and transition rules. However, the present results can be applied straightforwardly to full CafeOBJ specifications.

2.1 Algebraic Specification

Let S be a set. An S-sorted set A is a family $\{A_s \mid s \in S\}$ of sets indexed by elements of S. We may write $a \in A$ if $a \in A_s$ for some $s \in S$. S^* is the set of sequences of elements of S. The empty sequence is denoted by ε. S^+ is the set of non-empty sequences, i.e., $S^+ = S^* \setminus \{\varepsilon\}$. An (order-sorted) signature $(S, \leq, \Sigma)$ is a triple of a set S of sorts, a partial order $\leq \subseteq S \times S$, and S^+-sorted set Σ of operation symbols, where for $f \in \Sigma_{w\,s}$ ($w \in S^*$ and $s \in S$), $w\,s$ is referred to as the rank of f. When $w = \varepsilon$, f is referred to as a constant symbol. $(S, \leq, \Sigma)$ is occasionally abbreviated as Σ. Let $(S, \leq, \Sigma)$ be a signature and X an S-sorted set of variables. An S-sorted set $T(\Sigma, X)$ (abbr. T) of terms is defined as the smallest set satisfying the following: (1) $\Sigma_s \subseteq T_s$ for any $s \in S$, (2) $X_s \subseteq T_s$ for any $s \in S$, (3) $f(t_1, \ldots, t_n) \in T_s$ if $f \in \Sigma_{s_1 \cdots s_n\, s}$ and $t_i \in T_{s_i}$ $(i = 1, \ldots, n)$. (4) $T_{s'} \subseteq T_s$ if $s' \leq s$. An equation is denoted by $(\forall X)t = t'$, where X is a set of variables, $t, t' \in T(\Sigma, X)_s$ for some sort $s \in S$. We may omit $(\forall X)$ if no confusion exists. An (equational) specification is a pair of a signature and an axiom (a set of equations): $SP = (\Sigma, E)$. We write S_{SP}, $\leq_{SP}$, Σ_{SP}, and E_{SP} for the sets of the sorts, the partial order, the operation symbols, and the axiom of a specification SP. In addition, we also write $s \in SPCf \in SPCe \in SPCt \in SP$ if $s \in S_{SP}$, $f \in \Sigma_{SP}$, $e \in E_{SP}$, $t \in T(\Sigma_{SP}, X)$, respectively. We may omit the signature of a specification and the specification is referred to as simply the axiom E.

Example 1. The following specification $SP_{\mathbb{Z}}$ denotes integers.

$$\begin{aligned} S_{SP_{\mathbb{Z}}} &= \{\texttt{Zero}, \texttt{Int}\} \\ \leq_{SP_{\mathbb{Z}}} &= \{(\texttt{Zero}, \texttt{Zero}), (\texttt{Zero}, \texttt{Int}), (\texttt{Int}, \texttt{Int})\} \\ \Sigma_{SP_{\mathbb{Z}}} &:= (\Sigma_{SP_{\mathbb{Z}}})_{\texttt{Zero}} = \{0\}, (\Sigma_{SP_{\mathbb{Z}}})_{\texttt{Int Int}} = \{\texttt{s}, \texttt{p}\} \\ E_{SP_{\mathbb{Z}}} &= \{\texttt{s(p(X))} = \texttt{X},\ \texttt{p(s(X))} = \texttt{X}\} \end{aligned}$$

For a signature $(S, \leq, \Sigma)$, a Σ-algebra M is an algebra that consists of (1) an S-sorted carrier set M such that $M_s \subseteq M_{s'}$ if $s \leq s'$, (2) an element $M_c \in M_s$ for each $c \in \Sigma_s$, and (3) an operation (or a function) $M_f : M_{s_1} \times \cdots \times M_{s_n} \to M_s$ for each $f \in \Sigma_{s_1 \cdots s_n\, s}$. An assignment $a : X \to M$ is a map from an S-sorted variables set X to an S-sorted carrier set M such that $a(x) \in M_s$ if $x \in X_s$. By an assignment $a : X \to M$, a term $t \in T(\Sigma, X)$ can be interpreted as an element of M, denoted by $a(t)$, as follows: $a(t) = a(x)$ if $t = x \in X$, $a(t) = M_c$ if $t = c \in \Sigma$, and $a(t) = M_f(a(t_1), \ldots, a(t_n))$ if $t = f(t_1, \ldots, t_n)$. For a Σ-algebra M and an equation $e : (\forall X)t = t'$, we declare that M satisfies e, denoted by $M \models e$, iff $a(t) = a(t')$ for any assignment $a : X \to M$. For $SP = (\Sigma, E)$, a Σ-algebra that satisfies all equations in E is called an SP-algebra (or SP-model). We may omit SP- if no confusion exists. The set of all SP-algebras is denoted by $M(SP)$. For algebras A and B, a Σ-homomorphism $h : A \to B$ is an S-sorted homomorphism, which is a family of $\{h_s : A_s \to B_s\}_{s \in S}$, that satisfies the following: (M1) $h_s(x) = h_{s'}(x)$ for each $x \in A_s$ if $s \leq s'$. (M2) $h_s(A_f(a_1, \ldots, a_n))$ $= B_f(h_{s_1}(a_1), \ldots, h_{s_n}(a_n))$ if $f \in \Sigma_{s_1 \cdots s_n\, s}$ and $a_i \in A_{s_i}(i = 1, \ldots, n)$. The set of all Σ-homomorphisms is denoted by $H_{A,B}$. An initial SP-algebra is an SP-algebra I that has the unique Σ-homomorphism $h : I \to A$ for any SP-algebra

A. The set of all initial algebras is denoted by $IM(SP)$. Since initial algebras are isomorphic, we often identify one of the initial algebras with the set $IM(SP)$ of all initial algebras. Roughly speaking, an initial algebra I has the following properties: any element in I should be described in the signature of SP (no junk) and any equation in I should be deduced from the axiom of SP (no confusion).

Example 2. The following Z is an $SP_{\mathtt{Z}}$-algebra: $Z_{\mathtt{Zero}} = \{0\}$, $Z_{\mathtt{Int}} = \mathcal{Z}$, $Z_{\mathtt{0}} = 0$, $Z_{\mathtt{s}}(n) = n + 1$, $Z_{\mathtt{p}}(n) = n - 1$, where $\mathcal{Z}$ is the set of all integers. Z is initial ($Z \in IM(SP_{\mathtt{Z}})$). The real number algebra R with same interpretations and the Boolean algebra B with $B_{\mathtt{0}} = false$ $B_{\mathtt{s}} = B_{\mathtt{p}} = \neg$ can be $SP_{\mathtt{Z}}$-algebras; however, they are not initial. There is no term corresponding to the real number 3.1415, and although $B \models \mathtt{s(0)} = \mathtt{p(0)}$, it cannot be deduced from the axiom of `Z`.

2.2 CafeOBJ Algebraic Specification Language

We introduce CafeOBJ algebraic specifications language. Although in this paper we treat only CafeOBJ, other OBJ languages can be treated. The CafeOBJ specifications are described in a modular manner. The CafeOBJ module `Z` in Section 1 corresponds to $SP_{\mathtt{Z}}$ in Example 1: The declaration `[Zero < Int]` in `Z` corresponds to the sort set $\{\mathtt{Zero}, \mathtt{Int}\}$ and the reflexive transitive closure of the described order. An operation symbol is declared as `op f : A B -> C`, which stands for $\mathtt{f} \in \Sigma_{\mathtt{A\,B\,C}}$. By `ops`, we can declare two or more operation symbols with the same rank. $\Sigma_{\mathtt{A\,B\,C}}$ is the set of all operation symbols with the rank `A B C`. An equation is declared as `eq s(p(X:Int)) = X`, which stands for $(\forall X)\ \mathtt{s(p(X))} = \mathtt{X}$, where $X_{\mathtt{Int}} = \{\mathtt{X}\}$ and $X_s = \emptyset$ for any other $s \in S$. For a module MOD, the corresponding specification is denoted as SP_{MOD}. Denotations of CafeOBJ specifications represent the class of their algebras. In this section, we introduce specifications without explicit imports, called basic specifications (or basic modules). CafeOBJ basic specifications can be classified into specifications with a tight denotation and specifications with a loose denotation. A specification with a tight denotation is denoted as `mod!` and a loose specification is denoted as `mod*`. Hereinafter, each specification is assumed to have its denotation declaration and is referred to as $d(SP) = tight$ or $loose$. The denotation $[SP]$ of SP is defined as $IM(SP)$ if $d(SP) = tight$ and $M(SP)$ if $d(SP) = loose$. We refer to an element of $[SP]$ as a denotational model. We write $SP \models e$ if $M \models e$ for any $M \in [SP]$. Since `Z` is tight, $[SP_{\mathtt{Z}}] = IM(SP_{\mathtt{Z}})$. Thus, `Z` essentially denotes only the integer algebra Z. We next present an example of loose modules:

```
mod* FUN{ [Elt]
  op f : Elt -> Elt}
```

Since `FUN` is loose, $[SP_{\mathtt{FUN}}] = M(SP_{\mathtt{FUN}})$. Thus, `FUN` denotes all algebras, including at least one function on a set, e.g., they interpret f into, for example, the identity function on natural numbers, the sort function on arrays, a code refactoring, and a document editing.

The execution of CafeOBJ is based on the term rewriting system (TRS). The CafeOBJ system [3] is interactive. When starting CafeOBJ, we meet a prompt `CafeOBJ>`. After inputting a CafeOBJ module, e.g., `mod! TEST{...}`, by hand or through a file, we can select or open the module by `select TEST` or `open TEST`. A prompt will be changed to `TEST>` or `%TEST>`. We can then use the CafeOBJ reduction command `red`. Here, `red` takes a term constructed from the selected or opened module, and returns its normal form (in the default strategy) with respect to the TRS, the rewrite rules of which are left-to-right-oriented equations in the module. For example, `red s(p(p(0)))` returns `s(0)` for `Z`:

```
CafeOBJ> mod! Z{ ... }
-- defining module! Z...._..* done.
CafeOBJ> select Z
Z> red s(p(p(0))) .
-- reduce in Z : s(p(p(0)))
p(0) : Int
```

A special operation symbol `==` can be used for equational reasoning. The equality predicate `==` takes a pair of terms belonging to the same sort and returns `true` or `false`. When inputting `red` s `==` t, CafeOBJ reduces both terms into s' and t', and returns `true` if s' and t' are the same, and otherwise returns `false`:

```
Z> red s(p(0)) == p(s(0)) .
-- reduce in Z : s(p(0)) == p(s(0))
true : Bool
```

The equational reasoning with `red` (or `red _==_`) is sound, which means that if `red` t returns t' (or `red` t `==` t' returns `true`), then $SP \models t = t'$ holds. The equational reasoning is not complete for several reasons, for example, TRS may not be confluent, terms may include a variable, and a specification may not be tight. These reasons are discussed in Sections 3, 4, and 5.

2.3 Structured Specification

We briefly introduce the notion of specification imports. Details can be found in [8]. A specification can import a sub specification [1]. There are three import relations $\lhd_p$, $\lhd_e$, and $\lhd_u$, called protecting, extending, and using imports, respectively. $SP' \lhd_x SP$ means that SP imports SP' with mode x. We may use $\lhd$ as one of the three imports. Each imported specification is assumed to be declared with either the tight or loose denotation declaration. We present the properties of imports related to our research: (1) when SP imports SP' with protecting mode, any sort or operation symbol x in SP' is protected in SP, i.e. for any $M \in [SP]$, $M_x = M'_x$ for some $M' \in [SP']$, (2) the import relation is transitive, and the mode of the composed import is the weakest mode, where $\lhd_p$ is strongest and $\lhd_u$ is weakest, e.g., if $SP \lhd_p SP' \lhd_e SP''$, then $SP \lhd_e SP''$.

[1] SP' is a sub specification of SP, denoted by $SP' \subseteq SP$, iff $S_{SP'} \subseteq S_{SP}$, $\leq_{SP'} \subseteq \leq_{SP}$, $\Sigma_{SP'} \subseteq \Sigma_{SP}$ and $E_{SP'} \subseteq E_{SP}$.

In CafeOBJ, an import relation $SP' \lhd_p SP$ (or $SP' \lhd_e SP$, $SP' \lhd_u SP$) is described as pr(SP') (or ex(SP'), us(SP')). Note that import declarations should be irreflexive, e.g., CafeOBJ does not allow, for example, `mod! MOD{ pr(MOD)···}` and `mod! A{pr(B)···}` ··· `mod! B{pr(A)···}`. For a module with imports, SP_{MOD} includes, for example, the sorts, the operation symbols, and the equations described in the imported modules, as well as MOD itself. When declared only in MOD itself, the above are denoted as S_{MOD}, Σ_{MOD}, and E_{MOD}, respectively. Thus, when MOD imports $\overrightarrow{MOD_i}$ [2], $E_{SP_{MOD}} = E_{MOD} \cup \bigcup_i E_{SP_{MOD_i}}$, for example.

Example 3. The following is an example of specifications with imports:

```
mod! FUNN{ pr(Z) pr(FUN)
  op fn : Int Elt -> Elt
  var E : Elt   var X : Int
  eq fn(0, E) = E .
  eq fn(s(X), E) = f (fn(X, E)) .}
```

FUNN imports Z and FUN with the protecting mode. Thus, for example, $M_{\mathtt{Int}}$ is the set of integers (or its isomorphism) for any $M \in [SP_{\mathtt{FUNN}}]$. The operation symbol fn is interpreted into a function $M_{\mathtt{fn}}$ from $M_{\mathtt{Int}} \times M_{\mathtt{Elt}}$ to $M_{\mathtt{Elt}}$ satisfying $M_{\mathtt{fn}}(n, e) = f^n(e)$ if $n \geq 0$. Note that $M_{\mathtt{fn}}(n, e)$ can be any integer for $n < 0$.

3 Modular Equational Proof System

We next present an axiomatic semantics (Section 3) and an operational semantics (Section 4) for a modular algebraic specification language. The semantics presented in Sections 3 and 4 are similar to ordinary semantics, such as those presented in [8]. The difference is that we prepare notations to extract the part that corresponds to each submodule. The target language is the subset of CafeOBJ introduced in Section 2. The congruence relation $=_E$ for a set E of equations is defined as follows: $t =_E t'$ iff $t = t'$ can be derived from the reflexive, symmetric, transitive, congruent, and substitutive laws from E [8]. We redefine this congruence relation while maintaining the module structure. We define the congruence relation $=_{MOD}$ for each module MOD.

Definition 1. For a module MOD, the congruence relation $(\forall X)\_ =_{MOD} \_$ on $T(\Sigma_{SP_{MOD}}, X)$ (abbr. T) is defined as the smallest relation satisfying the following laws:

[reflexivity] [symmetry] [transitivity] For $s, t, u \in T$,

$$\frac{}{(\forall X)t =_{MOD} t} \quad \frac{(\forall X)s =_{MOD} t}{(\forall X)t =_{MOD} s} \quad \frac{(\forall X)s =_{MOD} u \quad (\forall X)u =_{MOD} t}{(\forall X)s =_{MOD} t}$$

[congruence] For $f \in (\Sigma_{SP_{MOD}})_{s_1 \cdots s_n\, s}$ and $t_i, t'_i \in T_{s_i}$ $(i \in \{1, \ldots, n\})$,

$$\frac{(\forall X)t_1 =_{MOD} t'_1 \quad \cdots \quad (\forall X)t_n =_{MOD} t'_n}{(\forall X)f(t_1, \ldots, t_n) =_{MOD} f(t'_1, \ldots, t'_n)}$$

[2] We write $\overrightarrow{a_i}$ instead of $a_1, a_2, \ldots, a_n$.

[substitutivity] For $(\forall Y)t = t' \in E_{MOD}$ and $\theta : Y \to T$,

$$\overline{(\forall X)\theta(t) =_{MOD} \theta(t')}$$

[import] For modules MOD that import MOD' and $s, t \in T$, if $(\forall X)s =_{MOD'} t$, then

$$\overline{(\forall X)s =_{MOD} t}$$

The last two laws can be a leaf of a proof tree. **[substitutivity]** is an instance of an equation e that belongs to MOD itself. By **[import]**, any equation derived from the submodule is also derivable.

Example 4. Figure 1 is a proof tree for $(\forall\emptyset)\texttt{mod2(s(s(p(s(0)))))} =_{\texttt{FUNN}} \texttt{0}$. We omit $(\forall X)$ for each equation, where $X_{\texttt{Elt}} = \{\texttt{E}\}$. Note that the left-most leaf comes from $\texttt{s(p(s(0)))} =_{\texttt{Z}} \texttt{s(0)}$.

$$\dfrac{\dfrac{\dfrac{}{\texttt{s(p(s(0))))} =_{\texttt{FUNN}} \texttt{s(0)}}}{\texttt{fn(s(p(s(0))),E)} =_{\texttt{FUNN}} \texttt{fn(s(0),E)}} \qquad \dfrac{\dfrac{}{\texttt{fn(s(0),E)} =_{\texttt{FUNN}} \texttt{f(fn(0,E))}} \quad \dfrac{\dfrac{}{\texttt{fn(0,E)} =_{\texttt{FUNN}} \texttt{E}}}{\texttt{f(fn(0,E))} =_{\texttt{FUNN}} \texttt{f(E)}}}{\texttt{fn(s(0),E)} =_{\texttt{FUNN}} \texttt{f(E)}}}{\texttt{fn(s(p(s(0))),E)} =_{\texttt{FUNN}} \texttt{f(E)}}$$

Fig. 1. A proof tree for $\texttt{fn(s(p(s(0))),E)} =_{\texttt{FUNN}} \texttt{f(E)}$

3.1 Soundness and Completeness of MEPS

We show the soundness of the modular equational proof system (abbr. MEPS), i.e., $s =_{MOD} t \Rightarrow SP_{MOD} \models s = t$, and gives a sufficient condition under which MEPS is complete, $s =_{MOD} t \Leftarrow SP_{MOD} \models s = t$. Let MOD be a module, and let E be the set of all equations in MOD and its imported modules, i.e., $E_{SP_{MOD}}$. It is trivial that $=_{MOD}$ and $=_E$ are exactly the same binary relation. Thus, the following properties hold [8].

Proposition 1. Let MOD be a module, $s, t \in T(\Sigma_{SP_{MOD}}, X)$. If $(\forall X)s =_{MOD} t$, then $SP_{MOD} \models s = t$.

Proposition 2. Let MOD be a tight and basic, i.e., with no explicit imports, module. Let $s, t \in T(\Sigma_{SP_{MOD}}, \emptyset)$. Then, $SP_{MOD} \models s = t \Leftrightarrow s =_{MOD} t$.

4 Modular Term Rewriting System

For a specification (Σ, E) and an equation $l = r \in E$, if l is not a variable and all variables in r occur in l, (Σ, E) (or just E) is called a TRS. In a TRS, equations are used as left-to-right rewrite rules. We may write $l \to r$ and R instead of $l = r$ and E when emphasizing rewrite rules. We propose an extension of TRSs for the module system, called a modular TRS (or MTRS), and an MTRS rewrite relation.

Definition 2. MTRSs are defined recursively as follows: an MTRS $\mathcal{R}$ is a pair $((\Sigma, R), A)$ of a TRS R and a set A of MTRSs satisfying the following: $\Sigma' \subseteq \Sigma$ for each MTRS $((\Sigma', R'), A') \in A$.

For a module MOD, the set E_{MOD} of equations described in MOD corresponds to the TRS of the first argument (Σ, R), and imported modules correspond to the second argument A. Since the rewrite rules (equations) in a module are constructed from the operation symbols declared in the module itself and *imported modules*, the condition $\Sigma' \subseteq \Sigma$ is needed. Basic modules correspond to MTRSs in which the second arguments are empty.

In order to assign an MTRS rewrite relation $\rightarrow_{\mathcal{R}}$, we introduce a positions set $O(t)$, a subterm $t|_p$ and a replacement term $t[u]_p$ as follows: $O(x) = \{\varepsilon\}$ and $O(f(t_1, \ldots, t_n)) = \{\varepsilon\} \cup \{i.p \in \mathcal{N}_+{}^* \mid p \in O(t_i)\}$. $t|_\varepsilon = t$ and $f(t_1, \ldots, t_n)|_{i.p} = t_i|_p$. $t[u]_\varepsilon = u$ and $f(t_1, \ldots, t_n)[u]_{i.p} = f(\ldots, t_{i-1}, t_i[u]_p, t_{i+1}, \ldots)$. The set of all maps from A to B is denoted by B^A. The reflexive transitive closure of $\rightarrow$ is denoted by $\rightarrow^*$.

Definition 3. Let $\mathcal{R} = (R, \{\mathcal{R}_i\}_{i=1,\ldots,n})$ be an MTRS. The MTRS rewrite relation $\rightarrow_{\mathcal{R}}$ is defined as follows:

$$s \rightarrow_{\mathcal{R}} t \overset{\text{def}}{\Longleftrightarrow} \begin{cases} \exists (\forall X) l \rightarrow r \in R, \theta \in T^X, p \in O(s).(s|_p = \theta(l) \wedge t = s[\theta(r)]_p) \\ \text{or } \exists i \in \{1, \ldots, n\}.s \rightarrow_{\mathcal{R}_i} t. \end{cases}$$

The first part is the definition of the ordinary TRS rewrite relation $\rightarrow_R$ for a TRS R, and the latter part $(\exists i \in \{1, \ldots, n\}.s \rightarrow_{\mathcal{R}_i} t)$ corresponds to the rewrite relation of the imported modules.

Example 5. MTRSs $\mathcal{R}_{\mathtt{Z}} = ((\Sigma_{\mathtt{Z}}, E_{\mathtt{Z}}), \emptyset)$ and $\mathcal{R}_{\mathtt{FUN}} = ((\Sigma_{\mathtt{FUN}}, \emptyset), \emptyset)$ correspond to modules `Z` and `FUN`. MTRS $\mathcal{R}_{\mathtt{FUNN}} = ((\Sigma_{\mathtt{FUNN}} \cup \Sigma_{\mathtt{Z}} \cup \Sigma_{\mathtt{FUN}}, E_{\mathtt{FUNN}}), \{\mathcal{R}_{\mathtt{Z}}, \mathcal{R}_{\mathtt{FUN}}\})$ corresponds to the modules `FUNN`. `s(p(s(0)))` $\rightarrow_{\mathcal{R}_{\mathtt{Z}}}$ `s(0)` holds. Thus, `fn(s(p(s(0))),E)` $\rightarrow_{\mathcal{R}_{\mathtt{FUNN}}}$ `fn(s(0),E)` $\rightarrow_{\mathcal{R}_{\mathtt{FUNN}}}$ `f(fn(0,E))` $\rightarrow_{\mathcal{R}_{\mathtt{FUNN}}}$ `f(E)` holds.

Let MOD be a module importing $\overrightarrow{MOD_i}$. MTRS $\mathcal{R}_{MOD}$ is defined as the pair $(E_{MOD}, \overrightarrow{\mathcal{R}_{MOD_i}})$. We write $\mathcal{R}, \overrightarrow{\mathcal{R}_i}$ instead of $\mathcal{R}_{MOD}, \overrightarrow{\mathcal{R}_{MOD_i}}$ if no confusion exists. We hereinafter assume the existence of a corresponding module for each MTRS.

4.1 Soundness and Completeness of MTRS

When a (possibly infinite) sequence $\overrightarrow{s_i}$ of terms satisfies $s_i \rightarrow_{\mathcal{R}} s_{i+1}$ for each $i = 0, 1, 2, \ldots$, the sequence is referred to as a rewrite sequence, denoted by $s_0 \rightarrow_{\mathcal{R}} s_1 \rightarrow_{\mathcal{R}} s_2 \rightarrow_{\mathcal{R}} \cdots$. If ($s \rightarrow^* t$ andjt $\rightarrow u$ does not hold for any $u \in T$, t is called a $\rightarrow$-normal form (of s). We often omit $\rightarrow$. For a binary relation $\rightarrow$ written as an arrow, we define $\leftarrow = \{(a, b) \mid b \rightarrow a\}$ and $\leftrightarrow = \rightarrow \cup \leftarrow$. The reflexive and transitive closure of $\leftrightarrow_{\mathcal{R}}$ coincides with $=_{MOD}$. Terms a and b are joinable, and are denoted by $a \downarrow b$ when there exists c such that $a \rightarrow^* c$ and $b \rightarrow^* c$. $\rightarrow$ is confluent iff $b \downarrow c$ whenever $a \rightarrow^* b$, $a \rightarrow^* c$. $\rightarrow$ is terminating iff there is no infinite rewrite sequence $s_0 \to s_1 \to \cdots. \to$ is convergent iff it is confluent and terminating. We define *equational reasoning by MTRS* as the following procedure: take terms s and t, reduce them into their $\to_{\mathcal{R}}$ normal forms, and return true if they are the same, and otherwise return false.

We show the soundness of the MTRS equational reasoning ($s \downarrow_{\mathcal{R}} t \Rightarrow s =_{MOD} t$) and the sufficient condition under which the MTRS equational reasoning is complete ($s \downarrow_{\mathcal{R}} t \Leftarrow s =_{MOD} t$). Let $\mathcal{R}$ be a MTRS, and let R the TRS union of all TRSs, including $\mathcal{R}$. It is trivial that the MTRS rewrite relation $\to_{\mathcal{R}}$ and the ordinary TRS rewrite relation $\to_R$ are exactly the same binary relation. Thus, the following properties hold [14,15].

Proposition 3. If $s \downarrow_{\mathcal{R}_{MOD}} t$, then $(\forall X) s =_{MOD} t$.

Proposition 4. Let MOD be a module such that $\to_{\mathcal{R}_{MOD}}$ is convergent. Let $s, t \in T(\Sigma_{SP_{MOD}}, X)$. Then, $(\forall X) s =_{MOD} t \Leftrightarrow s \downarrow_{\mathcal{R}_{MOD}} t$.

5 Equality Predicate

In CafeOBJ, we can use the equality predicate `_==_` not only in verification, but also in description as an operation symbol. t_1 `==` t_2 is a term for $t_1, t_2 \in T_s$. The equality predicate is included in a built-in module `BOOL`. The built-in module `BOOL` has a sort `Bool`, constants `true` and `false`, and operations such as `_and_`, `_or_`, and `_==_`. [3]. The rank of `_==_` is s s `-> Bool` for any sort s. It is not an ordinary operation symbol because it is polymorphic. In addition, the equality predicate `_==_` has another special quality in that it cannot be defined by equations or a TRS (even if the target sorts are fixed). Although we can give `eq X:`s `== X = true` for true cases, `eq X:`s `== Y:`s `= false` does not give false cases because t `==` t can be an instance of `X == Y`. The reduction command for a term including `_==_` is defined as follows: for a pattern s `==` t, reduce both terms, i.e., `red` s and `red` t, and replace the term with `true` if the results are same, and otherwise replace the term with `false`. The equality predicate denotes the equality of model values, i.e., $M_{==}(x, y) = (x = y)$ [8]. If we use the equality predicate as an operation symbol in the axiom, the equational reasoning is no longer sound because Propositions 2 and 4 do not hold without the assumptions. We next show examples in which $SP \models s = t$ does not hold, even if `red s == t` returns `true`.

Confluence: Consider SP with `eq a = b` and `eq a = c`. `red b == c` returns `false` because `b` and `c` are normal forms. Thus, `red (b == c) == false` returns `true`. However, $SP \models$ `b == c` $=$ `false` do not hold because `b = a = c`.

Denotation: For the loose module `FUN` (See Section 2.2), `red (f(E:Elt) == E) == false` returns `true` because `f(E)` and `E` are normal forms. However, $SP_{\texttt{FUN}} \not\models$

[3] We define a basic module (or specification) as a module without *explicit* imports. The *explicit* import means that the module has no import declaration, and does not use anything belonging to `BOOL`, i.e., the sort `Bool`, operations `true`, `false`, `_and_`, etc. Such modules can be considered as modules with no imports.

$(\forall\{\mathtt{E}\})$ `(f(E) == E)` = `false` because there exists $M \in [SP_{\mathtt{FUN}}]$, which interprets `f` into the identity function, i.e., $M_{\mathtt{f}}(x) = x$ for all $x \in M_{\mathtt{Elt}}$.

Verification: Even if the specification is convergent as a TRS and is declared with a tight denotation, equational reasoning is still unsound for a specification with the equality predicate. Before showing a problematic example, we introduce a proof score, which is a basis for CafeOBJ verifications. Consider the following module: `mod! PROOF{ pr(Z) op n : -> Int }`. Since `Z` is protected, the constant `n` should be an integer. Then, the reduction command `red s(p(n)) == p(s(n))` in `PROOF` returns `true`, which means that $M \models$ `s(p(n))` = `p(s(n))` for any $M \in [SP_{\mathtt{PROOF}}]$ from Proposition 1 and 3. For any integer $n \in Z_{\mathtt{Int}}$, there exists $M \in [SP_{\mathtt{PROOF}}]$ such that $M_{\mathtt{n}} = n$. Thus, $Z_{\mathtt{s}}(Z_{\mathtt{p}}(n)) = Z_{\mathtt{p}}(Z_{\mathtt{s}}(n))$ holds for any $n \in Z_{\mathtt{Int}}$. The theory of a proof using a constant as an arbitrary element, called *Theorem of Constants*, can be found in [11]. By the `open` command, we can declare a nameless module that imports the opened module with the protect mode. The following code, called a proof score, has the same meaning as the above proof:

```
CafeOBJ> open Z
-- opening module Z.. done.
%Z> op n : -> Int .
%Z> red s(p(n)) == p(s(n)) .
-- reduce in %Z : s(p(n)) == p(s(n))
true : Bool
```

Consider the following proof score for the module `ZERO` with the equality predicate (Section 1).

```
CafeOBJ> open ZERO
-- opening module ZERO.. done.
%ZERO> op n : -> Int .
%ZERO> red zero(n) == false .
-- reduce in %ZERO : zero(n) == false
true : Bool
```

The proof score means that `zero`(n) = `false` for any integer n. However, this does not hold because 0 is an integer. The literature [11] mentions the problem of the equality predicate (Section 2.1.1). One solution given by [11] is to give a user-defined equality predicate for each sort needed. For example, the equality predicate `_is_` on `Nat`, which is defined as `0 : -> Nat` and `s : Nat -> Nat`, is defined by the four equations: `(0 is 0) = true`, `(s(N) is 0) = false`, `(0 is s(N)) = false`, and `(s(M) is s(N)) = M is N`, where `M` and `N` are variables [11]. However, it is not always possible for the user to find a suitable definition. For example, how should `_is_` be defined on `Int` for the specification `Z`? The equation `(s(N) is 0) = false` does not hold for `N` = `p(0)` on `Int`. Moreover, the user should prove that each user-defined equality predicate actually denotes the equality on its target set.

5.1 Local Equality Predicate

To solve the problems of the equality predicate, we propose a new equality predicate, called the local equality predicate (LEP). The equality predicate implemented in CafeOBJ is hereinafter referred to as the global equality predicate (GEP). The LEP is defined for the specification language without the global equality predicate, which we introduced in Section 2, 3 and 4. For a module MOD, the specification SP_{MOD} is redefined as follows:

Definition 4. Assume that MOD imports $\overrightarrow{MOD_i}$. The specification SP_{MOD} is redefined by replacing the definition of $\Sigma_{SP_{MOD}}$ as follows: $\Sigma_{SP_{MOD}} = \Sigma_{MOD} \cup \bigcup_i \Sigma_{MOD_i} \cup \{$`op _=`$MOD_i$`=_ : s s -> Bool` $\mid$ `s` $\in S_{MOD_i}\}$. $E_{SP_{MOD}} = E_{MOD} \cup \bigcup_i E_{MOD_i} \cup \{$`eq (X:s =`$MOD_i$`= X) = true` $\mid$ `s` $\in S_{MOD_i}\}$. The other parts, such as $S_{SP_{MOD}}$, are not changed.

Denotation: For any SP_{MOD}-algebra M, LEP `op _=`MOD_i`=_ : s s -> Bool` is interpreted in the equality on $M_{\mathtt{s}}$.

MEPS: Add the following to Definition 1:

[LEP] For module MOD, which imports MOD' and $s, t \in T(\Sigma_{SP_{MOD}}, \emptyset)$, if $(\forall X) s \neq_{MOD'} t$, then

$$\frac{}{(\forall X)(s \texttt{ =}MOD'\texttt{= } t) =_{MOD} \texttt{false}}$$

MTRS: Add the following condition to Definition 2: MTRS $((\Sigma, R), A)$ satisfies the following: `op _=`MOD_i`=_ : s s -> Bool` $\in \Sigma$ for each $s \in S_{MOD_i}$ and $\mathcal{R}_i \in A$, and `eq (X:s =`MOD_i`= X) = true` $\in R$ for each $\mathcal{R}_i \in A$ for each $s \in S_{MOD_i}$ and $\mathcal{R}_i \in A$. Replace Definition 3 with the following:

$$s \to_{\mathcal{R}} t \overset{\text{def}}{\iff} \begin{cases} \exists (\forall X) l \to r \in R, \theta \in T^X, p \in O(s).(s|_p = \theta(l) \wedge t = s[\theta(r)]_p) \\ \text{or } \exists i \in \{1, \ldots, n\}. s \to_{\mathcal{R}_i} t \\ \text{or } \exists p \in O(s).(s|_p = (u \texttt{ =}MOD_i\texttt{= } v) \wedge t = s[\texttt{false}]_p \wedge u \not\downarrow_{\mathcal{R}_i} v) \end{cases}$$

Note that for both MEPS and MTRS, the `true` cases are given by simply adding an ordinary equation `eq X =`MOD_i`= X = true`.

5.2 Soundness of the Local Equality Predicate

Here, we present properties on the soundness of LEP. These properties can be proved from Proposition 2 and 4, and the proofs are omitted.

Theorem 1. **[Soundness of MEPS with LEP]** Let MOD be a module such that for any occurrence of `=`MOD_i`=` in MOD, the module MOD_i is basic, tight, and imported with the protecting mode. Let $s, t \in T(\Sigma_{SP_{MOD}}, X)$. Then, $SP_{MOD} \models s = t$ if $(\forall X) s =_{MOD} t$.

Theorem 2. **[Soundness of MTRS with LEP]** Let MOD be a module such that for any occurrence of `=`MOD_i`=` in MOD, the rewrite relation $\to_{\mathcal{R}_i}$ is convergent. Let $s, t \in T(\Sigma_{SP_{MOD}}, X)$. Then, $(\forall X) s =_{MOD} t$ if $s \downarrow_{\mathcal{R}} t$.

Corollary 1. Equational reasoning by MTRS for specifications with LEP is sound under the assumption of Theorems 1 and 2.

5.3 Sound Verification System

We next introduce a sound verification system (or rewrite engine) for specifications with LEP. Consider the assumption of Corollary 1 (i.e., Theorems 1 and 2). The tight denotation, the basic module, and the protecting import can be easily checked. Consider an MTRS $(R, \emptyset)$ corresponding to a basic module. $(R, \emptyset)$ can be regarded as an ordinary TRS R. For an ordinary TRS, many useful sufficient conditions and tools for termination have been proposed [14,15,10,1,4,6], and when assuming termination, the confluence property is decidable and can be proved using the critical pair method [14,15]. Thus, we can obtain a decidable procedure P to check the assumption of Corollary 1 by using termination provers. The reduction command for LEP is defined as follows. s =MOD_i= t is rewritten as follows: Reduce s and t into their normal forms s' and t', respectively. If s' and t' are same, then replace the equation with `true`. If s' and t' are not same, then check the conditions (1) $s', t' \in T(\Sigma_{SP_{\mathtt{MOD}_i}}, \emptyset)$ and (2) $P(MOD_i)$. If the conditions hold, then replace the equation with `false`, and otherwise return the equation as is. Then, from Corollary 1, the obtained reduction command is sound.

Example 6. We show the experiences of the reduction command for specifications with local equality predicates [4]. We modify `ZERO` as follows:

```
mod! ZERO{ pr(LEP-Z)
  op zero : Int -> Bool
  eq zero(X:Int) = (X =Z= 0) .}
```

where `LEP-Z` is the module having the local equality predicate `_=Z=_` on `Z` (Omit the definition). In the new `ZERO`, the global equality predicate `_==_` has been replaced with `_=Z=_`. For the terms `zero(s(p(0)))` and `zero(s(p(s(0))))`, the CafeOBJ system returns the correct answers `true` and `false`. We again try the proof score shown in Section 5 as follows:

```
CafeOBJ> open ZERO
-- opening module ZERO.. done.
%ZERO> op n : -> Int .
%ZERO> red zero(n) == false .
-- reduce in %ZERO : zero(n) == false
false : Bool
```

As a result of the LEP, an incorrect `true` is not returned for the above proof score. Note that `false` does not mean a disproof. The following is a proof score of `n` $\neq$ `0` $\Rightarrow$ `zero(n)` = `false`, and returns `true`. Thus, it holds for any $M \in [SP_{\mathtt{M2}}]$.

```
ZERO> open ZERO
-- opening module ZERO.. done.
%ZERO> op n : -> Int .
%ZERO> eq n =Z= 0 = false .
```

[4] We have implemented each local equality predicate in CafeOBJ manually by using order sorts.

```
%ZERO> red zero(n) == false .
-- reduce in %ZERO : zero(n) == false
true : Bool
```

6 Applications

6.1 Application to Full CafeOBJ

The CafeOBJ specifications in the above sections are restricted in order to focus on the essential part of the problem of GEP. LEP can be applied to full CafeOBJ (or OBJ languages) straightforwardly, which include, for example, conditional equations, parameterized modules, behavioral specifications, and rewrite specifications.

6.2 Application of LEP

The assumption of Corollary 1 is not so restrictive. The tight denotation and the protecting import are necessary conditions. The convergence property is one of the properties that any algebraic specification is expected to satisfy. In particular, Maude, one of the OBJ languages, requires its functional modules (corresponding to CafeOBJ tight modules specifying a data type of a target system) to be convergent in order to obtain a sound rewriting engine for system specifications [5]. Since the import relation is transitive, the basic module is not so restrictive. For example, `_=Z=_` can be used in a module, which imports `FUNN` with the protecting mode, where `FUNN` imports `Z` with the protecting mode. The following `TREE` is an example outside the assumption:

```
mod! TREE{ pr(Z) [Int < Tree]
  op __ : Tree Tree -> Tree  }
```

This is a specification of trees having leaves that are integers: Term `s(0)` is a tree from `[Int < Tree]`. Term `(p(0) s(0)) p(0)` is another example of trees. `TREE` is not basic, and `Tree` is defined in `TREE`. The LEP on trees is outside the assumption of Corollary 1. However, if necessary, we can describe the corresponding basic specification satisfying the assumption as follows:

```
mod! TREE{ [Zero < Int < Tree]
  op 0 : -> Zero
  op s p : Int -> Int
  op __ : Tree Tree -> Tree
  eq s(p(X:Int)) = X .
  eq p(s(X:Int)) = X .}
```

6.3 Applications of MEPS and MTRS

MEPS and MTRS are useful not only for dealing with the equality predicates, but also for the introduction of several functions to modular specification languages. For example, built-in modules are treated well by our framework rather than the ordinary framework. Some built-in modules have only signatures and do not have equations (axioms), thus, the ordinary TRS does not treat them directly. The meaning of operation symbols are implemented in other low-level languages, e.g., Common Lisp for CafeOBJ built-in modules. For example, a built-in module `NAT` has constants `0`, `1`, `2`, ..., operation symbols, such as `_+_`, `_*_`, and the expression x `+` y, for example, is reduced to the result of the evaluation of the Common Lisp expression `(+` x y`)`. In our modular framework, we simply define $=_{\mathtt{NAT}}$ and $\rightarrow_{\mathtt{NAT}}$ from the implementation of `NAT` in order to obtain the axiomatic and operational semantics of specifications with the built-in module `NAT`. Similarly, our framework can be used while implementing a specification. When we have implemented submodules of a given large specification, we may obtain a specification combined with those implementations and can perform some execution tests for the ongoing implementation, or verifications for the semi-implemented specification. Integrating other verification techniques, such as model-checking, with a rewriting-based verification is another possible use of our framework.

7 Conclusion

We proposed the modular equational proof system and the modular term rewriting system, which are suitable for algebraic specification languages with a module system. We also proposed the local equality predicate and showed its soundness (Corollary 1 and Section 5.3). The problem of the global equality predicate is well-known in the CafeOBJ community, and it has not been used in the recent practical specifications. The current CafeOBJ system also supports another equality predicate `=`, which is implemented by simply `eq (X = X) = true`, where `X` is a variable. Many case studies have been succeeded with the above simple equality predicate. However, because it does not support false cases, we have to manually provide false cases needed for verification. The local equality predicate solves the problem of the equality predicate while maintaining its advantages.

For the TRS area, MTRS with LEP is related to the conditional TRS (CTRS) with negative conditions. A conditional rewrite rule in CTRS is written as $l \rightarrow r$ if $\bigwedge l_i = r_i$. When $l_i \downarrow_R r_i$, an instance of l is replaced with the instance of r (there are several definitions of CTRS rewrite relations. See [14,15]). If a negative equation is included in the condition part, it is not easy to prove the soundness of the CTRS. A conditional rewrite rule can be described in CafeOBJ as a conditional equation in which the condition is a term of the sort `Bool`. We can give a `Bool` condition term as $(u_1 =$ `M1` $= \mathtt{v}_1)$ `and` $\cdots$ `and` $(u_n =$ `Mn` $= \mathtt{v}_\mathtt{n})$ for positive equations and `not`$(\mathtt{u}'_1 =$ `M1`$' = \mathtt{v}'_1)$ `and` $\cdots$ `and` `not`$(\mathtt{u}'_\mathtt{n} =$ `Mn`$' = \mathtt{v}'_\mathtt{n})$ for negative equations. We can say that MTRS with the local equality predicate gives one solution of the difficulty of dealing with negative conditions in CTRS.

References

1. AProVE, `http://www-i2.informatik.rwth-aachen.de/AProVE/`
2. BOBJ, `http://www.cs.ucsd.edu/groups/tatami/bobj/`

3. CafeOBJ, http://www.ldl.jaist.ac.jp/cafeobj/
4. CiME, http://cime.lri.fr/
5. Maude, http://maude.cs.uiuc.edu/
6. Tyrolean Termination Tool, http://cl2-informatik.uibk.ac.at/ttt/
7. Burstall, R.M., Goguen, J.A.: The Semantics of CLEAR, A Specification Language. In: Bjorner, D. (ed.) Abstract Software Specifications. LNCS, vol. 86, pp. 292–332. Springer, Heidelberg (1980)
8. Diaconescu, R., Futatsugi, K.: CafeOBJ Report. World Scientific, Singapore (1998)
9. Futatsugi, K., Goguen, J.A., Jouannaud, J.-P., Meseguer, J.: Principles of OBJ2. In: POPL. Proceedings of the 12th ACM Symposium on Principles of Programming Languages, pp. 52–66. ACM Press, New York (1985)
10. Giesl, J., Thiemann, R., Schneider-Kamp, P., Falke, S.: Automated Termination Proofs with AProVE. In: van Oostrom, V. (ed.) RTA 2004. LNCS, vol. 3091, pp. 210–220. Springer, Heidelberg (2004)
11. Goguen, J.A., Malcolm, G.: Algebraic Semantics of Imperative Programs, Massachusetts Institute of Technology (1996)
12. Goguen, J.A., Winkler, T., Meseguer, J., Futatsugi, K., Jouannaud, J.-P.: Software Engineering with OBJ: Algebraic Specification in Action. Kluwers Academic Publishers, Boston, MA (2000) (chapter Introducing OBJ*)
13. Meinke, K., Tucker, J.V.: Universal Algebra. In: Abramsky, S., Gabbay, D.M., Maibaum, T.S.E. (eds.) Handbook of Logic in Computer Science: Background - Mathematical Structures, vol. 1, pp. 189–411. Clarendon Press, Oxford (1992)
14. Ohlebusch, E.: Advanced topics in term rewriting. Springer, Heidelberg (2002)
15. Terese: Term Rewriting Systems. Cambridge Tracts in Theoretical Computer Science, vol. 55. Cambridge University Press, Cambridge (2003)
16. Wirsing, M.: Algebraic Specification. In: Handbook of Theoretical Computer Science. Formal Models and Sematics (B), pp. 675–788 (1990)

Data-Distributions in *PowerList* Theory

Virginia Niculescu

Faculty of Mathematics and Computer Science
Babeş-Bolyai University, Cluj-Napoca
vniculescu@cs.ubbcluj.ro

Abstract. *PowerList* theory is well suited to express recursive, data-parallel algorithms. Its abstractness is very high and ensures simple and correct design of parallel programs. We try to reconcile this high level of abstraction with performance by introducing data-distributions into this theory. One advantage of formally introducing distributions is that it allows us to evaluate costs, depending on the number of available processors, which is considered as a parameter. The analysis of the possible distributions for a certain function may also lead to an improvement in the design decisions. Another important advantage is that after the introduction of data-distributions, mappings on real parallel architectures with limited number of processing elements can be analyzed. Case studies for Fast Fourier transform and rank-sorting are given.

Keywords: parallel computation, abstraction, design, distribution, data-structures.

1 Introduction

PowerLists are data structures introduced by J. Misra [9], which can be successfully used in a simple and provably correct, functional description of parallel programs, which are *divide and conquer* in nature. They allow work at a high level of abstraction, especially because index notations are not used. To ensure methods that verify the correctness of the parallel programs, algebras and structural induction principles are defined on these data structures. Based on the structural induction principles, functions and operators representing the parallel programs, are defined.

The second section briefly describes this theory.

PowerList theory can be considered the basis for a model of parallel computation with a very high level of abstraction. In order to be useful, a model of parallel computation must address both issues, abstraction and effectiveness, which are summarized in the following set of requirements: abstractness, software development methodology, architecture independence, cost measures, no preferred scale of granularity, efficiently implementable [13]. The first three requirements are clearly fulfilled by *PowerList* theory.

Mappings on hypercubes have been analyzed for the programs specified based on *Power* notations [9,7]; they are based on Gray code.Thus, we may agree that the requirement of efficient implementation is also fulfiled. The most practical

C.B. Jones, Z. Liu, J. Woodcock (Eds.): ICTAC 2007, LNCS 4711, pp. 396–409, 2007.

approach of bounded parallelism has to be introduced, and so, the distributions. The cost measures have to be more rigorously defined, as well.

Section 3 presents the way in which distributions may be defined on these special kinds of data structures, and also how the functions defined on them could be transformed to accept distributions. Time-complexity is analyzed, and examples are given for Fast Fourier Transformation, and Rank-sorting.

For other models, these kinds of enhancement have been analyzed, as well. There is a clear necessity to reconcile abstraction with performance, as is it stated by S. Gorlatch in [3].

The BMF formalism [1,3] is also based on recursion, and there the notion of homeomorphism is essential. The distributions have been introduced as simple functions that transform a list into a list of lists. But, since few of the key distributions, such as block decomposition, can be defined in this calculus, so various hybrid forms, often called *skeletons* [2] have been introduced to bridge the gap.

Shape theory [4] is a more general approach. Knowledge of the shapes of the data structures is used by many cost models [5]. Static shape analysis can be applied to those programs for which the shape of the result is determined by that of inputs, i.e. the *shapely programs*. PowerList theory allows us to define shapely programs, but in a very elegant and simple way. It has proved to be highly successful in expressing computations that are independent of the specific data values. By introducing data distributions in this theory, we enhance its power of expressivity.

We will define distributions in the same way as we define functions representing programs (based on pattern matching). Hence, distribution properties could be proved by induction as well. Also, choosing a distribution strongly depends on initial function definition: it depends on the decomposition operator that is used.

The analysis of time-complexity is done on the hypothesis of a PRAM model (shared memory), or a complete interconnection network (distributed memory).

2 *PowerList* Theory

PowerList

A *PowerList* is a linear data structure whose elements are all of the same type. The length of a *PowerList* data structure is a power of two. The type constructor for *PowerList* is:

$$PowerList : Type \times \mathbb{N} \rightarrow Type \tag{1}$$

and so, a *PowerList* with 2^n elements of type X is specified by $PowerList.X.n$ ($n = loglen.l$). A *PowerList* with a single element a is called *singleton*, and is denoted by $[a]$. If two *PowerList* structures have the same length and elements of the same type, they are called *similars*.

Two *similar PowerLists* can be combined into a *PowerList* data structure with double length, in two different ways:

- using the operator *tie* $p \mid q$; the result contains elements from p followed by elements from q
- using the operator *zip* $p \natural q$; the result contains elements from p and q, alternatively taken.

Therefore, the constructor operators for *PowerList* are:

$$\begin{aligned}
&[.] : X \rightarrow PowerList.X.0 \\
&.|. : PowerList.X.n \times PowerList.X.n \rightarrow PowerList.X.(n+1) \\
&.\natural. : PowerList.X.n \times PowerList.X.n \rightarrow PowerList.X.(n+1).
\end{aligned} \quad (2)$$

Functions are defined based on the structural induction principle. For example, the high order function *map*, which applies a scalar function to each element of a *PowerList* is defined as follows:

$$\begin{aligned}
&map : (X \rightarrow Z) \times PowerList.X.n \rightarrow PowerList.Z.n \\
&map.f.\,[a] = [f.a] \\
&map.f.\,(p\natural q) = map.f.p \natural map.f.q \text{ or } map.f.\,(p \mid q) = map.f.p \,|\, map.f.q
\end{aligned} \quad (3)$$

A special case of the *map* is obtained if function f is an application of a binary operator ($\odot$), provided that the first argument (z) is given :

$$< z\odot > .l.p = map.(z\odot).p. \quad (4)$$

Another example is the function *flat* that is applied to a PowerList with elements which are in turn PowerLists, and it returns a simple PowerList:

$$\begin{aligned}
&flat : PowerList.\,(PowerList.X.n)\,.m \rightarrow PowerList.X.(n*m) \\
&flat.\,[l] = l \\
&flat.\,(p\natural q) = flat.p \natural flat.q \quad \text{or } flat.\,(p \,|\, q) = flat.p \,|\, flat.q
\end{aligned} \quad (5)$$

Associative operators on scalar types can be extended to *PowerList*, as well.

3 Distributions

The ideal method to implement parallel programs described with *PowerLists* is to consider that any application of the operators *tie* or *zip* as deconstructors, leads to two new processes running in parallel, or, at least, to assume that for each element of the list there is a corresponding process. That means that the number of processes grows linearly with the size of the data. In this ideal situation, the time-complexity is usually logarithmic (if the combination step complexity is a constant), depending on *loglen* of the input list.

A more practical approach is to consider a bounded number of processes n_p. In this case, we have to transform the input list, such that no more than n_p processes are created. This transformation of the input list corresponds to a data distribution.

Definition 1. *$D = (\delta, A, B)$ is called a (one-dimensional) distribution if A and B are finite sets, and δ is a mapping from A to B; set A specifies the set of data objects (an array with n elements that represent the indices of data objects), and set B specifies the set of processes, which is usually $\overline{p}$. Function δ assigns each index $i (0 \leq i < n)$, and its corresponding element, to a process number [11].*

One advantage of *PowerList* theory is that it is not necessary to use indices, and this simplifies very much reasoning and correctness proving. Thus, we will introduce distributions not as in the definition above, but as functions on these special data structures.

The distribution will transform the list into a list with n_p elements, which are in turn sublists; each sublist is considered to be assigned to a process.

3.1 *PowerList* Distributions

We consider *PowerList* data structures with elements of a certain type X, and with length such that $loglen = n$. The number of processes is assumed to be limited to $n_p = 2^p$ $(p \leq n)$.

Two types of distributions – linear and cyclic, which are well-known distributions, may be considered. These correspond in our case to the operators *tie* and *zip*. Distributions are defined as *PowerList* functions, so definitions corresponding to the base case and to the inductive step have to be specified:

- linear

$$\begin{array}{l} distr^l.p.(u|v) = distr^l.(p-1).u|distr^l.(p-1).v, \text{ if } loglen.(u|v) \geq p \wedge p > 0 \\ distr^l.0.l = [l] \\ distr^l.p.x = [x], \text{ if } loglen.x < p. \end{array} \tag{6}$$

- cyclic

$$\begin{array}{l} distr^c.p.(u \natural v) = distr^c.(p-1).u \natural distr^c.(p-1).v, \text{ if } loglen.(u \natural v) \geq p \wedge p > 0 \\ distr^c.0.l = [l] \\ distr^c.p.x = [x], \text{ if } loglen.x < p. \end{array} \tag{7}$$

The base cases transform a list l into a singleton, which has the list $[l]$ as its unique element.

Examples. If we consider the list $l = [1\ 2\ 3\ 4\ 5\ 6\ 7\ 8]$, the lists obtained after the application of the distribution functions $distr^l.2.l$ and $distr^c.2.l$ are:

$$\begin{array}{lcl} distr^l.2.l &=& distr^l.1.[1\ 2\ 3\ 4] \mid distr^l.1.[5\ 6\ 7\ 8] = [[1\ 2]\ [3\ 4]\ [5\ 6]\ [7\ 8]] \\ distr^c.2.l &=& distr^c.1.[1\ 3\ 5\ 7] \natural distr^c.1.[2\ 4\ 6\ 8] = [[1\ 5]\ [2\ 6]\ [3\ 7]\ [4\ 8]] \end{array}$$

Properties. If we consider $u \in PowerList.X.n$, then $distr.n.u = \overline{u}$, where $\overline{u}$ is obtained from the list u by transforming each of its elements into a singleton list. (This could be easily proved by structural induction.)

We also have the trivial property $distr.0.u = [u]$.
The result of the application of a distribution $distr.p$ to a list $l \in PowerList.X.n$, $n \geq p$ is a list that has 2^p elements each of these being a list with 2^{n-p} elements of type X. (This property could be proved by induction on p.)

The properties are true for both linear and cyclic distributions.

3.2 Function Transformation

We consider a function f defined on $PowerList.X.n$ based on operator tie with the property that

$$f.(u|v) = \Phi(f.x_0, f.x_1, \dots, f.x_m, u, v), \tag{8}$$

where $x_i \in PowerLists.X.k, k = loglen.u$, and $x_i = e_i.u.v, \forall i : 0 \leq i \leq m$, and e_i and Φ are expressions that may use scalar functions and extended operators on powerlists. If the function definition Φ is more complex and uses other functions on $PowerLists$, then these functions have to be transformed first, and the considered function after that.

A scalar function fs has zero or more scalars as arguments, and its value is a scalar. The function fs is easily extended to a PowerList by applying fs "pointwise" to the elements of the PowerList. A scalar function that operates on two arguments could be seen as an infix operator, and it can also be extended to PowerLists.

The extensions of the scalar functions on PowerLists could be defined by using either operator tie or zip. Some properties of these functions can be found in [9]. For the sake of clarity, we will introduce the notation fs^1, which specifies the corresponding extended function on PowerLists of the scalar function fs defined on the scalar type X. For the case of one argument the definition is:

$$\begin{aligned} &fs^1 : Powerlist.X.n \to Powerlist.X.n \\ &fs^1.[a] = [fs.a] \\ &fs^1.(p|q) = fs^1.p|fs^1.q \;\text{ or }\; fs^1.(p\natural q) = fs^1.p\natural fs^1.q \end{aligned} \tag{9}$$

Further, fs^2 (which is the notation for the extension of fs on PowerLists with elements which are in turn PowerLists) could be defined:

$$\begin{aligned} &fs^2 : Powerlist.(PowerList.X.m).n \to PowerList.(PowerList.X.m).n \\ &fs^2.[l] = [fs^1.l] \\ &fs^2.(p|q) = fs^2.p|fs^2.q \;\text{ or }\; fs^2.(p\natural q) = fs^2.p\natural fs^2.q \end{aligned} \tag{10}$$

This represents, in fact, an extension from functions defined on $PowerLists$ with depths equal to 1 to those defined on $PowerLists$ with depths larger than 1.

We intend to show that

$$f.u = flat \circ f^p.(dist^l.p.u),$$

where

$$\begin{aligned} &f^p.(u|v) = \Phi^2(f^p.x_0^{'}, f^p.x_1^{'}, \dots, f^p.x_m^{'}, u, v) \\ &f^p.[l] = [f^s.l] \\ &f^s.u = f.u \\ &x_i^{'} = e_i^2.u.v, \forall i : 0 \leq i \leq m \end{aligned} \tag{11}$$

Function f^p corresponds to parallel execution, and function f^s corresponds to sequential execution.

Lemma 1. *Given a scalar function $fs : X \to X$, and a distribution function distr.p, defined on PowerList.X.n, then the following equality is true*

$$dist.p \circ fs^1 = fs^2 \circ dist.p \tag{12}$$

Proof. To prove this lemma we use induction on p.

We give the proof only for the case of the linear distribution, but the case of the cyclic distribution is similar.

Base case$(p = 0)$

$$\begin{aligned}
& fs^2.(dist^l.0.u) \\
= & \{p = 0 \Rightarrow dist^l.p.u = [u]\} \\
& fs^2.[u] \\
= & \{fs^2 \text{ definition}\} \\
& [fs^1.u] \\
= & \{distr^l.0 \text{ definition}\} \\
& distr^l.0.(fs^1.u)
\end{aligned}$$

Inductive step

$$\begin{aligned}
& fs^2.(dist^l.p.(u|v)) \\
= & \{ \text{ definition of } distr^l\} \\
& fs^2.(dist^l.(p-1).u|dist^l.(p-1).v) \\
= & \{fs^2 \text{ definition}\} \\
& fs^2.(dist^l.(p-1).u)|fs^2.(dist^l.(p-1).v)) \\
= & \{\text{induction assumption}\} \\
& distr^l.(p-1).(fs^1.u)|distr^l.(p-1).(fs^1.u) \\
= & \{distr^l \text{ definition}\} \\
& distr^l.p.(fs^1.u|fs^1.v) \\
= & \{fs^1 \text{ definition}\} \\
& distr^l.p.(fs^1.(u|v))
\end{aligned}$$

The previous result is naturally extended to scalar functions with more arguments, such as infix operators.

Scalar binary associative operators $(\oplus)$ could also be extended on PowerLists as reduction operators – $red(\oplus)$. They transform a PowerList into a scalar. For them, similar extensions as for scalar functions may be done.

$$\begin{aligned}
& red^1(\oplus) : Powerlist.X.m \to X \\
& red^1(\oplus).[a] = a \\
& red^1(\oplus).(p|q) = red^1(\oplus).p \oplus red^1(\oplus).q
\end{aligned} \tag{13}$$

$$\begin{aligned}
& red^2(\oplus) : Powerlist.(PowerList.X.m).n \to PowerList.X.0 \\
& red^2(\oplus).[l] = [red^1(\oplus).l] \\
& red^2(\oplus).(p|q) = [red^1(\oplus).\left(red^2(\oplus).p|red^2(\oplus).q\right)]
\end{aligned} \tag{14}$$

For this, a similar property in relation to distribution is obtained:

$$distr.p \circ red^1(\oplus) = red^2(\oplus) \circ distr.p \tag{15}$$

Theorem 1. *Given a function f defined on PowerList.X.n as Eq. 8, a corresponding distribution $distr^l.p, (p \leq n)$, and a function f^p defined as in Eq. 11, then the following equality is true*

$$f = flat \circ (f^p \circ dist^l.p) \tag{16}$$

Proof. We will prove the following equation

$$\begin{array}{l} (distr^l. \circ f).u = (f^p \circ dist^l.p).u \\ \text{for any } u \in PowerList.X.n \end{array} \tag{17}$$

which implies the equation 16. To prove this, we use induction on p again.

Base case$(p = 0)$

$$\begin{array}{l} \quad f^p.(dist^l.0.u) \\ = \{p = 0 \Rightarrow dist^l.p.u = [u]\} \\ \quad f^p.[u] \\ = \{f^p \text{ definition}\} \\ \quad [f^s.u] \\ = \{f^s \text{ and } distr^l.0 \text{ definitions}\} \\ \quad distr^l.0.(f.u) \end{array}$$

Inductive step

$$\begin{array}{l} \quad f^p.(dist^l.p.(u|v)) \\ = \{ \text{ definition of } distr^l\} \\ \quad f^p.(dist^l.(p-1).u|dist^l.(p-1).v) \\ = \{f^p \text{ definition, scalar functions properties}\} \\ \quad \Phi^2(f^p.(e_0^2.(dist^l.(p-1).u).(dist^l.(p-1).v)), \ldots, \\ \qquad\qquad f^p.(e_m^2.(dist^l.(p-1).u).(dist^l.(p-1).v)), dist^l.(p-1).u, dist^l.(p-1).v) \\ = \{e_i \text{ are simple expressions -- use scalar functions}\} \\ \quad \Phi^2(f^p \circ\ distr^l.(p-1).(e_0.u.v), \ldots, \\ \qquad\qquad f^p \circ\ distr^l.(p-1).(e_m.u.v), dist^l.(p-1).u, dist^l.(p-1).v) \\ = \{\text{induction assumption, and scalar functions properties}\} \\ \quad (distr^l.p \circ \Phi)(f.(e_0.u.v), \ldots, f.(e_m.u.v), u, v) \\ = \{f \text{ definition}\} \\ \quad distr^l.p.(f.(u|v)) \end{array}$$

For cyclic distribution the proof is similar; the operator *tie* is replaced with the operator *zip*.

3.3 Time Complexity

Considering a function f defined on *PowerList* representing a program, and a distribution $distr.p.\cdot$, time-complexity of the resulting program is the sum of the parallel execution time and the sequential execution time:

$$T = \Theta + T(f^p) + T(f^s)$$

where Θ reflects the costs specific to parallel processing (communication or access to shared memory).

The evaluation considers that the processor-complexity is 2^p ($O(2^p)$ processors are used).

Example 1. (**Constant-time combination step**) If the time-complexity of the combination step is a constant $T_s(\Phi) = K_c, K_c \in \mathbb{R}$, and considering that the time-complexity of computing the function on singletons is equal to K_s ($K_s \in \mathbb{R}$ also a constant), then we may evaluate the total complexity as being:

$$T = \Theta + K_c p + K_c(2^{n-p} - 1) + K_s 2^{n-p} \quad (18)$$

If $p = n$, we achieve the cost of the ideal case (unbounded number of processors).

For example, for **reduction** $red(\oplus)$ the time-complexity of the combination step is a constant, and $K_s = 0$; so we have

$$T_{red} = \Theta + K_{\oplus}(p + 2^{n-p} - 1) \quad (19)$$

For extended operators $\odot$ the combination constant is equal to 0, but we have the time needed for the operator execution on scalars reflected in the constant K_s. We have a similar situation for the high order function *map*. In these cases, the time-complexity is equal to

$$T = \Theta + K_s 2^{n-p} \quad (20)$$

Example 2. (**Fast Fourier Transform**) As proved by J. Misra[9], the function for the computation of Fast Fourier Transform on N points is:

$$\begin{aligned} &fft.[x] = [x] \\ &fft.(p \natural q) = (fft.p + u \times fft.q) | (fft.p - u \times fft.q) \\ &\text{ where } u = powers\ p \end{aligned} \quad (21)$$

The powerlist definition for the function *powers* is:

$$\begin{aligned} &powers.[x] = [1] \\ &powers.(p|q) = (powers.p)^2 \natural (< w * > (powers.p)^2) \\ &\text{ where } w \text{ is the } N\text{th principal root of } 1 \end{aligned} \quad (22)$$

The extended operators $+, -, \times$ were used.

The computation of the function fft could be carried out in $O(logN)$ time using $O(N)$ processors (N is the length of the initial list).

The function could be transformed for bounded parallelism, to be a distributed PowerList function, using Theorem 1. Thus, we obtain

$$\begin{aligned} &fft^p.[l] = [fft^s.l] \\ &fft^p.(p \natural q) = (fft^p.p \ +^2\ v\ \times^2\ fft^p.q) \mid (fft^p.p\ -^2\ v\ \times^2\ fft^p.q) \\ &\text{ where } v = powers^p\ p \end{aligned} \quad (23)$$

In the first stage, each of the 2^p processors executes a sequential computation of a Fourier Transformation (fft^s), and the time-complexity is $O\left((n-p)2^{(n-p)}\right)$. For the execution of fft^p there are p steps, and each one could be executed in $O\left(2^{(n-p-1)}\right)$ time. At the level $k, 0 \le k < p$, the operators $+, -, \times$ are applied to lists of length equal to $2^{n-p+(p-k-1)}$ using 2^{p-k} processors; based on Eq. 20 this can be executed with a time-complexity equal to 2^{n-p-1}. Because the function *powers* is also defined based on extended operators, it needs the same time-complexity $O(2^{(n-p-1)})$ at each level. (But this time could still be improved since the result of the function *powers* depends only on the length of the argument list.)

So, the total time-complexity is

$$T = \Theta + T^p + T^s = \Theta + O\left(\frac{N}{P}\log N\right) + O\left(\frac{N}{P}(\log N - \log P)\right)$$

where $N = 2^n$ and $P = 2^p$. Θ could be approximated to $O\left(\log P \frac{N}{P}\right)$. If $p = n$ then the time-complexity is $O(\log N)$.

Example 3 (**Rank Sorting**)
The idea of the rank sort algorithm is as follows: determine the rank of each element in the unsorted sequence and place it in the position according to its rank. The rank of an element is equal to the number of elements smaller than it [6].

Rank sort is not exactly a good sequential sorting algorithm because the time complexity in the sequential case is: $O(N^2)$ (N is the length of the sequence). But this algorithm leads to good parallel algorithms.

We will consider the special case of a sequence with $N = 2^n$ elements. The type of the elements is X, on which we have defined an order relation $\le$.

By using the definition of the method, we arrive to the following simple *PowerList* function:

$$\begin{aligned}
&rank : PowerList.X.n \to PowerList.\mathbb{N}.n\\
&rank.l = map.(count.l).l\\
\\
&count : PowerList.X.n \times X \to \mathbb{N}\\
&count.l.x = (red(+) \circ map.(f\ x)).l\\
\\
&f : X \times X \to \mathbb{N}\\
&f.x.y = \begin{cases} 1, & \text{if } x \ge y\\ 0, & \text{if } x < y\end{cases}
\end{aligned} \tag{24}$$

A simple transformation can be made:

$$red(+) \circ map\ (f\ x)\ l = red(+)\ (map\ (f\ x)\ l) \stackrel{not}{=} redmap(+, f.x).l \tag{25}$$

which simple means that the application of the function $f.x$ is made in the same step with the reduction, not in a separate sequent step. Function composition leads to sequential composition.

We proved by induction on the *loglen* of the list, that for any associative operator $\oplus$ and any scalar function f we have

$$redmap(\oplus, f).(p|q) = redmap(\oplus, f).p \;\oplus\; redmap(\oplus, f).q$$

(Operator *zip* could also be used.)

Base case $loglen.p = loglen.q = 0$

$$\begin{aligned}
& redmap(\oplus, f).[a\ b] \\
= & \{redmap \text{ definition}\} \\
& red.(\oplus).(map.f.[a\ b]) \\
= & \{map \text{ definition}\} \\
& red.(\oplus).[f.a\ f.b] \\
= & \{red \text{ definition}\} \\
& f.a \oplus f.b \\
= & \{map, red, \text{ and } redmap \text{ definition}\} \\
& redmap(\oplus, f).[a] \;\oplus\; redmap(\oplus, f).[b]
\end{aligned}$$

Inductive step

$$\begin{aligned}
& redmap(\oplus, f).(p|q) \\
= & \{redmap \text{ definition}\} \\
& red.(\oplus).(map.f.(p|q)) \\
= & \{red \text{ and } map \text{ definition}\} \\
& red.(\oplus).map.f.p \;\oplus\; red.(\oplus).map.f.q \\
= & \{\text{induction hypothesis }\} \\
& redmap(\oplus, f).p \;\oplus\; redmap(\oplus, f).q
\end{aligned}$$

We may consider that the function *redmap* is a special kind of reduction.

Ideally, for computing the first function *map* of the *rank* definition, we need a number of processors equal to the length of the input list – n. Each application of the function *count* l is a reduction that can be computed with $O(\log n)$ time complexity and $O(n)$ processor complexity. So, for whole program the unbounded time complexity is $O(\log n)$, with the processor complexity equal to $O(n^2)$.

For bounded parallelism we need to transform the program by imposing that the number of processors be equal to 2^p, and using Theorem 1.

As it may be noticed in the specification, the algorithm contains two phases: one represented by the function *map*, and the other represented by the function *count*, each of them having the input list l as an argument. A distribution function *dist.p* simple divides the argument list into 2^p balanced sublists. So, we may apply it for the computation of the function *map*, or for the computation of the function *count*, or for both.

There are two cases that we have to take into account:

- A. Case $p \leq n$.
- B. Case $n < p \leq 2n$.

A. Case $p \le n$ If the number of processors is less or equal to the size of the list, than a distribution function can be applied only once: for the function *map*, or for the function *count*.

In the first sub-case we obtain the following transformation:

$$\begin{aligned} rank.l &= (flat \circ map^p.(count^s.l) \circ dist^l.p).l \\ map^p.(count^s.l).[p] &= map^s.(count^s.l).p \\ count^s.l.u &= redmap^s(+, f.x).l \end{aligned} \tag{26}$$

This means that each processor sequentially computes the ranks for 2^{n-p} elements.

If we apply the function *dist* to the function *count*, we obtain the following transformation of the function *rank*:

$$\begin{aligned} &rank.l = map^s\ (flat \circ count^p.l).l \\ &count^p.l.x = (redmap^p(+, f.x) \circ dist^l.p).l \\ &redmap^p(+, f.x).(p|q) = [red(+).(redmap^p(+, f.x).p|redmap^p(+, f.x).q)] \\ &redmap^p(+, f.x).[p] = [redmap^s(+, f.x).p] \end{aligned} \tag{27}$$

This program sequentially computes the ranks of the elements, but each rank is computed in parallel using 2^p processors. For computing the rank of an element x, the processors compare x to all their 2^{n-p} local elements, and compute local ranks; then the local ranks are added.

The two sub-cases reflect different ways for algorithm decomposition in sub-steps, which can be computed with 2^p processors. Based on equations 19 and 20, the time complexities of the two sub-cases are:

1. $\Theta_1 + 2^{n-p}(2^n + 2^n - 1) = \Theta_1 + 2^{2n-p+1} - 2^{n-p}$ for the first case, and
2. $2^n * (\Theta_2 + p + 2^{n-p} - 1 + 2^{n-p}) = 2^n\Theta_2 + 2^{2n-p+1} + p2^n - 2^n$ for the second.

Obviously, if we ignore the Θ times, the first is the best.

In order to implement the program on a *shared memory* (SM) architecture, the list l is shared by all processors, so normally we will choose the first sub-case with the better time complexity.

If we analyze the number of accesses to the shared memory, we have the following situation, in the first sub-case: Each processor makes 2^{2n-p} readings and 2^{n-p} writings from/in the shared memory. On a CREW architecture, Θ_1 will be $\alpha(2^{2n-p} + 2^{n-p}))$, where α is the unit time for shared memory access.

On a *distributed memory* (DM) architecture, the second alternative is better since we have the list distributed over the processors. An element is broadcasted to all the processors during the step that computes its rank - so there are 2^n steps. Each processor compares the current received element to the local elements and computes a local rank. Local ranks are summed using a tree like computation that represents the reduction. If we consider β the unit time for communication, and the constant b reflects the time for a broadcast, then Θ_2 is given by the following expression: $\beta(p + b)$. So, for good values of β and b, the result could be better than that of the SM architecture case.

B. Case $n < p \leq n^2$ If we have more than n processors and $p = q + r$ ($q < n$ and $r < n$), we may use the distribution function for both stages of computations. Thus, we arrive to the following transformation of the program:

$$\begin{aligned} rank.l &= (flat \circ map^p.(flat \circ count^p.l) \circ dist.p).l \\ count^p.l.x &= (redmap^p(+, f.x) \circ dist.p).l \end{aligned} \tag{28}$$

The time complexity for this case is $\Theta_1 + 2^{n-q}(\Theta_2 + r + 2^{n-r} - 1 + 2^{n-r})$.

For a DM architecture, the processors could be arranged on a $2^q \times 2^r$ mesh, and the data distribution of the first line may be replicated on the other lines of processors. Each line computes the ranks of the elements of a sublist with 2^{n-q} elements.

We have obtained three variants, two for the case $p \leq n$ and one for the case $n < p \leq n^2$.

Remark. The functions *map* and *red* could be defined based on operator *tie*, but also based on operator *zip*. So, in order to obtain distributed functions we may also use cyclic distribution.

Rank sorting algorithm is one that shows that a poor sequential algorithm for a problem may lead to very good parallel algorithms. It has been considered especially for sorting on shared memory architectures [14]. We have shown here in a formalized way that we may successful use it for distributed architectures, as well. We have also formally analyzed the case when the number of processors p is between n and n^2.

The abstract design using PowerList notation can comprise different cases that may appear at the implementation phase: shared memory versus distributed memory, and different numbers of processors. Thus, the abstractness of this formalism does not exclude performance.

3.4 Further Work

If we want to work with matrices, it is possible to use *PowerList*, whose elements are in turn, *PowerList*. But this is not the natural way to work with multidimensional structures, and also by using this kind of structures it would be very difficult to define specific functions – for example matrix transposition. For these reasons a new notation, specific to multidimensional structures, has been introduced – *PowerArray* [9]. Distributions could also be introduced for these multidimensional structures. (The limited space did not allow us to present their case, here.) For *PowerArray* data structures, Cartesian distributions could be defined.

A distribution is generally defined as simple mapping between the input data and the processors numbers. A special case of distributions is represented by the set-distributions [10], which are defined using set-mappings between the input data and the processors numbers. They are used when we want to assign a datum to more than one processor. We may introduce this special case of distribution into the abstract model of *Power* theories by transforming the functions defined on *PowerLists* into functions defined on *PowerArrays*, where the arrays are obtained by replicating the lists on new dimensions.

Beside *PowerList* notation, other two have been developed for one-dimensional data structures: *ParList*, and *PList* [7]. They consider the case when the lists don't have lengths which are powers of two, and respectively, the case when the division could be done into more than two parts. This kind of analysis, based on distribution, could be done for *ParList*, *PList* theories as well, and so the model would not be restricted to special structures with lengths equal to powers of two, and to divide&conquer programs, where division is done always into two parts.

4 Conclusions

The synthesis and analysis of a parallel algorithm can be carried out under the assumption that the computational model consists of p processors only, where $p \geq 1$ is a fixed integer. This is referred to as *bounded parallelism.* In contrast, *unbounded parallelism* refers to the situation in which it is assumed that we have at our disposal an unlimited number of processors.

From a practical point of view algorithms for bounded parallelism are preferable. It is more realistic to assume that the number of available processors is limited. Although parallel algorithms for unbounded parallelism, in general, use a polynomially bounded number of processors (e.g. $O(n^2)$, $O(n^3)$, etc.) it may be that for very large problem sizes the processors requirement may become impractically large. However, algorithms for unbounded parallelism are of great theoretical interest, since they give limits for parallel computation and provide a deeper understanding of a problem's intrinsic complexity.

Consequently, the right way to design parallel programs is to start from unbounded parallelism, and then transform the algorithm for bounded parallelism. The *PowerList* functions represent programs which usually reflect the unbounded parallelism.

The *PowerList* notation has been proved to be a very elegant way to specify divide&conquer parallel algorithms and prove their correctness. The main advantage of this model is that it offers a simple, formal and elegant way to prove correctness. Their abstractness is very high, but we may reconcile this abstractness with performance by introducing bounded parallelism, and thus distributions. The necessity of this kind of reconciliation for parallel computation models is argued by Gorlatch in [3], and also by Skillicorn and Talia in [13].

We have proved that the already defined *PowerList* functions could be easily transformed to accept bounded parallelism, by introducing distributions. The functions defined based on operator *tie* have to use linear distributions, and the functions defined based on operator *zip* have to use cyclic distributions.

The presented case studies of Fast Fourier Transform and Rank-Sorting emphasize the advantages of using distributions, and the way in which design may be improved based on distribution analysis.

There are several advantages of formally introducing the distributions; the first is that it allows us to evaluate costs, depending on the number of available processors - as a parameter. The analysis of the possible distributions for a certain function may lead to an improvement in the design decisions, too. Another advantage is that we may control the parallel decomposition until a certain level of tree decomposition has been achieved; otherwise parallel implementation of this kind of programs could be done, for example, in a 'deep-first' manner, which could be disadvantageous. Also, after the introduction of the distributions functions, mapping on real architectures with limited number of processing elements (e.g. hypercubes) could be analyzed.

References

1. Bird, R.: Lectures on Constructive Functional Programming. In: Broy, M. (ed.) Constructive Methods in Computing Science. NATO ASI Series F: Computer and Systems Sciences, vol. 55, pp. 151–216. Springer, Heidelberg (1988)
2. Cole, M.: Parallel Programming with List Homomorphisms. Parallel Processing Letters 5(2), 191–204 (1994)
3. Gorlatch, S.: Abstraction and Performance in the Design of Parallel Programs. In: CMPP'98 First International Workshop on Constructive Methods for Parallel Programming (1998)
4. Jay, C.B.: A semantics for shape. Science of Computer Programming 25(2), 251–283(33) (1995)
5. Jay, C.B.: Costing Parallel Programs as a Function of Shapes. Science of Computer Programming 37(1), 207–224 (2000)
6. Knuth, D.E.: The Art of Computer Programming. In: Sorting and Searching, vol. 3, Addison-Wesley, Reading (1973)
7. Kornerup, J.: Data Structures for Parallel Recursion. PhD Thesis, Univ. of Texas (1997)
8. Kornerup, J.: PLists: Taking PowerLists Beyond Base Two. In: MIP-9805, 9805th edn. First International Workshop on Constructive Methods for Parallel Programming, pp. 102–116 (1998)
9. Misra, J.: PowerList: A structure for parallel recursion. ACM Transactions on Programming Languages and Systems 16(6), 1737–1767 (1994)
10. Niculescu, V.: On Data Distributions in the Construction of Parallel Programs. The Journal of Supercomputing 29(1), 5–25 (2004)
11. Niculescu, V.: Unbounded and Bounded Parallelism in BMF. Case-Study: Rank Sorting. Studia Universitatis Babes-Bolyai, Informatica XLIX(1), 91–98 (2004)
12. Skillicorn, D.B.: Structuring data parallelism using categorical data types. In: Programming Models for Massively Parallel Computers, pp. 110–115. Computer Society Press (1993)
13. Skillicorn, D.B., Talia, D.: Models and Languages for Parallel Computation. ACM Computer surveys 30(2), 123–136 (1998)
14. Wilkinson, B., Allen, M.: Parallel Programming Techniques and Applications Using Networked Workstations and Parallel Computers. Prentice-Hall, Englewood Cliffs (2002)

Quasi-interpretation Synthesis by Decomposition
An Application to Higher-Order Programs

Guillaume Bonfante, Jean-Yves Marion, and Romain Péchoux

Nancy-Université, Loria, Carte team, B.P. 239, 54506 Vandœuvre-lès-Nancy Cedex, France, and École Nationale Supérieure des Mines de Nancy, INPL, France
Guillaume.Bonfante@loria.fr Jean-Yves.Marion@loria.fr
Romain.Pechoux@loria.fr

Abstract. Quasi-interpretation analysis belongs to the field of *implicit computational complexity (ICC)* and has shown its interest to deal with resource analysis of first-order functional programs, which are terminating or not. In this paper, we tackle the issue of program decomposition wrt quasi-interpretations analysis. For that purpose, we use the notion of modularity. Firstly, modularity decreases the complexity of the quasi-interpretation search algorithms. Secondly, modularity increases the intentionality of the quasi-interpretation method, that is the number of captured programs. Finally, we take advantage of modularity conditions to extend smoothly quasi-interpretations to higher-order programs.

We study the modularity of quasi-interpretations through the notions of constructor-sharing and hierarchical unions of programs. We show that, in both cases, the existence of quasi-interpretations is no longer a modular property. However, we can still certify the complexity of programs by showing, under some restrictions, that the size of the values computed by a program remains polynomially bounded by the inputs size.

1 Introduction

1.1 Certifying Resources by Quasi-interpretations

The resources control of memory, space or time is a fundamental issue when considering critical systems. This paper, which deals with static analysis of first-order functional programs, is a contribution to that field and, in particular, to the field of *implicit computational complexity (ICC)*. The control of resources is studied by the *ICC* community in four distinct approaches that we briefly review. The first one deals with linear type disciplines in order to restrict computational time and began with the seminal work of Girard [13] on Light Linear Logic. The interested reader should consult the recent results of Baillot-Terui [4], Lafont [22] and Coppola-Ronchi [8]. The second approach is due to Hofmann [15,16], who introduced a resource atomic type, into linear type systems, for higher-order functional programming. The third one considers imperative programming languages and is developed by Niggl-Wunderlich [26], Jones-Kristiansen [20] and

C.B. Jones, Z. Liu, J. Woodcock (Eds.): ICTAC 2007, LNCS 4711, pp. 410–424, 2007.

Marion-Moyen [24]. The fourth approach is the one on which we focus in this paper. It concerns term rewriting systems and quasi-interpretations.

A comprehensive introduction to quasi-interpretations is given in [6]. Basically, a quasi-interpretation of a first-order functional program provides an upper bound on the size of any value computed by the program. Combined with recursive path orderings, it characterizes complexity classes such as the set of polynomial time functions or yet the set of polynomial space functions. The main features of quasi-interpretations (abbreviated QI) are the following:

1. QI analysis includes a broad class of algorithms, even some that have an exponentially length derivation but denote a polynomial time computable function using dynamic programming techniques. See [23,5].
2. Resource verification of bytecode programs is obtained by compiling first-order functional and reactive programs which admit quasi-interpretations. See for example [2,3,9].
3. In [7], the synthesis of QI was shown to be decidable in exponential time for polynomial quasi-interpretations of bounded degree over real numbers.

1.2 Modularity

The issue of modularity of term rewriting systems has been introduced by Toyama in [30]. Nowadays, it is a classical approach to solve problems like confluence [31], termination [21,14] or completeness [19] by dividing the problem into smaller parts. The interested reader should consult Middeldorp [25], Klop [19] and, more recently, Ohlebusch [27] to read an overview on this subject. In the literature, modularity is studied with respect to the way programs are divided. In this paper, we consider two distinct program decompositions. The first one is the *constructor-sharing union* in which functions defined by programs can share constructors. The second one is the *hierarchical union*, where constructors of one program are defined function symbols of another program.

1.3 More Intentionality

We show that in both cases QI are not modular, but we can still use QI in order to predict resource bounds for *constructor-sharing unions*. Moreover, we are able, under some syntactical restrictions, to analyze resource bounds in the *hierarchical* case. The consequence is that we analyze the complexity of more programs. We obtain new characterizations of the sets of polynomial time and polynomial space functions. Last but not least, the hierarchical union of two programs can be considered as a way to deal with higher-order programs. Up to now, the QI method only applies to first-order functional programs. A way to deal with higher-order programs is to transform a higher-order definition into a hierarchical union of programs using higher-order removal methods. As a result, we obtain new higher-order characterizations of the sets of polynomial time and polynomial space functions.

1.4 Modularity as a Way to Improve QI Synthesis

The problem of the QI synthesis, which was introduced by Amadio in [1], consists in finding a QI for a given program. In a perspective of automatic analysis of the complexity of programs, such a problem is fundamental. We have shown in [7] that the QI synthesis for a program having n variables, has a time complexity in 2^{n^α}, for some constant α, as long as we take polynomial QI with degrees smaller than an arbitrarily fixed constant. On one hand we have a very general procedure, on the other hand the procedure has a high cost. The question of modularity of QI is central as long as one considers a divide and conquer strategy to find QI. Take a program and divide it into k sub-programs having n_j variables for j from 1 to k. Then the complexity of the QI synthesis decreases from $2^{(\sum_{j=1}^{k} n_j)^\alpha}$ to $\sum_{j=1}^{k} 2^{n_j^\alpha}$, for some constant α. Such results allow the improvement of a software called CROCUS, available at `http://libresource.inria.fr//projects/crocus`, that we are currently developing and which finds QI using some heuristics.

1.5 Plan of the Paper

The paper is organized as follows. Section 2 describes the syntax and semantics of considered programs. After introducing the notion of QI, it briefly reviews their main properties. Sections 3 and 4 are devoted to the study of constructor-sharing and, respectively, hierarchical unions. Finally, Section 5 is an application of the complexity results obtained in the case of a hierarchical union to higher-order programs.

The full paper with the proofs and more examples is available at the address `http://hal.inria.fr`

2 Quasi-interpretations of First-Order Functional Programs

2.1 Syntax and Semantics of First-Order Programs

A program is defined formally as a quadruple $\langle \mathcal{X}, \mathcal{C}, \mathcal{F}, \mathcal{R} \rangle$ with $\mathcal{X}, \mathcal{F}$ and $\mathcal{C}$ finite disjoint sets which represent respectively the variables, the function symbols and the constructors symbols and $\mathcal{R}$ a finite set of rules defined below:

$$\begin{array}{llll}
\texttt{(Values)} & \mathcal{T}(\mathcal{C}) \ni v & ::= & \mathbf{c} \mid \mathbf{c}(v_1, \cdots, v_n) \\
\texttt{(Terms)} & \mathcal{T}(\mathcal{C}, \mathcal{F}, \mathcal{X}) \ni t & ::= & \mathbf{c} \mid x \mid \mathbf{c}(t_1, \cdots, t_n) \mid \mathtt{f}(t_1, \cdots, t_n) \\
\texttt{(Patterns)} & \mathcal{P} \ni p & ::= & \mathbf{c} \mid x \mid \mathbf{c}(p_1, \cdots, p_n) \\
\texttt{(Rules)} & \mathcal{R} \ni r & ::= & \mathtt{f}(p_1, \cdots, p_n) \to t
\end{array}$$

where $x \in \mathcal{X}$, $\mathtt{f} \in \mathcal{F}$, and $\mathbf{c} \in \mathcal{C}$.

The set of rules induces a rewriting relation $\to$. The relation $\xrightarrow{*}$ is the reflexive and transitive closure of $\to$. Throughout the paper, we only consider programs having disjoint and linear patterns. So each program is confluent [17].

The domain of computation of a program $\langle \mathcal{X}, \mathcal{C}, \mathcal{F}, \mathcal{R} \rangle$ is the constructor algebra $\mathcal{T}(\mathcal{C})$. A substitution σ is a mapping from variables to terms and a ground substitution is a substitution which ranges over values of $\mathcal{T}(\mathcal{C})$. Given a term t and a ground substitution σ, we define the notation $[\![t\sigma]\!]$ by if $t\sigma \xrightarrow{*} w$ and w is in $\mathcal{T}(\mathcal{C})$ then $[\![t\sigma]\!] = w$, $[\![t\sigma]\!] = \perp$ otherwise.

The size $|t|$ of a term t is defined to be the number of symbols of arity strictly greater than 0 occurring in t. We define $|\perp| = 0$.

2.2 Recursive Path Orderings

Given a program $\langle \mathcal{X}, \mathcal{C}, \mathcal{F}, \mathcal{R} \rangle$, we define a *precedence* $\geq_{\mathcal{F}}$ on function symbols and its transitive closure, that we also note $\geq_{\mathcal{F}}$, by $\mathtt{f} \geq_{\mathcal{F}} \mathtt{g}$ if there is a rule of the shape $\mathtt{f}(p_1, \cdots, p_n) \to \mathsf{C}[\mathtt{g}(e_1, \cdots, e_m)]$ with $\mathsf{C}[\diamond]$ a context and $e_1, \cdots, e_m$ terms. $\mathtt{f} \approx_{\mathcal{F}} \mathtt{g}$ iff $\mathtt{f} \geq_{\mathcal{F}} \mathtt{g}$ and $\mathtt{g} \geq_{\mathcal{F}} \mathtt{f}$. $\mathtt{f} >_{\mathcal{F}} \mathtt{g}$ iff $\mathtt{f} \geq_{\mathcal{F}} \mathtt{g}$ and not $\mathtt{g} \geq_{\mathcal{F}} \mathtt{f}$.

We associate to each function symbol $\mathtt{f}$ a status $st(\mathtt{f})$ in $\{p, l\}$ and which satisfies if $\mathtt{f} \approx_{\mathcal{F}} \mathtt{g}$ then $st(\mathtt{f}) = st(\mathtt{g})$. The status indicates how to compare recursive calls. When $st(\mathtt{f}) = p$, the status of $\mathtt{f}$ is said to be product. In that case, the arguments are compared with the product extension of $\prec_{rpo}$. Otherwise, the status is said to be lexicographic.

Definition 1. *The product extension $\prec^p$ and the lexicographic extension $\prec^l$ of $\prec$ over sequences are defined by:*

- $(m_1, \cdots, m_k) \prec^p (n_1, \cdots, n_k)$ *if and only if (i)* $\forall i \leq k, m_i \preceq n_i$ *and (ii)* $\exists j \leq k$ *such that* $m_j \prec n_j$.
- $(m_1, \cdots, m_k) \prec^l (n_1, \cdots, n_l)$ *if and only if* $\exists j$ *such that* $\forall i < j$, $m_i \preceq n_i$ *and* $m_j \prec n_j$

Definition 2. *Given a precedence $\preceq_{\mathcal{F}}$ and a status st, we define the recursive path ordering $\prec_{rpo}$ as follows:*

$$\frac{u \preceq_{rpo} t_i}{u \prec_{rpo} f(\ldots, t_i, \ldots)}\ f \in \mathcal{F} \bigcup \mathcal{C} \qquad \frac{\forall i\ u_i \prec_{rpo} f(t_1, \cdots, t_n) \qquad g \prec_{\mathcal{F}} f}{g(u_1, \cdots, u_m) \prec_{rpo} f(t_1, \cdots, t_n)}\ g \in \mathcal{F} \bigcup \mathcal{C}$$

$$\frac{(u_1, \cdots, u_n) \prec_{rpo}^{st(f)} (t_1, \cdots, t_n) \qquad f \approx_{\mathcal{F}} g \qquad \forall i\ u_i \prec_{rpo} f(t_1, \cdots, t_n)}{g(u_1, \cdots, u_n) \prec_{rpo} f(t_1, \cdots, t_n)}$$

A program is ordered by $\prec_{rpo}$ if there are a precedence $\preceq_{\mathcal{F}}$ and a status st such that for each rule $l \to r$, the inequality $r \prec_{rpo} l$ holds.

A program which is ordered by $\prec_{rpo}$ terminates [11].

2.3 Quasi-interpretations

An assignment of a symbol $b \in \mathcal{F} \bigcup \mathcal{C}$ of arity n is a function $(\!|b|\!) : (\mathbb{R}^+)^n \to \mathbb{R}^+$.

An assignment satisfies the *subterm property* if for any $i = 1, n$ and any $X_1, \cdots, X_n$ in $\mathbb{R}^+$, we have

$$(\!|b|\!)(X_1, \cdots, X_n) \geq X_i$$

An assignment is *weakly monotone* if for any symbol b, $(\!|b|\!)$ is an increasing (not necessarily strictly) function with respect to each variable. That is, for every symbol b and all $X_1, \cdots, X_n, Y_1, \cdots, Y_n$ of $\mathbb{R}$ with $X_i \leq Y_i$, we have $(\!|b|\!)(X_1, \cdots, X_n) \leq (\!|b|\!)(Y_1, \cdots, Y_n)$.

We extend assignment $(\!|-|\!)$ to terms canonically. Given a term t with m variables, the assignment $(\!|t|\!)$ is a function $(\mathbb{R}^+)^m \to \mathbb{R}^+$ defined by the rules:

$$(\!|b(t_1, \cdots, t_n)|\!) = (\!|b|\!)((\!|t_1|\!), \cdots, (\!|t_n|\!))$$
$$(\!|x|\!) = X$$

where X is a fresh variable ranging over reals.

Definition 3 (Quasi-interpretation). *A quasi-interpretation $(\!|-|\!)$ of a program $\langle \mathcal{X}, \mathcal{C}, \mathcal{F}, \mathcal{R} \rangle$ is a weakly monotonic assignment satisfying the subterm property such that for each rule $l \to r \in \mathcal{R}$, and for every ground substitution σ*

$$(\!|l\sigma|\!) \geq (\!|r\sigma|\!)$$

Definition 4. *Let **Max-Poly**$\{\mathbb{R}^+\}$ be the set of functions defined to be constant functions over $\mathbb{R}^+$, projections,* max, $+$, $\times$ *and closed by composition. An assignment $(\!|-|\!)$ is said to be polynomial if for each symbol $b \in \mathcal{F} \bigcup \mathcal{C}$, $(\!|b|\!)$ is a function in **Max-Poly**$\{\mathbb{R}^+\}$. A quasi-interpretation $(\!|-|\!)$ is polynomial if the assignment $(\!|-|\!)$ is polynomial.*

Now, say that an assignment of a symbol b of arity $n > 0$ is additive if

$$(\!|b|\!)(X_1, \cdots, X_n) = \sum_{i=1}^{n} X_i + \alpha \text{ with } \alpha \geq 1$$

An assignment $(\!|-|\!)$ of a program $\mathtt{p}$ is *additive* if $(\!|-|\!)$ is polynomial and each constructor symbol of $\mathtt{p}$ has an additive assignment. *A program is additive if it admits a quasi-interpretation which is an additive assignment.*

Example 1. Consider the program which computes the logarithm function and described by the following rules:

$\mathtt{log}(\mathbf{0}) \to \mathbf{0}$	$\mathtt{half}(\mathbf{0}) \to \mathbf{0}$
$\mathtt{log}(\mathbf{S}(\mathbf{0})) \to \mathbf{0}$	$\mathtt{half}(\mathbf{S}(\mathbf{0})) \to \mathbf{0}$
$\mathtt{log}(\mathbf{S}(\mathbf{S}(y))) \to \mathbf{S}(\mathtt{log}(\mathbf{S}(\mathtt{half}(y))))$	$\mathtt{half}(\mathbf{S}(\mathbf{S}(y))) \to \mathbf{S}(\mathtt{half}(y))$

It admits the following additive quasi-interpretation:

$$(\!|\mathbf{0}|\!) = 0$$
$$(\!|\mathbf{S}|\!)(X) = X + 1$$
$$(\!|\mathtt{log}|\!)(X) = (\!|\mathtt{half}|\!)(X) = X$$

2.4 Key Properties of Quasi-interpretations

Lemma 1 (Fundamental Lemma). *Assume that* $\langle \mathcal{X}, \mathcal{C}, \mathcal{F}, \mathcal{R} \rangle$ *is a program admitting an additive quasi-interpretation* $(\!|-|\!)$. *There is a polynomial* P *such that for any term* t *which has* n *variables* $x_1, \cdots, x_n$ *and for any ground substitution* σ *such that* $x_i\sigma = v_i$, *we have*

$$|[\![t\sigma]\!]| \leq P^{|t|}(\max_{i=1..n} |v_i|)$$

where $P^1(X) = P(X)$ *and* $P^{k+1}(X) = P(P^k(X))$.

A proof of the Lemma is written in [23]. Notice that the complexity bound just depends on the inputs and not on the term t which is of fixed size. Lemma 1 and the subterm property of QI imply that each intermediate call in a computation is performed on values whose size is polynomially bounded by the input size.

Theorem 1 ([23]). *The set of functions computed by additive programs ordered by* $\prec_{rpo}$ *where each function symbol has a product status is exactly the set of functions computable in polynomial time.*

The proof is fully written in [23]. It relies on the fundamental Lemma, combined with a memoization technique à la Jones [18].

Theorem 2 ([5]). *The set of functions computed by additive programs ordered by* $\prec_{rpo}$ *is exactly the set of functions computable in polynomial space.*

3 Constructor-Sharing and Disjoint Unions

Two programs $\langle \mathcal{X}_1, \mathcal{C}_1, \mathcal{F}_1, \mathcal{R}_1 \rangle$ and $\langle \mathcal{X}_2, \mathcal{C}_2, \mathcal{F}_2, \mathcal{R}_2 \rangle$ are constructor-sharing if

$$\mathcal{F}_1 \cap \mathcal{F}_2 = \mathcal{F}_1 \cap \mathcal{C}_2 = \mathcal{F}_2 \cap \mathcal{C}_1 = \emptyset$$

In other words, two programs are constructor-sharing if their only shared symbols are constructor symbols. The constructor-sharing union of two programs $\langle \mathcal{X}_1, \mathcal{C}_1, \mathcal{F}_1, \mathcal{R}_1 \rangle$ and $\langle \mathcal{X}_2, \mathcal{C}_2, \mathcal{F}_2, \mathcal{R}_2 \rangle$ is defined as the program

$$\langle \mathcal{X}_1, \mathcal{C}_1, \mathcal{F}_1, \mathcal{R}_1 \rangle \bigsqcup \langle \mathcal{X}_2, \mathcal{C}_2, \mathcal{F}_2, \mathcal{R}_2 \rangle = \langle \mathcal{X}_1 \cup \mathcal{X}_2, \mathcal{C}_1 \cup \mathcal{C}_2, \mathcal{F}_1 \cup \mathcal{F}_2, \mathcal{R}_1 \cup \mathcal{R}_2 \rangle$$

Notice that the semantics for constructor-sharing union is defined since the confluence is modular for constructor-sharing unions of left-linear systems [28].

Proposition 1 (Modularity of $\prec_{rpo}$). *Assume that* $\mathtt{p}_1$ *and* $\mathtt{p}_2$ *are two programs ordered by* $\prec_{rpo}$ *then* $\mathtt{p}_1 \bigsqcup \mathtt{p}_2$ *is also ordered by* $\prec_{rpo}$, *with the same status.*

We are showing a negative result for the modularity of quasi-interpretations in the case of constructor-sharing union:

Proposition 2. *The property of having an additive quasi-interpretation is not a modular property w.r.t. constructor-sharing union.*

Proof. We exhibit a counter-example. We consider two programs $\mathtt{p}_0$ and $\mathtt{p}_1$. Both constructor sets $\mathcal{C}_0$ and $\mathcal{C}_1$ are taken to be $\{\mathbf{a}, \mathbf{b}\}$, $\mathcal{F}_0 = \{\mathtt{f}_0\}$ and $\mathcal{F}_1 = \{\mathtt{f}_1\}$. Rules are defined respectively by:

$$\begin{array}{l|l} \mathtt{f}_0(\mathbf{a}(x)) \to \mathtt{f}_0(\mathtt{f}_0(x)) & \mathtt{f}_1(\mathbf{b}(x)) \to \mathtt{f}_1(\mathtt{f}_1(x)) \\ \mathtt{f}_0(\mathbf{b}(x)) \to \mathbf{a}(\mathbf{a}(\mathtt{f}_0(x))) & \mathtt{f}_1(\mathbf{a}(x)) \to \mathbf{b}(\mathbf{b}(\mathtt{f}_1(x))) \end{array}$$

$\mathtt{p}_0$ and $\mathtt{p}_1$ admit the respective additive quasi-interpretations $(\!|-|\!)_0$ and $(\!|-|\!)_1$ defined by:

$$\begin{array}{r|r} (\!|\mathbf{a}|\!)_0(X) = X + 1 & (\!|\mathbf{a}|\!)_1(X) = X + 2 \\ (\!|\mathbf{b}|\!)_0(X) = X + 2 & (\!|\mathbf{b}|\!)_1(X) = X + 1 \\ (\!|\mathtt{f}_0|\!)_0(X) = X & (\!|\mathtt{f}_1|\!)_1(X) = X \end{array}$$

Ad absurdum, we prove that $\mathtt{p}_0 \bigsqcup \mathtt{p}_1$ admits no additive quasi-interpretation. Suppose that it admits the additive quasi-interpretation $(\!|-|\!)$. Since $(\!|-|\!)$ is additive, let $(\!|\mathbf{a}|\!)(X) = X + k_{\mathbf{a}}$ and $(\!|\mathbf{b}|\!)(X) = X + k_{\mathbf{b}}$, with $k_{\mathbf{a}}, k_{\mathbf{b}} \geq 1$. For the simplicity of the proof, suppose that the polynomial $(\!|\mathtt{f}_0|\!)$ can be written without max operation. For the first rule of $\mathtt{p}_0$, $(\!|\mathtt{f}_0|\!)$ has to verify the following inequality:

$$(\!|\mathtt{f}_0|\!)(X + k_{\mathbf{a}}) \geq (\!|\mathtt{f}_0|\!)((\!|\mathtt{f}_0|\!)(X))$$

Now, write $(\!|\mathtt{f}_0|\!)(X) = \alpha X^d + Q(X)$, where Q is a polynomial of degree strictly smaller than d. Observe that $(\!|\mathtt{f}_0|\!)(X + k_{\mathbf{a}})$ is of the shape $\alpha X^d + R(X)$, where R is a polynomial of degree strictly smaller than d, and that $(\!|\mathtt{f}_0|\!)((\!|\mathtt{f}_0|\!)(X))$ is of the shape $\alpha^2 X^{d^2} + S(X)$, where S is a polynomial of degree strictly smaller than d^2. For X large enough, the inequality above yields the following inequalities $d \geq d^2$ which gives $d = 1$. So, we can compare leading coefficient, $\alpha \geq \alpha^2$. So that, $\alpha = 1$ and, in conclusion, $(\!|\mathtt{f}_0|\!)(X) = X + k$. By symmetry, the same result holds for $(\!|\mathtt{f}_1|\!)(X) = X + k'$.

Now the last two rules imply the inequalities:

$$k_{\mathbf{b}} + k \geq 2k_{\mathbf{a}} + k$$
$$k_{\mathbf{a}} + k' \geq 2k_{\mathbf{b}} + k'$$

Consequently, $k_{\mathbf{a}} = k_{\mathbf{b}} = 0$, which is a contradiction with the requirement that $k_{\mathbf{a}}, k_{\mathbf{b}} \geq 1$. □

However, the complexity bounds remain correct even if the constructor-sharing union does not admit a quasi-interpretation. We establish that the Fundamental Lemma holds:

Theorem 3. *Given* $\mathtt{p}_1 = \langle \mathcal{X}_1, \mathcal{C}_1, \mathcal{F}_1, \mathcal{R}_1 \rangle$ *and* $\mathtt{p}_2 = \langle \mathcal{X}_2, \mathcal{C}_2, \mathcal{F}_2, \mathcal{R}_2 \rangle$*, two programs having an additive quasi-interpretation, there is a polynomial* P *such that for any term* t *of* $\mathtt{p}_1 \bigsqcup \mathtt{p}_2$ *which has* n *variables* $x_1, \cdots, x_n$*, and for any ground substitution* σ *such that* $x_i\sigma = v_i$*:*

$$|[\![t\sigma]\!]| \leq P^{|t|}(\max_{i=1..n} |v_i|)$$

Proof. The proof is a consequence of Lemma 1, by observing that there is no call between the two programs p_1 and p_2 of a constructor-sharing union $p_1 \bigsqcup p_2$. □

Together with the fact that $\prec_{rpo}$ is modular, Theorem 3 implies:

Corollary 1 (TIME and SPACE for constructor-sharing union)

- *The set of functions computed by constructor-sharing union of additive programs ordered by $\prec_{rpo}$ where each function symbol has a product status is exactly the set of functions computable in polynomial time.*
- *The set of functions computed by constructor-sharing union of additive programs ordered by $\prec_{rpo}$ is exactly the set of functions computable in polynomial space.*

Theorem 3 analyzes more programs like the counter-example built in the proof of Proposition 2. In fact, there are several meaningful examples based on coding/encoding procedures which are now captured, but which were not previously, by dividing the QI analyzing on subprograms of the original one. So, the time/space characterization that we have established, is intentionally more powerful than the previous ones. Moreover, it gives rise to an interesting and simple strategy for synthesizing quasi-interpretations, which consists in dividing a program into two sub-programs having disjoint sets of function symbols, and iterating this division as much as possible.

4 Hierarchical Union

Two programs $\langle \mathcal{X}_1, \mathcal{C}_1, \mathcal{F}_1, \mathcal{R}_1 \rangle$ and $\langle \mathcal{X}_2, \mathcal{C}_2, \mathcal{F}_2, \mathcal{R}_2 \rangle$ are hierarchical if

$$\mathcal{F}_1 \cap \mathcal{F}_2 = \mathcal{F}_2 \cap \mathcal{C}_1 = \emptyset \text{ and } \mathcal{C}_1 \cap \mathcal{C}_2 \neq \emptyset \text{ and } \mathcal{F}_1 \cap \mathcal{C}_2 \neq \emptyset$$

where symbols of $\mathcal{F}_1$ do not appear in patterns of $\mathcal{R}_2$. Their hierarchical union is defined as the program:

$$\langle \mathcal{X}_1, \mathcal{C}_1, \mathcal{F}_1, \mathcal{R}_1 \rangle \ll \langle \mathcal{X}_2, \mathcal{C}_2, \mathcal{F}_2, \mathcal{R}_2 \rangle = \langle \mathcal{X}_1 \cup \mathcal{X}_2, \mathcal{C}_1 \cup \mathcal{C}_2 - \mathcal{F}_1, \mathcal{F}_1 \cup \mathcal{F}_2, \mathcal{R}_1 \cup \mathcal{R}_2 \rangle$$

Notice that the hierarchical union is no longer a commutative operation in contrast to constructor-sharing union. Indeed, the program $\langle \mathcal{X}_2, \mathcal{C}_2, \mathcal{F}_2, \mathcal{R}_2 \rangle$ is calling function symbols of the program $\langle \mathcal{X}_1, \mathcal{C}_1, \mathcal{F}_1, \mathcal{R}_1 \rangle$ and the converse does not hold. In other words, the hierarchical union of programs $p_1 \ll p_2$ corresponds to a program p_2 which can load and execute libraries of p_1.

The hypothesis that patterns in $\mathcal{R}_2$ are over $\mathcal{C}_2 - \mathcal{F}_1$ symbols entails that there is no critical pair. Consequently, confluence is a modular property of hierarchical union and the semantics is well defined.

Proposition 3 (Modularity of $\prec_{rpo}$). *Assume that $\langle \mathcal{X}_1, \mathcal{C}_1, \mathcal{F}_1, \mathcal{R}_1 \rangle$ is a program ordered by $\prec_{rpo}$ with a status function st_1 and a precedence $\preceq_{\mathcal{F}_1}$ and $\langle \mathcal{X}_2, \mathcal{C}_2, \mathcal{F}_2, \mathcal{R}_2 \rangle$ is a program ordered by $\prec_{rpo}$ with a status function st_2 and a precedence $\preceq_{\mathcal{F}_2}$, then $\langle \mathcal{X}_1, \mathcal{C}_1, \mathcal{F}_1, \mathcal{R}_1 \rangle \ll \langle \mathcal{X}_2, \mathcal{C}_2, \mathcal{F}_2, \mathcal{R}_2 \rangle$ is ordered by $\prec_{rpo}$*

Since the constructor-sharing union is a particular case of hierarchical union , the following holds:

Proposition 4. *The property of having an additive quasi-interpretation is not a modular property w.r.t. hierarchical union.*

Moreover, contrarily to what happened with constructor-sharing union, the Fundamental Lemma does not hold. That is why we separate both cases. Here is a counter-example:

Example 2. The programs $\mathtt{p}_1$ and $\mathtt{p}_2$ are given by the rules:

$\mathtt{d}(\mathbf{S}(x)) \to \mathbf{S}(\mathbf{S}(\mathtt{d}(x)))$	$\exp(\mathbf{S}(x)) \to \mathtt{d}(\exp(x))$
$\mathtt{d}(\mathbf{0}) \to \mathbf{0}$	$\exp(\mathbf{0}) \to \mathbf{S}(\mathbf{0})$

$\mathtt{p}_1$ and $\mathtt{p}_2$ are ordered by $\prec_{rpo}$ with product status and admit the following additive quasi-interpretations:

$(\!\vert\mathbf{0}\vert\!)_1 = 0$	$(\!\vert\mathbf{0}\vert\!)_2 = 0$
$(\!\vert\mathbf{S}\vert\!)_1(X) = X+1$	$(\!\vert\mathbf{S}\vert\!)_2(X) = (\!\vert\mathtt{d}\vert\!)_2(X) = X+1$
$(\!\vert\mathtt{d}\vert\!)_1(X) = 2 \times X$	$(\!\vert\exp\vert\!)_2(X) = X+1$

$\mathtt{d}$ can be viewed as a constructor symbol whose quasi-interpretation is additive in $\mathtt{p}_2$ whereas it is a function symbol whose quasi-interpretation is affine in $\mathtt{p}_1$. The exponential comes from the distinct kinds of polynomial allowed for $\mathtt{d}$.

From now on, some restrictions which preserve the Fundamental Lemma are established. In order to avoid the previous counter-example, we put restriction on the shape of the polynomials allowed for the quasi-interpretations of the shared symbols in a criteria called Kind preserving.

For that purpose, define an *honest polynomial* to be a polynomial, without the max operation, whose coefficients are greater or equal to 1. By extension, define the QI $(\!\vert-\vert\!)$ to be honest if $(\!\vert b\vert\!)$ is honest for every symbol b. Honest polynomials are very common in practice because of the subterm property.

Given n variables $X_1, \cdots, X_n$ and n natural numbers $a_1, \cdots, a_n$, define a monomial m to be a polynomial of one term, of the shape $m(X_1, \cdots, X_n) = X_1^{a_1} \times \ldots \times X_n^{a_n}$ where some $a_j \neq 0$. Given a monomial m and a polynomial P, define $m \sqsubseteq P$ iff $P = \sum_{j=1}^{k} \alpha_j \times m_j$, with α_j constants and m_j pairwise distinct monomials, and there is $i \in \{1, k\}$ s.t. $m_i = m$ and $\alpha_i \neq 0$. The coefficient α_i, also noted $\mathtt{coef}_P(m)$, is defined to be the multiplicative coefficient associated to m in P.

Definition 5. *Assume that $\langle \mathcal{X}_1, \mathcal{C}_1, \mathcal{F}_1, \mathcal{R}_1 \rangle \ll \langle \mathcal{X}_2, \mathcal{C}_2, \mathcal{F}_2, \mathcal{R}_2 \rangle$ is the hierarchical union of two programs with respective polynomial QIs $(\!\vert-\vert\!)_1$ and $(\!\vert-\vert\!)_2$. We say that $(\!\vert-\vert\!)_1$ and $(\!\vert-\vert\!)_2$ are* ***Kind preserving*** *if $\forall b \in \mathcal{C}_2 \cap \mathcal{F}_1$:*

1. *$(\!\vert b\vert\!)_1$ and $(\!\vert b\vert\!)_2$ are honest polynomials*
2. *$\forall m,\ m \sqsubseteq (\!\vert b\vert\!)_1 \Leftrightarrow m \sqsubseteq (\!\vert b\vert\!)_2$*

3. $\forall m,\ \mathtt{coef}_{(\!|b|\!)_2}(m) = 1 \Leftrightarrow \mathtt{coef}_{(\!|b|\!)_1}(m) = 1$

Two Kind preserving QIs $(\!|-|\!)_1$ *and* $(\!|-|\!)_2$ *are called* ***additive Kind preserving*** *if the following conditions are satisfied:*

- $(\!|b|\!)_1$ *is additive for every* $b \in \mathcal{C}_1$,
- $(\!|b|\!)_2$ *is additive for every* $b \in \mathcal{C}_2 - \mathcal{F}_1$.

Notice that $(\!|b|\!)_2$ is not necessarily additive for $b \in \mathcal{C}_2 \cap \mathcal{F}_1$. The QI $(\!|-|\!)_1$ and $(\!|-|\!)_2$ of example 2 are not additive Kind preserving since we have $(\!|\mathtt{d}|\!)_1(X) = 2 \times X$ and $(\!|\mathtt{d}|\!)_2(X) = X + 1$.

Consequently, an interesting restriction for preserving the Fundamental Lemma might be to force the quasi-interpretations of a hierarchical union to be additive Kind preserving. However, this restriction is not enough as illustrated by the following program:

Example 3. Consider the following respective programs $\mathtt{p}_1$ (on the left) and $\mathtt{p}_2$:

$\mathtt{g}(t) \rightarrow \mathbf{S}(\mathbf{S}(t))$	$\mathtt{f}(\mathbf{S}(x), \mathbf{0}, t) \rightarrow \mathtt{f}(x, t, t)$
	$\mathtt{f}(x, \mathbf{S}(z), t) \rightarrow \mathtt{f}(x, z, \mathtt{g}(t))$
	$\mathtt{f}(\mathbf{0}, \mathbf{0}, t) \rightarrow t$

Their hierarchical union $\mathtt{p}_1 \ll \mathtt{p}_2$ computes an exponential function. Using the notation $\underline{n}$ for $\underbrace{\mathbf{S}(\ldots\mathbf{S}(\mathbf{0})\ldots)}_{n \text{ times } \mathbf{S}}$, we have $\underline{[\![\mathtt{f}]\!](\underline{n}, \underline{m}, \underline{p}) = 3^n \times (2 \times m + p)}$.

$\mathtt{p}_1$ and $\mathtt{p}_2$ are ordered by $\prec_{rpo}$ with lexicographic status and admit the following additive Kind preserving quasi-interpretations:

	$(\!|\mathbf{0}|\!)_2 = 0$
$(\!|\mathbf{S}|\!)_1(X) = X + 1$	$(\!|\mathbf{S}|\!)_2(X) = (\!|\mathtt{g}|\!)_2(X) = X + 1$
$(\!|\mathtt{g}|\!)_1(X) = X + 2$	$(\!|\mathtt{f}|\!)_2(X, Y, Z) = \max(X, Y, Z)$

The problem of the above counter-example comes directly from the fact that the number of alternations between rules of both programs used during the evaluation depends on the inputs. A way to deal with Kind preserving QIs is to bound the number of alternations by some constant. For that purpose, we also put some syntactic restrictions over the considered programs, considering a notion of flat programs introduced by Dershowitz in [12], where it was used in order to ensure modularity of completeness of hierarchical unions.

Definition 6. *The hierarchical union* $\langle \mathcal{X}_1, \mathcal{C}_1, \mathcal{F}_1, \mathcal{R}_1 \rangle \ll \langle \mathcal{X}_2, \mathcal{C}_2, \mathcal{F}_2, \mathcal{R}_2 \rangle$ *is called stratified if*

- *For all rule* $f(p_1, \cdots, p_n) \rightarrow e$ *in* $\mathcal{R}_2$, *we have: For each* $g(e_1, \cdots, e_n)$ *subterm of* e *such that* $g \approx_{\mathcal{F}_2} f$, *no (shared) function symbols of* $\mathcal{C}_2 \cap \mathcal{F}_1$ *occurs in the arguments* $e_1, \cdots, e_n$ *of* g.
- *The program* $\langle \mathcal{X}_2, \mathcal{C}_2, \mathcal{F}_2, \mathcal{R}_2 \rangle$ *is flat: For every rule* $f(p_1, \cdots, p_n) \rightarrow e$ *of* $\mathcal{R}_2$, e *has no nesting of function symbols. In other words,* e *is a term without composition of function symbols in* $\mathcal{F}_2$.

The examples of this paper (see in particular Section 5) illustrate the fact that the restriction on the stratified union is not harsh.

Theorem 4. *Given two programs* $p_1 = \langle \mathcal{X}_1, \mathcal{C}_1, \mathcal{F}_1, \mathcal{R}_1 \rangle$ *and* $p_2 = \langle \mathcal{X}_2, \mathcal{C}_2, \mathcal{F}_2, \mathcal{R}_2 \rangle$ *having additive Kind preserving quasi-interpretations* $(\!-\!)_1$ *and* $(\!-\!)_2$ *and their stratified union* $p_1 \ll p_2$, *the Fundamental Lemma holds:*

There is a polynomial P *such that for any term* t *of* $p_1 \ll p_2$ *which has* n *variables* $x_1, \cdots, x_n$, *and for any ground substitution* σ *such that* $x_i \sigma = v_i$:

$$\| [\![t\sigma]\!] \| \leq P^{|t|}(\max_{i=1..n} |v_i|)$$

Proof. The proof relies on two Lemmas.

The first Lemma states that every stratified union is evaluated using a strategy of the shape $t \xrightarrow{*}_2 u_1 \xrightarrow{*}_1 v_1 \ldots \xrightarrow{*}_2 u_k \xrightarrow{*}_1 v_k$ with the number of alternations k between rules of p_1 and rules of p_2 bounded by some constant.

The second Lemma states that given two Kind preserving QIs $(\!-\!)_1$ and $(\!-\!)_2$, there exist two polynomials Q and P such that for every term t we have $(\!t\!)_1 \leq P((\!t\!)_2)$ and $(\!t\!)_2 \leq Q((\!t\!)_1)$.

Combined with Lemma 1, we obtain:

$$|v_k| \leq (\!v_k\!)_2 \leq (Q \circ P)^k (P((\!t\!)_2)) \leq (Q \circ P)^k (P(S(\max_{i=1..n} |w_i|)))$$

for some polynomial S and some inputs $w_1, \cdots, w_n$. $\qquad\qquad\square$

Example 4. Consider the following programs p_1 and p_2:

$$\mathbf{d(S}(x)) \to \mathbf{S(S(d}(x))) \qquad\qquad \mathbf{sq(S}(x)) \to \mathbf{S(add(sq}(x), \mathbf{d}(x)))$$
$$\mathbf{d}(\mathbf{0}) \to \mathbf{0} \qquad\qquad\qquad\qquad \mathbf{sq(0)} \to \mathbf{0}$$

- - - - - - - - - - -

$$\mathbf{add(S}(x), y) \to \mathbf{S(add}(x, y))$$
$$\mathbf{add}(\mathbf{0}, y) \to y$$

Their hierarchical union $p_1 \ll p_2 = \langle \mathcal{X}, \mathcal{C}, \mathcal{F}, \mathcal{R} \rangle$ computes the square of a unary number given as input. For the precedence $\geq_{\mathcal{F}}$, we have $\mathbf{sq} >_{\mathcal{F}} \{\mathbf{add}, \mathbf{d}\}$. Moreover the program p_2 is flat since there is no composition of function symbols in its rules. Consequently, $p_1 \ll p_2$ is a stratified union, since the argument of the recursive call $\mathbf{sq}(x)$ is a variable. Both p_1 and p_2 are ordered by $\prec_{rpo}$ with product status. Define the quasi-interpretations $(\!-\!)_1$ and $(\!-\!)_2$ by:

$$\begin{aligned} (\!\mathbf{0}\!)_1 &= 0 \\ (\!\mathbf{S}\!)_1(X) &= X + 1 \\ (\!\mathbf{d}\!)_1(X) &= 2 \times X \\ (\!\mathbf{add}\!)_1(X, Y) &= X + Y \end{aligned} \qquad\qquad \begin{aligned} (\!\mathbf{0}\!)_2 &= 0 \\ (\!\mathbf{S}\!)_2(X) &= X + 1 \\ (\!\mathbf{d}\!)_2(X) &= 2 \times X \\ (\!\mathbf{add}\!)_2(X, Y) &= X + Y + 1 \\ (\!\mathbf{sq}\!)_2(X) &= 2 \times X^2 \end{aligned}$$

$(\!-\!)_1$ and $(\!-\!)_2$ are additive Kind preserving QIs, so that the program $p_1 \ll p_2$ computes values whose size is polynomially bounded by the inputs size.

Moreover, the program division can be iterated on p_1 by separating the rules for function symbols $\mathbf{add}$ and $\mathbf{d}$, thus obtaining a constructor-sharing union.

Corollary 2 (TIME **and** SPACE **for hierarchical union of Kind preserving QIs).** *The set of functions computed by a hierarchical union of two programs* $\mathtt{p}_1$ *and* $\mathtt{p}_2$ *such that*

1. $\mathtt{p}_1 \ll \mathtt{p}_2$ *is a stratified union,*
2. $\mathtt{p}_1$ *and* $\mathtt{p}_2$ *admit the respective additive Kind preserving QIs* $(\!|-|\!)_1$ *and* $(\!|-|\!)_2$*,*
3. $\mathtt{p}_1$ *and* $\mathtt{p}_2$ *are ordered by* $\prec_{rpo}$ *and each function symbol has a product status,*

is exactly the set of functions computable in polynomial time.

Moreover, if condition (3) is replaced by: $\mathtt{p}_1$ *and* $\mathtt{p}_2$ *are ordered by* $\prec_{rpo}$ *then we characterize exactly the class of polynomial space functions.*

Proof. Again, this result is a consequence of the fact that we have the Fundamental Lemma in Proposition 4 and the $\prec_{rpo}$ ordering with product status. □

We have established a new decomposition of programs, called stratified union, which guarantees that the Fundamental Lemma remains correct. Such a decomposition is a necessary condition in order to preserve the polynomial bound, as illustrated by the above counter-examples. Thus, we obtain a new way of dividing programs in a synthesis perspective which is more flexible than in the constructor-sharing case. Consequently, it improves the time complexity of the QI search algorithm.

5 Application to Higher-Order Programs

Resource control of higher-order programs by QI is a tricky task, because we should deal at first glance with higher-order assignments. However, higher-order mechanisms can be reduced to an equivalent first order functional program by *defunctionalization*, which was introduced by Reynolds [29]. Defunctionalization consists in two steps. First, a new constructor symbol is substituted to every higher-order function declaration. Second, each function application is eliminated by introducing a new function symbol for application. We refer to Danvy [10] which investigates works related to defunctionalization and Continuation-Passing style and gives a lot of references.

Now, we show how to use modularity of QI in order to control resources of higher-order programs. Since this is an application of the previous Sections and due to the lack of space, we illustrate the key concepts without formalizing higher-order programs.

Example 5. Suppose that $\mathtt{g}$ is defined by a program $\mathtt{q}_3$. Consider the following higher-order program $\mathtt{p}$.

$$\begin{aligned} \mathtt{fold}(\lambda x.\mathtt{f}(x), \mathbf{nil}) &\to \mathbf{0} \\ \mathtt{fold}(\lambda x.\mathtt{f}(x), \mathbf{c}(y,l)) &\to \mathtt{f}(\mathtt{fold}(\lambda x.\mathtt{f}(x), l)) \\ \mathtt{h}(l) &\to \mathtt{fold}(\lambda x.\mathtt{g}(x), l) \qquad \text{for } \mathtt{g} \text{ defined in } \mathtt{q}_3 \end{aligned}$$

$\mathtt{h}(l)$ iterates g such that $[\![\mathtt{h}]\!](l) = [\![\mathtt{g}]\!]^n(0)$ where n is the number of elements in the list l. From $\mathtt{p}$, we obtain $\hat{\mathtt{p}}$ by defunctionalization:

$$\mathtt{q}_1 = \begin{cases} \hat{\mathtt{fold}}(\mathbf{nil}) \to \mathbf{0} \\ \hat{\mathtt{fold}}(\mathbf{c}(y,l)) \to \mathbf{app}(\mathbf{c}_0, \hat{\mathtt{fold}}(l)) & \mathbf{c}_0 \text{ is a new constructor} \\ \hat{\mathtt{h}}(l) \to \hat{\mathtt{fold}}(l) \end{cases}$$

$$\mathtt{q}_2 = \{\, \mathbf{app}(\mathbf{c}_0, x) \to \mathbf{g}(x)$$

We are now able to use QI to higher-order programs by considering their first-order transformations. In fact, the above example illustrates the fact that a defunctionalized program $\hat{p}$ is divided into three parts: the programs $\mathtt{q}_1$ and $\mathtt{q}_2$ above and a program $\mathtt{q}_3$ which computes $\mathbf{g}$. Notice that the hierarchical union of $\mathtt{q}_2 \ll \mathtt{q}_1$ is stratified. Moreover, it admits the following additive Kind preserving QIs:

$$\begin{aligned} (\!|\hat{\mathtt{fold}}|\!)_1(X) = (\!|\mathtt{h}|\!)_1(X) &= X \\ (\!|\mathbf{c}|\!)_1(X,Y) &= X+Y+1 \\ (\!|\mathbf{0}|\!)_1 = (\!|\mathbf{c}_0|\!)_1 = (\!|\mathbf{nil}|\!)_1 &= 0 \\ (\!|\mathbf{app}|\!)_1(X,Y) &= X+Y+1 \end{aligned} \qquad \Bigg| \qquad \begin{aligned} (\!|\mathbf{g}|\!)_2(X) &= X+1 \\ (\!|\mathbf{c}_0|\!)_2 &= 0 \\ (\!|\mathbf{app}|\!)_2(X,Y) &= X+Y+1 \end{aligned}$$

Now, the results on modularity that we have previously established, allow us to give a sufficient condition on the QI of $\mathbf{g}$ defined in $\mathtt{q}_3$, in order to guarantee that the computation remains polynomially bounded. Indeed, Proposition 4 implies that $(\!|\mathbf{g}|\!)_3$ should be Kind preserving. That is, $(\!|\mathbf{g}|\!)_3(X) = (\!|\mathbf{g}|\!)_2(X)+\alpha = X+\alpha+1$, where α is some constant. Notice that $(\!|\mathbf{g}|\!)_2$ is forced by $(\!|\mathbf{app}|\!)_2$, and on the other hand $(\!|\mathbf{app}|\!)_2$ is forced by $(\!|\mathbf{app}|\!)_1$.

Example 6. Consider the following program $\mathtt{p}$, which visits a list l in Continuation-Passing style.

$$\begin{aligned} \mathtt{visit}(\mathbf{nil}, \lambda x.\mathtt{f}(x), y) &\to \mathtt{f}(y) \\ \mathtt{visit}(\mathbf{c}(z,l), \lambda x.\mathtt{f}(x), y) &\to \mathtt{visit}(l, \lambda x.\mathtt{g}_1(\mathtt{f}(x)), y) \\ \mathtt{h}(l) &\to \mathtt{visit}(l, \lambda x.\mathtt{g}_0(x), 0) \end{aligned}$$

where $\mathtt{g}_0$ and $\mathtt{g}_1$ are defined by some program $\mathtt{q}_3$ which admits an additive QI $(\!|\_|\!)_3$. We have $[\![\mathtt{h}]\!](l) = [\![\mathtt{g}_1]\!]^n([\![\mathtt{g}_0]\!](0))$ where n is the number of elements in the list l. We obtain $\hat{\mathtt{p}}$

$$\mathtt{q}_1 = \begin{cases} \hat{\mathtt{visit}}(\mathbf{nil}, k, y) \to \mathbf{app}(k, y) \\ \hat{\mathtt{visit}}(\mathbf{c}(z,l), k, y) \to \hat{\mathtt{visit}}(l, \mathbf{c}_1(k), y) \\ \mathtt{h}(l) \to \hat{\mathtt{visit}}(l, \mathbf{c}_0, 0) & \mathbf{c}_0 \text{ and } \mathbf{c}_1 \text{ are new constructors} \end{cases}$$

$$\mathtt{q}_2 = \begin{cases} \mathbf{app}(\mathbf{c}_0, x) \to \mathbf{g}_0(x) \\ \mathbf{app}(\mathbf{c}_1(k), x) \to \mathbf{g}_1(\mathbf{app}(k, x)) \end{cases}$$

The hierarchical union $\mathtt{q}_2 \ll \mathtt{q}_1$ is stratified and admits the following additive Kind preserving QIs:

$$(\!|\hat{\mathtt{visit}}|\!)_1(X) = (\!|\mathtt{h}|\!)_1(X) = X+1 \qquad (\!|\mathbf{g}_1|\!)_2(X) = (\!|\mathbf{g}_0|\!)_2(X) = X+1$$
$$(\!|\mathbf{c}_1|\!)_1(X,Y) = (\!|\mathbf{c}|\!)_1(X,Y) = X+Y+1 \qquad (\!|\mathbf{c}_1|\!)_2(X) = X+1$$
$$(\!|\mathbf{0}|\!)_1 = (\!|\mathbf{c}_0|\!)_1 = (\!|\mathbf{nil}|\!)_1 = 0 \qquad (\!|\mathbf{0}|\!)_2 = (\!|\mathbf{c}_0|\!)_2 = 0$$
$$(\!|\mathsf{app}|\!)_1(X,Y) = X+Y+1 \qquad (\!|\mathsf{app}|\!)_2(X,Y) = X+Y+1$$

Now, suppose that we have two QI $(\!|\mathbf{g}_0|\!)_3$ and $(\!|\mathbf{g}_1|\!)_3$, which are two resource certificates for $\mathbf{g}_0$ and $\mathbf{g}_1$ wrt $\mathtt{q}_3$. Proposition 4 states that we are sure to remain polynomial if the QI of $\mathbf{g}_0$ and $\mathbf{g}_1$ are Kind preserving. In other words, $(\!|\mathbf{g}_0|\!)_3(X) = X+\alpha$ and $(\!|\mathbf{g}_1|\!)_3(X) = X+\beta$ for some constants α and β.

So, a modular approach is a way to predict safely and efficiently if we can apply a function in a higher-order computational mechanism.

Finally, we state the following characterizations:

Theorem 5 (Modularity and higher-order programs). *The set of functions computed by a higher-order program* $\mathtt{p}$ *such that the defunctionalization* $\hat{\mathtt{p}}$ *is defined by hierarchical union* $\mathtt{p}_1 \ll \mathtt{p}_2$ *of two programs* $\mathtt{p}_1$ *and* $\mathtt{p}_2$ *satisfying:*

1. $\mathtt{p}_1 \ll \mathtt{p}_2$ *is a stratified union,*
2. $\mathtt{p}_1$ *and* $\mathtt{p}_2$ *admit the respective additive Kind preserving QIs* $(\!|-|\!)_1$ *and* $(\!|-|\!)_2$*,*
3. $\mathtt{p}_1$ *and* $\mathtt{p}_2$ *are ordered by* $\prec_{rpo}$ *and each function symbol has a product status,*

is exactly the set of functions computable in polynomial time.

Moreover, if condition (3) is replaced by: $\mathtt{p}_1$ *and* $\mathtt{p}_2$ *are ordered by* $\prec_{rpo}$ *then we characterize exactly the class of polynomial space functions.*

References

1. Amadio, R.: Max-plus quasi-interpretations. In: Hofmann, M.O. (ed.) TLCA 2003. LNCS, vol. 2701, pp. 31–45. Springer, Heidelberg (2003)
2. Amadio, R., Coupet-Grimal, S., Dal-Zilio, S., Jakubiec, L.: A functional scenario for bytecode verification of resource bounds. In: Marcinkowski, J., Tarlecki, A. (eds.) CSL 2004. LNCS, vol. 3210, pp. 265–279. Springer, Heidelberg (2004)
3. Amadio, R., Dal-Zilio, S.: Resource control for synchronous cooperative threads. In: Gardner, P., Yoshida, N. (eds.) CONCUR 2004. LNCS, vol. 3170, pp. 68–82. Springer, Heidelberg (2004)
4. Baillot, P., Terui, K.: A feasible algorithm for typing in elementary affine logic. In: Urzyczyn, P. (ed.) TLCA 2005. LNCS, vol. 3461, pp. 55–70. Springer, Heidelberg (2005)
5. Bonfante, G., Marion, J.-Y., Moyen, J.-Y.: On lexicographic termination ordering with space bound certifications. In: Bjørner, D., Broy, M., Zamulin, A.V. (eds.) PSI 2001. LNCS, vol. 2244, Springer, Heidelberg (2001)
6. Bonfante, G., Marion, J.-Y., Moyen, J.-Y.: Quasi-interpretation a way to control resources. Submitted to Theoretical Computer Science (2005), `http://www.loria.fr/~marionjy`
7. Bonfante, G., Marion, J.-Y., Moyen, J.-Y., Péchoux, R.: Synthesis of quasi-interpretations. In: LCC2005, LICS affiliated Workshop (2005), `http://hal.inria.fr/`

8. Coppola, P., Rocca, S.R.D.: Principal typing for lambda calculus in elementary affine logic. Fundamenta Informaticae 65(1-2), 87–112 (2005)
9. Dal-Zilio, S., Gascon, R.: Resource bound certification for a tail-recursive virtual machine. In: Yi, K. (ed.) APLAS 2005. LNCS, vol. 3780, pp. 247–263. Springer, Heidelberg (2005)
10. Danvy, O.: An analytical approach to programs as data objects, Doctor Scientarum degree in Computer Science. BRICS. Departement of Computer Science. University of Aarhus (2006)
11. Dershowitz, N.: Orderings for term-rewriting systems. Theoretical Computer Science 17(3), 279–301 (1982)
12. Dershowitz, N.: Hierachical termination. In: Lindenstrauss, N., Dershowitz, N. (eds.) CTRS 1994. LNCS, vol. 968, Springer, Heidelberg (1995)
13. Girard, J.-Y.: Light linear logic. Information and Computation 143(2), 175–204 (1998)
14. Gramlich, B.: Generalized sufficient conditions for modular termination of rewriting. In: Kirchner, H., Levi, G. (eds.) ALP 1992. LNCS, vol. 632, pp. 53–68. Springer, Heidelberg (1992)
15. Hofmann, M.: A type system for bounded space and functional in-place update. Nordic Journal of Computing 7(4), 258–289 (2000)
16. Hofmann, M.: The strength of Non-Size Increasing computation. In: POPL, pp. 260–269 (2002)
17. Huet, G.: Confluent reductions: Abstract properties and applications to term rewriting systems. Journal of the ACM 27(4), 797–821 (1980)
18. Jones, N.D.: Computability and complexity, from a programming perspective. MIT Press, Cambridge (1997)
19. Klop, J.W.: Term rewriting systems. In: Handbook of logic in Computer Science, vol. 2, pp. 1–116. Oxford University Press, Oxford (1992)
20. Kristiansen, L., Jones, N.D.: The flow of data and the complexity of algorithms. In: Cooper, S.B., Löwe, B., Torenvliet, L. (eds.) CiE 2005. LNCS, vol. 3526, pp. 263–274. Springer, Heidelberg (2005)
21. Kurihara, M., Ohuchi, A.: Modularity of simple termination of term rewriting systems with shared constructors. Theoretical Computer Science 103, 273–282 (1992)
22. Lafont, Y.: Soft linear logic and polynomial time. Theoretical Computer Science 318, 163–180 (2004)
23. Marion, J.-Y., Moyen, J.-Y.: Efficient first order functional program interpreter with time bound certifications. In: Parigot, M., Voronkov, A. (eds.) LPAR 2000. LNCS (LNAI), vol. 1955, pp. 25–42. Springer, Heidelberg (2000)
24. Marion, J.-Y., Moyen, J.-Y.: Heap analysis for assembly programs. Technical report, Loria (2006)
25. Middeldorp, A.: Modular properties of term rewriting Systems. PhD thesis, Vrije Universiteit te Amsterdam (1990)
26. Niggl, K.-H., Wunderlich, H.: Certifying polynomial time and linear/polynomial space for imperative programs. SIAM Journal on Computing 35(5), 1122–1147 (2006)
27. Ohlebusch, E.: Advanced Topics in Term Rewriting. Springer, Heidelberg (2002)
28. Krishna Rao, M.R.K.: Modular proofs of completeness of hierarchical term rewriting systems. Theoretical Computer Science 151, 487–512 (1995)
29. Reynolds, J.C.: Definitional interpreters for higher-order programming languages. In: ACM, pp. 717–740. ACM Press, New York (1972)
30. Toyama, Y.: Counterexamples for the direct sum of term rewriting systems. Information Processing Letters 25, 141–143 (1987)
31. Toyama, Y.: On the church-rosser property for the direct sum of term rewriting systems. Journal of the ACM 34(1), 128–143 (1987)

Composing Transformations to Optimize Linear Code

Thomas Noll and Stefan Rieger

RWTH Aachen University
Software Modeling and Verification Group
52056 Aachen, Germany
{noll,rieger}@cs.rwth-aachen.de

Abstract. We study the effect of an optimizing algorithm for straight–line code which first constructs a directed acyclic graph representing the given program and then generates code from it. We show that this algorithm produces optimal code with respect to the classical transformations known as Constant Folding, Common Subexpression Elimination, and Dead Code Elimination. In contrast to the former, the latter are also applicable to iterative code containing loops. We can show that the graph–based algorithm essentially corresponds to a combination of the three classical optimizations in conjunction with Copy Propagation. Thus, apart from its theoretical importance, this result is relevant for practical compiler design as it potentially allows to exploit the optimization potential of the graph–based algorithm for non–linear code as well.

1 Introduction

Literature on optimizing compilers describes a wide variety of code transformations which aim at improving the efficiency of the generated code with respect to different parameters. Most of them concentrate on specific aspects such as the elimination of redundant computations or the minimization of register usage. There are, however, also combined methods which integrate several optimization steps in one procedure.

In this paper we compare several classical optimizing transformations for straight–line code with a combined procedure which first constructs a directed acyclic graph (DAG) representing the given program and then generates optimized code from it. The basic version of the latter has been introduced in [3], and the authors claim that it produces optimal results[1] regarding the length of the generated code. However the DAG procedure cannot directly be applied to iterative code containing loops, which on the other hand is possible for most of the classical transformations.

Although our analysis is limited to straight–line code in this contribution we have plans to extend it to iterative programs in the future.

In this paper we first present a slightly modified version of the DAG algorithm that in addition supports constant folding. We do not consider algebraic

[1] The optimality is given w.r.t. strong equivalence, see Sec. 2.

C.B. Jones, Z. Liu, J. Woodcock (Eds.): ICTAC 2007, LNCS 4711, pp. 425–439, 2007.

optimizations though, since our framework is independent of the interpretation of operator and constant symbols. Our results thus hold for arbitrary interpretations over any domain. We show that the DAG algorithm integrates the following three classical transformations:

Constant Folding, corresponding to a partial evaluation of the program with respect to a given interpretation of its constant and operation symbols;
Common Subexpression Elimination, aiming to decrease the execution time by avoiding multiple evaluations of the same (sub-)expression; and
Dead Code Elimination, removing computations that do not contribute to the actual result of the program.

It will turn out that these transformations are not sufficient to completely encompass the optimizing effect of the DAG algorithm. Rather a fourth transformation, *Copy Propagation*, has to be added, which propagates values in variable–copy assignments. This does not have an optimizing effect on its own but generally enables other transformations such as Common Subexpression Elimination and Dead Code Elimination, thus it is treated separately in an extra section.

Our investigation will be carried out in a framework in which we develop formal definitions for concepts such as linear programs and their semantics, (optimizing) program transformations, their correctness and their equivalence, etc. These preliminaries will be presented in Sec. 2, followed by the definition of the three classical transformations and of the DAG–based algorithm in Sec. 3 and 4, respectively. The subsequent Sec. 5 constitutes the main part of this paper, establishing the equivalence between the DAG procedure and the composition of the classical transformations.

To support the experimenting with concrete examples, a web–based implementation of the optimizing transformations is available at the URL [8].

Moreover we would like to mention that this paper is a condensed version of our technical report [7] which presents complete proofs for all of the propositions and includes more details and examples regarding the algorithms presented here.

2 SLC–Programs and Their Properties

Straight–line code (SLC) constitutes the basic blocks of the intermediate code of iterative programs. In particular it is contained in loop bodies whose efficient execution is crucial.

Syntax

An SLC–program consists of a sequence of assignments using simple arithmetic expressions without branching or loops.

A *signature* is a pair $\Sigma = (F, C)$ consisting of a finite set of *function symbols* (or: *operation symbols*) $F := \bigcup_{i=1}^{\infty} F^{(i)}$ where $F^{(i)}$ denotes the set of i–ary function symbols, and a set of *constant symbols* C. Furthermore $V := \{x, y, z, \ldots\}$ denotes a possibly infinite set of variables.

An *SLC–program* is a quadruple $\pi = (\Sigma, \boldsymbol{v}_{in}, \boldsymbol{v}_{out}, \beta)$ with a signature $\Sigma = (F, C)$, a vector of *input variables* $\boldsymbol{v}_{in} = (x_1, \ldots, x_s)$ $(x_i \in V)$, a vector of *output variables* $\boldsymbol{v}_{out} = (y_1, \ldots, y_t)$ $(y_i \in V)$ where all input and output variables are pairwise distinct, and a *block* $\beta = \alpha_1; \alpha_2; \ldots; \alpha_n$ with *instructions* α_i of the form $x \leftarrow e$ where $x \in V$ and $e \in (V \setminus \{x\}) \cup C \cup \{f(u_1, \ldots, u_r) \mid f \in F^{(r)}$ and $\forall j \in \{1,..,r\} : u_j \in V \cup C\}$.

In addition every program is assumed to be *complete* in the sense that every variable is defined before being used (with the understanding that every input variable x_i is defined in the beginning while every output variable y_j is used in the end).

Moreover we introduce the following denotations: V_{in} and V_{out} denote the *sets* of input/output variables of π, C_π and V_π the sets of constant symbols and variables occurring in π, respectively, and V_α and V_e stand for the set of variables in the instruction α and in the expression e, respectively. Finally, $\mathcal{SLC}$ denotes the set of all SLC–programs.

Figure 1 shows a simple SLC–program over the signature $\Sigma_\mathbb{Z} := (\{+^{(2)}, *^{(2)}, -^{(2)}\}, \mathbb{Z})$. For simplicity we employed the usual infix notation.

$$
\begin{array}{rll}
\boldsymbol{v}_{in}: & (x, y) & \\
\beta: & u & \leftarrow 3; \\
 & v & \leftarrow x - y; \\
 & w & \leftarrow u + 1; \\
 & x & \leftarrow x - y; \\
 & v & \leftarrow w - 1; \\
 & u & \leftarrow x - y; \\
 & z & \leftarrow u * w; \\
 & u & \leftarrow 2 * u; \\
\boldsymbol{v}_{out}: & (u, v) &
\end{array}
$$

Fig. 1. An SLC–program

Semantics

The semantics of an SLC–program depends on the domain of the variables and on the interpretation of the operators and constant symbols. These are formally given by a Σ–algebra $\mathfrak{A} := (A, \varphi)$ with *domain (universe)* A and *interpretation function* $\varphi : F \cup C \cup A \to \bigcup_{i=0}^{\infty} \{\delta \mid \delta : A^i \to A\}$ where $\varphi(f) : A^r \to A$ for every $f \in F^{(r)}$, $\varphi(c) \in A$ for every $c \in C$, and $\varphi(a) = a$ for every $a \in A$.[2]

The current state in the computation of an SLC–program can be expressed as a mapping of the program's variables to their values: $\sigma : V_\pi \to A$. This induces the *state space* $S := \{\sigma \mid \sigma : V_\pi \to A\}$.

Now every instruction $\alpha = x \leftarrow e$ determines a transformation $\mathfrak{A}[\![\alpha]\!] : S \to S$ of one state into another: the variable x is associated with the value resulting from the evaluation of the expression e. By composing the transformations of the instructions in a program π we obtain its semantics as a function that maps a vector representing the input values to a vector that contains the values of the output variables, that is, $\mathfrak{A}[\![\pi]\!] : A^s \to A^t$.

Note that the semantics is defined independent of the variable names, only the order of the variables in the input/output vectors is relevant. Moreover due to the completeness conditions on programs it suffices to give the values of the input variables; non–input variables can be initialized arbitrarily.

Equivalence and Optimality

For optimizations program equivalence is of high significance since programs have to be transformed in such a way that their semantics is preserved.

[2] Requiring the latter will turn out to be useful for constant folding; see Sec. 3 for details.

Two SLC–programs π_1 and π_2 over some signature Σ are called *$\mathfrak{A}$–equivalent* for a Σ–algebra $\mathfrak{A}$ ($\pi_1 \sim_{\mathfrak{A}} \pi_2$) iff $\mathfrak{A}[\![\pi_1]\!] = \mathfrak{A}[\![\pi_2]\!]$. If this holds for all interpretations $\mathfrak{A}$ then they are called *strongly equivalent* ($\pi_1 \sim \pi_2$).

Note that (strong) equivalence of two programs requires that both have the same number of input and of output variables. The $\mathfrak{A}$–equivalence of two programs is generally undecidable [5]. This, however, is not the case for strong equivalence [7].

Assessing the quality of an optimization requires a notion of cost. As standard cost functions we will use the number of instructions and the number of operations (that is, instructions of the form $x \leftarrow f(u_1, \ldots, u_r)$).

In general the optimality of a given program w.r.t. a cost function is undecidable (this follows from the undecidability of $\mathfrak{A}$–equivalence). Therefore from now on we will concentrate on transformations that *improve* programs instead of really *optimizing* them. (Nevertheless we will still call these "optimizations".)

3 Classical Optimizations

After discussing the formal basis we will now focus on optimization algorithms for SLC–programs. In this section we will introduce the "classical optimizations". Those are algorithms that are widely known and used in today's compilers. Optimizations typically consist of an *analysis* and a *transformation* step. For an optimizing transformation of SLC–programs we require the following properties:

Definition 3.1. *A function $T : \mathcal{SLC} \to \mathcal{SLC}$ is called an* $\mathfrak{A}$–program transformation *for an interpretation $\mathfrak{A}$ if, for every $\pi \in \mathcal{SLC}$, $T(\pi) \sim_{\mathfrak{A}} \pi$ (*correctness*) and $T(T(\pi)) = T(\pi)$ (*idempotency*). If T is correct for every interpretation, then we call it a* program transformation.

Dead Code Elimination

Dead Code Elimination removes instructions that are dispensable because they do not influence program semantics. An instruction $x \leftarrow e$ represents *dead code* if x is not used until it is redefined or if it is used only in instructions which are themselves dead code.

The transformation is based upon the *Needed Variable Analysis* which determines, for each instruction, those variables whose values are still required. It is a *backward analysis*, i.e., starting from the set of output variables the set of needed variables is computed for each instruction.

Definition 3.2 (Needed Variable Analysis). *Let $\pi := (\Sigma, \boldsymbol{v}_{in}, \boldsymbol{v}_{out}, \beta) \in \mathcal{SLC}$ with $\beta = \alpha_1; \ldots; \alpha_n$. For every instruction $\alpha = x \leftarrow e$ we define the transfer function $t_\alpha : 2^{V_\pi} \to 2^{V_\pi}$ as follows:*

$$t_\alpha(M) := \begin{cases} (M \setminus \{x\}) \cup V_e & \text{if } x \in M \\ M & \text{else} \end{cases}$$

The $t_{\alpha_n}, \ldots, t_{\alpha_1}$ determine, beginning with V_{out}, the sets of needed variables*:*

$$NV_n := V_{out} \quad \text{and} \quad NV_{i-1} := t_{\alpha_i}(NV_i) \text{ for } i \in \{n, \ldots, 2\}.$$

Using the sets of needed variables computed during the analysis step we can now define Dead Code Elimination.

Definition 3.3 (Dead Code Elimination). *For* $\pi = (\Sigma, \boldsymbol{v}_{in}, \boldsymbol{v}_{out}, \beta) \in \mathcal{SLC}$ *with* $\beta = \alpha_1; \ldots; \alpha_n$*, the transformation* $T_{DC} : \mathcal{SLC} \to \mathcal{SLC}$ *is given by:*

$$T_{DC}(\pi) := (\Sigma, \boldsymbol{v}_{in}, \boldsymbol{v}_{out}, \beta') \text{ with } \beta' := t_{DC}(\alpha_1); \ldots; t_{DC}(\alpha_n)$$

$$t_{DC}(x \leftarrow e) := \begin{cases} x \leftarrow e & \text{if } x \in NV_i \\ \varepsilon & \text{else} \end{cases}$$

This means all instructions $x \leftarrow e$ for which x is not in the set of needed variables are removed. A computation of NV_0 could be used for removing dispensable input variables. This would however conflict with our definition of the program semantics.

In Tab. 1 the analysis sets and the computation result of a T_{DC}–application to the program from Fig. 1 are shown.

Table 1. Application of the classical transformations to the program from Fig. 1

i	α_i	NV_i	d.c.?	AE_i	$vr(i)$	$T_{CS}(\pi)$	$RD_i(u,v,w,x,y,z)$	$T_{CF}(\pi)$
1	$u \leftarrow 3;$	$\{u,x,y\}$	No	$\emptyset$	$\emptyset$	$u \leftarrow 3;$	$(\bot,\bot,\bot,\bot,\bot,\bot)$	$u \leftarrow 3;$
2	$v \leftarrow x - y;$	$\{u,x,y\}$	Yes	$\emptyset$	$\{4\}$	$t_2 \leftarrow x - y;$ $v \leftarrow t_2;$	$(3,\bot,\bot,\bot,\bot,\bot)$	$v \leftarrow x - y;$
3	$w \leftarrow u + 1;$	$\{w,x,y\}$	No	$\{2\}$	$\emptyset$	$w \leftarrow u + 1;$	$(3,\bot,\bot,\bot,\bot,\bot)$	$w \leftarrow 4;$
4	$x \leftarrow x - y;$	$\{w,x,y\}$	No	$\{2,3\}$	$\emptyset$	$x \leftarrow t_2;$	$(3,\bot,4,\bot,\bot,\bot)$	$x \leftarrow x - y;$
5	$v \leftarrow w - 1;$	$\{v,x,y\}$	No	$\{3\}$	$\emptyset$	$v \leftarrow w - 1;$	$(3,\bot,4,\bot,\bot,\bot)$	$v \leftarrow 3;$
6	$u \leftarrow x - y;$	$\{u,v\}$	No	$\{3,5\}$	$\emptyset$	$u \leftarrow x - y;$	$(3,3,4,\bot,\bot,\bot)$	$u \leftarrow x - y;$
7	$z \leftarrow u * w;$	$\{u,v\}$	Yes	$\{5,6\}$	$\emptyset$	$z \leftarrow u * w;$	$(\bot,3,4,\bot,\bot,\bot)$	$z \leftarrow u * 4;$
8	$u \leftarrow 2 * u;$	$\{u,v\}$	No	$\{5,6,7\}$	$\emptyset$	$u \leftarrow 2 * u;$	$(\bot,3,4,\bot,\bot,\bot)$	$u \leftarrow 2 * u;$

T_{DC} is correct and idempotent and thus a program transformation [7]. It should be noted that there are *non–idempotent* variants of Dead Code Elimination based on a so–called "Live–Variable Analysis" (see e.g. [4,6]).

Common Subexpression Elimination

Unlike Dead Code Elimination, Common Subexpression Elimination is using a forward analysis, the *Available Expressions Analysis*, which computes for each instruction the (indices of the) operation expressions whose value is still available and whose repeated evaluation can be avoided therefore.

Definition 3.4 (Available Expressions Analysis). *Let* $\pi := (\Sigma, \boldsymbol{v}_{in}, \boldsymbol{v}_{out}, \beta) \in \mathcal{SLC}$ *with* $\beta = \alpha_1; \ldots; \alpha_n$ *and* $\alpha_i = x_i \leftarrow e_i$ *for every* $i \in \{1, \ldots, n\}$*. An expression* e *is* available *at position* i *if* $e_j = e$ *for some* $j < i$ *and* $x_k \notin V_e$ *for every* $j \leq k < i$.

The $t_{\alpha_i} : 2^{\{1,\ldots,n\}} \to 2^{\{1,\ldots,n\}}$ *are given by* $t_{\alpha_i}(M) := kill_{\alpha_i} \circ gen_{\alpha_i}$ *where*

$$gen_{\alpha_i}(M) := \begin{cases} M \cup \{i\} & \text{if } e_i = f(u_1, \ldots, u_r) \text{ and } \forall j \in M : e_j \neq e_i \\ M & \text{else} \end{cases}$$

$$kill_{\alpha_i}(M) := M \setminus \{j \in M \mid x_i \in V_{e_j}\}$$

This yields the sets of available expressions $AE_i \subseteq \{1, \ldots, n\}$ *for* $i \in \{1, \ldots, n\}$*:*

$$AE_1 := \emptyset \quad \text{and} \quad AE_{i+1} := t_{\alpha_i}(AE_i) \text{ for } i \in \{1, \ldots, n\}$$

Definition 3.5 (Common Subexpression Elimination). *For each instruction, the function* $vr : \{1, \ldots, n\} \to 2^{\{1,\ldots,n\}}$ *yields the* valid recurrences *of the corresponding expression:* $vr(i) := \{j \in \{i+1, \ldots, n\} \mid i \in AE_j, e_i = e_j\}$.

The program transformation[3] $T_{CS} : \mathcal{SLC} \to \mathcal{SLC}$ *works as follows: for every* $i \in \{1, \ldots, n\}$ *with* $vr(i) \neq \emptyset$*, select* $t_i \in V \setminus V_\pi$ *and*

1. *replace* $\alpha_i = x \leftarrow e$ *by* $t_i \leftarrow e;\ x \leftarrow t_i$ *and*
2. *for all* $j \in vr(i)$*, replace* $\alpha_j = y \leftarrow e$ *by* $y \leftarrow t_i$*.*

Table 1 shows both the available expressions, the valid recurrences, and the result of eliminating common subexpressions in the program from Fig. 1.

Again it is possible to show that Common Subexpression Elimination is a program transformation. Please refer to [7] for details.

Constant Folding

Constant Folding is a partial evaluation of the input program with constant propagation. It avoids the redundant evaluation of constant expressions at runtime. In contrast to Dead Code and Common Subexpression Elimination the optimization is incorporating the program semantics as this is necessary for evaluating constant expressions.

During the program analysis we determine for every instruction the known values of the variables. For this the definition of the semantics (Sec. 2) is extended to allow the "evaluation" of expressions with unknown variable values (represented by the symbol $\bot$ in Tab. 1). If at least one argument of a function is an unknown variable also the evaluation result is unknown. Special properties of operations, such as $\forall x \in \mathbb{R} : 0 \cdot x = 0$, are ignored.

The evaluation of constant expressions potentially causes the introduction of new constants (not contained in C). Therefore the signature of the target program needs to be adapted.

Definition 3.6 (Constant Folding). *For* $\pi = (\Sigma, v_{in}, v_{out}, \beta) \in \mathcal{SLC}$, $\Sigma = (F, C)$, $\beta = \alpha_1; \ldots; \alpha_n$, $\alpha_i = x_i \leftarrow e_i$ *and* $\mathfrak{A} = (A, \varphi)$*, the transformation* $T_{CF} : \mathcal{SLC} \to \mathcal{SLC}$ *is defined by:*

$$T_{CF}(\pi) := ((F, A), v_{in}, v_{out}, \beta') \text{ with } \beta' := x_1 \leftarrow \overline{RD}_1(e_1); \ldots; x_n \leftarrow \overline{RD}_n(e_n)$$

where $\overline{RD}_i$ *replaces all variables known to be constant by the respective values, and evaluates constant expressions (see [7] for the formal definition).*

[3] For a proof of this property refer to [7].

Example 3.7. When applying T_{CF} to the program from Fig. 1 employing the usual arithmetic interpretation we get the result depicted in Tab. 1. As we can see, Constant Folding potentially produces dead code: the first instruction is dispensable since u is not used anymore until its redefinition in the sixth instruction.

For establishing the correctness of Constant Folding the particular interpretation has to be taken into account; thus strong equivalence is generally not preserved. We show in [7]:

Lemma 3.8. *For every $\pi = (\Sigma, \boldsymbol{v}_{in}, \boldsymbol{v}_{out}, \beta) \in \mathcal{SLC}$ and every interpretation $\mathfrak{A}$ of Σ, $\pi \sim_{\mathfrak{A}} T_{CF}(\pi)$ and $T_{CF}(T_{CF}(\pi)) = T_{CF}(\pi)$.*

4 DAG Optimization

The DAG optimization for SLC–programs is based on the construction of a *directed acyclic graph* (DAG). A basic version of this optimization has been introduced in [3]. We will present a modified version which, however, does not consider the register allocation problem since we focus on intermediate code.

Definition 4.1 (DAG). *A* DAG *is an acyclic graph $G = (K, L, lab, suc)$ with a set of* nodes K *and a set of* labels L, *a* labeling function $lab : K \to L$ *and a partially defined* successor function $suc :\subseteq K \times \mathbb{N} \to K$.

A DAG represents the result and the operands of expressions by (different) nodes that are linked by the successor function.

The DAG of an SLC–Program

The DAG of an SLC–program is a graphical representation of the program with *sharing* of identical subterms. Furthermore a partial evaluation of expressions (similar to Constant Folding) is performed (extending the algorithm in [3]).

In addition to the DAG we need a valuation function $val :\subseteq V_\pi \times \mathbb{N} \to K$ with $val(x, i) = k$ iff the subgraph rooted at k represents the value of the variable x after i computation steps.

Algorithm 4.2 (DAG Construction). *Let $\pi := (\Sigma, \boldsymbol{v}_{in}, \boldsymbol{v}_{out}, \beta) \in \mathcal{SLC}$ with $\Sigma = (F, C)$, $\beta = \alpha_1; \ldots; \alpha_n$ and $\mathfrak{A} = (A, \varphi)$. The DAG G and the valuation function val are inductively constructed as follows where the set of labels is defined by $L := F \cup V_{in} \cup A$:*[4]

Select $K := V_{in} \cup \varphi(C_\pi)$ with $lab(k) = k$ $\forall k \in K$ as initial nodes[5] *and set $val(x, 0) := x$ for all $x \in V_{in}$ where $\varphi(C_\pi) := \{\varphi(c) \mid c \in C_\pi\}$.*

Assuming that G and val are already constructed for $\alpha_1; \ldots; \alpha_i$ and letting $\alpha_{i+1} = x \leftarrow e$, we distinguish different cases depending on the type of the expression e:

[4] Nodes that represent complex expressions will be labeled by the corresponding function symbols whereas variable/constant nodes will be labeled by themselves.

[5] Alternatively one could add the constants later "on demand".

1. $e = y \in V$:
According to the induction hypothesis, $val(y,i) \in K$ *is already representing the current value of* y*. Thus* G *is not extended; set*

$$val(x, i+1) := val(y,i) \quad \text{and} \quad val(x', i+1) := val(x', i) \text{ for } x' \neq x$$

In the following $\mathbf{update}(x, i+1, y)$ *will be used to abbreviate the above two assignments.*

2. $e = c \in C$:
$\varphi(c) \in K$ *already exists. Therefore only:* $\mathbf{update}(x, i+1, \varphi(c))$.

3. $e = f(u_1, \ldots, u_r)$, $u_j \in V \cup C$, $f \in F^{(r)}$. *We distinguish further subcases:*

(a) for all $j \in \{1, \ldots, r\}$, $u_j \in C$ *or* ($u_j \in V$ *and* $val(u_j, i) \in A$).
Then let $a := \varphi(f)(u'_1, \ldots, u'_r) \in A$ *with*

$$u'_j := \begin{cases} \varphi(u_j) & \text{if } u_j \in C \\ val(u_j, i) & \text{if } u_j \in V \end{cases}$$

- $a \in \varphi(C_\pi)$: *no extension of* G*, set* $\mathbf{update}(x, i+1, a)$.
- $a \notin \varphi(C_\pi)$: $K := K \cup \{a\}$ *and* $\mathbf{update}(x, i+1, a)$.

(b) $\exists j \in \{1, \ldots, r\}$ *with* $u_j \in V$ *and* $val(u_j, i) \notin A$.

- $\exists k \in K$ *with* $lab(k) = f$ *and*

$$suc(k, j) = \begin{cases} \varphi(u_j) & \text{if } u_j \in C \\ val(u_j, i) & \text{if } u_j \in V \end{cases}$$

  No modification of G*; the value of* e *is already represented by* k*. Set* $\mathbf{update}(x, i+1, k)$.
- *Otherwise: insert a node* k_{i+1}:

$$K := K \cup \{k_{i+1}\}$$
$$lab(k_{i+1}) := f$$
$$suc(k_{i+1}, j) := \begin{cases} \varphi(u_j) & \text{if } u_j \in C \\ val(u_j, i) & \text{if } u_j \in V \end{cases}$$
$$\mathbf{update}(x, i+1, k_{i+1})$$

Example 4.3. Figure 2 shows the DAG of the program from Fig. 1. The square nodes are the nodes already present before processing the instructions. The others were created later according to the above definition. For better clarity the *val*–table only shows those entries that represent changes.

The DAG construction incorporates aspects of Common Subexpression Elimination (node sharing for expressions already represented by a node in the DAG) and Constant Folding (partial evaluation of expressions based on constant information, i.e. no node represents a constant expression).

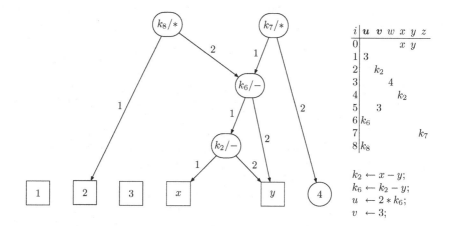

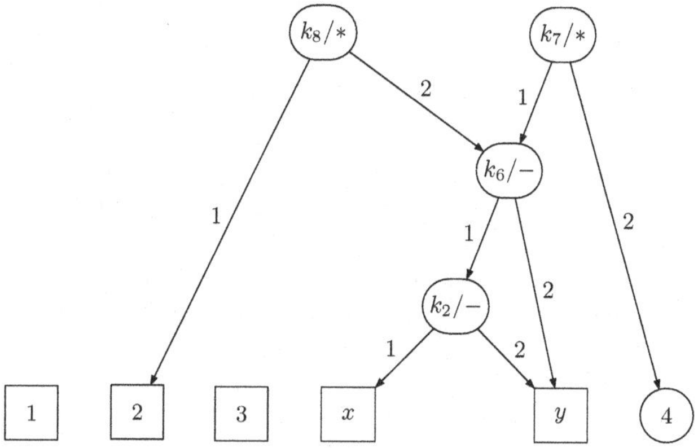

i	u	v	w	x	y	z
0				x	y	
1	3					
2		k_2				
3			4			
4				k_2		
5		3				
6	k_6					
7						k_7
8	k_8					

$k_2 \leftarrow x - y;$
$k_6 \leftarrow k_2 - y;$
$u \leftarrow 2 * k_6;$
$v \leftarrow 3;$

Fig. 2. DAG, *val*–function and optimized program for π from Fig. 1

Code Generation from a DAG

For generating code from a DAG only the nodes that are reachable from an "output node" are required. We will call these nodes *output relevant.* The others are not considered during code generation, thus implementing Dead Code Elimination.

With regard to the processing order of the nodes the following restriction has to be observed. Before creating an instruction for a node k all successors of k have to be processed first. In the following we will present a simple *nondeterministic* algorithm for code generation using our example.

Example 4.4. Let π be the program from Fig. 1 and G its DAG which is depicted in Fig. 2. Then code generation can be done as follows:

1. The set of output–relevant nodes is $\{2, 3, x, y, k_2, k_6, k_8\}$, as they are all reachable from k_8 (except 3 which itself is output–relevant).
2. Since the constants and input values are immediately available an operation node is the first node to process. This can only be k_2 because the other operation nodes depend on it. The instruction $\boldsymbol{k_2 \leftarrow x - y}$ is created (according to the node label and the node's successors).
3. The next node to process is k_6 because the node k_8 depends on it. For k_6 we obtain $\boldsymbol{k_6 \leftarrow k_2 - y}$.
4. For the last remaining operation node k_8 we add $\boldsymbol{u \leftarrow 2 * k_6}$. Here we do not use a temporary assignment variable but the output variable u because this will be the final value of u. Otherwise we would have to insert a copy instruction later on.
5. Now all the operation nodes are processed but the output variable v is still undefined. Since $val(v, 8) = 3$ we have to add the instruction $\boldsymbol{v \leftarrow 3}$.

Thus we get the result shown in Fig. 2.

This "naive" code generation technique has several disadvantages increasing the complexity of the correctness proof:

- The algorithm is nondeterministic, multiple choices for the next node to process are possible. Hence the output depends on the node ordering, and thus the order of the assignments may differ between the input and the optimized program. (In our example, the order of the assignments to the variables u and v is reversed.)
- The idempotency is violated because after eliminating output–irrelevant nodes in the first application of T_{DAG}, the second application will introduce new node names.

In [7] an extended algorithm avoiding the above problems is introduced. It works similarly and will be denoted by T_{DAG} in the sequel.

In programs obtained from the DAG code generation for every assignment a new, previously undefined variable is used; this normal form is called *Static Single Assignment (SSA) form* in the literature.

Note that if the number of available registers is limited, the optimal code generation from a DAG is NP–complete [2]. The code generation from expression *trees*, however, is also in this case efficient [1].

Intuitively it is clear that the DAG algorithm is working correctly. Proving this correctness, however, is not trivial. We show in [7]:

Theorem 4.5. *Let* $\pi = (\Sigma, v_{in}, v_{out}, \beta) \in \mathcal{SLC}$ *and* $\mathfrak{A}$ *be an interpretation of* Σ*. Then* $\pi \sim_{\mathfrak{A}} T_{DAG}(\pi)$ *and* $T_{DAG}(T_{DAG}(\pi)) = T_{DAG}(\pi)$.

5 Composing the Simple Transformations

After formally introducing the different optimizing program transformations we will analyze the relations between them. We call two optimizations equivalent if every transformation is optimal with respect to the other:

Definition 5.1. *Let* $T_1, T_2 : \mathcal{SLC} \to \mathcal{SLC}$ *be program transformations.*

- T_2 *is called* T_1–optimal $(T_1 \leq T_2)$ *iff* $\forall \pi \in \mathcal{SLC} : T_1(T_2(\pi)) = T_2(\pi)$.
- T_1 *and* T_2 *are called* equivalent $(T_1 \sim T_2)$ *iff* $T_1 \leq T_2$ *and* $T_2 \leq T_1$.

In previous examples we have seen that the DAG algorithm has a higher "optimizing potential" than the classical transformations. A generalization of this observation yields (proven in [7]):

Theorem 5.2. $T \leq T_{DAG}$ *for every* $T \in \{T_{DC}, T_{CS}, T_{CF}\}$.

In the following we will examine the reverse direction, that is, the question whether the classical transformations can be applied in a certain order such that the result is equivalent to the DAG–optimized program.

Copy Propagation

Our first observation is that the classical transformations alone do not suffice for "simulating" the DAG optimization.

Theorem 5.3. *There exists a program* $\pi \in \mathcal{SLC}$ *such that* $\pi = T(\pi)$ *for every* $T \in \{T_{DC}, T_{CS}, T_{CF}\}$, *but* $\pi \neq T_{DAG}(\pi)$.

Proof. Consider the program depicted in Fig. 3. It is optimal w.r.t. all three classical transformations. An application of T_{DAG}, however, produces a much shorter version. □

In the example Dead Code Elimination would yield an optimizing effect if one would replace e.g. the occurrences of u on the right–hand side of the instructions 2 and 3 by x. For this problem we will now introduce a new algorithm, *Copy Propagation*, which is no direct improvement but a *pre-processing* step enabling other optimizations.

Our version of Copy Propagation does not only substitute a variable used after a copy instruction with its original variable but also traces back transitive dependencies for copy chains. During the analysis step we collect the *valid copies* for each instruction. These are basically pairs of variables that have the same value at a given point (due to copy instructions). A third value – the *transitive depth* which represents the length of a copy chain – is used to guarantee determinism and idempotency of the transformation. Copy Propagation fulfills the requirements of a program transformation[6].

$$\begin{aligned} \boldsymbol{v}_{in} &: (x, y) \\ \beta &: u \leftarrow x; \\ & \quad y \leftarrow u + y; \\ & \quad v \leftarrow u; \\ & \quad u \leftarrow v * y; \\ & \quad v \leftarrow u + v; \\ \boldsymbol{v}_{out} &: (u, v) \end{aligned}$$

$$\downarrow T_{DAG}$$

$$\begin{aligned} v_1 &\leftarrow x + y; \\ u &\leftarrow x * v_1; \\ v &\leftarrow u + x; \end{aligned}$$

Fig. 3. Program with copy instructions and its DAG–optimized version

Definition 5.4 (Valid Copies). *Let* $\pi := (\Sigma, \boldsymbol{v}_{in}, \boldsymbol{v}_{out}, \beta) \in \mathcal{SLC}$ *with* $\beta := \alpha_1; \ldots; \alpha_n$. *For an instruction* $\alpha = x \leftarrow e$ *we define the transfer function* $t_\alpha : 2^{V_\pi^2 \times \{1,\ldots,n\}} \to 2^{V_\pi^2 \times \{1,\ldots,n\}}$ *by*

$$\begin{aligned} t_{x \leftarrow e}(M) := trans(M \setminus \{(y, z, d) \in M \mid d \in \{1, \ldots, n\},\ x \in \{y, z\}\} \\ \cup \{(x, e, 1) \mid e \in V_\pi \setminus \{x\}\}) \end{aligned}$$

Here $trans : 2^{V^2 \times \mathbb{N}} \to 2^{V^2 \times \mathbb{N}}$ *computes the* transitive closure *of the argument relation, taking the transitive depth into account. Now the analysis sets* $CP_i \subseteq V_\pi^2 \times \{1, \ldots, n\}$ *can be computed inductively:*

$$CP_1 := \emptyset \ \text{ and } \ CP_{i+1} := t_{\alpha_i}(CP_i) \text{ for } i \in \{1, \ldots, n-1\}$$

Based on the CP–sets we define the program transformation:

---

[6] Proven in [7].

Definition 5.5 (Copy Propagation). *The transformation* $T_{CP} : \mathcal{SLC} \to \mathcal{SLC}$ *for* $\pi = (\Sigma, V_{in}, V_{out}, \beta) \in \mathcal{SLC}$ *with* $\beta = x_1 \leftarrow e_1; \ldots; x_n \leftarrow e_n$ *and* $\Sigma = (F, C)$ *is given by*

$$T_{CP}(\pi) := (\Sigma, \boldsymbol{v}_{in}, \boldsymbol{v}_{out}, \beta') \textit{ with } \beta' := x_1 \leftarrow \overline{CP}_1(e_1); \ldots; x_n \leftarrow \overline{CP}_n(e_n)$$

where $\overline{CP}(e)$ *with* $CP \subseteq V_\pi^2 \times \{1, \ldots, n\}$, $c \in C$, $x \in V_\pi$ *and* $f \in F^{(r)}$ *is defined as follows:*

$$\overline{CP}(c) := c$$

$$\overline{CP}(x) := \begin{cases} y \textit{ if } \exists y \in V, \exists d \in \{1, \ldots, n\} \textit{ with } (x, y, d) \in CP \\ \quad\quad \textit{and } \forall (x, y', d') \in CP: \; d' \leq d \\ x \textit{ else} \end{cases}$$

$$\overline{CP}(f(u_1, \ldots, u_r)) := f(\overline{CP}(u_1), \ldots, \overline{CP}(u_r))$$

The selection of the tuple with the highest transitive depth for the substitution ensures that the copy chains are traced back completely and that the algorithm works deterministically.

Example 5.6. Applying Copy Propagation to the program of Fig. 3 yields:

i	α_i	CP_i	new instruction α'_i
1	$u \leftarrow x;$	$\emptyset$	$u \leftarrow x;$
2	$y \leftarrow u + y;$	$\{(u, x, 1)\}$	$y \leftarrow x + y;$
3	$v \leftarrow u;$	$\{(u, x, 1)\}$	$v \leftarrow x;$
4	$u \leftarrow v * y;$	$\{(u, x, 1), (v, u, 1), (\boldsymbol{v}, \boldsymbol{x}, \mathbf{2})\}$	$u \leftarrow x * y;$
5	$v \leftarrow u + v$	$\{(v, x, 2)\}$	$v \leftarrow u + x;$

In instruction 4 the tuple printed in boldface results from the computation of the transitive closure. The transitive depth is needed to decide which substitution to use for v in instruction 4.

Execution Order

Now we will analyze the relations between the simple algorithms. Of particular interest is the following property:

Definition 5.7. *Let* $T_i : \mathcal{SLC} \to \mathcal{SLC}$, $i \in \{1, 2\}$ *be two program transformations. If there exists a* $\pi \in \mathcal{SLC}$ *such that*

$$T_1(\pi) = \pi \textit{ and } T_1(T_2(\pi)) \neq T_2(\pi)$$

then T_2 *is called* T_1–enabling *(*$T_2 \to T_1$*).*

Thus intuitively a transformation enables another if it "produces" additional optimization potential w.r.t. the other. The enabling relationships holding for our transformations are given in Fig. 4. Here an arrow means that the transformation labeling the row enables the transformation indexing the column, whereas a dash indicates the absence of an enabling effect.

	T_{DC}	T_{CS}	T_{CF}	T_{CP}
T_{DC}		-	-	-
T_{CS}	-		-	$\to$
T_{CF}	$\to$	$\to$		-
T_{CP}	$\to$	$\to$	-	

Fig. 4. Enabling relations

- T_{DC} does not enable any of the other transformations because it eliminates instructions and therefore does not create new available expressions, copy instructions, or constant variables.
- T_{CS} enables Copy Propagation due to the insertion of copy instructions. It has no influence on Constant Folding and Dead Code Elimination.
- We have already seen in Ex. 3.7 that Constant Folding "produces" additional Dead Code. One can easily construct examples in which the substitution of variables by constants creates common subexpressions.
- From Ex. 5.6 it is clear that T_{CP} is T_{DC}–enabling. Similarly to Constant Folding the substitution of variables by others can create common subexpressions.

Between Copy Propagation and Common Subexpression Elimination there is a mutual dependence. Thus a repeated application of both is generally unavoidable.

Lemma 5.8. *There exists a sequence* $(\pi_n)_{n\in\mathbb{N}\setminus\{0\}}$ *such that* $T := T_{CP} \circ T_{CS}$ *has to be applied at least* n *times to* π_n *for reaching a fixed point.*

Proof. $\pi_n := (\Sigma, (x), (y, z), \beta_n)$ with $\Sigma = (F, \emptyset)$ and $F = \{f^{(2)}\}$ where β_n is given by

$$\begin{aligned} \beta_1 := y &\leftarrow f(x, x); \\ z &\leftarrow f(x, x); \end{aligned} \qquad \begin{aligned} \beta_{n+1} := \beta_n&; \\ y &\leftarrow f(y, x); \\ z &\leftarrow f(z, x); \end{aligned}$$

obviously fulfills the requirement. □

The maximum number of iterations is bounded by the number of instructions since every application of Common Subexpression Elimination that provokes a change reduces the number of operation expressions of the program, and since the number of operation expressions is limited by the number of instructions (see also [7]).

In practice it is certainly not advisable to "blindly" use the worst–case iteration number; rather a demand–driven method should be employed.

Definition 5.9. *For* $\pi \in \mathcal{SLC}$ *and* $T := T_{CP} \circ T_{CS}$ *the transformation* $T_{CPCS} : \mathcal{SLC} \to \mathcal{SLC}$ *is be defined by:*

$$T_{CPCS}(\pi) := \begin{cases} \pi & \textit{if } T(\pi) = \pi \\ T_{CPCS}(T(\pi)) & \textit{else} \end{cases}$$

From the previous observations as represented in Tab. 4, we can now derive an order for the simple transformations to achieve a good optimization effect:

1. Constant Folding (cannot be enabled by the other transformations)
2. Application of Common Subexpression Elimination and Copy Propagation in alternation (T_{CPCS})
3. Dead Code Elimination (enabled by T_{CP} and T_{CF})

Table 2. Application of T_{COPT} to π from Fig. 1

$T_{CF}(\pi)$	$T_{CS}(T_{CF}(\pi))$	$T_{CP}(T_{CS}(T_{CF}(\pi)))$	$T_{DC}(T_{CP}(T_{CS}(T_{CF}(\pi))))$
$u \leftarrow 3;$	$u \leftarrow 3;$	$u \leftarrow 3;$	
$v \leftarrow x - y;$	$\mathbf{t_2 \leftarrow x - y;}$	$t_2 \leftarrow x - y;$	$t_2 \leftarrow x - y;$
	$v \leftarrow \mathbf{t_2;}$	$v \leftarrow t_2;$	
$w \leftarrow 4;$	$w \leftarrow 4;$	$w \leftarrow 4;$	
$x \leftarrow x - y;$	$x \leftarrow \mathbf{t_2;}$	$x \leftarrow t_2;$	
$v \leftarrow 3;$	$v \leftarrow 3;$	$v \leftarrow 3;$	$v \leftarrow 3;$
$u \leftarrow x - y;$	$u \leftarrow x - y;$	$u \leftarrow \mathbf{t_2} - y;$	$u \leftarrow t_2 - y;$
$z \leftarrow u * 4;$	$z \leftarrow u * 4;$	$z \leftarrow u * 4;$	
$u \leftarrow 2 * u;$	$u \leftarrow 2 * u;$	$u \leftarrow 2 * u;$	$u \leftarrow 2 * u;$

Definition 5.10. *The* compositional transformation *incorporating the classical optimizations and Copy Propagation is given by* $T_{COPT} := T_{DC} \circ T_{CPCS} \circ T_{CF}$.

Example 5.11. Table 2 shows an exemplary computation of T_{COPT} for our example program from Fig. 1 starting from the T_{CF}–optimized program from Ex. 3.7. Already one application of $T_{CP} \circ T_{CS}$ suffices here to reach the fixed point (this is clear because in $T_{CP}(T_{CS}(T_{CF}(\pi)))$ all operation expressions are distinct).

The resulting program is identical to the DAG–optimized program from Fig. 2 except for variable naming and the instruction order[7]. Also for the example from Fig. 3 we would get the same results "modulo" variable names.

Simulation of the DAG Transformation

For achieving a T_{DAG}–optimal transformation we obviously need to rename the variables in the output program. This can be done via a variable renaming transformation. The T_{DAG}–equivalence is even then not fulfilled for the compositional T_{COPT}–optimization, there remain two minor issues:

- Under some circumstances Copy Propagation does not allow the propagation of a variable name even though the old assignment is still valid. This problem can be circumvented by transforming the input program in SSA form (T_{SSA} is formally defined in [7]) before applying T_{COPT}.
- Copy Assignments to output variables cannot be removed using the previously introduced transformations. They occur especially due to Common Subexpression Elimination. A specialized algorithm (T_{RC}; see [7]) solves this problem.

Finally we obtain an extended compositional transformation:

Definition 5.12. *For* $\pi \in \mathcal{SLC}$ *the* extended compositional transformation $T_{XOPT} : \mathcal{SLC} \to \mathcal{SLC}$ *is defined by* $T_{XOPT} := T_{SSA} \circ T_{RC} \circ T_{COPT} \circ T_{SSA}$.

[7] The advanced DAG–algorithm does not have the reordering issue.

The final application of T_{SSA} is only required to ensure a variable naming "compatible" to the advanced DAG algorithm. Approximately we have $T_{XOPT} \approx T_{COPT}$ and according to [7]:

Theorem 5.13. $T_{XOPT} \sim T_{DAG}$.

6 Conclusion and Future Work

We have shown that the DAG procedure can essentially be characterized as a combination of Copy Propagation and the three classical transformations. More concretely it corresponds to a repeated application of Common Subexpression Elimination and Copy Propagation in alternation, preceded by Constant Folding and followed by Dead Code Elimination:

$$T_{DAG} \approx T_{DC} \circ (T_{CP} \circ T_{CS})^* \circ T_{CF}.$$

Apart from its theoretical importance, this result is also relevant for practical compiler design as it potentially allows to exploit the optimization potential of the DAG–based algorithm for non–linear code as well. Certainly our results cannot be transferred directly to iterative code, but the basic composition of the transformations should turn out to be effective. This matter is the main point for future investigation.

Furthermore it would be interesting to analyze whether Copy Propagation and Common Subexpression Elimination can be merged into one algorithm to avoid the iterative application procedure.

References

1. Aho, A.V., Johnson, S.C.: Optimal code generation for expression trees. J. ACM 23(3), 488–501 (1976)
2. Aho, A.V., Johnson, S.C., Ullman, J.D.: Code generation for expressions with common subexpressions. J. ACM 24(1), 146–160 (1977)
3. Aho, A.V., Sethi, R., Ullman, J.D.: A formal approach to code optimization. ACM SIGPLAN Notices 5(7), 86–100 (1970)
4. Aho, A.V., Sethi, R., Ullman, J.D.: Compilers: Principles, Techniques, and Tools. Addison–Wesley, London, UK (1986)
5. Ibarra, O.H., Leininger, B.S.: The complexity of the equivalence problem for straight–line programs. In: STOC'80. Proc. of the 12th Annual ACM Symp. on Theory of Computing, pp. 273–280. ACM Press, New York, NY, USA (1980)
6. Nielson, F., Nielson, H.R., Hankin, C.: Principles of Program Analysis. Springer, Heidelberg (1999)
7. Noll, T., Rieger, S.: Optimization of straight–line code revisited. Technical Report 2005–21, RWTH Aachen University, Dept. of Computer Science, Germany (2005), `http://sunsite.informatik.rwth-aachen.de/Publications/AIB/`
8. Rieger, S.: SLC Optimizer - Web Interface (2005), `http://aprove.informatik.rwth-aachen.de/~rieger/`

Building Extended Canonizers by Graph-Based Deduction

Silvio Ranise[1] and Christelle Scharff[2,*]

[1] LORIA & INRIA-Lorraine, France
ranise@loria.fr
[2] Seidenberg School of Computer Science and Information Systems, Pace University, USA
cscharff@pace.edu

Abstract. We consider the problem of efficiently building extended canonizers, which are capable of solving the uniform word problem for some first-order theories. These reasoning artifacts have been introduced in previous work to solve the lack of modularity of Shostak combination schema while retaining its efficiency. It is known that extended canonizers can be modularly combined to solve the uniform word problem in unions of theories. Unfortunately, little is known about efficiently implementing such canonizers for component theories, especially those of interest for verification like, e.g., those of uninterpreted function symbols or lists. In this paper, we investigate this problem by adapting and combining work on rewriting-based decision procedures for satisfiability in first-order theories and SER graphs, a graph-based method defined for abstract congruence closure. Our goal is to build graph-based extended canonizers for theories which are relevant for verification. Based on graphs our approach addresses implementation issues that were lacking in previous rewriting-based decision procedure approaches and which are important to argue the viability of extended canonizers.

1 Introduction

An increasing number of verification tools, e.g., software model-checkers, require the use of Satisfiability Modulo Theories (SMT) solvers [14] (in first-order logic) to implement the back-ends for the automatic analysis of specifications and properties. This is so because verification problems require to solve satisfiability problems, e.g., checking if an abstract trace yields a spurious concrete trace can be reduced to a satisfiability problem modulo the theory of the data structures manipulated by the program. The availability of efficient SMT solvers becomes a crucial pre-requisite for automating the various verification tasks. To make the situation more complex, most verification problems involve several theories, e.g., programs manipulate composite data structures such as arrays and integers for their indexes, so that methods to combine theories are also required.

* This work is supported by the National Science Foundation under grant ITR-0326540.

C.B. Jones, Z. Liu, J. Woodcock (Eds.): ICTAC 2007, LNCS 4711, pp. 440–454, 2007.

The lazy approach to build SMT solvers is currently the most popular and most successful in terms of run-time performance. It consists in reducing a theory solver to its essence by separating generic Boolean reasoning from theory reasoning. The common practice is to write theory solvers just for sets of ground literals (i.e. atomic formulas and their negation). These simple procedures are then integrated with an efficient Boolean solver, allowing the resulting system to accept (possibly quite large) arbitrary Boolean combinations of ground literals. In the *lazy* approach, reasoning modules for a background theory obtained as the union of several simpler theories may be modularly built by writing procedures for each component theory and then use the solvers cooperatively via well-known combination schemas (see, e.g., [13] for an overview). As a consequence, the problem of building (a) *efficient* and (b) *easily combinable* theory solvers for conjunctions of literals in selected theories is central to the task of building SMT solvers which can be profitably integrated in larger verification tools. More in general, the problem of building and combining theory solvers is important for automated deduction and constraint programming since their use allows one to automatically reason on a computation domain, improve efficiency, and reduce user-interaction.

Theory solvers for selected theories (such as the theory of uninterpreted function symbols, the theory of lists, the theory of arrays) are usually built in *ad hoc* ways and their proofs of correctness depend on specific model-theoretic arguments (see, e.g., [9]). The rewriting-approach in [2] proposes a uniform methodology to build solvers which consists in showing the termination of a completion process of a refutation complete calculus on a set of formulae obtained as the union of the axioms of the background theory T and a (finite) set S of ground literals in T. A drawback of [2] is that it is difficult to derive a precise characterization of the complexity of the resulting theory solvers because of the abstraction notion of computation (i.e. a logical calculus) used. In this paper, we adapt the rewriting approach in [2] to use SER graphs [16], which provide a graph-based completion procedure to solve the word problem of (ground) equational theories, so as to build efficient theory solvers. SER graphs combine the key ideas of completion [7] and abstract congruence closure [4], and can be seen as a specialization of SOUR graphs [8], which were developed for general completion. The choice of a particular and compact data structure to represent terms and literals allow us to derive precise characterizations of the worst-case behavior for the synthesized theory solvers. We will see that, for the theories of uninterpreted function symbols and lists, such a worst-case behavior is the same of the best theory solvers available in the literature.

The adaptation of the rewriting-approach to SER graphs allows us to fulfill desideratum (a) for theory solvers to be used in lazy SMT tools. Regarding the possibility to easily combine solvers—cf. desideratum (b) above—more work is required. In [1], a modularity result for rewriting-based solvers in unions of theories is derived. On the one hand, it is possible to adapt this result to SER graphs. On the other hand, some theories (e.g., Linear Arithmetic) do not admit solvers based on rewriting and come with *ad hoc* procedures, that can be combined with others via well-known combination schemas, such as Nelson-Oppen [10] and Shostak [17]. Both combination schemas are based on exchanging logical formulae between the solvers so as to synchronize their states. Since Shostak assumes the existence of certain interface functionalities—called the canonizer and the solver—to efficiently derive the facts needed for synchronization, it is believed to give better performances than Nelson and Oppen. Unfortunately, as clearly shown in [5], Shostak is not modular. A further drawback is that the theory of uninterpreted function symbols (which is present in virtually any verification problems) does not admit a solver and Shostak must be amended to incorporate the theory. To find a better trade-off between the modularity of Nelson and Oppen and the efficiency of Shostak, a new combination method has been proposed in [13]. The schema combines *extended canonizers*, i.e. procedures capable of computing normal forms not only with respect to a background theory (as it is the case for canonizers in Shostak) but also with respect to (ground) sets of equalities. In [13], it is also sketched how to obtain extended canonizers for the theory of uninterpreted function symbols and for theories with (finitely many) commutative function symbols. However, the discussion is sketchy and does not address complexity and implementation issues which are important to argue the viability of the proposed concept. The **main contribution** of this paper is showing how to build efficient extended canonizers by adapting the rewriting-based approach to use SER graph. We notice that extended canonizers are easily combinable as a by product of the fact that they are the basic modularity notion underlying the combination schema in [13].

Plan of the paper. In Section 2, we give some background notions and recall the formal definition of extended canonizer from [13]. In Section 3, we show how to build theory solvers and compute extended canonizers for the theory of equality and the theory of lists *à la* Shostak. In Section 4, we argue the correctness of the extended canonizers described in the previous section. In Section 5, we illustrate the internal workings of an extended canonizer on an example. Finally, in Section 6, we give some conclusions and discuss lines for future work.

2 Background

We assume the usual first-order syntactic notions of signature, term, position, and so on. Let Σ be a signature containing only function symbols with their arity and X a set of variables. A 0-arity symbol is called a constant. A Σ-term is a term built out of the symbols in Σ and the variables in X. A Σ-term is flat if its depth is 0 or 1. If l and r are two Σ-terms, then $l \approx r$ is a Σ-equality and $l \not\approx r$ is a Σ-disequality. A Σ-literal is either a Σ-equality or a Σ-disequality. For a literal, $depth(l \bowtie r) = depth(l) + depth(r)$, where $\bowtie$ is either $\approx$ or $\not\approx$. A Σ-equality is flat if its depth is at most 1 (i.e., it is of the form $c = d$, for c, d constants, or $f(c_1, ..., c_n) \approx c_{n+1}$, for $c_1, ..., c_n, c_{n+1}$ constants). A Σ-disequality is flat if its depth is 0 (i.e., it is of the form $c \not\approx d$, for c, d constants). A Σ-formula is built in the usual way out of the universal and existential quantifiers, Boolean connectives, and symbols in Σ. A Σ-formula φ is ground if $Var(\varphi) = \emptyset$ (where

$Var(\varphi)$ is the set of variables occurring in φ) and a sentence if it has no free variables.

We also assume the usual first-order notions of interpretation, satisfiability, validity, logical consequence, and theory. A Σ-theory is a set of sentences. In this paper, we consider theories with equality, meaning that the equality symbol $\approx$ is always interpreted as the identity relation. A Σ-structure $\mathcal{A}$ is a model of a Σ-theory T if $\mathcal{A}$ satisfies every sentence in T. A Σ-formula is satisfiable in T (or, equivalently, T-satisfiable) if it is satisfiable in a model of T. Two Σ-formulae φ and ψ are equisatisfiable in T if for every model $\mathcal{A}$ of T, $\mathcal{A}$ satisfies φ iff $\mathcal{A}$ satisfies ψ. The satisfiability problem for a Σ-theory T amounts to checking whether any given (finite) conjunction of Σ-literals (or, equivalently, any given finite set of Σ-literals) is T-satisfiable or not[1]. A satisfiability procedure for T is any given algorithm that solves the satisfiability problem for T. (When checking the T-satisfiability of a conjunction Γ of Σ-literals, the free variables Γ can be regarded as Skolem constants.) The uniform word problem for a theory T amounts to checking whether $T \models \Gamma \Rightarrow e$ where Γ is a conjunction of Σ-equalities and e is a Σ-equality, and all the variables in $\Gamma \Rightarrow e$ are implicitly universally quantified.

Definition 1 (Extended canonizer [13]). *Let T be a Σ-theory and Γ a conjunction of ground Σ-equalities. If Γ is T-satisfiable, then an* extended canonizer *for T is a computable function $ecan(\Gamma) : T(\Sigma, X) \to T(\Sigma \cup K, X)$ such that for any Σ-terms s, t we have $T \models \Gamma \Rightarrow s \approx t$ iff $ecan(\Gamma)(s) = ecan(\Gamma)(t)$, where K is a set of constants such that $K \cap \Sigma = \emptyset$.*

The existence of an extended canonizer for a theory T implies the decidability of the uniform word problem for T. The notion of extended canonizer can be seen as a generalization of the concept of canonizer for the theory of equality defined in [15]. An important difference is that the extended canonizer defined above can be modularly combined as shown in [13]. However, [15] describes a solution to the problem of combining the theory of uninterpreted function symbols with some classes of theories by an interesting generalization of Shostak combination schema.

In the rest of this paper, for simplicity, we only consider convex theories. A Σ-theory is convex iff all the conjunctions of Σ-literals are convex. A conjunction Γ of Σ-literals in a theory T is convex iff for any disjunction $x_1 = y_1 \vee \cdots \vee x_n = y_n$ (where x_i, y_i are variables for $i = 1, ..., n$) we have that $T \cup \Gamma \models x_1 = y_1 \vee \cdots \vee x_n = y_n$ iff $T \cup \Gamma \models x_i = y_i$ for some $i \in \{1, ..., n\}$. If a theory T admitting an extended canonizer is also convex, then it is always possible to build a satisfiability procedure for T by recalling that $\Gamma \wedge \neg e_1 \wedge \cdots \wedge \neg e_n$ (for $n \geq 1$) is T-unsatisfiable iff there exists some $i \in \{1, ..., n\}$ such that $\Gamma \wedge \neg e_i$ is unsatisfiable or, equivalently, $T \models \Gamma \Rightarrow e_i$, where $e_1, ..., e_n$ (for $n \geq 1$) are equalities.

The theory of uninterpreted function symbols is the set of sentences which are logical consequences of the empty set of axioms (in first-order logic with equal-

[1] The satisfiability of any ground formula can be reduced to the satisfiability of sets of literals by well-known techniques.

ity). The theory of lists *à la* Shostak [17] is the set of sentences which are logical consequences of the following axioms: $car(cons(X,Y)) \approx X$, $cdr(cons(X,Y)) \approx Y$, and $cons(car(X), cdr(X)) \approx X$, where X and Y are implicitly universally quantified variables. Notice that both theories are convex.

3 SER Graphs for Extended Canonizers

In this section we describe how to combine and adapt work from [13,16] to build decision procedures and compute extended canonizers for the theory of equality and the theory of lists *à la* Shostak. In particular we show how SER graphs represent the state of the procedures whose computations are described by a suitable set of transition rules ST (applied on an initial SER graph) and how to compute extended canonizers from saturated SER graphs. Preliminary, we illustrate how the rewriting-approach of [2] can be adapted to compute normal forms on a simple example (which will be used also in Section 5).

Let us consider the theory of lists *à la* Shostak and the following set of literals:

$$\Gamma := \left\{ \begin{array}{l} (1)\ car(c_9) \approx c_5, (2)\ cdr(c_9) \approx c_7, (3)\ cons(c_1, c_2) \approx c_4, \\ (4)\ d \approx c_6, (5)\ e \approx c_8, (6)\ k \approx c_3, (7)\ i \approx c_1, (8)\ j \approx c_2, (9)\ c \approx c_9, \\ (10)\ c_5 \approx c_6, (11)\ c_7 \approx c_8, (12)\ c_4 \approx c_3 \end{array} \right\}$$

where equalities are oriented from left to right. In view of building extended canonizers, we consider the problem of showing that $car(c) \approx d$ by normalizing the terms $car(c)$ and d with respect to Γ and the theory of lists. It is well-known that a (ground) convergent term-rewriting system can be obtained from Γ by detecting all possible critical pairs (i.e. selected logical consequences which "patch" non-confluent chains of rewriting) in Γ and the axioms of the theory of lists [7]. This can be done as follows. First, all critical pairs are derived between two equalities in Γ and added to the set of equalities (i.e. considering only the theory of uninterpreted function symbols). Second, compute a critical pair between an axiom of the theory of lists and an equality in Γ (i.e. considering suitable instances of the axioms of the theory of lists). Go back to the first step until no more critical pairs can be derived. For Γ, we derive the following equalities:

- (13) $cons(c_6, c_8) \approx c_{12}$ and (14) $c_{12} \approx c_9$ by axiom $cons(car(X), cdr(X)) \approx X$, (10), (1), (2) and (11);
- (15) $car(c_3) \approx c_{10}$ and (16) $c_{10} \approx c_1$ by axiom $car(cons(X,Y)) \approx X$, (3), and (12);
- (17) $cdr(c_4) \approx c_{11}$ and (18) $c_{11} \approx c_2$ by axiom $cdr(cons(X,Y)) \approx Y$, (3), and (12).

Notice how we have introduced fresh constants (namely, c_{10}, c_{11}, and c_{12}) to maintain the set of equalities flat. Technically, this simplifies the task of building a ground convergent term-rewriting system and it is compatible with the notion of extended canonizer (cf. Definition 1), which permits to return normal forms over a signature extended with extra constants. No more critical pairs can be detected and it is not difficult to see that (1)—(17) form a (ground) convergent term-rewriting system (assuming that equalities are oriented from left to right). At this point, we can find the normal form for $car(c)$:

$$car(c) \overset{(9)}{\approx} car(c_9) \overset{(1)}{\approx} c_5 \overset{(10)}{\approx} c_6.$$

Indeed, $d \approx c_6$ by (4). Hence, we are entitled to conclude that $T \models \Gamma \Rightarrow car(c) \approx d$, where T is the theory of lists *à la* Shostak. Below, we will show how to adapt this completion process for computing normal forms to use a particular data structure to represent terms and equalities, called SER graphs, so as to build efficient extended canonizers.

In the rest of this paper, let Γ be a set set of ground equalities built on a signature Σ, and $\mathcal{K}$ be a set of constants such that $\Sigma \cap \mathcal{K} = \emptyset$. We call Σ the (basic) *signature*, and $\Sigma \cup \mathcal{K}$ the *extended signature*. T denotes a *theory* defined by a set of *axioms* $Ax(T)$.

3.1 SER Graphs

Directed (SER) graphs that support full structure sharing are used to represent (ground) terms and equalities of Γ. Each vertex v is labeled by (i) a function symbol of Σ denoted by $Symbol(v)$, and (ii) a constant of $\mathcal{K}$ denoted by $Constant(v)$. The vertices labeled by constants of $\mathcal{K}$ represent terms or more generally equivalence classes of terms. Edges carry information about sub-term relationships between terms (S), unordered equalities (E) and rewrite rules (R). Sub-term edges are labeled by an index, and we write $u \rightarrow_S^i v$ for a sub-term edge between vertices u and v. Informally, this sub-term edge indicates that v represents the i-th sub-term of the term represented by u. We write $u -_E v$ and $u \rightarrow_R v$ to denote equality and rewrite edges respectively. This graph structure provides a suitable basis for computing (abstract) congruence closures as graph transformation rules as described in [16]. The efficiency of SER graphs crucially depends on the use of a simple ordering (that needs to be defined only on $\mathcal{K}$), rather than a full term ordering.

Initial SER Graph. An *initial* SER graph, $DAG(\Gamma)$, represents a set of equalities Γ as well as the sub-term structure of terms in Γ. It is characterized by the following conditions: (i) If $Symbol(v)$ is a constant, then v has no outgoing sub-term edges; and (ii) if $Symbol(v)$ is a function symbol of arity n, then there is exactly one edge of the form $v \rightarrow_S^i v_i$, for each i with $1 \leq i \leq n$.

The term $Term(v)$ *represented* by a vertex v over the signature Σ is recursively defined as follows: If $Symbol(v)$ is a constant of Σ, then $Term(v) = Symbol(v)$; if $Symbol(v)$ is a function symbol of Σ of arity n, then $Term(v) = Symbol(v)(Term(v_1), \ldots, Term(v_n))$, where $v \rightarrow_S^i v_i$, for $1 \leq i \leq n$. Evidently, $Term(v)$ is a term over the signature Σ. We require that distinct vertices of $DAG(\Gamma)$ represent different terms. Moreover, we insist that $DAG(\Gamma)$ contain no rewrite edges and that each equality edge $u -_E v$ correspond to an equality $s \approx t$ of Γ (with u and v representing s and t, respectively), and vice versa.

The vertices of the graph $DAG(\Gamma)$ also represent flat terms over the extended signature $\Sigma \cup \mathcal{K}$. More specifically, if $Symbol(v)$ is a constant of Σ, then

$ExtTerm(v) = Constant(v)$, and if $Symbol(v)$ is a function symbol of Σ of arity n, then $ExtTerm(v) = Symbol(v)(Constant(v_1), \ldots, Constant(v_n))$, where $v \rightarrow_S^i v_i$, for $1 \leq i \leq n$.

SER Graph Transformations Rules. Let ST denote a set of mandatory and optional SER graph transformation rules. For a theory T with axioms $Ax(T)$ the rules of ST_T are designed to handle the theory of equality and the axioms $Ax(T)$ simulating extension rules for T that reduce the satisfiability problem of T to the theory of equality. ST_{eq} is the set of graph transformation rules for the theory of equality. Note that $ST_{eq} \subseteq ST_T$. In this paper we instantiate ST to ST_{eq} and ST_{ls} to compute extended canonizers in the theory of equality and in the theory of lists *à la* Shostak respectively. The graph transformations for these theories are showed on Figures 1 and 2. The SER graph transformation rules are also formally defined as pairs of tuples of the form $(E_s,\ E_e,\ E_r,\ V,\ \mathcal{K},\ KC,\ C,\ M) \rightarrow (E_s',\ E_e',\ E_r',\ V',\ \mathcal{K}',\ KC',\ C',\ M')$, where the individual components specify a graph, an extended signature, an ordering on constants, a function that associates a constant of the basic and extended signature to a vertex, and a marking function, before and after rule application. More precisely, if $(E_s,\ E_e,\ E_r,\ V,\ \mathcal{K},\ KC,\ C,\ M)$ is a configuration, then:

- E_s, E_e, and E_r describe the sets of sub-term, equality, and rewrite edges, respectively;
- V is the set of vertices[2];
- $\mathcal{K}$ describes the (partial) ordering on constants. Specifically, KC is a set of "ordering constraints" of the form $\{c_i \succ c_j \mid c_i,\ c_j \in \mathcal{K}\}$. (A set of such constraints is considered *satisfiable* if there is an irreflexive, transitive relation on $\mathcal{K}$ that satisfies all of them);
- C is the function that associates a constant of $\mathcal{K}$ and a constant of Σ to a vertex of the graph. The signature of C is $V \rightarrow \mathcal{K} \times \Sigma$. C is updated the following way. Let $dom(C)$ be the domain of C and $update(C, v, c)$ be a function C' which is identical to C for every value v in $dom(C)$ except for c for which $C'(v) = c$. Indeed, $dom(update(C, v, c)) = dom(C) \cup \{v\}$; and
- M is the function that associates a tuple of size $|ST|$ to a vertex of the graph. For each rule r of ST this tuple records if r was applied on v. The signature of M is $V \rightarrow (\mathcal{B} \times \cdots \times \mathcal{B})$, where $\mathcal{B} = \{0, 1\}$.

The *initial state* we are starting with is $(E_s,\ E_e,\ E_r = \emptyset,\ V,\ \mathcal{K},\ KC = \emptyset,\ C,\ \emptyset)$, where V are the vertices of $DAG(\Gamma)$, E_s, E_e and E_r are the S, E and R edges of $DAG(\Gamma)$, $\mathcal{K}$ are the set of constants disjoint from Σ labeling the vertices of V, and C is constructed to associate to each vertex of V a pair composed of a constant of $\mathcal{K}$ and a symbol of Σ.

A graph G is *saturated* with respect to the rules of ST if there are no more transformation rules that can be applied on G. Note that saturated graphs contain only sub-term and rewrite edges. A state $(E_s,\ E_e,\ E_r,\ V,\ \mathcal{K},\ KC,\ C,\ M)$ is called *final* if no transformation rule is applicable on that state. Note that during

[2] Note that, in the theory of equality, vertices can be deleted. In the theory of lists *à la* Shostak vertices can be added or deleted.

the saturation process (and on the saturated graph) each vertex v represents a term on the extended signature but not on the basic signature (see [16]).

The rewrite system over the extended signature extracted from a SER graph is obtained by reading D-rules, C-rules and C-equalities from the graph [4]. Note that on a saturated graph there are only D-rules and C-rules. A *D-rule* on $\Sigma \cup \mathcal{K}$ is a rewrite rule $f(c_1, \ldots, c_n) \rightarrow c_0$, where $f \in \Sigma$ is a function symbol of arity n and $c_0, c_1, \ldots, c_n$ are constants of $\mathcal{K}$. A *C-rule* on $\Sigma \cup \mathcal{K}$ (respectively, a *C-equality*) is a rule $c_0 \rightarrow c_1$ (respectively, an equality $c_0 \approx c_1$), where c_0 and c_1 are constants of $\mathcal{K}$. Intuitively, the constants in $\mathcal{K}$ will essentially serve as names for equivalence classes of terms. Thus, an equation $c_i \approx c_j$ indicates that c_i and c_j are two names for the same equivalence class.

3.2 Extended Canonizers

Computing an extended canonizer $ecan(\Gamma)(s)$ of a term $s \in \mathcal{T}(\Sigma)$ considering a set of ground equalities Γ and a theory T (defined by a set of axioms $Ax(T)$) is performed in four steps.

- The first step consists of the saturation of the initial SER Graph $DAG(\Gamma)$ w.r.t. a set of graph transformation rules ST to obtain a graph G'.
- The second step integrates (recursively) s to the saturated graph G' and adds a marker # to point to the vertex v representing s.
  - If s is a constant c of Σ and c labels a vertex v of G', v represents s.
  - If s is a constant c of Σ that is not present on G', a new vertex v labeled by c and a new constant c_{new} is added to G' to represent s.
  - If $s = f(s_1, \ldots, s_n)$, a new vertex v labeled by f and a new constant c_{new} is added to G' to represent s. The terms s_i representing v_i are recursively integrated to the graph such that there is exactly one S edge of the form $v \rightarrow^i_S v_i$, for each i with $1 \leq i \leq n$.
    It is possible to dispense with this case by adding the equality $c_s = f(s_1, \ldots, s_n)$ to Γ, where c_s is a fresh constant. In this way, it is sufficient to find the normal form of a constant.
- The third step consists of the saturation of G' w.r.t. the same set of transformation rules ST after the addition of s to obtain a graph G''.
- The fourth (and last) step consists of computing $ecan(\Gamma)(s)$ on G'' by following the marker #.
  - If the marker points to a vertex with a chain of outgoing R edges ending with a vertex w, $ecan(\Gamma)(s) = Constant(w)$ [3].
  - Otherwise, $ecan(\Gamma)(s) = ExtTerm(v)$.

While the termination of the second and fourth steps above is obvious, the analysis of the exhaustive application of the rules of the SER graphs will offer the argument for the termination of the first and the third steps.

[3] Note that during the saturation process # may point to a vertex different from the initial v vertex in particular due to the fact that the SER graphs support full structure sharing. If v is deleted and merged with a vertex u then # will point to u.

3.3 Extended Canonizers for the Theory of Equality

To build an extended canonizer for the theory of equality the set of SER graph transformation rules ST is instantiated by $ST_{eq} = \{Orient, SR, RRout, RRin, Merge\}$. Figure 1 depicts the graph transformations with their specific conditions of application graphically and formally as transformation rules. *Orient*, replaces an equality edge, $v -_E w$, by a rewrite edge, $v \rightarrow_R w$, provided $Constant(v) \succ Constant(w)$. The ordering $\succ$ needs to be defined on constants in $\mathcal{K}$ not on terms over $\Sigma \cup \mathcal{K}$. The *SR* rule replaces one sub-term edge by another one. In logical terms it represents the simplification of a sub-term by rewriting, or, equivalently, the simultaneous simplification of all occurrences of a sub-term, if the graph presentation encodes full structure sharing for terms. The *RRout* and *RRin* rules each replace one rewrite edge by another. They correspond to certain equational inferences with the underlying rewrite rules (namely, critical pair computations and compositions, which for ground terms are also simplifications). The *RRin* rule is useful for efficiency reasons, though not mandatory. If the rule is applied exhaustively, the resulting rewrite system will be a right-reduced rewrite system over the extended signature. The *Merge* rule ensures full structure sharing; it collapses two vertices that represent the same term over the extended signature into a single vertex. For example, if two vertices v and w represent the same flat term (over the extended signature), the *Merge* rule can be used to delete one of the two vertices, say v, and all its outgoing sub-term edges. All other edges that were incident on v need to be redirected to w, with the proviso that outgoing rewrite edges have to be changed to equality edges.

The transformation rules can then be applied non-deterministically, and are only applied if they result in a *new* edge.

The component M is not modified by the rules in ST_{eq}. It will be updated by those presented in the next section, since we need to extend the graphs with sufficiently many ground instances of the axioms of the theory of lists in a fair way.

3.4 Extended Canonizers for the Theory of Lists *à la* Shostak

To build an extended canonizer for the theory of lists *à la* Shostak, the set of SER graph transformation rules ST is instantiated by $ST_{ls} = \{CrdCons, CarCons, CarCdrCons\} \cup ST_{eq}$. Figure 2 depicts the graph transformations with their specific conditions of application graphically and formally as transformation rules. The set ST_{eq} has been defined in Section 3.3. Rewriting and computing critical pairs in the presence of the axioms of the theory of lists *à la* Shostak requires extending the equalities of Γ [6]. These extension computations are implemented by the *CrdCons*, *CarCons* and *CarCdrCons* rules each corresponding to one of the axioms of the theory of lists *à la* Shostak $cdr(cons(X,Y)) \approx Y$, $car(cons(X,Y)) \approx X$ and $cons(car(X), cdr(X)) \approx X$ respectively.

The transformation rules can then be applied non-deterministically. They are only applied once on a particular vertex; this is guaranteed by the marking function M that controls the number of applications of each rule on a vertex. When

Orient Rule (mandatory)

$(E_s,\ \{v_1 -_E v_2\} \cup E_e,\ E_r,\ V,\ \mathcal{K},\ KC,\ C,\ M)$
$\rightarrow_{Orient}$
$(E_s,\ E_e,\ \{v_1 \rightarrow_R v_2\} \cup E_r,\ V,\ \mathcal{K},\ \{c_1 \succ c_2\} \cup KC,\ C,\ M)$
if $\{c_1 \succ c_2\} \cup KC$ is satisfiable.

SR Rule (mandatory)

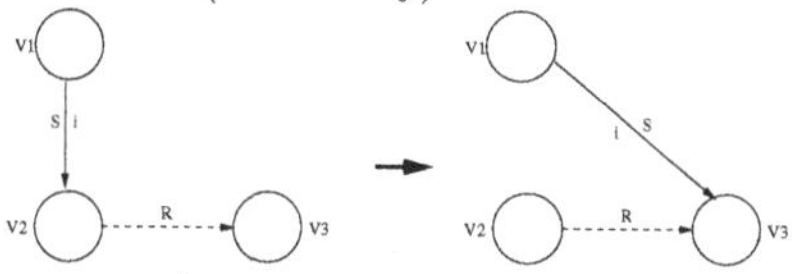

$(\{v_1 \rightarrow_S^i v_2\} \cup E_s,\ E_e,\ \{v_2 \rightarrow_R v_3\} \cup E_r,\ V,\ \mathcal{K},\ KC,\ C,\ M)$
$\rightarrow_{SR}$
$(\{v_1 \rightarrow_S^i v_3\} \cup E_s,\ E_e,\ \{v_2 \rightarrow_R v_3\} \cup E_r,\ V,\ \mathcal{K},\ KC,\ C,\ M)$

RRout Rule (mandatory)

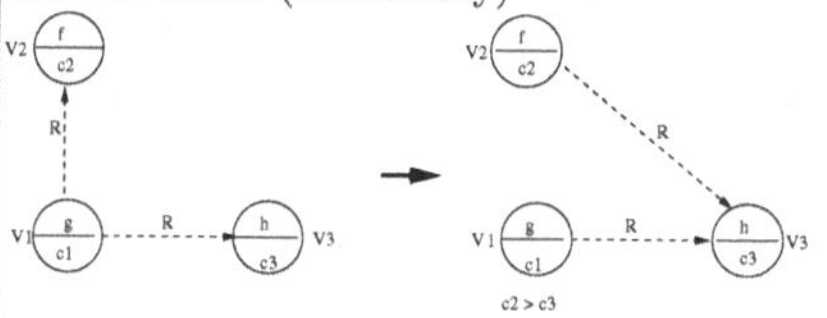

$(E_s,\ E_e,\ \{v_1 \rightarrow_R v_2,\ v_1 \rightarrow_R v_3\} \cup E_r,\ V,\ \mathcal{K},\ KC,\ C,\ M)$
$\rightarrow_{RRout}$
$(E_s,\ E_e,\ \{v_2 \rightarrow_R v_3,\ v_1 \rightarrow_R v_3\} \cup E_r,\ V,\ \mathcal{K},\ \{c_2 \succ c_3\} \cup KC,\ C,\ M)$

RRin Rule (optional)

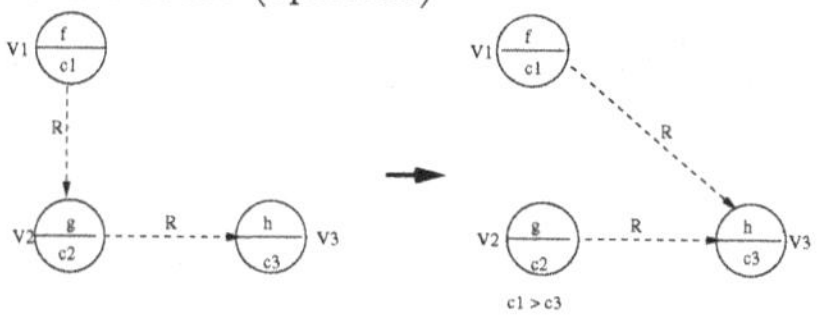

$(E_s,\ E_e,\ \{v_1 \rightarrow_R v_2,\ v_2 \rightarrow_R v_3\} \cup E_r,\ V,\ \mathcal{K},\ KC,\ C,\ M)$
$\rightarrow_{RRin}$
$(E_s,\ E_e,\ \{v_1 \rightarrow_R v_3,\ v_2 \rightarrow_R v_3\} \cup E_r,\ V,\ \mathcal{K},\ \{c_1 \succ c_3\} \cup KC,\ C,\ M)$

Merge Rule (mandatory)

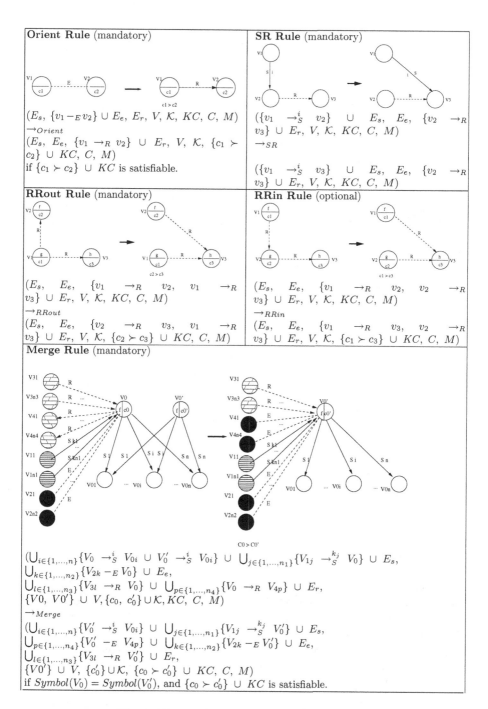

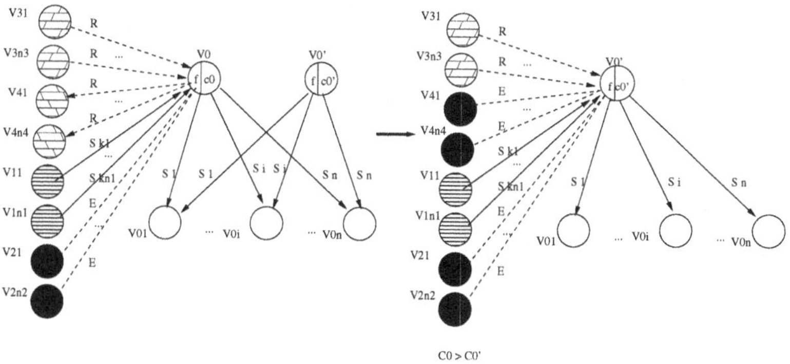

$(\bigcup_{i\in\{1,\dots,n\}}\{V_0 \rightarrow_S^i V_{0i} \cup V_0' \rightarrow_S^i V_{0i}\} \cup \bigcup_{j\in\{1,\dots,n_1\}}\{V_{1j} \rightarrow_S^{k_j} V_0\} \cup E_s,$
$\bigcup_{k\in\{1,\dots,n_2\}}\{V_{2k} -_E V_0\} \cup E_e,$
$\bigcup_{l\in\{1,\dots,n_3\}}\{V_{3l} \rightarrow_R V_0\} \cup \bigcup_{p\in\{1,\dots,n_4\}}\{V_0 \rightarrow_R V_{4p}\} \cup E_r,$
$\{V0,\ V0'\} \cup V, \{c_0,\ c_0'\} \cup \mathcal{K}, KC,\ C,\ M)$
$\rightarrow_{Merge}$
$(\bigcup_{i\in\{1,\dots,n\}}\{V_0' \rightarrow_S^i V_{0i}\} \cup \bigcup_{j\in\{1,\dots,n_1\}}\{V_{1j} \rightarrow_S^{k_j} V_0'\} \cup E_s,$
$\bigcup_{p\in\{1,\dots,n_4\}}\{V_0' -_E V_{4p}\} \cup \bigcup_{k\in\{1,\dots,n_2\}}\{V_{2k} -_E V_0'\} \cup E_e,$
$\bigcup_{l\in\{1,\dots,n_3\}}\{V_{3l} \rightarrow_R V_0'\} \cup E_r,$
$\{V0'\} \cup V,\ \{c_0'\} \cup \mathcal{K},\ \{c_0 \succ c_0'\} \cup KC,\ C,\ M)$
if $Symbol(V_0) = Symbol(V_0')$, and $\{c_0 \succ c_0'\} \cup KC$ is satisfiable.

Fig. 1. The graph transformation rules in ST_{eq}

CdrCons Rule (mandatory)

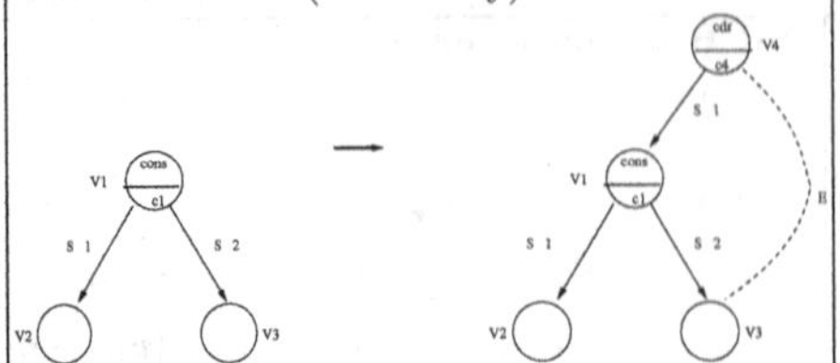

$(\{v_1 \rightarrow^1_S v_2, v_1 \rightarrow^2_S v_3\} \cup E_s, E_e, E_r, V, \mathcal{K}, KC, C, M)$
$\rightarrow_{CdrCons}$
$(\{v_1 \rightarrow^1_S v_2, v_1 \rightarrow^2_S v_3, v_4 \rightarrow^1_S v_1\} \cup E_s, \{v_4 -_E v_3\} \cup E_e, E_r, \{v_4\} \cup V, \{c_4\} \cup \mathcal{K}, KC, update(C, v_4, (c_4, cdr)), M')$
if $Symbol(v_1) = cons$ and $\#1\ M(v1) = 0$
$Symbol$ is extended such that $Symbol(v_4) = cdr$
M' is M extended with $\#1\ M(v1) = 1$, $\#1\ M(v4) = 1$, $\#2\ M(v4) = 1$ and $\#3\ M(v4) = 1$

CarCons Rule (mandatory)

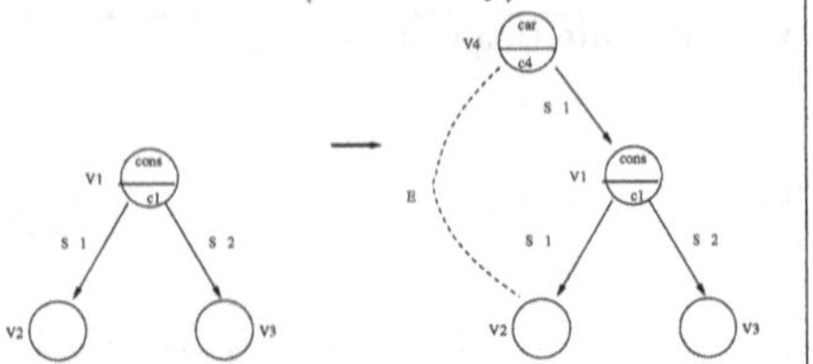

$(\{v_1 \rightarrow^1_S v_2, v_1 \rightarrow^2_S v_3\} \cup E_s, E_e, E_r, V, \mathcal{K}, KC, C, M)$
$\rightarrow_{CarCons}$
$(\{v_1 \rightarrow^1_S v_2, v_1 \rightarrow^2_S v_3, v_4 \rightarrow^1_S v_1\} \cup E_s, \{v_4 -_E v_2\} \cup E_e, E_r, \{v_4\} \cup V, \{c_4\} \cup \mathcal{K}, KC, update(C, v_4, (c_4, car)), M')$
if $Symbol(v_1) = cons$ and $\#2\ M(v1) = 0$
$Symbol$ is extended such that $Symbol(v_4) = car$
M' is M extended with $\#2\ M(v1) = 1$, $\#1\ M(v4) = 1$, $\#2\ M(v4) = 1$ and $\#3\ M(v4) = 1$

CarCdrCons Rule (mandatory)

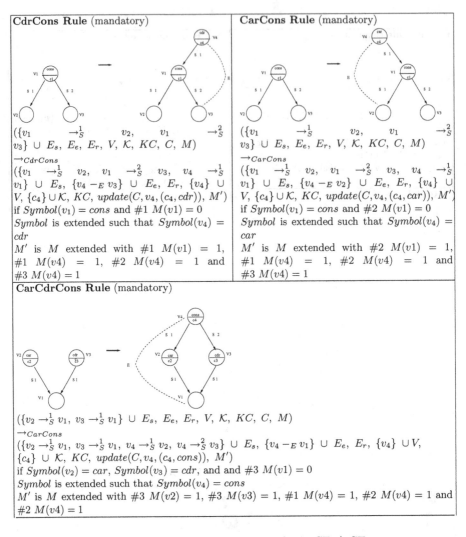

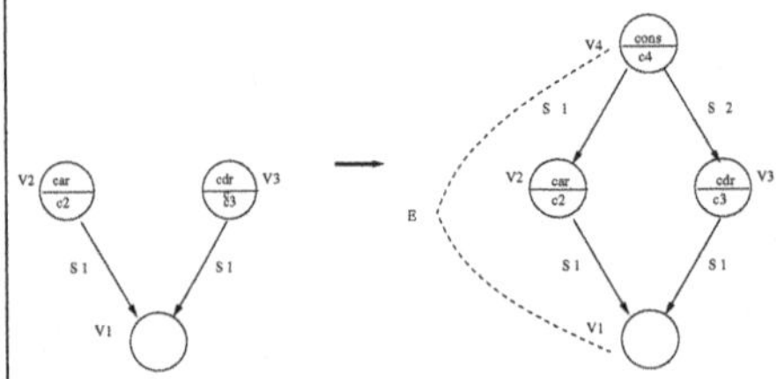

$(\{v_2 \rightarrow^1_S v_1, v_3 \rightarrow^1_S v_1\} \cup E_s, E_e, E_r, V, \mathcal{K}, KC, C, M)$
$\rightarrow_{CarCons}$
$(\{v_2 \rightarrow^1_S v_1, v_3 \rightarrow^1_S v_1, v_4 \rightarrow^1_S v_2, v_4 \rightarrow^2_S v_3\} \cup E_s, \{v_4 -_E v_1\} \cup E_e, E_r, \{v_4\} \cup V, \{c_4\} \cup \mathcal{K}, KC, update(C, v_4, (c_4, cons)), M')$
if $Symbol(v_2) = car$, $Symbol(v_3) = cdr$, and and $\#3\ M(v1) = 0$
$Symbol$ is extended such that $Symbol(v_4) = cons$
M' is M extended with $\#3\ M(v2) = 1$, $\#3\ M(v3) = 1$, $\#1\ M(v4) = 1$, $\#2\ M(v4) = 1$ and $\#2\ M(v4) = 1$

Fig. 2. The graph transformation rules in $ST_{ls} \setminus ST_{eq}$

a rule is applied on a vertex that vertex is marked w.r.t. that rule. Additionally, the vertices added by the rule are marked w.r.t. all the rules. The signature of M is $V \rightarrow (\mathcal{B} \times \mathcal{B} \times \mathcal{B})$ where $\mathcal{B} = \{0, 1\}$ where V is the set of vertices of the considered graph, and $M(v)$ is a tuple of size three such that $\#1\ M(v)$, $\#2\ M(v)$, and $\#3\ M(v)$[4] record if the rule *CrdCons*, *CarCons* and *CarCdrCons* were applied on v respectively. Figure 2 presents the transformation rules *Crd-Cons*, *CarCons* and *CarCdrCons*. For clarity, we did not add the marker to the rules.

[4] $\#i\ t$ denotes the ith component of the tuple t.

4 Correctness

By assigning a suitable weight to graphs that decreases with each application of a transformation rule (as shown in [16]), it is possible to show that the exhaustive application of the rules in ST_{eq} terminates. This implies that the first and the third steps in the construction of the extended canonizer (cf. Section 3.2) for the theory of equality also terminate. As already observed in Section 3.2, the termination of the second and fourth steps is trivial. The correctness of the extended canonizer for the theory of equality is a straightforward consequence of the results in [16]. Exhaustive application of the graph transformation rules in ST_{eq} is *sound* in that the equational theory represented over Σ-terms does not change with respect to the given set of equations Γ. Completeness follows from the fact that the term rewriting system over the extended signature extracted from the graph saturated by ST_{eq} is convergent. If $RRin$ is applied the resulting rewrite system over the extended signature is right-reduced. The proofs are based on associating a triple $(\mathcal{K}, Ex, Rx)$ with each SER graph tuple $(E_s, E_e, E_r, V, \mathcal{K}, KC, C, M)$, where Ex is the set of C-equalities and Rx is the set of D and C-rules extracted from the SER graph. Thus, with the initial graph we associate a triple $(\mathcal{K}_0, Ex_0, Rx_0)$, where $Rx_0 \cup Ex_0$ represents the same equational theory over Σ-terms (by construction). This property is preserved by the application of the transformation rules in ST_{eq}. The triple $(\mathcal{K}_n, Ex_n, Rx_n)$ representing a saturated SER graph is such that Ex_n is empty and Rx_n is a convergent rewrite system over the extended signature. Additionally, it is possible to prove that the extended canonizer runs in quadratic time in the number of sub-terms of the input set of literals by adapting the argument in [9].

Property 1. There exists an $O(n^2)$ extended canonizer for the theory of equality, where n is the number of sub-terms in the input set of literals.

The termination and correctness of the extended canonizer for the theory of lists *à la* Shostak is only slightly more complex. As for the theory of equality, we only need to prove the termination of the first and the fourth steps in the construction of the extended canonizer. This can be argued as follows. The termination of the exhaustive application of the rules in ST_{ls} can be easily seen by observing that the rules in $ST_{ls} \setminus ST_{eq}$ (cf. Figure 2) can only be applied a linear number of time in the number of the sub-terms represented in graph (because of the proviso in the rules about the function M). M is built in such a way that the rules in $ST_{ls} \setminus ST_{eq}$ are not applied on vertices added by the same set of rules.

Property 2. If we would apply rules of $ST_{ls} \setminus ST_{eq}$ on initial vertices and apply rules of the same set of rules to the resulting vertices generating new vertices, the latter vertices and the initial vertices would eventually be merged.

Indeed, the rules in $ST_{ls} \setminus ST_{eq}$ simulate extension rules for the theory of lists *à la* Shostak and equalities generated by extension rules are not extended themselves.

The rules in ST_{eq} terminates and do not create any new vertex to which the rules in $ST_{ls} \setminus ST_{eq}$ can be applied. This allows us to conclude the termination of the exhaustive application of the rules in ST_{ls}. For correctness, we observe that the exhaustive applications of the rules in ST_{ls} simulates the exhaustive applications of the superposition calculus to the flat set of literals corresponding to the initial set of equalities represented in the graph (see [2] for details). As a consequence, the term rewriting system over the extended signature in the final graph is ground convergent.

Property 3. There exists an $O(n^2)$ extended canonizer for the theory of lists *à la* Shostak, where n is the number of sub-terms in the input set of literals.

The quadratic complexity can be seen by observing that at most a linear number $k = O(n)$ of new vertices is created by the rules in $ST_{ls} \setminus ST_{eq}$ while the exhaustive application of those in ST_{eq} can be done in $O(k^2) = O(n^2)$.

5 A Worked Out Example

Figure 3a presents the construction of $DAG(\Gamma)$, where $\Gamma = \{car(c) \approx d,\ cdr(c) \approx e,\ cons(i,j) \approx k\}$ and $\mathcal{K} = \{c_1, \ldots, c_9\}$. We apply all the transformations described below on $DAG(\Gamma)$ using the ordering $\{c_5 \succ c_6, c_7 \succ c_8, c_{12} \succ c_9, c_{10} \succ c_1, c_{11} \succ c_2, c_4 \succ c_3\}$[5] on the constants of $\mathcal{K}' = \mathcal{K} \cup \{c_{10}, c_{11}, c_{12}\}$.

- *Orient* orients the E edge between c_5 and c_6 into an R edge from c_5 to c_6 ($c_5 \succ c_6$), and the E edge between c_7 and c_8 into an R edge from c_7 to c_8 ($c_7 \succ c_8$).
- *CarCdrCons* adds a vertex labeled by c_{12} and *cons*, two S edges from c_{12} to c_5 and from c_{12} to c_7, and an E edge between c_{12} and c_9.
- *SR* replaces the S edge from c_{12} to c_5 by an S edge from c_{12} to c_6.
- *SR* replaces the S edge from c_{12} to c_7 by an S edge from c_{12} to c_8.
- *Orient* orients the E edge between c_{12} and c_9 into an R edge from c_{12} to c_9 ($c_{12} \succ c_9$)
- *CarCons* transformation adds a vertex labeled by c_{10} and *car*, an S edge from c_{10} to c_4 and an E edge between c_{10} and c_1.
- *CdrCons* adds a vertex labeled by c_{11} and *cdr*, an S edge from c_{10} to c_4 and an E edge between c_{10} and c_2.
- *Orient* orients the E edges between c_{10} and c_1, c_{11} to c_2 and c_4 to c_3 into an R edges from c_{10} to c_1 ($c_{10} \succ c_1$), c_{11} to c_2 ($c_{11} \succ c_2$), and c_4 to c_3 ($c_4 \succ c_3$).
- *SR* replaces the S edge from c_{10} to c_4 by an S edge from c_{10} to c_3.
- *SR* replaces the S edge from c_{11} to c_4 by an S edge from c_{11} to c_3.

No more transformation rules can be applied on the graph. We obtain the saturated graph on Figure 3b. The convergent rewrite system over the extended signature $\mathcal{K}'$ is $\{c_{12} \rightarrow c_9,\ c_5 \rightarrow c_6,\ c_7 \rightarrow c_8,\ c_{10} \rightarrow c_1,\ c_{11} \rightarrow c_2,\ c_4 \rightarrow$

[5] This ordering is constructed "on the fly."

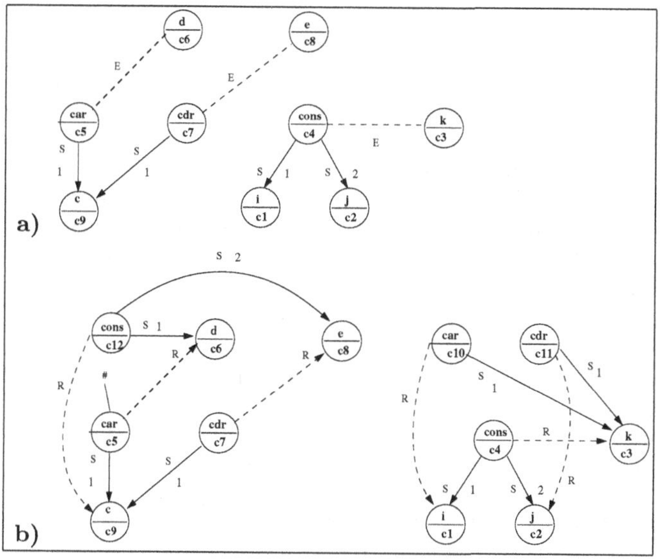

Fig. 3. a) Initial DAG for $\Gamma = \{car(c) \approx d,\ cdr(c) \approx e,\ cons(i,j) \approx k\}$, b) Saturated graph on the extended signature

c_3, $cons(c_6, c_8) \to c_{12}$, $car(c_9) \to c_5$, $cdr(c_9) \to c_7$, $car(c_3) \to c_{10}$, $cdr(c_3) \to c_1$, $cons(c_1, c_2) \to c_4\}$.

Using the graph we can now prove that $T \models \Gamma \Rightarrow car(c) \approx d$, where T is the theory of lists *à la* Shostak, by proving that $ecan(\Gamma)(car(c)) = ecan(\Gamma)(d) = c_6$.

- To compute $ecan(\Gamma)(car(c))$, we add a vertex v labeled by c_{13} and an S edge from v to the vertex labeled by c_9. c_{13} and c_5 are merged and the marker to the vertex representing $car(c)$ points to c_5 (cf. Figure 3b). As there is an R edge from c_5 to c_6, $ecan(\Gamma)(car(c)) = c_6$.
- $ecan(\Gamma)(d) = c_6$ because d and c_6 label the same vertex.

6 Discussion

We have presented a graph-based method for building decision procedures and extended canonizers for the theory of equality and the theory of lists *à la* Shostak. The method combines the key ideas of the rewriting-based approach to build satisfiability procedures and SER graphs. It also allows us to obtain a precise characterization of the computational complexity of the resulting procedures. We believe that our approach allows for efficient implementations and a visual presentation that better illuminates the basic ideas underlying the construction of decision procedures for convex theories and the computations of extended canonizers. We plan to apply our method to other theories for which the rewriting approach does not work, e.g., the theory of acyclic lists [11], by designing suitable rules on the graph data structure in order to take into account the infinitely many axioms for acyclicity.

References

1. Armando, A., Bonacina, M.P., Ranise, S., Schulz, S.: On a rewriting approach to satisfiability procedures: extension, combination of theories and an experimental appraisal. In: Gramlich, B. (ed.) Frontiers of Combining Systems. LNCS (LNAI), vol. 3717, Springer, Heidelberg (2005)
2. Armando, A., Ranise, S., Rusinowitch, M.: A rewriting approach to satisfiability procedures. J. of Information and Computation 183(2), 140–164 (2003)
3. Baader, F., Nipkow, T.: Term rewriting and all that. Cambridge University Press, Cambridge (1998)
4. Bachmair, L., Tiwari, A., Vigneron, L.: Abstract congruence closure. J. of Automated Reasoning 31(2), 129–168 (2003)
5. Conchon, S., Kristic, S.: Canonization for disjoint unions of theories. Information and Computation 199(1-2), 87–106 (2005)
6. Jouannaud, J., Kirchner, H.: Completion of a set of rules modulo a set of equations. SIAM J. on Computing 15(4), 1155–1194 (1986)
7. Knuth, D.E., Bendix, P.B.: Simple word problems in universal algebras. In: Computational Problems in Abstract Algebra, pp. 263–297. Pergamon Press, Oxford (1970)
8. Lynch, C., Strogova, P.: SOUR graphs for efficient completion. Journal of Discrete Mathematics and Theoretical Computer Science 2(1), 1–25 (1998)
9. Nelson, C.G., Oppen, D.C.: Fast Decision Procedures based on Congruence Closure. Journal of the ACM 27(2), 356–364 (1980)
10. Nelson, C.G., Oppen, D.C.: Simplification by cooperating decision procedures. ACM Trans. on Programming Languages and Systems 1(2), 245–257 (1979)
11. Oppen, D.C.: Reasoning About Recursively Defined Data Structures. J. ACM 27(3), 403–411 (1980)
12. Rusinowitch, M.: Theorem-proving with resolution and superposition. J. Symb. Comput. 11(1-2), 21–49 (1991)
13. Ranise, S., Ringeissen, C., Tran, D.: Nelson-Oppen, Shostak and the Extended Canonizer: A Family Picture with a Newborn. In: Liu, Z., Araki, K. (eds.) ICTAC 2004. LNCS, vol. 3407, pp. 372–386. Springer, Heidelberg (2005)
14. Ranise, S., Tinelli, C.: Satisfiability Modulo Theories. IEEE Magazine on Intelligent Systems 21(6), 71–81 (2006)
15. Ruess, H., Shankar, N.: Deconstructing Shostak. In: Proceedings of the 16th Annual IEEE Symposium on Logic in Computer Science, Boston, Massachusetts, USA, pp. 19–28. IEEE Computer Society, Los Alamitos (2001)
16. Scharff, C., Bachmair, L.: On the Combination of Congruence Closure and Completion. In: Buchberger, B., Campbell, J.A. (eds.) AISC 2004. LNCS (LNAI), vol. 3249, pp. 103–117. Springer, Heidelberg (2004)
17. Shostak, R.E.: Deciding Combinations of Theories. Journal of the ACM 31, 1–12 (1984)

A Randomized Algorithm for BBCSPs in the Prover-Verifier Model

K. Subramani*

LDCSEE,
West Virginia University,
Morgantown, WV
ksmani@csee.wvu.edu

Abstract. In this paper we introduce a Prover-Verifier model for analyzing the computational complexity of a class of Constraint Satisfaction problems termed Binary Boolean Constraint Satisfaction problems (BBCSPs). BBCSPs represent an extremely general class of constraint satisfaction problems and find applications in a wide variety of domains including constraint programming, puzzle solving and program testing. We establish that each instance of a BBCSP admits a coin-flipping Turing Machine that halts in time polynomial in the size of the input. The prover **P** in the Prover-Verifier model is endowed with very limited powers; in particular, it has no memory and it can only pose restricted queries to the verifier. The verifier on the other hand is both omniscient in that it is cognizant of all the problem details and insincere in that it does not have to decide *a priori* on the intended proof. However, the verifier must stay consistent in its responses. Inasmuch as our provers will be memoryless and our verifiers will be asked for extremely simple certificates, our work establishes the existence of a simple, randomized algorithm for BBCSPs. Our model itself serves as a basis for the design of zero-knowledge machine learning algorithms in that the prover ends up learning the proof desired by the verifier.

1 Introduction

This paper analyzes a class of constraint satisfaction problems called Boolean Binary Constraint Satisfaction problems (BBCSPs) within the framework of a Prover-Verifier model. The principal goal of the analysis is to establish that BBCSPs can be decided by simple and efficient randomized algorithms. A BBCSP is characterized by a conjunction of binary constraints over boolean bi-valued variables. To recapitulate, a binary constraint is one which is defined by exactly two variables, while a boolean variable is one which can assume at

* This research is supported in part by a research grant from the Air-Force Office of Scientific Research under contract FA9550-06-1-0050. A portion of this research was conducted at the Stanford Research Institute, where the author was a Visiting Fellow.

C.B. Jones, Z. Liu, J. Woodcock (Eds.): ICTAC 2007, LNCS 4711, pp. 455–466, 2007.

most two values. The conjunction of binary constraints over boolean variables constitutes a BBCSP.

BBCSP instances arise in a wide variety of domains, including Real-Time Scheduling [13], program verification [1] and even constraint-based puzzle solving.

It is important to note that BBCSPs permit constraints that combine several theories as opposed to typical constraint systems which focus on a single theory. This feature is particularly important in the modeling and specification of problems in domains such as robotics. BBCSPS are not known to be polynomial-time solvable and on account of their generality, the design of a general-purpose polynomial time algorithm appears challenging at the very least. In this paper, we present a simple and efficient randomized algorithm for the class of BBCSPs. Randomized algorithms have a number of advantages in terms of robustness, simplicity, and space efficiency and the Constraint Solving literature is replete with the successful application of local search based on randomized strategies towards global optimization problems [11].

The principal contributions of this paper are as follows:

(a) Definition of a new class of Constraint Satisfaction problems called BBCSPs.
(b) Design and Analysis of a randomized polynomial time algorithm for BBCSPs.
(c) Development and Analysis of a Prover-Verifier Model for the analysis of Constraint Satisfaction problems.

The rest of this paper is organized as follows: Section 2 provides a formal definition of the class of BBCSPs. The Prover-Verifier model and its application to the analysis of Constraint Satisfaction problems are discussed in Section 3. In Section 4, the motivation for our work is detailed; related approaches in the literature are presented in Section 5. The randomized algorithm for BBCSP is described in Section 6, followed by a detailed analysis in Section 7. We conclude in Section 8, by summarizing our contributions and pointing out avenues for future research.

2 Statement of Problem

We begin with some preliminary definitions.

Definition 1. *A program variable (or variable) is a placeholder for values from a specified set, which is called its* domain.

Definition 2. *A variable is said to be* boolean, *if its domain has cardinality* 2.

Definition 3. *A* binary *constraint is defined as a predicate of the form:* $f(x_a, x_b) \leq c$, *where* x_a, x_b *are program variables,* c *is a real constant and* $f()$ *is an arbitrary binary function.*

A Constraint Satisfaction Problem (CSP) is defined by the triplet $\langle \mathcal{X}, \mathcal{D}, \mathcal{C} \rangle$, where $\mathcal{X} = \{x_1, x_2, \ldots, x_n\}$ denotes a set of program variables, $\mathcal{D} = \{D_1, D_2, \ldots D_n\}$ denotes the set of their respective domains and $\mathcal{C} = \{C_1, C_2, \ldots, C_m\}$ denotes a set of constraints over the program variables.

Definition 4. *An assignment to a CSP* $R = \langle \mathcal{X}, \mathcal{D}, \mathcal{C} \rangle$ *is any mapping* $g : \mathcal{X} \rightarrow \mathcal{D}$*, which assigns to each variable* $x_i \in \mathcal{X}$*, a values from the domain* D_i*.*

Definition 5. *An assignment* $g : \mathcal{X} \rightarrow \mathcal{D}$ *to the CSP* $R = \langle \mathcal{X}, \mathcal{D}, \mathcal{C} \rangle$*, satisfies a constraint* $f(x_a, x_b) \leq c$*, if* $f(g(x_a), g(x_b)) \leq c$*.*

Definition 6. *An assignment* $g : \mathcal{X} \rightarrow \mathcal{D}$ *to the CSP* $R = \langle \mathcal{X}, \mathcal{D}, \mathcal{C} \rangle$*, is said to be a valid (or consistent) assignment, if it satisfies all the constraints in* $\mathcal{C}$*. In this case, we write* $g \models R$*.*

If a CSP assignment does not have a valid assignment, it is said to be *infeasible* or *inconsistent*; otherwise it is feasible or satisfiable.

Definition 7. *Given an assignment* $g_1 : \mathcal{X} \rightarrow \mathcal{D}$ *which does not satisfy the CSP* $R = \langle \mathcal{X}, \mathcal{D}, \mathcal{C} \rangle$*, we define* $\oplus g_1$ *to be the disjunction of the negations of all the assignments in* g_1*. Note that* $\oplus g_1$ *is a* constraint*; further* R *is satisfiable, if and only if* $R \wedge \oplus g_1$ *is.*

For instance, consider the constraint $l_1 : x_1 - x_2 \leq 0$, with $x_1, x_2 \in \{2, 4\}$. The assignment $g_1 : x_1 = 4$, $x_2 = 2$ clearly violates l_1. It is not hard to see that l_1 is feasible if and only if $l_1 \wedge \oplus g_1 = l_1 \wedge (x_1 \neq 4 \vee x_2 \neq 2)$ is.

Definition 8. *A CSP* $R = \langle \mathcal{X}, \mathcal{D}, \mathcal{C} \rangle$ *is said to be a Boolean Binary Constraint Satisfaction Problem (BBCSP) if every program variable* $x_i \in \mathcal{X}$ *is boolean and every constraint* $C_i \in \mathcal{C}$ *is binary.*

Definition 9. *Given a BBCSP* $R = \langle \mathcal{X}, \mathcal{D}, \mathcal{C} \rangle$ *and an assignment* $g_1 : \mathcal{X} \rightarrow \mathcal{D}$*, such that* $g_1 \not\models R$*, the operation* $\bigtriangledown(g_1, x_i)$ *creates a new assignment* g_1'*, which differs from* g_1 *only on variable* x_i*. Since* x_i *has precisely two values, the* $\bigtriangledown$ *operation is well-defined.*

The application of the $\bigtriangledown$ operator to a variable in an assignment is referred to as *flipping* that variable in that assignment.

Any CSP R defines a natural relation over the ordered tuples over its domain $\mathcal{D}$, viz., the relation that is constituted of precisely those tuples that satisfy the CSP. This relation is called the inclusion relation corresponding to that CSP and is denoted by $\mathcal{R}_{in}$.

When dealing with CSPs in which program variables belong to bounded domains, it is important to distinguish between *extensional* and *intensional* constraint representations. A constraint is in intensional form, if it is represented implicitly; it is in extensional form if the tuples that satisfy it are explicitly enumerated. For instance, let $x_1, x_2 \in \{2, 4\}$ denote two program variables. Consider the constraint $x_1 - x_2 \leq -1$; this representation is the intensional. To represent the same constraint in extensional form, we would list the tuples that satisfy the constraint; in this case, there is only one such tuple, viz., $\langle 2, 4 \rangle$. The results of this paper do not make any assumption about the form in which the constraints are represented.

It is important to note that the framework of CSPs permits only conjunctive theories; in other words, a valid assignment must satisfy all constraints. This is not a restriction in general, since a pair of constraints which need to be satisfied in the disjunctive sense only can be conjunctively linked using a boolean variable. For instance, the disjunctive constraint specification: $(x_1 - 3 \cdot x_2 \geq 7) \vee (3 \cdot x_4 - 7 \cdot x_5 \leq 4)$ can be converted into the conjunctive specification: $(x_1 - 3 \cdot x_2 \geq 7 - y \cdot M) \wedge (3 \cdot x_4 - 7 \cdot x_5 \leq (1 - y) \cdot M + 4)$, $y \in \{0, 1\}$ and M is a sufficiently large number that relaxes the constraint. It is important to note though that this technique *does not* preserve the structure of BBCSPs since the constraints are no longer binary. Accordingly, BBCSPs are somewhat restrictive in the scope of the constraints that are permitted, in that the constraint specifications must be conjunctively linked.

In this paper we are concerned with the following problem: Given a BBCSP $R = \langle \mathcal{X}, \mathcal{D}, \mathcal{C} \rangle$, determine a valid assignment for R or establish its infeasibility. Alternatively, we can define the BBCSP problem as follows: Given a BBCSP $R = \langle \mathcal{X}, \mathcal{D}, \mathcal{C} \rangle$, check if $\mathcal{R}_{in} = \emptyset$. **It is crucial to note that the entire constraint set is not provided to the algorithm (prover), but only responses to queries are provided.** The following section clarifies this issue.

3 The Prover-Verifier Model

In this section, we discuss the Prover-Verifier Model, which will serve as the framework in which our algorithm for BBCSPs will be analyzed.

The model is best understood through the mechanics of the following two-person game:

(i) The BBCSP $R = \langle \mathcal{X}, \mathcal{D}, \mathcal{C} \rangle$ is known to player **V** (the verifier).
(ii) Player **P** (the prover) knows $\mathcal{X}$ and $\mathcal{D}$. It is **P**'s job to determine a valid assignment $g()$ for R.
(iii) In each round of the game, player **P** provides a *proof* to R. The proof is nothing more than an assignment function, which maps the variables in $\mathcal{X}$ to the domain $\mathcal{D}$.
(iv) If player **V** finds **P**'s proof satisfactory, i.e, the assignment provided by **P** satisfies all the constraints in R, then **P** wins and the game is over.
(v) If player **V** is dissatisfied with **P**' s proof, then he provides a certificate which serves to convince **P** that his proof was incorrect. Two distinct certificates (i.e., certificates provided during distinct rounds of the game) are said to be inconsistent, if they are inconsistent on at least one variable. For instance, if **V** declares that the sub-proof $x_1 \geq 2$ is incorrect in one certificate and that the sub-proof $x_1 < 2$ is incorrect in another certificate, then these two certificates are inconsistent.
(vi) Player **P** can use the certificates obtained up to the current juncture to formulate a new proof and the protocol continues. If **P** can access only the current certificate, before he makes his next move, then he is said to be *memoryless*.
(vii) At any point in the game, **P** can decide that R is an inconsistent constraint set and terminate the game.

(viii) At the end of each round player **V** can augment the constraint set $\mathcal{C}$ of the BBCSP R in response to **P**'s proofs, as long as the new constraints that are added are consistent with R. For instance, if **V** has responded negatively to **P**'s subproof $x_1 \geq 2$, then he can add the constraint $x_1 < 2$ to R, if $x_1 < 2$ is consistent with R.

We make the following important observations:

(a) Under the above protocol, player **P** is not required to provide a proof, establishing the inconsistency of R; if such a proof were to be provided, whenever **P** terminates with a declaration of inconsistency, then **P** is said to be a *complete* prover.
(b) It is understood that if R is feasible, then **V** will provide a consistent sequence of certificates to **P** during the game. Indeed, **P** can use the inconsistency of certificates provided by **V** as a valid proof that R is inconsistent.
(c) **V** is not bound to a specific consistent assignment for R; this feature is important when R has multiple consistent assignments. Accordingly, if **P** presents **V** with a proof g_1 that is consistent with R, **V** could choose to declare that g_1 is incorrect, if $R \wedge \oplus g_1$ is satisfiable by an alternate proof g_2. If player **V** fixes the assignment he is interested in, before the game begins, then we say that he is *sincere*; otherwise, we say that he is insincere.

As part of rejecting the prover's current proof, the verifier can provide four types of certificates, viz.,

(i) Type 0 Certificate - This type of certificate (also called *value certificate*) targets a specific variable in the assignment. For instance, in case of a SAT instance, the prover could provide the proof ($x_1 = \textbf{true}, x_2 = \textbf{false}$) to the verifier. The verifier could reject the proof with the certificate $x_1 = \textbf{false}$.
(ii) Type 1 Certificate - This type of certificate (also called *order certificate*) targets some ordering property that is violated in the current proof. For instance, in case of an integer programming problem, the proof $x_1 = 1, x_2 = 2$ could be rejected with the certificate $x_1 \geq 2$ or even $x_1 > x_2$.
(iii) Type 2 Certificate - This type of certificate (also called *aggregate certificate*) targets some aggregate measure which is violated in the current proof. For instance, in case of an integer programming problem, the proof $(x_1 = 1, x_2 = 2)$ could be rejected with the certificate $(x_1 + x_2) \geq 10$.
(iv) Type 3 Certificate - This type of certificate (also called *membership certificate*) targets the proof as a whole and returns as a certificate one of the constraints that is violated by the current proof. In other words, the verifier establishes the incorrectness of the current proof, by explicitly providing a constraint which precludes the current assignment from being a tuple in $\mathcal{R}_{in}$.

Let T_v^i denote the time taken by a verifier to provide a certificate of Type i. It is not hard to see that $T_v^0 \geq T_v^1 \geq T_v^2 \geq T_v^3$.

In this paper, we shall be considering verifiers which provide certificates of Type 3 only, i.e., the prover does not have access to the entire constraint set.

It must be noted that in the traditional computational model in which all the constraints are part of the input, BBCSPs can be reduced to 2CNF satisfiability and are therefore solvable in linear time [2]. However, our computation model is different from the traditional RAM model.

4 Motivation

Our work in this paper is motivated by two orthogonal considerations:

(A) Tools for practical applications - As mentioned before, BBCSPs arise in a number of interesting domains, including but not limited to real-time scheduling [14], program analysis [1], constraint solving [6,10] and program testing [3].

(i) Real-Time Scheduling - [16] describes a real-time scheduling problem called Totally Clairvoyant scheduling, which is characterized by two non-standard features, viz., the existence of relative timing constraints among jobs (for instance, Job J_4 should start 7 units after job J_2 ends) and non-constant execution times (for instance, the execution time e_1 of job J_1 belongs to $[7, 10]$). There also exist applications in which job execution time is not a continuous range, but one of two values, e.g., $\{7, 10\}$. Such a problem can be directly modeled as a BBCSP.

(ii) BoolIPD(2) - A conjunctive theory that arises often in constraint-based analysis of programs is BoolIPD(2).
Let $\mathbf{A} \cdot \boldsymbol{x} \leq \boldsymbol{b}$ denote a polyhedron in which the support of each row is at most 2, i.e., at most two non-zero variables per row. Let $\mathbf{C}\boldsymbol{x} \neq \boldsymbol{d}$ denote an open region, in which the support of each row is at most 2. The mathematical programming problem

$$\exists \boldsymbol{x} \in \mathcal{Z}\ \mathbf{A} \cdot \boldsymbol{x} \leq \boldsymbol{b} \wedge \mathbf{C} \cdot \boldsymbol{x} \neq \boldsymbol{d}$$

is an instance of IPD(2), i.e., integer programming with at most two non-zero variables per constraint with disequalities. If in addition, each program variable is boolean, then we have an instance of BoolIPD(2). Modern day SMT (Satisfiability Modulo Theory) solvers such as YICES [5], ICS [3] and the one described in [12], solve BoolIPD(2) instances using additional variables and disjunction; however, this destroys the binary nature of BoolIPD(2) constraints. Inasmuch as BoolPD(2) problems form a subclass of BBCSPs, the randomized algorithm that we describe in this paper can be directly used for solving them. Additionally, it would be worthwhile to investigate the exact complexity of BoolIPD(2).

(B) Alternative mode(l)s of computation - The typical approach to constraint solving problems is deterministic in nature; however, randomized approaches have been found to be fairly robust and effective in identifying solutions to CSPs [7]. While it is true that the randomized algorithm discussed here works for only selected class of CSPs, viz., BBCSPs, the insights from this algorithm can be used for guided testing and bounded model checking for a more general class of constraints. Our technique embodies a number of search paradigms:

(i) Search through Verification - [4] proposes a randomized, linear-time algorithm for identifying the Minimum Spanning Tree (MST) of an undirected, weighted graph using a verification subroutine; in other words, the search for the desired structure is achieved through verification. Our algorithm is similar in that the search for a solution is achieved through a number of Type 3 certificates.

(ii) Learning with Zero Knowledge - In Valiant's PAC model of learning [17], a concept is learned through a sequence of positive and negative examples. Each example causes the algorithm to reformulate its hypothesis about the concept. In our approach, we learn a solution to the BBCSP through a sequence of negative examples only; it is important to note that the algorithm never formulates a hypothesis, but still succeeds in learning the concept with a probability better than one-sixth.

5 Related Work

Papadimitriou [8] gave the first randomized algorithm for the 2SAT problem, which had provable polynomial time convergence and bounded error was presented. Their strategy is easily modeled as a one dimensional random walk with one absorbing barrier and one reflecting barrier. Applications of the random walk strategy to harder versions of satisfiability with detailed implementation profiles are described in [18]. In particular, they consider the efficacy of biasing the process of selecting the clause which is satisfied in the next round. [15] extended the ideas presented by Papadimitriou [8] to derive a randomized algorithm for the Q2SAT problem. Local search through random walks has also been studied for harder Satisfiability problems [11].

6 The Randomized Algorithm

Algorithm (6.1) represents the randomized algorithm for solving BBCSPs. The algorithm itself is a variant of the technique described in [8] for solving 2SAT instances.

Observe that the algorithm is extremely local in its approach and does not advocate any form of constraint propagation, which is standard in sophisticated CSP solvers. Indeed not only does it not exploit any specific constraint theory, it is completely oblivious to the constraint set $\mathcal{C}$ itself. and therefore does not require random access to the constraint base.

The algorithm commences with an initial assignment g_0 on which the constraints are evaluated. In each round, the algorithm picks an arbitrary constraint that is falsified and flips one of the variables that define that constraint.

If the algorithm fails to find a satisfying assignment in $3 \cdot n^2$ rounds (where $n = |\mathcal{X}|$), it declares that R is unsatisfiable. In the next section, we shall show that such a declaration has a probability $\frac{5}{6}$ of being correct.

Function BBCSP-SOLVE($R = \langle \mathcal{X}, \mathcal{D}, \mathcal{C} \rangle$)
1: Let g_0 be an arbitrary assignment to $\mathcal{X}$.
2: **if** ($g_0 \models R$) **then**
3: (R is satisfiable.)
4: **return**(g_0)
5: **end if**
6: $count = 0$; $n = |\mathcal{X}|$.
7: **while** (a constraint in $\mathcal{C}$ is violated **and** ($count \leq 3 \cdot n^2$)) **do**
8: Arbitrarily select a violated constraint $C_r \in \mathcal{C}$.
9: Let x_a and x_b denote the two variables associated with C_r.
10: Flip a fair coin to pick one of x_a and x_b.
11: **if** (x_a is selected) **then**
12: Set $g_{count+1}$ to $\bigtriangledown(g_{count}, x_a)$
13: {The flipping operation is well-defined.}
14: **else**
15: Set $g_{count+1}$ to $\bigtriangledown(g_{count}, x_b)$
16: **end if**
17: **if** $g_{count+1} \models R$ **then**
18: (R is satisfiable.)
19: **return**($g_{count+1}$)
20: **else**
21: $count = count + 1$.
22: **end if**
23: **end while**
24: **return**("R is probably unsatisfiable.")

Algorithm 6.1. Randomized algorithm for an arbitrary BBCSP

We observe that the algorithm does not build a copy of the constraints; accordingly it does not need to know all of the constraints in $\mathcal{C}$ or even all of the broken constraints in $\mathcal{C}$, under the current assignment. All it needs is the variables associated with a single broken constraint, that could be chosen by an adversary. This observation is especially useful in the adversarial analysis of online algorithms.

7 Analysis of Correctness

Observe that if Algorithm (6.1) claims that the input constraint system R is satisfiable, by executing Line (3) or Line (18), then it the assignment $g()$ that is provided along with the claim, is proof positive that R is indeed satisfiable. In other words, the algorithm does not create a false positive.

On the other hand, other hand, if Algorithm (6.1) claims that the input instance R is not satisfiable, then it is possible that there exists an assignment $g : \mathcal{X} \to \mathcal{D}$, such that $g \models R$, and which was not discovered in the $3 \cdot n^2$ iterations; we now show that the probability that this occurs over all the random choices made by the algorithm is less than one-sixth.

We analyze the case of false negatives within the framework of the Prover-Verifier model discussed in Section 3. Assume that the BBCSP R is satisfiable and let us focus on a particular satisfying assignment $\hat{T}$. Let T denote the current assignment to the variables x_i, $i = 1, 2, \ldots, n$. The prover **P** provides T to the verifier **V**. If T is a satisfying assignment and meets with **V**'s approval, the game is over with **P** winning. If it is not, then there is at least one constraint in R which is broken by T; let $C_r = f(x_i, x_j)$ denote a broken constraint, where the function $f()$ models the fact that the constraint C_r is dependent on x_i and x_j only. **V** *provides only the variables (say x_i and x_j) that are involved in the broken constraint to* **P**.

P flips a fair coin to decide which variable to flip; assuming that the coin picks x_i, **P** computes $\bigtriangledown(T, x_i)$ and returns this assignment to **V**. We observe that in $\hat{T}$, either x_i has been set incorrectly or x_j has (If both variables were set correctly, the constraint would not have been broken!). Since both x_i and x_j are bi-valued, and the variable to be flipped is chosen by **P**, uniformly and at random, after the variable flip, with probability one-half, T agrees with $\hat{T}$ in one more variable and with probability one-half, T agrees with $\hat{T}$ in one less variable. (In order to simplify the analysis, we ignore the possibility that both x_i and x_j are incorrectly set, in which case T moves closer to $\hat{T}$ with probability one.)

Let $t(i)$ denote the expected number of variable flips for Algorithm (6.1) to take the current assignment T to the satisfying assignment $\hat{T}$, assuming that T differs from $\hat{T}$ on i variables. Note that $t(0) = 0$, since if the current assignment differs from $\hat{T}$ on 0 variables, then it is already a satisfying assignment. Likewise, $t(n) = 1 + t(n-1)$, since if the current assignment differs from $\hat{T}$ on all n variables, with probability 1, the new assignment will agree with $\hat{T}$ on at least one assignment.

We need the following technical lemma that helps us to compute the expectation of a random variable by conditioning it on a different random variable. This lemma has been proved in [9].

Lemma 1. *Let X and Y denote two random variables; let $\mathbf{E}[X \mid Y]$ denote that function of the random variable Y, whose value at $Y = y$ is $\mathbf{E}[X \mid Y = y]$. Then,*

$$\mathbf{E}[X] = \mathbf{E}[\mathbf{E}[X \mid Y]]. \tag{1}$$

In other words,

$$\mathbf{E}[X] = \sum_y \mathbf{E}[X \mid Y = y] \cdot \mathbf{Pr}[Y = y]. \tag{2}$$

Based on the above discussion, we note that the prover **P** is executing a one-dimensional random walk with one absorbing barrier (at 0) and a reflecting barrier (at n). Accordingly, we use Lemma (1) to derive the recurrence relations for the expected number of variable flips assuming that **P** is currently at position i of the walk.

$$\begin{aligned} t(0) &= 0 \\ t(i) &= \frac{1}{2} \cdot t(i-1) + \frac{1}{2} \cdot t(i+1) + 1, \; 0 < i < n \\ t(n) &= t(n-1) + 1 \end{aligned} \tag{3}$$

System (3) can be solved using induction (among other techniques) to give $t(n) = n^2$. In other words, the expected number of variable flips before the prover **P** translates an arbitrary assignment, which does not satisfy R to a particular assignment $\hat{T}$, which is approved by the verifier **V** (i.e., $\hat{T} \models R$ is n^2.

We need another technical lemma known as Chebyshev's inequality, proved in [9] among other places.

Lemma 2. *Let X be a non-negative random variable, with variance σ^2 and mean $\mathbf{E}[X]$. Given an arbitrary constant $a > 0$,*

$$\mathbf{Pr}[|X - \mathbf{E}[X]| \geq a \cdot \mathbf{E}[X]] \leq \frac{\sigma^2}{a^2(\mathbf{E}[X])^2}$$

It has been established that the variance of the random walk described by System (3) is at most $\frac{2}{3}n^4$.

If X denotes the random variable corresponding to the number of steps taken by Algorithm 6.1, we have,

$$\begin{aligned}
\mathbf{Pr}[X \geq 3 \cdot n^2] &= \mathbf{Pr}[X - n^2 \geq 2 \cdot n^2] \\
&\leq \mathbf{Pr}[|X - n^2| \geq 2 \cdot n^2] \\
&= \mathbf{Pr}[X - \mathbf{E}[X]| \geq 2 \cdot n^2] \\
&\leq \frac{\frac{2}{3}n^4}{(2n^2)^2}, \text{ using Chebyshev's inequality} \\
&= \frac{1}{6}
\end{aligned}$$

We conclude that the probability that the prover **P** has not identified $\hat{T}$ after $3 \cdot n^2$ rounds of the game is less than one-sixth.

8 Conclusions

The main contributions of this paper were as follows:

(a) The isolation of a class of constraint satisfaction problems, called Boolean Binary Constraint Satisfaction problems (BBCSPs) - BBCSPs are restrictive in the nature of constraints that they admit; however, as we have seen in Section 2 and Section 4, they can be used to model constraint satisfaction problems in a number of interesting domains.

(b) The design a Monte Carlo algorithm for BBCSPs - We detailed a simple, randomized algorithm for BBCSPs, with a probability of error of at most one-sixth.

From our perspective, the following open problems are interesting for future research:

(a) Can the constraint size be included in the analysis? - The weakness of the analysis in this paper is that neither the expected convergence time nor the probability of error account for the number of constraints in the BBCSP instance. Clearly, if the number of constraints is small in a satisfiable BBCSP instance, with respect to the number of program variables, the number of variable flips should be small as well. Likewise, if the number of constraints is large, we should have a higher degree of confidence in a negative answer than the one afforded by the Chebyshev inequality.

(b) Can the analysis be extended to the case where the program variables are multi-valued as opposed to boolean? - The boolean nature of program variables was crucial in the current analysis; relaxing this requirement leads to a larger class of problems. We have had some success in modeling a randomized algorithm for difference constraints as a 2-dimensional random walk.

References

1. Aiken, A.: Introduction to set constraint-based program analysis. Science of Computer Programming 35(2), 79–111 (1999)
2. Aspvall, B., Plass, M.F., Tarjan, R.: A linear-time algorithm for testing the truth of certain quantified boolean formulas. Information Processing Letters 8(3), 121–123 (1979)
3. de Moura, L.M., Owre, S., Ruess, H., Rushby, J.M., Shankar, N.: The ics decision procedures for embedded deduction. In: Basin, D., Rusinowitch, M. (eds.) IJCAR 2004. LNCS (LNAI), vol. 3097, pp. 218–222. Springer, Heidelberg (2004)
4. Karger, D.R., Klein, P.N., Tarjan, R.E.: A randomized linear-time algorithm to find minimum spanning trees. Journal of the ACM 42(2), 321–328 (1995)
5. Khachiyan, L.G.: A polynomial algorithm for linear programming. *Soviet Math. Doklady*, vol. 20, pp. 191–194 (1979) (Russian original in Doklady Akademiia Nauk SSSR 244, 1093–1096)
6. Marriott, K., Stuckey, P.J.: Programming with Constraints: An Introduction. The MIT Press, Cambridge (1998)
7. Motwani, R., Raghavan, P.: Randomized Algorithms. Cambridge University Press, Cambridge, England (1995)
8. Papadimitriou, C.H.: On selecting a satisfying truth assignment. In: IEEE (ed.), Proceedings: 32nd annual Symposium on Foundations of Computer Science, San Juan, Puerto Rico, pp. 163–169, October 1–4 (1991), 1109 Spring Street, Suite 300, Silver Spring, MD 20910, USA. IEEE Computer Society Press, Los Alamitos (1991)
9. Ross, S.M.: Probability Models, 7th edn. Academic Press, Inc., San Diego (2000)
10. Schlenker, H., Rehberger, F.: Towards a more general distributed constraint satisfaction framework: Intensional vs. extensional constraint representation. In: 15. WLP, pp. 63–70 (2000)
11. Schöning, U.: New algorithms for k-SAT based on the local search principle. In: MFCS: Symposium on Mathematical Foundations of Computer Science (2001)
12. Sheini, H.M., Sakallah, K.A.: From propositional satisfiability to satisfiability modulo theories. In: Biere, A., Gomes, C.P. (eds.) SAT 2006. LNCS, vol. 4121, pp. 1–9. Springer, Heidelberg (2006)
13. Subramani, K.: An analysis of zero-clairvoyant scheduling. In: Katoen, J.-P., Stevens, P. (eds.) ETAPS 2002 and TACAS 2002. LNCS, vol. 2280, pp. 98–112. Springer, Heidelberg (2002)

14. Subramani, K.: An analysis of totally clairvoyant scheduling. Journal of Scheduling 8(2), 113–133 (2005)
15. Subramani, K.: Cascading random walks. International Journal of Foundations of Computer Science (IJFCS) 16(3), 599–622 (2005)
16. Subramani, K.: Totally clairvoyant scheduling with relative timing constraints. In: Emerson, E.A., Namjoshi, K.S. (eds.) VMCAI 2006. LNCS, vol. 3855, pp. 398–411. Springer, Heidelberg (2005)
17. Valiant, L.G.: A theory of the learnable. Communications of the ACM 27(11), 1134–1142 (1984)
18. Wei, W., Selman, B.: Accelerating random walks. In: Van Hentenryck, P. (ed.) CP 2002. LNCS, vol. 2470, pp. 216–232. Springer, Heidelberg (2002)

On the Expressive Power of QLTL*

Zhilin Wu

State Key Laboratory of Computer Science, Institute of Software,
Chinese Academy of Sciences, P.O. Box 8718, Beijing, China, 100080
Graduate School of the Chinese Academy of Sciences,
19 Yuquan Street, Beijing, China
wuzl@ios.ac.cn

Abstract. LTL cannot express the whole class of ω-regular languages and several extensions have been proposed. Among them, Quantified propositional Linear Temporal Logic ($QLTL$), proposed by Sistla, extends LTL by quantifications over the atomic propositions. The expressive power of LTL and its fragments have been made relatively clear by numerous researchers. However, there are few results on the expressive power of $QLTL$ and its fragments (besides those of LTL). In this paper we get some initial results on the expressive power of $QLTL$. First, we show that both $Q(U)$ (the fragment of $QLTL$ in which "Until" is the only temporal operator used, without restriction on the use of quantifiers) and $Q(F)$ (similar to $Q(U)$, with temporal operator "Until" replaced by "Future") can express the whole class of ω-regular languages. Then we compare the expressive power of various fragments of $QLTL$ in detail and get a panorama of the expressive power of fragments of $QLTL$. Finally, we consider the quantifier hierarchy of $Q(U)$ and $Q(F)$, and show that one alternation of existential and universal quantifiers is necessary and sufficient to express the whole class of ω-regular languages.

1 Introduction

Linear Temporal Logic (LTL) was first defined by the philosopher A. Prior in 1957 [9] as a tool to reason about the temporal information. Later, in 1977, A. Pnueli introduced LTL into computer science to reason about the behaviors of reactive systems [8]. Since then, it has become one of the most popular temporal logics used in the specification and verification of reactive systems.

Expressive power is one of the main concerns of temporal logics. Perhaps because of their popularity, the expressive power of LTL and its fragments have been made relatively clear by numerous researchers. A well-known result is that an ω-regular language is LTL-definable iff it is first order definable iff it is ω-star free iff its syntactic monoid is aperiodic [5,4,14,15,7]. Since the class of ω-star-free languages is a strict subclass of the class of ω-regular languages,

* Partially supported by the National Natural Science Foundation of China under Grant No. 60223005 and the National Grand Fundamental Research 973 Program of China under Grant No. 2002cb312200.

C.B. Jones, Z. Liu, J. Woodcock (Eds.): ICTAC 2007, LNCS 4711, pp. 467–481, 2007.

some natural temporal properties such as the property that the proposition p holds at all even positions cannot be expressed in LTL [18]. Consequently several extensions of LTL have been proposed to define the whole class of ω-regular languages. Among them we mention Extended Temporal Logic (ETL) [19], linear μ-calculus (νTL)[17] and Quantified propositional Linear Temporal Logic ($QLTL$, also known as $QPTL$) [11].

$QLTL$ extends LTL by quantifications over atomic propositions. While the expressive power of LTL and its fragments have been made relatively clear, there are few results on the expressive power of $QLTL$ and its fragments (besides those of LTL). A well-known result is that ω-regular languages can be expressed by X, F operators and existential quantifiers in $QLTL$ [2,12], which, nevertheless, is almost all we know about the expressive power of $QLTL$ and its fragments besides those of LTL. We do not even know whether several natural fragments of $QLTL$, e.g. $Q(U)$ (the fragment of $QLTL$ in which "Until" is the only temporal operator used, without restriction on the use of quantifiers) and $Q(F)$ (similar to $Q(U)$, with temporal operator "Until" replaced by "Future"), are expressively equivalent to $QLTL$ or not. Consequently we believe that the expressive power of $QLTL$ could be made clearer, which is the main theme of this paper.

In this paper, we first give a positive answer to the question whether $Q(U)$ and $Q(F)$ can define the whole class of ω-regular languages. Then we compare the expressive power of various fragments of $QLTL$ in detail and get a panorama of the expressive power of fragments of $QLTL$. In particular, we show that the expressive power of $EQ(F)$(the fragments of $QLTL$ containing formulas of the form $\exists q_1 ... \exists q_k \psi$, where ψ is the LTL formula in which "Future" is the only temporal operator used) is strictly weaker than that of LTL; and the expressive power of $EQ(U)$ (the fragments of $QLTL$ containing formulas of the form $\exists q_1 ... \exists q_k \psi$, where ψ is the LTL formula in which "Until" is the only temporal operator used) is incompatible with that of LTL. Finally, we consider the quantifier hierarchy of $Q(U)$ and $Q(F)$, and show that one alternation of existential and universal quantifiers is necessary and sufficient to express the whole class of ω-regular languages.

Compared to ETL and νTL, $QLTL$ is more natural and easier to use for those people already familiar with LTL. As it was pointed out in [6,3], $QLTL$ has important applications in the verification of complex systems because quantifications have the ability to reason about refinement relations between programs.

However, the complexity of $QLTL$ is very high: $QLTL$ is not elementarily decidable [12]. So from a practical point of view, it seems that it is unnecessary to bother to clarify the expressive power of $QLTL$. Our main motivation of the exploration of the expressive power of $QLTL$ is from a theoretical point of view, that is, the analogy between $QLTL$ and $S1S$ [16], monadic second order logic over words.

The formulas of $S1S$ are constructed from atomic propositions $x = y$, $x < y$ and $P_\sigma(x)$ (P_σ is the unary relation symbol for each letter σ in the alphabet of words) by boolean combinations, first and second order quantifications. $S1S$ defines exactly the class of ω-regular languages. $QLTL$ can be seen as a variant of $S1S$ because the quantifications over atomic propositions in $QLTL$ are essentially second order quantifications over positions of the ω-words.

In $S1S$, second order quantifications are so powerful that the first order vocabulary can be suppressed into the single successor relation ("$S(x, y)$") since the linear order relation ("<") can be defined by the successor relation with the help of second order quantifications:

$$x < y \equiv \neg(x = y) \wedge \forall X((X(x) \wedge \forall z \forall z'(X(z) \wedge S(z, z') \to X(z'))) \to X(y)).$$

Then, analogously we may think that in $QLTL$ the LTL part (the first order part) can also be suppressed to the temporal operator X ("Next"), the counterpart of successor relation $S(x, y)$. However, because in $S1S$ the positions of words can be referred to directly by first order variables while in $QLTL$ they cannot, it turns out that in $QLTL$ the LTL part cannot be suppressed into the single temporal operator X (As a matter of fact, the fragment of $QLTL$ with only X operators used has the same expressive power as the fragment of LTL with only X operator used). However, we still want to know to what extent the LTL part of $QLTL$ can be suppressed. So we consider $Q(U)$ and $Q(F)$, the fragment of $QLTL$ with only U and F operator used respectively, to see whether they can still express the whole class of ω-regular languages. When we find out that they can do so, we then want to know whether they can also do so when only the existential quantifiers are available. The answer is negative, and naturally, we then consider the quantifier hierarchy of $Q(U)$ and $Q(F)$ to see how many alternations of existential and universal quantifiers are necessary and sufficient to express the whole class of ω-regular languages.

The rest of the paper is organized as follows: in Section 2, we give some notation and definitions; then in Section 3, we recall some relevant results on the expressive power of $QLTL$ and its fragments; in Section 4, we establish the main results of this paper; finally in Section 5, we give some conclusions.

2 Notation and Definitions

2.1 Syntax of QLTL

Let $\mathcal{P}$ denote the set of propositional variables $\{p_1, p_2, ...\}$. Formulas of $QLTL$ are defined by the following rules:

$$\varphi := q(q \in \mathcal{P}) \mid \varphi_1 \vee \varphi_2 \mid \neg\varphi_1 \mid X\varphi_1 \mid \varphi_1 U \varphi_2 \mid \exists q \varphi_1 (q \in \mathcal{P})$$

Let φ be a $QLTL$ formula, the subformulas of φ is denoted by $Sub(\varphi)$, and the closure of φ, denoted by $Cl(\varphi)$, is $Sub(\varphi) \cup \{\neg\psi | \psi \in Sub(\varphi)\}$.

Let φ be a $QLTL$ formula. The free-variables-set and bound-variables-set of φ, denoted by $Free(\varphi)$ and $Bound(\varphi)$ respectively, are defined similar to that of first order logic.

The set of variables occurring in a formula φ, denoted by $Var(\varphi)$, is $Free(\varphi) \cup Bound(\varphi)$.

In the remaining part of this paper, we assume that all $QLTL$ formulas φ are well-named: i.e., for all φ, $Free(\varphi) \cap Bound(\varphi) = \emptyset$, and for any $q \in Bound(\varphi)$, there is a unique quantified formula $\exists q\psi$ in $Cl(\varphi)$.

We define several abbreviations of $QLTL$ formulas as follows: $true = q \vee \neg q (q \in \mathcal{P})$, $false = \neg true$, $\varphi_1 \wedge \varphi_2 = \neg(\neg\varphi_1 \vee \neg\varphi_2)$, $\varphi_1 \rightarrow \varphi_2 = \neg\varphi_1 \vee \varphi_2$ $F\varphi_1 = trueU\varphi_1$, $G\varphi_1 = \neg F \neg \varphi_1$, $\forall q \varphi_1 = \neg(\exists q(\neg\varphi_1))$.

Moreover, we introduce the following abbreviations. Let AP be a given nonempty finite subset of $\mathcal{P}$. Then, for $a \in 2^{AP}$,

$$\mathcal{B}(a)^{AP} = \left(\bigwedge_{p \in a} p\right) \wedge \left(\bigwedge_{p \in AP \backslash a} \neg p\right);$$

and for $A \subseteq 2^{AP}$,

$$\mathcal{B}(A)^{AP} = \bigvee_{a \in A} \mathcal{B}(a)^{AP}.$$

2.2 Semantics of QLTL

$QLTL$ formulas are interpreted as follows. Let $u \in \left(2^{\mathcal{P}}\right)^{\omega}$. Denote the suffix of u starting from the i-th position (the first position is 0) as u^i and the letter in the i-th position of u as u_i.

- $u \models q$ if $q \in u_0$.
- $u \models \varphi_1 \vee \varphi_2$ if $u \models \varphi_1$ or $u \models \varphi_2$.
- $u \models \neg\varphi_1$ if $u \not\models \varphi_1$.
- $u \models X\varphi_1$ if $u^1 \models \varphi_1$.
- $u \models \varphi_1 U \varphi_2$ if there is $i \geq 0$ such that $u^i \models \varphi_2$ and for all $0 \leq j < i$, $u^j \models \varphi_1$.
- $u \models \exists q \varphi_1$ if there is some $v \in \left(2^{\mathcal{P}}\right)^{\omega}$ such that v differs from u only in the assignments of q (namely for all $i \geq 0$ and for all $q' \in \mathcal{P} \backslash \{q\}$, $q' \in v_i$ iff $q' \in u_i$) and $v \models \varphi_1$.

Let $AP \subseteq AP' \subseteq \mathcal{P}$. If $a \in 2^{AP}$, $a' \in 2^{AP'}$, and $a' \cap AP = a$, then we say that the restriction of a' to AP is a, denoted by $a'|_{AP} = a$. If $A \subseteq 2^{AP}$, $A' \subseteq 2^{AP'}$, and $A = \{a'|_{AP} |\ a' \in A'\}$, then we say that the restriction of A' to AP is A, denoted by $A'|_{AP} = A$. If $u \in \left(2^{AP}\right)^{\omega}$, $u' \in \left(2^{AP'}\right)^{\omega}$ and for all $i \geq 0$, $u'_i|_{AP} = u_i$, then we say that the restriction of u' to AP is u, denoted by $u'|_{AP} = u$. Let $L \subseteq \left(2^{AP}\right)^{\omega}$ and $L' \subseteq \left(2^{AP'}\right)^{\omega}$, we say that the restriction of L' to AP is L, denoted by $L'|_{AP} = L$, if $L = \left\{u \in \left(2^{AP}\right)^{\omega} | \exists u' \in L', u'|_{AP} = u\right\}$.

Proposition 1. *Let AP be a nonempty finite subset of $\mathcal{P}$ and φ be a $QLTL$ formula such that $Free(\varphi) \subseteq AP$. Then, for any $u, v \in \left(2^{\mathcal{P}}\right)^{\omega}$ with $u|_{AP} = v|_{AP}$, we have that $u \models \varphi$ iff $v \models \varphi$.*

Let φ_1, φ_2 be two $QLTL$ formulas. φ_1 and φ_2 are said to be equivalent, denoted by $\varphi_1 \equiv \varphi_2$, if for all $u \in \left(2^{\mathcal{P}}\right)^{\omega}$, $u \models \varphi_1$ iff $u \models \varphi_2$.

Proposition 2. *Let AP be a nonempty finite subset of $\mathcal{P}$, φ_1 and φ_2 be two formulas such that $Free(\varphi_1), Free(\varphi_2) \subseteq AP$. Then $\varphi_1 \equiv \varphi_2$ iff (for all $u \in (2^{AP})^\omega$, $u \models \varphi_1$ iff $u \models \varphi_2$).*

For a $QLTL$ formula, the bound variables are usually seen as auxiliary variables. Consequently if AP is the set of propositional variables that we are concerned about, and if we want to use $QLTL$ formula φ to define a language of $(2^{AP})^\omega$, naturally we may require that $Free(\varphi) \subseteq AP$ and $Bound(\varphi) \cap AP = \emptyset$. So we introduce the following definition.

Definition 1 (Compatibility of AP and φ). *Let AP be a given nonempty finite subset of $\mathcal{P}$ and φ be a formula of $QLTL$. AP and φ are said to be compatible if $Free(\varphi) \subseteq AP$ and $Bound(\varphi) \cap AP = \emptyset$.*

Let AP be a nonempty finite subset of $\mathcal{P}$ and φ be a formula such that AP and φ are compatible. The language of $(2^{AP})^\omega$ defined by φ, denoted by $\mathcal{L}(\varphi)^{AP}$, is $\{u \in (2^{AP})^\omega | u \models \varphi\}$.

Proposition 3. *Let AP be a nonempty finite subset of $\mathcal{P}$ and $\varphi = \exists q_1 ... \exists q_k \psi$ be a formula such that AP and φ are compatible. Let $AP' = AP \cup \{q_1, ..., q_k\}$, then AP' and ψ are compatible and $\mathcal{L}(\varphi)^{AP} = \mathcal{L}(\psi)^{AP'}|_{AP}$.*

2.3 Fragments of QLTL and Expressive Power of Logics

Let $O_1, O_2, ... \in \{X, F, G, U\}$. We use $L(O_1, O_2, ...)$ to denote the fragment of $QLTL$ containing temporal operators $\{O_1, O_2, ...\}$ but containing no quantifiers, and use $Q(O_1, O_2, ...)$ to denote the fragment of $QLTL$ containing both temporal operators $\{O_1, O_2, ...\}$ and quantifiers. Moreover we denote the fragment of $QLTL$ containing exactly formulas of the form $\exists q_1 ... \exists q_k \psi$ (or $\forall q_1 ... \forall q_k \psi$), where $\psi \in L(O_1, O_2, ...)$, as $EQ(O_1, O_2, ...)$ (or $AQ(O_1, O_2, ...)$).

For instance, LTL is $L(X, U)$ and $QLTL$ is $Q(X, U)$.

Let φ be a formula in $QLTL$ and $\mathcal{SL}$ be one fragment of $QLTL$. We say that φ is expressible in $\mathcal{SL}$ iff there is a formula ψ in $\mathcal{SL}$ such that $\varphi \equiv \psi$.

Let AP be a nonempty finite subset of $\mathcal{P}$, $L \subseteq (2^{AP})^\omega$, and $\mathcal{SL}$ be one fragment of $QLTL$ (e.g., $Q(F)$). We say that L is expressible in $\mathcal{SL}$ if there is a formula φ in $\mathcal{SL}$ such that AP and φ are compatible and $\mathcal{L}(\varphi)^{AP} = L$.

Let $\mathcal{SL}_1$ and $\mathcal{SL}_2$ be two fragments of $QLTL$. We say that $\mathcal{SL}_1$ is less expressive than $\mathcal{SL}_2$, denoted by $\mathcal{SL}_1 \leq \mathcal{SL}_2$, if for any formula $\varphi_1 \in \mathcal{SL}_1$, there exists a formula $\varphi_2 \in \mathcal{SL}_2$ such that $\varphi_1 \equiv \varphi_2$, and we say that $\mathcal{SL}_1$ and $\mathcal{SL}_2$ are expressively equivalent, denoted by $\mathcal{SL}_1 \equiv \mathcal{SL}_2$, if $\mathcal{SL}_1 \leq \mathcal{SL}_2$ and $\mathcal{SL}_2 \leq \mathcal{SL}_1$. Moreover we say that $\mathcal{SL}_1$ is strictly less expressive than $\mathcal{SL}_2$, denoted by $\mathcal{SL}_1 < \mathcal{SL}_2$, if $\mathcal{SL}_1 \leq \mathcal{SL}_2$ but not $\mathcal{SL}_2 \leq \mathcal{SL}_1$. Finally we say that the expressive power of $\mathcal{SL}_1$ and $\mathcal{SL}_2$ are incompatible, denoted by $\mathcal{SL}_1 \perp \mathcal{SL}_2$, if neither $\mathcal{SL}_1 \leq \mathcal{SL}_2$ nor $\mathcal{SL}_2 \leq \mathcal{SL}_1$, namely there are two formulas $\varphi_1 \in \mathcal{SL}_1$ and $\varphi_2 \in \mathcal{SL}_2$ such that there exists no formula in $\mathcal{SL}_2$ equivalent to φ_1 and there exists no formula in $\mathcal{SL}_1$ equivalent to φ_2.

2.4 Büchi Automaton and ω-Languages

A Büchi automaton $\mathcal{B}$ is a quintuple $(Q, \Sigma, \delta, q_0, T)$, where Q is the finite state set, Σ is the finite set of letters, $\delta \subseteq Q \times \Sigma \times Q$ is the transition relation, $q_0 \in Q$ is the initial state, and $T \subseteq Q$ is the accepting state set. Let $u \in \Sigma^\omega$, a run of $\mathcal{B}$ on u is an infinite state sequence $s_0 s_1 ... \in Q^\omega$ such that $s_0 = q_0$ and $(s_i, u_i, s_{i+1}) \in \delta$ for all $i \geq 0$. A run of $\mathcal{B}$ on u is accepting if some accepting state occurs in it infinitely often. u is accepted by $\mathcal{B}$ if $\mathcal{B}$ has an accepting run on u. The language defined by $\mathcal{B}$, denoted by $\mathcal{L}(\mathcal{B})$, is the set of ω-words accepted by $\mathcal{B}$.

An ω-language is said to be ω-regular if it can be defined by some Büchi automaton.

An ω-language $L \subseteq \Sigma^\omega$ is said to be stutter invariant if for all $u \in \Sigma^\omega$ and function $f : \mathbf{N} \to \mathbf{N} \backslash \{0\}$ ($\mathbf{N}$ is the set of natural numbers), we have that $u \in L$ iff $u^{f(0)} u^{f(1)} ... \in L$.

Let $L \subseteq \Sigma^\omega$ be ω-regular. The syntactic congruence of L, denoted by $\approx_L$, is a congruence on Σ^* defined as follows: let $u, v \in \Sigma^*$, then, $u \approx_L v$ if for all $x, y, z \in \Sigma^*$, ($xuyz^\omega \in L$ iff $xvyz^\omega \in L$) and ($x(yuz)^\omega \in L$ iff $x(yvz)^\omega \in L$). The syntactic monoid of L, denoted by $M(L)$, is the division monoid $\Sigma^* / \approx_L$.

An ω-language $L \subseteq \Sigma^\omega$ is said to be non-counting if there is $n \geq 0$ such that for all $x, y, z, u \in \Sigma^*$, ($xu^n yz^\omega \in L$ iff $xu^{n+1} yz^\omega \in L$) and ($x(yu^n z)^\omega \in L$ iff $x(yu^{n+1} z)^\omega \in L$).

A monoid M is said to be aperiodic if there is $k \geq 0$ such that for all $m \in M$, $m^k = m^{k+1}$.

Let $L \subseteq \Sigma^\omega$. It is not hard to show that $M(L)$ is aperiodic iff L is non-counting.

3 Known Results on the Expressive Power of $QLTL$ and LTL

In the remaining part of this paper, we always assume that AP is a nonempty finite subset of $\mathcal{P}$.

Proposition 4 ([2,12]). *An ω-language is ω-regular iff it is expressible in $QLTL$.*

Corollary 1. $Q(X, U) \equiv EQ(X, F)$.

Proposition 5 ([1])

(i) Xp_1 is not expressible in $L(U)$;
(ii) Fp_1 is not expressible in $L(X)$;
(iii) $p_1 U p_2$ is not expressible in $L(X, F)$.

In the following we recall three propositions characterizing the expressive power of LTL(namely $L(X, U)$), $L(U)$ and $L(F)$ respectively.

In the remaining part of this subsection, we assume that $L \subseteq (2^{AP})^\omega$.

Proposition 6 (Characterization of LTL, [5,4,14,15,7]). *Suppose that L is ω-regular, then the following two conditions are equivalent:*

- *L is expressible in LTL;*
- *The syntactic monoid of L, $M(L)$, is aperiodic.*

Proposition 7 (Characterization of $L(U)$, [10]). *Let φ be a formula in $L(X,U)$ and $Free(\varphi) \subseteq AP$. Then φ is expressible in $L(U)$ iff $\mathcal{L}(\varphi)^{AP}$ is stutter invariant.*

Definition 2 (Restricted ω-regular set). *L is said to be a restricted ω-regular set if it is of the form*

$$S_1^* s_1 S_2^* s_2 ... S_{m-1}^* s_{m-1} S_m^\omega, \tag{1}$$

where $S_i \subseteq 2^{AP}$ $(1 \le i \le m)$, and $s_i \in S_i \backslash S_{i+1}$ $(1 \le i < m)$.

For instance, let $AP = \{p_1\}$, then, $\left(2^{AP}\right)^\omega$ and $\left(2^{AP}\right)^* \{p_1\}\emptyset^\omega$ are both restricted ω-regular sets.

Definition 3. *Let $s_0 \in 2^{AP}$ and $S' \subseteq 2^{AP}$. We define $L_{inf(S')}^{init(s_0)}$ as follows:*

$$L_{inf(S')}^{init(s_0)} = \{u \in L | u_0 = s_0, \textit{ each element of } S' \textit{ occurs infinitely often in } u\}$$

Proposition 8 (Characterization of $L(F)$, [13]). *Let L be nonempty. Then, L is expressible in $L(F)$ iff L is a finite union of nonempty languages of the form $M_{inf(S')}^{init(s_0)}$, where $M \subseteq \left(2^{AP}\right)^\omega$ is a restricted ω-regular set, $s_0 \in 2^{AP}$ and $S' \subseteq 2^{AP}$.*

For instance, let $AP = \{p_1\}$, then, $\mathcal{L}(Fp_1)^{AP} \subseteq \left(2^{AP}\right)^\omega$ is exactly the union of languages $(L_1)_{inf(\emptyset)}^{init(\{p_1\})}$, $(L_1)_{inf(\{\{p_1\}\})}^{init(\emptyset)}$, and $(L_2)_{inf(\emptyset)}^{init(\emptyset)}$, where $L_1 = \left(2^{AP}\right)^\omega$ and $L_2 = \left(2^{AP}\right)^* \{p_1\}\emptyset^\omega$.

4 Our Results on the Expressive Power of $QLTL$ and Its Fragments

According to Proposition 4, $Q(X,U)$, $Q(X,F)$, $EQ(X,U)$ and $EQ(X,F)$ are all expressively equivalent, which, nevertheless, is almost all we know about the expressive power of $QLTL$ besides those of LTL. For instance, we do not know whether several natural fragments of $QLTL$, e.g., $Q(U)$ and $Q(F)$, can define the whole class of ω-regular languages or not.

In this section, we first give a positive answer to the above question, namely, we show that $Q(U)$ and $Q(F)$ can define the whole class of ω-regular languages. Then, since $EQ(X,U)$ and $EQ(X,F)$ can also do so, analogously, we want to know whether $EQ(U)$ and $EQ(F)$ can do so or not. However, the answer is negative. As a matter of fact, we show that $EQ(F) < LTL$ and $EQ(U) \perp$

LTL. Furthermore, we compare the expressive power of $EQ(U)$ and $EQ(F)$ with that of other fragments of $QLTL$ and get a panorama of the expressive power of various fragments of $QLTL$ (Fig. 1). Since neither $EQ(U)$ nor $EQ(F)$ can express the whole class of ω-regular languages, we want to know how many alternations of existential and universal quantifiers are necessary and sufficient to do that. The answer is one, which will be shown in the end of this section.

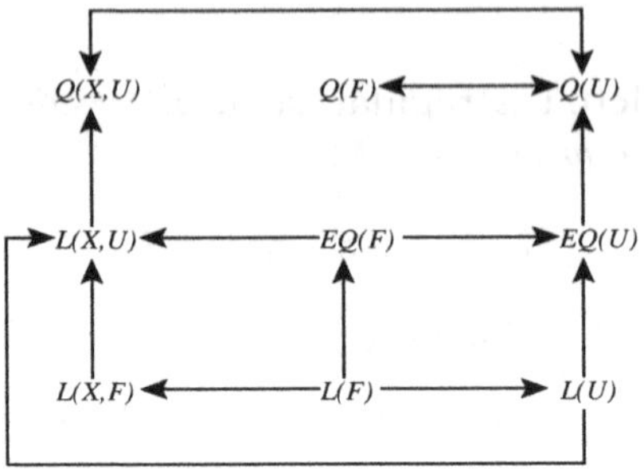

Fig. 1. Expressive power of $QLTL$ and its fragments

Remark 1 (Notation in Fig. 1). Let $\mathcal{L}_1$ and $\mathcal{L}_2$ be two nodes in Fig. 1. If $\mathcal{L}_2$ is reachable from $\mathcal{L}_1$ but not vice versa, then $\mathcal{L}_1 < \mathcal{L}_2$, e.g. $EQ(F) < EQ(U)$. If neither $\mathcal{L}_2$ is reachable from $\mathcal{L}_1$ nor $\mathcal{L}_1$ is reachable from $\mathcal{L}_2$, then $\mathcal{L}_1 \perp \mathcal{L}_2$, e.g. $EQ(F) \perp L(U)$. If $\mathcal{L}_1$ and $\mathcal{L}_2$ are reachable from each other (namely, in the same Strongly Connected Component), then $\mathcal{L}_1 \equiv \mathcal{L}_2$, e.g. $Q(U) \equiv Q(F)$. □

4.1 Expressive Power of $Q(U)$ and $Q(F)$

In the following we will show that, with the help of quantifiers, the operator X can be expressed by the operator U and the operator U can be expressed by the operator F.

Lemma 1. *Let $\varphi \in QLTL$, $q_1, q_2 \in \mathcal{P}\backslash Var(\varphi)$ and $q_1 \neq q_2$. Then*

$$X\varphi \equiv \big(\varphi \wedge \exists q_1 \left(\neg q_1 \wedge (\varphi \wedge \neg q_1)\ U\ (\varphi \wedge q_1)\right)\big) \vee \big(\neg\varphi \wedge \neg\exists q_2 \left(\neg q_2 \wedge (\neg\varphi \wedge \neg q_2)\ U\ (\neg\varphi \wedge q_2)\right)\big).$$

Lemma 2. *Let φ_1 and φ_2 be two formulas of $QLTL$ and $q \in \mathcal{P}\backslash(Var(\varphi_1) \cup Var(\varphi_2))$. Then*

$$\varphi_1 U \varphi_2 \equiv \exists q \left(F(\varphi_2 \wedge q) \wedge G(\neg q \rightarrow G\neg q) \wedge G(\varphi_1 \vee \varphi_2 \vee \neg q)\right).$$

From Lemma 1 and Lemma 2, we have the following theorem.

Theorem 1. $Q(X, U) \equiv Q(U) \equiv Q(F)$.

4.2 Expressive Power of $EQ(F)$ and $EQ(U)$

Both $EQ(X,U)$ and $EQ(X,F)$ can define the whole class of ω-regular languages (Corollary 1). Then a natural question to ask is whether this is true for $EQ(U)$ and $EQ(F)$ as well. We will give a negative answer to this question in this subsection. Moreover, in this subsection, we will compare the expressive power of $EQ(F)$ and $EQ(U)$ with that of other fragments of $QLTL$.

We first show that $EQ(F)$ cannot define the whole class of ω-regular languages. In fact we show that $EQ(F)$ is strictly less expressive than LTL.

Lemma 3. *Let $AP \subseteq AP' \subseteq \mathcal{P}$ and $L \subseteq \left(2^{AP'}\right)^{\omega}$. If L is a restricted ω-regular set, $s_0 \in 2^{AP'}$, $S' \subseteq 2^{AP'}$ and $L_{inf(S')}^{init(s_0)} \neq \emptyset$, then, $\left(L_{inf(S')}^{init(s_0)}\right)\Big|_{AP} = (L|_{AP})_{inf(S'|_{AP})}^{init(s_0|_{AP})}$.*

Lemma 4. *For any formula $\varphi = \exists q_1 ... \exists q_k \psi \in EQ(F)$, there exists some formula $\theta \in L(X,U)$ such that $\varphi \equiv \theta$.*

Proof of Lemma 4.
Suppose that $\varphi = \exists q_1 ... \exists q_k \psi \in EQ(F)$, where $\psi \in L(F)$.
Suppose that φ and AP are compatible and $AP' = AP \cup \{q_1, ..., q_k\}$.

Then, according to Proposition 3, we have that ψ and AP' are compatible, and $\mathcal{L}(\varphi)^{AP} = \mathcal{L}(\psi)^{AP'}|_{AP}$.

If $\mathcal{L}(\psi)^{AP'} = \emptyset$, then $\varphi \equiv false$. So we assume that $\mathcal{L}(\psi)^{AP'} \neq \emptyset$.

According to Proposition 8, $\mathcal{L}(\psi)^{AP'}$ is a finite union of nonempty languages of the form $L_{inf(S')}^{init(s_0)}$, where $L \subseteq \left(2^{AP'}\right)^{\omega}$ is a restricted ω-regular set, $s_0 \in 2^{AP'}$ and $S' \subseteq 2^{AP'}$.

In the remaining part of the proof of this lemma, we always suppose that L is a restricted ω-regular set, specifically, $S_1^* s_1 S_2^* s_2 ... S_{m-1}^* s_{m-1} S_m^{\omega}$, where $S_i \subseteq 2^{AP}$ $(1 \leq i \leq m)$, and $s_i \in S_i \backslash S_{i+1}$ $(1 \leq i < m)$.

From Lemma 3, we know that $\mathcal{L}(\varphi)^{AP} = \mathcal{L}(\psi)^{AP'}|_{AP}$ is a finite union of nonempty languages of the form $(L|_{AP})_{inf(S'|_{AP})}^{init(s_0|_{AP})}$.

In the following we will show that there is a formula ξ in $L(X,U)$ such that $Var(\xi) = Free(\xi) \subseteq AP$ and $\mathcal{L}(\xi)^{AP} = (L|_{AP})_{inf(S'|_{AP})}^{init(s_0|_{AP})}$. Let θ be the disjunction of all these ξ's. Then $\mathcal{L}(\varphi)^{AP} = \mathcal{L}(\theta)^{AP}$. Because $Free(\varphi) \subseteq AP$ and $Free(\theta) \subseteq AP$, according to Proposition 2, we conclude that φ and θ are equivalent.

In order to define ξ, we define a sequence of formulas η_i $(1 \leq i \leq m)$ as follows:

$$\eta_i = \begin{cases} G\left(\mathcal{B}\left(S_m|_{AP}\right)^{AP}\right) & \text{if} \quad i = m \\ \mathcal{B}\left(S_i|_{AP}\right)^{AP} \ U \ \left(\mathcal{B}(s_i|_{AP})^{AP} \wedge X\eta_{i+1}\right) & \text{if} \quad 1 \leq i < m \end{cases}$$

It is not hard to show that for all $1 \leq i \leq m$,

$$\mathcal{L}(\eta_i)^{AP} = \left(S_i|_{AP}\right)^* \left(s_i|_{AP}\right) ... \left(S_m|_{AP}\right)^{\omega}.$$

Thus, $L|_{AP} = \mathcal{L}(\eta_1)^{AP}$.

We can define ξ by the formula

$$\mathcal{B}\left(s_0|_{AP}\right)^{AP} \wedge \eta_1 \wedge \bigwedge_{a \in (S'|_{AP})} GF\left(\mathcal{B}(a)^{AP}\right).$$

□

Lemma 5. *Let φ be a formula in $EQ(U)$ and AP be compatible with φ. Then for any $u \in (2^{AP})^\omega$, any function $f : \boldsymbol{N} \to \boldsymbol{N} \backslash \{0\}$, if $u \models \varphi$, then, $u_0^{f(0)} ... u_i^{f(i)} ... \models \varphi$.*

Lemma 6. *Let $AP = \{p_1\}$. Then Xp_1 is not expressible in $EQ(U)$.*

Proof of Lemma 6.
To the contrary, suppose that Xp_1 is expressible in $EQ(U)$.

We know that $\emptyset\{p_1\}^\omega \models Xp_1$, then according to Lemma 5, we have that $\emptyset^2\{p_1\}^\omega \models Xp_1$, a contradiction. □

Theorem 2. *$EQ(F) < LTL$.*

Proof.
It follows directly from Lemma 4 and Lemma 6. □

Theorem 3. *$EQ(F) \perp L(X, F)$.*

Proof.
From Lemma 2, we know that p_1Up_2 is expressible in $EQ(F)$. While it is not expressible in $L(X, F)$ according to Proposition 5.

Xp_1 is not expressible in $EQ(F)$ according to Lemma 6.

So, $EQ(F) \perp L(X, F)$. □

From Lemma 6, we already know that $EQ(U)$ cannot define the whole class of ω-regular languages. In the following, we will show that the expressive power of $EQ(U)$ and LTL are incompatible.

Lemma 7. *Let $AP = \{p_1\}$ and*

$$L = \{u \in \left(2^{AP}\right)^\omega | (\emptyset\{p_1\}) \text{ occurs an odd number of times in } u\}.$$

L is expressible in $EQ(U)$, while it is not expressible in LTL.

Remark 2. A language similar to L in Lemma 7 is used in Proposition 2 of [2]. □

Theorem 4. *$EQ(U) \perp LTL$.*

Proof.
It follows from Lemma 6 and Lemma 7. □

Now we compare the expressive power of $EQ(F)$ and $EQ(U)$ with that of $L(F)$ and $L(U)$.

Lemma 8. *Let $AP = \{p_1\}$. Then*

$$L = \{\emptyset, \{p_1\}\}^* \{p_1\}\{p_1\} \{\emptyset, \{p_1\}\}^* \emptyset^\omega \subseteq \left(2^{AP}\right)^\omega$$

is expressible in $EQ(F)$, while it is not expressible in $L(U)$.

The following theorem can be derived from Lemma 8 easily.

Theorem 5. *$L(F) < EQ(F)$ and $L(U) < EQ(U)$.*

But how about the expressive power of $EQ(F)$ and $L(U)$? In Lemma 8, we have shown that there is a language expressible in $EQ(F)$, but not expressible in $L(U)$. In the following we will show that there is a language expressible in $L(U)$, but not expressible in $EQ(F)$.

Lemma 9. *Let $AP = \{p_1, p_2, p_3\}$ and*

$$L = (\{p_1\}\{p_1\}^*\{p_2\}\{p_2\}^*\{p_3\}\{p_3\}^*)^\omega .$$

Then L is expressible in $L(U)$, while it is not expressible in $EQ(F)$.

Proof of Lemma 9.
We first define the formula φ in $L(U)$ such that AP and φ are compatible and $\mathcal{L}(\varphi)^{AP} = L$:

$$\begin{aligned}\varphi \equiv \mathcal{B}(\{p_1\})^{AP} \wedge G\left(\mathcal{B}(\{p_1\})^{AP} \rightarrow \mathcal{B}(\{p_1\})^{AP}\ U\ \mathcal{B}(\{p_2\})^{AP}\right) \wedge \\ G\left(\mathcal{B}(\{p_2\})^{AP} \rightarrow \mathcal{B}(\{p_2\})^{AP}\ U\ \mathcal{B}(\{p_3\})^{AP}\right) \wedge \\ G\left(\mathcal{B}(\{p_3\})^{AP} \rightarrow \mathcal{B}(\{p_3\})^{AP}\ U\ \mathcal{B}(\{p_1\})^{AP}\right) .\end{aligned}$$

Now we show that L is not expressible in $EQ(F)$.

To the contrary, suppose that there is an $EQ(F)$ formula $\psi = \exists q_1 ... \exists q_k \xi$ such that ψ and AP are compatible and $L = \mathcal{L}(\psi)^{AP}$.

Let $AP' = AP \cup \{q_1, ..., q_k\}$. Then, according to Proposition 3, we have that ξ and AP' are compatible, $\mathcal{L}(\psi)^{AP} = \mathcal{L}(\xi)^{AP'}|_{AP}$.

According to Proposition 8, $\mathcal{L}(\xi)^{AP'}$ is a finite union of nonempty languages of the form $M^{init(s_0)}_{inf(S')}$, where M is a restricted ω-regular set, $s_0 \in 2^{AP'}$, $S' \subseteq 2^{AP'}$.

From Lemma 3, we know that $L = \mathcal{L}(\xi)^{AP'}|_{AP}$ is a finite union of nonempty languages of the form $(M|_{AP})^{init(s_0|_{AP})}_{inf(S'|_{AP})}$.

Let $u = (\{p_1\}\{p_2\}\{p_3\})^\omega \in L$. Then, $u \in (M|_{AP})^{init(s_0|_{AP})}_{inf(S'|_{AP})}$ for some restricted ω-regular set M, $s_0 \in \left(2^{AP'}\right)^\omega$ and $S' \subseteq \left(2^{AP'}\right)^\omega$.

Suppose that $M = S_1^* s_1 ... S_{m-1}^* s_{m-1} S_m^\omega$, where $S_i \subseteq 2^{AP}$ $(1 \leq i \leq m)$, and $s_i \in S_i \backslash S_{i+1}$ $(1 \leq i < m)$. Then,

$$M|_{AP} = (S_1|_{AP})^* (s_1|_{AP}) ... (S_{m-1}|_{AP})^* (s_{m-1}|_{AP}) (S_m|_{AP})^\omega .$$

Since $\{p_1\}$, $\{p_2\}$ and $\{p_3\}$ occur infinitely often in $u \in M|_{AP}$, we have that $\{\{p_1\}, \{p_2\}, \{p_3\}\} \subseteq S_m|_{AP}$.

If $m = 1$, then $M|_{AP} = (S_m|_{AP})^\omega$. In this case, let

$$u' = \{p_1\}\{p_2\}\{p_3\}(\{p_2\}\{p_1\}\{p_3\})^\omega.$$

Evidently $u' \in M|_{AP}$. Moreover, $u_0 = u'_0$, and the elements of 2^{AP} occurring infinitely often in u and u' are the same. So, $u' \in (M|_{AP})^{init(s_0)}_{init(S')} \subseteq L$, a contradiction.

Now we assume that $m > 1$.

Since $u \in M_{AP}$, we have that $u = x(s_{m-1}|_{AP})y\left(\{p_1\}\{p_2\}\{p_3\}\right)^\omega$, where

$$x \in (S_1|_{AP})^* (s_1|_{AP}) ... (S_{m-1}|_{AP})^* \text{ and } y\left(\{p_1\}\{p_2\}\{p_3\}\right)^\omega \in (S_m|_{AP})^\omega.$$

Let $u' = x(s_{m-1}|_{AP})y\left(\{p_2\}\{p_1\}\{p_3\}\right)^\omega$.

Then, $u' \in (S_1|_{AP})^* (s_1|_{AP}) ... (s_{m-1}|_{AP}) (S_m|_{AP})^\omega$. Moreover, $u'_0 = u_0$ and the elements of 2^{AP} occurring infinitely often in u and u' are the same. So, $u' \in (M|_{AP})^{init(s_0)}_{inf(S')} \subseteq L$, a contradiction as well.

So, we conclude that L is not expressible in $EQ(F)$. □

Theorem 6. $L(U) \perp EQ(F)$.

Proof.
It follows from Lemma 8 and Lemma 9. □

Also we have the following theorem according to Lemma 9.

Theorem 7. $EQ(F) < EQ(U)$.

The expressive power of $QLTL$ and its fragments are summarized into Fig. 1.

4.3 Quantifier Hierarchy of $Q(U)$ and $Q(F)$

In Subsection 4.2, we have known that $EQ(F)$ and $EQ(U)$ can not define the whole class of ω-regular languages. It follows easily that $AQ(F)$ and $AQ(U)$ can not define the whole class of ω-regular languages as well. Moreover since $\neg Xp_1 \equiv X(\neg p_1)$ is not expressible in $EQ(U)$ (similar to the proof of Lemma 6), Xp_1 is not expressible in $AQ(U)$ or in $AQ(F)$. Consequently Xp_1 is expressible in neither $EQ(U) \cup AQ(U)$ nor in $EQ(F) \cup AQ(F)$. Thus we conclude that alternations of existential and universal quantifiers are necessary to define the whole class of ω-regular languages in $Q(U)$ and $Q(F)$. A natural question then occurs: how many alternations of existential and universal quantifiers are sufficient to define the whole class of ω-regular languages? The answer is one.

Now we define the quantifier hierarchy in $Q(U)$ and $Q(F)$.

The definitions of hierarchy of Σ_k, Π_k and $\triangle_k$ in $Q(U)$ and $Q(F)$ are similar to the quantifier hierarchy of first order logic. Σ_k (Π_k resp.) contains the formulas of the prenex normal form such that there are k-blocks of quantifiers and the quantifiers in each block are of the same type (all existential or all universal); the consecutive blocks are of different types; the first block is existential (universal resp.). $\triangle_k = \Sigma_k \cap \Pi_k$, namely $\triangle_k$ contains those formulas both equivalent to some Σ_k formula and to some Π_k formula. In addition, we define $\triangledown_k = \Sigma_k \cup \Pi_k$.

Lemma 10. *Σ_2^U and Σ_2^F define the whole class of ω-regular languages.*

Proof of Lemma 10.
Let $\mathcal{B} = (Q, 2^{AP}, \delta, q_0, T)$ be a Büchi automaton. Suppose that $Q = \{q_0, ..., q_n\}$, $\mathcal{L}(\mathcal{B})$ can be defined by the following formula φ.

$$\varphi := \exists q_0 ... \exists q_n \left(q_0 \wedge G \left(\bigwedge_{i \neq j} \neg(q_i \wedge q_j) \right) \wedge \right.$$
$$\left. G \left(\bigvee_{(q_i, a, q_j) \in \delta} (q_i \wedge \mathcal{B}(a)^{AP} \wedge X q_j) \right) \wedge \left(\bigvee_{q_i \in T} GF q_i \right) \right)$$

Let $AP' = AP \cup Q$. If we can find a formula ψ in Π_1^U (Π_1^F, resp.) such that ψ and AP' are compatible and

$$\psi \equiv G \left(\bigvee_{(q_i, a, q_j) \in \delta} (q_i \wedge \mathcal{B}(a)^{AP} \wedge X q_j) \right),$$

then, we are done.

We first show that such a ψ in Π_1^U exists.

We observe that $\bigvee_{(q_i, a, q_j) \in \delta} (q_i \wedge \mathcal{B}(a)^{AP} \wedge X q_j)$ can be rewritten into its conjunctive normal form and the conjunctions can be moved to the outside of "G":

$$G \left(\bigvee_{(q_i, a, q_j) \in \delta} (q_i \wedge \mathcal{B}(a)^{AP} \wedge X q_j) \right)$$

$$\equiv \bigwedge_{\substack{i_1, ..., i_k \\ a_1, ..., a_l \\ j_1, ..., j_m}} G \left(q_{i_1} \vee ... \vee q_{i_k} \vee \mathcal{B}(a_1)^{AP} \vee ... \vee \mathcal{B}(a_l)^{AP} \vee X q_{j_1} \vee ... \vee X q_{j_m} \right)$$

It is sufficient to show that there is a Π_1^U formula such that the formula and AP' are compatible and the formula is equivalent to

$$G \left(q_{i_1} \vee ... \vee q_{i_k} \vee \mathcal{B}(a_1)^{AP} \vee ... \vee \mathcal{B}(a_l)^{AP} \vee X q_{j_1} \vee ... \vee X q_{j_m} \right). \qquad (2)$$

The negation of the formula (2) is of the form $F(\varphi_1 \wedge X\varphi_2)$, where φ_1, φ_2 are boolean combinations of propositional variables in AP'. If we can prove that for any formula of the form $F(\varphi_1 \wedge X\varphi_2)$, there is a formula ξ in Σ_1^U such that ξ and AP' are compatible, and $\xi \equiv F(\varphi_1 \wedge X\varphi_2)$, then, we are done.

Let

$$S_i = \left\{ a \in 2^{AP'} \middle| a \text{ satisfies the boolean formula } \varphi_i \right\}, \text{ where } i = 1, 2.$$

Then, for any $u \in \left(2^{AP'}\right)^\omega$,

$$u \models F(\varphi_1 \wedge X\varphi_2) \text{ iff } u \models F\left(\mathcal{B}(S_1)^{AP'} \wedge X\mathcal{B}(S_2)^{AP'}\right).$$

From Proposition 2, we know that

$$F(\varphi_1 \wedge X\varphi_2) \equiv F\left(\mathcal{B}(S_1)^{AP'} \wedge X\mathcal{B}(S_2)^{AP'}\right).$$

Let $q' \in \mathcal{P}\backslash AP'$, and $AP'' = AP' \cup \{q'\}$, $S_1' = S_1$, and $S_2' = \{a \cup \{q'\} \big| a \in S_2\}$. We have that $S_i'|_{AP'} = S_i$ $(i = 1, 2)$ and $S_1' \cap S_2' = \emptyset$.

Then, Σ_1^U formula

$$\chi := \exists q' F\left(\mathcal{B}(S_1')^{AP''} \wedge \mathcal{B}(S_1')^{AP''}\ U\ \mathcal{B}(S_2')^{AP''}\right)$$

satisfies that χ and AP' are compatible, and

$$\chi \equiv F\left(\mathcal{B}(S_1)^{AP'} \wedge X\mathcal{B}(S_2)^{AP'}\right) \equiv F\left(\varphi_1 \wedge X\varphi_2\right).$$

Now we show that there is also a formula $\chi' \in \Sigma_1^F$ equivalent to $F(\varphi_1 \wedge X\varphi_2)$.

According to Lemma 2, there are $q'' \in \mathcal{P}\backslash AP''$ and $\xi \in L(F)$ such that $\exists q''\xi \equiv \mathcal{B}(S_1')^{AP''}\ U\ \mathcal{B}(S_2')^{AP''}$.

Let

$$\chi' := \exists q' \exists q'' F\left(\mathcal{B}(S_1')^{AP''} \wedge \xi\right).$$

Then $\chi' \in \Sigma_1^F$, χ' and AP' are compatible and

$$\chi' \equiv \chi \equiv F\left(\varphi_1 \wedge X\varphi_2\right).$$

□

The following theorem is a direct consequence of Lemma 10.

Theorem 8. *$Q(U) \equiv \Sigma_2^U \equiv \Pi_2^U \equiv \Delta_2^U \equiv \nabla_2^U$ and $Q(F) \equiv \Sigma_2^F \equiv \Pi_2^F \equiv \Delta_2^F \equiv \nabla_2^F$.*

5 Conclusions

In this paper, we first showed that $Q(U)$ and $Q(F)$ can define the whole class of ω-regular languages. Then we compared the expressive power of $EQ(F)$, $EQ(U)$ and other fragments of $QLTL$ in detail and got a panorama of the expressive power of fragments of $QLTL$. In particular, we showed that $EQ(F)$ is strictly less expressive than LTL and that the expressive power of $EQ(U)$ and LTL are incompatible. Furthermore, we showed that one alternation of existential and universal quantifiers is necessary and sufficient to express the whole class of ω-regular languages.

The results established in this paper can be easily adapted to the regular languages on finite words.

There are several open problems. For instance, since we discovered that neither $EQ(U)$ nor $EQ(F)$ can define the whole class of ω-regular languages, a natural problem is to find (effective) characterizations for those languages expressible in $EQ(U)$ and $EQ(F)$ respectively.

We can also consider similar problems for the other temporal operators, such as the strict "Until" and "Future" operators.

Acknowledgements. I want to thank Prof. Wenhui Zhang for his reviews on this paper and discussions with me. I also want to thank anonymous referees for their comments and suggestions.

References

1. Emerson, E.A., Halpern, J.Y.: "Sometimes" and "not never" revisited: On branching versus linear time temporal logic. Journal of the ACM 33(1), 151–178 (1986)
2. Etessami, K.: Stutter-invariant languages, ω-automata, and temporal logic. In: Halbwachs, N., Peled, D.A. (eds.) CAV 1999. LNCS, vol. 1633, pp. 236–248. Springer, Heidelberg (1999)
3. French, T., Reynolds, M.: A Sound and Complete Proof System for QPTL. Advances in Modal Logic 4, 127–147 (2003)
4. Gabbay, D.M., Pnueli, A., Shelah, S., Stavi, J.: On the Temporal Analysis of Fairness. In: POPL'80. Conference Record of the 7th ACM Symposium on Principles of Programming Languages, pp. 163–173. ACM Press, New York (1980)
5. Kamp, H.W.: Tense Logic and the Theory of Linear Order. PhD thesis, UCLA, Los Angeles, California, USA (1968)
6. Kesten, Y., Pnueli, A.: A Complete Proof Systems for QPTL. In: LICS, pp. 2-12 (1995)
7. Perrin, D.: Recent results on automata and infinite words. In: Chytil, M.P., Koubek, V. (eds.) Mathematical Foundations of Computer Science 1984. LNCS, vol. 176, pp. 134–148. Springer, Heidelberg (1984)
8. Pnueli, A.: The temporal logic of programs. In: 18th FOCS, pp. 46–51 (1977)
9. Prior, A.N.: Time and Modality. Clarendon Press, Oxford (1957)
10. Peled, D., Wilke, T.: Stutter-invariant temporal properties are expressible without the next-time operator. Information Processing Letters 63, 243–246 (1997)
11. Sistla, A.P.: Theoretical issues in the design and verification of distributed systems. PHD thesis, Harvard University (1983)
12. Sistla, A.P., Vardi, M.Y., Wolper, P.: The complementation problem for Büchi automata with applications to temporal logic. TCS 49, 217–237 (1987)
13. Sistla, A.P., Zuck, L.D.: Reasoning in a restricted temporal logic. Information and Computation 102, 167–195 (1993)
14. Thomas, W.: Star-free regular sets of ω-sequences. Inform. and Control 42, 148–156 (1979)
15. Thomas, W.: A combinatorial approach to the theory of ω-automata. Inform. and Control 48, 261–283 (1981)
16. Thomas, W.: Automata on Infinite Objects. In: Van Leeuwen, J. (ed.) Handbook of Theoretical Computer Science, pp. 133–191. Elsevier Science Publishers, Amsterdam (1990)
17. Vardi, M.Y.: A temporal fixpoint calculus. In: POPL'88. Proceedings of the 15th Annual ACM SIGACT-SIGPLAN Symposium on Principles of Programming Languages, pp. 250–259 (1988)
18. Wolper, P.: Temporal logic can be more expressive. Inform. and Control 56, 72–99 (1983)
19. Vardi, M.Y., Wolper, P.: Yet another process logic. In: Clarke, E., Kozen, D. (eds.) Logics of Programs. LNCS, vol. 164, pp. 501–512. Springer, Heidelberg (1984)

Author Index

Author Index

Lecture Notes in Computer Science

Sublibrary 1: Theoretical Computer Science and General Issues

For information about Vols. 1–4446
please contact your bookseller or Springer

Vol. 4770: V.G. Ganzha, E.W. Mayr, E.V. Vorozhtsov (Eds.), Computer Algebra in Scientific Computing. XIII, 460 pages. 2007.

Vol. 4743: P. Thulasiraman, X. He, T.L. Xu, M.K. Denko, R.K. Thulasiram, L.T. Yang (Eds.), Frontiers of High Performance Computing and Networking ISPA 2007 Workshops. XXIX, 536 pages. 2007.

Vol. 4742: I. Stojmenovic, R.K. Thulasiram, L.T. Yang, W. Jia, M. Guo, R.F. de Mello (Eds.), Parallel and Distributed Processing and Applications. XX, 995 pages. 2007.

Vol. 4736: S. Winter, M. Duckham, L. Kulik, B. Kuipers (Eds.), Spatial Information Theory. XV, 455 pages. 2007.

Vol. 4732: K. Schneider, J. Brandt (Eds.), Theorem Proving in Higher Order Logics. IX, 401 pages. 2007.

Vol. 4731: A. Pelc (Ed.), Distributed Computing. XVI, 510 pages. 2007.

Vol. 4711: C.B. Jones, Z. Liu, J. Woodcock (Eds.), Theoretical Aspects of Computing – ICTAC 2007. XI, 483 pages. 2007.

Vol. 4710: C.W. George, Z. Liu, J. Woodcock (Eds.), Domain Modeling and the Duration Calculus. XI, 237 pages. 2007.

Vol. 4708: L. Kučera, A. Kučera (Eds.), Mathematical Foundations of Computer Science 2007. XVIII, 764 pages. 2007.

Vol. 4707: O. Gervasi, M.L. Gavrilova (Eds.), Computational Science and Its Applications – ICCSA 2007, Part III. XXIV, 1205 pages. 2007.

Vol. 4706: O. Gervasi, M.L. Gavrilova (Eds.), Computational Science and Its Applications – ICCSA 2007, Part II. XXIII, 1129 pages. 2007.

Vol. 4705: O. Gervasi, M.L. Gavrilova (Eds.), Computational Science and Its Applications – ICCSA 2007, Part I. XLIV, 1169 pages. 2007.

Vol. 4703: L. Caires, V.T. Vasconcelos (Eds.), CONCUR 2007 – Concurrency Theory. XIII, 507 pages. 2007.

Vol. 4700: C.B. Jones, Z. Liu, J. Woodcock (Eds.), Formal Methods and Hybrid Real-Time Systems. XVI, 539 pages. 2007.

Vol. 4697: L. Choi, Y. Paek, S. Cho (Eds.), Advances in Computer Systems Architecture. XIII, 400 pages. 2007.

Vol. 4688: K. Li, M. Fei, G.W. Irwin, S. Ma (Eds.), Bio-Inspired Computational Intelligence and Applications. XIX, 805 pages. 2007.

Vol. 4684: L. Kang, Y. Liu, S. Zeng (Eds.), Evolvable Systems: From Biology to Hardware. XIV, 446 pages. 2007.

Vol. 4683: L. Kang, Y. Liu, S. Zeng (Eds.), Intelligence Computation and Applications. XVII, 663 pages. 2007.

Vol. 4681: D.-S. Huang, L. Heutte, M. Loog (Eds.), Advanced Intelligent Computing Theories and Applications. XXVI, 1379 pages. 2007.

Vol. 4672: K. Li, C. Jesshope, H. Jin, J.-L. Gaudiot (Eds.), Network and Parallel Computing. XVIII, 558 pages. 2007.

Vol. 4671: V. Malyshkin (Ed.), Parallel Computing Technologies. XIV, 635 pages. 2007.

Vol. 4669: J.M. de Sá, L.A. Alexandre, W. Duch, D. Mandic (Eds.), Artificial Neural Networks – ICANN 2007, Part II. XXXI, 990 pages. 2007.

Vol. 4668: J.M. de Sá, L.A. Alexandre, W. Duch, D. Mandic (Eds.), Artificial Neural Networks – ICANN 2007, Part I. XXXI, 978 pages. 2007.

Vol. 4666: M.E. Davies, C.J. James, S.A. Abdallah, M.D Plumbley (Eds.), Independent Component Analysis and Blind Signal Separation. XIX, 847 pages. 2007.

Vol. 4665: J. Hromkovič, R. Královič, M. Nunkesser, P. Widmayer (Eds.), Stochastic Algorithms: Foundations and Applications. X, 167 pages. 2007.

Vol. 4664: J. Durand-Lose, M. Margenstern (Eds.), Machines, Computations, and Universality. X, 325 pages. 2007.

Vol. 4649: V. Diekert, M.V. Volkov, A. Voronkov (Eds.), Computer Science – Theory and Applications. XIII, 420 pages. 2007.

Vol. 4647: R. Martin, M. Sabin, J. Winkler (Eds.), Mathematics of Surfaces XII. IX, 509 pages. 2007.

Vol. 4646: J. Duparc, T.A. Henzinger (Eds.), Computer Science Logic. XIV, 600 pages. 2007.

Vol. 4644: N. Azémard, L. Svensson (Eds.), Integrated Circuit and System Design. XIV, 583 pages. 2007.

Vol. 4641: A.-M. Kermarrec, L. Bougé, T. Priol (Eds.), Euro-Par 2007 Parallel Processing. XXVII, 974 pages. 2007.

Vol. 4639: E. Csuhaj-Varjú, Z. Ésik (Eds.), Fundamentals of Computation Theory. XIV, 508 pages. 2007.

Vol. 4638: T. Stützle, M. Birattari, H. H. Hoos (Eds.), Engineering Stochastic Local Search Algorithms. X, 223 pages. 2007.

Vol. 4628: L.N. de Castro, F.J. Von Zuben, H. Knidel (Eds.), Artificial Immune Systems. XII, 438 pages. 2007.

Vol. 4627: M. Charikar, K. Jansen, O. Reingold, J.D.P. Rolim (Eds.), Approximation, Randomization, and Combinatorial Optimization. XII, 626 pages. 2007.

Vol. 4624: T. Mossakowski, U. Montanari, M. Haveraaen (Eds.), Algebra and Coalgebra in Computer Science. XI, 463 pages. 2007.

Vol. 4621: D. Wagner, R. Wattenhofer (Eds.), Algorithms for Sensor and Ad Hoc Networks. XIII, 415 pages. 2007.

Vol. 4619: F. Dehne, J.-R. Sack, N. Zeh (Eds.), Algorithms and Data Structures. XVI, 662 pages. 2007.

Vol. 4618: S.G. Akl, C.S. Calude, M.J. Dinneen, G. Rozenberg, H.T. Wareham (Eds.), Unconventional Computation. X, 243 pages. 2007.

Vol. 4616: A. Dress, Y. Xu, B. Zhu (Eds.), Combinatorial Optimization and Applications. XI, 390 pages. 2007.

Vol. 4613: F.P. Preparata, Q. Fang (Eds.), Frontiers in Algorithmics. XI, 348 pages. 2007.

Vol. 4600: H. Comon-Lundh, C. Kirchner, H. Kirchner (Eds.), Rewriting, Computation and Proof. XVI, 273 pages. 2007.

Vol. 4599: S. Vassiliadis, M. Berekovic, T.D. Hämäläinen (Eds.), Embedded Computer Systems: Architectures, Modeling, and Simulation. XVIII, 466 pages. 2007.

Vol. 4598: G. Lin (Ed.), Computing and Combinatorics. XII, 570 pages. 2007.

Vol. 4596: L. Arge, C. Cachin, T. Jurdziński, A. Tarlecki (Eds.), Automata, Languages and Programming. XVII, 953 pages. 2007.

Vol. 4595: D. Bošnački, S. Edelkamp (Eds.), Model Checking Software. X, 285 pages. 2007.

Vol. 4590: W. Damm, H. Hermanns (Eds.), Computer Aided Verification. XV, 562 pages. 2007.

Vol. 4588: T. Harju, J. Karhumäki, A. Lepistö (Eds.), Developments in Language Theory. XI, 423 pages. 2007.

Vol. 4583: S.R. Della Rocca (Ed.), Typed Lambda Calculi and Applications. X, 397 pages. 2007.

Vol. 4580: B. Ma, K. Zhang (Eds.), Combinatorial Pattern Matching. XII, 366 pages. 2007.

Vol. 4576: D. Leivant, R. de Queiroz (Eds.), Logic, Language, Information and Computation. X, 363 pages. 2007.

Vol. 4547: C. Carlet, B. Sunar (Eds.), Arithmetic of Finite Fields. XI, 355 pages. 2007.

Vol. 4546: J. Kleijn, A. Yakovlev (Eds.), Petri Nets and Other Models of Concurrency – ICATPN 2007. XI, 515 pages. 2007.

Vol. 4545: H. Anai, K. Horimoto, T. Kutsia (Eds.), Algebraic Biology. XIII, 379 pages. 2007.

Vol. 4533: F. Baader (Ed.), Term Rewriting and Applications. XII, 419 pages. 2007.

Vol. 4528: J. Mira, J.R. Álvarez (Eds.), Nature Inspired Problem-Solving Methods in Knowledge Engineering, Part II. XXII, 650 pages. 2007.

Vol. 4527: J. Mira, J.R. Álvarez (Eds.), Bio-inspired Modeling of Cognitive Tasks, Part I. XXII, 630 pages. 2007.

Vol. 4525: C. Demetrescu (Ed.), Experimental Algorithms. XIII, 448 pages. 2007.

Vol. 4514: S.N. Artemov, A. Nerode (Eds.), Logical Foundations of Computer Science. XI, 513 pages. 2007.

Vol. 4513: M. Fischetti, D.P. Williamson (Eds.), Integer Programming and Combinatorial Optimization. IX, 500 pages. 2007.

Vol. 4510: P. Van Hentenryck, L.A. Wolsey (Eds.), Integration of AI and OR Techniques in Constraint Programming for Combinatorial Optimization Problems. X, 391 pages. 2007.

Vol. 4507: F. Sandoval, A.G. Prieto, J. Cabestany, M. Graña (Eds.), Computational and Ambient Intelligence. XXVI, 1167 pages. 2007.

Vol. 4501: J. Marques-Silva, K.A. Sakallah (Eds.), Theory and Applications of Satisfiability Testing – SAT 2007. XI, 384 pages. 2007.

Vol. 4497: S.B. Cooper, B. Löwe, A. Sorbi (Eds.), Computation and Logic in the Real World. XVIII, 826 pages. 2007.

Vol. 4494: H. Jin, O.F. Rana, Y. Pan, V.K. Prasanna (Eds.), Algorithms and Architectures for Parallel Processing. XIV, 508 pages. 2007.

Vol. 4493: D. Liu, S. Fei, Z. Hou, H. Zhang, C. Sun (Eds.), Advances in Neural Networks – ISNN 2007, Part III. XXVI, 1215 pages. 2007.

Vol. 4492: D. Liu, S. Fei, Z. Hou, H. Zhang, C. Sun (Eds.), Advances in Neural Networks – ISNN 2007, Part II. XXVII, 1321 pages. 2007.

Vol. 4491: D. Liu, S. Fei, Z.-G. Hou, H. Zhang, C. Sun (Eds.), Advances in Neural Networks – ISNN 2007, Part I. LIV, 1365 pages. 2007.

Vol. 4490: Y. Shi, G.D. van Albada, J.J. Dongarra, P.M.A. Sloot (Eds.), Computational Science – ICCS 2007, Part IV. XXXVII, 1211 pages. 2007.

Vol. 4489: Y. Shi, G.D. van Albada, J.J. Dongarra, P.M.A. Sloot (Eds.), Computational Science – ICCS 2007, Part III. XXXVII, 1257 pages. 2007.

Vol. 4488: Y. Shi, G.D. van Albada, J.J. Dongarra, P.M.A. Sloot (Eds.), Computational Science – ICCS 2007, Part II. XXXV, 1251 pages. 2007.

Vol. 4487: Y. Shi, G.D. van Albada, J.J. Dongarra, P.M.A. Sloot (Eds.), Computational Science – ICCS 2007, Part I. LXXXI, 1275 pages. 2007.

Vol. 4484: J.-Y. Cai, S.B. Cooper, H. Zhu (Eds.), Theory and Applications of Models of Computation. XIII, 772 pages. 2007.

Vol. 4475: P. Crescenzi, G. Prencipe, G. Pucci (Eds.), Fun with Algorithms. X, 273 pages. 2007.

Vol. 4474: G. Prencipe, S. Zaks (Eds.), Structural Information and Communication Complexity. XI, 342 pages. 2007.

Vol. 4459: C. Cérin, K.-C. Li (Eds.), Advances in Grid and Pervasive Computing. XVI, 759 pages. 2007.

Vol. 4449: Z. Horváth, V. Zsók, A. Butterfield (Eds.), Implementation and Application of Functional Languages. X, 271 pages. 2007.

Vol. 4448: M. Giacobini (Ed.), Applications of Evolutionary Computing. XXIII, 755 pages. 2007.

Vol. 4447: E. Marchiori, J.H. Moore, J.C. Rajapakse (Eds.), Evolutionary Computation, Machine Learning and Data Mining in Bioinformatics. XI, 302 pages. 2007.